Wasco, Illinois: A History

by Adam D. Gibbons

Old Adage Press

Geneva, Illinois

First Edition

2018

Wasco, Illinois: A History

Copyright ©2018, Adam D. Gibbons

All rights reserved. No part of this book may be reproduced in any form or by any electronic or mechanical means including information storage and retrieval systems without permission in writing from author, except by a reviewer who may quote passages in a review. Requests for permission should be addressed in writing to the author, Adam D. Gibbons, 33W777 Hill Road, Geneva, IL 60134.

Printed in the United States of America

Publisher's Cataloging-in-Publication Data

Gibbons, Adam D., 1975-
    Wasco, Illinois: A History /Adam D. Gibbons
    Includes surname index.
    ISBN 978-1-7327016-0-1
    Library of Congress Control Number: 2018955186

This book is dedicated to the people of Wasco, both past and present.

Table of Contents

Acknowledgements 5
Introduction 6
Wasco's Origins 8
A Brief Decade-by-Decade History of Wasco 13
    Initial Settlement (1880s) 13
    The 1890s 18
    The 1900s 21
    The 1910s 26
    The 1920s 31
    The 1930s 34
    The 1940s 38
    The 1950s 41
    The 1960s 46
    The 1970s 51
    The 1980s 55
    The 1990s 58
    The 2000s 65
    The 2010s 69
Community Institutions 74
    The Wasco Depot 74
    Wasco Baptist Church 79
    Wasco School 87
    The Whitney Cemetery 107
    Some Wasco Firsts 109
Important Wasco Families 111
    The Austin Family 111
    The Edward Swanson Family 118
    The Bergland Family 120
    The Gustaf Swanson Family 133

The John Swanson Family	136
The Higgins Family	138
The Hawkins Family	141
The Peterson Family	147
The Charles Anderson Family	149
The Bell Family	153
The Rice Family	157
The Whitney Family	160
The Leonard White Family	164
The Millen Family	167
The Bert Brown Family	172
The Waterhouse Family	177
The Carpenter Family	179
The Fischer Family	181
The Isaac Johnson Family	185
The George Brown Family	195
The Stevens Family	196
The Mather Family	197
The Erickson Family	201
The Denker Family	204
The Bowgren Family	207
The Ekstrom Family	213
The Jay Family	216
The Langrill Family	218
The Vanderhoof Family	219
The Lathrop Family	221
The Hagaman Family	221
The Anderson/Barber Family	225
The Chrystal Family	227
The Harold Anderson Family	228
The Ross Family	231
The Theodore Johnson Family	232
The Two Olson Families	233

Some Wasco Houses 236
    Northwest Quarter 236
    Southwest Quarter 280
    Northeast Quarter 304
    Southeast Quarter 326

Significant Institutions & Places of Business 345
    The Bergland/Hummel Lumberyard 345
    The Original Bergland Store 348
    The Bergland/Hummel Store 352
    Erickson's Blacksmith Shop 360
    The Wasco Blacksmith Shop 366
    Johnson's Store/Larson's Garage/Mather's Gas Station 368
    The Wanzer Dairy/King's Mill 376
    Travis Tavern/Bohr's Tavern/Denny's Den 378
    The Wasco Inn 380
    The Wasco Garage 382
    The Farm Restaurant 383
    White Brothers Trucking 389
    Wasco Nursery 390
    Fox River & Countryside Fire & Rescue 393
    Trellis Farm & Garden 394
    Trailside Automotive Repair 394
    Country Gas/Suburban Propane 395

Local Sports 397
    Boys Baseball 397
    Girls Softball 402

Important Social Organizations 406
    The Wasco History Club 406
    Modern Woodmen of America 406
    The Woman's Christian Temperance Union 407
    The Christian Endeavor Society 408
    Wasco Ladies Aid 409
    The Pollyanna Club 415

- The Wasco Glad Game Club 415
- Wasco Mothers' Club 416
- The Wasco Home Bureau 418
- The Wasco/Campton 4-H Club 419
- The Wasco Community Club 421
- The Fortnightly Card Club 422
- The Shrinking Matrons 422
- The U-Go-I-Go Club 423
- The Pure Milk Association (Wasco Local) 424
- The Wasco American Legion 425

Bibliography 429

Surname Index 458

About the Author 468

Acknowledgements

Until now, there has never been a comprehensive history of Wasco, Illinois, compiled and published. The original idea for creating this book came from two individuals, both of whom are as closely connected with Wasco as anyone living. Thank you, Christine ("Chris") Brauer and George Bergland, for planting the seed for this work. I hope you both find the result interesting, accurate, and informative. My sincere thanks go out to all the other contributors to this work, including Don Swanson, Joan Bowgren, Tom Corron, Neal Anderson, the Campton Township Assessors Office, several members of Wasco Ladies Aid, and the office staff at Wasco Elementary School. I also owe a debt of gratitude to Skylar Zimny, who put in countless hours carefully reading and improving the manuscript. Thank you to my family, especially to Heidi for helping with the book cover, to Evelyn for her encouragement, and to Tobias for his help cleaning up the index. Without all of you, completing this work would not have been possible.

The Chicago Great Western Railroad Depot at Wasco, as it appeared in the 1950s

Introduction

The village of Wasco is not, strictly speaking, a village. This is not to say that it cannot be located on a map, however – it has not changed locations, in fact, in its one hundred and thirty-two years of existence. What we all know as Wasco is, with certainty, located in the northern half of Section 23, in the eastern part of Campton Township. The township itself, first permanently settled in the mid-1830s, is located in the central part of Kane County, Illinois. Few would deny that the very center of Wasco is the intersection of the present Route 64 and Old LaFox Road, although Wasco's extent in any direction from this point is open to debate. Because Wasco is not, and has never been, incorporated, its boundaries are defined by tradition, and not by statute. Since 2007, when the village of Campton Hills was officially incorporated, Wasco has been a part of this municipality, but Wasco is not contiguous with Campton Hills by any means. Depending upon who is speaking, Wasco's "borders" can shift in all cardinal directions. For the purposes of this work, Wasco's boundaries are not and cannot be exact, but will more or less correspond to those implied by the "Wasco" columns in early local newspapers – those found in the *Elburn Herald* and the *St. Charles Chronicle* in particular. For example, the Carpenter family home on the present Wasco Road was "in" Wasco but the Norris farm was considered to be "east of Wasco." The Johnson brothers' farm was usually described as being "in" Wasco, but the Campton Town Hall was "near" it. The Frank Vanderhoof farm on Burlington Road near Corron Road was "north of Wasco," while the August Johnson and A. J. Mongerson farms were "south of" the village. Overall, it seems, for most of its history, only the few dozen buildings located within roughly a half-mile radius of the Wasco post office were generally considered to comprise Wasco.

Happily for your author and all local historians, early Kane County deeds, almost without exception, state the residences of both the grantors and grantees. Those living in Wasco were most often said to be "of Campton Township," since this locality has legally-defined boundaries, and has since 1850. Fairly often, however, the buyers and sellers are said to have been "of the village of Wasco," and occasionally, "of the town of Wasco." A few deeds even exist which include the phrase "of the city of Wasco" but these are rare exceptions. Throughout this work, Wasco will be called and considered a village, when a label is both appropriate and necessary. By tradition, villages contain a group or groups of houses and related buildings (often a church, store, and school, at minimum) and are larger than hamlets, but smaller than towns. Regardless of how the reader defines Wasco, however, it is hoped that this work will serve to illustrate a small part of its rich, varied, and fascinating history.

An aerial view of Wasco, taken in 1987

Welcome to Wasco!

Wasco's Origins

At noon, on Wednesday, 29 December 1886, the long-awaited first construction train on the Minnesota & Northwestern Railroad reached the center of the city of St. Charles. This event was widely celebrated, and was heralded as a new beginning for the city and for Kane County. The train arrived almost thirty-seven years to the day after the very first locomotive came into St. Charles over the old branch line. On the third-last day of 1886, the engine pulling the train coming into the city arrived there safely. The engine was designated Number 33, and weighed forty-two tons. It had been built in Paterson, New Jersey, by the Cooke Locomotive and Machine Works. For more than thirty years, the people of St. Charles had "looked anxiously for a railroad over the old grade." A newspaper account from the period boasted that "To-day it is here. The track is laid; a fine iron bridge spans the river over the old piers, and everything betokens a new resurrection for the long waiting city."

Citizens of St. Charles surprised the M. & N. W. railroad employees and contractors by organizing an oyster supper to celebrate the memorable occasion of the train's arrival. The relationship between the local citizens and the railroad's officials and employees had been very pleasant over the period of planning and construction, and sufficient money was raised by railroad boosters to pay for "all who might accept the tendered hospitality." Locals felt that "the era of prosperity which the new road brings to our doors [was] worth rejoicing over." A total of ninety-three men connected with the railroad sat down to "a steaming supper at the Hotel Billings" on the evening of the 29th, and "enjoyed themselves as hungry men know how." An excellent feeling prevailed over the feast, and all present sensed the importance of that day.

One of the men present at that celebratory supper was Mr. G. A. Kyle, resident engineer for the railroad. Less than a month later, in January 1887, two citizens of Campton Township began circulating a petition to name the new station being completed west of St. Charles in his honor. The 1885 St. Charles city directory and census report listed no one with the surname Kyle living in town, and indeed George Allan Kyle, who was listed as a civil engineer in the 1900 census of Auburn, King County, Washington, moved around a fair amount during his railroad career. He was born in Clermont County, Ohio, on 21 September 1857, and should not be confused with the two men by that name (with different occupations) who resided in Illinois at the turn of the twentieth century. The Kyle for whom the railroad petition was circulated traveled to South Africa in 1895, remained there for three years, and resided in Canada in 1901 and 1902. He went to China in 1916 (see his passport photo on the next page) to "engage in civil engineering for the Chinese government." His employer at that time, as a point of interest, was A. G. Hoagland, Chief Engineer of the Great Northern Railway.

Although "Kyle" was not accepted by the community at large to replace the newly-built station's original and short-lived name - Graystock (apparently chosen by the railroad company) - the station would soon get a new name after all. The new train station located east of the center of Campton Township, and the community which would quickly grow around it, would soon be designated "Wasco." For information on the naming of Wasco, see "Important Wasco Families – The Austin Family" later in this work.

Apparently, there was some contention over the naming of the railroad station west of St. Charles from the very beginning. On 14 January 1887, a local brief in a newspaper published by St. Charles pioneer Samuel W. Durant stated under the heading "North Campton," that "We are told that the name of the M. & N. W. station on Mr. Carpenter's place is Graystock, that of the next one west being Campton." The "Campton" train station referred to here was located at what is now Lily Lake. The editor went on to state that "There is some dispute about the name; some claiming it will be Kyle, and others Gretna." Incidentally, the name Gretna (whose name was ultimately taken from a town in southern Scotland) would be used for another station on the M. & N. W. railroad line – one located several miles to the east, in Milton Township, DuPage County. The name Kyle was not used for a train station or community in Kane County, or anywhere else in Illinois.

George A. Kyle as he appeared in 1916 - many Campton Township citizens favored naming the train station at Wasco in his honor, and circulated a petition to this effect in January 1887

The first known mention of the controversy over the name of the new station at Wasco

Simon E. Chaffee was Campton Township Supervisor when the village of Wasco was founded and surveyed. Other local government officials were F. B. Hitchcock, who was Town Clerk, and A. D. Chaffee, who was Assessor at the time. Isaac Barber, William Beith, and John Worth were the town's three Highway Commissioners. In early 1887, Supervisor Chaffee was one of the two men (the other being C. L. Probert) that circulated the petition "asking that the M. & N. W. station on Mr. Carpenter's place be named Kyle" which was referred to earlier. In other local news that January, the locomotives along the new line were rolling "from Chicago well into Virgil . . . their advent [bringing] to hope a new immigration."

The railroad depot at Lily Lake, the next stop west of Wasco, was erected in April 1887. A St. Charles newspaper reported on the fifteenth of that month that "depot buildings are being built on the M. & N. W. R. R. near Canada Corners. Telegraph poles have been erected." Trains were to be running regularly within ten weeks. A milk car was to be run from that depot. More than six months earlier, on 17 September 1886, an article in a St. Charles newspaper stated that "A depot has been located on the road leading from Canada Corners to Blackberry. It will be on the west side of the road. Grading is progressing rapidly." The engineers had examined the ground there in early September, when work on the railroad itself was "being pushed rapidly." Locally, it was extremely hot that month. Plowing for winter rye was underway in Campton Township when the depot sites were chosen. Graystock, referred to earlier, never caught on as a local place name. Instead, the new depot at Wasco was sometimes referred to the "east depot" during the winter and spring of 1887, while locals argued about its ultimate designation. One of the few references to Graystock in Campton Township records occurs in the 4 June 1887 minutes of the Commissioners of Highways, who refer to the new village as "Gray Stock." The ditch on the "new road" (now the northern section of Old LaFox Road) "running by the new depot" had just been completed at that time, and was soon inspected by the township's Board of Commissioners.

Simon E. Chaffee, Campton Township Supervisor when Wasco was founded in 1886

The exact site of the Wasco train station was selected during the autumn of 1886, amidst an historic regional drought. A lack of rain of that scope and severity had not been seen in Campton Township for almost a generation. After months of dry weather, some rain finally fell in Kane County at the end of August 1886. Throughout that month, the railroad was speedily paying various sums to Campton Township landowners for rights-of-way through their properties to be used for the actual path of the railroad track. By the end of the third week of August, the Minnesota & Northwestern Railroad had secured a continuous right of way all the way through Campton Township, "with perhaps one or two exceptions." The township was then (and still is) six miles in width, and rights had to be secured from scores of local landowners before construction could begin in earnest.

Despite the lack of rain in the autumn of 1886, oats and rye were turned out rather well, and Kane County farmers continued their laborious harvest work as usual. Construction on the M. & N. W. railroad tracks began amid and in fact continued throughout the course of several lawsuits brought against the railroad all that season. These cases were being decided in Geneva, the county seat, as progress on the road moved steadily westward. By the twentieth of August, those in St. Charles learned "that the location of the depot [at the future site of Wasco] has been settled. There will be one on Norman Carpenter's farm, in the east part of town," with the other station in Campton Township being located just south of what is now the center of Lily Lake, on property owned by Renalwin Outhouse.

Landowners in Campton Township who were paid sums by the railroad in the fall of 1886 included: Alexander Anderson ($589); Harriet Eddy ($406); Peter Alfred Peterson ($400); C. L. Probert ($400); Catherine Anderson ($375); James Powell ($365); John S. Swanson ($325); John Ross ($300); David Hamilton ($200); LaFayette Anderson ($183); C. M. Vandervolgen ($125); Susan Crosby ($100); Alonzo D. Chaffee ($61); Charles Baldwin ($60); Lewis P. Walker ($50); Andrew Mongerson ($31); and Nicholas Fuller ($18). Nearly all of these landowners' farms, which span the entire width of the township, can be found delineated on the 1892 Campton Township map.

By October 1886, work was "well advanced" along the Minnesota & Northwestern Railroad west of St. Charles. Track laying was about to commence at that time, and grading was nearly complete. The site of "the new station on the Carpenter place" at Wasco was to be

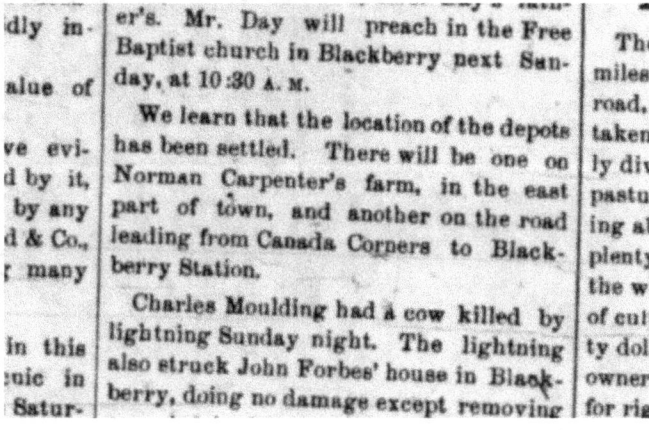

The site of the Wasco station was selected in August 1886

"leveled and ready for buildings" in the very near future. Locals understood by then that "a considerable tract of land [would] be laid out into village lots." Grading on the railroad was completed in Campton Township in the middle of November 1886. The Wasco depot was no doubt under construction at that time. It was then predicted that the railroad would soon be "one of the important lines of the continent." While the railroad was being built, farmers were finding a ready market for their hay and grain.

To illustrate the quick pace of progress on the railroad itself, it is apparent that by March 1887 farmers whose property adjoined the path of the railroad were already feeling anxious about the lack of fencing along the line. Cattle and other livestock represented significant monetary investments, and no farmer wished to see his assets destroyed in railroad collisions. Before trains began moving along the line, work building fences along the railroad's path was undertaken in the winter months of 1887. Local residents also saw ahead and asked for local governments to create new wagon roads toward the depots. For example, there was a petition presented that March (which was a rather snowy month that year in Kane County) to lay out a new road to the "east depot" at Wasco – passenger and freight trains along the railroad had not yet begun to run, but soon would. Minnesota & Northwestern Railroad Depot buildings were completed at Sycamore and Canada Corners in the spring of 1887, and those elsewhere along the line followed immediately afterward.

On 8 December 1887, the newly-incorporated Chicago, St. Paul & Kansas City Railway acquired the Minnesota & Northwestern. The railroad was known by this designation for just over four years before it acquired its more familiar name, the Chicago Great Western. Alpheus Beede Stickney, a railroad executive from St. Paul, incorporated the Chicago Great Western Railway, which in the winter of 1892 acquired the assets of the Chicago, St. Paul & Kansas City Railway. The train line running through Wasco was known as the Chicago Great Western for the remaining decades of its existence. Stickney served as the president of the C. G. W. from its creation until his retirement in 1909.

Advertisement for the Chicago Great Western Railway from 1907

A Brief Decade-by-Decade History of Wasco

Initial Settlement (1880s)

In the spring of 1886, Wasco did not yet exist. The region which would soon become the village was then owned by the Higgins, Rice, Hagaman, and Carpenter families. The closest dwelling to the center of the future village was the original Pattee/Higgins house, a quarter-mile west (see the map below). David Pattee, a carpenter by trade, who came to Kane County from Grafton County, New Hampshire, built the house in the first half of the 1840s, most likely in 1843. Remarkably, this home was still standing in the 1930s, though it had been long-since abandoned. The old dwelling, thought to have been used for a time as an outbuilding, was taken down some time later by the Hawkins family, who owned the property. The road which ran east-west through the Wasco village site (part of which is now designated Route 64 and another part which is known as Wasco Road) was in the 1880s known most often known as "the St. Charles-Lily Lake Road," although it was occasionally called "Rice Road" for the family who had owned a farm on its south side since the 1850s.

As has already been stated, the Minnesota & Northwestern Railroad Company (not yet known as the Chicago Great Western) began purchasing its right of way from locals in August of 1886, spurring regional development. Several early Kane County deeds which conveyed the lands to the railroad specified that the sales were to be null and void "unless the lands hereby conveyed shall be used for erecting and maintaining thereon a Passenger and Freight Station of the Railroad Company hereinafter named." This railroad, of course, was rapidly built, and it is no exaggeration to state that Wasco came into existence because of it. The "Wasco Station Road" (part of which is now Old LaFox Road, north of the present Route 64) was built across the Austin, Carpenter, and Whitney properties in 1886-1887.

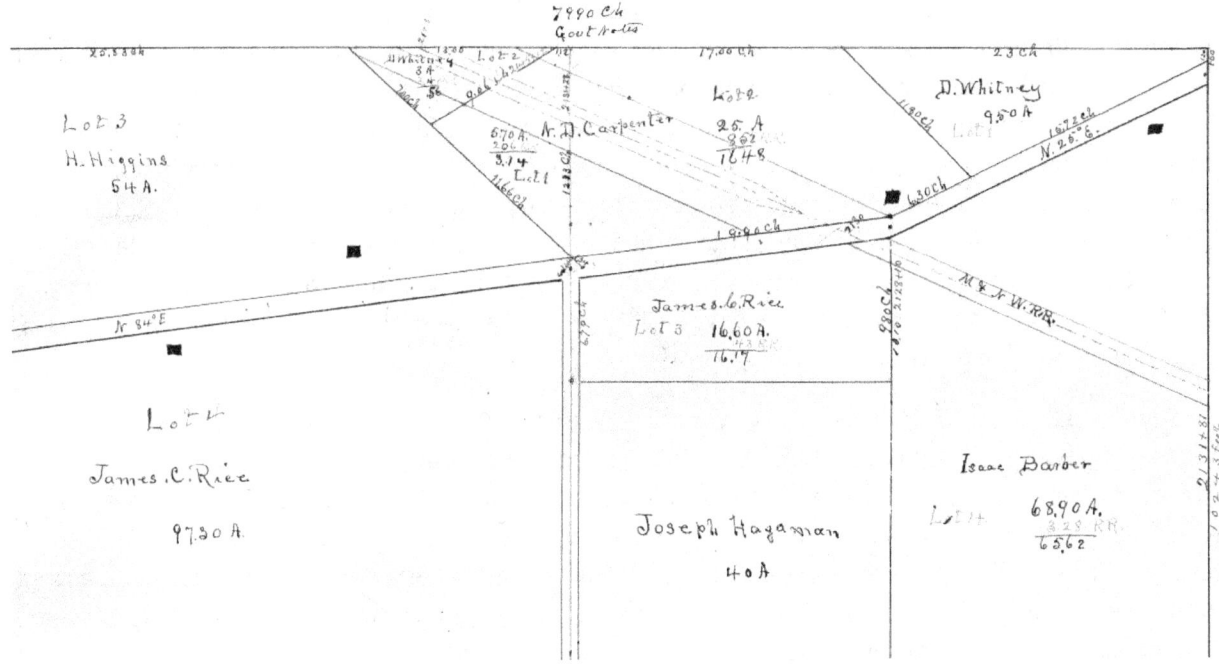

The Wasco vicinity in 1886, just before the railroad built through the area. The railroad right-of-way is visible near the top of the map, running at an angle to the east-southeast.

The first mention of Wasco by its present name in the region's largest newspaper, the *Chicago Tribune*, occurred on 9 September 1887. Its first mention in the *Elgin Advocate* dates to 6 August, when there was a notice that the "Byron accommodation train" which had just begun passenger service on the first of the month, left Lily Lake at 8:22 AM, "and Wasco at 8:35." Wasco was mentioned by its present name on 19 August 1887, in the local (St. Charles) paper, the *Valley Chronicle*. Newspapers and their readers, though, were far less concerned with the new station's appellation than with the region's disagreeable weather. During the summer of 1887, just prior to the renaming of Wasco, vegetation throughout Campton Township was suffering for lack of rain. There had been less than two inches of rain between February and June, and pastures were rapidly drying up. The hay crop was "nearly a failure," and the region was experiencing a marked decrease in the milk supply. On 20 May 1887, the local newspaper stated that "Those who have never prayed before are now practicing on a petition for rain." Then, the nascent "village" (consisting of the train depot and perhaps two or three houses) was being called Graystock.

One of the first two residents of Graystock ever mentioned in the *Valley Chronicle* (both of whom were included in a list of attendees at Dayton Ward's sixty-ninth birthday party!) was "William" [actually Charles Wilson] Millen, whose house is thought to have been completed within half a year of Wasco's initial settlement. Millen was a carpenter by trade, and is sometimes credited as being Wasco's first permanent resident. The other pioneer settler mentioned as a resident of Graystock was John Bell (see "The Bell Family").

Tracks were being laid for the Minnesota & Northwestern Railroad during the summer of 1887. This followed the completion of grading, which took many months. By early that summer the portion of the present Old LaFox Road north of Route 64 had been surveyed and laid out – it was then alternately known as either "Wasco Depot Road" or "New Depot Road." Norman L. Carpenter, whose property was negatively impacted by cutting the new road, was awarded $390 that April for the damage his property suffered as the road was put through. The road was first proposed in March 1887.

As the local drought persisted into June and July, some farmers allowed their cows to graze in their meadows, due to the nearly non-existent hay crop. The barley and oats crops were also light. Temperatures reached "95 degrees in the shade" that summer. On the first of July, local farmers stated frankly that "Our main dependence is [now] corn. If that shall fail our cattle will starve." Thankfully, the region received a modest rainfall later that month. Also at that time, a petition was put together (which unlike that to rename Graystock "Kyle") successfully renamed the depot and post office in the western part of Campton Township. The new name given to this settlement, initially known as "Campton," was Lily Lake. The new (and present) name was selected by the family of George and Renalwin Outhouse, after a large lily-filled pond located on their property.

On Sunday, 31 July 1887, at 8:45 PM, the very first passenger train on the Minnesota & Northwestern Railway reached St. Charles from Chicago. The trip took an hour and twenty minutes, and the train consisted of an engine (No. 42) and five "elegant coaches," some of "the finest coaches ever seen in the west." Several hundred people were present to mark the occasion, and never before had St. Charles residents witnessed such a scene. Locals felt that "truly we have entered upon a new era." The advent of the line meant "much more to St. Charles . . . than the most sanguine can foresee." The "happy event" also marked a beginning for the next station to the west – Wasco.

By the middle of August 1887, farmers along the line of the Minnesota & Northwestern railroad were already shipping milk to Chicago. Rates were lower than those on the competing line, the Chicago &

Northwestern, and farmers paid just twelve cents a can, a savings of approximately four cents for every can shipped. A well was being dug at the new Lily Lake station that month, and the days were extremely hot, occasionally reaching one hundred degrees when milk shipments began. More than seventy cans of milk were being shipped daily "from Wasco" (the first mention of that locality by its present name in print) with forty cans from Lily Lake by late in the month. Cattle yards had already been erected, and the new wells at both Wasco and Lily Lake were finished. Fred Moody built a store at the Lily Lake Station in September and October 1887, and opened for business immediately. Beginning on 3 October, the railroad began carrying the mail to and from Wasco on a daily basis. George C. Bergland was appointed Wasco's first postmaster on the twentieth of that month.

By mid-September 1887, traffic on the newly-opened rail line through Wasco was "increasing fast." The milk business was growing every month – by early October eighty-five cans of milk were placed aboard the morning train at Wasco every day, destined for pasteurization in River Forest and for quick resale in Chicago. The number of cans of milk shipped daily reached one hundred by the 11th of November, less than four months after the very first trains ran on the M. & N. W. line. Milk prices remained low at that time, however, and there was "great need of combination among farmers" to increase and stabilize the prices they could obtain from milk sales. Watson Kelley was the conductor of the Chicago-bound milk train, which departed from Lily Lake at 8:00 AM, and from Wasco a short time later. Frances (Bergland) Peterson later astutely wrote that "the milk train that ran to St. Charles from the west was the life of the thriving rural community" of Wasco.

The first known "Wasco" column in any local newspaper appeared in the 17 December 1887 issue of the *Elgin Advocate*. The railroad had recently begun regular service, and that month for "the first time ever known hereabouts," farmers were shipping hay to Chicago. In the Wasco area, the Chaffee brothers were among the first to take advantage of this commerce. Wasco was described as a "thriving little station on the Minnesota & Northwestern railroad" then, with one hundred and ten cans of milk shipped daily to Chicago from the depot. There was some talk of moving the "town house to the station" which the *Elgin Advocate* editors considered "a good idea." Charles Hurd, the first Wasco station agent, was yet unmarried, so a sister was "to preside over his house." Late rains in December had "filled up the wells" causing the local dairyman "to rejoice." Temperatures plummeted by January, though, reaching between ten and twenty-four degrees below zero. It was so cold that month in fact that canvas coverings and "wraps of all descriptions" were used to keep the milk in the cans from condensing aboard the trains.

Some of the earliest dairy farmers in the Wasco area who were shipping their milk on the trains from Wasco by December 1887 were: Charles Probert, Edward and Jefferson Garfield, Simon and Alonzo Chaffee, Gunnar Anderson, Frank Watkins, J. B. Ward, James McDonald, D. W. Stevens, John Brown, George Bergland, Frank Heath, Ben Lake, and George Shaver.

In January 1888, the snow that had fallen in Wasco that week made for "splendid sleighing" and 'Wills' Kelley of Campton Township had just secured the position of milk conductor on the Minnesota & Northwestern railroad. Mr. and Mrs. John W. Bell had just celebrated their tenth anniversary, and thirty relatives and friends surprised them on this occasion. A number of "useful presents" were given to the couple at the celebration. That May, a "load of Wascoites" traveled to a dance in South Elgin together. Will Plummer of Wasco "gave a dance at the Gray Willow hall" that month also, and "quite a good time was had" by those in attendance.

By February 1888, the Campton Township Highway Commissioners were referring to the nascent village as Wasco Station (as in the reference to the "new road laid at Wasco Station") and all further references to the short-lived Graystock were dropped from the official records. By 1890 or earlier, some Kane County documents were using the name Wasco Station to refer to the settlement as well. The name Wasco alone (without the word "Station") was in widespread usage by 1889 however and has been used continuously and invariably since then.

In 1888, sleighing in Campton Township was still good in mid-February. A few local dairymen were taking stock in the new Milk Trust, but others were skeptical that it could help boost milk prices. There was an over-supply of milk in Chicago at that time. Farmers were desperate for assistance. Many were paying farm laborers as much as $20 per month – a local St. Charles paper stated that "They want men who know how to milk cows." Nor was the weather cooperating - as of February, there had not been "a drop of water to be found at Wasco," as it had not rained in three months. Those visiting the village were "compelled to go to St. Charles for a drink." There was a heavy rainfall in late March, but the rain tapered off significantly in May and June of that year. Road scrapers, which the township had just purchased for a tidy sum, were proving "nearly worthless" at the time due partly to the adverse weather and partly to the machines' flawed manufacture.

*A typical locomotive that would have passed through Wasco in the 1890s –
a "Brooks Tandem Compound" used on the Chicago Great Western*

Sidewalks had not yet been built in Wasco by May 1888, despite local residents having been discussing their construction for more than a year. In February of that year, those looking for sidewalks in the village were humorously told that "they were in the lumber woods as yet." By May, Mark Dunham of Wayne, a very prominent and wealthy landowner and businessman, "took in the sights at Wasco." Because of the lack of sidewalks, Mr. Dunham "rolled up his pants and walked in the mud." A subscription of $45 was raised to install a sidewalk from the Wasco depot to the post office that season.

As early as the 1880s, buildings of all types were being fairly regularly moved within the township and in nearby areas – one Mr. Caustin moved a house near Elburn for L. E. Bartlett in the spring of 1888, and a newspaper man stated that Caustin, "in moving buildings, we never saw excelled." According to oral tradition, some of the very earliest buildings in Wasco were not built on site; rather, they were moved to the village from nearby farms.

Interest in local politics varied somewhat when Wasco was first settled, but when the village was young political participation was not as strong as it would later become. Just one hundred and fifty voters cast ballots in the April 1888 local elections in Campton, for example. Weather, more than politics, continued to rank foremost among the first settlers' interests, and many were publicly and loudly thankful that May when cool weather prevailed as the potato crop was being planted.

From the very beginning of the settlement, all Wasco settlers utilized the daily mail, and kept in regular touch with friends and relatives, many of whom lived "out East." The Minnesota & Northwestern Railroad had become the Chicago, St. Paul, & Kansas City by then, and it continued to carry the daily mail both into and out of Wasco and points east and west.

A selection of events which occurred locally in 1888 may serve to set Wasco's early years in a proper context. William Beith, well-known farmer of Campton Township, planted more than four thousand trees (mostly European larch) in the spring of that year and the hay crop was very good that summer. Some of the corn failed in early June, though, and had to be replanted. In May, a new "milk station" was created on the railroad three miles west of Lily Lake, and was named Foote's Crossing. The Beers & Leggett Company's landmark publication *Commemorative Biographical and Historical Record of Kane County* was published in the summer of 1888, was purchased by several local families, and was found to be "much freer from errors than that of 1878." Most dairy farmers in Wasco and the surrounding area in the late 1880s sold and shipped their milk to one "Mr. Newton" (probably Samuel Dexter Newton) an influential Chicago milk dealer. In March 1888, the pupils of the red schoolhouse south of Wasco presented their teacher, Mr. Waite, with a copy of Milton's poems as their class gift. A spelling bee was held at the red school that month, with John Chaffee emerging as the champion speller.

The Whitney/White school house near Wasco, as it appeared in 2017

Political sentiment in Wasco in the late 1880s was heavily Republican, although at that time the G. O. P. was by far the more liberal of the two major American parties. Local residents debated issues such as the protective tariff, the benefits of temperance, and women's participation in business. Several Campton Township citizens attended the Republican Convention in Chicago in June 1888. The St. Charles *Valley Chronicle* offered the opinion that "we must wrest the government from the hands of those who overtook to overthrow it and perpetuate slavery" by which they meant the Democratic Party and its supporters. All readers at the time understood that the (conservative) Democrats were in control of nearly all Southern state governments, but that this control threatened Republicans and their political agenda. Historians later called this rhetorical technique of reminding voters of Civil War-era political factions "waving the bloody shirt," and it worked quite well in Wasco, throughout Kane County, and in much wider circles still. Incidentally, Campton Township residents Garrit Norton, William White, J. P. Bartlett and many others proudly (and publicly!) made known their intention of voting for Benjamin Harrison that fall; the Republican nominee went on to defeat Democrat Grover

Cleveland by a narrow margin nationwide. In Kane County as a whole, in 1888, Harrison received 7,572 votes to Cleveland's 4,386.

Winter rye fared well in Wasco in the summer of 1888, and farmers were then "very busy haying and harvesting." Miss B. Coughlin was the teacher at the "white school house" just east of Wasco; she had less than a score of pupils. That fall was another season without much rain, and in late September farmers were still "cutting their corn as fast as possible." Threshing had been underway since August, and oats were yielding sixty bushels per acre in the Wasco vicinity. By December 1888, Wasco-area farmers were receiving between $1.10 and $1.15 for each can of milk shipped to Chicago. Nearly 160 cans of milk left Wasco daily by February 1889.

Prior to the construction of the Wasco Baptist Church in 1891, religious services in Wasco were held in local schools, especially the Whitney school east of the village. On Sunday evenings in October 1889, for example, evening worship services were "held at the white school house." Sunday School took place at the schoolhouse at 10:30 AM on Sundays, throughout the summer of 1889. There was preaching that took place at the school most Sundays at 3:00 PM.

The most disastrous storm ever seen in Campton Township passed through Wasco at 5:00 PM on 27 July 1889. A local observer noted that "everybody was terrified" and during the storm objects just six feet away could not be seen. The loss "to the growing crops is beyond any estimate," said a contemporary observer, and both corn and oats "were leveled to the ground, and then beaten by hail." Trees were uprooted and carried several hundred feet in any given direction. Almost every local farmer lost his windmill. C. W. Bolcum, in fact, lost two windmills – "a total wreck." Daniel Whitney and Gust Swanson lost their brand-new windmills, valued at several hundred dollars apiece, and "Mr. Whitney's barn, 100 feet long, was moved on its foundation and left in bad shape." Supervisor S. E. Chaffee's barn was completely unroofed, and Kane County farmers at all points west of St. Charles were all "heavy losers." A brakeman on the Chicago, St. Paul, & Kansas City railroad, Mr. Baker, was stuck by lightening during the storm and was instantly killed.

George Bergland was "fitting up his warehouse" in Wasco September 1889. He was "putting in [grain] elevators, and otherwise making it convenient." The building may have been the first on the lumberyard site, and was almost certainly located immediately adjacent to the railroad tracks. George Eddy of Campton Township bought a "new engine" in August 1889, and expected "to do all the threshing" in the Wasco area because of the purchase.

The 1890s

As has already been stated, the village of Wasco, located approximately five miles west-northwest of downtown St. Charles, grew around the present Route 64 (most often called the "Wasco & Lily Lake road" around the turn of the twentieth century) near its intersection with what is now Wasco Road, the Chicago Great Western Railroad, and Old LaFox Road. By 1891, the village of Wasco was already fairly-well settled. Dairy farms covered Campton Township from end to end, and the regional population was on the increase. There was a steady stream of Swedish immigrants coming to central Kane County in the 1890s, and several of these families settled in Wasco. Local newspaper articles from 1890 state that Campton Township had "good hay weather" all through the summer, with an above-average crop of winter wheat, and a much better cherry harvest than in years past.

In 1892, the largest landowners in the village of Wasco and its immediate surroundings were the Rice, Higgins, Carpenter, Austin, Hagaman, Bergland, and Whitney families. The Wasco Baptist Church was already completed, as were the blacksmith shop and the old Bergland store. There were fewer than ten dwellings in the village that year. In 1893, the Austin family began to subdivide its large landholdings in the northern part of Wasco. A handful of lifelong Wasco residents were born in the new village that year, including Edmund Swanson and Edna Carpenter. Bergland Hall, which used to stand a bit north of the Wasco Church, was likely built in 1893. The Higgins family sold several residential lots in the northwest part of Wasco in 1894, and several houses were built there immediately afterward. The horse stables at the Wasco Church were also thought to have been built that year. Glen W. Bell, George Vanderhoof, and C. W. Millen were all born in or very near Wasco in 1895. Jennie Denker and Paul Waterhouse, although not Waco natives, were born that year as well, and were associated with the village for nearly their whole lives.

The vicinity of Wasco in the year 1892

In 1896, Wasco was described in the *Kane County Directory* as being "a small village, five miles northwest of St. Charles, east of the center of Campton township, on the line of the C. G. W. R. R." containing "a Baptist church, general store, lumber and coal yard, feed mill, U. S. express office, [and a] blacksmith shop." The population of the village was seventy-five. That year, the Baptist church held Sunday services at both 10:30 am and 7:30 pm, with Sunday School at noon. Rev. T. Ketman was the local pastor. He regularly hosted prayer meetings on Fridays. There were fifty-six members of the congregation, which was the only one in Wasco.

In the late 1890s, Wasco was the site of the "Maple Leaf Camp" of the Knights of the Maccabees, a fraternal organization formed in 1878 in London, Ontario. The group met monthly and was known for providing low-cost insurance to its members; certain branches supported society cemeteries. Local members included Chester W. Bolcum and Edward Chaffee (whose name is misspelled "Schaffee" in the directory) as well as more than two dozen others. The group faded greatly in importance and size after the turn of the previous century.

Wasco also boasted a second fraternal organization in the 1890s – namely, Lodge no. 1771 of the Modern Woodmen of America. J. V. Millen and D. W. Stevens were active in this group, which met the second and fourth Saturdays of every month. This organization was founded in Lyons, Iowa, in 1883, and its large membership was spread across twelve states by the early twentieth century. Members were men between the ages of eighteen and forty-five; the Wasco chapter had thirty-three members in 1896.

There were thirteen heads of household living in Wasco in 1896 that were listed in that year's Kane County directory. They were: John W. Bell, an agricultural statistician; George C. Bergland, a dealer in feed, coal, and lumber; A. A. Burr, a carpenter and farmer; Charles E. Hurd, an agent for the Chicago Great Western Railroad and an employee of the U. S. Express Company; Will Johnson, whose occupation was given as "can laundry"; E. P. Lathrop, a partner with George Bergland; C. W. Millen, a carpenter; James C. Rice, postmaster; Ed Selden, a laborer; Charles Simon, a blacksmith; Gus Swanson, a retired farmer; Leonard White, a teamster; and Merrill Whitney, a farmer. Short biographical sketches of most of these men are found later in this work.

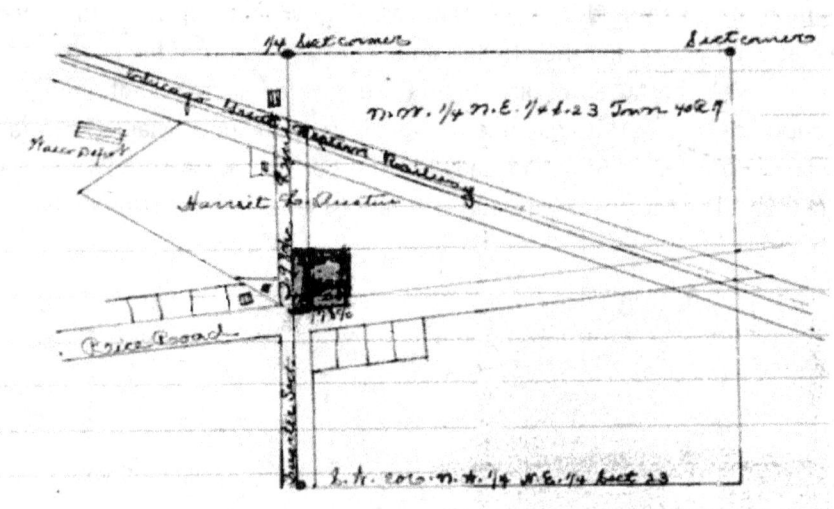

A sketch of Wasco as it appeared in April 1896 – note the Depot, and the lots on the present Route 64 (then known as "Rice Road")

One of these early residents, A. A. Burr, was a carpenter and farmer, and was crucial in Wasco's early history. This pioneer's full name was Algernon A. Burr – he was born in the northwestern part of St. Charles Township on 1 August 1846, just thirteen years after that town's very first permanent settlement. His parents, James and Mary Burr, were natives of New York State, and settled in Kane County in 1837, when the region was still "an unbroken wilderness." Algernon Burr married Cornelia L. Bartlett on 3 October 1872, and they lived in St. Charles through the remainder of that decade, and the 1880s. He and his wife built a "fine home" in Wasco in the mid-1890s; the structure cost $5000 and was considered a very "handsome residence." The home was just west of the Bergland house, which was narrowly saved from destruction during a 1901 fire "by the most heroic efforts on the part of the villagers." Both homes were on the north side of the present Route 64. The Burr house was considered "a very good one for a small town." Sadly, the Burr residence burned to the ground in April 1901. The cause of the fire was not known with certainty, but it was thought to have been started by burglars ransacking the home in the middle of the night.

The Burr family's pioneer log house, built in 1837 or 1838 in St. Charles Township

Burr never rebuilt in Wasco; this fact was considered by contemporaries as a serious loss to the village, which had suffered from several fires in the first years of its existence. Algernon Burr, who barely managed to escape his burning home by means of a ladder raised to a second-story window, later died "while leading a horse at his farm" in St. Charles Township (about two miles east of Wasco) on 23 April 1903.

In April 1897, the Wasco Cemetery Association was formed. Its incorporators were Carrie J. Peterson, Vesta P. Bell, and Isaac Barber. The Association was formally organized on 30 October of the following year, with Vesta Bell being elected its first President. The other founding members of the Wasco Cemetery Association were D. W. Stevens, Carrie Peterson, and Mr. and Mrs. L. Barber.

By the middle of 1899, Wasco area dairy farmers had been suffering from low milk prices for two years. Farmers were profiting under two cents per quart of milk sold, once the costs of washing and steaming their cans and the freight costs of the product were factored in. It then took a dairy of sixty well-managed cows to produce ten cans of milk per day. A "good new milch cow" cost $50 at that time, and farmers were obliged to purchase large quantities of bran "to balance the corn ration which he raises." Milk distributors in Chicago were then making as much money per can of milk as the actual milk producer, and had significantly less capital invested in the enterprise.

The 1900s

Popular social events in Wasco during the first decade of the twentieth century included church picnics, musical events, ice cream socials, recitations, dances, Fraternal gatherings, formal teas, house weddings, housewarming parties, and candy pulls. The first automobiles appeared in the area and a small number of telephones were installed in Wasco homes and businesses during this decade. Roadways throughout the township were being improved in the 1900s, and the Chicago Great Western Railway was operating more than one hundred and fifty miles of track in the state, including the line through Wasco. The consolidation of "country" schools was a regional trend which affected Wasco during the decade of the 1900s; in 1906 three small schools near Wasco were closed and the new school was built in the village.

Members of the Wasco Baptist Church decorated a Christmas tree in December 1902, and there was a masquerade ball held at Bergland Hall, just north of the church, in January 1903. Perhaps not coincidentally, Wasco's pastor spoke on the "anti-saloon subject" later that same month. The Modern Woodmen of America held an oyster supper at Bergland Hall in January 1904, and the same year the White family's fifteenth anniversary party was also held at that venue. All Wasco families received out-of-town visitors on a regular basis, thanks in part to the local train, which had affordable daily passenger service during that era. Many from Wasco attended the farmer's institute at Geneva in February 1905, and locals were active in organizations such as the Christian Endeavor Society, the Modern Woodmen of America, the Woman's Christian Temperance Union, and Wasco Ladies Aid throughout the decade.

Political sentiment in the decade of the 1900s remained (as it had been since the founding of the village) heavily Republican. In the November 1900 election, Campton Township voters cast approximately four-and-a-half times the number of votes for the Republican Presidential and gubernatorial candidates as for their Democratic challengers. In the November 1904 election, in Campton Township, votes for Republican candidates for both local and national office outnumbered those for their Democratic challengers eight-

or even nine-to-one. In the early twentieth century, it was almost unheard of for any Democratic candidate to garner more than sixty votes for any office across the entire township's electorate. Republicans, however, had no difficulty tallying three or four hundred votes in a regular election.

The first "Wasco News" column appeared in the *St. Charles Chronicle* on Friday, 1 March 1901. The very first item in this first column read: "Mrs. Chauncey Agnew is ill." This referred to Mattie A. (Millen) Agnew, who was born in 1881, and who was then just recently married. Mattie Agnew later moved to Ohio, and would live until 1956. Typical items in the column stated who was visiting Chicago, who had relatives in town, who was ill, where the Ladies Aid Society was meeting (Mrs. C. W. Millen's house that week), and which farmers were renting which property (Nels Hawkins moved onto Bergland's farm "near Wasco" that week). The item of perhaps the most interest that week was the fact that several Wasco residents "enjoyed a sleigh ride to Lily Lake" where they attended a WCTU event.

On Sunday, 17 January 1903, a disastrous train accident occurred one mile east of Wasco, on the Great Western Railway. Train No. 5, west-bound, was the one that "took the fatal plunge," resulting in the death of its engineer (Mr. J. D. Leahy) and the injury of many more. The injured "were taken to near by farm houses, where they were cared for" until they could be sent on to their various destinations. The bridge near the site of the accident "was badly wrecked" while the cars "were piled and jumbled into a hopeless wreck." The five men uninjured in the crash succeeded in pulling the passengers through the car windows, and one of them walked the distance to Wasco, telegraphing Sycamore for assistance. Shortly afterward, the injured were brought to hospitals in St. Charles and Sycamore.

Train accident just east of Wasco, in January 1903

Agricultural items continued to take precedence in the Wasco community in the first years of the twentieth century. Many from Wasco attended the Farmers' Institute at Geneva in February 1905, and several Wasco agriculturalists (including members of the Brown, Whitney, Fischer, Vanderhoof, and Lake families) attended the "fat stock shows" in Chicago in late 1904, 1905, and 1906. Many Wasco residents attended the eighth annual Farmers' Institute at Geneva in January 1906. Local dairy herds continued to increase in size. To accommodate this growth, Peter A. Peterson was building a new barn near Wasco in the fall of 1907, and to learn the latest in agrarian innovation, several Wasco families attended Corn Exposition in Chicago that season. Charles O. Johnson began renting the Andrew Peterson farm in February 1908, but bought the former Simon Chaffee farm in March 1909. The Swanson brothers, Frank Vanderhoof, and the Johnson brothers were shipping steers, cattle, and hogs from the Wasco stock yards adjacent to the depot with some frequency. A "good many" from Wasco again attended the Farmers' Institute in Geneva in January 1909.

Miss Kathryn Flinn of Elburn contracted to teach at the Whitney/White School near Wasco for the 1904-1905 school year. In the spring of 1904, members of Wasco Ladies Aid presented a play entitled "Breezy Point" (with thirteen female characters) in Bergland's Hall. It was a "jolly entertainment," and helped the Ladies Aid increase its treasury by the respectable sum of $35. In early April 1905, there was an "old-fashioned spelling school" held at the same venue in Wasco. Attendees were asked to dress appropriately, in 'old-fashioned' clothing. The spelling contest attracted attendees from throughout the township and from adjacent towns as well.

Accidents occurred from time-to-time throughout Wasco's history, and were sometimes linked to unusual weather events. Frank Walker of Campton Township was tragically killed when he was stuck by lightening at 4:30 PM on Wednesday, 29 May 1905. He was harrowing with four horses, three of which were also killed when the bolt struck. Frank Lake, who lived a mile and a half north of Wasco, was stricken unconscious by the same lightening blast, but Lake slowly recovered.

During the 1905-1906 school year, Florence Smith served as the very last teacher at the White schoolhouse just east of Wasco. By then the building had been open for more than fifty years. Smith's instruction there occurred just before the local district was consolidated with those of three other rural schools to form the Wasco School, which opened in the fall of the latter year. Two Wasco students graduated from St. Charles High School in June 1906 – Esther Bolcum and Ellen Mongerson.

Frank Lake, who was struck by lightning in the summer of 1905

Wasco was only the third locality in Illinois to consolidate its schools. This consolidation took place in 1906, and the achievement, which was widely heralded in the local press, was reported to have made Wasco "the envy of rural communities everywhere." The new school meant "better equipment for all" as well as meaning "graduation and the better work that follows it." See "Community Institutions – Wasco School" for more information on this accomplishment.

Railroad incidents and accidents were rather frequent occurrences in the first decade of the new century. The 1903 derailment has already been mentioned, but there was another railroad accident in Wasco during the first week of March 1906. Then, eighteen cars carrying cattle and hogs jumped the track, and were crushed. Livestock was "thrown in every direction," with fatal effect for much of the cargo, and the chaotic scene of the wreck took several days to clear. The following winter, on 5 February 1907, at 10:00 AM, Charles Newberry was hit by the eastbound Chicago Great Western fast passenger train while driving across the railroad tracks in Wasco. He was instantly killed, as was one of his horses. Newberry had just delivered his milk to the Wasco creamery, and was driving home when he was struck. The train itself was fully an hour late, and "came thundering in at terrific speed." Newberry was bundled up because of the severe weather and may not have heard the train until it was too late. The impact left Newberry's wagon "splintered into kindling wood." Charles Newberry was born in Sweden on 22 November 1843, and came to the United States in 1869. His family, which was comprised his wife and three children, owned the old Muller farm a mile north of Wasco. One of his daughters, Esther Newberry, was then a teacher in St. Charles.

Advertisement for the Chicago Great Western from the St. Charles Chronicle, June 1906

Two short-lived social groups meeting in Wasco in 1907 were the "China club," hosted by Mrs. C. W. [Cassie] Bolcum, and the Social Circle, hosted by Mr. and Mrs. Charles Ekstrom. A very popular social event that year was 'Buffalo Bill's Wild West Show,' which was held in Aurora in August, drawing many Wasco citizens of all ages. Another popular regional event that fall was the Chautauqua conference (also held in Aurora) which was attended by the Browns, Millens, Fischers, and Bolcums, among others. The Campton Township Sunday School convention was held at the Wasco Church that month as well.

A very unusual Wasco social event took place at the Wasco Church on 23 August 1907, and seems to have been repeated for several years afterward. This was the so-called "Hard Tymes" party, which (in 1907 at least) featured brown bread, beans, ham sandwiches, pickles, cottage cheese, ginger bread, coffee, and donuts. The front-page article advertising the event in the *St. Charles Chronicle* was intentionally misspelled, with such instructions as: "every woman that kums must ware a calaker dres an apern, both well patched," and "You alls and yourn friends are axed tew a soshul that the A. B. C.'s of the Wasco Aid society air goin to hav."

A rare photograph of a Wasco "Hard Tymes" party - this one took place in 1911

In other matters of local interest, Florence Anderson was taking a business course in Elgin and Mrs. Fred Swanson was visiting her parents in Aurora in 1908. In May of that year, the high school students of Wasco, "assisted by the Wasco orchestra," presented a play entitled "Al Martin's Country Store." Mildred Swanson was confirmed that month as well, and Fred Lake returned from his honeymoon in Niagara Falls. In the summer of 1908, Olive Bolcum undertook an "extended visit in the east." She was one of the eight daughters of C. W. and Cassie Bolcum. Aunt Bessie Bolcum accompanied Olive for some of the trip. Several Wasco residents again visited "Buffalo Bill's Wild West Show" when it came to Elgin that season. Frank Chaffee celebrated his thirty-first birthday in August. A. J. Mongerson had a silo built that autumn, and William Wanzer of Chicago made several trips to Wasco on business then. With his wife, Rev. D. M. Hand of the Wasco Baptist Church offered a reception to honor their fifth wedding anniversary that July. Cake and ice cream were served, and the church choir presented them with a souvenir spoon that evening (as well as a song composed in their honor). There was a Republican rally held in Bergland's Hall in late October, with music by the "Wasco band." The Wasco Baptist church offered a Halloween social, and Old Neighbors' Day was well-attended, despite the rain. Mrs. E. Hagaman relocated to her winter home in Chicago, and Gust Malmberg took on a new position at the Wanzer Creamery. The Modern Woodmen of America and the History Club remained popular social organizations in the village.

Between 1907 and 1909, active members of the Wasco Ladies Aid included Nettie Anderson (elected President of that organization in 1908, and re-elected in 1909), Mrs. J. W. Bell (Vice-President during the same period), Mrs. H. S. Higgins (Secretary and Treasurer), Mrs. N. L. Carpenter (Chairman of the Work Committee), Mrs. George Bergland, Mrs. B. F. Lake, Mrs. C. W. Millen, Mrs. H. S. Higgins, Mrs. L. White, Mrs. Fred Swanson, Mrs. C. J. Waterhouse, Mrs. Merrill Whitney, Mrs. J. I. Ellsworth, and Mrs. F. Vanderhoof. They met every other week for much of the year, most often at the Baptist Church. Mrs. Millen was elected Chairman of the Sewing Committee in January 1909.

Nettie Anderson was caring for Harry Carlson at her home in 1909, and R. V. Austin (who was living in the Rice residence) resumed his former position at the local creamery. Andrew Erickson had visitors from Rockford, and the Millen family entertained relatives from St. Charles. Fred Swanson and his wife spent Christmas with relatives in Aurora. The Woman's Christian Temperance Union had broad local support, and met frequently at the Wasco Baptist Church, as well as in private homes. The Wasco Mothers' Club was also active then, and they occasionally met in homes of the Millen, McGowan, or Brown families (see "Important Social Organizations" for further information).

In April 1909, members of the Wasco Ladies Aid performed a play entitled "Mrs. Briggs of the Poultry Yard." This was a comedy in three acts, which was written in 1905. The title character, "a woman of business," was played by Emma White. Her family members were played by: Elmer Peterson, Floyd Bergland, Evelyn Whitney, and Grace Vanderhoof. Silas Green was played by C. J. Waterhouse, and Mr. Lee, "a wealthy neighbor," was played by George Chrystal. Genevieve Coy played Genevieve Lee, his daughter, and Alberta Thurber played "Mrs. O'Connor, with no liking for goats." Selma Meager, in the role of Daisy Thornton, rounded out the cast. The Wasco orchestra furnished the music.

In 1909, Nathan H. Warren, a Wasco dairy farmer, wrote two fascinating letters which were printed in the *Chicago Tribune*. He stated firmly that any dairyman who did not thoroughly clean his stable on a daily

Nathan H. Warren, Wasco dairy farmer, as he appeared in 1904

basis, and provide his cows with a fresh bed of clean straw "should be driven out of the business." There was a public outcry at the time about the poor conditions of some dairies in Kane and DuPage Counties, but Mr. Warren wanted to stand up for his Campton Township neighbors, who kept clean facilities. He wrote of the dairy cow's intelligence, and contended that "at the risk of being considered weak in the upper story for the belief, I think very many of them seem to try to give as much milk as possible, because they think it pleases their caretaker, who does so much for their comfort." Warren also stated the known benefits of milk for the physical development of children, and his hope that they could be "supplied with pure, healthful milk, and at a moderate price."

Although many dairy farmers refused to sign the rate agreement offered by the Chicago Milk Dealers' Association in the autumn of 1909 (more than sixty farmers in St. Charles refused to accept the prices, for example, which they considered far too low), those at Wasco almost all agreed to renew their contracts. The Kee & Chappel Company "renewed [milk] contracts with practically all of its old connections" in Wasco at that time. In the first decade of the twentieth century, quite a few farmers founded local butter factories as alternative outlets for their milk, since sales to the Chicago market were still scarcely (at best) earning a profit.

The 1910s

The second decade of the twentieth century was one of great significance for Wasco. The local school and church were well-established by this time, and several businesses thrived in the village. Milk production remained high and the railroad's milk train meant reliable access to a vast market of consumers for all local farmers. The first garages appeared in the area in the 1910s as automobiles became more and more common, and farming methods began to shift toward more mechanized production. Beginning in 1915, immediately following the passage of the "Registration of Farm Names Act" by the Illinois legislature, dozens of farms in the Wasco area were named by their owners, and these names were registered with both the county and the state. Farms immediately surrounding Wasco were given names such as Daniel Whitney's "Pleasant Knoll Farm," or Frank Brown's "Woodside Farm." The First World War, fought during this decade, impacted Wasco as much as any other similar-sized community, and many of its citizens enlisted or were conscripted into the armed forces in 1917 and 1918. Local residents contributed to the war effort by purchasing "War Stamps" and bonds or by volunteering with the Red Cross. Electricity began to be installed in a handful of Wasco homes that decade, although the vast majority of dwellings remained without power for another decade or more.

The first notable event in Wasco in the 1910s was the funeral of Harry Carlson, just a few days into January in the first year of that decade. Carlson had lived with Nettie Anderson, and the funeral was conducted from her home. Harry was just twenty-five years old, and had been in the United States for five years. Two of his brothers, Christ and Ollie Carlson, were also living in Wasco. Harry Carlson had passed away after fifteen months "of severe suffering."

A handful of Wasco residents purchased automobiles in the summer of 1910, including C. W. Bolcum, and the Johnson brothers. One of the closest automobile sales shops to Wasco was run by Ekdahl & Skoglund of Geneva, and may have supplied the vehicles to many of the early Wasco purchasers. Not all new purchases of modes of transportation were of the mechanized variety, however, for the "Wasco News Items" column in the *St. Charles Chronicle* from June 1910 also notes that Elmer Ekstrom acquired a new Shetland pony! Wasco residents graduating from St. Charles High School that month were Gertrude Ethel Bolcum, Myrtle Jane Bolcum, and Floyd H. Bergland. Those graduating from "the Consolidated School here" (Wasco School) were Mildred Swanson and Selma Meager. Those graduating from Wasco School had completed tenth grade, while those graduating from St. Charles had completed twelfth. Gertrude Bolcum, mentioned here, followed a career in education, and even ran her own school for a time. Those familiar with the family may recall that Gertrude's sister Myrtle became a well-known golfer, and married Lester Shrader.

Entertainment for Wasco residents was not hard to find. A series of barn dances were held at the B. F. Lake farm near Wasco during the summer of 1913. The dances were run by George Chrystal of Campton Township, and occurred several times that season. In October 1913, the "Old Neighbors Day" festival in Wasco drew nearly two hundred people. Nettie Anderson was the presiding officer, and the day was billed as "the annual harvest home event." Many attendees came from St. Charles, Batavia, Geneva, Aurora, and DeKalb, though most were from Wasco and Campton Township. Rev. Hartman of the Wasco Baptist Church gave the invocation at 11:00 AM, followed by a musical selection featuring Harry Burr on violin, Zilpha Brown on piano, and her husband Bert Brown on cornet. This was followed by a recitation from Charles Dickens by Mrs. Arthur [Zoe] Bolcum, and children's stories by Clara Powell. Other events included Daniel Whitney playing "The Virginia Reel" on his violin, and songs by N. H. Warren. Warren and Whitney had been known for their music since the 1860s, when they performed at various local dances and political events. Dinner at the conclusion of the day was "composed of all the good things those Wasco women are famous at preparing."

Several Wasco farmers attended a plowing match in Big Rock in the fall of 1913. That season, a four-foot-wide cement sidewalk was under construction in Wasco, which was staunchly promoted by the Young People's Christian Association of the Wasco Baptist Church. The walkway ran from the church to the depot. Unusually for that time, not one but three Wasco boys (Norvid Swanson, George Vanderhoof, and Floyd Bergland) were attending the University of Illinois that fall.

Although by means of near-constant effort most area farmers earned a (nominally) profitable living, they faced constant obstacles in their path, including periodic sickness in their livestock. There was an outbreak of hoof and mouth disease in the Wasco area in between December 1914 and February 1915, which hurt many in the area. The initial local quarantine, which was the preferred method of fighting the disease, was placed upon the Carlson farm one mile east of Wasco when forty head of cattle were found to be afflicted. Within two months, local farmer E. H. Allen had thirty-three cattle and eight hogs infected, which together were valued at over $2400. Gust F. Carlson had forty-three ill cattle, while W. J. Close was most negatively impacted. He had fifty-six cattle and twenty-two hogs stricken by the disease; the animals' value was estimated to be $3332.45.

Food crops fared better than livestock that year. During the summer of 1915, three young Wasco-area farmers were praised for producing one-hundred-and-thirteen and one-hundred-and-fifteen bushels of corn per acre on their farms. These young men were Lawrence McGowan, Harold McGowan, and Earl Johnson. The boys were honored for "their splendid achievement" by the Top-Notch Farmers' Club of Illinois. Most young farmers still found time for both school and fun. In May 1915, the graduating class of Wasco high school had a social at the William Osborne home, on the Isaac Mongerson farm southeast of the village. Girls attending the function were "requested to bring two caps that match and lunch for two."

On Memorial Day, 1915, N. H. Warren, mentioned earlier, gave an "excellent address" to the veterans gathered at Lily Lake. After returning to his son's home near Wasco, Mr. Warren passed away a few hours later, at the age of eighty-seven. He was survived by a widow, two sons, and three daughters. N. H. Warren's body was taken to Hinsdale for burial.

The people of Wasco put on a country fair on 26 August 1915. There were exhibits of poultry, farm products, fruits, jellies, and "a lot of needle work." A musical program took place that evening, following a supper from 6:00 to 9:00 PM. In October 1915, many Wasco residents attended the eleventh annual ball hosted by the Elburn Fire Department. Just prior to the dance, the ladies of St. Gall parish "served a delicious supper to fully two hundred well pleased patrons."

Grace Vanderhoof with Roy McGowan (the small boy) and an unnamed gentleman, about 1913. The photo was taken on the present Old LaFox Road, looking north. Nettie Anderson's house and barn are visible at left, and the edge of the old Bergland store is also visible behind the man's shoulder

Florence (Bergland) Peterson wrote in her sketch of Wasco that in 1917, a "terrible cyclone swept up the west side of Fox River Valley, shearing off the tree tops and homes, causing many deaths in Elgin. The Silver Glen school was leveled." The year 1917, sadly, was one of both natural and manmade disasters.

In August 1917, the first soldiers from Wasco were called up for service in the U. S. Army to fight in the First World War, which had begun in Europe three years earlier. Those living in the village at the time of the draft, who were not exempted from conscription, were: George L. Vanderhoof, Frank F. Anderson, Frank Richmond, and Hugo Denker. Those Wasco men who were examined for inclusion into the military reserves were: Oscar Soderquist, Alvie Austin, Andrew Johnson, and John Lind.

In December 1917, eighteen local women volunteered at the Wasco branch of the Red Cross to help the war effort. The women worked "at the gauze tables, and two sewing machines were kept busy." Some photographs were shown at the meeting, including some taken by J. H. Burr "the morning Lieut. Floyd Bergland left for American Lake, Wash." One of the photos, and the only one known, is shown below.

Floyd H. Bergland was commissioned 2nd Lieutenant in the Corps of Cadets while attending the University of Illinois. He was commissioned at a similar rank on 15 August 1917, with the Officer Reserve Corps of the U. S. Army. Bergland was made a First Lieutenant in the U. S. Army itself on 24 August 1918. When he left Wasco for Camp Lewis, in Washington State, the farewell event at the Wasco depot was very largely attended.

Floyd Bergland is in uniform, left of center, with his sister Florence and their mother beside them. The building in the background is the Wasco Depot, and the year of the photograph was 1917

The 1918 *Prairie Farmer's Reliable Directory of Farmers and Breeders* for Kane County listed businesses in each county village. There were three listed for Wasco: Bergland & Company (general store, coal, & mill feeds); Andrew Erickson (blacksmith shop); and Elmer T. Peterson (implements store). A handful of Wasco residents owned automobiles at the time. These included: John Coombes, who owned a Saxon; Robert M. Corron, who owned a Briscoe; Fred Ekstrom, who owned an Empire; Otto Ekstrom, who owned a Ford;

Peter Holmquist, who owned a Studebaker; Alex Johnson, who owned a Ford; Charles O. Johnson, who owned a Buick; Solomon Johnson, who owned a Ford; Jacob Kaiser, who owned a Rumley; Alfred Peterson, who owned an Empire; Carl Peterson, who owned a Ford; P. A. Peterson, who owned an Overland; L. S. Richmond, who owned an Overland; Roy C. Sharp, who owned a Briscoe, and Frank Vanderhoof, who owned a Saxon.

Fundraising efforts for the Great War were at a height in the year 1918. An article from the *Elburn Herald* from May of that year asserted that the Wasco Red Cross was attempting to raise $175 (while the much-larger chapter in Batavia had $4000 as it goal). Those advocating for the fundraising wrote that "we must forget our halves and dollars, and think in fives, tens and up. Don't get the idea into your mind that this is begging. It is the greatest opportunity for the expression of service and patriotism the world has ever known."

In June 1918, fourteen enlisted men in and around Wasco were given a farewell party, under the auspices of the women of the G. A. R. and the women of the Red Cross. Each of the men had been recently drafted, and were being sent to Camp Grant, near Rockford, for training. The local men were: C. O. Littlejohn (formerly a teacher); Arthur Larson; Glen Bell; John Duddridge; Joe Bagge; Carl Carlson; Bert Holmquist; Joseph Ekstrom; Albert Johnson; Andrew Johnson; Rudolph Mongerson; Charles Hempt; Charles Hedberg; and Frank Jenson.

Camp Grant, near Rockford, where many Wasco men trained during World War I

The roads leading westward from Wasco were improved during the fall of 1918, not long after these men left for their training. Just prior to the road work, a $6000 bond issue was approved for the road machinery required to accomplish the longed-for and much-needed improvements.

Like any other industry, agriculture continued to evolve throughout the early twentieth century. In the late 1910s, some of the popular brands of livestock on the farms around Wasco were Polled Durham cattle, Holstein cattle, Dorset sheep, Poland China pigs, Duroc pigs, and White Wyandotte and Speckled Sussex chickens. Jersey and Brown Swiss cattle became more popular locally in the 1920s and later. Farming also continued to mechanize. A typical farm auction held in the Wasco area in the 1910s had the following items for sale, in addition to livestock: a McCormick corn harvester, a grain binder, a Champion mower, a steel hay rake, a Clean Sweep hay loader, a Corn King manure spreader, a Deere riding plow, a walking plow, two corn cultivators, a two-row cultivator, a four-horse pulverizer, a grain drill, a corn planter, a harrow, a gang plow, a fanning mill, a lumber wagon, a three-spring wagon, a double-seated surrey, a light wagon, three heavy harnesses, thirty milk cans, a milk cart, five hundred bushels of oats, barley, corn, hay, silage, straw, oak fence posts, strainers, tools, and miscellaneous small tools and other articles.

Many Wasco farmers attended F. A. Read's farm auctions in the 1910s. One popular auction (held in Lily Lake) in February 1919 featured named herd boars, and the names the area farmers chose for the animals helps illustrate the agriculturalists' creativity and even humor. Some of the boars at that particular auction included 'Great Big Ben' (son of Big Ben), 'Smooth Bob' (third-prize junior yearling of 1918), 'Great Mastodon' (son of Model Mastodon), 'Model Bob Jones' (son of Leonard's Big Jones) and 'Long King Joe.'

The 1920s

The decade of the 1920s was a difficult one for most American farmers. An agricultural depression impacted rural communities of all sizes during the years preceding the much more well-known Great Depression, and Wasco suffered noticeably in this era. In most cases, the entire span of the 1920s was one of struggle for the Midwestern farmer, and although individuals in Kane County and the surrounding area survived and even thrived, success and high prices for farm products were not easy to achieve. Businesses continued to function in Wasco during the decade, but those more closely linked to farming struggled. To make matters worse, a typhoid fever epidemic struck Wasco in the fall of 1921, resulting in the death of at least three area residents, and the sickness of far more. By the summer of 1924 there was significant financial trouble throughout Campton Township, including in Wasco. A proposal to raise additional revenue for local projects was voiced by Wasco-area farmer Frank W. Hagaman, but the motion failed. Supervisor (and Wasco resident) Elmer T. Peterson reported that anyone owed money by the town for work already performed should "wait . . . until there should be sufficient money in the treasury" before requesting payment. Very little building was done in Wasco in the 1920s, although existing structures were updated and maintained. Social organizations during this era, however, continued to thrive.

One of the numerous social organizations meeting in Wasco throughout the 1920s was the "Helping Hand Club," sometimes known as the Helping Hand Society. Thirty members of the Wasco Helping Hands went to Geneva for a picnic in September 1920. Later that month, several citizens from Wasco attended the "Cow Testing Association Picnic" held in Pottawatomie Park, St. Charles. The short-lived "Teen Age Club" met at Verner Bowgren's house in July 1923. Organizations such as the Pollyanna Club, the Glad Game Club, the WCTU, and the Wasco Ladies Aid were each popular during that decade as well.

During the last week of August 1920, Carl Oscar Peterson of Wasco (who lived on the Nettie Anderson farm just west of the village) married "Mrs. Johnson, his housekeeper." Peterson's bride, who was briefly something of a local 'celebrity,' was "one of the few survivors" of the 1912 *Titanic* disaster, according to a contemporary article in the *Elburn Herald*. Her full name was Alice V. (Backberg) Johnson, and she lived on Sixth Avenue in St. Charles in 1910. Mrs. Johnson was indeed aboard the *Titanic* in April 1912, and she and her two children were thought to have escaped using one of the aft starboard lifeboats. After recovering in St. Luke's Hospital in New York, Alice returned to St. Charles. Her husband Oscar died there on 31 October 1917. Carl Peterson was born in Kungsbaka, Sweden, on 28 March 1885, and came to the U. S. in 1902. He worked for the Vanderhoof family on their farm just north of Wasco in 1910. The Petersons moved to DuPage County the spring of 1927.

Alice Johnson and her children, who survived the 1912 Titanic sinking. Mrs. Johnson married a Wasco man in 1920

Regional farming troubles were already quite evident in 1921. That January, members of the Kane County Farm Advisors met with concerned citizens at seven locations, including the Bergland Store in Wasco, "to talk over their problems" and to assist locals in filling out income tax forms. The same year saw many other changes locally, most for the worse. Esther Johnson, a long-time teacher at Wasco School, resigned early in 1921 due to ill health. She would later come back to teaching, though, benefitting many. Local farmer John Larson left the area then, and moved with his family to Marshalltown, Iowa, where he rented a farm.

Team sports had been gaining popularity with the local youth since the late 1880s, with baseball being the most played and followed in the Wasco area (see "Local Sports"). Local basketball, though it would never match baseball's following, enjoyed a spike in popularity in the post-World War I years. By 1921, there were not one but two basketball teams in Wasco. One was the "High school basket ball team" and the other was the "Independent team." Both teams traveled to Maple Park that February, but were soundly defeated.

The road through Wasco which is now known as Route 64 received the earliest version of its current name in 1924. The roadway was then designated "State aid route 64." This name referred to the sequential number of the state-issued bond series designated to pay for the road's improvement. The route has commonly been known as Route 64 since that time.

In 1924, *the Kane County Rural and Business Directory* listed the following individuals, together with their occupations (when given), as residents of Wasco: Miss Frances Anderson (saleslady); Miss Nettie G. Anderson (Member Board of Education); Alvie C. Austin (trainman) and wife Ethel; Mrs. H. L. Austin; Floyd H. Bergland (Bergland & Company); Mrs. Louise Bergland; Wilmer Besser; George I. Brown (President, Board of Education) and wife Lottie; Gertrude Byerhoff (teacher); Miss Edna Carpenter; Mrs. Emma Carpenter; John Coombs (general work) and wife Annie; Marshall Carlson (painter and paper hanger); Albert Eddy (farm hand); Charles M. Eddy (farmer) and wife Mary; Miss Gertrude V. Eddy (student); Miss Harriet M. Eddy (teacher); Andrew J. Erickson (blacksmith); Andrew Erickson (blacksmith) and wife Grace; Miss Bertha Hawkins (student); Joy Hawkins (farmer); Nels Hawkins (farmer); Mrs. Martha C. Higgins; William A. Hill (painter and paper hanger) and wife Anna; Miss Ruth M. Isaacson; Alex Johnson (farmer) and wife Ellen; Elmer Johnson (general work) and wife Mildred; Mrs. Marie Johnson; Solomon Johnson (farmer and member, Board of Education) and wife Fern; Thomas Langrill (cement worker); Anders G.

Lofgren (retired farmer) and wife Johanna C. Most of these citizens listed here are mentioned at various points throughout this work.

Also in Wasco that year were: Arnold G. Mather (implement dealer) and wife Grace; Lawrence McGowan (garage); Mrs. Sarah McGowan; Mrs. Augusta Meissner; C. W. Millen (carpenter) and wife Mary; Andrew Mongerson (retired farmer) and wife Augusta; Isaac Mongerson (retired) and wife Mary; Elmer T. and Florence Peterson (store); Mrs. Rachel C. Probert; Miss Lotten Swanberg; D. W. Stevens (farmer, Township Assessor, and Justice of the Peace); Claus Swanson (retired farmer) and his wife Emma C.; Charles J. Swanson (retired farmer); Ed Swanson (creamery); Fred Swanson (farm hand) and wife Carrie; Harry Travis (garage); Paul Waterhouse (station agent) and wife Ethel M.; John Wessberg (carpenter) and wife Alma; Walter H. Wheadon (painter) and wife Nealy B.; Leonard White (carpenter) and wife Emma; Merrill Whitney (painter); and Morris Whitney (student).

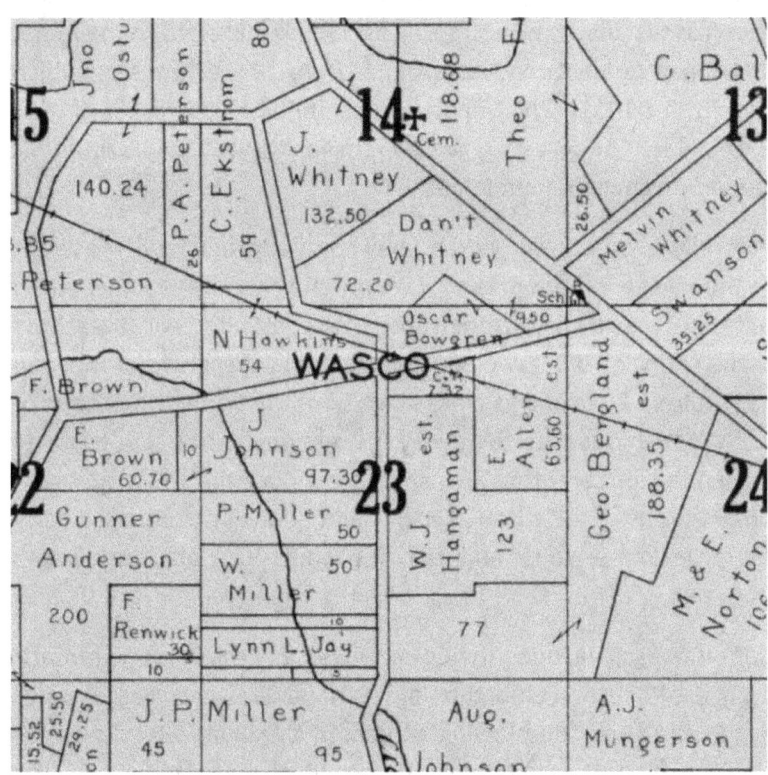

Landowners in the vicinity of Wasco, 1927

In 1927, there were some two dozen farms within a mile of the center of Wasco. The farms' owners were members of the Allen, Anderson, Bergland, Bolcum, Bowgren, Brown, Ekstrom, Fisher, Hagaman, Hawkins, Jay, Johnson, Miller, Norton, Oslund, Peterson, Renwick, Swanson, and Whitney families.

Throughout most of the twentieth century, farmers in Wasco would often begin harvesting corn in late September and would continue the harvest during the first weeks of October. Spring oats would precede corn and would be harvested typically in late July and early August. Winter wheat (so named because of its having been planted in October, before the onset of winter) was being actively harvested in the Wasco area in early July. For decades, many Wasco residents fondly remembered the noon meals prepared by local wives and mothers at the time of the grain harvests – the early afternoon "dinner" (evening meals were referred to as supper) would often consist of ham, chicken, beef, potatoes, various vegetables, pies and cakes for dessert, with coffee, water, or milk to drink. Neighbors would often help one another at harvest time, and a collaborative atmosphere was prevalent.

The decade of the 1920s, which was a time of difficulty for most Wasco residents, did not end well. In mid-March 1929, a severe windstorm did "considerable damage in and around Wasco." Those few Wasco residents with investments lost much when the New York stock market crashed in October of that year. This event, of course, heralded the beginning of the Great Depression, which impacted every Wasco resident without exception.

The 1930s

In the early 1930s, Wasco children enjoyed exploring the swampland on the Solomon Johnson farm south of Route 64, and playing in the large gravel pit at the corner of Old Burlington and Bolcum Roads. They spent time tossing horseshoes behind Nettie Anderson's house, or watching Paul Waterhouse tap messages on his telegraph key at the depot. They loved playing on the Wasco School playground or in one another's yards. During the summer, young boys in Wasco often went fishing in Ferson Creek, and in the winter many of the boys and girls went sledding. They often gathered to watch Andrew Erickson shape horseshoes and metal implements at his local blacksmith shop. Most families listened to the radio, actively following such programs as Little Orphan Annie (broadcast from 1930 to 1942), Tom Mix (which debuted in 1933), Jack Armstrong (from 1933 to 1951), The Shadow radio series (1937 to 1954), and Captain Midnight (which ran from 1938 to 1948). On occasion, Wasco families would take a trip to St. Charles to see a movie at the Arcada Theater, which opened in 1926.

In the 1930s, as in previous decades, literally everyone in Wasco knew one another, and most felt comfortable visiting the other houses in the village unannounced. Everyone in the village knew when someone was sick or in need of help, and there was a very strong sense of community. Local teachers were widely respected and even loved. In the spring of 1933, two popular Wasco teachers (Esther Johnson and Harriet Eddy) attended a teachers' institute in Elburn, and were always improving their methods of instruction. Because this decade is almost synonymous with the Great Depression, quite a lot of money was placed into the "Pauper Fund" by the leaders of Campton Township throughout the 1930s, in order to support the town's poor. Part of the money was raised through a special road tax implemented early in the Depression. The fund was created in December 1931, and its first payouts took place that same month.

In 1930, the most active social organizations in Wasco included the Community Club, the Wasco Dramatic Club, the Home Bureau, the Glad Game Club, the Pollyanna Club, the Helping Hand Club, and Wasco Ladies Aid. Several local families traveled to Big Rock to see the plowing contest in October 1930. The next month, there was a free "cooking school" given at the Wasco Baptist Church, which was often called "the Community church" during the Depression. The Wasco teachers were entertained at a pancake supper that month as well; this event was hosted by Mr. and Mrs. L. E. Wickizer. During the summers of 1930 and 1931, the Wasco baseball team played most of their games on the "Brown diamond" at The Farm. During the summer months in the early years of the Depression some of the teachers at Wasco School held other jobs. Gertrude Eddy, for example, worked at the A & P store in St. Charles in 1931.

Eric Olson built a new barn on the John Whitney farm in the summer of 1932. Just a few months before, the 1840s "Old Red School House" burned down south of Wasco. It had been moved to the George Eddy farm (later the Lynn Jay farm) following the 1906 school consolidation. "Home" Baseball games continued to be played that season on the Brown diamond, but the Wasco players traveled to Kaneville, Virgil, Aurora, Elburn, LaFox, Plano, Nelson Lake, St. Charles, and many other locations for their "away" games. The Wasco School play that year was "Beads on a String," and in May an ambitious "Spring Music Festival" was held at the school. Many cases of influenza hit Wasco in December 1932, affecting the Wickizer, Richmond, Mongerson, Johnson, McGowan, and Barber families, among others. Just six months earlier, dozens of cases of the measles were found in and around Wasco.

Between July 1933 and September 1935, tens of thousands of businesses across the nation displayed the National Recovery Administration's Blue Eagle symbol in their windows to show their compliance with the National Industrial Recovery Act specifically, and with President Roosevelt's New Deal program more generally. The Mather Service Station in Wasco was one of a number of local businesses to do so. In the 1930s, the daily routine of local farmers was also shifting. By late in the decade, trucks had largely replaced the daily trains which delivered milk to Chicago. These milk trains had been picking up their namesake product in Wasco since the 1880s. Although the trucks transported the milk to the same locations, the prices farmers were paid for the milk did not always even meet expenses. In the 1930s, some local farmers began raising more cash crops instead of dairy cows, and the number of dairy farms in the township, though not yet declining, would no longer see increases over a long period. Political events also contributed to this shift in focus.

In the fall of 1935, during the depths of the Depression, many dairy farmers in northern Illinois, including many in and near Wasco, participated in a picket whose aim was to increase milk prices. Large amounts of milk (nearly 70,000 gallons) were kept from the market in early October of that year. Picket lines were "thrown across roadways and around the country depots of large Chicago dairy companies" while over thirty thousand gallons of milk were dumped on the ground to call attention to the extremely low prices farmers were then receiving for their dairy products. Most of the farmers participating were members of the Pure Milk Association, and the Bowman Dairy Company was particularly affected.

On a much less confrontational note, the Centennial Queen contest took place in July 1935, to commemorate the one hundredth anniversary of the permanent settlement of Campton Township. A memorable series of events took place then, including the dedication of an historic boulder, softball and baseball games, an evening dance, the singing of patriotic songs, an oral history of the township, airplane and parachute stunts, the scattering of five thousand pennies for the children, and a large parade. The Centennial Queen herself, Gladys Bowgren, was a Wasco resident. Other contestants were also Wasco residents, including Jewel Brown, Faith Austin, and Irma Erickson. One side of the township's float read "Campton – the Hub of Kane County," due to the township's central location.

The Centennial Queen float, in July 1935

Frances Johnson, contestant for Centennial Queen, with her attendants Ruth Anderson (left) and Virginia Richmond, 1935

Bonnie Bergland, outside the Bergland playhouse (featured in the 1935 Centennial parade)

A series of massive snowstorms struck the Wasco area in February 1936. School was cancelled, no milk was shipped because all roads were blocked, and some cars became stuck for several days at a time. Many feet of snow fell in a matter of days, and many Wasco families became stranded in their homes. Even snow plows were temporarily immobilized, so teams of young men (working in shifts around the clock) were enlisted to clear paths for the plows. Reports in local newspapers called the storms "heavy and unusual," with one storm that month called "the most severe within the recollection of most inhabitants." Many Wasco-area homes were filled with stranded motorists, and snow drifts frequently reached over ten feet in height.

As they had from the beginning of the line, harrowing accidents continued to occur in the vicinity of the railroad crossing in Wasco. In May 1936, Mr. and Mrs. John L. Benson and their daughter Eleanor (age ten) of Wasco narrowly escaped death "when a Chicago and Great Western passenger train struck their auto in the village." The Bensons were treated for cuts and bruises, but survived the accident.

Mary's Nell of Foxwood Farm - a grand champion in the mid-1930s

Local farmers continued to take pride in their herds in the 1930s and engaged in friendly competition with other dairymen across the state. In 1937, Mary's Nell of Foxwood Farm (a Brown Swiss cow) near Wasco had her butterfat record broken. Mary's Nell had produced 1109 pounds of butterfat in a single year, but was surpassed by Illini Nellie, a cow in the University of Illinois herd at Urbana.

Several Wasco citizens attended enjoyable regional events such as the WLS Barn Dance in West Chicago in April 1937, or farmers' exhibitions in Cook or DuPage Counties. The Farm, just west of Wasco, drew tremendous crowds during its motorcycle and automobile races held in the 1930s (see "Significant Institutions & Places of Business").

In December 1937, the Wasco Home Bureau gave one presentation on family photographs and another on "Food Cookery." Tomato rarebit was prepared by Della Scott, and a light lunch was served after the lessons. The previous month, the "Wasco Girls Club" gave a bridal shower for Helen Jay at the home of Gladys Bowgren. Miss Jay was "to be married soon." On 29 May 1938, the Baccalaureate services for that year's graduating class from Wasco School were held in the church. Rev. Arthur Enquist delivered the address to the assembled crowd. Later that year, Mrs. Louise Bergland, "venerable octogenarian of Wasco," whose family was among the first to settle in the village, died as the result of a fall.

In September 1939, farmers met at Wasco for the 2nd annual Kane County Milk Day. "Free milk, chocolate or white" was given to all who attended. The event was held at The Farm, one mile west of Wasco, and was sponsored by the Pure Milk Association. There were games and contests all day, with $1000 in prizes split among the winners.

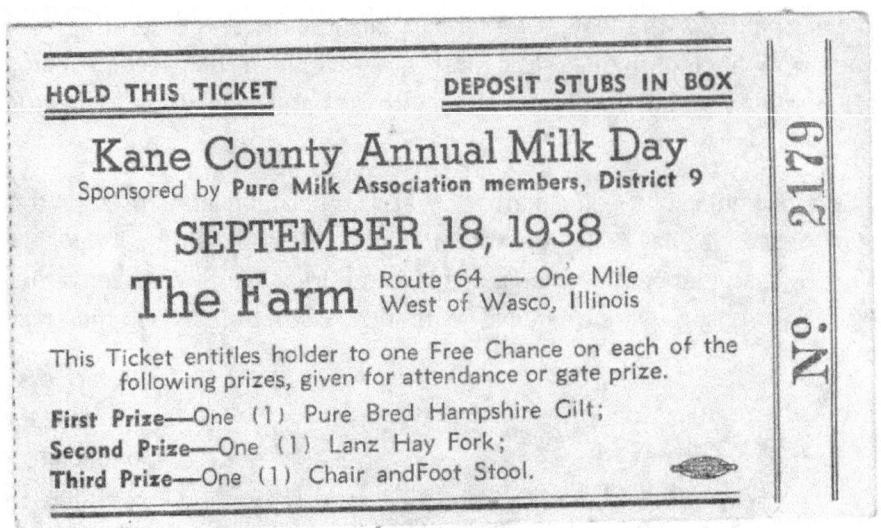

Ticket from the First Annual Milk Day, 1938

The 1940s

All areas of life American during the first half of the 1940s were of course dominated to a greater or lesser extent by the events of the Second World War. This fact was as true in Wasco as it was in any other American community which might be considered. During this era, local citizens both enlisted in the armed services and volunteered from home to support the war effort. Scores of Wasco women filled out "enrollment for Civilian Defense Duty" cards beginning in December 1941, and local young men flocked to Kane County enlistment offices. Local men and women purchased war bonds and raised or prepared food to help the war and those enlisted men fighting to win it. During the war years, Wasco citizens used ration coupons just like their fellow citizens across the nation. Pro-war cartoons and editorials were ubiquitous in local newspapers, and events such as a statewide blackout in June 1943 achieved 100% compliance. Life "at home on the farm" continued as before, however, and the Wasco area remained primarily agricultural. As in the previous two decades, little new construction took place in the village during the 1940s. Before the decade was over, though, Wasco saw a wave of marriages take place, and a new generation of postwar children soon came along to swell the local population.

In September 1940, more than a year before the United States entered the war, several Wasco farmers participated in the annual Lily Lake plowing match. A horse team driven by Oliver Anderson of Wasco won the light weight pulling contest, moving 4500 pounds twenty-four feet. Plowing matches at Lily Lake had been going on for years, but ceased altogether by the war's end.

The Wasco Baptist Church celebrated its fiftieth anniversary in October 1941. The event was observed with the "ringing of the new bell which weighs 700 pounds and which was placed in the belfry by willing hands about the community." Rev. Wickenden, who was the pastor of the church in 1920, came back to the area for the occasion, and gave the sermon at the celebration. A quartet consisting of Gertrude Eddy, Ruth Perch, Frank Bolwahnn, and Morris Whitney sang at the event.

During World War II, an "Honor Board" was erected at the corner of LaFox Road and Route 64 in Wasco. It listed all the men and women serving in the Armed Forces from Campton Township. As was true nationally, local families with someone in the various branches of the military would display a small flag in their front window indicating their loved one's service. These flags had blue stars in a white field, with a red border, and gold fringe across the bottom.

During the war years (1941-1945) gasoline, rubber tires, shoes, sugar meat, and many other items were rationed. It was common for families to save newspapers, tin cans, watermelon rinds, and other items. Most local residents planted Victory Gardens, which often included tomatoes, potatoes, green beans, peas, sweet corn, carrots, beets, and more. The vegetables grown in these gardens would be eaten or canned for use during the winter months. To finance the war, savings bonds were sold in various denominations. Savings stamps were sold to school children; those students purchasing the stamps would paste them into a book until the booklet was complete. These books could then be taken to banks and exchanged for a savings bond.

Due to gasoline rationing, automobile trips taken by Wasco families between 1942 and 1945 were more limited than previously or just afterward. The war certainly impacted local families strongly, and many area young men were killed or injured during the war itself. The first area casualty was Keith Jennings, whose father Dwight was the rural postal carrier in St. Charles. Keith was killed at Pearl Harbor on 7 December 1941, while serving aboard the U. S. S. Arizona. St. Charles High School had many more females than males in the upper grades during the war, due to enlistments and the implementation of the draft.

In November 1942, the scrap drive in Campton Township brought in fifty tons of scrap metal for the war effort. Kane County schools engaged in intense scrap drives during that time, benefiting Midwestern steel mills in particular and the war effort in general. Earl Johnson left for Fort Sheridan that month, following his induction into the Army. He had been working at the Berglands' Foxwood Farm for the previous decade. Also that month, Earl Shott, "the cook for the Chicago Great Western railroad men," who were then installing signal lights at Wasco, was inducted into the Army.

Red Cross offices collected older sewing machines during the war. This was done in an effort to increase production of garments and blankets which would assist the civilian victims of war abroad. Members of local 4-H clubs raised money to benefit hospitals used by convalescing soldiers. One of many Wasco residents to serve during World War II was Charles K. ("Babe") Bowgren, who was with the Marine Corps for twenty-eight months during the war. In mid-December 1945, he returned to Wasco from Okinawa, Japan, a city which he had left more than a month before. Howard Mather of Wasco also returned from his service around the same time, by way of California. Members of the local community participated in can drives then, largely to aid war-devastated areas.

Babe Bowgren with his son Ken, shortly after the war's end

Interest in local politics waned during and immediately after the war, and beginning in 1942, the annual Campton Township meetings which had gone on for decades while attracting a healthy crowd of interested local residents, were now often attended solely by officials. The 1946 meeting, in fact, had just two attendees – the moderator and the Town Clerk! Elections did of course continue in the post-war years. In 1947, two Wasco men were elected to local office: Gordon Swanson as Highway Commissioner; and Stanley Bowgren as Township Assessor.

In 1948, there were close to thirty houses in Wasco, along with another twenty or so farmhouses close to the village. Local roads and bridges, however, had fallen into a state of disrepair by then. That year and again in 1949, the "township road problem" was raised at all local meetings and quite a few social gatherings. Those in Wasco and the surrounding community asked both Kane County the State of Illinois for road gravel and blacktop, or money for these items, yet little aid was forthcoming.

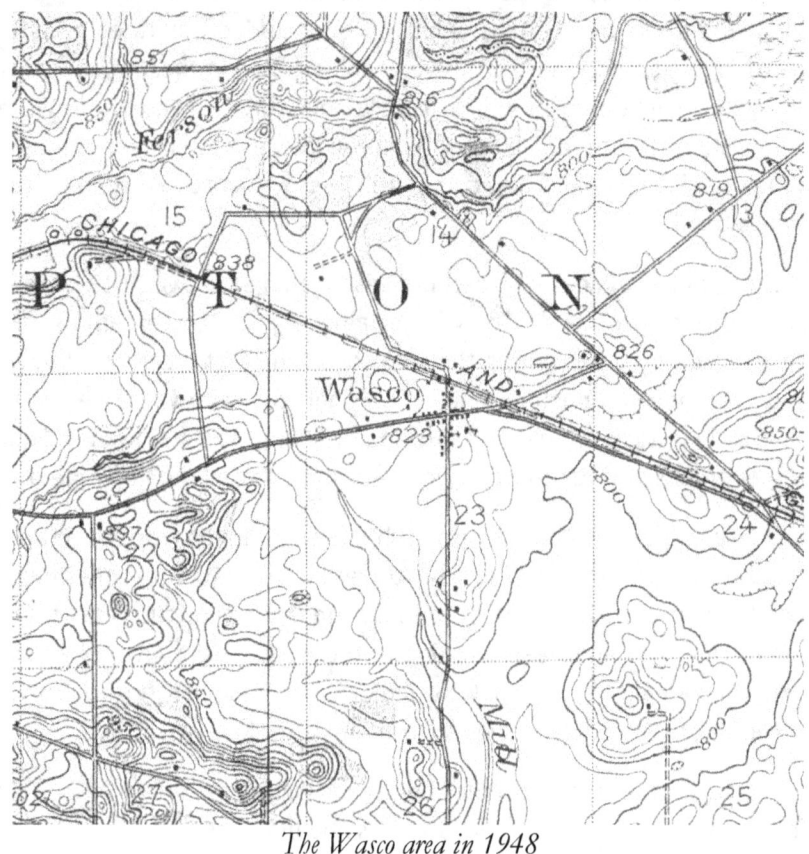

The Wasco area in 1948

In 1949, some Wascoites often mentioned in local newspapers included Calvin and Edna Cray, Solomon Johnson, George Brown, George Hawkins, Helen Hawkins, Don Hagaman, Hugo Denker, Andrew Erickson, Rev. Dalton Ward, Elmer Peterson, Olive Bergland, and John Olson. The Campton 4-H Club Basketball Team was new then, and the Wasco Community Club was meeting regularly. The Wasco Church Missionary Society was rather active, and there were dozens of school activities taking place year-round.

The Wasco Legion Post was organized during this era, and held its very first party in October 1949. The Legion created a bonfire on Halloween night that year, and a large crowd turned out to enjoy "the huge fire, the games, and had plenty of hot dogs, candy, cider and apples." Those attending "went home voting the Legion a real asset to the Wasco community."

The last Chicago Great Western steam locomotive in Illinois (Engine No. 465) made its final run on 9 July 1949. The switchover to diesel locomotives across the entire railroad had taken place over the preceding two-and-a-half years, beginning in December 1946. Trains would continue to be seen on the line until the 1970s.

About seventy people, mostly locals, attended the Pure Milk Association Banquet held at the Wasco Church in mid-December 1949. Mr. Thomsen of Denmark was the evening's speaker.

The 1950s

The decade of the 1950s was one of great change for Wasco and the surrounding region. In 1950, the groundwork was laid for the very first suburban-style development close to the village when Morris and Martha Whitney of Geneva (but formerly of Wasco) sold property near Lake Campton to the St. Charles Building Corporation. What would become Unit 1 of the King's Mill subdivision was bordered on Empire Road, Burlington Road, and Lake Campton, and contained twenty-six lots and two new roads (King's Mill Drive and Crooked Lane) by 1955. The oldest section of this first subdivision was platted in November 1955; it is located just one mile north of the village of Wasco. Bill Fisher, a local businessman, was the chief developer of this subdivision. The second unit of the King's Mill subdivision, containing thirteen lots and located on the south side of Lake Campton, was platted in August 1957. The Campton Ridge subdivision in the northeast quarter of Section 15, a bit northwest of Wasco, adjoined King's Mill to the west. It contained eight lots on the south side of Empire Road, and was platted in May 1957. These subdivisions and others like them marked the beginning of the first large-scale influx of new families into the Wasco area since shortly after its creation.

The significant increase in the local population had multiple effects. One of the most important of these was the pressing need to expand the number of classrooms in the Wasco School. This was accomplished by the construction of two separate additions onto the building in the 1950s. Another significant change for Wasco late in the decade was the closure of the historic Wasco Depot in the fall of 1959, after more than seventy years of continuous service. Rex Pelley was the depot's last station agent.

On 6 January 1950, the Wasco Post of the American Legion gave its first annual dinner; the gathering was held at "The Farm" on Route 64, just west of Wasco. The speaker was Col. Charles H. Edwards, who investigated concentration camps in Germany during the war. His topic was "Man's inhumanity to man." In 1950, Rev. Dalton Ward (who was then newly-married) was the pastor of the Wasco Church.

Four young men at the Illinois Training School for Boys escaped that facility on foot in January 1950. One of the boys, after scaling a twelve-foot fence, broke into Grace Mather's house in Wasco. The family notified the Sheriff's office, and the teenage escapee was promptly captured by Deputy Sheriff (and Wasco resident) Wesley Johnson and his friend and neighbor Lee Mather. The youth was located hiding in the Mather basement, behind a washing machine.

Political affiliations in Campton Township and Wasco had not changed much over the preceding decades. Of the 556 total voters in the township in November 1950, 295 voted a straight Republican ticket, while just 44 voted a straight Democratic ticket. Republican candidates for state and county offices generally received about four times as many votes as their Democratic counterparts. The most pressing local political issue in the early 1950s continued to be the condition of local roads and bridges, which were in severe need of improvement and maintenance. A successful referendum to increase the road tax thankfully succeeded, and the problem was gradually solved.

On 7 April 1950, there was a large railroad accident just east of Wasco. Twenty-six freight cars on the Chicago Great Western railroad track, containing lumber, automobiles, and linseed oil, "piled up on the crossing of the Burlington Blacktop east of the village," leading to Wasco's being a temporary "attraction for many visitors." The wreck was caused by a broken draw-bar coupling.

The Campton 4-H Club (which was renamed the Wasco 4-H Club in December 1950, though it was called by its former name for years afterward) was quite active throughout the decade, and occasionally held meetings and activities at the Wasco School. Jerry Hagaman, Elwood Hultine, Dean Richmond, and Dexter Norton Jr. were among the group's leaders in the early '50s. Most meetings opened with the Pledge of Allegiance followed by the 4-H Pledge. Mrs. Synnott, Mrs. Bullock, Mrs. Dibblee, and Mr. and Mrs. Palmer Johnson were some of the group's adult leaders in 1954 and 1955. Rummage sales brought in a fair amount of money for the club during this time period.

In July 1950, five boys from Wasco were involved in a rescue of nine-year-old Peter J. Bohr, who nearly drowned in Ferson's Creek near St. Charles. Bohr was saved by Dennis McKay, Ralph Swanson, Terry Bowgren, Jimmy White, and Dick Swanson. Peter's parents were Peter J. and Jane M. (Carden) Bohr. The Bohrs later moved to Aurora, and then to Batavia.

The boys involved in the aforementioned rescue - Ralph Swanson, Dennis McKay, Peter Bohr, Terry Bowgren, and Jimmy White. Dick Swanson is not pictured.

In April 1951, Wasco resident Frank Hagaman made a motion at the Annual Campton Town Meeting requesting that a memorial to World War I and World War II veterans be placed on the Town Hall grounds. Supervisor Robert Corron chose a committee to design the memorial itself. Many other local officials that year were Wasco residents: Wesley Johnson and Calvin Cray were Constables; and Paul Waterhouse was a Justice of the Peace. Later that same month, the Wasco Community Club ran an event at the Wasco School with the help of the St. Charles Chamber of Commerce. The event was named "St. Charles Night in Wasco."

Andrew Mongerson of Wasco passed away during the first week of November 1951, at the age of ninety-one. He came to the United States in 1871, had lived in the Wasco area since 1886, and retired from farming in 1917. His funeral services were held at Bethlehem Lutheran Church in St. Charles; hymns sung at his funeral included "He Leadeth Me" and "Sweet Hour of Prayer." He was survived by three sons, two daughters, and four grandchildren. See "Some Wasco Houses – Southwest Quarter" for further information on the family.

A film entitled "God of the Atom," produced by the Moody Bible Institute of Chicago, was shown at the Wasco Baptist Church on 29 June 1952. The film was "proof that atomic energy is not too technical to understand or too dangerous to talk about." The color motion picture was commended by the Atomic Energy Commission and the film concluded with "a summary of the world crisis caused by the discovery of atomic power." Surely, the showing of this film represents one of the most significant times that the early Cold War and its global implications was discussed in a public forum in Wasco.

The new addition to the Wasco School was dedicated on 15 November 1952. The open house that day attracted "a large number of visitors" and those attending were entertained by music from the fifth and sixth graders, led by Nancy Potter. Paul Waterhouse spoke of the "Wasco School of the Past" and Superintendent G. E. Thompson told of "the New Wasco School."

While crossing Route 64 one morning in December 1953, Nettie Anderson, one of Wasco's oldest residents, was tragically killed in an automobile accident (see "The Anderson/Barber Family" for further information on Nettie and her family). This was not the only sudden death which shocked Wasco in 1953, however. Earlier that year, Gerry Daum, one of the two proprietors of The Farm just west of Wasco, died of influenza at the age of forty-five (see "The Farm Restaurant").

Augusta and Andrew Mongerson, in the 1930s

Rev. David J. Klasing, who was pastor of the Wasco Baptist Church in the early 1950s, was one of the most popular ministers in the church's history. He created a ran a series of community events during his years in Wasco, and showed a wide variety of films which piqued local interest. In January 1954, Rev. Klasing extended an invitation to the public to attend the showing of a new documentary film entitled "The Street," which featured authentic scenes (in color) of Chicago's "Skid Row." The film told the story of a young alcoholic who turned to God "out of the depths of spiritual and physical need."

In July 1954, Jennie Denker of Wasco introduced a local effort to raise money for a new wing of Community Hospital in Geneva. The new beds and facilities were urgently needed at that time; the fundraising effort reached all areas served by the hospital, including Wasco. The contract for building the new west wing of the hospital was signed with the LaSalle Construction Company of Chicago in March 1955.

A proposal to install the first street lights in Wasco was introduced at the 1955 annual meeting, and passed, but Supervisor Corron received a letter from the State's Attorney shortly afterward stating that town funds could not be used for such a project. The effort to install the street lights was beset with legal difficulties since Wasco was unincorporated and had no tax funds available unto itself for such work.

Rudolph and Anne Mongerson celebrated their Silver wedding anniversary in November 1955. The couple entertained two hundred friends and relatives at an open house in the Wasco School auditorium on that memorable occasion. Following the open house, they offered a buffet supper at their home for family and out-of-town guests. Their son John Mongerson was on duty with the U. S. Army in Germany at that time, but their daughter, who was a senior at the University of Illinois, was able to attend the event.

The Wasco American Legion Post 1195 held a donation and consignment auction sale on the White Brothers' Trucking Company property in June 1955. During the auction, the Wasco Legion Auxiliary hosted a rummage and bake sale at the same site. The Legion had another sale at the same location that October. Items such as farm machinery, tools, horse equipment, and furniture were sold there. In November 1959, the Wasco American Legion sponsored a dance at Wasco School, with the "Gene Victor Band" furnishing the music. The party lasted until midnight, and attracted a large crowd.

The Chicago Great Western Railroad discontinued passenger service in 1956. The C. G. W., like nearly all railroads nationwide, had experienced a significant decline in both passenger and freight traffic during the preceding several decades. Total railroad mileage, in fact, had peaked in the United States as early as the 1910s, and thereafter the industry faced increased competition from other modes of transportation (most notably from the automobile and slightly later from commercial airlines) which became more and more appealing and cost effective. Freight service on the local C. G. W. R. R. line continued, however, past 1967-68, when the railroad merged with the Chicago & Northwestern. Most of the railroad's lines in Illinois, including those in Wasco, were abandoned and removed in the 1970s and 1980s.

There was a popular series of evangelistic services held at the Wasco Church in February and March 1956. The series was brought to the area by Rev. Klasing, and featured special musical entertainment from students at Wheaton College. The guest speaker was Dr. Peter R. Joshua, who had toured many nations while preaching the Gospel.

Julian Verhaeghe, who lived on the "old Bolwahnn farm on the St. Charles Burlington Blacktop Road" three miles northwest of Wasco, decided to "quit dairying" in February 1957. He sold off his herd of forty-nine Holstein dairy cattle, plus all his dairy equipment, at an auction held that month. That spring, Dan Rediger was drilling wells in the Wasco area, and Hummel & Company was having a sale on plywood, plaster board, and ceiling tile. The store also sold fence posts, barbed wire, woven wire, feed, coal, and more. The 1957 Deckert family reunion drew a crowd of sixty-five people, most of whom lived in Wasco and the surrounding area. The LaFox Farmers Club held their Thanksgiving supper in the Wasco gymnasium on 24 November 1957. Joseph White, co-founder of White Brothers Trucking of Wasco, died earlier that month, at the age of thirty-seven.

The vicinity of Wasco in 1957, at the beginning of its suburbanization

In March 1958, the LaFox Farmers Club sponsored a card party at Wasco School. Attendees had their choice of playing "Five Hundred, Pinochle, or Canasta." There was a Bingo game for the children. The Club awarded prizes and served refreshments. Admission was seventy-five cents for adults.

The Brookside Subdivision, just west of Wasco, was created in June 1959. It is located on the north side of Route 64, at its intersection with Town Hall Road, and west, on the former Charles Westbrook farm. It contained twenty-seven lots, and new roads: Griffin Lane; Circle Drive; and Brookside West Drive. Two of the first families to build there, soon after November 1959, were Mr. and Mrs. Malcolm Ball and Mr. and Mrs. John Schmidt.

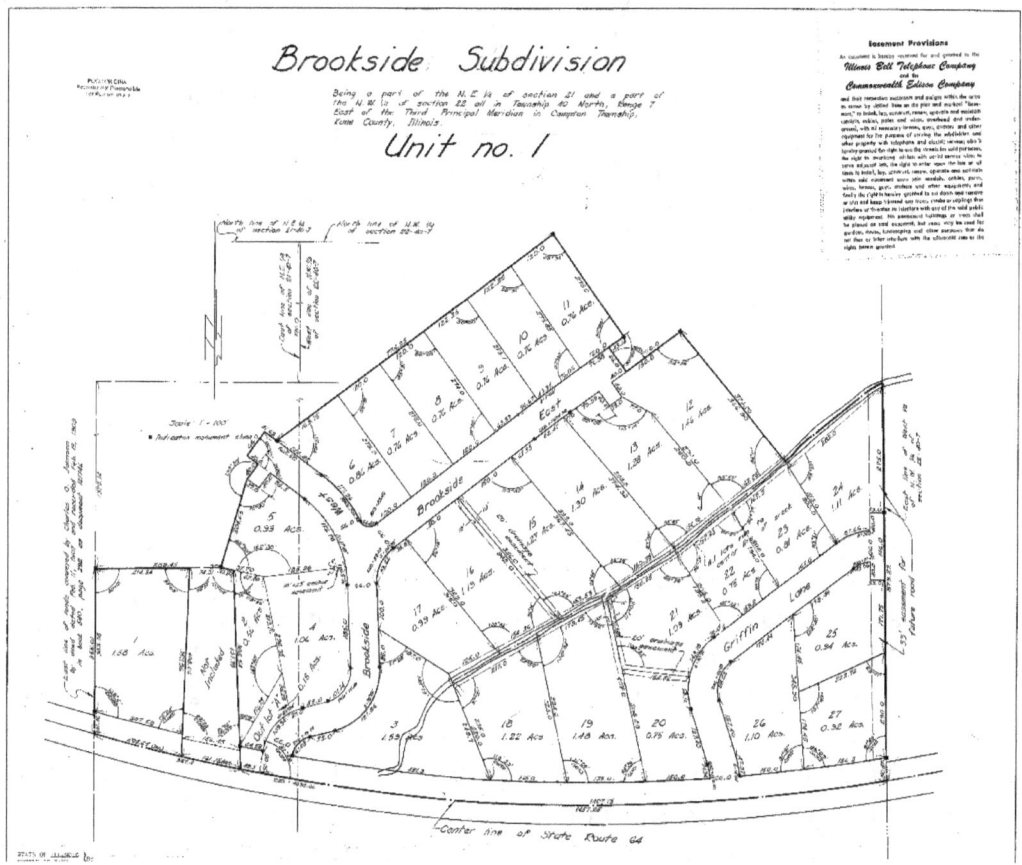

The original plat of the Brookside Subdivision, 1959

Baseball was the most popular sport locally in the 1950s. During the summer of 1959, the Wasco American Legion purchased equipment for a new elementary school-age baseball team. Gloves, mitts, balls, bats, helmets, bases, and a catcher's outfit were all provided, as were T-shirts and caps. The Legion Auxiliary hired Don Hagaman to coach the boys, who played two games most weeks. Their practices were held every Wednesday and Saturday afternoon on the school grounds. There was no charge to join the team, which drew players from Wasco and the surrounding region.

In September 1959, a private plane carrying three passengers landed unexpectedly in Solomon Johnson's hay field in Wasco. The pilot had been searching for the DuPage County Airport, but the heavy fog made the destination impossible to find. The passengers disembarked and walked to the Little House, where they spent an hour and a half waiting for the fog to clear. During the same month, the new addition to Wasco School was delayed, when it was found that the pre-stressed beams to be used for the two new classrooms were all too short, and new ones had to be ordered. The new classrooms, "which were needed last year," were not ready for the start of school. The basement was remodeled that year, and Carole Prendergast took over as the new first grade teacher, upon the retirement in June of Ethel Waterhouse.

In a decision with profound local consequences, the Illinois Commerce Commission voted to close the Wasco Depot in the late fall of 1959, three years after discontinuing passenger service on the Chicago Great Western line through the village. The building would soon be acquired by the Wasco American Legion, and would be relocated a short distance away (see "The Wasco Depot"). The last station agent there, Rex Pelley, moved to Colonial Village south of Batavia in November 1959, soon after the Wasco station was closed. He and his wife had lived in the Vanderhoof apartment in Wasco for almost nine years. The Pelleys "regret[ted] their going" but stated that "changes come with the times."

Construction was on the increase in the Wasco area in the second half of the 1950s. Several new houses were constructed in the village then, and the first subdivisions went in during those years also. By the end of 1959, there was a regular "parade of gravel trucks going through Wasco" carrying material to nearby developments such as Silver Brook Farm, King's Mill, or Brookside.

One of the last events to take place in Wasco during the 1950s was the Christmas party held at Wasco School under the auspices of the LaFox Farmers Club during the last week of December 1959. There were songs and recitations by "the little ones," and Santa distributed gifts to all the children in attendance.

The 1960s

The expansion of housing developments in the Wasco area was a marked trend in the 1960s. While the developments of the late 1950s contained a handful of houses each, those of the following decade tended to be larger in scale. In Wasco, traffic increased, the school's enrollment continued to climb, and more and more new families moved to the area. The number of farms in the immediate area around Wasco began to fall as several were subdivided and developed. Quite a number of the remaining farmers sold their dairy herds in the 1960s, and either retired from the business altogether or shifted to a different form of agricultural production. Unlike population trends of the late nineteenth and early twentieth century, Wasco's population was now steadily increasing from year to year. The region began losing its primarily rural 'character' at this time and continued to shift toward a more suburban one. An obvious symbol of this social shift was the location in which Campton Township public meetings were conducted. All of the Annual Town Meetings of the 1960s took place not in the diminutive but quaint Town Hall, as was typical for the previous ninety years, but rather in the ever-expanding Wasco School. These buildings, of course, are vastly different in size, but also in purpose.

Voters attending the 1960 Campton Town Meeting saw the changes that were happening in the Wasco area clearly, stating at the meeting that the township was "rapidly changing from a predominately agricultural to [a] residential area." Due to the large number of new houses, the system of property tax assessments modernized, by shifting (in 1961) to a card-based system for each parcel. Evidence of the influx of new families to the area can be easily seen by reading the list of attendees at meetings in the 1960s – a smaller and smaller percentage of "old" Wasco surnames are found as the decade progresses.

In 1960, the former Charles White residence in Wasco was functioning as a bakery and coffee shop (see "Some Wasco Houses – Northwest Quarter"). The Wasco branch of the Home Bureau was active then, and several locals attended a flower show in Chicago that spring. A card club met regularly on Wednesdays. Members of the Wasco American Legion Post were busy discussing the logistics of moving the former Depot building, and would accomplish that task later in the year. The Browns, Vanderhoofs,

Hawkinses, Mongersons, Bowgrens, Johnsons, and many other long-time residents were active in the village's social events then.

Some long-time residents moved away from Wasco in the early 1960s. In February 1961, for example, Ed Mongerson and his sisters Ellen and Florence moved to a home on South 13th Street in St. Charles. They had purchased the home the previous December. All three had been lifetime residents of the Wasco area. Their farm tenant, Pete Peterson, moved into the old Mongerson home at that time. David and Joanne Allen also moved from Wasco to St. Charles in 1961. George and Hilda Hawkins moved to Mooseheart that year, and Rose, Effie, and Esther Johnson moved from Wasco to Batavia later in 1961.

A new club known as TOPS (which stood for "taking off pounds sensibly") began meeting in Wasco in November 1961. The group got together over "black coffee" and met twice a month. The first two meetings took place at the homes of Mrs. John Schaefer and Mrs. Clarence Raasch. Those interested in joining were invited to phone Mrs. Raasch at JU 4-4033. In April 1962 TOPS met at the home of Christine Hatzis and Elaine Raasch. Anne Van Bogaert was a host late in 1962. The group may have evolved into the Shrinking Matrons, who had a similar purpose and membership, and who began meeting locally by 1963 (see "Important Social Organizations").

In April 1962, the Wasco American Legion and the Legion Auxiliary were collecting donations for their annual auction, which was to be held during the first week of May at the Legion Home "just north of Wasco." The Legion Home, relocated two years previously, was formerly the Wasco Depot.

Baseball was becoming more and more popular in the area in the 1960s. The Wasco Little League baseball team played five games in June 1962. Their opponents that season were the teams from Huntley, Burlington, Sugar Grove, and Hampshire. The Babe Ruth League of Wasco began their 1963 season with two victories. Pitchers during those games were Bob Corron

Wasco and its immediate vicinity in 1964

and Wayne Heuertz. That spring, the Wasco American Legion sold tickets to their all-you-can-eat ham dinner, which was held on 23 March. The proceeds of the dinner purchased uniforms and equipment for the baseball team. By 23 May 1963, the men of the Legion had "about finished a new baseball diamond" behind their building. The infield had by then been sodded, and the backstop erected.

By 1962, the Cub Scouts were actively meeting in Wasco, and featured a significant local membership. The Wasco Mothers and Teachers Club voted to sponsor the Scouts in October 1962. Wasco Cub Pack 150's membership charter was presented to the vice president of the Wasco Mothers Club by Scout Executive Bill Downs in February 1963. There were three dens in the local pack that year.

Wasco Cub Scouts, 1964

In 1964, zip codes had been newly introduced, and postmasters across Illinois were encouraging their use. Wasco was given the zip code 60183 by the end of that year. That was also the year that the last of the local elm trees were lost to Dutch elm disease, leading a local correspondent to write that although new trees were being planted that spring it was to be "many long years before these will give beauty and shade to our village."

In December 1964 the LaFox Farmers Club held their annual Christmas party at the Wasco School. Attendees sang carols, enjoyed refreshments, and were visited by Santa Claus. The party lasted until 11:00 PM. That month, Wasco was nicely decorated for the holiday both "In the homes and outside" and looked "very festive at night especially." The LaFox Farmers Club's Christmas party was held in the same place in 1965 as it was the prior year, but the usual long children's program was cut short since so many young Wascoites were home with colds, flu, or measles. Homemade cookies were served in addition to sandwiches and ice cream. There was a gift grab-bag at the party as well.

In late July 1965, Wasco defeated Sugar Grove in two consecutive baseball games to win the Little League Championship. Willy Crook was the winning pitcher, and Jeff Swanson hit a two-run homer in the first game. The players on both teams were aged twelve and under. In July 1966, the Twilight Little League's Wasco baseball team had a record of 7-1, the second-best record of the league's nine clubs. The previous month, Jon Ball of Wasco had pitched a no-hit no-run game versus Sugar Grove, striking out thirteen batters. Wasco's coach was Don Hagaman.

There was flooding in Wasco in May 1966, during which many local basements took on water. The Wasco School was also significantly impacted by this sudden influx of water, which occurred just weeks before the end of the school year. The following November, which was also characterized by weather extremes, the Wasco Parent & Teachers Club (later the PTO) held an ice cream social at the Wasco School. Posters advertising the event were created by the fifth and sixth-grade students. The winner of the fifth-grade contest was Judy Gordon, and the sixth-grade winner was Rhonda Hanson.

Cal Corron and his Wasco Little League team - note the former Wasco Train Station in the background

During the winter of 1966-67, which was remembered for its extreme weather conditions, Lester Swanson's new snowmobile was only half-jokingly considered the "best transportation in town."

The Wasco community was saddened by the sudden death of Conrad Hibbeler in November 1966. His widow Ruth survived until 1981. Joe Hawkins (a longtime resident of Wasco) moved to the Bowes Nursing Home in Elgin at that time, and Norm Skala of Wasco was convalescing at home "from an accident with a young colt."

The Kane County Flea Market has its roots in Wasco. In April 1967, Helen Robinson, the matriarch of the Kane County Flea Market, held her first flea market at the American Legion Hall in Wasco. She had fourteen dealers then, and four hundred customers. An article from that time called the sale "a grand success" with many of the exhibitors expressing interest in conducting such a sale monthly. Many said that "they had not sold so much in one location as they did there." The following year, in August 1968, the Wasco American Legion and its Auxiliary, again with the help of Helen Robinson, conducted a large-scale antique flea market at the Kane County Fairgrounds. The project turned out to be "a huge success financially" and all agreed that Chairman Robinson "did a tremendous job" with the sale. George Vanderhoof of Wasco manned the gates and parking lot at the 1968 flea market. Assistance in the kitchen was given by Babe Bowgren, Jack Van De Veire, and John Jorgenson, with other assistance from Wes Johnson, Bill Spalten, JoAnn Jay, Ernie Begerman, Karen Hagaman, Dorothy Corron, Donna Crook, Miriam O'Connell, and others. The sale at the Kane County Fairgrounds evolved into the Kane County Flea Market.

In March of 1967, Richard Swanson of Wasco was elected President of the Fox Valley Truckers Association. The next month witnessed a local election in the village – there were "not too many votes cast" since there was only one person (J. L. McGowan for Road Commissioner) on the ballot! Wasco School had a

"Spring Sing" that year, which was well-attended and enjoyed by all. Don Swanson and William Zobjeck both visited Wasco during their furloughs from military service that season. In August 1967, Wasco Baptist Church held an "Evangelistic Crusade" with a preacher from St. Petersburg, Florida, as the evangelist. Wes Johnson of Wasco was installed as Kane County American Legion Commander the previous month. He and his wife were then building a new home in Wasco. The annual Barbeque Supper was held in the Wasco School gymnasium on 2 December 1967.

New post office boxes were installed in the Wasco Post Office in 1967. There were just over forty members of the Wasco Post that year, nine of whom owned post office boxes in the local post office. These owners were: Charles Bowgren (Box #43); Harold Ekstrom (Box #5); Wes Johnson (Box #107); Adrian Landreth (Box #2); Clarence Raasch (Box #63); Frank Richmond (Box #1); James Sanderson (Box #14); David Sleeman (Box #87); and George Vanderhoof (Box #94).

In the spring of 1968, there were twenty-one young men from Campton Township in the U. S. Armed Services, most of whom were serving in Vietnam. Some of those from Wasco were Leo G. Untz, James A. Untz, Ronald R. Leathers, Donald C. Swanson, Keith Bowgren, and Kenneth Bowgren. An article in the *Chicago Tribune* from that time stated that two-thirds of the fifty or so houses in Wasco were then flying the American flag. In May 1968, the Wasco American Legion Post and the Legion Auxiliary sponsored another spring auction at the Legion Home. A rummage and bake sale were again held in conjunction with the auction. Junior Girl Scout Troop #37 of Wasco created and packed care packages for the local servicemen in December 1968. The packages included cookies baked by the Scouts, personal articles, canned meats, and candy. The troop was directed by Mrs. Edward Ledbetter and Mrs. John Basic.

Celebrations in Wasco continued during the Vietnam years. In the fall of 1968, a very large fortieth wedding anniversary party was held in Wasco. This was for Elmer and Hazel Ekstrom, parents of Carl and Darlene. Over one hundred and twenty-five guests attended the reception, which featured a "serving table . . . beautifully arranged with a floral centerpiece of yellow and white chrysanthemums, and tall tapers in silver candelabra." Their niece Eileen Strom circulated the guest book. Harold Peterson, who was in the wedding party in 1928, also participated in the celebration. In the fall of 1968, the Wasco American Legion held their annual baseball picnic. The "food was plentiful and delicious" and "a good time was had by all." At the picnic, the Little League played the Mothers, and the Babe Ruth League played the Fathers. In August of that year, Henry Verhaeghe purchased a home in Wasco from James ("Sandy") Sanderson, at which time the Sandersons moved to the Russell farm (formerly the Ekstrom farm). In June 1969, the Wasco School PTO honored Miss Margaret Johnson, who had just completed her twenty-fifth consecutive year of teaching at the school. The previous month, friends and neighbors of Eric Olson had helped him celebrate his seventy-fifth birthday. Also that year, the local women's social group known as the "Shrinking Matrons" closed out its season with a luncheon held at The Terrace on Route 64.

The "Windings of Ferson Creek," a large housing development a mile and a half west of Wasco, was platted in the summer of 1969. The subdivision comprises a large portion of Section 16 of Campton Township, an area which was heavily wooded through the early part of the twentieth century. Many old trees were left when the area was developed, as part of the "winding greenbelt" planned from the beginning of the subdivision.

A wide array of social events took place during the last years of the 1960s. The Shrinking Matrons continued to meet. Mrs. George Vanderhoof and Mrs. Robert A. Anderson were frequent hosts of this group in 1968 and 1969. The LaFox Farmers Club met regularly at Wasco School, and had a Halloween party there in October 1969. The next month, there was a Veteran's Day potluck dinner held at the American Legion Home. The Wasco Ladies Aid held their Christmas party at the home of Mrs. Raymond Fischer in December 1969, two weeks before the decade came to an end.

The 1970s

Many more farmers in the Wasco area sold their property to developers in the 1970s, and the regional population continued to climb. The number of dairy farms still in operation by the end of the decade was a fraction of its Depression-era size, and reached the single digits within two miles of the village. Several Wasco men were fighting in Vietnam in the early part of the decade, and the Wasco American Legion Post became the site of the annual Campton Town Meetings starting in 1970. Many of the children of the first generation of Wasco settlers who had remained in the area began to pass away during this decade, and the proportion of "old families" active in local affairs continued to shrink. On a positive note, more and more Wasco women became active in political meetings during the 1970s, and the Wasco Legion Auxiliary remained very active throughout the decade. Concern for the environment and its protection also grew during the '70s, and the Campton Forest Preserve began just two years after the first Earth Day was celebrated.

In January 1970, John Brown, who lived just west of the village, quit farming. He and Clif Bowgren had a large farm sale on the last day of January. That year, Anita Bumgarner was Rehabilitation Chairman of the Wasco Legion Auxiliary. She and other Auxiliary members would regularly travel to Elgin State Hospital that year to visit the veterans, and to bring them clothing and food. In February 1970, Kenny Bowgren of Wasco received his commercial pilot's license. Local resident Robert Leathers left for Vietnam in mid-March 1970, less than two weeks after his wedding. Around the time that Robert left, his brother Ronnie returned from the same country. Lois M. (Fleming) Spalten of Wasco, former President and Treasurer of the Wasco American Legion Auxiliary, passed away on 20 March 1970, at the age of forty-eight. A memorial service was held for her at the Post Home, during which the Auxiliary Charter was draped in black.

Cub Pack 150 of Wasco was reorganized in November 1970, and they conducted a membership drive that winter. Bob Darflinger was one of the chief organizers of the group, which invited boys between the ages of eight and ten that lived in the Wasco School District to join. Besides Mr. Darflinger, the group's leaders then were: Glenn Johnson (Cubmaster); Ted Thull (Assistant Cubmaster); Sam Gray (Representative); Gary Claus (Webelo leader); Anita Bumgarner (Den Mother); Joan Darflinger (Secretary); and George Einwich (Treasurer). The Pack put on a popular Christmas Bazaar at Wasco School in 1974, where gifts suitable for all family members were for sale at affordable prices. Hot homemade bread was also for sale, and many hand-crafted items were available. Pack 150 repeated the event the following year, and held their third annual "Mothers' Bazaar" fundraiser in the Wasco School gymnasium in December 1976.

The Wasco Legion Auxiliary hosted a series of family pot luck suppers at Legion Hall in the early 1970s, which drew large crowds. The dinner in November 1970 drew more than eighty people. The Wasco School Parents and Teachers Club (later the PTO) enjoyed excellent membership numbers in this era also.

In the early 1970s, the first home one would pass on Route 64 driving west into Wasco was that of the Raasch family. The yard was known for having an eagle perched on a brass ball, next to an American flag. The Raasches left Wasco in the spring of 1980, and moved to Florida.

In May 1971, Wasco residents voted in favor of creating their own municipal sewer system. The proposal passed by "a large majority." Route 64 in Wasco was resurfaced that summer, and several local construction projects were then underway.

In August 1972, the Campton Forest Preserve, located immediately southwest of Wasco, was begun with the acquisition of 166 acres of land. The first parcel acquired here was the Minnette Barber farm with frontage on both Town Line Road and Route 64. Eve S. Johnson, founder of Garfield Farm, was an important figure in bringing this purchase about. Four years later, another eighteen acres was added, and twenty-six more were acquired in 1979. There were other additions to the preserve in the 1990s and the early 2010s.

The Campton Forest Preserve near Wasco, which was begun in 1972

Little League baseball continued to enjoy widespread popularity in Wasco in the 1970s. In July 1973, more than four hundred people attended the Little League family picnic, held on the Legion Field. The event was sponsored by the Women's Auxiliary of Wasco American Legion Post 1195. The afternoon program included softball games between the younger boys and their mothers and the older boys and their fathers. Little League Director Cal Corron served as master of ceremonies following a pot luck supper. There was both a Wasco Legion League and a "City League" that summer, and several teams including the Sox, Tigers, and Pirates, plus the newly-formed girls team "the Wascoettes." Wasco baseball teams during the 1974 season included the aforementioned groups plus the As, Braves, Cardinals, Mets, and Cubs. Local sponsors that year included the Wasco Garage, Hummel & Company, and the Wasco Blacksmith Shop.

The Denny family moved to Wisconsin after selling Denny's Tavern in Wasco in the spring of 1973 (see "Travis Tavern/Bohr's Tavern/Denny's Den"). The Wasco Winners 4-H Club held their springtime outing and picnic at LeRoy Oakes Forest Preserve that season. Sherry Critchfield was one of the group's leaders that year. Although Wasco had always been a very safe community, there was a wave of vandalism in Campton Township, including in Wasco, in 1974. Lights had been shot out repeatedly at intersections, stop signs knocked down, and mailboxes damaged. Every resident was urged to "be on the alert to help apprehend the guilty parties."

The year 1974 also witnessed several successful flea markets held at the Wasco Legion Post. The Legion Hall was newly-remodeled and enlarged that spring. Admission to the flea markets was free, and each seller was charged just $1 to set up. Lunch was available for purchase, and vendors could "buy, sell, or trade anything." Construction on the 1500-square-foot addition to the Hall began in May 1973. The Wasco School's 4th Graders took a bus trip to the state capitol in November 1974. They visited Lincoln's home, and New Salem; more than sixty children and their teachers participated in the trip.

When the LaFox Farmers Club met at the Wasco School in April 1975, there was no heat in the building so "everyone wore his coat all evening." Each attendee brought a 'white elephant' gift which was sold at a silent auction. The proceeds increased the club's treasury. Sandwiches and coffee were enjoyed by the members, and many rounds of cards were played, as usual. The old Eddy house in Wasco, located just north of the railroad crossing on LaFox Road, was torn down during the spring of 1975, one of the first homes to be demolished in Wasco in many years.

Tom, Ned, Myron, and Cal Corron. Cal was Little League Director in Wasco in the late 1960s and early 1970s

On 15 May 1976, the annual barbeque at Wasco Elementary School had a "Revolutionary" theme. The food was prepared by the cooks at the Wasco Inn, and the event was chaired by Mr. and Mrs. David Gross. There was a "Star-Spangled Carnival Tent" which featured games of chance, and the Wasco Girl Scouts sold cookbooks and baked goods at the event. The Cub Scouts ran a "patriotic popcorn stand." Red, white, and blue banners made by the Wasco students decorated the cafeteria.

In June 1976, Campton Township celebrated the U. S. Bicentennial with a series of community events. There was a parade held whose route ran from the Wasco School to the Wesley Johnson Memorial Legion Hall. The route was "lined all the way with spectators and their cars." Pastor Aldridge of the Wasco Baptist Church gave the invocation, and the St. Charles Bicentennial Band played the Star-Spangled Banner to open the program. Frank Richmond and Zilpha Brown were given plaques honoring their achievement of longest period of residence in the township – both had been born there in 1888. After the floats were judged, "all adjourned to eat their picnic lunches." The Wasco Baptist Church float had a replica of their building, complete with a functioning bell. Edna Cray, the longest-serving member of the church, rode on the float. The event was judged to be "the greatest day in Wasco since the parade in 1935." Food and drink was served by the Wasco Ladies Aid and the Boy Scouts.

The Wasco Baptist Church float, in the 1976 parade

On Friday, 23 April 1977, the last train accident in Wasco took place. On that date, a Chicago & Northwestern train derailed just east of the village. Three cars were thrown into the ditch, and the vibrations from the derailment were felt for a wide distance in all directions. The tracks themselves were permanently abandoned and removed not long afterward.

The Garfield Farm Museum, located just two miles south of Wasco, was created in 1977 when Elva Ruth Garfield, a third-generation Campton Township resident, donated one hundred and sixty-three acres of her farm and its buildings to the newly-established non-profit organization as part of an effort to teach visitors about America's prairie farm heritage. The Museum is now located on more than three hundred and sixty contiguous acres, and offers an amazing variety of educational events such as the Rare Breeds Show, archaeological field sessions, prairie walks, agricultural seminars, and much more.

An image of the last train accident in Wasco, 1977

In September 1977, the family of Mrs. Theo Scott, formerly of Wasco, celebrated her eightieth birthday. The Verkler family of Wasco harvested "a bountiful crop of everbearing strawberries" that season. Not all local news was so pleasant that season, however. Traffic had been on the increase in the area for many year, and Wasco even suffered a power outage when a utility pole at Brown Road and Route 64 was hit by a car.

There was a severe blizzard in January 1978 which impacted Wasco and thousands of other communities across the Midwest and Northeast. Wasco suffered "blinding snow," high winds, and zero visibility during the storm. Heavy equipment was required to remove tons of snow from the roads. During the winter of 1978-79, the Kane County Forest Preserve built a warming shelter, a parking lot, and an unloading area at the Campton Forest Preserve near Wasco. A new entrance to the preserve was opened on Town Hall Road that winter. Gardening and rototilling began in Wasco in mid-April 1979 after the "hard winter." The Wednesday Card Club continued to meet that season, as did the LaFox Farmers Club, Wasco Ladies Aid, and the Wasco American Legion Post and Auxiliary.

The 1980s

The regular "Wasco & LaFox" column of the *Elburn Herald*, which had existed in one form or another for the better part of a century, was discontinued after the fall of 1980. The region had been rapidly changing for many years, and with the large increase of new arrivals in Campton Township, the sense of Wasco as a single community was, for some, being lost. Campton Township was then the fastest-growing township in Kane County, and its population had increased more than 170% in the previous ten years. As an unincorporated place, Wasco's exact population cannot be precisely known, but it certainly increased apace. Despite the rapid growth, several community institutions remained, of course, and some persisted even until the present day. Among these are the Wasco Ladies Aid, which enjoyed a healthy membership in the 1980s, the Wasco Baptist Church, and Wasco Elementary School, which continued to exist (and thrive in some cases) in part because of the population increase. Other groups which survived the 1980s, but which are no longer extant, include the Wednesday card club, the Wasco Winners 4-H Club, the LaFox Farmers Club, and the Wasco American Legion Post and Auxiliary.

In the 1980s and '90s, Patrick Henry Collins Jr., a native of Roundup, Montana, ran the Collins General Store in Wasco with his wife Julie. Julie Collins was a former accountant, and Pat worked for the Kane County Department of Transportation before acquiring the store in 1980. The Collinses lived just four houses away from the post office. The store was open for twenty-one years, and was located in the Bergland/Hummel building. It closed in October 2001, and was replaced by Kathy Munyon's The Corner Store. Pat Collins was a life member of the Kane County Farm Bureau and was active in the Wasco American Legion. He passed away in September 2017, at the age of ninety.

A small tornado passed through the Wasco area in June 1980. Some trees lost limbs, but no buildings were damaged. That month, both the Bowgren family reunion and the Ekstrom family reunion were held in the Elburn Forest Preserve. John Karametsos, the owner of the Wasco Inn, was killed in an automobile accident in June. The Wasco Inn was remodeled that summer, and the renovated dining room opened in August.

The Wasco Scouts hosted an all-you-can-eat "pizza bash" fundraiser at Wasco Elementary School on 11 April 1981. Admission was $3 for adults, or $10 for a family of four or more. A drink and dessert was included with the meal, which was followed by a "treasures and trash" auction. Wasco was also hosting important regional groups in this era. For example, on 23 September 1981, the Fox River Chapter of the American Women Business Association held their monthly meeting at the Wasco Inn.

The Wasco Winners 4-H Club earned an "A" rating for its act entitled 'The Wizard of 4-H,' which they presented at the Illinois State Fair's "Share the Fun" talent competition in August 1982. Many Kane County 4-Hers exhibited projects at the fair that year, ranging from horticulture, to decorating, to arts and crafts. The previous month, Kathy Farr of Wasco won two prizes for her market lambs at the Kane County Fair. The Wasco Blacksmith Shop celebrated its thirtieth anniversary in September 1983. There were refreshments, door prizes, and demonstrations, as well as discounts on all types of equipment from riding lawnmowers to chainsaws. Their slogan at the time was "The business that service built."

A description of Wasco from 1983 stated that "there is one of everything in Wasco," including one school, one church, one grocery store, one post office, one Legion hall, and so on. Wasco was hailed as "a good place to be outside on a summer day," and like today it was "rather difficult to determine where the community actually ends."

Wasco's last World War I veteran, George Vanderhoof, died on 28 May 1985, at the age of eighty-nine. He had lived in the township for his entire life, and his wife Margaret was the Wasco correspondent for the Elburn Herald from 1959 to 1980. They are mentioned frequently throughout this work.

On 7 September 1985, the citizens of Campton Township celebrated the 150th anniversary of the town's permanent settlement. A parade took place to celebrate the occasion – it began at The Farm restaurant, just west of Wasco. There were games and wagon rides following the parade; pony rides, concessions, and a square dance took place later in the day. Events were held at the Campton Forest Preserve near Wasco. The parade was coordinated by Cal Corron and Bob Johnson. At the parade, Melvin Peterson of the Wasco Blacksmith Shop won first prize for the float he created, which featured a birthday cake for the township. Students from Wasco Elementary School marched in the parade, as did members of the Wasco Cub Scouts. Norm Skala served as Master of Ceremonies.

A scene from the September 1985 Campton Township parade, just west of Wasco near Brown Road

One of Wasco's most popular restaurants is The Lodge, located at 41W379 Route 64. This restaurant is located on property that once belonged to the Brown family. The Olde Farm Inn (beginning in January 1989) and the Silverado Bar and Grill are among the Lodge's previous incarnations. The restaurant, previously called The Farm Inn, had been shut down by federal agents in February 1985 because the building had been used to launder drug money. The restaurant's owner prior to the seizure was Donald R. Thompson, who (in 1988) was convicted of laundering drug profits for his brother Raymond's "elaborate Florida smuggling operation" through his Wasco restaurant. After its reopening, the Olde Farm Inn restaurant (under Bruce and Valerie Jablonski) featured dishes such as Yankee pot roast, sole Rockefeller, marinated lobster tail, fried chicken, and homemade soups and desserts.

Calvin M. Corron passed away at Community Hospital, Geneva, on 4 May 1986. He was born in Elgin on 7 May 1925, was a lifelong Campton Township resident, and was a graduate of Northwestern University. He served on the Board of Directors of the Campton Township Cemetery Association, was active in Indian Guides and Cub Scouts, and was once Supervisor of Campton Township. Cal Corron was Director of Wasco Little League Baseball and served as a coach for that group for many years. He worked as an executive for the U. S. Steel Corporation. He was survived by his wife Dorothy, four children, and two grandchildren. Dorothy ("Dee") Corron became Chief Deputy Kane County Recorder in 1984. She had worked in that office for ten years, and was in the County Clerk's office prior to that. Dee was a graduate of Elgin High

School, the University of Illinois, and the Ellis Business School of Elgin. She was the co-chairman of the annual barbeque at Wasco School and was a Den Mother for the Wasco Cub Scouts.

The historic Rice/Johnson house in Wasco "burned to a shell" in July 1987. The home was built in the early 1870s, and had been owned by the Johnson family for eighty years prior to its destruction (see "Some Wasco Houses – Northwest Quarter").

Peter A. Peterson, formerly of Wasco, passed away on 19 August 1987, at the age of fifty-six. He was born in Aurora, but farmed in the Wasco area for most of his life. Pete Peterson was President of Garfield Cemetery Association, was a 4-H leader, and was a former President of the Kane County Livestock Breeders Association. Peterson coached basketball at Wasco Grade School, and was a baseball coach for the Wasco American Legion team. Pete Peterson was a member of Bethlehem Lutheran Church, and was survived by his wife Eleanor, as well as four children and three grandchildren.

Cal Corron at his family's homestead, 1985

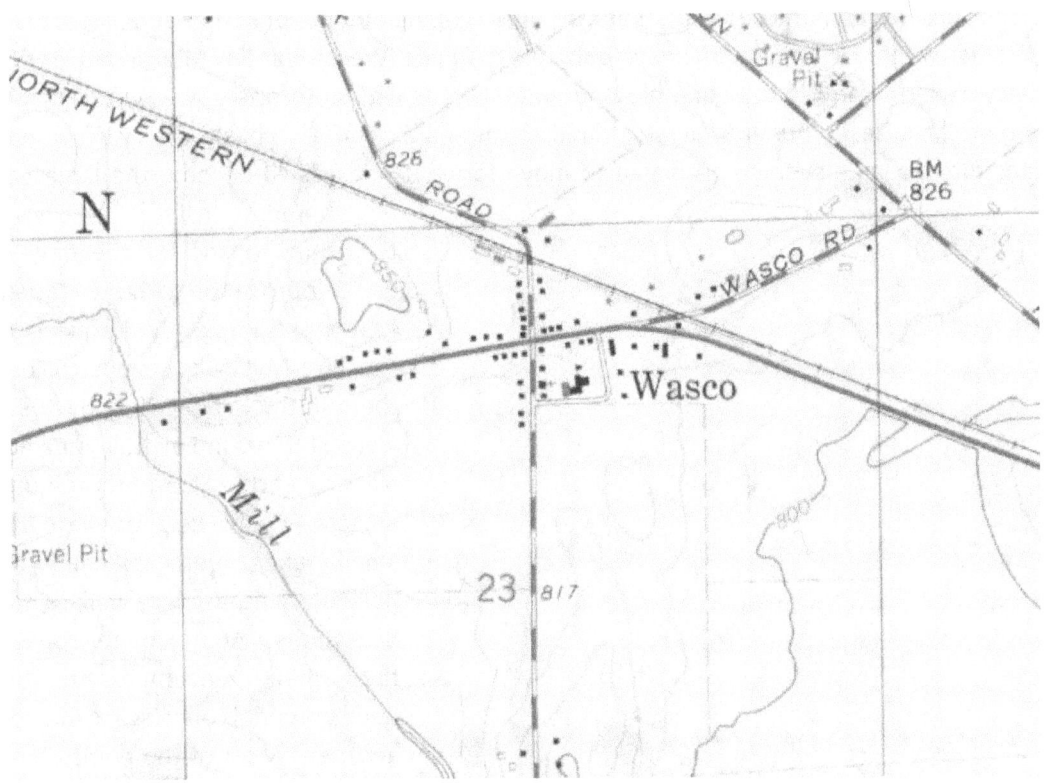

Topographic map of Wasco, with 1981 revisions

The theme of the August 1988 Vacation Bible School at Wasco Baptist Church was "My Wonderful Lord." The instructor was the church's summer missionary Sarah Pepple; the program was designed for children between the ages of four and twelve. The church offered a weekly "Friday Kids' Club" for children aged six to fourteen that year. The pastor was John Feldmann then, and the youth directors were Les and Sharon Pepple.

In June 1988, the Kane County Board passed a Preservation Ordinance which promoted the preservation of the county's surviving rural historic structures. This action was taken following a comprehensive report of the county's Historic Preservation Study Committee. This ordinance was the first of its kind passed in Illinois, and has helped protect a small number of historic properties in the Wasco area.

During the summer of 1989, Wasco American Legion Girls Softball remained very popular. The group fielded three "City League" teams that year in the 10-12 age bracket and two teams in the 7-9 bracket. They also had an Instructional League. The following year, their goal was to field a girls' traveling team of thirteen to fifteen-year-olds, and to begin playing under "fast-pitch" rules (see "Local Sports"). The Orange Crushers dominated the City League that year, winning the Rural Kane County Girls Softball Association Championship, while the Wasco White Sox and the Wasco Cubs both had winning records in the Instructional League.

The 1990s

By 1990, Campton Township's overall population exceeded seven thousand people, and Wasco continued to grow. The decade was marked by a dramatic expansion of the number of homes and places of business in the immediate area. First among the developments to impact Wasco was Fox Mill. In January 1990, St. Charles lawyers Jerry Boose and Kenneth Blood, operating as B&B Enterprises, were in negotiations to purchase more than seven hundred acres of land south and east of Wasco. In the last few months of 1991, plans for this large subdivision began to move forward – it was to become the largest housing development in the history of the township. Plans for the development were approved in 1992. Eventually, this vast and complex undertaking became the Fox Mill subdivision. Sales began there in the fall of 1994. By 1997, there were 686 lots in Fox Mill, ranging in size from a quarter-acre to three-quarters of an acre. Twelve neighborhood parks and small lakes were planned for this development, as were walking trails and bike paths. Approximately one-third of the area encompassed by the development is open space of one kind or another. Most of the homes built there in the 1990s used elements of traditional architectural styles popular in Illinois,

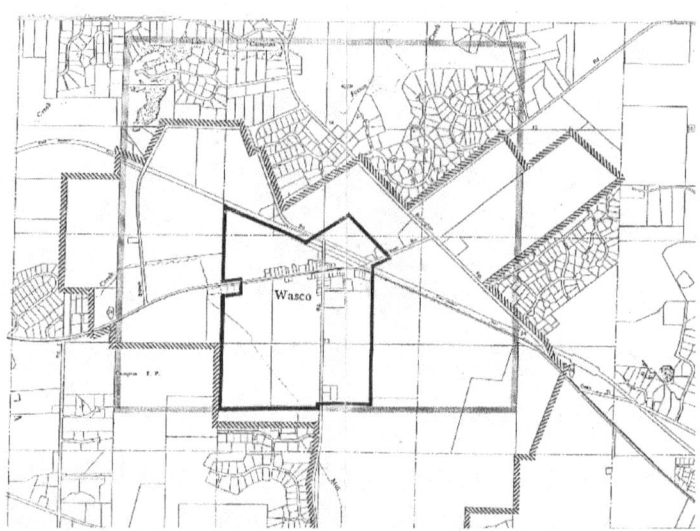
Map of the Wasco Sanitary District, 1990. Existing boundaries are indicated by the dark line, and the study area boundary by the dashed line

such as Prairie style, Italianate, Tudor, and Greek Revival. Many of the roads in Fox Mill are named for famous American poets and authors. Fox Mill is located in Sections 23, 24, 25, and 26 of Campton Township.

In May 1990, the Wasco Sanitary District created a proposed addendum to their 1980 facilities plan. Local landowners and residents were invited to a public meeting regarding these changes; the meeting took place at Wasco Elementary School on 12 July 1990. A significant local issue in the year 1990 was the at-times overwhelming accumulation of water in a play area near Wasco Elementary School. Every time it rained and significant water would build up there, local parents would call it "Wasco Lake." Storm water from much of Wasco was draining onto the school's property, and more residents began pointing out that the water possibly contained runoff from septic systems. The water was later tested, and found to be free from sewage, but the question helped prompt the vast expansion and modernization of the Wasco Sanitary District.

Lord of Life Lutheran Church held regular Sunday services in Wasco Elementary School throughout the years 1990, 1991, and 1992, while their permanent building at the corner of Route 38 and LaFox Road was under construction.

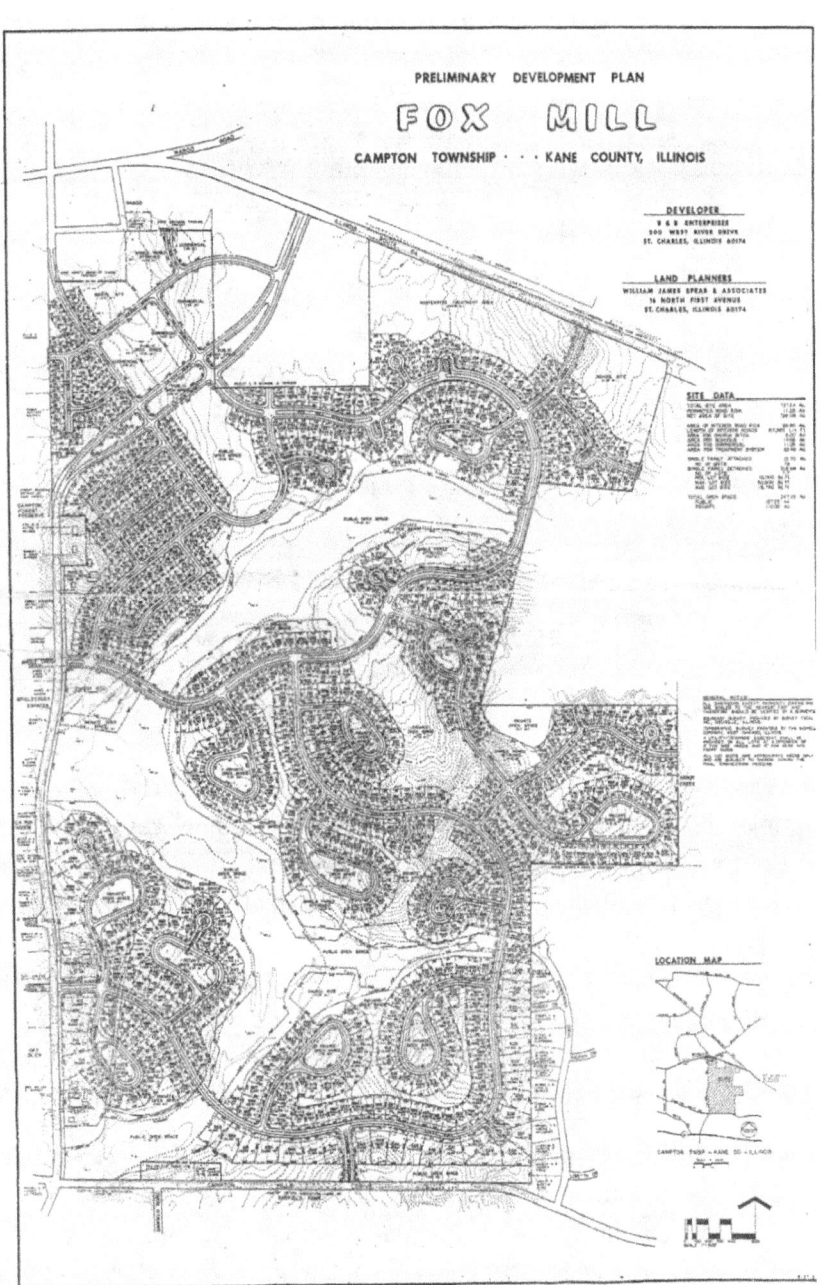

The original plan for the Fox Mill development, from 1992

The first service at the school took place early in 1989. During the summer of 1992, the church held vacation Bible school at Evergreen Valley Farm, on Brown Road in Wasco.

In March 1992, the Wasco Sanitary District put forward a referendum seeking the development of a waterworks system. The referendum passed with twenty-six votes in favor and twenty-one against. In

April 1994, the Wasco Sanitary District Board (at a very heavily-attended meeting) annexed the Fox Mill subdivision, and approved an agreement with the development's builders, B&B Enterprises.

In October 1993, an episode of "The Untouchables" television series was filmed in Wasco. The Bergland/Hummel store was featured prominently in the shooting. The location was "discovered" by Betsy Horning, a location coordinator with Paramount Pictures. Some filming also took place at the Ellis Johnson barn in Wasco on Route 64, and at Potter's General Store in LaFox.

A scene from "The Untouchables," filmed in Wasco in 1993

In 1994, Wasco Road was permanently bisected when the new realignment of Burlington Road was completed. Road construction there began in June and was completed by November. The intersection of Route 64 and Burlington Road was given left turn lanes and traffic signals, where none existed previously. In the fall of 1994, sales began at Fox Mill on the east side of Wasco. The first section of the development was known as the Hamlet, and consisted of nearly one hundred home sites. Models there opened in the spring of 1995. Fox Mill covers more than seven hundred and thirty acres of land east of LaFox Road, north of Campton Hills Road, and south of Route 64. It includes twenty acres of commercial development at its northern end, and a wastewater treatment plant at its southern end. Plans for the subdivision were approved by the Kane County Board in September 1992.

Sue McMahon began her job as Wasco's postmaster in the late 1980s, and is still serving in that capacity. In 1994, she maintained five hundred post boxes, plus a waiting list. McMahon worked in the Elgin post office before coming to Wasco. McMahon stated in an interview then that "there is no local government here [in Wasco] so when anyone wants to know anything, they call the post office."

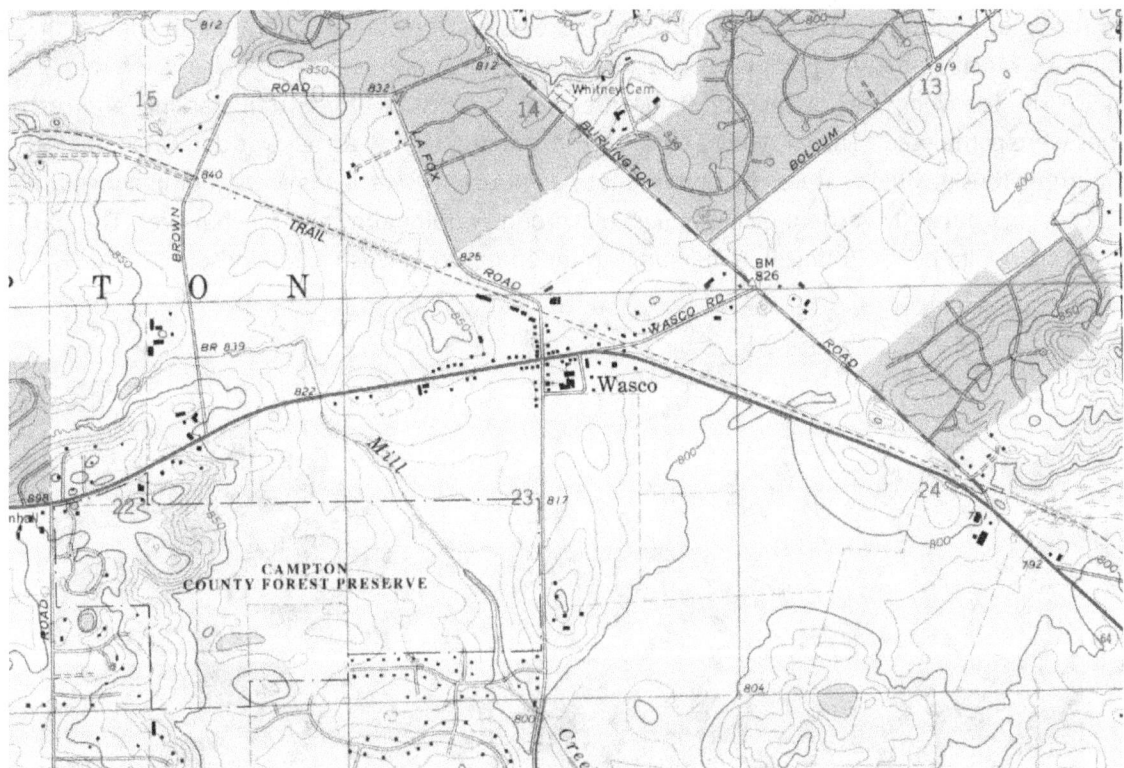
Wasco and the surrounding area in 1993, just before Fox Mill began construction

On 24 February 1994, there was a large propane explosion at Country Gas in Wasco, near the corner of Wasco Road and Route 64. Employee Russ Mazur was seriously injured in the accident. Kane County Deputy Steve Yahnke, who was off duty at the time of the explosion but was standing nearby when it occurred, alerted employees at the King's Mill furniture refinishing shop to call 9-1-1. Yahnke then found Mazur, and helped to extinguish fire in the victim's clothing. Two Country Gas employees quickly shut off the gas valves and electricity at the facility, and a potentially much worse disaster was averted.

The explosion at Wasco's Country Gas, in 1994

Campton Community Park, located on the west side of Wasco, was being developed in the mid-1990s. Land for the park, which was first primarily intended for baseball and softball fields, had been purchased in the fall of 1992 from Robert and Dolores Anderson. The park was later renamed in honor of the Anderson family. Money for the purchase came from many sources, both public and private, and numerous Wasco-area residents donated their time and talents to make the park a reality in the 1990s.

In the spring of 1996, the park's well and septic systems were installed, and most of the grading was completed. Much landscape planting was also accomplished that year, and Phase II for the site was planned. The following year, a baseball field, three soccer fields, a fitness trail, parking, and restroom facilities were completed. The forty-acre park (later expanded to fifty acres) was dedicated in 1997, and now features (besides the features just mentioned) an education wetlands area, multiple jogging trails, tennis courts, a butterfly garden, picnic tables, playground equipment, and much more. The park was renamed in 2007 to honor Robert P. Anderson, former Campton Township Supervisor.

Part of Anderson Park in Wasco, as it appears today

The St. Charles District 303 School Board put plans in place in September 1996 which projected more than three thousand new students entering the district in the next few years. This projection was in part based on discussions with five residential developers, who expected to build five thousand homes in the district over the same period. During the preceding three years, the district had already built one new middle school, and had added additions to one high school and six elementary schools. Wasco Elementary School's addition was built in 1998. The buildings' renovations and additions were largely funded through a successful 1993 referendum.

By May 1997, there were one hundred houses completed in the Fox Mill subdivision. The new water and sewer system was being connected to area homes then, and new fire hydrants were installed in Wasco soon afterward. The St. Charles and Elburn Fire Departments still served Wasco at that time. A new 400,000 gallon water tower had just then been completed, which was vital to the functionality of the new water system in Wasco.

Beginning in July 1998, Premier Development Group of Arlington Heights presented conceptual plans for the 44.5-acre site on the east side of Wasco located between the northern edge of Fox Mill and Route 64. Initial plans called for a retail center, an office complex, and forty-five homes. Campton Township Trustee Barb Wojnicki described the conceptual plan as "virtually building a brand-new Wasco." This parcel became known as the Campton Crossing development; construction began here in earnest during the fall of 2001. The initial plan for the property was rejected by the Campton Township Trustees in March of 1999. At that time, Wasco's only restaurant was the Wasco Inn, and its only convenience store was Collins General Store; the only stoplight in town was located at the intersection where Campton Crossing was built. Campton Square, which contains eighteen office and retail buildings, comprises the eastern part of the Campton Crossing development. The newest buildings in Campton Square were completed in 2005.

One of the nicely-landscaped entrances to Fox Mill, in Wasco

In September 1998, the St. Charles School District approved the construction of a new elementary school on a 10.5-acre parcel at the northeastern edge of Fox Mill. This building is now known as Bell-Graham Elementary. The Fox Mill subdivision was then "almost complete." By 2000, about two hundred and eighty homes had been finished in Fox Mill. Nearby subdivisions at Arbor Creek and Renault Manor were then underway.

A portion of the Campton Centre, located on the west side of LaFox Road in Wasco

In the summer of 1998, the new Congregational United Church of Christ of St. Charles opened at its new location just south of Wasco. The congregation, one of the oldest in Kane County, was established in 1837 with nine charter members, and its church on Walnut Street in St. Charles was dedicated in 1848. The congregation received a gift of land in Fox Mill in July 1995, during the pastorate of Rev. William L. Nagy. The congregation's new building was dedicated on 8 November 1998, exactly one hundred and fifty years after the dedication of the earlier building. The current church is located at 40W451 Fox Mill Boulevard, in Campton Hills. The church had 1,031 members in 2016. Rev. David E. Pattee has been the congregation's minister since January of that year.

The southern end of the Campton Square development in Wasco as it appears today

The Wasco Diamonds girls fast-pitch softball team continued to gain popularity in the late 1990s. In August 1998, tryouts were held at the Campton Township Community Park on Brown Road. There were twelve-and-under and fourteen-and-under teams, as well as younger teams not subject to tryouts that year. Some of the teams' sponsors then included local businesses such as Collins' Store, Wasco Nursery, Campton Excavating, and Kane County Bank. The league offered both instructional and recreational softball for girls ages five to sixteen. By early July 1998, all of the 8U and 6U teams had perfect 8-0 records, and the 14U traveling team won back-to-back tournaments that month. The League held its annual indoor winter clinic in March 1999, featuring instruction in proper batting, fielding, base running, and throwing technique. An additional class that April included an introduction to pitching. As of the third week of June 1999, all seven of the 6U and 8U Wasco Girls Fastpitch teams were undefeated, and one each of the 10U and 12U teams also had perfect records.

Campton Township officials purchased the old Wasco Great Western Depot in 1999 (see "Community Institutions – The Wasco Depot") and late in 2000 they solicited bids for both exterior and interior construction work on the building.

The 2000s

In the 2000s, a new wave of building took place in Wasco and the surrounding region, with new businesses coming to the heart of the village. The construction of Fox Creek, the building of a new elementary school nearby, and the completion of Campton Square and Fox Mill were all part of this trend. The Wasco area also embraced technology during this decade, as Campton Township's local government began using a new website to inform the public about important issues in the region. Internet usage increased dramatically, and some Wasco businesses began promoting themselves on social media sites and installed wireless routers for WiFi access near the end of the decade. The passage of two Open Space referenda during the 2000s added significant green space and protected land throughout the township, and the expansion of Anderson Park benefitted Wasco greatly. The restoration of the Campton Township Community Center took place in the early 2000s, after it was acquired for the use of the public. Also, the creation of the Village of Campton Hills in 2007 greatly affected Wasco.

Bell-Graham Elementary School, just east of Wasco, opened on 5 September 2000, and was dedicated on the first of October that year. The school is named in honor of retired educators Charles Bell and Kenneth and Robert Graham. Bell had been a teacher at Wasco Elementary School beginning in 1967. He later served as Principal of Richmond School; for the last eleven years of his career in the district, Bell was Principal of Munhall School. Robert and Kenneth Graham, who are twin brothers, began working for the district in 1966 at Wasco and Wild Rose Elementary Schools, respectively. The school's architect was Hestrup & Associates, and Dr. Cheryl Troyer was the school's first principal. The current enrollment of Bell-Graham, which is located on Fox Mill Boulevard and Route 64, is approximately four hundred students; Nathan Jarot is its Principal.

Soon after August 2000, the Campton Township Board began the restoration and expansion of the former Wasco Depot, which was purchased from the American Legion the previous year. It was also then that Township Supervisor Ed Malek formed a committee to explore the possibility of establishing an open space program in Campton Township. This committee was chaired by Kathleen Judy. In August, after presenting a petition with over nine hundred signatures favoring the establishment of such a program, the Town Board directed the committee to prepare an open space plan; this plan was presented in September 2000.

The entrance of Bell-Graham Elementary School, in 2018

The "Horton-Burnidge" building at 40W450 Route 64 was built in the year 2000. Today, the building houses several businesses, including the Urban Elegance Salon in the west half of the structure and Pizza Cucina (which opened in May 2001) in the east half. Sweet Dream Desserts, a cupcake and baked goods company based in Sycamore, opened a store in the building in 2010. Bean Appétit coffeehouse, owned by Kimberly Day, opened in the building in June 2001. Cup of Joy Café, a business which donated ten percent of its revenue to a local mission or ministry, was in the building in the late 2000s. A Perfect U salon, which also opened in 2001, preceded Urban Elegance in this building.

Campton Township voters approved an $18.7 million Open Space referendum in April 2001. The previous year, supporters of the referendum presented a petition to buy and preserve land for active and passive recreational purposes. Purchasing the land for these uses was made possible through the passage of the Township Open Space Act. A second open space referendum passed in 2005, which set aside $28.2 million for further land acquisition. Over 1,300 acres of land have been preserved to date, including Brown Road Meadows and the Campton Community Center property in Wasco.

Early in the spring of 2001, Campton Township purchased an additional five acres of land for the expansion of Anderson Park (then Community Park) in Wasco. The Anderson family then donated an additional five-acre adjoining parcel, part of which was used for prairie restoration. This combined ten-acre addition brought the park to fifty acres, its current size.

In 2002, the Fox Creek development was proposed in the southwest quarter of Wasco. The property was purchased by Fox Creek Limited Partnership in two parcels, the first in July 2003 and the second in June 2004, and construction began during the latter year. Many of the homes here were built in 2005 and 2006, although quite a few are newer. The major roads in the development are Fox Creek Drive, Blue Lake Circle, and Ellis Johnson Lane, the last of which is named for the property's long-time owner. The development comprises the major portion of the Rice/Johnson farm, mentioned many times throughout this work.

Fox Creek marketing map from 2002

From 2002 until November 2007, Sage Creek, a Fox Valley home décor and gift store, operated at the southeast corner of Route 64 and LaFox Road, in the Campton Crossing development. At the end of 2007, Sage Creek opened their new store at 1920 West Main Street, St. Charles, and the Wasco location closed its doors. Sage Creek was operated by Christina and Mark Kwasniewski.

Campton Township Trustees looked into creating an historic district in Wasco in the fall of 2002. Supervisor Neal Anderson was part of this effort, which began in earnest when the township's History and

Preservation committee approached the Board with the question of supporting a district similar to that created in the village of LaFox, which was the first unincorporated historic district in Illinois. Sam Santell, a Wasco resident who was then Kane County Director of Planning, was also a supporter of the creation of the historic district. The old Erickson blacksmith shop and two homes just east of the former Mather's Service Station had recently been razed, prompting some local officials to try and preserve Wasco's remaining historic buildings. Despite this support, the Wasco historic district was never created.

The Wasco Diamonds 18U team completed their 2003 season with a second-place finish in the AAA National Championships held in Kissimmee, Florida. The team advanced to the championship game for the first time in the program's history. They had finished the regular season with thirty wins, and had done so for the previous four years as well. The Diamonds hosted their first annual golf outing fundraiser in August 2003.

In 2004, District 303 was experiencing overcrowding in many of its schools. With 751 additional students that school year, the district saw the largest single-year growth in its history. The total enrollment at the end of the 2003-04 school year was 13,056. Two new elementary schools opened at the beginning of that school year, which helped to alleviate overcrowding in the other buildings.

On 1 June 2004, Wasco Corner Butchers opened at 40W484 Route 64, near the northeast corner of Route 64 and Old LaFox Roads. The business was located in the newly-constructed "Westbound Station" building, immediately east of (and adjoining) the former Mather building. The business was owned and operated by Chris Tope of Elburn. The retail portion of the business consisted of freshly-cut meats and seafood, as well as a deli and a dry goods grocery. Two smokehouses located on site allowed the business to sell their own smoked ribs and jerky. The storefront was vacant for several years after the Corner Butchers closed. In 2014, Spa La Vie, a popular and highly-rated organic skin spa, opened in the location previously occupied by Wasco Corner Butchers.

The Wasco Sanitary District had fewer than fifty voters cast ballots in its elections in the early 1990s. By November 2004, after the construction of Fox Mill and the vast expansion of the district's borders, budget, and scope, nearly one thousand voters cast ballots, an increase of over 2000%. In December 2004, the Wasco Sanitary District's water was judged to be the best tasting in the region, beating out competitors from nine other municipalities. The new ion exchange water treatment plant that became functional in March of that year was credited in part with the district's good-tasting water.

By 2005, the Fox Valley Astronomical Society, which is based in Wasco, had thirty-one members. The amateur stargazers' organization was founded in 1944, and its members meet monthly at Peck Farm Park in Geneva. The group's president in the 2000s was Herman Zwirn. Development in Wasco continued at that time. In May 2005, the Wasco Business Center plan was created. The owner/developer was the TAB Construction Company; the 3.34-acre site is located between Wasco Road, the Great Western Trail, and Burlington Road. A commercial building was built on the site in 2007.

The Wasco Diamonds 12U team placed first in the Woodstock Girls Softball Tournament held in July 2005. Tryouts for the 10U "Gems," a new Diamonds program, were held in August 2005 in Campton Township Community Park in Wasco. The program continued to grow, and by the end of the 2008 season the Diamonds had sent a total of forty teams to compete in national championship tournaments. In 2008, the 10U team finished second at the Northern Nationals in South Bend, Indiana, and the 11U team won their first national championship in St. Louis, Missouri. That year the Diamonds had girls participating the program from more than forty Fox Valley towns and villages, including (of course) Wasco.

The second annual "Bean There . . . Run That 5K" run took place in Wasco in October 2005. The event was sponsored by the Bean Appetit Coffee House, and proceeds raised benefited the Fox River Chapter of the American Red Cross.

In April 2006, Campton Township acquired significant property on the east side of Brown Road in Wasco, using $6.19 million of the money raised by the 2005 Open Space referendum. This parcel, which is eighty-five acres in size, is sometimes called Brown Road Meadows. It adjoins the Great Western Trail, and is located across from Anderson Park. The first controlled burn to encourage growth of native plant species took place there in 2011, and there were even found to be surviving prairie remnants near the former railroad tracks.

The Village of Campton Hills, which is approximately seventeen square miles in size, and which covers a bit less than half of the total territory of Campton Township, was created on 14 May 2007. The referendum to create the village, which is roughly centered around Wasco, appeared on the 17 April 2007 ballot. The Kane County Board approved a petition requesting the referendum that January. The population of the new village of Campton Hills three years after its incorporation was 11,131, with 3,492 households counted within the village's borders. A bit more than four thousand one hundred residents cast ballots in the referendum for incorporation. One-third of the village's population was under the age of nineteen, a significantly higher percent than in the region as a whole. Patsy Smith was Campton Hills' first village President; the first election for Campton Hills Village Board took place on 5 February 2008. There were five zip codes being used in the village that year, including Wasco's, 60183. Smith served as the village's president until 2015. She had served as chairwoman of the Campton Hills Incorporation Committee leading up to the referendum itself.

The Village of Campton Hills' offices are located at 40W270 LaFox Road

One very popular restaurant in Wasco today is the Old Towne Pub and Eatery, located at 40W290 LaFox Road. This location opened in 2005, through the efforts of Jason and Chris Cellini, who had earlier operated another Old Towne Pub in Geneva. The rapid growth of Fox Mill near Wasco spurred the brothers to open their second restaurant location. The site is adjacent to the Fox Mill Square commercial area, and the building was erected by Tracy Burnidge, who had also constructed several other buildings in the area. Old Towne Pub installed a full music stage in February 2015, and since that time has become a very popular local music venue. Kim Weiss is the restaurant's general manager in 2018. Another nearby eatery, Mel's Diner, located at 40W160 Campton Crossings Drive in Wasco, opened in the fall of 2008.

According to a Kane County estimate, some 20,095 people lived within a three-mile radius of the center of Wasco in 2006. The median age of those residents was just over thirty-seven years. In 2007, there was some discussion of whether the Wasco Sanitary District would remain independent, due to the incorporation of Campton Hills. The district did not dissolve as many predicted it would, though, since not all of its territory was inside the new village's boundaries.

The one-story commercial building at the Wasco Business Center was built in 2007

In 2007 and later, thousands of ash trees in and around Wasco were killed by the emerald ash borer. One hundred ash trees located near the entrance to the Campton Forest Preserve on Town Hall Road, just southwest of Wasco, were removed in March 2008. To make matters worse, a devastating storm destroyed over one thousand trees in Campton Township in August 2008. Many dozens of these trees were in the Wasco area. The Highway District's crew picked up debris for nearly a month afterward; the storm resulted in almost two hundred truckloads of wood ships, quadruple a typical amount for brush pickup dates.

The number of new structures built in Wasco (and the entire township) slowed down significantly in 2008, due to the economic downturn, and did not increase significantly for almost a decade afterward. Some residents wondered if Wasco would continue to exist as an unincorporated place at that time, since it's "territory" was by then entirely subsumed by Campton Hills. Therefore, in April 2009, there was an advisory referendum on the ballot in Campton Hills, asking if voters wished to "preserve [the] identity of Wasco." The measure passed, with 1,577 votes in favor of keeping Wasco's identity, and 549 against.

The 2010s

Wasco today is a fascinating mix of new and old, with buildings built more than a century apart standing side-by-side. Businesses continue to draw visitors and customers to the area, and Wasco's residents (now formally part of the Village of Campton Hills) contribute to the region's culture in every way imaginable.

Wasco Baseball and the Wasco Diamonds are amazingly successful local sports programs, which involve record numbers of participants every year.

In May 2010, after the Illinois Attorney General filed a pollution complaint against the Wasco Sanitary District, the district agreed to pay a penalty of $12,500 to the Environmental Protection Trust Fund to settle the complaint without admitting wrongdoing. The district affirmed its commitment to abide by pollution control laws and to strictly comply with its own operating permits.

Beginning in the spring of 2011, a series of public meetings were held to discuss updating the Village of Campton Hills' comprehensive growth plan. Conceptual plans for the area included a mix of open space, residential units, retail shopping, civic buildings, light industrial sites, row homes, and more. The meetings held at Wasco Elementary School that October and November were both very well-attended, and partly focused on a planned "town center" in Wasco.

The Corron Farm Preservation Society Board, in August 2017

The inaugural "Old Wasco Days" festival was held on Sunday, 3 July 2011, at Corron Farm, north of Wasco. It was sponsored by the Corron Farm Preservation Society, and the event was both free and open to the public. The Society's mission continues to be "to preserve, increase, and enrich knowledge of the history of the Corron farm and Campton Township." See the Society's website at www.corronfarm.org for details about the CFPS's events, membership information, and much more.

In July 2012, the Village of Campton Hills published its Comprehensive Plan. Patsy Smith was the Village President at the time. The plan represented the "cumulative effort of many individuals, including residents and stakeholders who attended public meetings and workshops" and who provided their expertise in identifying the municipality's top priorities for the future. Protecting local natural resources proved to be a top priority for many of the plan's more than two hundred contributors.

In March 2012, an advisory referendum asked Campton Hills voters if they wished to "push to keep" the post office in Wasco. The measure passed with 1,060 voters in favor and 706 against. The post office remains open to this day, as it has since the beginning of the village. In April 2012, a Great Western Trail clean-up event (in honor of Earth Day) took place in Wasco as well as both east and west of the village.

In July 2012, construction began on the Marathon gas station on the east side of Wasco (now 40W299 Route 64) and continued until the business opened the following year. At that time, the gas station was the only one of its kind on Route 64 between St. Charles and Sycamore. It was the first station opened by Carls Oil in Kane County. The company's plans were approved by the Campton Hills Village Board in a five-to-one vote. The gas station site was vacant for several years prior to construction, but once was the location of a dwelling (the Raasch home). Carls Oil is based in Hinkley, DeKalb County, Illinois.

The "Outpost" store at the Marathon gas station in Wasco, in 2018

The near-mint-condition 1948 Allis-Chalmers tractor on the grounds of the Marathon gas station in Wasco. The vehicle was restored by the Carls family in recent years. The image dates to 2018.

Wasco Nursery continued to conduct its annual spring open houses throughout the current decade, and every year the nursery offers interesting seminars such as butterfly gardening, new perennial introductions, and using native plants in landscaping. Wasco Nursery was voted the best garden center in the Fox Valley in July 2014. The nursery celebrated its 90th anniversary in 2015 with a series of spring open houses that April, which included guest speakers, raffle prizes, and a beautiful Morton Arboretum Photographic Society exhibit. The nursery's third annual Fall Family Fest will take place on 29-30 September 2018.

By 2014, the Wasco Girls Fastpitch Softball League was open to all area girls from kindergarten through twelfth grade. Spring training, including pitching and catching clinics, drills and conditioning, typically begins in April for the spring/summer season. Competitive 10U, 12U, and 14U teams require tryouts. Practices for the fall season begin in early August and the season concludes with the Susan G. Komen tournaments in mid-October. In October 2013, the 14U Wasco Team 4 won first place in the fourth annual "Pretty in Pink" tournament sponsored by the WGFSL. Pitcher Grace Sobieski threw five perfect innings, closed the third inning with a double play, and stole five bases during the championship game. Beginning in 2013, many clinics were offered in partnership with the Elite Sports Training Center in St. Charles. Tryouts for the all-star teams, the Wasco Warriors, begin in January. The thirteenth annual Wasco Diamonds golf outing took place on 18 September 2015 at Kishwaukee Country Club. The sixteenth annual golf outing is scheduled for 21 September 2018. The fourteenth annual WD Memorial Day Classic is scheduled for 24-26 May 2019.

Vegetables grown at Wasco Nursery, July 2018

One option put forward to the School District 303 Board of Education in the fall of 2015, in an effort to cut costs amid declining enrollment, was to close Wasco School. Lincoln School was also threatened with closure, but due in large part to vociferous community outcry at the possibility of either building closing, both of these elementary school buildings remain open to this day. Wasco Elementary School had 377 students at that time, and Lincoln had 245. In January 2016 the District 303 School Board voted unanimously to keep both schools open.

Since 2015, the Chicago-based Skyline Council of Landmarks Illinois has been working on advocating for the preservation and restoration of the historic Whitney schoolhouse, just east of Wasco. It is one of only two remaining nineteenth-century schoolhouses in Campton Township, and dates to 1852. Later in 2018, the building may be stabilized and relocated to the Gray Willows property owned by Campton Township, and may be ultimately restored into a usable building. See www.landmarks.org/skyline-council for further information on the preservation effort.

The Whitney school, near Wasco, as it appeared in the early 2000s

In 2017, the Wasco School Parent Teacher Organization held its seventeenth-annual bake sale to benefit the school's numerous programs and extracurriculars. Some popular activities for the 2017-18 school year included chess club, junior strings orchestra, band, and charitable events such as the Spirit Club's Toys for Kids event held in November and December. Also in 2017, Janice Stahl, a Chicago native who served as school secretary for Wasco Elementary for twenty-five years, passed away. School opened this year on Wednesday, 22 August 2018. Barbara Stokke is in her eleventh year as the principal of Wasco Elementary School.

In April 2017, with little fanfare, the Village of Campton Hills celebrated its tenth anniversary of incorporation. Harry Blecker is the current (2018) Village President. In January 2018, The Lodge on 64 hosted the sixth annual "Model Car Indoor Cruise In" for model car enthusiasts. The event, which featured 1:24 and 1:18 scale models of diecast cars, trucks, and motorcycles, was also held at The Lodge three years earlier, and was well-attended. The eleventh annual Prairie Fest took place at Corron Farm, north of Wasco, on 23 September 2017. This year's event is scheduled for 22 September, rain or shine. The eighth-annual Campton Hills Fall Fest will take place on 8 September 2018, at the Congregational United Church of Christ, just south of Wasco. The family-friendly event features live music, an outdoor movie, fireworks, a bags tournament, and other activities. Pulled pork, beef brisket, and many other food and drink options are available for purchase at the event.

Community Institutions

The Wasco Depot

The Wasco train station was one of the most important buildings in the village from its absolute beginning. Its early history, including its construction in 1887, has been covered already (see "Initial Settlement"). The depot building was located on the north side of the railroad tracks, not far from the northern edge of the Bergland lumberyard. The station master sent all messages from the depot either by telegraph, or by writing messages on paper that were then passed to the train engineer via a long, triangular stringed device on a forked pole as the train passed the station. Local children enjoyed playing on the box cars and coal cars left temporarily on the rail siding near the lumberyard, across from the depot. When trains would pass the station, they would normally not stop, but would either throw off a mail sack or pick up messages while passing along. When trains did stop, they would drop off or pick up packages held for delivery in the depot storage area. Sometimes they would leave freight cars filled with lumber, feed, or coal, to be unloaded into the adjacent Bergland & Company lumber yard.

The Chicago Great Western railroad (named such beginning in 1892) offered extensive passenger service in the late 19th and early 20th century. In local newspapers, the railroad was constantly advertising excursions from the Chicago area to Dubuque, Kansas City, Omaha, St. Paul, Des Moines, and other locations along their routes westward. As more and more farmers in the Wasco area purchased automobiles, however, passenger service began to decline. Charles Hurd was Wasco's first station agent, in the late 1880s. G. H. Martin was the Wasco station agent in 1905 and into 1906, when he took the agency of the Chicago Great Western station in Sycamore. He was succeeded in May 1906 by Charles Waterhouse of Byron, Illinois, whose son Paul succeeded his father in this position.

The earliest known dated photo of the Wasco Depot, from 1907

In 1907, the Chicago Great Western Railway offered one-way passenger rates to Minnesota, the Dakotas, and the Canadian Northwest. They also offered rates to Montana, Oregon, California, and "Homeseekers' Excursions to the Northwest, West, Southwest, and South." Tickets could be purchased from all local agents, including the agent at Wasco.

Beginning in the mid-1910s, Paul Waterhouse was the Great Western Railroad depot agent at Wasco. He worked in that capacity until the 1940s, and then worked as station agent in St. Charles until his retirement in August 1963. Waterhouse was also a Campton Township auditor in the 1940s and '50s and served as Township

Assessor in the 1960s. Often Paul Waterhouse's shifts at the Wasco depot would last until several hours after midnight. At 6:00 PM, the mail train would stop at the Wasco station to pick up the mail collected daily at the nearby Bergland Store. Besides the mail, there were often one or two cream containers being shipped to the Bowman Dairy in River Forest. In the late 1930s and early 1940s, Don Swanson would assist Mr. Waterhouse in pulling the wagon from the depot storage area into position alongside the railroad tracks. When the train arrived, the cans of cream and the mail were placed into the baggage car. The train (which consisted of the locomotive, fuel car, baggage car, and passenger car) was affectionately called "The Dinky." It would pull out of the station a few minutes after 6:00, on its way to St. Charles, and then to Chicago. Freight trains also ran along the route, and could have fifty cars or more. Among the cars being hauled then were refrigerator cars, carrying fruits and vegetables to the Chicago market. The perishables were kept cool by means of large slabs of ice placed along the outside walls of the cars. During the Depression, quite a few homeless men (and some women) rode in the empty boxcars.

The Wasco Depot, in 1914

Another item of interest relating to the Wasco Depot was the means of communication between agents and engineers during the early years. Local depot agents would tie handwritten notes to pieces of string, which would then be placed on wire triangles attached to a long handle. When passing by, the train engineer would extend his arm out of a locomotive window and would grab the messages by putting his arm through the triangle and pulling the messages in. Outside the station, there was a tall pole where several paddles of varying colors (often red, white, or green) could be placed to signal information to a passing train. Next to the depot agent's office was a door into a freight storage area. A window in the west side wall of the depot was used to transact ticket sales. Also, at the north end of the waiting room inside the station, there was an area where a ticket agent would sell tickets to individuals needed to board the trains to Chicago.

The Wasco Depot, as it appeared around World War I

The Wasco Depot in 1921 or earlier

Rex A. Pelley was the last station agent at the Wasco Depot. He was employed there beginning in 1950, and continued his employment until the fall of 1959 when the station was closed. Pelley was born in Delaware County, Iowa, on 27 March 1907. He and his wife lived in the Vanderhoof apartment in Wasco for almost nine years, and moved to Batavia in November 1959. He was station agent in DeKalb in 1962, but was still living in Batavia in the late 1960s. Pelley died in Palm Beach, Florida, on 1 January 1982.

Late in 1959, the Wasco Depot was purchased by the American Legion, and the following year it was moved a short distance west-northwest of its original location. In January 1960, the Legion had "nearly completed plans for transforming the defunct Great Western depot into a Legion Hall for use by the Post." The building was to be moved to a lot on the Ekstrom farm which the Legion had already purchased. In February 1960 it was reported that "many offers of help have been received and gratefully accepted" relating to the relocation and remodeling of the former Great Western Depot building. In the fall of 1960, the retiring officers of the Legion Post were: Clarence Raasch (Commander); John Schaefer (Vice Commander); Hillis Barber (Sergeant); Kenneth Johnson (Finance Officer); George Vanderhoof (Chaplain); and Dean Clopton (Adjutant). The building was "finally settled onto its new foundation" in mid-September 1960. The American Legion and Auxiliary sponsored an auction at the newly-restored building in May 1962, and in subsequent years. A new baseball diamond was built behind the Hall in May 1963.

The Wasco Depot in 1960

The Wasco Depot in the mid-1960s

The former Wasco Depot as it appeared in the 1970s

The Legion sponsored public dances in December 1965, November 1966, and December 1967. In April 1966 they sponsored a pancake and sausage supper at the Legion Home to benefit the baseball team. In 1974, the American Legion added onto the existing building, nearly doubling its size. Legion members and their wives enjoyed a fondue supper that April to celebrate the building's expansion. In August 1979, the Post sponsored a steak dinner for the Auxiliary in honor of their twenty-fifth anniversary. The building was used for the monthly Legion meetings, for the Annual Town Meetings in the 1970s, and for a wide variety of Lodge and community events in the 1980s and '90s.

In 1999, the Campton Township Board purchased the Wasco American Legion property. After receiving grant funding from both Kane County at the State of Illinois, the Board sought bids on the restoration and expansion of the building. This project was developed through the town's Land and Building Committee, chaired by Dan Dowling. The restoration and expansion of the building began in January 2001, and was completed that April. The $167,400 restoration project was coordinated by general contractor Howard Wallin of St. Charles, and by the Campton Community Center Committee. The building now functions as the Wasco Community Center, and houses the offices of the Campton Township Assessor. Township Board meetings are held there, which are open to the public. There are two baseball fields on the property, and the center's

A rare photograph of the interior of the Wasco Depot, from 1960, just after the American Legion purchased the building

parking lot offers access to the Great Western Trail. The main room of the building may be rented for small groups for a nominal fee.

The Wasco Community Center, formerly the Wasco Depot

Wasco Baptist Church

In 1890, Pastor William K. Lane of the Campton Baptist Society of Canada Corners (Lily Lake) saw the need for another church building in Campton Township. Lane had been holding services in various school buildings and houses of worship in the vicinity, and favored the construction of a church in or near Wasco, which by then had only been settled for a few years. Pastor Lane immediately began a subscription for a building fund, and this effort was quite successful. On 24 December 1890, Wasco farmer James C. Rice and his wife Maria sold a parcel of land to the Trustees of the Baptist Church of Wasco and their successors. Trustees at the time were J. W. Francisco, Albert Gilbert, J. C. Rice, J. A. Garfield, and D. W. Stevens. The purchase price for the lot was $1, a symbolic amount. The deed specifies that if the site should ever be abandoned for church purposes, the title is to revert to the Rice heirs, "as fully as if [the] indenture had never been made."

Organizational meetings for what would become the Wasco Baptist Church had been held in September and October 1890. The church's first pastor was Rev. Donald Hugh McGillivray, who was called in 1891. Rev. McGillivray was born in Lancaster, Ontario, on 13 August 1856. He came to the United States from Canada in 1890. Rev. McGillivray had three daughters (Margaret, Anna, and Abbie) born while he was a pastor in Wasco. Shortly before 1900, the family moved to Rock Island County, Illinois. For years after his pastorate was over, Rev. McGillivray visited Wasco, and stayed with old friends from the congregation. During his August 1907 visit, McGillivray brought his three daughters to town, and stayed with Mr. and Mrs. A. D. Chaffee.

On 22 July 1891, thirteen members of the Baptist church in Lily Lake petitioned to leave that congregation "for the purpose of uniting in the formation of a new Church at Wasco." Four of the founders were members of the Stevens family, and three were Garfields. Franklin E. Chaffee was also a church founder, though his letter of dismissal came from the Elgin Baptist Church. D. W. Stevens was elected the congregation's first deacon, R. K. Garfield was chosen as church clerk, and Jennie E. Garfield was elected church treasurer.

The charter members of the Wasco Baptist Church, 1891

The D. W. Stevens family, several of whom were among the founders of the Wasco Baptist Church in 1890. The back row has Mabel, Edith, Cyrenus, John, and Fred Stevens, with Lottie, D. W., Clara, Amelia, and Pary Stevens in front. The photo dates to about 1896.

The Wasco Baptist church was built in 1891, with the cornerstone being laid early that summer. The cost to construct the building was $2773, and the principal builders were brothers Charles W. and Daniel B. Millen. The main door to the building was (and still is) located in the base of the three-story bell tower, on the structure's west side. The new church edifice was dedicated on 8 November 1891. A celebratory dinner and supper were served in the Wasco Depot. The Wasco Church Sunday School was organized on 29 November 1891, with D. W. Stevens as Superintendent. Rev. D. H. McGillivray was the congregation's first pastor. The first choir was made up of Mr. and Mrs. C. E. Hurd, Clara Fischer, Carolyn Peterson, and Mrs. Isaac Barber. A five-person orchestra (composed of Angie and Julia Garfield, Arthur and Harry Burr, and C. E. Hurd) frequently furnished music during regular worship in the early years of the congregation.

The Wasco Ladies Aid was organized in 1890, before the church itself was built (see "Important Social Organizations") and included most of the wives and mothers in the small settlement. Rev. Lane was the person credited with the group's organization, and it was he that wrote the Ladies Aid's first constitution and bylaws. Mrs. A. D. [Phoebe] Chaffee was elected the first president of Wasco Ladies Aid. From the very beginning the Ladies Aid has helped furnish and maintain the Wasco Baptist Church, even contributing to some pastors' salaries. For further information on the Ladies Aid, see "Important Social Organizations."

The Baptist Young People's Union was organized on 12 November 1892 and continued through the early decades of the twentieth century. In 1894, twelve horse stalls were built near the Wasco church. These stalls (after 1906) were shared with the Wasco School, and stood for several decades afterward. The Wasco Baptist Church had fifty-six members in 1896, during the pastorate of Rev. T. Ketman. The building could accommodate up to three hundred congregants. Services were held at 10:30 AM and 7:30 PM, with Sunday School at noon, and prayer meetings on Fridays.

Sometime in the 1890s, Minnie Garfield (who was in her twenties at the time) was said to have been the first person baptized at the Wasco Baptist Church. Interestingly, the first wedding in the church itself did not occur until 29 July 1941! The first church organ was purchased in the 1890s for a cost of $55. A dining room was built in the church very early on, and a kitchen was installed a short time later. A furnace was installed before the first years of the twentieth century. All funds to pay for these improvements were raised by the Wasco Ladies Aid. The church grew consistently during its first decade of existence, and reached a record forty-two adult members by 1903. Most of the early ministers came either from the University of Chicago, Wheaton College, or the Baptist Theological Seminary.

In the year 1900, the Wasco Church held Sunday School each week at 10:00 AM. Preaching services were an hour later, and the "young people's prayer meeting" was held Sunday evening at 7:00. Evening services were held at 7:45 PM. During the decade of the 1900s, various members of the congregation (such as Grace Chaffee in late March 1901 or Edna (Allen) Kimble a month later) took turns leading the young people's prayer meeting. The Farther Lights Society was also active at that time.

The Wasco Church, in the very early years of the twentieth century, likely circa 1908

"Children's day exercises" took place at the Wasco Church on 11 June 1905. Christian Endeavor meetings were held at the church at 7:30 every Sunday evening beginning in 1905, or slightly earlier. Nettie Anderson entertained the Wasco Church Sunday School at her home in December 1905. The party featured a tree, a visit from Santa, and candy for the children. In February 1906, Rev. N. J. Peterson of the Wasco Church accepted a call to Verona, Wisconsin, and left the region. The following month, one of the largest baptisms ever to take place in the church occurred, with nine baptized candidates; Rev. Dent of Joliet baptized each of the new members.

Work began on improvements to the Wasco Baptist Church on 24 September 1906. The improvements entailed the installation of a "basement and furnace" according to a newspaper published at that time. A musical entertainment was held in the church (managed by Mrs. N. H. [Minerva] Warren) to raise funds for the improvements. There were no services held at the church in October 1906, while repairs were underway. In fact, all donations made toward the construction of the new basement were turned over to the Ladies Aid treasurer. Once the basement was completed the Ladies Aid furnished it with tables and chairs, a coal-burning stove, a water heater, a kitchen floor, curtains for the windows, and more. The Wasco Ladies Aid held a banquet in the new basement of the church on 3 May 1907, shortly after its completion. At this celebration, Mrs. Higgins sang, Mrs. Warren served as "toastmistress," and a twenty-five cent supper was served.

In January 1907, members of the Wasco Church elected their new slate of Sunday School officers. These included: J. I. Ellsworth (Superintendent); Flossie Austin (Assistant Superintendent); Floyd Bergland (Secretary); Olive Bolcum (Treasurer); Esther Bolcum (Librarian); and Florence Peterson (Organist). Rev. Hand of the University of Chicago was called to minister to the Wasco church in March 1908, and immediately organized a chorus class upon his arrival. Esther Bolcum (one of eight daughters of C. W. and Cassie Bolcum) taught a Sunday School class at the church in 1909.

The Wasco Church (as it was commonly known) hosted an "Old Neighbor's Day" on 24 February 1910. Dinner was provided by the Ladies Aid. Addresses by D. W. Stevens, A. D. Chaffee, and N. H. Warren made up a portion of the program. On 10 August 1913, the Campton Township Sunday School Convention was held in the Wasco church. Several of the Sunday School officers throughout Kane County had important parts to play in the program. Later that month, Eugenie St. John of Salina, Kansas, spoke at the church. She was "a very forceful speaker and an enthusiastic worker in . . . social reform."

The Wasco Baptist Church, in 1917

Something of a local scandal took place in Wasco in the mid-1910s. In September 1914, Rev. Ira Harkness of the Wasco Baptist Church quit his job, "to enter the employ of a 5 and 10 cent store in Quincy, Ill." Deacons of the Wasco Church said that their minister "resigned on account of the greater promises in a commercial career." However, "gossips" in town declared "that a kissing episode which created no end of excitement in the village" was actually responsible for the resignation!

On 2 February 1918, the Wasco Baptist Church broke tradition in allowing "all Christians," including women, to vote in calling the new pastor of the church. The congregation also extended communion to all evangelical denominations at that time, fostering a spirit of ecumenism and cooperation. Because it was the only church in the community, the Wasco Baptist Church promoted a sense of tolerance from the early days, and in 1926 it adopted resolutions making it less burdensome to be accepted into church membership. Church leaders promoted "tolerance and unity" and the church then "sought to meet the needs of those who were faithful attendants and gave their talents in support to the church." Throughout its history, the church building has been open for Bible study and to other denominations for services and funerals.

The Baptist Young People's Union was locally organized in 1922 and continued to exist well into the 1940s. Scores of local residents were active in the Wasco congregation in the 1920s and '30s. These included members of the following families, among others: Bagg, Bergland, Bowgren, Carlson, Corron, Crook, Erickson, Goldenstein, Jay, Johnsen, Johnson, Mather, Osborne, Potter, Wilkison, and Wynthein. Joseph Vasil Deletkanic was the pastor in Wasco in 1933 and 1934, during the depths of the Depression.

The "old Wasco church sheds" were torn down in May 1935, according to a statement in the *Elburn Herald* from early in that month. These were presumably the same stalls constructed behind the church in the mid-1890s. The church shared the stalls and barn with the nearby Wasco School starting in 1906, when that building was completed.

Throughout the 1930s, young divinity students from the University of Chicago would come to Wasco to preach. They would always have dinner with the Bergland family, and sometimes with other local families as well. The first wedding within the Wasco Baptist Church itself did not take place until 29 July 1941. Rev. Harold R. Elliott of Wheaton served as minister at that time. Edna Fischer re-organized the Sunday School on 4 May 1941; Flora Norton was appointed the Assistant Superintendent then, with the following teachers to assist: Lillian Elliott, Harold Elliott, Judith Richmond, Ethel Waterhouse, Josephine Cavoltsky, Gertrude McKay, and Flora Norton. No minister had served the Wasco Baptist Church for more than three consecutive years as of the outbreak of World War II.

The Wasco Baptist Church's float in the 1935 Campton Centennial parade

In the fall of 1941, Cal Cray (a Wasco handyman) installed the new bell in the bell tower of the Wasco Baptist Church. The bell was acquired "through the efforts of Paul Waterhouse." To install the bell, Cray nailed planks on the west side of the tower, which extended from the ground to the steeple. With a series of ropes and pulleys, the bell was hoisted to the top of the tower, where it was installed. Following its installation, the bell ran on Sunday mornings to call Wasco's residents to worship. The bell was considered by the community as a source of great pride. D. W. Stevens, Nettie G. Anderson, and Floyd H. Bergland were church Trustees at the time of the bell's installation. The 1941 bell still resides in the church tower today. The rope attached to the bell hangs through a hole in the ceiling.

The pulpit, altar, and baptismal font are located in the sanctuary of the church. A coat room and gathering room are located on the main floor, and a large community room is located downstairs. This space was often used for Sunday School and for lunches, dinners, or other community events. A kitchen was added on the north side of this room; this renovation was paid for by the Wasco Ladies Aid.

More than two hundred people attended the congregation's Fiftieth Anniversary dinner on 17 October 1941. Beatrice Johnson played piano selections both before and after the special program. Pastor Harold R. Elliott (of Wheaton) led the anniversary service on the Sunday following the dinner. The new church bell was rung fifty times for the occasion. Lottie (Stevens) Brown was the only charter member present at the event, though her father D. W. Stevens, at the age of ninety-eight, was still living at the time. The services were closed with the song "Blest Be the Tie That Binds." Jess Horan played for the opening and closing of the service. One of the singers at the event was Mrs. P. G. Plummer of Michigan, who had sung in the first church choir in 1891. Elva Garfield of Geneva played two piano selections, and Irma Erickson sang a vocal solo at the congregational celebration.

At the end of World War II, in 1945, Deacons of the Wasco Baptist Church were Bud Wynthein, Henry Verhaeghe, and Fern Johnson. Trustees were John Goldenstein, Raymond Fischer, and Nettie Anderson. Esther Johnson was Church Treasurer, while Judith Richmond was Chairman of the Supper Committee. The church was improved at that time with the installation of new carpet, an altar rail, electrical work, a new roof, and paint and plasterwork throughout the structure. David J. Klasing became pastor in June 1950, and emphasized an annual Sunday School Christmas program throughout his six-year tenure, the longest of any Wasco pastor up to that time. These programs were among the most well-attended in the history of the church. In May 1951, Rev. Klasing's message for a special "4-H Sunday" program was "God's Message in the Mess Age." The congregation had over forty ministers in its first half-century of existence, but just eleven over its second fifty years.

The Wasco Baptist Church in 1934

In 1955, the Rice heirs (including Louise Swarthout, Louella (Rice) Tappan, Alice M. Swarthout, Florence Swarthout, Irene Rice, and Byrd Rice) quit their claim to the Wasco Baptist Church property. The church's trustees then were Julius Wynthein, Stanley Bowgren, and Roscoe Pierce. New pews were installed in the church in May 1955. The Hammond organ and pulpit furniture were new at that time. The Wasco Baptist Church purchased the house to its immediate south as a parsonage in November 1955 (see "Some Wasco Houses – Southeast Quarter"). The congregation has had full-time pastors since 6 March 1957, when Rev. Elmer Davis began his pastorate. The congregation adopted a new constitution on 13 April 1959, in which the church's mission was declared to be "to promote the worship of God by preaching the Gospel of the Lord Jesus Christ at home and abroad, trusting that, as a result, sinners shall be saved and believers edified and built up in the faith." Between 1959 and 1967 the congregation was affiliated with the Conservative Baptist Association, but thereafter its affiliation became independent.

Wasco Sunday School Class, about 1958. The teacher was Ethel Waterhouse, and the students included Christine Johnson, Roberta Bates, Sally Corron, Nancy Jay, John Wynthein, and Ron Leathers

The church vestibule and auditorium were remodeled in February 1966. That March, Rev. Richard Paige gave his farewell sermon, and was given a sendoff party by the congregation. A new cement floor was laid in the church basement in 1967, and the parsonage was completely redecorated and improved that year. The church nave was also updated and redecorated then. Evergreen trees, donated by the Wasco Nursery, were newly-planted at that time, and new sidewalks were laid in front of the church and parsonage then as well. As of 1967, Edna Cray was the congregation's longest-serving member and had been attending regularly for fifty-two years. The next-longest-serving members were Julius Wynthein and Mr. and Mrs. John Goldenstein. There were thirty-three active members then. Julius Wynthein had married Margaret Carlson in the Wasco Baptist Church in May 1945; this was one of the first marriages to take place in the building.

During the first week of November 1967, the congregation celebrated its (slightly belated) seventy-fifth anniversary. Seven former pastors attended the event. Rev. G. William Bauerlein was pastor then, and Deacons were Dan Rediger and Dale Schaefer. Brenda Wiegel played the organ at the celebration service, and Palma Bauerlein played the piano. Rev. Bauerlein came to the congregation at the end of February, 1967, from Dolton, Wisconsin. That year, Ann Brown was church treasurer, and the Trustees were Roscoe Pierce, Julius Wynthein, and Garfield Harley. Other church officers included Donna Rees (Clerk) and Margaret Johnson (Financial Secretary). Some missions supported by the congregation in the late 1960s were the Sudan Interior Mission, the Gospel Missionary Union, the Baptist World Mission, the Moody

Bible Institute, and the Rural Bible Crusade. The church held a regular evening service in the late 1960s, for both prayer and Bible study.

The Wasco Baptist Church in 2018

In the fall of 1970, B & B Builders repaired the roof of the Wasco Baptist Church, and performed many other needed repairs. Two church organizations (the Women's Fellowship and the youth group) were both quite active in the 1970s. In January 1975, Mrs. Garfield Harley entertained seventeen ladies of the Wasco Baptist Church Fellowship in her home. Pastor John Hyde was appointed to minister to the congregation in March 1979. The church youth group held its bowling party in Aurora in September 1979. The family of Pastor John Hyde was honored at a potluck dinner in March 1980 to celebrate his first anniversary as pastor of the Wasco Baptist Church.

Pastor John Feldmann of Elgin was the church's full-time minister beginning in August 1981. In 1987, there were worship services at 11:00 AM and 7:00 PM every Sunday. Youth directors that year were Les and Sharon Pepple. There was also a "Kids Club" that met at the church every Friday; it was open to youth from the ages of six to fourteen. A Vacation Bible School was held each August. In June 1989, an area north of the church building was paved for off-street parking. Pastor Feldmann of Elgin broke the record for longest ministry in the church's history, when he passed his ten-year mark at the time of the church centennial. The church bell was rung one hundred times at the Centennial Service in 1991. The support beams beneath the bell were replaced in 2009. The church parsonage is open to missionaries visiting the United States. Currently the church, which is located at 4N783 Old LaFox Road, maintains a small but dedicated and close-knit core of worshippers. In 2015, the Wasco Baptist Church celebrated its 125th anniversary. Pastor Bruce Miller is the church's current minister. Worship is held in the church each Sunday morning at 11:00.

Wasco School

The Wasco School was and is the most important educational institution in central Campton Township and has been open since 1906. The original building was a two-story red brick structure, located on the present school site. The property on which the school was built was sold by James C. and Lucy M. Rice to the Trustees of Schools of Township 40 North Range 7 East of the Third Principal Meridian on 19 October 1905. The price paid was $574.50, and the size of the parcel was two-and-a-half acres, plus a public road along the southern and eastern boundary of the lot. Wasco was said to be the third locality in Illinois to form a consolidated school. One of the most tireless and vocal supporters of the creation of a consolidated school at Wasco was D. W. Stevens, Campton Township Supervisor and School Trustee.

Initial meetings regarding the possible consolidation of the four rural school districts in and near Wasco were held as early as March 1905. That month, prospects for the consolidation were rated "good" in the local newspapers. The district consolidation itself was approved the following month, and the formal meeting to elect a school board for the "newly-consolidated district" in Wasco took place in Bergland's Hall, Wasco, on 13 May 1905. The first three school trustees were A. D. Chaffee, E. S. Sharp, and Frank Vanderhoof. Although for decades only primary schools were supported by public tax dollars in Illinois, school reform became a priority during the Progressive era, and by the first years of the twentieth century a great number of local residents agitated for the expansion of public education. This movement included the construction of secondary schools, especially high schools. Chautauquas, adult education meetings mentioned elsewhere in this work, were quite popular in Campton Township in the first years of the 1900s and offered another means for supporters of the reform school movement to learn about and further the cause.

Wasco School prior to 1910 - note the lack of trees on the grounds

On 3 June 1905, there was a vote held on where to build the new Wasco School. Two sites were voted upon – the present school site "adjoining the church east," and the "H. Higgins site," on the west side of the village. The present site received fifty-six votes, and the Higgins site twenty-eight. On the same day, local voters passed a $6000 bond to fund the school's construction, by a vote of seventy-one to twenty-nine. The two-and-a-half-acre Rice site was purchased on 5 October 1905, for $574.50. Construction work began the following spring; the new school's foundation was completed on 8 June 1906.

The newly-completed school building in Wasco opened on Monday, 1 October 1906, with sixty-seven total pupils. All elementary and the first two high school grades were taught at the school. The teachers then were: Alberta Thurber (principal, who taught the upper grades); Ella C. Adams (who taught the intermediate grades); and Jennie Garfield (who taught the primary grades). Miss Garfield had previously taught at the Old Red Schoolhouse south of Wasco. The Wasco School's formal dedication took place on Saturday, 10 November 1906. One among the three hundred people attending the dedication was the elderly Delia (Quackenbush) Wilkinson, who had been the very first teacher at the White schoolhouse east of Wasco when it opened in the early 1850s.

The dedication exercises for the Wasco School lasted the entire day and were "devoted to discussions, histories, addresses presenting library decorations and fixtures, recitations and music." The Honorable Frank Hall, who was hailed by some as "the best country school teacher in the United States," and State Superintendent Bayless gave the principal addresses. Histories of the three rural districts which had consolidated (the White School, the Stone School, and the Red School) were given as part of the program. A tree was planted outside of the building, and many regional district superintendents spoke to the assembled crowd. The singing, speeches, dinner, and conversation lasted "until early candle light" that evening, and the food served at the dedication ceremony "hardly could be surpassed."

Wasco's first substitute teacher was Ida Sharp, who filled in for Miss Garfield when she visited relatives in North Carolina the first winter that the school was open. When Miss Adams, the school's first intermediate-grade teacher, left Wasco to take a position in Fort Wayne, Indiana, in March 1907, she was replaced by Miss Sharp. Genevieve Coy joined the faculty at some point during the 1906-1907 school year as well.

The Wasco School as it appeared in the early 1910s

The first entertainment given at the newly-opened Wasco School took place on 20 February 1907, when a combination of dialogue, drills, and both vocal and instrumental music was presented. Admissions raised $25 to benefit the school that day. The event was "very largely attended by an appreciative audience." Pearl V. Webb was the first student to graduate from Wasco School in June 1907. Pearl was born in Campton Township on 19 November 1891, and was the daughter of Frank J. and Mertell (Whitney) Webb. Wasco also had two residents graduate from St. Charles High School that year – Arthur Bolcum and May Sharp.

On the west side of the school's interior there was a vestibule for handing hats and coats, along with a bench for lunches. The basement held (besides a boiler room) a multipurpose room used for indoor games during rainy or snowy days. For many years, first and second grades were taught in one room on the first floor of the building, with the third, fourth, and fifth grades being taught in another room. The sixth, seventh, and eighth grade room had a row of desks for each grade, with the younger children nearest the blackboard. The school also had a library. Early teachers included Alberta Thurber, Genevieve Coy, Esther Bolcum, Ada Bell, Gertrude Eddy, Harriet Eddy, Margaret Berg, Pauline Williams, and Esther Johnson. Various instructors (the last of which was Leonard Thompson) taught the high school grades in a room on the second floor while the school had such a program – this program existed until 1941. After this year nearly all Wasco students of high-school age continuing their education attended secondary school in St. Charles.

During the 1906-1907 school year, there were eight sixth-grade students at the Wasco School; eleven seventh-grade students; six eighth-grade students; and six ninth-grade students. Those in ninth grade that year were Lillian Kayner, Gertrude Bolcum, Myrtle Bolcum, Rose Johnson, Wilbur Mongerson, and Ernest Lofgren. Four of these students (Kayner, Johnson, and the Bolcum girls) were the first to graduate from the Wasco School's two-year high school program, on 1 June 1908. The Illinois Superintendent of Schools gave the address at the occasion, "which proved exceedingly interesting and practical," according to one observer. Good music "added greatly to the success of the program." The class colors that year were blue and yellow. Their motto was: "To be, and not to seem." Kane County Superintendent H. A. Dean awarded the diplomas to the four graduates. A local newspaper wrote that "much praise is allotted to our principal for the success of the day and we will all cherish these the first graduating exercises, as a pleasant memory." In early September 1908, the school opened with eighty pupils in total, across all grades. The second class of graduates from the high school grades at Wasco consisted (in 1909) of Bert Holmquist, Earle Mapes, George Anderson, Florence Bell, and Bernice Guthrie. The teachers during the 1909-1910 school year were Zoe Melville (of Wilmette), Esther Bolcum, and Esther Johnson, both of Wasco.

The Wasco School, probably in the late 1910s

The fourth annual commencement exercises of the "Wasco Consolidated School" took place on Thursday, 1 June 1911. The class colors (which during that era often varied from year to year) were light green and gold. Graduates were Albert Peterson, who read an essay on the Panama Canal, Amy Denker, who read an essay on Henry Bergh, and George Vanderhoof, who read an essay on irrigation. Jennie Denker's essay was entitled "Wanted: A Leader" and Adolph Mongerson's was on Luther Burbank. Misses Swanson and Webb performed a piano duet, and the high school quintet sang "Pretty Village Maiden."

Ada L. Bell taught first, second, third, and fourth grades at Wasco School in 1912. Esther Bolcum taught fifth, sixth, and seventh grades that year. In November 1913, the girls of Wasco high school organized a basketball team. There was a spelling bee conducted at the Wasco School in March 1915; school was canceled in Lily Lake because of the event, which invited spellers from across the township. The school lacked running water and a well in the early years, and therefore large water jugs were kept in the school building for both drinking and washing. During that era, first through fifth grades were taught in two classrooms on the first floor, and sixth through tenth grades were taught upstairs.

The upper grades of Wasco School in 1912. Front row: Lawrence McGowan, Clyde Crook, George Hawkins Earl Johnson, Harold McGowan, Wilfred Eddy. Middle row: Madge Osborne, Letha Wilcox, _____ Swanson, and Emil Swanson. Back row: Charlie Millen, Vern Nash, Evelyn Whitney, Rudolph Mongerson, Paul Scott, Marie Downey, Grace Vanderhoof, and Albert Wilson, principal

Students at the Wasco School in its early years, likely late 1910s

Ada L. Bell with her students at Wasco School, 1912. The front row has, left to right: Vera Carlson, Johnny Brown, Marian McGowan, Gertie Eddy, Harold Wilcox, Palmer Whitney, Dorothy Johnson, and Lillian Waterhouse. Second row: Robert Wilcox, Lola Millen, Ella Nash, Viola Carlson, Lavina Johnson, Mabel Harrison, Harriet Ellsworth, Johnnie Olson, and Frances Nash. Third row: George Olson, Lloyd Johnson, Hazel Johnson, Freeman Elvin, Marie Johnson, Frank Saelens, and Mildred Hawkins. Back row: Miss Bell, Frances Eddy, Mabel Travis, Elmer Ekstrom, and an unknown student

In February 1917, there was a "large attendance of basket ball enthusiasts" to witness the Elburn All-Stars play the Wasco high school basketball team. Whether the team consisted of boys or girls is not mentioned, but Wasco was soundly defeated, 42-7. In May 1918, as part of the regional war effort, the students at Wasco School sold $2795.50 in war savings stamps. Harriet Eddy sold the largest number of bonds, with almost one-third of the total amount raised.

On 24 April 1920, the "Little Ten" athletic conference of Kane County was formed in an effort "to boost athletics in the smaller high schools in Kane County." One of the founding schools was the Wasco Consolidated School. Others included the schools in Plato Township, Burlington, Lily Lake, Maple Park, Elburn, Kaneville, Hampshire, Big Rock, and Sugar Grove. The conference's first event was a track and field meet held in May. In September 1920, the teachers at the Wasco School were Jennie Denker, Esther Johnson, Alice Peterson, Irene Hawkins, and Ethel Waterhouse. Mr. Lively of Oblong, Illinois, was the new principal that year. Those graduating from Wasco School on 2 June 1922, after completing tenth grade, were: Johnny Olson; Gertrude Eddy; Lilly Larson; and Mabel Harrison. There was a Wasco School baseball team by 1923, and a diamond was already built near the school by the following fall.

Students at Wasco School, May 1921

Anne C. Askeland, who was born in Esmond, in DeKalb County, on 16 September 1906, graduated from Sycamore High School in 1923. After obtaining her teaching license and a degree from the Normal School in DeKalb four years later, she was offered a job at Wasco School. Miss Askeland married Adolph Mongerson on 22 November 1930, in Esmond. Her bridal shower was held at the Waterhouse home in Wasco, and was sponsored by the Wasco Dramatic Club. A two-course luncheon was served at the event, and the card game five hundred was played. The Mongersons spent their honeymoon at the Mammoth Caves in Kentucky. Anne's husband and his family were dairy farmers until 1940, when they "engaged in feeder operations." Since the time of their marriage, Adolph and Anne Mongerson lived in a house on the west side of the present LaFox Road, south of Wasco. Mrs. Mongerson kept a "profuse and beautiful" flower garden west of the home for many years. A 1946 article stated that Mrs. Mongerson's "teaching career was cut short by marriage and she has done her post-graduate work as a housewife." She later returned to teaching, however. Beginning in 1951, Anne (Askeland) Mongerson taught fourth grade at Lincoln School in St. Charles. Anne's daughter Nancy also taught at Wasco School for many years.

Games played during recess at Wasco School in the 1910s and '20s included tag, catch, jacks, hopscotch, baseball, and Pom Pom Pullaway. A swing and teeter-totter were installed in the playground by 1925. In the mid-1920s, the Wasco School averaged approximately eighty students in all ten grades combined. Teachers during that decade included Ethel Waterhouse, Esther Johnson, Harriet Eddy, and Lucy A. Pease. Mrs. Auer of St. Charles became the new music teacher at Wasco School in the fall of 1929.

A play performed at Wasco School in the mid-1920s

Ethel Waterhouse's "Daily Program" for her 1st-3rd grade classes, for the 1926-1927 school year

Teachers at Wasco in the late 1920s and early '30s included Anne Askeland (mentioned above) and Jess Horan, who was Wasco School's principal beginning in 1928. Five students graduated at the conclusion of the 1928-1929 school year. They were: Florence Olson, Rose Strom, Hilton Bowgren, Ellis Johnson, and

Eric Hawkins. The diplomas were presented by George Hawkins of Wasco. The class motto was "Rowing Not Drifting." Rev. C. B. Jenson gave an address to the graduates, and the program included songs by the boys' and girls' chorus. Due to the influenza epidemic during the winter of 1928/29, the Wasco School stayed closed until 7 January 1929, several days after its originally-scheduled opening. Even then, several Wasco residents were still sick with the flu.

Wasco School students (lower grades) in 1928

Wasco School graduates in the spring of 1930 were: Hazel Anderson, Leroy Lindquist, Doris Johnson, Frances Johnson, Ralph Wilkison, Paul Ross, and Dwight Bateman. The play that year was "The Little Clodhopper." In May 1931, the high school class play in Wasco was "Raspberry Red," which was a great success. Enrollment in the high school grades (ninth and tenth) at that time hovered at close to a dozen students. The school had a large boiler in the basement at that time, and the classrooms were all heated using steam radiators. Wasco Students seem to have been close to their teachers during the Depression. For example, the high school students threw Mr. J. C. Horan a surprise birthday party after school just before winter break in 1931. The following year, in November 1932, the ninth and tenth-grade students at the Wasco School "enjoyed a Halloween party at the Benson home" with Mr. Horan. Prizes were awarded to Helen Johnson, Elaine Ekstrom, George Marvin, and Gordon Swanson. Jess C. Horan took the high school pupils to Geneva in October 1933, where they enjoyed a picnic on Herrington Island in the Fox River. Mr. Horan even took his pupils to the Century of Progress World's Fair in Chicago in the fall of 1933.

In June 1933, the high school pupils at Wasco School presented a play entitled "One Minute to Twelve." The cast included Orvel Tarnow, George Marvin, Rose Wilkison, Elaine Ekstrom, Dorothy Benson, Edna Olson, Evelyn Jay, Helen Johnson, Gordon Swanson, and Gladys Bowgren. Mr. Horan directed the play. In February 1934, he was still serving as principal of Wasco School, and took the female high school students to see "Little Women." Mr. Horan later (by 1941) moved to Chicago, and then to Rockford, but continued to visit friends in Wasco until his untimely death in April 1951.

Wasco School as it appeared around 1930

An early play performed at Wasco School, probably in the late 1920s

Edna Olson and Erma Erickson were the only two students to complete tenth grade at Wasco School in 1934 – as was typical for Wasco students of that era, both women continued her studies at St. Charles High School, graduating from that institution two years later. During the Depression years of the mid-to-late 1930s, each of the eighty or so students enrolled in Wasco School would bring in one vegetable every day to be used in a large soup kettle. The vegetable soup made from the students' contributions was served daily for lunch. In July 1934, the Wasco 4-H Club sponsored a "basket social" in the school building. There were sixty-six pupils enrolled in the Wasco School during the 1934-1935 school year. In March 1935, the Wasco Dramatic Club presented "The Yellow Shadow," a mystery comedy in three acts, in the Wasco School auditorium. Some of the actors included Harold Erickson, Raymond Fischer, Blanche Allen, Margaret Berg, Edna Fischer, Arthur Brown, George Brown, Louis Bolwahnn, Irma Erickson, and Paul Waterhouse.

The Wasco School and its students in April 1931

Roller skating at Wasco School, March 1932. Shown are Orville Tarnow, George Marvin, Frances Schultz, Gordon Swanson, Gladys Bowgren, Elaine Ekstrom, and Dorothy Benson

On 29 May 1935, commencement ceremonies were held in the Wasco School auditorium. The featured speaker was O. V. Waters, principal of East Aurora High School. Those graduating from tenth grade and thus leaving Wasco School then were: Ethel Bell Johnson, Ester Wilkison, Doris Strom, Adeline Close, and Helen Jay. Graduating from eighth grade were: Louise Barrett, Roy Olson, Robert Carlson, George Olson, Doris Ekstrom, and Charles Bowgren.

A selection of the books read by the upper grades at Wasco School during the 1936-37 school year include: *Ben Hur, Ivanhoe, The Merchant of Venice, A Christmas Carol, Les Miserables, Tales of Wayside Inn, Hiawatha, Man Without a Country, Evangeline, David Copperfield,* and *The Courtship of Miles Standish*. Some books purchased for the students of Wasco School's lower grades during the 1938-39 school year included: *David's Friends at School, Susan's Neighbors, The Billy & Frisky Stories, In Rabbitville, The Teenie Weenies, Three Little Indians, Visit to Grandmother, The Sunbonnet Primer, The Quins' Book, Mickey Mouse, Shining Star,* and *Little Elephant Catches Cold*. There were seven high school graduates in the spring of 1938, and ten eighth-graders completing the school year. Commencement exercises were again held in the Wasco School auditorium. Rev. Armin Wing of the Holy Trinity Lutheran Church, Elgin, gave the address in 1938.

The Wasco School graduates of 1939 had as their class motto the phrase "Impossible is Un-American." Their class colors were green and white. Graduates that year were: Fredric Abrahamson Jr., Robert Paul Anderson, Betty Marie Carlson, Arlene Lillian Gustafson, Robert M. B. Jay, Jay Leroy Johnsen, Raymond Johnson, Lee Foch Mather, Elmer W. Nelson, Robert Osborne, Norman Charles Skala, and Julius Wynthein. Their class picnic was held in Pottawatomie Park, St. Charles.

A music festival under the direction of Mrs. Max Keller took place at the Wasco School on 17 May 1940. Two "numbers by the rhythm band" were followed by animal impersonations. In another room, "songs of foreign lands" were sung. The high school students presented an operetta entitled "Thirty Minutes with Stephen Foster." Ruth Anderson played the organ for the program. In 1940, the graduates from Wasco School were: Lavern L. Abrahamson, George R. Anderson, Charles E. Bagge, Willard Leroy Carlson, Calvin Morris Corron, Mary Ellen M. Ekstrom, Ruth E. Hatch, Kenneth Johnsen, Wesley A. Johnson, and Donald H. Nelson. The class colors were blue and white, and the class flower was the red rose.

Harriet Eddy (teacher) with Wasco School students Jerry Hagaman, Owen Richmond, Leona Olson, Billy Crook, Marjorie Jay, June Olson, George Bergland (all standing, L to R), Dorothy _____ , Phyllis Denker, Blanche Scott, Margaret Nelson, and Bonnie Bergland

Their motto was "when we build, let us build forever." Teachers at Wasco School in the late 1930s and early 1940s included Harriet M. Eddy, Esther Johnson, and Pauline (Williams) Peterson.

The final sophomore class to graduate from Wasco School did so on 28 May 1941. The two members of the class were Roger W. Ekstrom and Edward Van Bogaert. The class colors were blue and silver, and the class flower was the white rose. Leonard Thompson was the school's principal at the time. There were just seven total students in the high school grades then, including Virginia Richmond, John Goldenstein, Bruce Hatch, Eleanor Johnson, and Ken Carlson, in addition to the two graduates. The spring play in 1941 was "Toby Helps Out," a comedy in three acts. In April 1942, the pupils of Wasco School presented "Tom Sawyer," an operetta in three acts. School opened on 5 September in the year 1944. Esther Johnson taught sixth, seventh, and eighth grades that year, and Margaret Johnson of St. Charles taught third, fourth, and fifth. Mildred Cunningham taught the primary grades.

The Wasco Consolidated School gave its Christmas program in the school auditorium on 21 December 1945. The primary room presented an operetta "A Mischievous Mouse in Toyland" with actors John McDonald, Loretta Meyer, Mary Nichols, Warren Henry, John Johnson, Robert McDonald, Davis Brown, James Harley, Richard Harley, Richard Swanson, Calvin Calhoon, Gladys Aug, Janet Swanson, Mildred Wakeman, Wayne Wakeman, Ralph Swanson, Barbara Norton, and Kenneth Peters. A pageant entitled "The Story Beautiful" was also performed that evening.

A 1941 photo of Virginia Richmond, one of the last students to attend the high school program at Wasco

The Wasco School received a new school bus for use in their district in the early fall of 1946. Julius Verhaeghe was the first bus driver. He made two "runs" every morning, a "north run and a south run," the first of which began at 7:30 AM. The first bus stop was at the Elmer Ekstrom farm just north of the railroad tracks; the last children to be picked up on the northern route were Dexter Norton Jr. and his sister Barbara. The bus dropped the children off at school at 8:24 AM. The first student picked up on the south run was Robert Brown, who lived just west of Wasco. The last pickup on this route, at 8:58 AM, was Don Hagaman, who lived a short distance south of the school. Serving on the Wasco School Board that year were Frank Richmond, Adolph Mongerson, and Dexter Norton, all of whom had children enrolled at the school. On 28 May 1947, the Eighth Grade Commencement Exercises were held, as usual, at the Wasco School. Graduates that year were: Margaret Bergland, Peter Denker, Carl Ekstrom, Melvin Johnson, Barbara Larson, Richard Tredup, and Rene Verhaeghe. John Wredling, Kane County Assistant Superintendent of Schools, presented the diplomas. Speeches at the event included "We Would Be Farmers" by Rene Verhaeghe, and "What Baseball Does for a Boy" by Melvin Johnson.

There were three teachers at Wasco School in 1948 – Esther Johnson of Wasco, Margaret Johnson of St. Charles, and Margaret Rollins of Elburn. The following year, Ethel Waterhouse replaced Ms. Rollins as the school's first and second grade teacher. Stanley O. Bowgren began working as a custodian at the Wasco School in the late 1940s and served in that capacity for twenty-five years. Bowgren also coached basketball at the school and kept score at many sporting events. He also drove the school bus for thirty years, retiring from that role in 1980. In the late 1940s and into the 1950s, many Wasco School students enjoyed being in the upstairs classrooms, since the "tube fire escape" was located there. During fire drills, students would sometimes slide down the tube on large sheets of waxed paper!

Some of the young cast members of a play performed at Wasco School, likely 1940s

In 1950, Illinois eliminated two-year high schools throughout the state, and Wasco School became part of St. Charles School District 303. Subsequently, instruction at Wasco covered Kindergarten through sixth grade. Seventh and eighth grade students were bused to St. Charles to attend Junior High and beginning in ninth grade students from Wasco would attend St. Charles High School. In the early 1950s, attendance at Wasco School was significantly higher than in earlier years because of the postwar "baby boom," as well as due to an influx of young families moving to the new housing developments in Campton Township. Enrollment peaked at one hundred students, prompting discussions for a significant addition to the school building. Esther Johnson was then serving as Wasco School's principal.

Because there was no lunch room at Wasco School by 1950, students would each their lunches at their classroom desks as they had since the school opened. Milk for lunch was kept in a large cooler, under ice. This would soon change, however, with the substantial addition to the school constructed in 1951-52. In 1950, seventh and eighth-grade pupils at Wasco School began attending St. Charles Junior High School. In January 1951, the St. Charles School District approved a much-anticipated addition for the Wasco School. This addition was to include an all-purpose room, a kitchen, and a kindergarten. The school had three classrooms at that time. The addition, when built, contained three additional classrooms, a gymnasium, washrooms, and a kitchen. The addition was dedicated on 16 November 1952.

Frances Gustafson became Wasco School's first physical education teacher when the new gymnasium was built in 1952. Two more classrooms were added to the building between July and October of 1959, and the school's basement underwent a remodel, with the goal of including "a work room for mimeographing," a storage area, a lounge, an office, and a room "for use by the nurse and dentist." Carole Prendergast became the new first grade teacher at Wasco School in 1959. Ethel Waterhouse had retired that spring, with 12 May 1959 being celebrated as "Ethel Waterhouse Day." Special gifts were presented to Mrs. Waterhouse, and former students from near and far visited her and wished her well during her retirement. Some games played during recess at the school during that era included London Bridge, fox and geese, baseball, jumping rope, and crack-the-whip.

Margie Schafer, a graduate of Northern Illinois University, became the Wasco School's new fifth grade teacher in 1961. George Peterson was then the principal. In May 1965, Mr. Peterson left this position after twelve years, and began working at Haines Junior High in St. Charles. Margaret Johnson was teaching at the school during that decade, and in fact had begun her teaching career at Wasco School in the 1940s, when there were just three other teachers and a janitor employed in the building. She began teaching third, fourth, and fifth grades, at which time the principal taught sixth, seventh, and eighth. As has been mentioned, High School coursework had been discontinued by that time. Nancy (Mongerson) Warner began her teaching career in Wasco in 1963 and was with the school for twenty-seven years. Nancy attended Wasco School, as did both of her parents. In the 2000s Nancy's grandchildren became the fourth generation in the family to attend Wasco School. Her daughter served as co-president of the school's PTO in 2006.

George Peterson (center) who was principal of Wasco School from 1953 to 1965. He is standing with Bob and June (Olson) Henningson, the latter of whom graduated from Wasco in 1941 – the photo is from the 2006 centennial

During the spring and summer of 1964, the District 303 Board of Education began discussing plans for another large addition to Wasco School, which was to cost $150,000. In the spring of 1965, the original 1906 structure was demolished, though the 1950s addition was kept, and still stands today. A portion of the larger (present) school was then built in the old building's place; this addition was under construction by May 1965. By mid-September of the same year, the rooms in the new building were in use, although they were only partly finished, and lacked heat, water, and electricity.

Wasco School as it appeared in December 1965 - the new addition had just been completed

Herb Birk was the Wasco School's new principal in 1965. Early in that school year, while the addition was still being completed, the third grade classes were held in the gym, kindergarten classes met in the school office, and what once comprised the office was temporarily located on the stage! Heat was installed in mid-October, the rooms were painted by the following month, and furniture was installed by December. A new flag was presented to the school then by the local American Legion. Commander John Jorgenson "instructed the children in the proper way to fold the flag." The new building was truly completed in January 1966, after almost a year of work.

In May 1967, Principal Birk attended the National Convention of Elementary School Principals held in Boston, Massachusetts. Don Erdman was Principal of Wasco School in 1968, and Mrs. Gerald Hansen was Secretary. The teachers for the 1968-1969 school year were as follows: Judy Freundlich (Kindergarten); Barbara Merrell (1st Grade); Betty Harris (2nd Grade); Margaret Johnson (3rd Grade); Marie Stahl (4th Grade); Charles Bell (5th Grade); Nancy Warner (6th Grade). Each of the grades but two had between twenty-four and twenty-seven students apiece. Robert Graham (formerly of Munhall) replaced Erdman as Wasco School Principal in 1969, when Erdman took a position at Wild Rose School. In the spring of 1969, the sixth-grade class at Wasco School held a book sale to defer the costs of their upcoming field trip to Springfield. The LaFox Farmers' Club regularly met at Wasco School throughout the 1960s and 1970s.

The oldest portion of Wasco School, not long before its demolition in 1965

Throughout the 1960s and '70s, there was an annual Wasco Barbecue held in the school. The event, which was first held in 1958, was extremely well-attended throughout its run. More than seven hundred people attended the barbeque in March 1968. In November 1970, plans to expand the Wasco School again were approved. Six new classrooms plus a learning resources center were added to the western part of the building. The 1971 addition adjoined the 1950s section of the building. By that time, over four hundred students attended the school, many of whom were newcomers to the area. Still, by the 1970s there were also several examples of fourth-generation students of Wasco School. By that decade, the building was commonly known as Wasco Elementary School. In the early 1970s, enrollment at the school increased to more than 340 students. In April 1973, the annual barbeque, whose theme was "It's your barbeque Charlie Brown," raised money for the school's new playground. The price for attending that year's event was $1.75 for adults and $1 for children. The 1977 barbeque was known as the "Sunshine Bar-B-Que" and featured relishes, coleslaw, potato chips, ice cream, and homemade pies, besides the namesake dish.

Ms. Milton's class at Wasco School in 1977

Wasco Elementary School in the 1970s

Wasco School's annual "Heritage Days" took place every spring throughout the mid-to-late 1970s and into the next decade. Karen Morrison, former Miss U.S.A. from St. Charles, was the event's honorary chairperson in 1977. Judge William H. Ellsworth of Geneva was honorary chairman in 1981. One of the last annual "barbeque suppers" at Wasco School took place on 19 May 1979. As in previous years, it was open to the public and functioned as a fundraiser. Robert Graham was the principal of Wasco Elementary School for all of the 1970s, and most of the 1980s. He was succeeded by Karen Larsen, who was principal until 2002. Mrs. Marge Meanger was a kindergarten teacher at Wasco School throughout that decade; she retired in 1994.

Robert Graham and Karen Larsen, both of whom served as principals at Wasco School

In the summer of 1994, the Community Unit School District 303 Board of Education approved a plan to move several dozen students then attending Wasco Elementary School to Richmond School. The impacted students lived in the Arbor Creek subdivision. The Elementary Attendance Boundary Committee had a major role in the decision-making process. Other children were moved from Ferson Creek School to Wild Rose School to alleviate overcrowding.

The new addition and playground of the Wasco School were both dedicated at a ceremony held on 17 September 1998. This most recent addition added a classroom, a community room, a teacher's lounge, a staff workroom, and a music room to the building. The earlier playground items, which were replaced, had been installed in 1983. A survey conducted by the school's students in January and February 1998 was helpful in deciding what new equipment to install in the playground. Karen Larsen was principal of Wasco Elementary when the new playground was constructed.

The 1998 playground at Wasco Elementary School, as it appears today

In September 2005, second-grade students at Wasco Elementary put together a book entitled "How to Feel Better When You Are Sad," which they assembled for the children of New Orleans who were then suffering during Hurricane Katrina. The project, which was directed at helping the children who had been evacuated to the Astrodome, was conceived by teacher Lori Devitt. Wasco Elementary School celebrated its one hundredth anniversary with a ceremony held on 10 September 2006. Throughout the celebration, tours of the building were offered by the Wasco Spirit Club. Dr. David Abhalter was the building's principal beginning in 2002. He and Dr. Melanie Raczkiewicz, the school's Chief Academic Officer, both gave addresses at the school's centennial celebration. The Centennial Spirit Wheel was installed in front of the building at that time.

The Centennial Spirit Wheel, installed at Wasco School in 2006

In 2011, Wasco Elementary School won the Illinois State Board of Education Academic Excellence award for the fourth year in a row. St. Charles District 303 had seven of its elementary schools win that year, a remarkable achievement for any district. Dozens of local events take place in and around the school yearly. On 2 August 2011, for example, on National Night Out, the Forest Preserve hosted a bicycle safety event in the school parking lot. The school is truly a pillar of the local community, and has an excellent, experienced faculty. In April 2012, Beverly Taylor, a reading resource teacher at Wasco Elementary with more than thirty-six years of experience, was nominated for a Kane County Educator of the Year award. She was one of just seventeen educators, support staff, and administrators nominated across the county that year for this most prestigious award in local education.

Over the years, every conceivable community event has been held at Wasco School, which is truly the heart of the community. Events such as pot luck suppers, art shows, bake sales, lectures, community meetings, elections, dances, concerts, card games, auctions, game nights, agricultural meetings, sporting events, debates, and parties of every description represent the scope of uses the school has had over its long history. In addition, the community school has helped shape the lives of thousands of students. As one former student of Wasco School wrote in recent years, "it seemed like the world was always a happy place during my years as a student at Wasco School. Children were nurtured and taught in a caring and loving way," while the "welfare of the school children [was] always utmost in the neighborhood."

The older section of Wasco Elementary School as it appears today

The faculty and staff of Wasco Elementary School in 2012

At present, the Principal of Wasco Elementary School is Barbara Stokke. The 2018-2019 school year is her eleventh at Wasco, and her seventeenth as an administrator in District 303. Her passion is "helping students experience success within a challenging yet supportive environment." The school enrolls just under four hundred students, and enjoys very strong community support. Wasco Elementary School is located at 4N782 School Street in Wasco. For information on joining the school's PTO, see www.wascoschoolpto.org.

The main entrance to Wasco Elementary School, 2018

The Whitney Cemetery

Sometimes known as the Wasco Cemetery, the Whitney Cemetery is located near the center of Section 14, Campton Township, two-thirds of a mile north of the center of Wasco. The cemetery is on the north side of Burlington Road between Old LaFox and Bolcum Roads. There are over seven hundred burials in the cemetery, including a very large percentage of Wasco's early residents. The earliest burials date to the 1840s, although the cemetery was not formally created until 16 June 1855, when Maria Whitney sold just over a third of an acre of land to the Campton Cemetery Association. Simultaneously, John and Elsia Elliot sold three-fourths of an acre of land to the same organization. The Campton Cemetery Association was first created in June 1852. That decade, the present Burlington Road was known as "the road running from St. Charles to Genoa" or the "St. Charles-Genoa road." Mrs. Whitney sold her parcel of land to the association for $5, and the Elliotts sold their much larger parcel for twice that sum. The deeds marking the cemetery's creation note that the property was to be used for a "burying ground and nothing else."

There was once a log schoolhouse on the site of part of the Whitney Cemetery. The building was built in the fall of 1839 and was used until the early 1850s. Mrs. McClure was the first teacher there, followed by Sarah M. Chaffee, and then Ed Quackenbush. It was the first school building built in the township, though various classes met in private homes prior to its construction. The building was razed or moved prior to the Civil War. Elsia Elliot, daughter of John and Elsia, and the last surviving child of eleven siblings, attended the school in her youth. Elsia was born in Campton Township on 27 April 1841. When Eliza (Elliott) Murray was buried in the Whitney Cemetery in September 1926, it was on "the same ground where the Log School House stood where she first attended school."

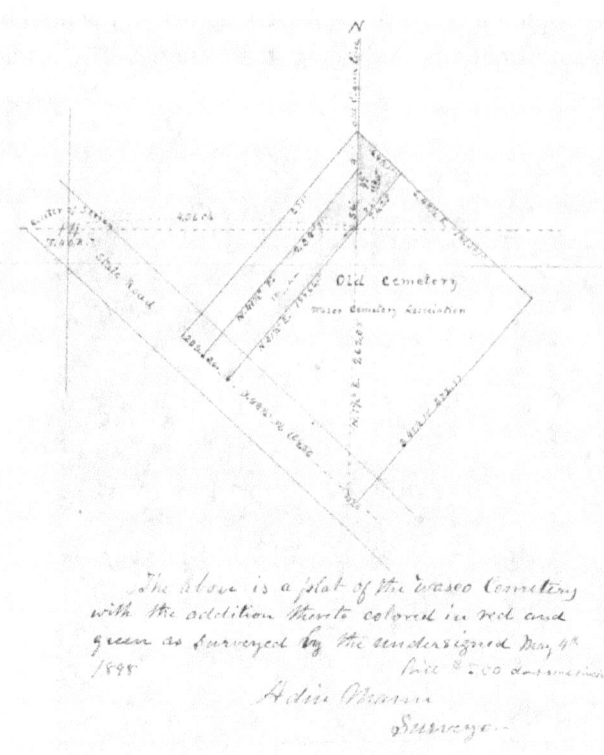

An 1898 survey of the Whitney Cemetery

The meeting organizing the Wasco Cemetery Association (as opposed to the Campton Cemetery Association) took place in the old Bergland store in the village on 30 October 1898. Daniel Whitney chaired that meeting, and Carrie Peterson acted as secretary. Both Vesta (Ward) Bell and D. W. Stevens moved that all five trustees of the new association be women, but this motion failed. The amended motion, which passed, stated that "three ladies and two men" constitute the trustees of the association. The original trustees, besides Mrs. Bell and Mr. Stevens, were Carrie Peterson, L. Barber, and Mrs. Barber. Many dozens of the burials which took place here are referred to throughout this work. A year prior to this meeting, in September 1897, the Board of Supervisors of Kane County quit their claim to any lands owned by the Trustees of the Wasco Cemetery Association. The cemetery itself was described as being located along the "road running from St. Charles to Genoa."

The cemetery trustees were authorized to levy a tax on lot owners, not to exceed $2 per lot annually, in order to pay for the upkeep of the cemetery grounds. Vesta Bell and Carrie Peterson drew up the bylaws for the cemetery association. On 21 May 1898, John Whitney sold a thirty-six by two-hundred-and-thirty-eight-foot strip of land to the Cemetery Association for the sum of $14. This parcel was along the western edge of the old cemetery. A fence and flowers were added to the cemetery from nearly the beginning, and a caretaker was hired prior to the First World War. On 17 April 1916, John Whitney sold a twenty-eight-and-one-half-foot-wide strip of land immediately northwest of the other parcel to the Trustees for the sum of $50. Both of these additions are outlined on the map above.

J. August Johnson was a member of the Wasco Cemetery Association from 1905 until his death in 1928. Lot assessments were raised to $2 per lot annually in 1922, during Johnson's term. In 1916,

Willard R. Austin's grave in the Whitney Cemetery. The photo dates to 1917, the year after his death.

at the request of C. W. Bolcum, Lot #20 in the cemetery was set aside as a "free lot" to be used by anyone unable to pay for burial. Loren E. Wickizer was Director of the Wasco Cemetery Association in 1932 and 1933, and was Treasurer in 1929. A. J. Erickson was the group's President that year, and George Vanderhoof was Secretary. Gust Swanson was the caretaker of the cemetery in the 1930s, when care of the property cost $85 per year. Florence Peterson was a member in 1945, and George Vanderhoof was President of the WCA from at least 1957 to 1970, when the association's property and assets were turned over to the newly-created Campton Township Cemetery Association. Paul Waterhouse was acting secretary then.

The Campton Township Cemetery Association, which now maintains the Whitney Cemetery, was formed in June 1970, with an annual budget of $1000. Maurice Craft was the group's first Treasurer. Dexter F. Norton and Carl D. Miller were the two other original Trustees. There have been two donations of land to the Whitney Cemetery in recent decades, which together have almost doubled its size. The first was made in August 1978, and the second in April 1988. The donors were John J. and Suzanne S. Hamer.

Some Wasco Firsts

It is said that the first wedding ever to take place in Wasco was that of Mattie Millen and Chauncey G. Agnew. This marriage took place at the home of C. W. Millen (the bride's father) on Wednesday, 2 January 1901, the second day of the twentieth century. The evening ceremony saw the bride "becomingly attired in a gown of white cashmere" and carrying white roses. Merna Whitney was the bridesmaid, and Earle Millen was best man. Rev. Clutterbuck officiated, and Mrs. Charles Tanner played the wedding march. Chauncey G. Agnew was born in Ogle County, Illinois, on 21 July 1875, and lived to be ninety years of age. He was an express messenger for the railroad, and he and Mattie moved (with their young daughter Norma H. Agnew) to Marion, Ohio, around 1905. Mattie Millen was born in Campton Township on 27 August 1881, and died in Marion County in 1956. The Agnews lived in Chicago in the summer of 1903, when they spent a month visiting with their Wasco relatives. Though the Wasco Baptist Church had been standing for a decade by the time of the Millen/Agnew wedding, no marriage ceremony had yet taken place in the building. Couples who resided in Wasco in its earliest years were often married at the various churches then standing in St. Charles or Geneva.

The Millen house, site of the first marriage in Wasco, as it appeared around 1910

The first person to reach the age of one hundred in Wasco was DeVolois W. Stevens, Civil War veteran, whose centennial birthday was celebrated in the village on 21 March 1943. He came to Illinois in 1865, soon after he was discharged from the U. S. Army. During the war, he took part in the battles of Fredericksburg and Gettysburg, and was wounded at the battle of the Wilderness. He was the guest of honor at the Decoration Day ceremonies on 30 May 1939, when a flag ceremony was held at the Wasco School. At the time of his centennial birthday, five of his grandsons were fighting in World War II. On the occasion of Mr. Stevens' 100th birthday, students were dismissed early from school, and they and their teachers sang "Happy Birthday" and presented Mr. Stevens with a large basket of flowers. Stevens' home was decorated with red, white, and blue bunting and flags, and residents of Wasco presented the honoree a series of birthday cards. Some two hundred and fifty guests attended the two-day celebration of his centennial birthday. A dramatization of his life was given on the WLS radio station on Saturday, 27 March 1943. Incidentally, Stevens was not the first centenarian in all of Campton Township – this honor belongs to Asenath Miller, who turned one hundred on 12 August 1887.

On Friday, 24 August 1917, the first Wasco "County Fair" took place. Local residents presented "a home talent entertainment," and local ladies brought exhibits of fancy work, flowers, and home cooking. Prize fruits and vegetables were exhibited, and candy and ice cream were sold. The event replaced an earlier local celebration, "Old Neighbors' Day." That celebration took place at least as early as February 1910, and included events such as songs, addresses, lectures, literary selections, duets, and dinner (served by Wasco Ladies Aid). In October 1913, Nettie Anderson presided at Old Neighbors' Day, which by then was considered an annual event "always looked forward to with keen interest and great pleasure."

D. W. Stevens, Wasco's first Centenarian

What is thought to be the first piano in Wasco was purchased by George C. Bergland, in 1891. It is not known if the piano was sold by Mr. Bergland at his store, or if the instrument was for the family's personal use. The Bergland house in the village was not built until 1894, however. Since the piano likely arrived in Wasco by rail, it was either moved to the Bergland's farm home one mile east of the train station, or was exhibited at the Old Bergland Store, and was sold from that location.

The first automobile in Wasco was very likely purchased between 1900 and 1905, although its owner is not known with certainty. The very first automobile in St. Charles, though, belonged to W. B. Ullman, President of Moline Malleable Iron Company. He purchased it in Chicago in August 1900. The newspaper stated that "the machine," which was powered by both gasoline and steam, ran "as smoothly as a bicycle"! By the outbreak of World War I, more than a dozen families in Wasco owned automobiles.

The first known reference to a ghost in Wasco dates to October 1889. That month, according to a contemporary newspaper account, "a number of people report seeing [the ghost] at the place of the late railroad accident. What next, we wonder?" No further references to this apparition are known.

Important Wasco Families

The Austin Family

Although the fact was either unknown or forgotten for more than half a century, the Austin family may be credited with the naming of the village of Wasco, and therefore they appear first in this work. Willard Richard Austin was a New York native, and was the individual who, in 1887, first suggested the name Wasco for the new village in central Campton Township. He was born in the town of Penfield, located just east of Rochester, in Monroe County, New York, on 25 August 1836. His parents were Amasa Comstock and Roba ("Ruby") (White) Austin. Amasa Austin was said to be a veteran of the War of 1812, and his family had lived in the United States since its founding, and in the American colonies prior to that. The Austins were married in Syracuse in 1826 and began to raise a family there. Shortly after the birth of Willard's sister Pamelia (in Monroe County) in June 1842, the family came to Illinois, first settling in Sugar Grove, and shortly afterward in Geneva, in Kane County. There, the father and Willard's older brothers worked as laborers; Willard's younger siblings William and Charlotte Austin were born in Kane County. Amasa C. Austin died in DeKalb County in 1866; his widow lived until 1885. Remarkably, Amasa C. Austin of DeKalb County enlisted as a Private in Company K, 42nd Illinois Infantry, in August 1861, at the age of sixty-three! He was 5' 10" tall, had brown hair, and gray eyes, a light complexion, and his occupation was given as "farmer." Mr. Austin was discharged from the U. S. Army in January 1862 "by order of General Fremont."

Willard R. Austin, during the Civil War

Willard R. Austin got the idea for the name Wasco during the pre-Civil War years, when he resided in Wasco County, Oregon. At the time, this region of north-central Oregon was the only locality in the United States with the name Wasco. Austin lived in "the other" Wasco following a much-longer residence in Campton Township, Kane County, to which his family had moved when he was a child. Willard Austin later returned to Campton Township to live, and with his wife, the former Harriet L. Higgins (who by the time of the village of Wasco's creation had lived in the immediate vicinity for over a decade) owned land on the site of the future village. Besides the various Wasco place names in Oregon, there are no other pre-1880 settlements named Wasco in other parts of the country. All Wasco place names in Oregon derive for the Wasco tribe of Native Americans, a Chinookan people who live primarily in Oregon near the banks of the Columbia River. Traditionally, the Wasco people were sedentary, lived in plank houses, and heavily relied on fishing to survive. They were also able traders, and were visited by Lewis and Clark in 1805. In the 1820s and after, the Wasco suffered periodic smallpox and measles epidemics which dramatically reduced their population. The Warm Springs Reservation, located partly in the Wasco's traditional tribal area, was created in 1855 after the federal government forced the tribe to relinquish most of their lands. The Wasco tribe's name (meaning "small bowl" or "cup") derives from a bowl-shaped rock located in their principal village near The Dalles, Wasco County, Oregon. This is exactly where Willard R. Austin lived prior to the outbreak of the Civil War. He would have both seen the namesake rock and interacted with the Wasco on a frequent basis during his residence there.

In the late 1850s, the Austin family moved to the city of DeKalb, but some of the children moved to Sycamore in later years. Willard, who was then yet unmarried, moved much further west, winding up in The Dalles, the seat of Wasco County, Oregon. The Dalles is located on the south bank of the Columbia River, eighty miles east of Portland. W. R. Austin is found on the 1860 census list of Wasco County, and was then working as a master carpenter. Soon after the outbreak of the Civil War, he began working as a miner. During the conflict, Willard Austin fought for the Union as part of the 3rd Regiment, Colorado Infantry, and then in Company L, 2nd Colorado Cavalry. His brother William also enlisted in the Union cause, but from DeKalb County, Illinois. In the fall of 1862, Willard R. Austin's regiment was organized and posted at Camp Weld, in Denver, and the following spring they rode and marched to Fort Leavenworth, Kansas. Willard, who was twenty-six at the time of his enlistment in September 1862, enlisted in the regiment at Central City, Colorado.

Maude and Flossie Austin of Wasco, daughters of Willard

The 3rd Colorado was relocated to St. Louis, and were on duty at Pilot Knob, Potosi, and Ironton Till, Missouri, during the autumn of 1863. The unit was then consolidated with the 2nd Colorado Cavalry. That winter, Austin and his regiment marched to Fort Riley, Kansas, and then to Kansas City, Missouri. An early twentieth century biography stated that Austin's regiment "assisted in driving Price out of Missouri." This is a reference to Confederate Major General Sterling Price, known for his ill-fated Missouri Campaign. For most of 1864, Austin and his regiment were engaged with the enemy and were charged with protecting the borders of Kansas, especially from guerilla attacks. The unit took part in the Battles of Little Blue River, Westport, Mine Creek, Little Osage River, Newtonia, and many others. While in the Army, Willard R. Austin held the rank of Corporal, and worked as a saddler for the regiment. The 2nd Colorado was mustered out in Leavenworth, Kansas, in September 1865. Austin was "a faithful and loyal defender of the cause which he espoused, never faltering in the performance of any military duty assigned him."

On 2 April 1878, in Cortland, DeKalb County, Illinois, Willard R. Austin married Harriet L. Higgins. He was then a farmer, residing in Sycamore. It was the first marriage for both Willard and Harriet; Timothy Peck, Justice of the Peace, performed the ceremony. Harriet was born in DuPage County, Illinois, on 2 April 1848 (one source gives 1847), and was a daughter of Van Rensselaer and Lucy (Bingham) Higgins (see "The Higgins Family"). She had come to Campton Township in 1872. The couple had four children: Flossie, Maude, Rollie, and Alvie Austin. The Austins were living on their farm in Campton Township in 1880, at which time Willard was working as a "well borer." The farm was immediately west of the future site of Wasco. The Austins lived on the Higgins farm until they built their own home in Wasco in the late 1880s. This 'town' home is shown on the 1892 map, and was one of the first dozen dwellings built in the village.

On 3 April 1889, Harriet L. Austin "of the Town of Campton" purchased additional land in Wasco from Norman L. Carpenter. This parcel adjoined her family's land to the northeast, and had frontage on both "Wasco Station road" [Old LaFox] and "the road running from St. Charles to Lily Lake" [Route 64]. The land she acquired was bounded on the north by the Minnesota & North Western railroad tracks.

The oldest child in the family of Willard and Harriet was Flossie Birdell Austin, who was born in Campton Township on 13 January 1879. She attended the White school, just east of Wasco, and was living at home with her parents in 1908. She had "considerable musical talent," and often sang in local concerts and performances. Flossie received a new piano in December 1907 and played it daily. She never married, and lived with her parents and siblings during her lifetime. Flossie B. Austin died at the family home in Wasco on 19 or 20 February 1924 (her gravestone gives the former date, and her funeral card the latter).

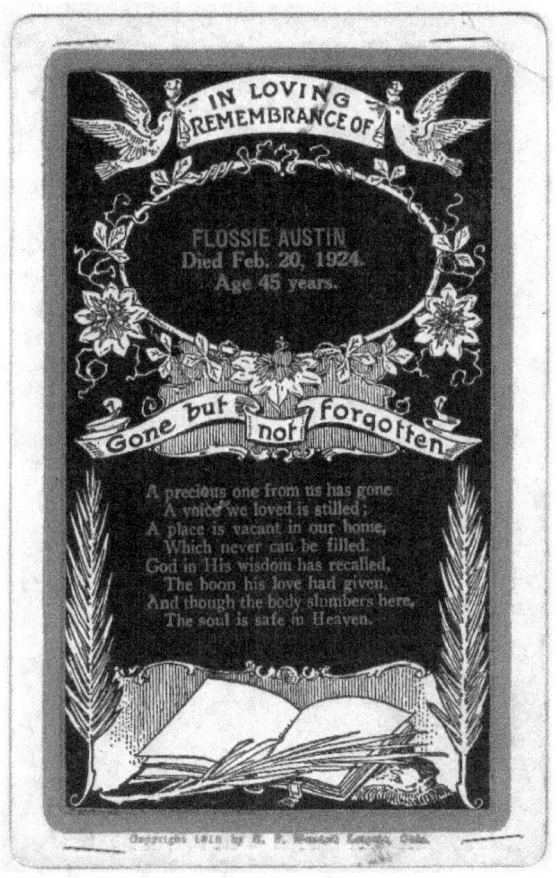

Flossie Austin's funeral card, from 1924

By 1892, Willard R. Austin owned five-and-a-half acres of land in Wasco, located between the railroad's lands and the "public road" (present Route 64). His holdings adjoined those of George C. Bergland to the northeast, and there was both a store and a blacksmith shop on the Austin land by that year. The 1900 census listed Willard Austin as a [milk] "can washer." All four of the Austin children were in the household at that time. In April 1903, the Austins celebrated their silver wedding anniversary. One hundred guests were present, and the party-goers left the happy couple "two handsome chairs [at the Austin house] as tokens of love and respect." Willard R. Austin was a Republican politically, and was affiliated with the G. A. R. Post No. 456 in St. Charles. Both he and his wife were "highly esteemed throughout the community," according to a 1908 biographical sketch, "the circle of their friends being almost coextensive with the circle of their acquaintances."

The Austin family was still living in Wasco at the time of the 1910 census. Willard was then aged seventy-four, and was a farmer. Harriet was sixty-two, and kept a boarding house. Flossie B. Austin was at home, as was her brother Alvie. Both were single, and were aged thirty-one and twenty-one, respectively. Two boarders were also in the household that year. Flossie often visited her sister Maude, who lived in Maple Park in the 1910s. Flossie Austin lived alone in 1920, when she was listed on the census near her widowed mother, but in a separate household. Her father Willard R. Austin died in Wasco at the age of eighty, on 28 December 1916.

Harriet (Higgins) Austin passed away at the family home in Wasco on 18 September 1929. She was survived by three of her children – Rollie, who lived in Chicago, as well as Maude (Austin) Swanson, and Alvie Austin of Wasco. There were eleven grandchildren. Harriet's obituary stated that she was "a good mother and wife and a Christian woman." She and her husband were both buried in the Whitney Cemetery.

Harriet (Higgins) Austin, a Wasco pioneer

Rollie Van Rensselaer Austin was born in Campton Township (in what would later become Wasco) on 16 January 1883. He attended high school in 1900, probably in St. Charles. On 18 November 1903, in St. Charles, Rollie V. Austin married Mary Arvilla Johnson, who was a native of Michigan. Mary Arvilla, who was born on 3 January 1884, was a daughter of John C. and Mary E. (Nash) Johnson, who were married in Kent County, Michigan on 7 February 1867. The Johnsons had eight children, and later moved to Wasco. J. C. Johnson died in Wasco on 4 November 1906 "after a long suffering of many weeks from a tumorous growth in the throat." He was sixty-four years old at the time of his death. Johnson was a member of the Odd Fellows and the Masons.

Rollie Austin worked at a creamery in the early years of the twentieth century. After a brief residence in Chicago, the Austins returned to Wasco in March 1907, when they moved into the W. A. Hiser house. R. V. Austin worked for the Wasco Creamery at that time. He and Mary remained in Illinois for the birth of their first three children: Alden P., who was born on 26 June 1905; Olive L., who was born in Chicago on 5 January 1907; and Cora A. Austin, who was born in Wasco in 1909. Rollie Austin's children attended the Wasco School shortly after its opening, but the family moved to Wisconsin when the children were young.

Around 1914, Rollie and Mary Austin, along with their three children, moved to Waukesha County, Wisconsin, where Rollie got a job with the railroad. Their youngest daughter Flossie was born there in 1915. The family was in Sussex, Wisconsin, in 1918. That year was a tragic one for the family, since their young daughter Mary Ellen died during the influenza epidemic then. The family moved back to Illinois in the mid-1920s. During the early years of the Depression, the family lived at #341 Garfield Boulevard, Chicago. Rollie was again working in the dairy industry at that time. In 1940, Rollie and his family lived at

#5611 S. Princeton Avenue, in the Washington Park neighborhood of Chicago. Mary A. Austin died in the city on 4 April 1946; her widower passed away just a few months later, on 30 July 1946.

Alvie Cyril Austin, the youngest of the four Austin children, was born in the nascent village of Wasco on 28 August 1888. He lived in that locality for nearly seventy-five years, longer than almost anyone else on record either before or since. On 1 July 1913, Alvie married Ethel Louise Hilburn; she was born near Cairo, Illinois, on 1 November 1890. The marriage took place in Wheaton, in DuPage County, where Alvie had moved around 1911. At the time of her marriage, Ethel's maiden name was mistakenly given as "Hillman" in the *Elburn Herald*. Ethel's parents were Herbert and Emma (Walters) Hilburn. In August 1913, Alvie and his wife moved into the house in Wasco which had been "recently vacated by Mr. and Mrs. E. S. Sharp." The Sharps moved to Elburn at that time; they purchased a home there from Mary Warne. The oldest child in the family, Irene Harriet Austin, was born in Wasco on 2 May 1915.

Rollie Austin, of Wasco

In 1918, Alvie was a milk car conductor on the Chicago Great Western Railroad. His World War I draft card states that he was then of medium height, stout build, and had blue eyes and light hair. His daughter Faith Elizabeth Austin began attending Wasco School just before her sixth birthday, in the fall of 1923. Alvie and Ethel had a son, Roy H. Austin, who was born on 10 April 1924, as well as three daughters. Roy later moved to Geneva. His sister Irene H. Austin married George Thomas Ramer of Elburn on 19 December 1934; they lived in Lily Lake, and later moved to Aurora. Faith E. Austin, who was born on 19 November 1917, was a contestant in Campton's "Centennial Queen" competition in 1935. She married Donald Rambow, and moved to Walworth, Wisconsin. Virginia Austin, the youngest child in the family, was born in Wasco in 1926. She married Albert Chapman, who along with her brother Roy Austin, lived in Geneva. See "Some Wasco Houses – Northwest Quarter" for further information on the Austins.

In 1935, Alvie Austin worked on the Meredith family's farm near Elburn. In 1937, he worked on the Mills Brothers' farm. During the late 1930s, as well as during the war years, Alvie drove a milk truck, and worked at various odd jobs. All of his children of course attended the Wasco School. By 1940, just Roy and Virginia remained at home with their parents. By 1942, Alvie and Ethel Austin had moved to #70 South Van Buren Street, Batavia, but after the war they returned to Wasco. In 1950, Alvie was a punch press operator for Hawley Products. Virginia, Alvie's daughter, was an employee of the Blue Goose Market in St. Charles that year, though she lived in Wasco. The Austins lived in a house on the west side of Old LaFox Road for many years, and in fact were Wasco residents until the year 1963. Ethel Austin died at Copley Memorial Hospital in Aurora on 21 November 1964. She had sixteen grandchildren, and six great-grandchildren. Rev. Peter Quist of the Fox Valley Bible Church presided at her funeral. Alvie later lived in Geneva, and died there on 20 September 1972. He and Ethel are buried in the Whitney Cemetery.

Alvie and Ethel Austin, of Wasco

Faith Austin (left) with the other contestants for Queen at the Campton Centennial Celebration, 1935

The Wasco home of the Austin family, circa 1910

Willard and Harriet Austin, with their children Flossie, Maude, Rollie, and Alvie, about 1892

The Edward Swanson Family

Maude Luella Austin, the second-oldest of the four Austin children, was born in Campton Township on 15 April 1881. In her youth, she attended the Whitney school just east of Wasco, as did her siblings. In February 1903 and again during the following autumn and winter, Maude Austin worked in the Elgin shirt factory. She lived with her parents on their farm until her marriage, which took place on 19 September 1906. Maude's husband was Edward Alvie Swanson, who was born on 30 October 1885. The Swansons owned the land between "the point," the local name for the land where the present Route 64 intersected with the railroad right-of-way, and the Higgins farm on the other side of the present LaFox Road. By 1903, they had two homes on their property, one on either side of LaFox Road, and rented the one on the west side of the road. In June 1903, Mr. and Mrs. W. C. Bryant of Chicago then occupied "the Swanson house." In March 1904, William Sarbaugh was soon going to "occupy the Swanson house in Wasco." August Bowgren "of Batavia" began renting Sarbaugh's farm at that time.

In February 1907, Mr. and Mrs. Ed Swanson of Wasco moved into the house "recently vacated by Edward Hawkins." Ed Swanson was then to "be in Mr. Hawkins' employ" according to the Wasco column of the *St. Charles Chronicle* from that time. In June of 1908 "Mr. & Mrs. Vanderbruggen of Chicago . . . moved into the Swanson house here [in Wasco] recently vacated by the teachers." Merrill Whitney "moved his family into the Swanson house" in March 1909.

In 1910, Edward and Maude Swanson, along with their oldest son Wallace, boarded with John O. Oslund, a Swedish-born farmer near Wasco. In fact, a February 1910 edition of the *St. Charles Chronicle* mentioned that just recently, "Mr. and Mrs. Ed. Swanson have moved on the farm with John Oslund." The property in question was located just northwest of the village. In March 1909, John Oslund had purchased the former Charles Probert farm in the northeast quarter of Section 15, located on the north side of the present Brown Road, just east of the curve. The Swansons had three sons in all: Wallace, Gordon, and Lester Swanson, and they remained in the vicinity. The 1920 census listed the Swansons next to the Austins, and by then they owned their own home. In the 1910s and later, Maude Swanson was a member of the Wasco Ladies Aid, was a director of the Wasco School, and was well-known throughout the community. For a time in the 1930s, she was also the Wasco

Maude Austin Swanson at her home in Wasco, with Flossie Austin, Edward Swanson and Harriet Higgins Austin. Jay and Leo Johnson, Mildred Swanson, and Mildred's mother Mrs. Johnson are also in the circa 1910 photo

correspondent for the *Elburn Herald* newspaper. In 1940, all the descendants of Edward and Maude Swanson were listed in three households, one after the next. Edward was then a road maintenance laborer, while his son Lester was a painter. Wallace Swanson was a scrap iron truck driver, while Gordon Swanson was a farm hand. Gordon and Rose had a young son, Richard, and Wallace and Louise had the following children: Wallace Jr. (see below); Donald Warren (a contributor to this work); Robert Kenneth; Charlene June; and Ralph Gerald Swanson. Their youngest child, Dorothy Lois, was born later that year.

Edward Alvie Swanson as a young man, and his wife Maude (née Austin) of Wasco

Gordon E. Swanson, the second son of Edward and Maude, was born in Wasco on 31 August 1916. He attended Wasco School, and in eleventh grade he lost his left arm in a farm accident. He married Rose Wilkison on 24 December 1935, and they moved to their long-time home in Wasco in 1947 (see "Some Wasco Houses – Northeast Quarter"). Gordon served as a Campton Township Road Commissioner in the late 1940s. When he was a young man he worked for Anderson Trucking Company, and then for Becker Iron and Metal in Geneva. He was a driver and mechanic for White Brothers Trucking in Wasco for eighteen years. Beginning in 1970, Gordon joined his son Richard in the latter's business, R. G. Swanson Trucking and Excavating. Later, Gordon worked with his nephew Wally Swanson Jr. at Abrahamson's in Lily Lake. Gordon Swanson died at Delnor Hospital, St. Charles, on 29 December 1983. He was survived by his son Richard G. Swanson, his daughter Linda L. (Swanson) Glasco, and four grandchildren. Burial was in the Whitney Cemetery. His widow Rose S. Swanson passed away at her home on 29 July 1989. Rose was born in Elburn on 20 November 1915 and grew up in Kaneland. Her husband lived in Geneva at the time of their marriage. Rose enjoyed bowling, and was a member of the LaFox Farmers Club.

Lester L. Swanson was born on 8 February 1919 at the family homestead in Wasco. He graduated from Wasco School, and worked for Howell's in St. Charles until the early 1940s. During World War II, Lester served in the U. S. Army in the European Theater. He joined his cousin Roy Austin in the gravel business upon returning from the front in 1945. Later, he drove for White Brothers Trucking Company, and retired from that job after thirty-five years. He enjoyed fishing and boating in Minnesota, riding his motorcycle, and outdoor sports. He had no children, and was not married, but was survived by five nephews and three nieces. He passed away on his birthday in 1996 and was buried in the Whitney Cemetery.

Wallace, Gordon, and Lester Swanson, with their mother Maude, about 1920

Wallace A. Swanson Jr. was born in St. Charles on 8 December 1930. He grew up with his parents, Wallace and Louise (Gerdau) Swanson in Wasco, and attended Wasco School and St. Charles High School. After graduating in 1949, Wally got a job at the St. Charles Post Office, and later worked for the Howell Company in St. Charles. He married Margaret Carlson at Lily Lake on 25 April 1953, and the following year began working with his father-in-law in an implement dealership. After moving to Lily Lake, he worked for Abrahamson's, and was involved in the plumbing, hardware, heating and air conditioning business for many years. Wally Swanson died in St. Charles on 21 February 1991, and was survived by his wife, his mother, an uncle, three brothers, two sisters, and three sons.

Since 1993, the descendants of the Austin and Higgins families of Wasco have had annual family reunions. These are often held in the Geneva home of Don and Joanne Swanson, contributors to this work. Your author had the distinct pleasure of being invited to the 2017 reunion as an "honorary Austin descendant"!

The Bergland Family

In the fall of 1939, Florence (Bergland) Peterson carefully recorded the history of the Bergland family in a thin, 5" x 8" olive-colored notebook. Florence was born in Campton Township on 15 February 1878, and personally remembered the beginnings of Wasco from the days of her youth. Florence's account of her family's history began with information on her paternal grandfather, Andrew Bergland, who was born in Knaggebo, in Jönköping County, Sweden, on 17 December 1817. He was said to be over six feet tall, dark complexioned, and handsome. His surname at birth was Nelson, but he was "given the name of Bergland when he entered the army." Two of these facts are confirmed in a journal entry from January 1909, when Andrew's grandson, Floyd H. Bergland, wrote that his great-aunt had told him that her brother Andrew had been over six feet tall, was a soldier, and "was fine looking." Florence, Floyd's sister, recorded that their grandfather Andrew Bergland was reportedly a member of "the Queen's bodyguard," although the queen in question is not stated. If the oral tradition is true, Bergland would have almost certainly guarded Désirée Clary, the wife of King Karl Johan, who ruled Sweden from 1818 until 1844.

Andrew Bergland married Louisa Benjamen (alternatively, Benjaminson), and they lived near the city of Jönköping. Andrew died of tuberculosis in middle life. He and Louisa had five children, two of whom (Augusta Olivia and Emma) died in infancy. Louisa (Benjamen) Bergland was a woman of "high intelligence" and "strong character." Following her husband's death, she came to the United States. This was in the year 1878, approximately a decade after her son's immigration. While in the U. S., Louisa married John Holst, a bachelor, and lived in DeKalb, and later in Rockford, Illinois. She died at the age of eighty-seven in 1905. The 1900 census of Rockford shows Louise Holst at age eighty-two, and her husband John (married for twenty-six years by then) living at #211 Twelfth Street. Although John was then eighty years old, he was nonetheless still employed in a furniture factory!

Louise (Benjamen) Bergland was not the first member of her immediate family to immigrate to the United States. She had a younger sister Charlotte, who had married a man by the name of Charlie Johnson in 1851. Charlotte and Charlie had preceded Louise to the United States by several years and had settled first in Lily Lake in 1853. After several decades of residence in Kane County, the Johnsons moved to Chicago. According to Florence's notes, Charlotte and Charlie had three children: Henry, Matilda ("Tillie"), and Charles Oscar Johnson. The 1860 census shows this couple living in Lily Lake, one of the first few Swedish families in Campton Township. Charlie was a blacksmith in that village, and later censuses show at least four children of this couple, including the three mentioned above, plus Alfred Gusta Johnson.

The Bergland Family Bible still exists, and confirms much early information on the family. It was printed in Stockholm, Sweden, in 1853, and is inscribed by "Anders Berglund." The inscription corroborates his date and place of birth. His wife's name is given as "Lovisa Beniamins Doter," and her date of birth is shown to be 16 May 1818. Their oldest child, "Claus Luddvig" (who was "called George Claus" according to another handwritten note in the Bible) was born on 27 April 1843 and was among the founders of Wasco.

George Claus Bergland was born in Mullsjö, in Jönköping County, Sweden, a town of about five thousand people, located northwest of the historic city of Jönköping. Mullsjö is also about nine miles west of Vättern, the sixth-largest lake in Europe and the second-largest in the nation. George's daughter described him as being of "medium stature, light complexioned" and as "ambitious, capable, quiet, and friendly." He was "given the name of Quick, while serving in the army in Sweden but later used the name Bergland." George C. Bergland came to the United States at the age of twenty-five, and first went to Minnesota. Following a brief residence there, he came to Campton Township, Kane County, Illinois, where he was "engaged in farming for a number of years." George Bergland was Naturalized as a U. S. citizen at the Kane County Courthouse in Geneva on 16 May 1878. The two citizens testifying to Bergland's "good moral character" and to his attachment to the principles of the Constitution were Gardner and Gillespie Bentley. Judge J. W. Ranstead of Kane County administered the Oath of Citizenship, in which Bergland renounced all allegiance to his former ruler, Oscar II, King of Sweden & Norway.

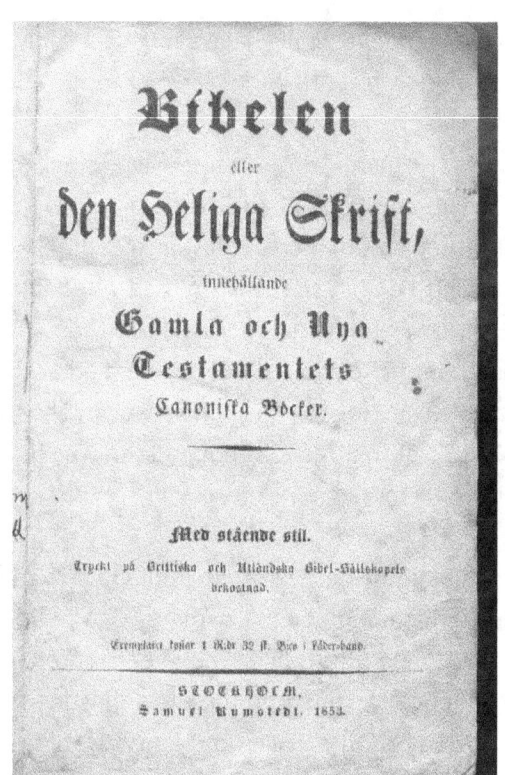 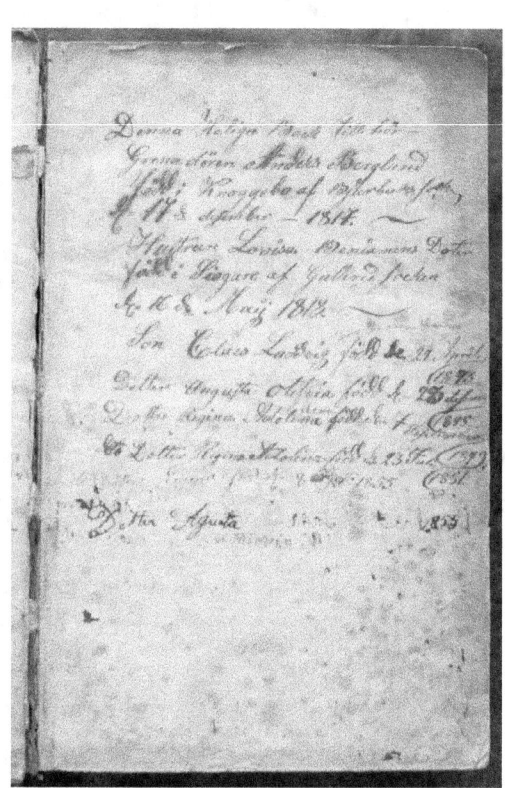

Title page and first inscription page from the Bergland Family Bible (1853)

This 1890s photograph shows George C. Bergland, one of the founders of Wasco. His wife Anne Louise (Swanson) Bergland is standing on the porch with a young boy, likely their son Floyd.

For two years in the late 1870s or early 1880s George C. Bergland ran a grocery store in St. Charles. The 1885 *St. Charles Biographical Directory* shows that the Berglands then lived at the northwest corner of West Cedar and Second Streets. This location is now [2018] the site of a parking lot. Bergland's occupation was given as "Teamster," and his political affiliation as Republican. He had come to St. Charles in 1870 and was a member of the Lutheran church. On 8 April 1876, he had married Anne Louise ("Louisa") Swanson, who had been born in Sweden on 10 May 1854. She had come to the United States with her parents and brothers at the age of ten. Louise lived in DeKalb until her marriage and then moved to the "Home Acres Farm" in Campton Township, where she and her husband lived for eight years. Early in the year 1885, the Berglands moved to the village of St. Charles.

George and Louise (Swanson) Bergland, as they appeared in the 1870s, around the time of their marriage

At the time the 1885 St. Charles city directory was compiled, the Berglands had one child – Florence Mabel, mentioned above. Not long afterward (in 1887) the family would relocate to the nascent village of Wasco, where they would live out the rest of their days. Anne Louise (Swanson) Bergland had a dark complexion, black hair, and was small in stature. Her granddaughter described her as a "capable and thrifty home-maker and an indulgent mother – unselfish, kind, and hospitable." Her obituary asserted that Louise and her husband lived busy, active lives, during which they won "the friendship and respect of their fellow man."

Religiously, Louise Bergland was raised as a Lutheran, but joined the Baptist Church as an adult. She was an active member of the congregation in Wasco from a very early date. Mrs. Bergland lived in Wasco for many years in the old Bergland home on the north side of the present Route 64. George and Louise had three children: Florence, Minnie, and Floyd. Their middle child, Minnie Lavinia Bergland, was born on 26 January 1882, and died at the age of twenty-four days, during a mild winter. She is buried in the Whitney Cemetery near her parents and siblings.

In 1887, when the Chicago Great Western Railroad was built and the village of Wasco began, George Bergland and his family moved to that locality, and opened a general merchandise business. He sold lumber, coal, and feed, among other commodities. Bergland was appointed Wasco's first Postmaster in October 1887. An 1888 biographical sketch noted that he had then "recently built a fine large store near Wasco Station on the line of the Minnesota and North-Western Railroad in which he is keeping a general country store and the post office." This was the old frame store (see "The Bergland/Hummel Store" section of this work) which was later replaced by the present brick building located on the same site. George C. Bergland suffered from poor health for a great number of years, but at the age of sixty-five, after a successful operation in Battle Creek, Michigan, performed by a local physician by the name of Dr. Kellogg, he recovered somewhat. The operation's outcome was reported in the St. Charles *Valley Chronicle* of 11 December 1908. By the year 1890, a full eighteen years before this surgery, George C. Bergland already owned two farms in Campton Township. The first was located on the north side of the present Empire Road, about a mile east of Lily Lake, and was 124.5 acres in size. This property was sold to Frank Swanberg in March 1901. The other Campton Township farm was just over 109 acres in extent, and adjoined the Norton farm less than a mile east of Wasco. This property grew in size over the decades, and most of the property comprising the old home farm remained in the Bergland family until the 1990s. George C. Bergland, the family's patriarch, died at the age of seventy-one from complications resulting from the flu.

Louise (Swanson) Bergland of Wasco, with her grandson George, about 1930

Florence (Bergland) Peterson, standing next to her mother, Louise (Swanson) Bergland, in August 1938

The original Bergland store in Wasco was built almost exactly along the border of the former Higgins and Carpenter farms.

The old claim line ran northwest from the intersection of the present Route 64 and Old La Fox Road, the latter of which ran along the exact center-line of Section 23. On an old map, the northern edge of the store is shown as nearly touching the property line; the land just to the north was owned by the Carpenter family when the railroad went through, and was sold shortly afterward to Harriet L. Austin. Mrs. Austin "and W. R. Austin, her husband" of the Town of Campton sold a triangular quarter-acre of land at the northwest intersection of the present Route 64 and Old LaFox Road to Charles Simon (also of Campton) on 7 November 1891. The purchase price was $50. The Higgins family owned all the land to the west, and the Austins owned the lands to the north and east at the time of the sale. Bergland himself bought the irregular parcel of land on which the old store was built from John and Charlotte Millen on 1 July 1892. Since he paid $1500, it is certain that the old store was on the property at that time. The old Bergland store is also shown on a map dating to that year, and is referenced in an earlier biographical sketch. The Simon family (who owned the property just north of the store, and whose land would be purchased by George Bergland in 1906) later moved to Republic Township, Marquette County, Michigan. Their children Bertha and Floyd were both born in Illinois. In September 1937, an elderly Melissa Simon returned to Wasco for a visit, taking her granddaughter along. Charles W. Simon died in Michigan in 1928; Melissa survived until 1956. Both are buried in the Republic Cemetery, in Michigan.

The first page of the handwritten text of George Bergland's obituary, November 1914

George Bergland established his feed mill, agricultural implement warehouse, and lumberyard in Wasco at various points in the 1890s. Though the lumberyard lasted the longest of these businesses, each was successful and functioned separately from the store and post office, which Bergland also ran simultaneously. In May 1901, a newspaper columnist for the *St. Charles Chronicle* asked locals, on behalf of George Bergland, to come in and "examine his display of buggies and road wagons." Bergland was then, beginning on 1 May, running his feed mill three days per week – Tuesdays, Thursdays, and Saturdays. George Bergland traveled to Sweden with Clark Swanson in the summer of 1903. They were gone for eleven weeks, and saw a number of friends and relatives while there. George and Louise Bergland spent several days at the St. Louis World's Fair in October of 1904. Bergland also traveled to Chicago and Elgin on business quite frequently, and sometimes visited relatives in Rockford. His health greatly improved after his 1908 surgery, which helped to alleviate his "bowel and stomach trouble." In December 1910, George C. Bergland purchased a third farm in Campton Township. This property, known as "Belle View," was located in Section 13, on what is now Bolcum Road, and contained 112 acres. The property adjoined the St. Charles Township border; the farm was tenanted in the 1910s by Otto and Helen (Carlson) Ekstrom. After a short trip to the West in the summer of 1914, George C. Bergland's health quickly declined. He passed away at his home in Wasco on 11 November 1914. George Bergland's funeral took place at the Wasco Baptist Church; Rev. N. J. Peterson preached the funeral sermon, using Romans 8:28 as his text. The songs sung at the service were "Nearer My God to Thee" and "No Need of Shadows." Pall bearers were Will Millen, Leonard White, August Johnson, Frank Vanderhoof, A. J. Mongerson, and C. W. Bolcum, all of whom were prominent Wasco residents. Bergland's obituary called him the "leading citizen of Wasco" and "the founder of the village." It was through his efforts that "all of the business enterprises" of Wasco were established. He was a Mason and a member of the Modern Woodmen of America. George Bergland was survived by his wife and their two children, as well as by a sister and "an aged aunt."

Elmer and Florence (Bergland) Peterson's wedding photo, from 1904

In November 1914, the estate papers for George Bergland were filed in the Kane County Probate Office. A schedule in the file shows that he died owning real estate valued at $55,000, and personal property worth $10,000. Adjusted for inflation, these sums would total just over $1.6 million today. Bergland's legal heirs were his widow and his two children, Floyd and Florence. Louise Bergland continued to live in Wasco following her husband's death. In fact, she survived long enough to witness the Campton Township Centennial celebration in 1935. In September 1938, she fell and broke her hip at her home in Wasco. The result of this injury caused her death, which occurred at the Community Hospital in Geneva, at noon on 11 October 1938. She was eighty-four years of age, and was survived by two children, two grandchildren, and her brother Claus A. Swanson. Louise's obituary eloquently stated that those she left behind were blessed "with the sweetest memories of a beautiful life."

Florence Mabel Bergland, who was born on the Bergland family's "Home Acres" Farm, married

Elmer T. Peterson of Campton Township on 22 June 1904. Her wedding dinner was served in "a tent on the lawn" of the Bergland home in Wasco. The bride's table was decorated with smilax and carnations. A quartet played at dinner; the musicians were Messrs. Brown and Lake, and Misses Fisher and Lake. Among her wedding presents was "a finely wrought china cabinet" from some church workers. Miss Bergland had been an organist in the Wasco Baptist Church for some years prior to her marriage. Her husband was described as "an energetic businessman of sterling qualities" whose "constant good nature" had won for him "the highest esteem" of Wasco's citizens. The event was described as "one of the prettiest home weddings ever witnessed in Wasco." There were some two hundred guests in attendance, and the ceremony was performed by Rev. J. Y. Atchison, a former pastor of the Wasco church. Mrs. I. Barber played Mendelsohn's grand wedding march on the piano, which announced the coming of the bridal party.

Florence Peterson attended high school on the east side of St. Charles, graduating in 1895. Florence (who was known to family members as "Auntie Lo") taught in a rural school for two years following her graduation. Although confirmed at the Lutheran church in St. Charles, in the year 1895 Florence and her immediate family joined the Wasco Baptist Church. She was a faithful member of that congregation for many years, and even taught Sunday School there, in addition to serving as church pianist. For many years, Florence would make a weekly trip to Hull House, the famous Chicago settlement house, and often invited friends of that institution (including some women who had known Jane Addams personally) to visit the Bergland and Peterson families in Wasco.

Florence (Bergland) Peterson was a partner in the Bergland Company business, first with her father, and later with her husband and her brother Floyd. She was employed there from May 1899 until January 1936, when she retired. She was industrious and thrifty, and possessed a keen business ability. Florence asserted that "faith and faithfulness were the key notes of her living." Her husband Elmer passed away in November 1942; they had no children. Florence died, suddenly, on 23 October 1951, due to a heart condition, and was survived by two nieces, one nephew, and several cousins.

Florence and Elmer Peterson, Louise Bergland, her son Floyd Bergland, and an unknown individual, likely 1910s

Floyd Harrison Bergland was born in the new village of Wasco on 12 April 1892. His middle name was chosen in honor of the Republican U. S. President at the time of his birth, Benjamin Harrison. Like his sister before him, Floyd attended St. Charles High School, and following his graduation he enrolled at the University of Illinois. He was outgoing and gregarious, and enjoyed developing local community entertainment when he was younger, occasionally writing plays which were performed in Wasco. One such play, entitled "One Hundred Thousand Dollars" featured a local cast of Margaret Berg, Harriet Eddy, Eddie Mongerson, George Perkins, and Morris Whitney.

Floyd Bergland's 1908 "Daily Reminder" still exists, which chronicles his day-to-day activities for much of that year and part of the next. In the journal, Floyd chronicled visits from his Aunt Minnie and Uncle Oscar, going hunting, attending church, watching games played by the Wasco "Basket ball team," playing pranks at the (then-new) Wasco School, and much more. Floyd pasted clips of Japanese proverbs, historic events, and President Lincoln's achievements onto several of the journal's pages. He considered *Treasure Island* a "certainly swell" read, and Winston Churchill's historical novel *The Crisis* a true "peach of a book." Floyd recorded when the local railroad went into receivership, which tests he had in school, and often noted the state of his father's health (poor for most of the year). Typical entries included lines such as "Went to school, nothing doing" or "Snowing like the dickens." Those individuals he mentions by name include Margaret Norton, Edna Bolcum, Villa Austin, Carrie Hurd, John Stewart, George Scott, Frank Lake, Elmer [Peterson], Norvid [Swanson], Mrs. Crook, Mrs. Higgins, Mrs. Allen, Messrs. Ellsworth, Hawkins, and Austin, among others. He often noted the form of transportation that he took to St. Charles (buggy, cutter, horseback, or train) and remarked on the weather. A favorite expression of the time was the phrase "to beat the band," which Floyd used most often to describe extreme weather phenomena, as in when it was "lightning & thundering out to beat the band" or "snowing and blowing to beat the band." He seemed quite excited when learning of the election of President Taft, the Republican Candidate, on 4 November 1908, and even had a heated political argument with Nathan Saperston the previous day, during which they called each other "all the names that are not in the dictionary"!

Shortly after the 1908 election, Floyd and most of the Wasco residents his age went "up to Vanderhoof's" for a social gathering given to benefit the local school. On 20 December 1908, Floyd went to Chicago to meet his father, who had just come in "on the Grand Trunk [railroad] at the Dearborn street Depot." George Bergland had successfully recovered from surgery in Battle Creek, Michigan, and was on his way home to Wasco. The family was active in several businesses enterprises at that time, including the store, the post office, the lumberyard, and a local feed lot adjoining the railroad tracks.

In 1914, the year of his father's death, Floyd Bergland became a partner with his sister in the family's business, Bergland & Company. In February 1917, Floyd and his sister Florence registered the name "Oakenwald" for their farm in the southeast quarter of Section 23, Campton Township. This farm was just south of Wasco, on the east side of LaFox Road, and was formerly owned by John and Mariam Hagaman. Floyd and Florence's father George C. Bergland had purchased this farm of seventy-seven and one-third acres from the Hagamans on 2 November 1907. The purchase price was $6000. The Hagamans had owned the land since 1844 and had occupied it for several years prior to their purchase. For most of the

1910s, Theodore and Hilma Johnson tenanted the farm, which was 118 acres in size then. In the 1930s, Eric and Fredrika Olson tenanted this farm, which had dairy cows for most of its existence.

At the same time "Oakenwald" was registered as a Kane County farm name, the Berglands also registered the name "Bergland Home Acres" for their property just east of Wasco, adjoining the Norton farm in the northwest quarter of Section 24, Campton Township. This property had been in the Bergland family's possession for much longer – George had purchased the original part on 30 October 1877, also from the Hagaman family. George Bergland "of the Town of Campton" paid $1700 to Elida Hagaman (John's older sister) for thirty-six acres on the south side of "the Griggs Road" [now Wasco Road] and "the St. Charles and Geneva Road" [now Route 64]. The farm was later expanded to more than one-hundred-and-nine acres. In the spring of 1903, Charles Johnson "moved onto the Bergland farm" near Wasco. In 1918, George and Lottie Brown were tenants on the Bergland farm in Section 24. Elnor Carlson tenanted the farm during the Depression years. This was a dairy farm, but corn was raised there for silage, and oats for feed. Some alfalfa and soybeans were also grown on Bergland Home Acres.

On 15 September 1914, Albert S. Burleson, U. S. Postmaster General, appointed Floyd H. Bergland as Wasco's Postmaster. More than a decade later (on 3 February 1925), Harry S. New reappointed Bergland to this office. During the intervening years (from 1917 to 1924) Floyd's brother-in-law, Elmer T. Peterson served as Postmaster. Floyd's father George was appointed the first Postmaster of Wasco on 20 October 1887, and was reappointed to that office on 6 September 1899, serving until his death. Although Floyd Bergland was officially Wasco's postmaster for years, most of the actual postal work (like waiting on customers or distributing mail to postal boxes) for much of that time was done by John Olson, according to Floyd's son George C. Bergland. Olson's wife Gladys was Floyd's secretary for several years. The bookkeeper was Elaine Ekstrom.

Floyd Bergland in his WWI Uniform

During the First World War, Floyd Bergland served as a First Lieutenant at Camp Lewis, Washington. He and several others from Wasco were given community send-offs at the depot building when they left to serve their country. Upon his discharge from the U. S. Army at the conclusion of World War I, Floyd Bergland left Fort Lewis and returned to Wasco. He took over control of Bergland & Company from his sister, who had run the business during the preceding four years. In 1924, Floyd Bergland was one of the founders of the St. Charles Country Club, and he stayed active with the group for many years. He and his wife Olive owned a Franklin automobile in 1928. They used it to bring their newborn son home from the Sherman Hospital in Elgin that August. In addition to running Bergland & Company at that time, Floyd Bergland was also a Director of the State Bank of St. Charles, and was President of the Board of Trustees of Delnor Hospital. He suffered from severe asthma (and generally poor health) but was very social with his business associates. During the Depression, Floyd Bergland and Lester Norris helped ensure that the Stewart Bank, on whose Board of Directors they both served, remained open by offering some of their personal capital to back up the bank's deposits. Early in the 1930s, Floyd Bergland acquired an ownership share in the Bergland-Stephens Lumber Company of Glen Ellyn, partly through the collection of a debt he had guaranteed for a business friend, Montelle Stephens.

In 1936, Floyd Bergland purchased his sister's and brother-in-law's interest in the family business and became its sole owner.

The certificate appointing Floyd H. Bergland as Wasco's Postmaster (1914)

He was an intelligent, capable executive. Floyd was also a 32nd Degree Mason, a Shriner, and was a member of the Scabbard and Blade, a military honor society. He was active in the Kiwanis Club also. Floyd married Olive Lillian Anderson on 6 October 1927, on her parents' Knollwood Farm, just west of Wasco. Floyd later served as Vice President of the St. Charles Country Club, and in the same capacity with the State Bank of St. Charles. In 1940, he fell from a horse and suffered a concussion, which quite negatively impacted his overall health. Floyd died of a cerebral hemorrhage on 10 May 1946, at the age of fifty-four.

Olive Lillian (Anderson) Bergland was born on Knollwood Farm, near Wasco, on 30 July 1901. She was the youngest daughter of CJ and Hilda Anderson (see "The Charles Anderson Family"). Olive attended St. Charles High School, and then Wheaton College, graduating from the latter institution in 1924. For three years, Olive taught in a Girls' School in Cedarhurst, Long Island. Her sister-in-law described her as possessing a "marked ability as a home maker and mother" with a "friendly and pleasing personality." She and Floyd had two children, George Charles Bergland (a contributor to this work) and Bonnie Louise Bergland. Olive was a member of various local clubs, and among her closest friends were Ann Mongerson, Fern Jordan, and Helen Keplar. Olive was a "people person," and lived in Wasco until her husband's

1927 wedding photo of Floyd & Olive (Anderson) Bergland

death in 1946. At that time, she sold the family's home there, and moved to a newly-built home at 1333 South Third Street, St. Charles. Some years later, Olive Bergland helped design a new home which was built at 311 Iroquois Avenue, St. Charles, where she would live until her death. She was a fine cook, and family favorites include her pecan and cinnamon rolls, Swedish meatballs, and rice pudding with raisins.

By 1943, Bergland and Company had been in business for fifty-six years, and was selling "tile, fence, hardware, feeds, seeds, hybrids," as well as building material and fuel. They offered "a complete service for farms and estates" according to their letterhead, and had two sales yards – one in Wasco, and the other in Glen Ellyn. Their phone numbers at the time were: "St. Charles 4065 R-1 and 3545." Floyd Bergland and his sister Florence jointly owned three farms in Campton Township at that time – Bergland Home Aces (on Old Burlington Road near the Whitney/Goldenstein property), Oakenwald on LaFox Road south of Wasco, and Belle View on Bolcum Road east of Denker. The first two of those properties are now part of the Fox Mill subdivision. Oakenwald was Floyd's favorite property of the three, and it was there that he kept his horses. A five-gaited Tennessee walking horse, Dixie, was bred there yearly. She was always ridden with an English saddle. In the late 1930s, the well-known philanthropist Edward J. Baker of St. Charles gave Floyd Bergland a coal-black riding horse, which Bergland named "EJ," for Baker's first two initials. The horse was given to Bergland along with a handsome silver-inlaid western saddle and bridle. Floyd's brother-in-law Elmer Peterson helped raise the horses on Oakenwald Farm for years. Elmer's wife Florence, besides being Floyd's sister, was his close friend throughout their lives.

Floyd Bergland, with his horse Dolly

The Bergland family in June 1938 – Olive, Bonnie, Louise, George, and Florence

The gambrel-roofed barn and silo at Oakenwald Farm, south of Wasco

Floyd Bergland riding EJ, in Wasco

One of the Berglands' horses, at Oakenwald

In 1940, Floyd Bergland was riding his horse EJ when he was stricken with a stroke. After Floyd's death from a cerebral hemorrhage six years later, Olive Bergland sold her husband's horses. Floyd's funeral services were held in the Wasco Baptist Church in May 1946. As was the local custom at that time, the body was displayed in the Bergland family's parlor in Wasco rather than in a funeral home. The Berglands are buried in the Whitney Cemetery.

Olive (Anderson) Bergland Hamilton passed away on 4 August 1984 in Hayward, Wisconsin, at the age of eighty-three. Her family had a cottage in Round Lake, some miles east of there, where Olive spent much time. Beginning in the early 1940s, she spent part of most summers there. Olive had been a resident of St. Charles since 1946. She was survived by two sisters, her children George and Bonnie, and seven grandchildren. Her funeral services were held in Bethlehem Lutheran Church in St. Charles, with Rev. Arthur Holmer officiating.

The Gustaf Swanson Family

Gustaf Swanson, the father-in-law of George C. Bergland, was born in Timmelhed, Västra Götaland, Sweden, on 3 February 1825. His granddaughter Florence described him as being small in stature, with a "Roman nose," black hair, and whiskers. He was ambitious, impulsive, and intelligent. He married Inga Lisa Peterson in Sweden, and they came to the United States "in a sail-boat in 1864." The voyage took eleven weeks. Inga (Peterson) Swanson was born on 6 October 1821, and was "slender in stature, kind, quiet . . . and courageous." The Swansons lived in DeKalb for fifteen years, and later bought a farm in Campton Township. They lived with Inga's sister Johannah, who was deaf, for many years. Gustaf had diabetes in adulthood, and died from apoplexy at the age of seventy-one. His wife Inga died of pneumonia at the age of seventy-five, on 24 October 1896. Gustaf died eight weeks later. Both are buried in the Whitney Cemetery just north of Wasco.

Gustaf and Inga Swanson had six children, two of whom died in infancy in Sweden. Another child, Oscar, died at the age of eight. Their son Claus August Swanson, who was born in Timmele, Västra Götaland, Sweden, on 10 March 1857, continued to live in Campton Township throughout most of his life. His niece described him as being thrifty and industrious, and a successful farmer. He had chronic bronchial trouble, but actively farmed until he was in his early eighties. He arrived in the United States in 1879. On 28 April 1888, in Chicago, C. A. Swanson married Emma Caroline Anderson of St. Charles. The couple had four children: Claude, Mildred, Norvid, and Ila. Local residents sometimes called him "Clark" Swanson, and he is often referred to in newspaper accounts by this name. Lutheran church records refer to him as Claes Aug. Svenson. In 1918, Clark and Emma Swanson owned a 160-acre farm in Section 24, Campton Township. They had been residents of Kane County since 1884, and owned a telephone. Their children Mildred and Norvid were in the household at that time. The farmhouse was located just southeast of (and across the street from) the Whitney Schoolhouse. Claus A. Swanson died of pneumonia on 3 June 1943, at the Community Hospital in Geneva. Two of the Swanson children (Claude and Ila) died while in their youth. Ila Elizabeth Swanson died in Wasco on 13 December 1896, aged five weeks. Claude passed away on 15 January 1901, at the age of eleven years, eleven months, and four days. Rev. E. C. Jessup preached the sermon at his funeral. Norvid R. Swanson married Louise M. Redborg of Batavia, and his sister Mildred married Carl H. Olson of St. Charles. Mildred was known for having a "pleasing personality and kindly disposition," and Norvid was successful in both business and farming. Besides being cousins of the Berglands, Norvid and Mildred Swanson and their spouses were also close friends with the members of that family.

Norvid Swanson, of Wasco, in 1910

Emma C. (Anderson) Swanson, widow of Claus, died on 17 September 1960, at the age of ninety-four. She had been born in Hycklinge, Östergötland, Sweden, on 25 August 1866, and came to St. Charles, Kane County, Illinois, with her parents when she was one year old. Her father was Andrew Anderson; he passed away in St. Charles on 21 March 1907. From that time until to her death on 22 September 1910, Emma's mother Anna S. Anderson lived with the Swansons on their farm east of Wasco. Emma C. Anderson joined Bethlehem Lutheran Church, St. Charles, in 1883, five years prior to her marriage. Emma's daughter Mildred Elvira Swanson, mentioned above, was born in Wasco on 12 April 1893. She and her family attended Bethlehem Lutheran Church for decades. Mildred married Carl Henry Olson, who was originally from Joliet, on 28 June 1917, at Salem Lutheran Church in Sycamore. They had a daughter Dorothy Jean Olson, who was born in Geneva on 23 October 1919. The family moved to St. Charles before 1930. Mildred underwent major surgery at Community Hospital, Geneva, in May 1941. In 1950 and 1956, she and her husband lived at #1211 South Fourth Avenue in St. Charles. They were on the same street in 1935 and 1940 as well. Carl was an insurance broker for many years. Mildred died in Minnesota on 23 May 1968, and her widower passed away in St. Charles in November 1970.

Mildred E. Swanson's Confirmation photo, from 1908 - Bethlehem Lutheran Church, St. Charles

Mildred's brother, Norvid Raymond Swanson, was born on the family farm just east of Wasco on 7 December 1894. His marriage took place in Kane County on 19 March 1921. He and his wife Louise lived in St. Charles early in their marriage, and then moved into the "Bergland cottage" in Wasco, during the winter of 1928/29. They entertained at their home in Wasco during the Depression years, and moved to the nearby Swanson brothers' farm in 1933. In 1936, they moved to St. Charles. Norvid and Louise Swanson later moved to Batavia. Norvid died there on 21 December 1972, and was survived by his widow, and a niece, Dorothy (Olson) Kemp.

Charles John Swanson, younger brother of Claus, also lived in Wasco. In fact, the brothers lived together for more than forty years, and worked their home farm jointly. He was a bachelor, and was patient, kind, and industrious, according to his niece, who remembered him well. Most references to the "Swanson Brothers" in early Wasco records refer to these two men - Charles J. and Claus August Swanson, whose large farm was located less than a mile east of the village. The house was on the north side of what is now Old Burlington Road, a short distance east of Wasco Road. Claus August Swanson purchased the majority of the property from Harry and Mary Eddy on 14 February 1879. The farm was over one hundred and eighty acres in extent in 1892, when it was still owned by "August" Swanson. In January 1906, a burglar broke into the Swanson farmhouse, but quickly made his escape when confronted by Charles Swanson. Charles never married. He passed away on the old farm on 2 April 1936, at the age of seventy-three. The cause of death was heart failure.

The John Swanson Family

A second Swanson family lived in Wasco from a very early date but does not seem to be closely related to the family mentioned above. This "set" of Swansons descended from John Smith Swanson, who was born in Falköping, Västra Götaland, Sweden, in August 1823. While still residing abroad, he married Elisa Anderson, and they came to the U. S. in 1869. The Swansons were already living in Campton Township by July 1870, when they were listed near the Higgins and Hagaman families in that year's census. John gave his occupation that year as "farmer and blacksmith," and the three children then in the household (Helman, Charles, and Alfred) were all natives of Sweden. The family would remain in the area for several generations, and when Wasco was founded the Swansons began to patronize the earliest businesses there. Alfred Swanson, who came to the country with his parents as a two-year-old, remained in the Wasco area for his entire life. Alfred's younger sister Amanda Swanson was born in Campton Township in May 1871. In 1897, Amanda married John C. Mungerson, son of Andrew and Carrie. He was born in Campton Township on 22 June 1862. The Mungersons later moved to North Aurora, and had children including Ethel, Edward, Edna, and Raymond. John died in Aurora Township on 9 May 1937, and is buried in the Lily Lake Cemetery.

Alfred and Alma Swanson of Campton Township, with their son Edmund

John S. Swanson of Campton Township was known as "John Smitt" in February 1873, when he purchased a small parcel of land from William H. Hess. In a 1909 affidavit, John S. Swanson stated that he was sometimes known as John Smitt "on account of his mail becoming confused with that of other Swansons . . . in the neighborhood having similar names." Later, on 28 December 1878, "Smitt" Swanson of St. Charles purchased the majority of his thirty-seven-acre Campton Township farm from William and Mary Hess. The purchase price was $400. The Swansons immediately took out a mortgage on this property, which was paid off by the end of 1881. The farm was located in the southeast quarter of Section 16, about 1 ½ miles west-northwest of the future site of Wasco. The Chicago Great Western Railroad cut through a portion of the John S. Swanson farm when it was constructed in 1886. A good portion of the property remained wooded in the 1890s and later. The home was north of the railroad tracks, on the north bank of a branch of Ferson creek. Access to the home could be gained via a long lane leading south from Empire Road.

In November 1909, John S. Swanson and his wife "Lizzie" conveyed their farm to their son Alfred. Neither of the Swansons were able to write their name, and instead made their marks on the deed. Elisa ("Lisa") Swanson died in Wasco in 1915, and John S. survived until 1 February 1917, when he passed away at the age of ninety-three. Alfred Swanson, their son, married Alma Olivia Johnson in Chicago on 4 October 1889. They were living with Alfred's parents in Campton Township in 1900. Alfred was a charter member of Grace Lutheran Church, Lily Lake, and was a member of their Board of Trustees for a number of years.

Alfred and Alma Swanson celebrated their fiftieth wedding anniversary in October 1939 at "their farm home" near Wasco. Seventy-five friends and relatives were present at the celebration. The couple was presented with a radio by those in attendance. Alfred passed away at his home on 23 June 1940, at the age of seventy-three. Alma died at the home "northwest of Wasco" on 30 December 1944. She had been in poor health "for a long time," and was cared for by her son for "some years." Alma's funeral services were held in Geneva. She was buried in the Whitney Cemetery.

Alfred and Alma's son Edmund A. Swanson was born near Wasco on 17 March 1893. Edmund was a long-time member of Grace Lutheran Church, Lily Lake. During the Great Depression, he worked on the William Parson farm in Campton Township. He lived in the area his entire life, and moved to a nursing home in Elgin shortly before his eightieth birthday. In the 1920s and '30s, Edmund Swanson would come to Wasco for his grocery supplies for the winter. Like so many customers, he would hitch his horse outside the Bergland store when making his purchases. He still used a horse and buggy long after automobiles became prevalent in the area. His home was that of his parents and grandparent, located far off of both Brown Road and Empire Road, near the railroad tracks. In 1942, Edmund was 5' 10" tall, weighed 185 pounds, had a ruddy complexion, and had blue eyes and black and gray hair. Edmund Alfred Swanson died in Elgin on 4 January 1975. He had no children.

Edmund Swanson, on the family farm near Wasco. He's shown here with a horse-drawn corn-binder

The Higgins Family

William Higgins "of the Town of St. Charles" purchased the large farm of David Pattee, comprising what would become the northwest quarter of Wasco, on 23 July 1869. The old Pattee farmhouse, built in the 1840s, was located on the north side of the present Route 64 and was the closest building to Wasco when the village was created in 1887. The purchase price for the Pattee farm was $5000. The farm was conveyed in two parcels, one being 62 ¼ acres in size and the other a bit over 65 ½ acres in extent. The second parcel was located across the road and to the west of the first, and later comprised a part of the Frank Brown farm. William and Mary Higgins immediately took out a mortgage from Pattee, for $4000.

William Higgins was born in New York City in 1825, and moved to Wales, Erie County, New York, in 1837. His wife Mary J. (née Babbage) was born in Genesee County, New York, in 1833. They were married by 1855, but as of then had no children. Michael Higgins, William's brother, was also born in New York City, in 1832. The family moved to Illinois shortly after the Civil War. They were all still in Wales, New York, when the 1865 State Census was taken; Michael had married Cynthia, a native of Erie County, by that time. William and Mary Higgins had three children by 1870: George, Mary, and Charles. The children were born in Erie County, New York, and came with their parents to Kane County in 1867 or 1868. William was a farmer, as was his younger brother Michael, who (in 1870) also lived in what would later become Wasco. Mary Jane (Babbage) Higgins passed away in 1874 and is buried in the Whitney Cemetery.

An 1880s tintype of George Higgins, of Wasco

George L. Higgins, a son of William and Mary, stayed in Wasco, and in 1880 he was a farm laborer in the household of James C. and Maria L. Rice, who lived across the street from the Higgins house, and slightly west. George was then aged twenty-four. George was born in Wales, Erie County, New York, on 21 November 1855; his wife's name was Flora (née Catnaugh) – she was from Byron, Illinois. George was a carpenter, and died in Sycamore, DeKalb County, Illinois, on 22 July 1923. His obituary called him "a good man and friend," prominent in the Odd Fellows, and a skilled carpenter. When he was thirteen years old, "the family became residents on a farm near Wasco, Kane County, Ill." There, George attended school and reached adulthood. In January 1888, "George Higgins and Wm. Denson [of Wasco] having become tired of rural life have found employment with the Illinois Central railroad." George then moved to Lindenwood, Ogle County, Illinois, and in 1895, he moved to Sycamore. On 11 May 1898, in Ogle County, he married Flora. She passed away in Sycamore in December 1906. George was survived by three siblings – Charles, Ida, and Mary, all of whom lived in Western New York at the time of his death.

William and Mary J. Higgins of the Town of Campton sold their two farms near the future village of Wasco to Lucy Higgins "of the Town of Bloomingdale, DuPage County, Illinois" on 29 October 1872. The purchase price was $4800. By 1877, William Higgins had moved back to Erie County, New York. The new owners of the Campton Township property were Lucy Higgins, and her husband, Van Rensselaer Higgins.

Van Rensselaer Higgins was possibly a relative of William, although their exact relationship is not immediately clear. These Higgins families were from very different parts of New York State, and they were certainly no closer than first cousins to one another. Van Rensselaer (named for the famous New York family, of which his mother was a member) was a New York native, and was a farmer. He was born in Homer, in Cortland County, in 1811, and was married twice. By his first wife, Van Rensselaer had a son Gilbert, who was born in Ohio in 1833. Gilbert's mother seems to have passed away soon afterward. In May 1834, Van Rensselaer married Lucy Bingham. They were very early settlers of DuPage County, arriving there in the late 1830s. Lucy (Van Rensselaer's second wife) was native of Tolland County, Connecticut. The 1850 census shows "Van R." Higgins as a farmer, living in Bloomindale Township. By 1860, he and Lucy had three children in the household: Letitia, Harriet, and Horace Higgins, all of whom were born in Illinois. The family was in Bloomindale Township at the outbreak of the Civil War, when William Higgins' family was still in Erie County, New York. Van Rensselaer and Lucy Higgins, along with their two children, were still living in Bloomindale, DuPage County, Illinois, in August 1870, although they moved to Kane County very soon afterward. Van Rensselaer Higgins died in Campton Township on 1 September 1873, aged sixty-two, and is buried in the Whitney Cemetery.

An 1860s tintype of Horace Higgins, with his father Van Rensselaer Higgins

Lucy (Bingham) Higgins, who was born on 29 January 1813, was living on the family's farm in the northwest quarter of Section 23, Campton Township, at the time of the 1880 census. She passed away in what would soon be Wasco, at 11:00 PM, on 21 January 1881. She died of pneumonia, after having resided in Illinois for more than forty-two years. All three of her children remained in the area. The oldest, Cornelia (Higgins) White, was born in 1838, possibly in Ohio, but probably in DuPage County.

On 22 September 1857, in DuPage County, Cornelia Higgins, who was sometimes known as Nellie, married Uriah C. White, a Civil War veteran and Massachusetts native. He was a musician for Company D, 105th Illinois Infantry, during the war. Uriah suffered from consumption, and passed away in Winfield, DuPage County, in May 1880. Nellie moved in with her widowed mother a short time after her husband's death; Nellie passed away in Wasco on 5 December 1889 and is buried in the Whitney Cemetery.

Lucy Higgins' death record, from 1881

Horace S. Higgins, a brother to Cornelia, was born in DuPage County, Illinois, on 17 March 1851. He moved to Campton Township with his family around 1870. His mother Lucy officially sold him the two Campton Township farms on 15 March 1877, for $4800. Beginning in 1890, Horace Higgins began selling small parcels near the eastern edge of his property line (in what had become Wasco) to various buyers. Higgins, then still a bachelor, sold several lots on the north side of the present Route 64 in 1894, including one to Leonard White, and another to Louise Bergland, both of whom built homes there at that time. In October 1898, Horace married Martha Clark Idleman. They had no children together, although Martha had a daughter from her first marriage. Martha Higgins was extremely active in the W. C. T. U. during the first decade of the twentieth century and was often meeting with the temperance organization's regional representatives.

Horace Higgins retained ownership of the Higgins farm in Wasco for many years, and was still a bachelor when he sold a right-of-way to the Chicago Great Western Railroad in July 1886. He was still the property's legal owner as late as 1903. In February of that year, Horace S. and Martha C. Higgins sold the farm in Section 22, Campton Township, consisting of just over sixty acres of land, to Emma J. Brown. H. S. Higgins moved from Wasco to Detroit in September 1906. He kept the old farm in Wasco, though, until 23 February 1910, when he sold it to Chester W. Bolcum for $7000. With his wife Cassie, Bolcum sold the land to Nels Hawkins (whose descendants still own the property) one week later for the sum of $7500. Horace died in Chicago on 12 April 1913 and is buried in the Whitney Cemetery. Horace's sister Harriet, who remained on the family farm, married Willard R. Austin (see "The Austin family" for further information on Harriet and her children).

The Hawkins Family

The first member of the Hawkins family to settle in the Wasco area was Nels Peter Hawkins, who was born in Kattarp, Skåne County, Sweden on 29 March 1873. His surname in Sweden was Håkansson, and his parents were Håkan Mårtensson and Johanna Nelson. Nels came to the United States in 1890, and settled in the northeastern part of Campton Township in 1892. Nels was married twice and had a total of six children, two of whom died young. Nels P. Hawkins became a member of Grace Lutheran Church, Lily Lake, on 16 August 1896. His wife Ellen M. (Abrahamson) Hawkins joined the same church on 15 May 1898.

In February 1903, shortly after the death of his six-month-old son Raymond from pneumonia, Nels Hawkins moved his family "to a farm east of St. Charles," but before long they returned to the vicinity of Wasco to live. His first wife, Mathilda Ellen (Abrahamson) Hawkins died in Wasco on 17 February 1904. She was only twenty-nine years old; they had been married for just six years. Nels Hawkins took a two-month-long trip to Sweden between December 1907 and February 1908, traveling there with Charles Ekstrom. They sailed to Europe aboard 'The Mauritania' and met with many friends and relatives while abroad. Before the Hawkinses purchased the old Higgins farm in Wasco in 1910, their Campton Township farm was located on Silver Glen Road, west of Corron Road, two-and-a-half miles north of Wasco. Edward and Emma Hawkins had purchased this land from the Tucker family in April 1903.

By the summer of 1910, Nels's brother Joel (who had come to the United States in 1901) was living on the Wasco farm with with Nels's son George and his daughter Mildred, along with Nels himself, who was then a widower. Nels married Amanda Wilhelmina Johnson/Scherman on 20 April 1911. Amanda was born on 24 May 1871, in Korsgården (now a part of Västra Götaland), Sweden, and she came to the United States in 1905. Her surname was Johnson, but to distinguish themselves from the many Johnsons in the area, she and her sister sometimes used their mother's maiden name, Scherman, in place of their father's surname. Nels and Amanda had two children: Eric Nels Hawkins, who was born in Wasco on 6 August 1911; and Bertha Erica Hawkins, who was born in Wasco on 18 September 1914.

Nels and Amanda Hawkins, with children George and Millie (from Nels's first marriage), and Eric

The "new" Hawkins house, Sionilli (see "Some Wasco Houses – Northwest Quarter"), was built during World War I, and the family moved into this home by 1918. In 1920, Nels and Amanda Hawkins were living on their dairy farm in Wasco with their children Eric and Bertha. After Amanda's death following an operation at

Colonial Hospital, Geneva, on 22 April 1921, her children Eric and Bertha went to live with their aunt and uncle Alfred and Alma Swanson, who raised them (see "The John Swanson Family"). Alma was Amanda's older sister, but emigrated later than Alma. Amanda (Johnson) Hawkins was forty-nine years old at the time of her death. She is buried in Union Cemetery, St. Charles.

Nels Hawkins died in Aurora on 17 February 1925. He had been living in that city for two months but had lived in Wasco for more than thirty years. Nels's youngest son, Eric N. Hawkins, married Iva Espel in Princeton, Illinois, in August 1934, and they soon moved to Rock Island. Eric was studying at Augustana College at that time. He and his wife later moved to California, and then to Texas. Eric was a Lutheran minister for many years; he passed away in Lead Hill, Arkansas on 26 August 1977. Eric's sister Bertha E. Hawkins also left Wasco and moved out of state in the 1930s. She married Arthur R. Franzen, and they lived in Kansas and later in Washington State. Bertha (Hawkins) Franzen died in Tacoma on 26 June 1999.

Brothers Joel, Ed, and Nels Hawkins, as young men

Nels Hawkins' son George was perhaps the last local farmer to deliver his milk from the farm to the milk station near the Wasco depot by means of horse and wagon. He did this until the late 1930s at least, by which time all other local farmers were delivering milk with their trucks.

George Edward Hawkins was born in Campton Township on 8 February 1899, and was a son of Nels Peter and Ellen Matilda (Abrahamson) Hawkins. His baptismal record at Grace Lutheran Church, Lily Lake, gave his name as "Joy Edward," and his date of baptism as 11 June 1899. George was a lifelong member of this congregation. George was also active in the Kane County Farm Bureau, and served on the Campton Township School Board. In 1918, George was working as a farmhand on Edward Hawkins's farm north of Wasco. He was tall, slender, and had gray eyes and light hair, according to his WWI Draft Registration card. In January 1929, George Hawkins gave "a most interesting talk before the high school agriculture class on his experience with dairy work." The following month, George took the member of the U Go I Go Club on a "sleighing party." They had supper at "the Log Cabin at St. Charles." On 20 November 1929, in Marquette County, Michigan, George E. Hawkins married Hilda Augustine K. Berglund, a native of the county.

In the 1930s, George was a Kane County representative for the Agricultural Adjustment Administration. He and Hilda lived in Wasco immediately following their marriage; the Lily Lake Luther League threw the couple a wedding shower in December 1929. In 1933, George Hawkins of Wasco was elected Trustee of Schools for Campton Township. In April 1934, George Hawkins (for the third time in a row) led the Kane County Dairy Herd Association for most productive Holstein cows. His herd of sixteen averaged 1,038 pounds of milk and 42.0 pounds of butter for March. George was President of the Campton Township School Trustees in 1946. He was injured both of his hands in a corn shredder in November of that year, breaking his left index finger, but he recovered from the injury. Richard Mann, a hired hand, lived in the Hawkins home from 1939 to 1945; Mann then moved to Maywood, Illinois. Both George and Hilda attended the annual meeting of the Pure Milk Association in Chicago in March 1950. The couple moved from Wasco to Mooseheart in 1961. George worked with the dairy cows there, and enjoyed the work greatly. Hilda Hawkins moved into the Valley Rest Home in St. Charles in September 1962. After a prolonged illness, Hilda died there on 13 June 1968. She was survived by her husband, their two children, and two grandchildren.

Even in her old age, Hilda Hawkins kept her hair long and braided around her head in the back. Hilda Hawkins's recipe for "Sweet Potato Surprise" (which your author is going to attempt to make this weekend!) appeared in the 1968 recipe book for Grace Lutheran Church, Lily Lake. Hilda passed away in June of that year; George died on 2 June 1991, at the age of ninety-two. They were survived by their son Leonard and their daughter Helen A. Hawkins, who lived in Urbana, Illinois.

Helen Arlene Hawkins, daughter of George and Hilda, was born in Community Hospital, Geneva, on 10 January 1931. Helen was baptized at the family's home in Wasco by Rev. V. J. Tengwald, on 15 August 1931. Her baptismal sponsors were Mr. and Mrs. Elmer Johnson. Helen's maternal grandfather made an extended visit to Wasco then – Mr. Berglund lived in Skandia Township, Marquette County, Michigan at the time. Helen was the valedictorian of the St. Charles High School class of 1947. She attended Northern Illinois State Teachers College beginning in the fall of that year. Due to the coal shortage at the school in February 1950, Helen returned home to Wasco for several weeks. In 1957, Helen was Assistant Dean of Women at the State Teachers' College at Charleston, Illinois. By 1964, she was Assistant Dean of Women at the University of Illinois. In 1970, Helen became the Associate Director of Camp Osoha in Boulder Junction, Wisconsin. She lived in St. Charles in 1990. Helen passed away in Elgin on 18 November 2011.

Leonard Otto Hawkins, Helen's younger brother, was born in Geneva on 28 January 1932. He was baptized at Grace Lutheran Church, Lily Lake, on 14 August of that year. The 1940 census shows him as an eight-year-old student, living at home with his parents and sister and a hired hand from Michigan. In May 1948, Leonard Hawkins, then a student at

George Hawkins, in the 1920s. The photo was taken in Wasco

St. Charles High School, was asked to compete in the upcoming State Contest for the Future Farmers of America. Later that year, he and his sister hosted an event for the Luther League of Lily Lake. Leonard was an usher for Grace Lutheran Church, Lily Lake, in the 1940s and '50s. In the spring of 1956 Leonard was ill at the hospital at Fort Leonard Wood, in Missouri, where he was undergoing basic training. He trained for the U. S. Army Reserve in July 1959, when he was at Camp McCoy, Wisconsin.

Leonard Hawkins and his wife Adele moved into his parents' farmhouse when George and Hilda moved to Mooseheart in 1961. All told, Leonard worked on the family farm in Wasco for more than forty years. In November 1967, the family of James and Kay Vandervolk (formerly of St. Charles) moved into the Leonard Hawkins house in Wasco. Leonard Hawkins was given an award for excellence in milk production at the annual Dairy Herd Improvement Association dinner in April 1969. Leonard had the "new" Hawkins house built beginning late in 1970 (see "Some Wasco Houses – Northwest Quarter"). After selling the old farmhouse, he and Adele moved into their new home (next door) in July 1971. In February 1970 Leonard was appointed resolutions committeeman for the newly-organized Fox Valley district of the Associated Milk Producers. Leonard Hawkins quit farming in February 1973 and sold all of his agricultural equipment located on his farm "at the edge of Wasco" at that time. He was elected Campton Township Assessor in the 1980s, after working in that office for more than a decade, and he served in that capacity until his untimely death on 9 December 1990. Leonard O. Hawkins was largely responsible for modernizing and computerizing the township's assessment records.

Elmer Johnson, of Wasco, in the summer of 1926

One of Nels Hawkins's daughters was Mildred Matilda Hawkins, who was born on the farm near Wasco on 15 August 1900. She was one of the first students to attend Wasco School. On 22 June 1918, Mildred married Josef Eckstrom, a recent arrival from Sweden. That same month, Josef was one of fourteen Wasco men drafted into military service during the First World War. He was sent to Camp Grant for training, and then to France. While there, Josef Eckstrom was gassed while on the Front, and suffered from the effects of this until his untimely death the next year. He and Millie had a daughter named Elaine J. Eckstrom, who was born in Wasco on 5 December 1918. Sadly, Elaine's father died in Chicago on 17 November 1919, less than a year after her birth. On 21 November 1923, in Geneva, Millie married Elmer Johnson, who had been born in Sweden in 1879. They lived in Wasco, where Elmer worked in the Bergland Lumber Yard. Elmer was six feet tall and had brown hair. Elmer Johnson of Wasco died in Community Hospital, Geneva, on 23 July 1936, as a result of injuries sustained in an automobile-truck collision "at the junction of Plato Center

Mildred ("Millie") née Hawkins and her husband Josef Eckstrom, in 1918

and Chicken Woods roads." This is the same accident that killed Oscar Bowgren, also of Wasco. Johnson was a passenger in the truck, which was carrying lumber from Bergland & Company, Johnson and Bowgren's employer. The truck burst into flames after overturning following the collision with an automobile driven by Albert Oberhart, a neighboring farmer near Chicken Grove (located in southwestern Plato Township, near the border with Campton Township).

Elaine Eckstrom of Wasco, in the 1940s

Elaine Eckstrom graduated from St. Charles High School in 1935, and worked as a stenographer and secretary for Bergland & Company between October 1935 and the years just after World War II. Later, she worked for General Mills. Elaine was widely known for playing the organ at Grace Lutheran Church, Lily Lake, for more than thirty years. She married Norman G. Lockhart, and lived in Kane County her entire life. Elaine passed away in March 2010, at the age of ninety-one.

Edward Hawkins, Nels's brother, was born in Sweden on 10 February 1870, and came to the United States in January 1889. In 1900, he was living on his brother's farm (near the Lake and Vanderhoof families, just north of Wasco), but in 1903 he acquired his own property further north, on Silver Glen Road. He married Emma Christina Hanson of Lily Lake on 28 February 1901, at Bethlehem Lutheran Church in St. Charles. She had immigrated with her parents in 1893. Edward and Emma had three daughters, all born between 1902 and 1909: Irene D., Esther Ruby, and Margaret Naomi Hawkins. Mr. and Mrs. Edward Hawkins and their daughter Irene attended the Illinois State Fair in Springfield in September 1920. Ed Hawkins retired in the late 1920s, and moved to South Third Street in St. Charles at that time with his wife and their two younger daughters. Edward Hawkins often visited his brother Joel (who was known as "Joe" by family members and some friends) in Wasco in the 1930s. Emma (Hanson) Hawkins died at her home in St. Charles on 20 September 1934. Many from Wasco attended her funeral, which was conducted from Grace Lutheran Church, Lily Lake. Both Esther and Margaret Hawkins worked as bookkeepers in 1940, when they were still living with their recently-widowed father in St. Charles. Edward Hawkins died in St. Charles on 13 May 1951.

Irene Dagmar Hawkins was born near Wasco on 9 January 1902. She was a teacher in 1920, and married Celest R. Spriet on 26 September 1923, in Kane County. Celest owned a garage in St. Charles in 1930; his parents were natives of Belgium. Celeste and Irene had a daughter Helen Spriet, who was born in 1926. Celest Spriet was an automobile dealer in 1940, when he and his family lived on State Street in St. Charles.

Their address in the 1940s, '50s and '60s was #520 State Street. Irene passed away in St. Charles in November 1976, and her husband died there in October 1981.

Esther Ruby Hawkins was born in Campton Township on 13 March 1905, and was confirmed at Grace Lutheran Church in July 1919. Esther moved to St. Charles with her family in the late 1920s. She was a stenographer for a real estate office in 1930, and worked as a bookkeeper for a cabinet manufacturer ten years later. She was active in the Luther League in the 1930s, and was the financial secretary for Grace Lutheran Church, Lily Lake, in the late 1940s. Esther Hawkins lived in St. Charles in 1950, when she was a bookkeeper (and later a secretary) for the Chronicle Publishing Company. She was living with her younger sister and their father at #1302 South Third Street at that time. Both Hawkinses remained in the home following their father's death. Esther was working as a secretary for the same company in 1960. She never married, and died in St. Charles on 23 January 1994.

Esther R. Hawkins, in 1919, and her sister Margaret N. Hawkins, in 1922

Margaret N. Hawkins, the youngest of the three Hawkins girls, was born on 24 April 1909 on the family farm on Silver Glen Road. While young, she enjoyed playing with the cats, dogs, and ponies on the farm. She attended Wasco School, and was part of the first graduating class of the "new" St. Charles High School (now Thompson Middle School). Margaret later taught Sunday School at Grace Lutheran Church in Lily Lake. The family moved to St. Charles in 1927, and became active members of Bethlehem Lutheran Church, where Margaret volunteered as a bookkeeper. She was a bookkeeper for a garage office in 1940, when she was living on South Third Street with her immediate family. She was a bookkeeper for the Chronicle Publishing Company in the 1950s and '60s. Margaret Hawkins never married. She passed away on 19 October 1998 and was survived by a niece and seven great-nieces and nephews.

The Peterson Family

Peter Alfred Peterson, one of the first Swedish residents of Campton Township, was born in Östergötland on 17 August 1834, came to the United States in 1858, and married Josephine Harroldson in Kane County on 25 December 1862. They moved to Moline, in Rock Island County, Illinois, and later (on 21 January 1876) purchased a farm near the future site of Wasco from James C. and Caroline Baird of St. Charles. The purchase price for this property was $3486. The Petersons immediately took out a mortgage on this property (from Baird) in the amount of $1486, payable over a period of eight years. The 1880 census of Kane County shows the Petersons living there, in Campton Township, close to the Eddy, Rice, Muir, Anderson, and Swanson families. Peter was a farmer, and was then in his mid-forties. He and Josephine had three children in the household at that time: Caroline J. Peterson, aged twelve; Lillian Matilda Peterson, aged nine; and Charles Elmer T. Peterson, aged three. The two older children attended school that year. The eighty-five acre farm belonging to Peter A. Peterson was located on the south side of what is now Brown Road, and the west side of the present Old LaFox Road, just north of Wasco. The barns and outbuildings were north of the farmhouse, and an orchard lay to the south of the home. The farm was later owned by Elmer and Harold Ekstrom. He is sometimes confused with Peter August Peterson, who lived nearby, but who was born in 1871 (see "The Harold Anderson Family").

In July 1886, for $400, Peter A. Peterson, "a single man," sold a one-hundred-foot-wide strip of land along the southern edge of his farm to the Minnesota & North Western Railroad, who would soon build a line through Wasco. Josephine Peterson had passed away on the family's farm earlier that year. In October 1889, Peter's son Elmer Peterson of Wasco went to Chicago for an operation on his eye. A local newspaper column from that month stated that "it will be remembered that Elmer P. is the little boy who was injured in a runaway last August." On 31 August 1892, Peter A. Peterson purchased an adjoining forty-acre parcel of land just north of his farm (across Brown Road) from Charles L. Probert for $2000.

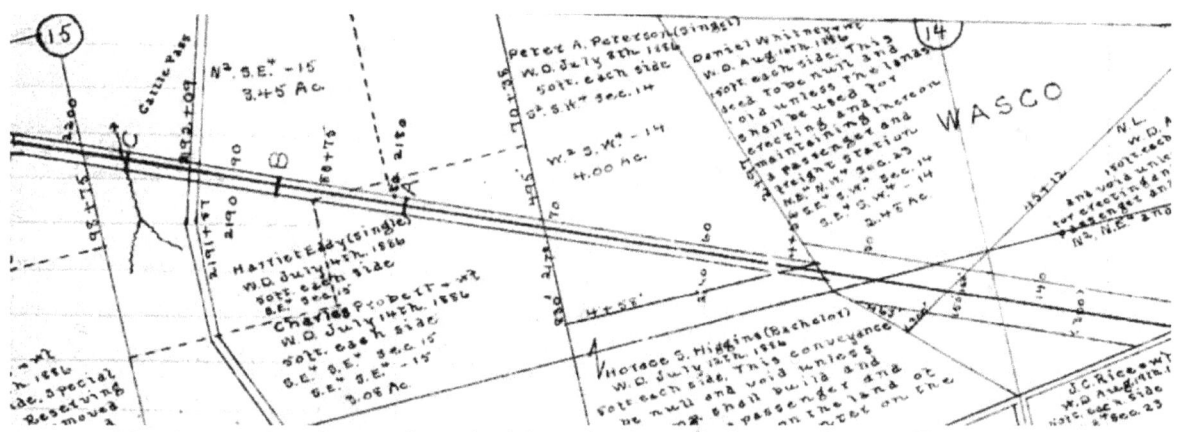
Map from 1893 indicating the path of the railroad over the Peter A. Peterson Farm in Wasco

The 1900 census includes Peter and Josephine Peterson's youngest daughter, Avice Eugenia Peterson, who was born on the family's farm near Wasco on 22 October 1882. Florence Peterson described Avice as being a leader, very active in social groups, possessing a charming personality, and being cheery and "full of fun." Avice's sister Carolyn (sometimes spelled Caroline) was still in the household in 1900; she was a dressmaker. She would later marry Philo G. Plummer, and lived until the age of eighty-nine. The Plummers lived in Lansing, Michigan for many years. Carolyn's sister-in-law Florence wrote of her that she (Carolyn Josephine Peterson) gladly used her talents "for country, church, and charity," was interested in current events, and was a very kind friend to all. Another sibling, Walter A. Peterson, who was born in 1873, died at the age of four. Lillian was described by her sister-in-law as being conscientious, unusually kind, loyal, patient, and cheerful. Most members of this family are buried in the Whitney Cemetery.

Elmer Peterson (left) as a young boy – the cabinet card was labeled with his name and the affectionate description "My Little Sweet-heart." Marriage notice (right) of Florence Bergland and Elmer Peterson, 1904

The four children of Wasco farmers Peter A. and Josephine Peterson: Caroline ("Carrie"), Avice, Elmer and Lillian Matilda ("Til"). The photo dates to August 1931.

Peter A. Peterson passed away at his daughter's house in Lansing, Ingham County, Michigan, on 29 November 1914. He is buried in the Whitney Cemetery. In February 1918, his daughters Caroline J. (Peterson) Plummer of Lansing and Lillian M. (Peterson) Martin of Genoa, Illinois, sold their half-interest in the family's farm to Charles P. Ekstrom of Campton Township for $11,500. The next month, Carl E. ("Elmer") Peterson and Avice (Peterson) Chaffee each sold their quarter-interest in the property to Ekstrom in separate deeds.

Caroline Peterson married Philo G. Plummer in Kane County on 29 June 1905. The couple moved to Lansing, Michigan, by 1910. Philo was a machinist that year, and was a salesman for the Advance-Rumely Thresher Company in 1916. By 1922, he was an agent for Avery Threshing Machines. Philo started his own business, the Plummer Machinery Company, in the mid-1930s. He and Caroline remained in Lansing through the 1940s at least. Philo George Plummer, who was born in Kane County in January 1872, died in Puyallup, Washington, on 6 November 1957. Caroline had passed away the previous year.

Lillian M. Peterson married George H. Martin in Kane County on 25 September 1894. By 1920, the Martins lived in the city of Genoa, in DeKalb County. George ran a jewelry store there. George H. Martin died in 1938, and Lillian passed away in 1957. She lived in Charlotte, Michigan, in 1939, and in St. Charles in 1945. Both she and her husband are buried in the Whitney Cemetery.

Elmer T. Peterson was born in Campton Township on 29 July 1876. He lived with the Bergland family in Wasco in the year 1900. At that time he was listed as a "servant" to the family and as a salesman by occupation. His future bride Florence Bergland was listed as a "Sales Lady." Elmer was appointed Wasco's Postmaster on 7 September 1917, and worked in that position for seven years. He ran for Campton Township Supervisor on the Republican ticket in April 1924 and April 1928, and served in that capacity until his retirement from politics in the spring of 1933. Elmer Peterson died in Wasco on 21 November 1942; his occupation was then given as "retired lumber merchant." For further information on Caroline, Lillian, and Avice's brother Elmer, see "The Bergland Family" and "Some Wasco Houses – Northwest Quarter."

Avice Laura Eugenia Peterson of Wasco was baptized at the Geneva Lutheran Church on 3 November 1882. She married Earle G. Chaffee in Chicago on 22 October 1903. Avice and Earle moved to Long Beach, California by 1907. They had a daughter Ona N. Chaffee who was born that year. In the early 1920s, the family relocated to Ontario, in San Bernadino County. In 1940, Avice's sister Lillian moved in with her but only stayed there for a short period. The Chaffees lived on Granada Court in Ontario from at least 1924 to 1960. Earle, who was an electrician, was born in 1881, and died in 1960. Avice passed away in San Bernadino on 28 April 1970.

The Charles Anderson Family

Charles and Hilda Anderson were farmers living two miles west of Wasco during the late nineteenth and early twentieth century. Charles John Anderson, or Carl Anderson as he was commonly known, was born in Västra Götaland, Sweden, on 24 July 1859, and was a son of Johannes and Katarina Rylander (later Anderson). Carl (who was sometimes known as "CJ" to family and friends) came to the United States with his parents in 1864, and spent nearly his entire working life farming. The family first settled into a log house east of Wasco, on or near the Norton property. Carl married Hilda C. Carlson in Kane County on 6

October 1883, and their oldest child, Avis Nellie Anderson, was born the following summer. Their second daughter, Clara Belle Anderson, was born in October 1885, and Anna Josephine followed in November 1886. In all, the family would have ten children, eight of whom (all daughters) survived childhood. Florence C. Anderson was born in 1890, Hattie E. in June 1892, and Julia E. in November 1895. Ebba E. Anderson was born in 1897 but died later that year. Her younger sister Frances H. Anderson was born in June 1899, and Olive joined her seven older sisters just after the turn of the twentieth century. Carl Anderson's sister Emma passed away in Rockford on 19 February 1909.

More than sixty guests from Rockford, Chicago, and Wasco surprised Mr. and Mrs. C. J. Anderson on 3 October 1903, in honor of their twentieth wedding anniversary. The occasion made for a "pleasant evening." In mid-June 1909, Charles J. Anderson began "the construction of a fine residence" near Wasco. They entertained friends in their new residence that December. In 1910, Charles J. Anderson ran a "general farm" in Campton Township, and was living with his wife of twenty-six years and seven of their eight surviving children. The children in the household were: Clara B., Anna J., Florence C., Edna H., Julia E., Frances H., and Olive L. Anderson. Marshall Carlson, a hired man, was a laborer on the farm and was also living there with the family.

Hilda Christina Carlson was born in Gränna Parish, Jönköping County, Sweden, on 19 July 1858. Her parents were Carl and Anna Britta Jonson; they came to the United States in 1879, settling in Kane County.

Hilda and Charles Anderson, at the time of their marriage in 1883

Hilda's maiden name was properly Carlson, as per the Swedish naming tradition, although it is sometimes given as Jonson or Johnson, deferring to the American tradition of using her father's surname at birth. Due to an illness, she was advised to move to "the country" not long after she arrived in the United States. Hilda's brother was then working as a hired hand for CJ Anderson in the eastern part of Campton Township, and it is there that she met her future husband, probably in 1881. Following her marriage to CJ in 1883, the Andersons rented the future "Brookside" farm on the north side of Route 64, just west of Campton Town Hall. This farm was owned by the Chaffee family and was known for its substantial two-story brick house. In October 1891, the Andersons purchased a farm further west and later named the property "Knollwood Farm." They acquired that one-hundred and twenty-acre property from Henry and Mary Hagaman; the farm was located on both sides of Route 64, one mile west of Town Hall Road.

In the post-World War I years, CJ and Hilda Anderson lived with seven of their daughters (and three hired men) on their farm. In the early 1910s, at least two of their nephews (Elmer and Alfred Peterson) went to the Dakotas to work, but later returned to Wasco. Most of the daughters left the household when they married, beginning with Avis, in 1912. By 1920, only the

Andersons' youngest daughter, Olive, was still in school. The other daughters were "at home" and the two oldest, Anna and Clara, were enumerated as housekeepers.

Avis Nellie Anderson, CJ's oldest daughter, was born on 16 July 1884. She married Harry G. Hamilton in Kane County on 28 August 1912; Harry was a "renegade horse-loving Irishman from Belfast" who later became a born-again Christian, and a very devoted Baptist preacher. He was a close follower of Billy Graham. The Hamiltons moved to Warsaw, Indiana not long after their marriage; their daughter, Ruth N. Hamilton, was born there. Prior to 1928, the family relocated to Austin, Minnesota. In 1944 the Hamiltons lived in Buffalo, New York. Still later (in 1947) they moved to Ft. Worth, Texas. In December 1949, the "Wasco" column of the *Elburn Herald* stated that "Dr. Harry Hamilton of Ft. Worth, Tex., spoke at the Wasco church last Sunday at 11 a.m. Dr. Hamilton is a former pastor of the church. His wife is the former Avis Anderson of Wasco." Avis died in that city on 29 July 1957, but her body was brought to Wasco for burial in the Whitney Cemetery.

Avis and her husband Harry G. Hamilton, who for a short time was a minister at the Wasco Baptist Church

Clara Belle Anderson, the second-oldest child of CJ and Hilda, was born in Campton Township on 24 October 1885. Like her siblings, Clara attended the Old Red Schoolhouse one mile south of Wasco (her family's farm was located in the extreme northwest corner of that district according to the 1904 Campton Township map). Clara lived on Knollwood farm until her family sold the property. She moved to St. Charles shortly thereafter, in 1930. Her obituary stated that "Clare was born in Wasco, moving from the farm to St. Charles with her father several years ago. Mrs. Olive Bergland and Mrs. Frances Denker of Wasco are sisters." Clara B. Anderson passed away at Community Hospital, in Geneva, on 29 August 1940. Rev. J. D. Ekstrom conducted her funeral services.

The Old Red Schoolhouse, located one and a half miles south of Wasco, and attended by the Anderson girls

Anna Josephine Anderson was born just west of Wasco, probably on the Chaffee farm, on 7 November 1886. She was one of the three Anderson sisters never to marry; along with her parents and two sisters, she moved to the Anderson house on South Fourth Street in St. Charles in 1930. When living on Knollwood farm, Anna raised bees. Her nephew George Bergland later took up this hobby.

Anna passed away in St. Charles in February 1969, at the age of eighty-two.

Florence C. Anderson, the fourth daughter in the family, was born in September 1890. She completed four years of high school, and moved with her parents and two sisters to St. Charles in 1930. Her nephew and niece knew her as "Aunt Pete." Florence also never married – she passed away in Kane County in 1955. In the late 1920s, Florence's brother-in-law Henry Torstenson, who was married to CJ's daughter Jewel, convinced his father-in-law to sell his farm west of Wasco, and to invest in Chicago real estate, which Mr. Anderson did. Because of severe economic conditions (and bad advice), CJ lost everything. In 1930, Torstenson, along with another of CJ's sons-in-law, Floyd Bergland, then built CJ a house in St. Charles, located at 1014 South Fourth Street. Charles and Hilda Anderson moved into their new house that year, and they lived there with their unmarried daughters Clara, Florence, and Anna. Hilda died in St. Charles on 21 January 1933, at the age of seventy-four.

The two-story brick farmhouse west of Wasco, built by the Chaffees, which the Andersons occupied for part of the 1880s

Edna H. Anderson, who was born just west of Wasco on 7 June 1892, attended Wasco School and then St. Charles High School. Edna went on to study at Northern Illinois Teachers College in DeKalb, and after graduating from there she taught in the Prescott School in Chicago for twenty years. Edna attended her sister Frances at her wedding in March 1927, when Frances married Hugo Denker. Edna was the Maid of Honor in her sister Olive's wedding in October 1927; the ceremony took place at the family's home, Knollwood Farm (later known as the Rainbow Dairy Farm after it was purchased by Fred Hummel). Edna visited her sister Nellie Hamilton in Austin, Minnesota in July 1928. She lived in St. Charles by November 1930, when she returned to Wasco to visit her sister Olive. She was still living there in April 1933 as well but would soon move to Chicago. Edna married Henric G. Spaak on 22 September 1933, in Chicago. Henric's mother Gerda was Swedish-born dressmaker; she lived on West Wellington Avenue in Chicago and worked at a department store in the city in the 1910s and '20s. Henric and Edna had no children. They lived in Chicago

Sisters Clara, Edna, and Florence Anderson, of Campton Township

for nearly all of their married life. Edna died in St. Joseph's Hospital, Chicago, on 16 November 1948. She was fifty-six years old, and was survived by her husband and six sisters. Just one of her sisters (Frances) lived in Wasco at the time (see "The Denker Family").

Hilda Anderson (left) holding her grandson, George Bergland. The photo was taken behind the Bergland home, in Wasco. Olive Anderson (right) at the time of her marriage to Floyd Bergland

Charles J. Anderson passed away at his home in St. Charles on Sunday, 5 November 1944. He was eighty-five years old. At the age of five, CJ had come to the United States from Sweden, and "farmed in the vicinity of Wasco until his retirement." He was formerly a member of Grace Lutheran Church of Lily Lake, but later joined Bethlehem Lutheran Church, St. Charles. Mr. Anderson was preceded in death by his wife and one daughter, and was survived by seven daughters and six grandchildren.

The Bell Family

John W. Bell, a native of Easington in northeastern England, was an agricultural statistician when he was listed as a Wasco resident in 1896. John Watson Bell's date of birth was 16 February 1852; as a child he was brought to the United States by his parents, Thomas and Mary (Gibson) Bell. The family initially settled in Ohio. In 1875, J. W. Bell came to Kane County. On 2 January 1878, John married Vesta P. Ward, a native of Campton Township. Her family's extensive farm was located in the west half of Sections 1 and 12, in the northeast part of the township. The southeast part of this property was, in later years, the Bell family's property. The Bell farm home was in Section 12, Campton Township, on the east side of what is now Denker Road, north of Bolcum Road. Two branches of Ferson Creek ran through Bell's lands, which contained some woods. In the late 1890s Bell sold the southeastern part of his farm to W. H. Sarbaugh, and the northwest part to Alice Warren, keeping the central portion for himself. John W. Bell was a staunch Republican, and although he never ran for office, he was frequently present at the party's meetings, events, and rallies.

The Bell family, including John W. and Vesta (Ward) Bell with their children Fern L. and John N. (back row) and Florence R. and Glen W. Bell (front)

Mr. and Mrs. John W. Bell celebrated their tenth anniversary in January 1888, and on that occasion "relatives and friends gave them a genuine surprise." Thirty people showed up for the celebration, and "hailed them with congratulations" and a number of presents. In the early 1890s, Vesta (Ward) Bell was among the founders of the Wasco Ladies Aid, and was very active in the Wasco Church from its founding until her death. She was an active member of the Whitney Cemetery Board, and was a former teacher at the Old Red Schoolhouse south of Wasco. Among her students were well-known Wasco residents Nettie Anderson and Emma White.

In November 1902, the new Bell family home was completed, and their friends from St. Charles, Elgin, Geneva, and elsewhere in Campton Township threw them a surprise house-warming party. The couple also celebrated their twenty-fifth wedding anniversary then, since the occasion was "near enough at hand." The organizers of the party were members of the Modern Woodmen of America. As presents, the Bells received a set of dining room chairs, a willow rocker, a Morris chair, a sewing machine, a buffet side board, a dinner set, and a parlor lamp! Rev. Eyles of Wasco made the presentation speech at the celebration.

John W. Bell met with "considerable loss" from a severe storm which passed through Wasco during the last days of March, 1904. The family was living on their seventy-three-acre farm in Section 12, Campton

Township. The property was on the east side of the present Denker Road, about halfway between Silver Glen and Bolcum Roads, and the family's home was just north of Ferson Creek. Mr. Bell was an active farmer, and in late July 1909 he proudly told the local newspaper of a twenty-acre field of corn he'd planted that was then shoulder high – every hill had three or four stalks. In 1910, the three younger Bell children lived with their parents on the farm near Wasco. Vesta Bell was the Treasurer of the Wasco Mothers' Club in 1911-1912. In the summer or fall of the latter year, Mrs. Bell gave what must have been an interesting presentation on "Early Settlers of Campton and [the] Growth of Wasco."

John W. Bell died suddenly at 9:50 in the evening on Saturday, 12 October 1916, of apoplexy. His widow, Mrs. Vesta P. (Ward) Bell, passed away at her home near Wasco on 14 November 1931, at the age of eighty. She had been ill for eleven days. She was born in Campton Township on 19 February 1851, a daughter of I. D. Ward, and according to her obituary, lived on only two adjoining farms her entire life. The Bells were survived by three children: John N. Bell, of St. Charles; Florence (Bell) Peterson, of Minooka; and Fern (Bell) Johnson of Wasco. There were eight grandchildren in the Bell family. Rev. McGillivray of Maywood, formerly the first pastor of the Wasco Baptist Church, conducted Vesta (Ward) Bell's funeral.

John N. Bell, in the 1890s

The youngest child in the family, Glen Ward Bell, was born in Wasco on 27 September 1895. He attended Wasco School, and his World War I draft card from 1917 reveals that he had blue eyes, brown hair, was tall, and had a medium build. He was then employed as a farm laborer for Albert Larson of Wasco. Glen Bell was living with his widowed mother Vesta on the family farm in 1920. He married Elna W. Frey on 9 August 1923. Sadly, Glen passed away not long into the marriage, on 27 August 1926. He died in Broadview, Cook County, Illinois, and was a railroad fireman at the time of his death. His widow Elna, who was born on 19 March 1904, lived with her mother-in-law in Campton Township after Glen's death. She and Glen had two children: John Alfred Bell (who was born on 3 March 1924); and Glen E. Bell (who was born on 19 November 1925). Elna and her children moved to St. Charles by 1940. She died there on 31 January 1979, and is buried in the Whitney Cemetery beside her husband.

Glen's sister Florence Rae (Bell) Peterson was born on 22 July 1892, and outlived her three siblings. When she was seventeen, Florence got a job as an inspector for the Western Electric Company, and she moved to Chicago to live with her brother John and his wife May. She married Henry P. Peterson, a conductor for the Chicago street railway, on 19 January 1914. Henry was a son of Swan and Tillie Peterson. After her marriage, she remained in Chicago. Their oldest son Paul Henry Peterson was born at the family's home on Avers Avenue in Chicago in 1915. Their second son, Forrest Glen Peterson, was born there the next year, and was followed by a sister, Lyla Bell in 1917. The youngest child, John Albert Peterson, was born in 1923. The family lived at #4853 Ferdinand Avenue in 1930. In 1935 and 1940, the Petersons lived at #4823 West Race Avenue in Chicago. Their sons Forrest and John were in the household at that time. Florence and her family lived in Minooka, Illinois, in July 1945, when Solomon Johnson and his family visited her there. In December 1945, Fern visited her sister Florence at Augustana Hospital in Chicago. Henry Peterson, who was born on 1 April 1891, passed away on 10 August 1957. In 1967, Florence suffered a stroke and was confined to the St. Joseph Hospital in Joliet. She recovered somewhat, but passed away on 26 October 1971. She is buried at the Aux Sable Cemetery in Minooka, Illinois.

John and Vesta (Ward) Bell, at their home on Denker Road

John Newman Bell of Wasco, the surviving son of John and Vesta, married May E. James of Chicago on Saturday, 27 February 1909. The wedding took place at the bride's home. John was born on 8 November 1878, in Huntley, McHenry County, Illinois. John Newman Bell was a farm laborer in 1900. He began working as a locomotive fireman for the railroad in November 1903 and was later a locomotive engineer. In August 1906, J. N. Bell was injured when a steam water bottle burst, causing cuts and burns to his head. He was then a fireman for the Chicago Northwestern railroad. By 1910, John and May Bell were living at #502 N. Hamlin Street in Chicago. John and May were then living with John's sister Florence R. Bell, who was seventeen. Florence was employed at that time as an inspector for the Western Electric Company. John N. Bell worked for the railroad for more than twenty-seven years. He moved to St. Charles some years later. He and his wife had no children; John died in Campton Township on 14 December 1933. His widow married James Thorpe after John's death.

Before her marriage to Solomon Johnson (see "The Isaac Johnson Family" section of this chapter) Fern L. Bell worked as the "Hello girl" (operator) at the Geneva Telephone Office beginning in November 1905. Fern was still living at home with her parents and two younger siblings in 1910. She was then aged twenty-four, was single, and listed no occupation. She got married the following summer, and moved into her husband's farm home on the west edge of Wasco.

John N. Bell's pension record, from 1933

The Rice Family

In the 1880s, James C. Rice, mentioned elsewhere in this work, owned fully half the land that would become part of Wasco. Rice's adjoining parcels of land essentially comprised the entire southern half of the village, being located on either side of the present LaFox Road, although the lands extended much further west than east. The Wasco Church, Wasco School, and any dwelling built on the south side of the present Route 64 were all built on former Rice land. The early 1870s Rice family farmhouse (their second dwelling on the same site) was one of just three homes within two-thirds of a mile of the center of Wasco when the village was created (the others being the Pattee/Higgins and the Slate/Carpenter houses).

Maria and James C. Rice, pioneers of Wasco

James C. Rice, a son of Joseph and Sarah (Caldwell) Rice, was born in Henniker, Merrimack County, New Hampshire, on 15 April 1823. When James was young, the family moved to Holland, Erie County, New York, where his younger brothers and sister were born. The Rices were farmers, and the children received their education in Western New York. James came to Kane County, Illinois, in June 1843, and his parents followed him two or three years later. The Rices rented a farm before purchasing the property near the future site of Wasco. In 1850, there were seven members of the Rice family living in Campton Township, six of whom were in one household. Joseph and Sarah Rice, who ran the farm, had four of their children at home then: James, aged twenty-seven; Dana, aged twenty; "Firena" [Virena], aged eighteen; and "Luellem" [Llewellyn], aged fourteen. Their older sister Leonora (Rice) Chaffee was living nearby. She was aged twenty-four and was also born in New York State. The Rice family was listed near the Chaffee and Hagaman families in that year's census. The agricultural census taken at that time indicates that the Rices then had twelve cattle, seventeen sheep, and nine pigs on the farm. They had forty acres of improved land, which had (that year) produced four hundred bushels of wheat and two hundred bushels of corn, but no rye.

By the late 1850s, the Rice farm comprised most of the northwest quarter of Section 23, Campton Township. On 18 April 1852, in Kane County, James C. Rice, the oldest son in the household, married Maria Bogue, a native of Ohio. The principal portion of the Rice farm (consisting of eighty acres of land) was purchased by the family from John R. and Margaret Tucker on 24 November 1852. The other portion of the farm had been acquired in March 1850 from David Pattee. During the Civil War, there were two males and four females in the Rice household. The family kept sheep then (producing 150 pounds of wool in 1865) and owned $160 worth of livestock. On 23 April 1858, for the sum of $1800, Joseph and Sarah Rice sold their family farm to their son, James C. Rice, and his wife Maria. On the same date, the younger Rices granted a Life Lease to Joseph and Sarah, who continued to live on the farm until their deaths. As part of the deed's conditions, James C. Rice agreed not to sell the lands without the consent of his parents. Maria Rice was sometimes known by her middle name - Lucy.

By the eve of the Civil War, the Rice family was living in a farmhouse on the south side of Route 64, a half-mile west of the future center of Wasco. James and Maria had three children: Emma Augusta, who was born on 24 February 1853; Hattie Eleanor, who was born on 28 August 1857; and Llewellyn Jackson Rice, who was born on 4 April 1861. After Emma's marriage in 1872 she moved to Geneva. Hattie became a school teacher and moved to Missouri soon after her marriage in 1880. After Llewellyn relocated to Iowa Falls later that decade, James and Maria remained on their Campton Township farm rather than moving in with one of their children.

The farm of James Rice, on the future site of Wasco - the map dates to 1860

In 1870, J. C. Rice owned 123 acres of cultivated land and forty acres of woodland – the property was valued at $7000 at that time. The agricultural census from that year shows that he owned nine horses, twelve cows, thirteen sheep, and twelve pigs. James Rice harvested 300 bushels of corn, 600 bushels of oats, and 206 bushels of barley that year. During the month of December 1872, the Rice family home burned to the ground. A new home (later known as "The House of Seven Gables") was rebuilt on the same site (see "Some Wasco Houses – Southwest Quarter").

James and Maria's daughter, Hattie E. Rice, was a school teacher by 1880. She was then twenty-two, and was living with her brother Llewellyn, their parents, and their grandmother, Sarah Rice, who was then aged eighty-four. J. C. Rice's sister, Mrs. L. Chaffee of Chicago, visited him in Wasco in January 1888. James C. Rice served as Wasco's postmaster for four years, beginning in September 1895. Although Joseph Rice passed away before there was a Wasco (he died on 29 September 1872, aged eighty-one) his widow Sarah Rice did live long enough to see the creation of the village. In December 1888, "Grandma Rice, mother of James Rice" fell "and broke her limb" according to a local newspaper. She was "not improving much" then. She died at the Rice farmhouse just west of Wasco on 19 May 1889, at the age of ninety-two. She was "a firm believer in spiritualism" as was her late husband. Joseph and Sarah Rice are both buried in the Whitney Cemetery.

James Rice continued to improve his farm in the last years of the nineteenth century. In the spring of 1888, he laid 6000 drainage tiles on the property, and followed suit with a similar number that summer. Mabel and Alice Swarthout of Geneva visited J. C. Rice, their grandfather, in January 1888, and frequently afterward. By 1900, just James and Maria Rice were living in the old farmhouse, although James was no longer listing his occupation as "farmer"; instead, he was a "Landlord." Seven years later, the Rices moved to Los Angeles, California. For $14,500, they sold their property to Solomon and Alex Johnson on 12 February 1908, shortly after James and Maria had already taken up residence in the far west.

Rice was still in Wasco in late 1902, and was reluctant to leave, since an article in the *St. Charles Chronicle* from November of that year stated that James Rice had "had offers of $100 per acre for his farm from two parties. With his newly wedded wife he occupied the farm upwards of fifty years ago, and the venerable couple hesitate to sever connection with the scene of so many happy and prosperous years."

In late November 1905, Mr. Morgan, a cartoonist for the *Chicago Examiner*, spent a weekend at the Rice house in Wasco. J. C. Rice came down with rheumatism in January 1906. Alice Swarthout of the DeKalb Normal Institute (now Northern Illinois University) visited her grandparents, Mr. and Mrs. J. C. Rice of Wasco, in March 1906. Mr. and Mrs. G. L. Higgins of Sycamore visited the Rice family in June of that year. Mrs. Williams of St. Joseph, Michigan, visited her sister (Mrs. Rice) in July. In August 1906, the Rices again enjoyed a visit by their granddaughter, Alice Swarthout of DeKalb. Florence Swarthout of Chicago visited the Rices in November. John Johnson, who had been a farmhand on the Rice farm, had a sale and left for Oklahoma late that same month. Not long afterward, the Rices sold their Wasco property to the Johnson brothers, and moved to California to live with their daughter.

James C. and Lucy Rice with their children, Emma, Llewellyn, and Hattie

The Rices were living with their daughter Hattie (and her husband Edwin P. Lathrop) in Alhambra, Los Angeles County, California, in 1910. James and Lucy had been married for fifty-eight years by then. James C. and Maria L. Rice both died in Los Angeles County, California, on 23 January 1911. Their remains were taken to Wasco for burial in the Whitney Cemetery.

Emma A. Rice married Walter H. Swarthout of LaFox on 3 March 1872. They moved to Geneva, and later relocated to Cumberland County, Pennsylvania, and Camden County, New Jersey. Walter was a traveling salesman. The Swarthouts had three daughters: Mabel, who was born on 22 May 1874; Alice, who was born on 28 June 1876; and Florence, who was born on 28 November 1881. They also had a son Charles A. Swarthout, who was born on 20 July 1879. The Swarthout family returned to Geneva in 1922, and Walter died there two years later. Emma Swarthout passed away at her home on Campbell Street in Geneva on 17 February 1940. She was survived by three children, and one granddaughter.

Hattie Rice, who taught school when in her early twenties, married Edwin P. Lathrop in Kane County on 15 December 1880. Edwin was a son of Alvin and Emma Lathrop, and was born in Kane County on 3 October 1853. The Lathrops lived in Missouri for six years, and then moved back to Kane County, but in 1907 they moved to California. They had no children. Edwin died in Los Angeles on 12 January 1918. In October 1946, Hattie moved back to Illinois, and moved in with her nieces, who lived at #116 Campbell Street in Geneva. Hattie passed away there on 10 July 1948, at the age of ninety. She was buried at Forest Lawn Cemetery in Glendale, California.

The youngest child in the family, Llewellyn J. Rice, married Clara M. Curtis in Putnam County, Indiana, on 19 January 1886. Clara was a native of Lake County, Indiana, having been born there on 28 May 1861. They moved to Algona, Iowa in 1887. All three of their children were born here. The oldest, Luella, was born in January 1887, and her sister Lulu Byrd Rice was born in May 1888. Their youngest son Milton Curtis Rice was born in Iowa on 3 November 1889, and died in Phoenix, Arizona on 17 May 1902. In 1900, the family lived in Maricopa County, Arizona. Llewellyn was an abstracter at that time. Between at least 1907 and 1915, Llewellyn Rice was a real estate agent living in the city of Los Angeles. Clara passed away in that city on 6 September 1917. Llewellyn was a title searcher in 1920, and was an assistant title officer in the same city in 1921. By 1936, Llewellyn had remarried, and was a title officer for the Security Title Insurance & Guarantee Company; the Rices were living in San Bernadino at that time. In 1940, Llewellyn and his second wife Irene (both of whom had attended four years of college) lived in Pasadena, California. Llewellyn died in Los Angeles County on 25 February 1949.

The Whitney Family

Floyd Bergland remembered John Whitney as being "only about five feet tall" but "as sharp as lightning." For many years, Whitney knew the names of "every race horse and prize fighter in the country of any worth whatever." John Whitney was born on the Whitney farm, east of the future site of Wasco, on 23 February 1846. In addition to farming, John Whitney dealt in stock for many years, and "his judgment of stock was considered excellent, and his opinion regarded as good as any in Kane County." John Whitney was one of seven children, and lived on the homestead for his entire lifetime, upwards of eighty-three years.

John's mother, Mariah (Blood) Whitney, came to Campton Township in 1839, just after her marriage. Her husband John Sr. first arrived in Kane County in 1836 or 1837, but made periodic trips back to Wyoming County, New York afterward. Mariah was born in Tompkins County, New York on 28 June 1812. Her husband was a native of Orange, Franklin County, Massachusetts, where he was born on 18 August 1804. John Whitney Sr. was one of the few Democrats in Campton Township at an early date. Religiously, he was a Baptist, although he did not live long enough to see the creation of the Wasco Church. He is listed on the 1840 and 1850 Kane County censuses, and was considered a true local pioneer. John Whitney Sr. died on his farm in November 1854, and is buried in his namesake cemetery. Mariah Whitney owned $7800 in real estate by 1860 and $2000 in personal property – both of these amounts are quite significant for the area at that time.

John Whitney lived with his niece, Harriet Martin, who was "assisted by Miss Nellie Westfield" which made it possible for Mr. Whitney "to remain in the old home." Marie Spence, a great-niece from Michigan, also lived in the home from her childhood until she was married. John Whitney was "a very interesting man" according to his 1929 obituary, and "old and young enjoyed visiting him. Although he was aged in years, he retained his sense of humor and enjoyed young people." Mr. Whitney passed away on 11 October 1929, after a short illness. Rev. Aiken of St. Charles officiated at his funeral.

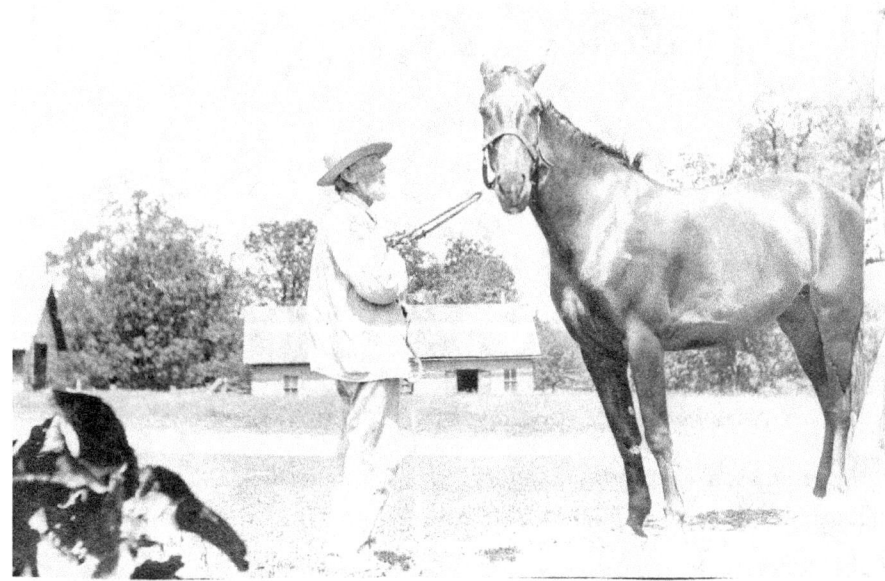
John Whitney with one of his horses, near Wasco

The only member of the Whitney family listed in the 1896 directory of Wasco was Merrill Whitney, who was then a farmer. Merrill was born in Campton Township (just east of the future site of Wasco) on 18 January 1867. He was the son of Daniel and Althea (Babbitt) Whitney, who were also very early settlers of the area. Daniel was another of the sons of John Whitney Sr., mentioned above. When Althea's mother died at her home in Chicago on 13 December 1902, her death was noted in the Wasco column of the *St. Charles Chronicle*. Mrs. Babbitt's grandson Merrill Whitney and his sister Mertell were listed with their parents in the 1870 Campton Township census. The farmhouse was located on the northwest corner of what is now Wasco Road and Old Burlington Road, very close to the 1852 Whitney school. In fact, in deeds dating to the 1860s, what is now Wasco Road was sometimes called the "highway from the School house." The two-story brick, hipped-roof Whitney farmhouse is built in an Italianate style, and is located just north of the former White/Whitney schoolhouse. By 1880, there were three children in the Daniel Whitney household, besides the parents: Mertell, Merrill, and Merritt. All attended school that year, and each had only steps to walk to get there. In the fall of 1886, it was said that "school at the white school house [was] flourishing under the proficient tutorage of Mr. Wait."

The Whitney house, near Wasco. It was built in the 1860s

The first member of the Whitney family to own land near Wasco was actually Daniel Whitney's father, John Whitney, mentioned previously. In the year 1850, the elder John Whitney purchased land just north of Wasco from David Pattee, the original owner of the north half of the northwest quarter of Section 23. By 1863, these lands were owned by the "heirs of the late John Whitney." The came into the possession of Daniel Whitney by the end of the Civil War. Daniel Whitney was born in Campton Township on 3 January 1840, and was the oldest in the family. His younger sister Rachel Whitney, who married Charles Probert, later moved to Wasco, and is mentioned elsewhere in this work. Daniel Whitney continued to improve his farm over the years. In June 1888, he built a sixteen-foot "Goodhue power wind mill" on the property, and installed drainage tile during that era and afterward.

The Daniel Whitney farm, near the future site of Wasco, in 1872

Althea Whitney's father Benjamin M. Babbitt came to live with her after his wife passed away in 1902. Mr. Babbitt, who was born in 1816, died at the Whitney home east of Wasco on 8 November 1903.

Althea's nephew Lester Babbitt was mentioned as being "formerly of Wasco" when me married Marie Volpp of Elgin in the summer of 1905.

Mertell ("Mertie") Whitney of Wasco, daughter of Daniel, married Frank J. Webb of Ohio on 24 April 1889, in Cook County. He worked for the Chicago, St. Paul, & Kansas City Railroad at that time. Mertie and Frank had one daughter, Pearl V. Webb, who was born on 19 November 1891. Mertie later married Loren E. Wickizer, on 26 May 1906, in Kenosha County, Wisconsin. Loren was born in Indiana in February 1870, and was a bartender in Gilman, Iroquois County, Illinois, prior to their marriage. By 1910, Loren and Mertell had moved into her father's farmhouse east of Wasco, and Loren was working there as a farm laborer.

In 1893, Merrill Whitney married Josephine L. Murphy. "Josie" Murphy was a teacher in a school west of Wasco when she met Merrill. She was born in Illinois in February 1872, and after their marriage they lived with Merrill's parents on the farm near Wasco. Mrs. Merrill Whitney entertained the "Soap Club," a short-lived Wasco social group, in early June 1905. In February 1907, Mr. and Mrs. Merrill Whitney celebrated their fourteenth anniversary, and received six cut glass tumblers as a present from their Wasco friends. In March 1909, Merrill Whitney moved his family into the Swanson (rental) house in Wasco, and "Albert Larson and wife will occupy the rooms over the store vacated by Mr. Whitney." This was very likely the Bergland store, at the center of Wasco. Clearly, Merrill had left the family farm prior to 1909.

By 1910, Merrill was working in the village of Wasco as a paper hanger. He and Josephine (who died on 19 May of that year, following an operation to remove a cancerous tumor, aged just thirty-eight) had one son – Morris W. Whitney, who was born on 16 September 1907. In 1920, Merrill was working as a home painter, and he and his son were boarding in Wasco with his aunt, Rachel (Whitney) Probert, an elderly widow. In 1924, Merrill Whitney and his friend C. M. Eddy attended a horseshoe-pitching competition in St. Charles. Six years after that, Merrill was retired and was still residing with Mrs. Probert, who was by then nearly ninety years of age. In March 1937, Merrill Whitney bought the "Mrs. Rachel Probert place" in Wasco. For a time, the Whitneys rented the apartment above the Bergland store. In fact, Morris Whitney was a very close friend of Floyd Bergland, who worked in the post office and store, and who lived just a few houses away. Morris and Merrill Whitney were still in Wasco in 1940, when the former was doing office work for a furniture company. For years, Merrill and Morris lived on the west side of LaFox Road three houses north of the Bergland/Hummel Store (see "Some Wasco Houses – Northwest Quarter"). Merrill passed away on 2 January 1944, and is buried in the Whitney Cemetery, named for his family.

Morris Whitney in a field in Wasco, early 1910s

In November 1939, Morris Whitney sang on WLS Radio with the Esquires Quartette of St. Charles. Morris Whitney married Martha Licher, and they moved to Geneva in 1941. That year, Whitney was one of the singers at the Fiftieth Anniversary Celebration of the Wasco Church. The new seven-hundred-pound bell was dedicated at a service in October of that year. Morris and his wife had no children. Morris Whitney was an active volunteer well into his eighties. He delivered meals to the elderly for the Salvation Army, volunteered for Delnor Hospital's Hi Hat Shop, and lobbied for the Geneva Senior Housing Corporation. Morris was chosen Man of the Year by the Geneva Park District in 1985. Morris Whitney passed away in Geneva on 20 April 1995.

Merritt Whitney's wife, Lillian Mae (Young) Whitney, was a highly-respected woman in the Wasco community. She was the sister of a successful businessman in Detroit, but struggled for some years because of her husband's lack of employment. Early in their marriage, Merritt (known as "Tip") and his wife lived at the intersection of Burlington Road and Corron Road, across from Lake Campton. They had three children. Quite early in their marriage (in the autumn of 1903) Merritt and Lillie Whitney and their family occupied the rooms over the old Bergland Store in Wasco. The Whitneys had two daughters (Evelyn and Althea) and a young son (Gerald) at that time; their son Palmer J. Whitney was born shortly afterward. Merritt Whitney was a house painter at that time.

John Goldenstein of Elgin purchased the former Daniel Whitney farm and home from Mr. and Mrs. L. E. Wickizer in March 1935. They had a housewarming party there on 2 April of that year, after moving to the house. Those present were Florence Carlson, Edna Fischer, Dora Johnson, Louise Swanson, Flora Norton, Maude Killoran, Anna Allen, Eric Olson, and Ida Bowgren.

The Leonard White Family

Emma Melissa (Scott) White was born in Campton Township on 15 June 1863. Her father, Lucien B. Scott, was a native of Madison County, New York, and her mother, Emma Jane (Blackman) Scott was born in Toronto, Ontario, Canada. In their youth, Emma and her brothers James, George, and Lou all attended the "Little Red School House" just south of the future site of Wasco. Emma's husband, Leonard White, was a day laborer and a carpenter. They were married in Kane County on 8 January 1889, and moved into their house in Wasco in the mid-1890s. Emma's widowed mother Eliza Jane Scott was living with them at the time. Jane was the mother of five children, and was born in 1832. She came to the United States in 1844. In late May 1901, Jane Scott celebrated her sixty-ninth birthday in Wasco (at the White home) with many "old school-mates and relatives." Leonard and Emma White had no children. Emma White was elected Vice President of the Wasco Ladies Aid in January 1910. She was one of the principal organizers for 'Old Neighbor Day' that February.

Charles Leonard White, who was known by his middle name, was born in Vergennes Township, Kent County, Michigan on 11 May 1861. His parents were Burtis and Delilah (Robinson) White. Leonard died in St. Charles, at the age of sixty-five, on 18 February 1927, and is buried in the Garfield Cemetery. In 1910, the Whites were living in their Wasco home with Emma's mother, her nephew Paul Scott, and a boarder, Wilbert R. Jewell, a telegraph operator. By 1920, only Leonard and Emma, along with Leonard's mother, were living in the home.

Leonard White, Emma's husband, was one of only thirteen Wasco residents listed in the 1896 Kane County Directory. He was a teamster at that time, and had come to the village the previous year. The White family came from Michigan to Kane County in 1886, and initially lived and worked on the Burr farm near LaFox (in Blackberry Township). Leonard's parents returned to Michigan, but Leonard himself remained in the area. The Scott/White home is located just west of the Bergland store, in Wasco, and predates the present store building (see "Some Wasco Houses – Northwest Quarter").

Paul H. Scott, a nephew of Eliza and Leonard, was living in the White home in 1900. Paul Scott and Leonard White attended the fat stock show in Chicago in late November 1904. James Scott was then living in Barton, North Dakota, and preached at the Wasco Church in mid-November that year. An article in the "Wasco Items" column of the *St. Charles Chronicle* from that same month mentioned that he would make his home in Wasco. James and Louis Scott (both of North Dakota) were visiting at the L. White residence in Wasco in December 1909. The household was composed of the same individuals in 1910 as it was a decade previously (although Leonard's mother-in-law's name was listed as Jane E., instead of Eliza J. as it appeared before), in addition to a boarder. An article in the *St. Charles Chronicle* from early February 1905 stated that "L. White will soon be ready to begin tax collecting." Leonard's occupation was given in 1910 as "Carpenter – odd jobs." A farewell dance was given in honor of Paul Scott in April 1918, just before he left for his training during the First World War. The event was held at the "club rooms" in LaFox.

Mrs. White, in Wasco - likely the "new" Bergland store at right

The 1920 census lists Leonard and Emma White near their neighbors the Berglands, Waterhouses, Stevenses, and Carpenters. Leonard then gave his occupation as house carpenter. His mother, Delilah (Robinson) White (an eighty-year-old widow from Michigan) was living in the household at that time. In 1925, Leonard White and James Rees (both Republicans) were the two Constables for Campton Township. In the early 1920s, H. I. Sharp and Leonard White sold choice sweet clover seed ("hulled and scarified") in

Wasco. White had one of the first telephones in the area. In July 1926, he was injured when a load of hay fell over and toppled him to the ground, resulting in multiple bruises on his head.

Leonard White died at the St. Charles hospital at 3:00 am on Tuesday, 15 February 1927, following an illness lasting several months. After White's death, Emma's brother Louis A. Scott moved into the White home in Wasco. A newspaper referred to the place (in 1927) as the "Emma White home." Emma and Louis's brother George Scott visited Wasco that year and several times afterward; George lived in LaFox during the late 1920s. In July and August 1929, Emma White traveled to Wyoming, Montana, and other western states with her brother Lou Scott. By 1930, Thomas Langrill was renting a room there. He was a bachelor in his late fifties, and worked odd jobs. Emma (Scott) White died in Wasco on 4 May 1938, at the age of seventy-four.

Miss Delia Scott, who passed away in Aurora in the fall of 1959, lived with the Whites in Wasco in the mid-1930s, "when the Little House was their home." Leonard Scott was a member of the St. Charles Masonic Lodge, the Eastern Star at Lily Lake, and the Modern Woodmen of America. His obituary described him as being "a good husband and respected neighbor." He and his wife Emma had been Wasco residents for thirty-two years.

Leonard and Emma White, in Wasco, circa 1915. The White home is at right, with the Bergland home at center, behind the trees – the view is looking west down the present Route 64

Emma Melissa (Scott) White was a lifelong resident of Campton Township. Her father, Lucian B. Scott, a native of Madison County, New York, was a Civil War veteran who joined the 58th Illinois Infantry in 1861. Emma was born on the family farm two miles southwest of the future site of Wasco, on what is now Beith Road. Emma's mother, Eliza Jane (Blackman) Scott, was born in Ontario, and died in Wasco on 19 January 1912, at the age of seventy-seven. After her husband's death, Emma White had many visitors at her home, was involved in various social events, and traveled rather frequently. She and her sister undertook a month-long trip to Wyoming in the summer of 1929 and traveled to Texas in the fall of 1930. She traveled with her brother to Iowa in the fall of 1931. In June 1936, Emma's friend and across-the-street neighbor Nettie Anderson threw her a surprise seventy-third birthday party, "with a gathering of old friends and neighbors." Emma (Scott) White passed away at her home in Wasco on 1 May 1938. Emma's niece, Miss Maybelle Scott of Aurora, cared for her during her final sickness.

The Millen Family

Charles Wilson ("Wil") Millen was among the very earliest settlers of the village of Wasco. He was born in New Jersey on 22 February 1853, although his younger siblings were Illinois natives. Soon after his birth, Charles's parents John V. and Charlotte Millen moved to Campton Township, Kane County, Illinois. The family lived in Gray Willow, in the northern part of the township, in 1870. On 8 December 1879, in Kane County, Wil Millen married Mary Ella Ward. She was born in Campton Township on 14 September 1862. Like his father, Charles W. Millen later became a skilled carpenter. He built the family's home at the southeast corner of what is now Route 64 and LaFox Road in the second half of the 1880s. His obituary stated that he had been a Wasco resident for forty-three years, and if accurate, he would have built his home in 1887-88, within six months of the very beginning of the village. Family tradition, which in this case is probably true, states that the home was built in 1887 (see "Some Wasco Houses – Southeast Quarter"). The home is shown on the 1892 Wasco map. Mr. Millen is said to have built the Bergland house as well, and the 1917 Johnson barn, both of which still stand [2018]. Mrs. Millen was a sister to Vesta P. Ward, the wife of John W. Bell.

Mary (Ward) Millen and her daughter, probably about 1906

Charlotte (Cooper) Millen of St. Charles frequently visited her son C. W. Millen of Wasco from the time he built his house there until the first years of the twentieth century. Mrs. Millen passed away in the second half of 1903 and is buried in the Whitney Cemetery. The Millens were thrown a surprise twenty-fifth anniversary party in December 1904 – their gift from those attending was a combination bookcase/writing desk. Two of Mrs. Millen's younger children were Daniel B. and Della Millen.

In September 1904, C. W.'s daughter Charlotte was attending school in Wheaton (almost certainly Wheaton Academy). Charlotte must have returned home for the summers, however, since in August 1904, Charlotte had received a watch "by the Mulvey Medicine show for receiving the most votes as being the most popular young lady in Wasco." She was again attending school in Wheaton in the spring of 1905. In February 1906, Charlotte obtained a job at D. C. Cook's publishing house in Elgin. She worked there only until that April, when she returned to Wasco "to stay." Charlotte was employed at the Wheaton Bank in August 1907.

Charles W. Millen gave his occupation as a building carpenter in 1930; he was still living at his home in Wasco then. He died at St. Charles city hospital on 11 May of that year. Charles W. Millen was survived by two sons – Earl V., of Elgin, and Charles W., of Chicago; and two daughters, Charlotte (Millen) Bartlett of Wyoming, and Mattie (Millen) Agnew of Ohio. Mattie had moved from Wasco to Marion, Ohio in July 1904, just three years after her marriage. When Mattie Millen celebrated her eighth birthday in August 1889, many of her classmates brought her "some pretty token" of their affection. Those celebrating with her included many familiar Wasco names: Flossie and Maude Austin, Grace and Florence Millen, Lottie and Vernie Whitney, Fern Bell, Amelia Eddy, Nettie Carpenter, Hazel Cherry, Johnny Bell, Sherman Wright, and Charlie and Alice Swarthout.

During the summer of 1931, the C. W. Millen home in Wasco was rented to Rev. and Mrs. V. J. Tengwald of Grace Lutheran Church, Lily Lake. Mary E. Millen moved to Elgin in the fall of 1932, and died there on 29 December 1937. She lived with her son Earl and his family during the last years of her life. Earl V. Millen continued to own the old family home in Wasco for a time, but he lived in St. Charles, and later in Elgin. The Millen home was occupied by "Mr. and Mrs. Joe Hawkins" beginning in February 1933. "Joe" Hawkins was Joel Hawkins, who was familiarly known by this nickname by locals and family members.

The Millen house in Wasco, as it appeared a century ago

The oldest child in the Millen family, Mattie A., was born in Campton Township on 27 August 1881. She moved to Wasco with her parents when she was a child. She attended the White School, just east of the village. Mattie married Chauncey George Agnew in Wasco on 2 January 1901. Their son Clifford R. Agnew died at birth in 1902. Their oldest daughter Norma Hope Agnew was born in Campton Township on 10 December 1903. Shortly afterward, they moved to Marion, Marion County, Ohio, where they resided by 1905. Chauncey Agnew was an express messenger for the steam railroad there. They remained in Marion in 1920, when there were three children in the household. By 1930, just their sons Ronald and Eugene remained at home. Chauncey was still in the same occupation then. Mattie Agnew passed away on 2 July 1956.

Earl VanLieu Millen was born in Campton Township on 14 November 1883. He married Ella May Wright in Kane County on 2 January 1905. She was a daughter of George and Addie Wright. Earl and Ella moved to First Street in St. Charles by 1910; he was a clerk in a lumber office at that time. They had children Dorothy, Violet, and Charlotte by then. For a short time in the early 1920s they lived in Kenosha, Wisconsin; Earl worked as a bookkeeper for a lumber yard at that time. In the 1930s and '40s, Earl was a carpenter/contractor, and lived on N. Worth Avenue in Elgin. His daughters Dorothy and Violet were stenographers by 1930. Phyllis was a younger daughter. Earl retired by 1950. He continued to live on North Worth Avenue, where he passed away on 29 September 1951.

Walter E. Bartlett at his home in California, around 1945

The "charm of Wasco," a "kind, much loved young lady," Miss Charlotte Wasco Millen, married Walter E. Bartlett of Elburn on 27 January 1909. She was born on 22 December 1887 and was indeed "the first baby of Wasco" - the first child born in the village (hence her middle name). The "Wasco" column in the *Elgin Advocate* from January 1888 stated that "Mr. and Mrs. C. W. Millen are the parents of the first baby girl born at Wasco." The village would have been made up of no more than three houses at that time (her father's being one) in addition to the train station. The wedding took place at the Millen home, "at high noon." Rev. Walton of Elburn performed the ceremony. Only the immediate families were present – the groom's mother, plus Mr. and Mrs. Henry Bartlett, Mr. and Mrs. Albert Bartlett, Mr. and Mrs. George Bartlett, Mr. and Mrs. C. G. Agnew, and Mr. and Mrs. Eric V. Millen. Locals mourned that "it is with regret that we must part with her after twenty-one years of friendship ties. But what is our loss is Walter's gain." Charlotte's friend Pearl Webb threw her wedding shower the week before the ceremony.

The newlyweds left soon after their marriage for Powell, Wyoming, their new home. Charlotte and Walter lived on a general farm in Garland Township, Park County, Wyoming, in 1910. They were still in that county in 1920, by which time they had three sons: Gerald, Donald, and Glen Bartlett. The farm was then described as a "stock farm." A fourth and final son, Lloyd Edgar Bartlett, followed in 1922. They were on a dairy farm in 1930. By 1940, Charlotte and Walter Bartlett had moved to the city of Cody, in the same county; their youngest son was still in the household then. Charlotte (Millen) Bartlett died in Park County, Wyoming, on her eightieth birthday.

Charlotte and Walter Bartlett, with sons Lloyd (in front), Don, Gerald, and Glenn

Will and Mary (Ward) Millen, whose daughter Charlotte was the first child born in Wasco

Charlotte W. (Millen) Bartlett, the first person born in Wasco

Charles Ward Millen was born in Campton Township on 22 September 1895. He was the youngest son in the family, and lived with his parents in Wasco until enlisting in the U. S. Army during World War I. By January 1919, Charles Millen was a Second Lieutenant at Camp Hancock, Georgia. He was discharged from the service at the end of the war, and visited his parents before leaving for North Dakota. There, Millen engaged "in Y.M.C.A. work." He married Evangeline Idarius in Chicago on 19 July 1919. They lived on North Lotus Avenue in the city of Chicago for many years. He worked as a steel worker in a factory in 1920, and a patent clerk in 1930. He and Evangeline had a son, Charles W. Millen Jr., who was born in Chicago on 9 May 1927. Charlie Millen worked for the William Wrigley Company in Chicago in 1942. He passed away in Florida in July 1963.

Lola Millen of Wasco, with her bicycle, in the mid-1910s

Lola A. Millen, the youngest daughter of Will and Mary, was born in Wasco on 28 July 1903, and attended the Wasco School. In June 1909, Lola Millen was one of several Wasco residents suffering from whooping cough. After her graduation from high school, she entered DeKalb Normal School and began training to become a teacher. She was described as being "of a kindly heart and sweet disposition," and was a member of the Wasco Church. Lola Almena Millen passed away at the age of seventeen, on 17 November 1920. She was living in the family home with her parents at that time; her death of course was a devastating loss to her mother and father.

Daniel B. Millen, C. W.'s younger brother, was born in Illinois in September 1854 or 1855. He married Celestia V. ("Lessie") Kinnear in Kane County on 22 January 1879. Celestia was born in Illinois in July 1858; her parents were from New Brunswick, Canada. D. B. Millen was a carpenter, and worked with his brother on many early buildings in Wasco. The couple lived in Wasco before moving to Cowley County, Kansas, in the 1890s. On 5 June 1888, Daniel Millen had twin sons. A local newspaper noted at the time that "the babes are vigorous" and that the father "rejoice[d] over the arrival." The twins were Herbert and Boyd Millen. Their older siblings, all of whom were born in Campton Township, were: Grace E. (born on 10 November 1880); Archie Wellington (born on 26 April 1883); and Florence V. Millen (born on 6 June 1885).

In 1900, Daniel B. and Celestia Millen were living in Kansas with their five children. Archie was a farm laborer, and Daniel was still a carpenter. In 1910, the Millens were living in Butler County, Kansas, and only the twins and their youngest brother Keith D. Millen (who was born on 18 May 1903) remained with their parents. The family moved to Sumner County by 1915, by which time only Keith was at home. In 1920, Keith Millen was a carpenter, and was living with his parents. All six children had moved out of the household by 1925. Daniel B. Millen died in the first few months of the year 1930, and is buried in Mulvane, Kansas. Celestia passed away on 15 January 1941.

In 1902, Grace E. Millen married William D. Nibel, an oil pipeline inspector. They first lived in Butler County, Kansas, but in the early 1920s they moved to Wichita, and stayed there for the rest of their lives. William died in 1935, and Grace passed away on 5 March 1960. They had no children. Grace's brother Archie W. Millen lived in Maple, Cowley County, Kansas for decades, and later moved to Udall, about forty miles to the northwest. He married, had a son, and worked as a farmer. Archie died near Udall on 2 July 1959, and is buried in the Mulvane Cemetery. His youngest brother Keith Millen moved to California by 1934. He worked in Costa Mesa as a carpenter during World War II, and died there on 29 April 1962. Boyd Millen moved to Mulvane, Kansas, where he worked as a house carpenter; he later worked for the Works Progress Administration. Boyd Elden Millen married and had four children; he passed away on 2 May 1954. His twin Herbert Leon Millen was also a house carpenter, and also lived in Mulvane. Herbert had three children, and passed away on 27 December 1966. Their sister Florence V. (Millen) Dabbs died in Costa Mesa, Orange County, California, on 12 April 1967.

The Bert Brown Family

Zilpha (Lake) Brown was a lifelong resident of Campton Township, and spent most of her life in Wasco. She was born just two miles northwest of Wasco on 29 November 1888 and was considered Wasco's oldest resident when she died in the summer of 1977. Zilpha's father, Benjamin F. Lake, was also born in Campton Township (on 21 March 1846) and was a son of some of the region's earliest pioneers. Benjamin F. Lake received his education at the Gray Willow school, and worked on his father's farm. At the age of nineteen, he began renting and operating other farms, and in the 1860s he began assembling a herd of dairy cattle. By the early twentieth century, B. F. Lake owned eighty-six cows, and bought and sold milk cows for the local market. Lake was "recognized as an authority on the quality and grade of dairy stock."

He married Phylantia ("Fannie") Vanderhoof, also of Campton Township, and they had three children: Frank, Fred, and Zilpha. Benjamin F. Lake was a School Trustee, and for a long period served as Supervisor of Campton Township. He was a supporter of the Republican party and was a member of the Modern Woodmen of America.

Frank John Brown, Zilpha's father-in-law, was born in St. Charles on 22 November 1858, and lived in Wayne, DuPage County, Illinois, for much of his youth. Frank married twenty-year-old Emma J. Royce in November 1880. Emma was born in Tolland County, Connecticut, on 28 April 1859. The Brown family home in the village of St. Charles was located on South Fifth Street, and is still standing. The Browns moved to Campton Township in the 1890s, and to Wasco in March 1903, soon after purchasing land in the north half of Section 22 from Horace S. and Martha C. Higgins. This parcel was just over sixty acres in size, and covered part of the intersection of the present Brown Road and Route 64. In February 1906, the Browns purchased the former O. Abrahamson farm just west of town, which adjoined the aforementioned land. The Browns' property, which grew to more than two hundred and sixty acres in size, was named "Woodside Farm" in the 1910s. Frank and Emma had one son, Herbert John ("Bert") Brown, who was born on 1 March 1884. He attended local schools and was both a farmer and an entrepreneur (see "The Farm Restaurant"). Frank and Emma Brown celebrated their silver wedding anniversary in 1905, and

Zilpha Lake of Campton Township, as a baby

were surprised by nearly one hundred friends, twenty of whom made the trip from St. Charles to Wasco. They received a China cabinet and an engraved spoon from those in attendance. M. T. Warren, a close friend of the family, even wrote a poem celebrating the occasion. Bert Brown, a member of the Wasco Orchestra then, helped furnish the music for entertaining the crowd. Frank Brown died at his home in St. Charles on 6 September 1928, at the age of sixty-nine. Emma Brown passed away on 21 March 1949.

The "new" house at the Brown farm in Wasco, in the 1910s

Four generations of the Brown family - John, Frank, Bert, and John, about 1909

Frank J. and Emma (Royce) Brown, in the year 1881

Benjamin F. and Fanny (Vanderhoof) Lake of Campton Township, grandparents of Jewel Brown

When he was twelve, Bert Brown was nearly killed in a runaway accident which occurred on "the Walnut street hill" in St. Charles. The accident took place on 6 July 1897, and was caused by the Brown family's wagon running onto the horses' feet, frightening them. Bert held onto the lines and held back the team the best he could, "but at the foot of the hill is the foundry fence and sheds, and in making the sharp turn to avoid crashing into this obstruction he was thrown out, and one of the heavy wheels passed over his head." W. P. Lillibridge happened to be nearby, and "seeing the boy beside the street ran over and picked him up." Bert was brought to his grandfather's house in town, and Dr. Bishop was summoned to care for him. According to the words of the *St. Charles Chronicle*, "It was a miracle that the boy was not killed outright." Days later, Bert was improving, but was still somewhat weak.

Bert Brown left for the Pan-American Exposition in Buffalo, New York, in early July 1901. President William McKinley was shot and killed at that event in mid-September, though Brown did not witness the tragic event. In early August 1904, the "Wasco orchestra" entertained locals at a lawn social at the home of Frank Brown, Bert's father. This lawn social featured ice cream, during which "a delightful time was enjoyed by all," was attended by some two hundred guests (more than the population of Wasco at the time). Herbert J. Brown and Zilpha K. Lake of Wasco were married on 19 February 1906, in Omaha, Nebraska. Immediately following the honeymoon, the Browns settled on Bert's mother's sixty-acre farm on the west side of Wasco. Their son John Lake Brown was born there on 18 November 1906.

In November 1904, Frank J. Brown purchased a 35 ½ acre parcel of land on the north side of Route 64 from James and Emma Chrystal. This parcel was bordered on the west by the present Brown Road, and was immediately north of the family's other property. In February 1910, the Chrystals sold the Browns an additional 11.92 acres of land in the northeast quarter of Section 22. The 1918 Farmers' Directory of Kane County listed H. J. Brown as a tenant on 267 acres of land owned by his father, Frank J. Brown. This land was located in two large parcels. The farm on the west edge of Wasco comprised just under 111 acres of land, and was formally sold to Herbert J. Brown by his father and mother on 10 November 1927. The land was sold for $1. Frank and Emma were living in the city of St. Charles at the time of the sale. When Route 64 was widened and paved in the spring and summer of 1928, the Browns sold a sliver of land to "the People of the State of Illinois" for the completion of this project. The land was owned by the family for many decades, and no part of it was sold until the 1970s, other than a small easement for the Northern Illinois Gas Company in November 1968. In February 1972, the property was split into two halves, one (57.87 acres in size) going to John L. and Anna C. Brown, and the other (52.74 acres in size) to John's sister Jewel (Brown) Bowgren and her husband Clifton.

Jewel A. Brown, the daughter of Herbert John and Zilpha, was born at Woodside Farm in Wasco on 16 June 1915. She attended Wasco School beginning in the fall of 1920 and had Ethel Waterhouse as her first teacher. Jewel then attended St. Charles High School. In 1935 she was one of the contestants in the Campton Township Centennial celebration. She worked as a waitress at The Farm for most of the 1930s. On 26 June 1940, in Wayne, Jewel married Clifton A. Bowgren (see "The Bowgren Family"). Jewel later worked as a waitress at The Little Traveler in Geneva. Jewel loved to entertain friends at her home, and was active in both Wasco Ladies Aid and the LaFox Farmers' Club.

The 1933 Elgin Rural Route Directory listed Bert and Zilpha Brown as renting 114 acres of land from Mrs. Emma Brown, and as the owners of the "Farm Barbeque," oil station, and tourist camp. Two years later, the Brown family's listing stated that they ran a "dairy farm also barbeque and cabins." Their son John L. Brown was listed as a farmhand that year. In 1937, Bert and Zilpha Brown were still proprietors of The Farm (then listed as a tavern) and were living on their property a half-mile west of Wasco. Their phone number that year was St. Charles 4063-J-2.

In 1939 and 1940, Jewel Brown was a waitress at The Farm tavern, which was still owned by her parents. They had started with a vegetable stand "at the edge of the woods, across the road from their farm" in 1925. By the late 1930s, Jewel's brother John L. Brown and his wife Anna were renting a 200-acre farm one-and-a-half-miles west of Wasco from F. K. Barber.

Jewel Brown and Frances Johnson at The Farm, early 1930s

John L. Brown of Wasco married Anna Charlotte Anderson of St. Charles on New Years' Day, 1935. Anna was born in Geneva on 23 July 1907, was a daughter of Martin and Signe Anderson, and graduated from St. Charles High School in 1925. After her marriage, which took place at the Geneva Baptist Church, Anna (Anderson) Brown and her husband moved to the Brown farm at the intersection of Brown Road and Route 64. Anna was an active member of the Wasco Baptist Church for many years. John and Anna Brown had three sons – Robert, William, and Bruce. John L. Brown retired from farming in 1970, but continued to love "farm life and working outdoors." He cultivated a large garden, and worked with surveying crews for Anderson Engineering. John L. Brown died in St. Charles at the age of eighty-five, on 20 December 1991. There were nine grandchildren in the family. Anna passed away on 27 March 1999, and is buried in Union Cemetery, St. Charles.

Bert and Zilpha (Lake) Brown in March 1954

Bert Brown retired in 1940. He was a member of the Blackberry Masonic Lodge and the Tebala Shriners Club of Rockford for more than fifty years. Bert passed away at Community Hospital in Geneva on 3 December 1970. His widow Zilpha K. Brown of Wasco died on 30 June 1977, at Delnor Hospital. She and her husband had farmed in the area for nearly fifty years. Zilpha was best known for her "kitchen artistry" at The Farm's restaurant, and was the second-oldest resident of Campton Township in the last years of her life. She was survived by her two children, six grandchildren, and fifteen great-grandchildren. Zilpha was buried in the North Cemetery in St. Charles, beside her husband.

The Waterhouse Family

Charles Jamison Waterhouse was one of the best-known men in Wasco soon after the turn of the twentieth century. He was a "popular and enterprising business man of Wasco," where he worked as a station agent and telegraph operator for many years, a position which was later held by his son Paul P. Waterhouse. Charles was born in Holton, Jackson County, Kansas, on 9 December 1869. His father, Robert J. Waterhouse, was a veteran of the Civil War, having served as a Lieutenant in the Twentieth Kansas Cavalry. Charles's mother, Martha A. (Spencer) Waterhouse, was born in Upper Stillwater, Maine, and was the daughter of a sea captain. Robert and Martha had two children – Charles and Edward. Edward J. Waterhouse left the family home in Kansas at the age of fourteen and was never heard from again.

Charles J. Waterhouse attended grade school and high school in Holton, Kansas, and spent his vacations doing railroad construction work. After high school, he entered Campbell Normal University in Holton, where he studied for two years. Then, he began working for the railroad and was an agent and a telegraph operator in various towns in Kansas, Missouri, Texas, Iowa, and Illinois. He was assigned to Wasco in 1906.

In the spring of 1893, Charles married Sarah A. ("Sallie") Allen of Shaw, Kansas. They had three children: Paul Preston Waterhouse, who was born on 9 April 1895; Lillian C. Waterhouse, who was born on 5 July 1905; and Ella M. Waterhouse, who was born on 16 September 1909. Paul was born in Kansas, but his youngest sister was born in Wasco. The Waterhouse family moved to Wasco in May 1906, when Mr. Waterhouse took over the station agency of the Chicago Great Western railroad from G. H. Martin. The Waterhouses initially lived in the former Martin house. In April 1908, Charles J. Waterhouse visited relatives in Kansas, and Earl Lamb temporarily took his place as Wasco's railroad agent. Charles Waterhouse never ran for office, but was a staunch Republican. He was a Mason and was a member of the Modern Woodmen of America, and the Order of Railway Telegraphers.

Paul Waterhouse, about 1913

Charles, Sarah, and Ella Waterhouse moved to Hillsborough, Florida before 1930. Charles continued to work as an operator for a telegraph company, while Ella became a teacher in the public schools. In the summer of 1933, Ella and Lillian Waterhouse, who lived in Florida, visited their brother Paul in Wasco. All three (later joined by their parents, who came up to visit in August) attended the Chicago World's Fair. Charles J. Waterhouse died in Tampa, Florida, on 3 November 1947.

Paul Preston Waterhouse was born in Shaw, Neosho County, Kansas, on 9 March 1895. In 1900, he was living with his parents in Rock Creek Township, Coffey County, Kansas. Like his father, he was a station agent for the Chicago Great Western Railroad. Paul was working in this capacity as early as 1917. In 1920, he listed his occupation as railroad telegrapher. He was newly-married to Ethel (née Coombes) at that time. Ethel was born in Blackberry Township on 5 April 1895 and was the daughter of John and Annie (Perkins) Coombes, both of whom had left Somersetshire, England, in the late 1880s. Ethel grew up on a farm and loved horses as a girl. Around 1908, her parents bought a farm in Section 7, St. Charles Township, just east of the Campton Township border. Ethel attended Wasco School, and completed her studies at Geneva High School, graduating in 1914. While there Mr. Harry Coultrap made a strong impression on her, and she decided to become a teacher. She began teaching at the Gray Willow School, and received her full teaching certificate in 1916. She married Paul Waterhouse very early in her career.

During her decades as a school teacher, Mrs. Waterhouse brought seeds to her students so that they could study the plants' growth and development. When one of her students had a birthday, she would draw a birthday cake on the blackboard with colored chalk, and the class would sing to the boy or girl. Her teaching extended to the weekends as well, for she taught Sunday School at the Wasco Baptist Church for almost twenty years. Mrs. Waterhouse was a kind person, an excellent teacher, and had no behavior problems in her classroom. Upon her retirement after forty-one years in the profession, a special program was presented in her honor. She retired at the end of the 1958-59 school year. Ethel Waterhouse, a beloved figure in Wasco, passed away on 7 August 1970 and was buried in the Whitney Cemetery.

When he was in his forties, Paul Waterhouse was 5' 9 ½" tall, weighed 145 pounds, and had blue eyes and gray hair. In the 1930s and '40s, his phone number was "St. Charles 4084-J-2." In the late 1940s, Paul took a job as station agent at the depot in St. Charles, and was replaced as agent in Wasco by Rex Pelley. In 1953, his post office box number in Wasco was 98. Waterhouse retired from his career as a station agent in 1963. In November 1967, Paul Waterhouse received his fifty-year Masonic pin. He retired as Campton Township Assessor in 1968. In 1969, he took over as treasurer of the Wasco Cemetery Association, when Lloyd Johnson retired.

There was an auction at the Waterhouse home in Wasco on 23 June 1973. Many antiques, collectibles, and tools were sold there, including a dining room set, a walnut wash stand, a writing desk, Depression glass, milk cans, and a clock from the old Wasco School. Paul moved to the Surrey Hill Apartments in St. Charles at that time, to the Geneva Retirement Center in 1974, and to the Holmstad in Batavia in 1977. Paul's sister Ella, who lived in Florida, visited him frequently when his health began to decline in the 1970s. Paul Waterhouse died in Batavia in February 1981. See "Some Wasco Houses – Northwest Quarter" for more information on the Waterhouses.

The Carpenter Family

Norman L. Carpenter was born in St. Lawrence County, New York, on 31 October 1842. By 1870, he and his wife Sarah (née Nichols, who was a native of Canada) were living in Campton Township on their farm on the future site of Wasco. Their oldest child, Nellie Viola Carpenter, was born in Wisconsin on 22 February 1868. Their other daughter, Nettie Gertrude Carpenter, was born in Campton Township on 31 May 1875. In 1880, Norman, who was a farmer, also worked in a cheese factory. William White, a nineteen-year-old farm laborer from New York, also lived with the Carpenters that year. Sarah Carpenter died at her home in Wasco on 10 February 1889. She had pneumonia, and was just forty-four years old. She was survived by her husband and two children. Rev. C. W. Thornton of St. Charles conducted the funeral, which was held from the family home. Well before her marriage to Norman Carpenter, Sarah Nichols had moved to St. Lawrence County, New York, at the age of fourteen, where she lived with her uncle. In 1865, Sarah went to Wisconsin, where she and Norman were married. After living there for three years, the Carpenters came to Campton Township. Following his wife's death, Carpenter rented his Wasco farm to "Mr. Kingsmill" of Elgin in the fall of 1889, with the intention of moving to Nebraska. It seems, however, that Carpenter either remained in the vicinity, or returned to Wasco in 1890.

On 2 December 1890, Norman L. Carpenter married a second time. His wife was Emma Norton of Campton Township. According to her obituary, she was born "in a log cabin on what is now [1946] the Dexter Norton farm east of Wasco." Her birth occurred on 5 December 1851; her father was Garrit Norton. Norman and Emma had one daughter, Edna R. Carpenter, who was born in August 1893. In 1900, the family lived on Second Street in Geneva, but in February 1903 they returned to their farm in Wasco. In 1910, the three Carpenters lived with Hal Wickizer, a laborer at a local creamery. Norman L. Carpenter died in Wasco in April 1914.

Nellie Carpenter lived on the family farm in Campton Township from her infancy through the time of her marriage. She attended the Whitney school in the 1870s and early '80s. On 4 May 1887, in Kane County, Nellie Viola Carpenter married William Lincoln Cherry. Will Cherry was a contractor on the Chicago,

Minnesota & Northwestern railroad in 1887, and took a contract with the Elgin, Joliet, & Eastern railroad in 1888. He and Nellie lived in Wasco at that time, although Will briefly lived in Kansas City during the winter of 1888. Their three children were all born in Kane County, and shortly after 1892, the Cherrys moved to Valparaiso, Porter County, Indiana. Their children were: Hazel N. Cherry (who was born in March 1888); Lester W. Cherry (who was born in December 1889); and Walter S. Cherry (who was born in August 1892). William Cherry was a house carpenter by trade. He was born in Ohio in March 1864. A touching column in the *Elgin Advocate* announced Hazel's birth this way: "although early in the season a young Cherry has appeared at Wasco. She will in the future call Will papa."

In September 1905, Mrs. Will Cherry and son Lester of South Chicago spent a week with the Carpenters at their home in Wasco. Nellie (Carpenter) Cherry again visited her family in November 1906, shortly after her father was injured "by the noon limited train" running through their farm. In July 1908, "Mrs. Will Cherry of East Chicago and daughter" were visiting their family, the Carpenters, in Wasco. The Cherry family is listed in the 1910 census of East Chicago, Lake County, Indiana. All three children were still in the household. Nellie remained for a time in East Chicago. In 1920, she was a saleswoman at a local store, and was living with her two sons at 4816 Olcott Avenue. By 1930, William and Nellie, with their son Walter, had moved to the city of Sonora, California. She was working as a housekeeper at a rooming house, and her husband was a building contractor. Walter was a timekeeper in a sawmill. All three Cherrys were registered Republicans. Nellie V. (Carpenter) Cherry died in Sonora on 13 February 1936. Her husband survived her by more than ten years.

Emma Carpenter, and her daughter Edna, both of whom lived in Wasco for many decades

Nettie G. Carpenter lived with Hylas and Mary Ward in St. Charles in 1900. Nettie married Henry F. VanWambeke in Kane County on 22 July 1903; they moved to Elgin soon afterward. Hazel Cherry visited the Carpenters in Wasco in August 1906. The St. Charles *Valley Chronicle* reported in July 1908 that Mr. and Mrs. "H. Vanwombeke [sic] and family of Elgin" were then visiting at N. L. Carpenter's. The family was listed in the 1910 census of the city of Elgin. H. F. had been married previously and had four sons and a daughter. By 1919, the VanWambekes had moved to San Francisco, California; they lived at 1005 Golden Gate Avenue that year. They were living at 1628 Steiner St., San Francisco, in 1923. Henry was a butcher by trade but later became a real estate salesman. By 1928, Nettie and Henry moved to Huntington Park City, Los Angeles County, California. They were both registered Democrats in 1936, when they were living at 3352 East Florence Avenue in Huntington Park City. By 1940, Nettie was a widow and was living with her step-daughter Sylvia Jackson, and Sylvia's son

Robert. Nettie died in Los Angeles County on 6 March 1945. She had several step-children but no children of her own.

With his second wife Emma (née Norton), Norman L. Carpenter had one child – a daughter – Edna R. Carpenter. She was born in Wasco on 9 August 1893, but for a short time in her youth she lived in Geneva, where she began her schooling. Edna briefly remained on her parents' farm in Wasco after her father's death, but soon moved into the house just west of Nettie Anderson's home (see "Some Wasco Houses – Southwest Quarter"). Edna was married twice. On 28 June 1913, according to the "Wasco Items" column of the *St. Charles Chronicle,* "Miss Edna Carpenter, daughter of Mrs. N. L. Carpenter . . . was married to Levi Chancellor of Davenport, Florida, where the young couple will make their home." The marriage may have been short-lived, since Edna was back in Wasco by 1920, and her marital status was again listed as "single." In 1927, Edna married Cal Cray, who was a railroad carpenter from Kansas, and the married couple lived in Wasco with Edna's mother. The couple were long-time Wasco residents and were known to all in the area.

Norman L. Carpenter died in Davenport, Florida (which was briefly the city in which his daughter Edna lived), on 16 April 1914, at the age of seventy-two. His remains were sent back to Wasco for burial. He was survived by his wife and three daughters (Edna, Nettie, and Nellie). His funeral was held at the Wasco Baptist Church with Rev. Harkness officiating.

The Fischer Family

The large August Fischer farm, which measured nearly three-hundred acres in extent in 1892, was located principally in Section 16, just north of Wasco. It was owned by the family for more than ninety years. The Whitney Cemetery was surrounded on three sides by Fischer property, and the farmhouse stood (and still stands) just southeast of the cemetery. August Fischer was born on 4 July 1838 in Hesse Kassel, Germany, and came to the United States in 1853, "with only two shillings in his pocket." Fischer first settled in Bloomingdale, and then in Elgin, in Kane County. While there, he worked as a farm laborer for ten years, earning between $10 and $12 per month. He married Hulda M. Miller on 26 November 1862. She was born in Saxony on 19 September 1843 and came to the U. S. with her parents in 1857; they first settled in Cook County. In 1869, the Fischers purchased their two-hundred and eighty-seven-acre farm north of Wasco, across the road from the Maria Whitney farm. The property was partly wooded and contained both a significant stream and ample fertile soil for planting.

On 22 September 1869, August W. Fischer "of the County of Cook" gave John Elliott (of Kane County) a bond to secure a deed for the soon-to-be Fischer farm in Campton Township. Elliott agreed to sell a large parcel of land to Fischer for $14,300. The warranty deed was executed for this property on 16 February 1870. One of the property boundaries in the deed (now Burlington Road) was called the "St. Charles and Rockford road." August's brother Theodore Fischer held a half-interest in the title to the family farm in Campton Township for just over three years. Theodore and his wife Eliza, of Kane County, sold their interest in the property to August W. Fischer (of the same place) on 22 March 1873. The price he paid for a half-interest in the land was $7150, a large amount for that time.

In the 1870s and '80s, August Fischer served as a Campton Township Road Commissioner, and also as a School Director. He was a Democrat politically, and was a member of the Lutheran Church. August and

Hulda had three children: Henry Theodore, John Gustaf, and Clara Amelia Fischer. The children were all born in Illinois and attended the Whitney school. August's younger brother Theodore Fischer also lived in the Wasco area for a time; both brothers were engaged in farming. David Plummer (a native of Indiana) worked as a farm hand on the August Fischer farm in 1880. By 1888, August Fischer had "about sixty head of steers, and some fine-blooded horses" on his farm, in which he took great pride. He was putting down "several cartloads of tile" that summer, and it was "hoped [that] others will follow suit."

Both Henry T. and John G. ("Gus") Fischer lived in St. Charles for many years. Their sister Clara married Horace R. Powell and moved to Oregon, although the Powells later returned to St. Charles. Mr. and Mrs. August Fischer had a home in Aurora in the very early twentieth century. They sold this home in July 1903, and soon afterward moved to a new house in St. Charles after briefly living with their son Theodore. In February 1907, August Fischer underwent an operation at Sherman Hospital in Elgin to treat his cancer. Daniel Whitney of Wasco visited him while in the hospital. August Fischer, who was a member of the Batavia Lutheran Church for many years, died on 27 May 1907, and is buried in the Whitney Cemetery "at Wasco, his old home." He was survived by three children and five grandchildren. August's widow Hulda survived until 18 September 1920. She passed away in St. Charles, at the home of her daughter Clara.

The August and Hulda Fischer farmhouse, in Section 14, Campton Township

August and Hulda Fischer of Wasco, in the 1890s

Henry Theodore Fischer was born on 30 November 1863, and came to Campton Township with his parents in 1869. Henry married Etta Belle Plummer on 28 November 1887. Rev. C. W. Thornton of St. Charles performed the ceremony. Carrie Peterson played the wedding march, and William Plummer and Clara Fischer attended the bride and groom. Etta was born on 6 February 1870, in St. Charles, and was a daughter of Daniel D. and Julia A. (Morgan) Plummer. Henry was a farmer. They had two children: Gladys Irene Fischer (who was born in August 1889); and Raymond Plummer Fischer (who was born in August 1898). Henry and Etta Fischer lived a mile south of Wasco in 1900, near the August Johnson farm. Etta's brother Frank P. Plummer lived with them at that time, and worked on the farm. They had moved to Fifth Avenue, St. Charles, by 1901, but briefly moved back to Wasco after that. Mr. D. Plummer of Arkansas visited his daughter, "Mrs. H. T. Fisher," in Wasco in August 1906. This gentleman sold his 125-acre farm 1 ¼ miles from Wasco, along the "new line of railroad" in the fall of 1888. The farm contained an apple orchard, good buildings, and two wells.

It was H. T. Fischer that purchased the former White schoolhouse east of Wasco in August 1906, shortly after it was permanently closed. The new brick school in Wasco was opened at that time. Gladys Fischer attended Elgin Academy in 1907. In

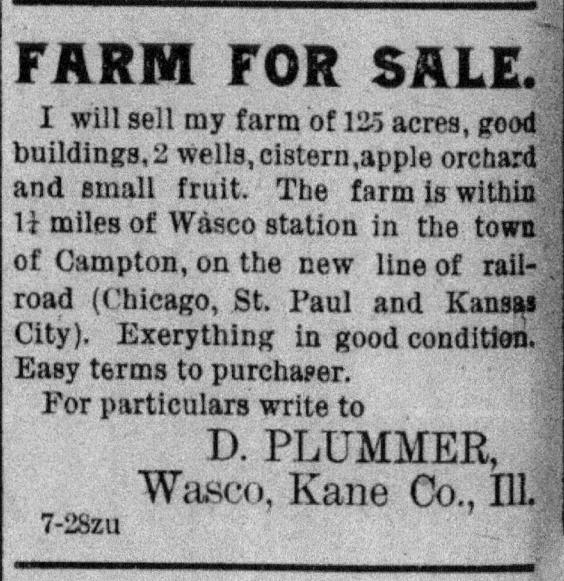

Daniel Plummer's advertisement for selling his farm near Wasco, August 1888

February 1908, the Fischers again moved to St. Charles, and remained there through at least 1920. Raymond Fischer attended school in Naperville in 1928. The Fischers left their farm in Campton Township in March 1929, and moved to Elgin. Their farm was rented by the George Simmons family of St. Charles. Edna Fischer was a substitute teacher in 1930, and her brother Raymond was working on a "fur farm." Raymond got married soon afterward, and he and his wife moved to St. Charles. The Fischers moved back to Campton Township by 1935, and in 1940 Raymond and Edna were living with their children Henry E. and Joy, as well as with Raymond's father Henry, in the old farmhouse.

Henry and Etta Fischer celebrated their twentieth wedding anniversary in December 1908. They had an orchestra entertain their guests, and readers at the celebration included Mrs. Allen, Gladys Fisher, and Floyd Bergland. Their gift was a hand-painted lemonade set "and a loving cup." John Larson moved to the Fischer farm near Wasco in February 1917; he likely worked there as a farm hand. Etta Fischer died in St. Charles on 31 May 1931, and her husband passed away in Campton Township on 15 January 1948. On 17 May 1946, H. Theo. Fischer deeded a 30' x 244' strip of land to the Wasco Cemetery Association.

Raymond P. Fischer, the son of Henry and Etta, retained ownership of the majority of his grandparents' farm until the summer of 1964. Once he and his wife sold the farm, they moved to Geneva. By the late 1950s, the northern eighty acres (in Section 11) had been sold to Lillian Fessenden, with Fischer retaining the property in the east half of Section 14 and in the extreme western portion of Section 13. The Fischer property was then 157.26 acres in size and fronted on Burlington and Bolcum Roads. Raymond and Edna Fischer sold the land to a trust in June 1964. Campton Oak Farms subdivision, surveyed in November

1965, was taken out of a portion of the former Fischer farm. The Deer Run Creek subdivision comprising the southern portion of the former Fischer farm was platted in October 1976.

Henry T. and Etta B. (Plummer) Fischer of Campton Township

Signature of H. Theo. Fischer from 1946, deeding land to the Wasco Cemetery Association

John Gustav Fischer was born in Kane County on 13 January 1867. His sister Clara A. Fischer was born in Campton Township on 20 June 1869. John G. Fischer was a cattle dealer in 1910, when he and his wife were living on Fifth Avenue in St. Charles with their eight-year-old son, Clarence. Clara (Fischer) Powell was next door, living with their mother. Clara's husband Horace was a telegrapher; they were married in 1897. She and Horace had three children: Esther, Theodore, and Ruth Powell. On 23 October 1925, John G. and his wife Emma, and Clara (Fischer) Powell and her husband Horace, all quit their claims to the Fischer farm in Campton Township, in favor of their brother H. Theo. Fischer, of the city of St. Charles. John and Emma lived in St. Charles then, and Clara and Horace lived in Portland, Oregon. In 1930, John Gustav and Emma Fischer were living on North Fifth Avenue in St. Charles, with their son Clarence, his wife Martha LaFern, and their grandson Jack. Clarence was a grocery store manager, and his wife was a clerk at the store. The same household members were together at the same address in 1940, when Clarence was an inspector at a radio manufacturing plant. Clarence's wife Fern was a coil winder at the same facility.

The Isaac Johnson Family

Solomon Johnson, one of the best-known citizens of Wasco, was born near the city of Jönköping, Sweden, on the shores of Lake Vättern, on 27 April 1877. His parents were Isaac and Mary (Peterson) Johnson. The Johnson family came to the United States in 1883, settling briefly in St. Charles before moving to Pingree Grove, northwest of Elgin. By the late 1880s, the family was again in St. Charles Township, where the children attended the Little Woods School a few miles north of the city of St. Charles. In 1900, the Johnson family was still on a farm in St. Charles Township, near those of Peter Benson, Walter Wilson, and Kirk Ferson. There were six members of the household, all of whom were born in Sweden. These were Isaac (who was born in December 1832) and Mary (born in October 1843) and four of their five surviving children (Solomon, Mathilda, Emma, and Alex). Family records collected by their daughter-in-law give the parents' dates of birth as 14 December 1832 and 16 October 1843. The Johnson children were all unmarried in 1900. Isaac and Alex were listed as farm laborers, and Solomon (who was considered the head of the household) was listed as a farmer. Isaac Johnson died soon after the census was taken, on 6 October 1900. His widow survived until 6 February 1928; both are buried in the North Cemetery, in St. Charles. Alex and Solomon Johnson were both naturalized as U. S. citizens in 1905.

Alex Johnson (left) and Solomon Johnson (right) of Wasco with their brother John Johnson (center)

The children of Isaac and Anna Marie ("Mary") Johnson were: John Magnus (who was born on 14 September 1873); Mathilda E. (who was born in April 1875); Solomon; Emma A. (who was born in January 1879); and Alex Johnson (who was born on 12 December 1881). After her husband's death, Mary Johnson went to Campton Township to live with her sons Solomon and Alex. She was listed in their household in 1910. By 1920, Mary had moved back to St. Charles Township, and was living with her other son John Johnson, and with her daughter Mathilda.

Upon coming to the United States, Solomon Johnson first lived in St. Charles, but then moved to Pingree Grove, Kane County. He lived there for three years, and then moved to a farm north of St. Charles, and subsequently to the Dan Murphy farm, where he lived for ten years. He was there for most of the 1890s. Next, Solomon moved to one of the Peck family's farms west of St. Charles, and finally (in 1908) to the farm in Wasco where he lived for the rest of his life. Solomon and Alex Johnson, both of whom were still bachelors at the time, purchased the Rice farm in the northwest quarter of Section 23 on 12 February 1908. The Rices had been on the Johnson brothers' property since the early 1850s.

Beginning in 1908, Solomon Johnson often "entertained the [Wasco] History club" at his home. He traveled to Minnesota and Iowa to purchase livestock beginning at that time as well. Upon moving to California to be with their daughter, James Rice gave his favorite rocking chair to Solomon upon his departure, telling the young Mr. Johnson that he was confident that "a lazy man [would not] sit in it."

The five Johnson siblings, in the 1890s - John, Mathilda ("Tillie"), Alec, Emma, and Solomon

On Thanksgiving Day, 1909, Alex Johnson of Wasco married Ellen Rasmussen of St. Charles. The wedding took place in Geneva, and the newlyweds enjoyed a ten-day-long honeymoon in Wisconsin. They then returned to Wasco to make their home. The 1910 census shows that Alex (who was just as often listed as Alec) and Ellen were aged twenty-eight and twenty-three then, and were living on the Johnson brothers farm. He was a general farmer, and his brother Solomon (who was then still single) was listed as a cattle buyer. Their mother Mary Johnson, aged sixty-six, was in the household with them. Also in the household was John Burgeson, a fifty-year-old farm laborer from Sweden. Throughout the 1910s, Alex Johnson (sometimes accompanied by his wife, such as in October 1913) traveled back and forth to locations such as Iowa and Nebraska to purchase stock.

Solomon Johnson married Fern Lillian Bell (see "The Bell Family") in Kane County on 3 June 1911. Fern was born in Campton Township on 7 April 1886. Rev. D. F. Bent of Elgin

Fern Bell Johnson, in the 1910s

performed the ceremony, which was held in the Bell home. Fern had her namesake plant in her bouquet, and the groom wore a boutonniere of Solomon's Seal on his lapel. The married couple took a trip by automobile (rare in 1911) to Wisconsin and New York and moved onto the Johnson farm upon their return. The couple lived their entire married lives on their farm (formerly the Rice farm) on the west side of Wasco. Fern worked for the Chicago Telephone Company at the time of her marriage. She was interested in history and genealogy. Fern was active in the Wasco Baptist Church, the Whitney Cemetery, and Wasco Ladies Aid. She enjoyed reading and had an extensive library which she generously shared with friends and neighbors alike.

Fourth of July celebration, 1917, with Solomon and Fern Johnson, Vesta Bell, and other local residents

In 1920, the Johnson brothers were listed in separate households in the census, though one was enumerated immediately after the other. It seems likely that they were separately occupying the two homes they owned, nearly across the street from one another, on the west side of town. Alex and Ellen had two young children then: Willis, who was aged nine; and Frances, who was aged four. Solomon and Fern Johnson had one son, Ellis, who was then aged six.

In 1930, the Johnson brothers were still living in separate, but nearby, homes. Solomon and Fern were aged fifty-three and forty-three, and were living with both of their children, Ellis (already mentioned) and Ethel (who was born in 1921). Alex and Ellen were living with their three children: Willis, Frances, and Raymond (who was born in 1923). Willis was working on the farm, and the other children were attending school that year.

The 1939 Elgin Rural Route Directory listed Solomon and Fern Johnson were taking their "mail at Wasco, P. O. Box 109." Their phone number was St. Charles 4084-W-1. He was a cattle dealer, living a quarter-mile west of Wasco, and he owned one hundred acres of land. Alex Johnson's listing was the same, but his phone number was St. Charles 4084-R-1, his residence was listed as a half-mile west of Wasco, and his occupation was given as "dealer in live stock." The 1940 census shows that Solomon and Fern Johnson were then living with children Ellis Ray and Ethel Bell. Ellis was listed as a farmer, and Ethel had then completed two years of college. Alex and Ellen's daughter Frances was then working as a private secretary, while Willis and Raymond were both working on the farm. Since Solomon's house was valued at $3000 and his brother's was valued at $2000, it seems likely that Solomon was living in the house on the south side of Route 64, and Alex in the house on the north, with their respective families.

Ellis Johnson and his first cousin, Frances Johnson, about 1920, outside of the House of the Seven Gables in Wasco

In June 1940, Fern (Bell) Johnson was one of the principal organizers of the Ward family reunion. The reunion, which was for descendants of Dayton Ward, was held on the sixteenth of that month at the Elburn Forest Preserve, and included relatives from Ohio, Wyoming, Iowa, and Illinois. Mrs. Johnson stayed in close touch with several Ward relatives over the years. In early July 1944, for example, Solomon and Fern Johnson and their children Ellis and Ethel attended the silver wedding anniversary celebration for Mr. and Mrs. Stephen Ward, in Aurora. Solomon Johnson passed away on 2 June 1963, and his widow died just over four months later, on 14 October. They were survived by one son, Ellis R. Johnson of Wasco, one daughter, Ethel (Johnson) Paetz of Florida, and three grandchildren. The Johnsons are buried in the Whitney Cemetery.

Ellis Ray Johnson was born in Wasco on 19 September 1913. In 1920, Ellis was living with his parents and with a hired man (a farm laborer from New York), Charles Kinney. Ellis Johnson graduated from Wasco School on 27 May 1927, and then attended St. Charles High School. In the 1930s, Ellis used post office box #109 in Wasco. In 1940, he and his sister Ethel were living with their parents in Wasco. Ellis Johnson was listed as a farmer that year. Ellis married Frances Davis in DeKalb County on 6 December 1941, the day before the infamous Japanese attack on Pearl Harbor, Hawaii. Frances (Davis) Johnson, daughter of Walter and Ida Davis of DeKalb, was born in Maple Park, Kane County, Illinois, on 9 April 1916. They lived on the Brown farm off of Burlington

Ellis Johnson of Wasco, about 1927

Road for a few years just after they were married. In March 1944, Ellis and Frances Johnson moved into their 'new' home on the old farm (see "Some Wasco Houses – Northwest Quarter"). In the 1950s, Ellis Johnson was a member of the District 303 School Board. Ellis and Frances had one daughter, who was an important contributor to this work.

Frances Johnson died at Community Hospital, Geneva, on 28 November 1977. She and her husband had been living in the "new" Johnson house on the south side of Route 64 since 1974. In July 1987, Ellis Johnson's childhood home, the historic "House of Seven Gables" built in the winter of 1872-73 by the Rice family, and purchased by Ellis' father and uncle in 1908, was destroyed by fire. Ellis Johnson lived next door at the time of the fire, and still owned the property, which was being rented to Ronald Dayton. The Dayton family was in Wisconsin when the fire occurred. Ellis R. Johnson passed away at Delnor Community Hospital on 7 November 1991, at the age of seventy-eight. A bit more than a decade later, Ellis Johnson Lane, located on his family's former farm, was named in his honor.

Ellis and Frances Johnson at their wedding, December 1941

Ellis Johnson had one sister, Ethel Bell Johnson, who was born on 25 January 1921. Ethel attended Wasco School, St. Charles High School, and the University of Illinois. She taught English, foreign language, and drama in Big Rock High School in the late 1930s and early 1940s. Ethel married Martin Charles Paetz on 6 October 1944, in Campton Township. He was at Fort Benning, Georgia, until the end of World War II. In 1949 the Paetzes lived in Plano, Illinois. They later moved to Florida, where she passed away on 14 July 1983.

Alex Johnson's wife Ellen was born in Wayne Township, DuPage County, Illinois, on 19 September 1887. Her father, Peter Rasmussen, was a Danish immigrant. The family later moved to a farm "near St. Charles" and then to the village, where they ran the St. Charles Hotel. After Ellen married Alex in 1909, she moved to the family farm in Wasco. They were there until 1942, when her husband retired from farming. They moved to St. Charles at that time. There were three children, all of whom attended Wasco School. The only daughter, Frances Johnson, was born on 25 June 1915. Ellen Johnson died at her home on South Third Street, St. Charles, on 19 January 1960. She was survived by seven grandchildren, and was buried in the North Cemetery in St. Charles.

Willis Johnson, the oldest child of Alex and Ellen, was born in Wasco in 1910. He attended Wasco School, and lived on his parents' farm for his childhood. He broke his leg in January 1927 while driving cattle near Lily Lake. He broke his right arm that August, while cranking an automobile. Willis saw the Stock Show in Chicago in December 1929. In 1930 he was living at home with his parents and two younger siblings; that year he worked as a farm laborer. In November 1930, Willis sprained his wrist badly while cranking a tractor. He attended four years of high school. He took a two-week trip to the "Eastern States" in August 1932. Willis was still living on the Wasco farm in 1940, with the same occupation. In fact, Willis remained there until the winter of 1961, when he and his wife and their son moved to Monticello, Iowa, where they bought a rest home and ran the business. Willis' brother Raymond then moved into the Johnson farmhouse with his family. In September 1959, a large tree "crashed through two ceilings" of the Willis Johnson farmhouse during a major storm in the area. Willis was married in the early 1940s – his wife Willa Mae (née Loop) was from Hopkinton, Iowa. The family lived in Delaware, Iowa, in 1974. Willis passed away in 1991, and Willa Mae died in 2000.

Ellis and Frances Johnson in the 1940s

Frances Johnson, daughter of Alex, married Andrez P. ("Pete") Ackerlund in the mid-1940s. Frances had been working for Hawley Products in St. Charles since at least 1935, and she met her future husband through work. Pete was vice-president of Hawley Products Company in 1950, when the family lived at #624 McKinley Avenue in Geneva. They lived at #908 North Third Avenue in St. Charles in 1956 and 1960. Frances (Johnson) Ackerlund later moved to Sun City, Arizona, where she lived in the early 1990s. She passed away in St. Charles on 2 April 2008, at the age of ninety-two.

Frances Johnson (left) with her friend Jewel Brown

Raymond Johnson, the youngest of Alex and Ellen Johnson's three children, was born in Wasco on 3 April 1923. He was a farm laborer in 1940, when he was still living at home. He was attending high school that year. Raymond moved to St. Charles with his family during the Second World War, and farmed with his brother Willis for several years. Raymond married Dorothy Dallesasse, and they had three children: Bruce, Janet, and Susan Johnson. Raymond worked for the City of St. Charles for fourteen years and worked part time for St. Charles Township for four years. He passed away in Manchester, Iowa, on 25 August 1992 and was buried in Union Cemetery, St. Charles. He was survived by six grandchildren and three great-grandchildren.

On 3 January 1940, John M. Johnson died at the Community Hospital in Geneva. He was a brother of Solomon and Alex Johnson, and was sixty-five years old. He had been in poor health for some time. He was a member of Bethlehem Lutheran Church in St. Charles. John was also survived by a sister, Emma (Johnson) Hawkins of Wasco, and two nephews, but John had no children of his own. His funeral was conducted in Geneva, and his burial took place in the North Cemetery in St. Charles.

Aerial view of the Solomon Johnson farm, looking southeast, likely 1960s

The Johnson brothers had two sisters – Emma, who married Joel Hawkins (see "The Hawkins Family"), and Mathilda, known as "Tillie" to her immediate family members. Mathilda Johnson was born in Sweden in April 1875 and came to the United States in 1883. By 1910, Tillie Johnson, already a widow, was living with her brother John M. Johnson in St. Charles Township. Tillie was aged thirty-five and listed no occupation. Her brother was a dairy farmer. She was still living with John in 1920. Their mother Mary Johnson was also in the household. Mathilda was then aged forty-four and was also living with her only son Arthur Johnson who was then nineteen years old (Arthur was listed as aged ten in the previous census, when he was living with his mother and uncle). In 1930, Mathilda Johnson was a housekeeper, and was living with John Peterson of Campton Township. She moved into her own newly-built home in 1935 (see" Some Wasco Houses – Southeast Quarter"). Mathilda Johnson died in 1964 and is buried in the North Cemetery, St. Charles.

Isak Arthur Johnson (who was always known by his middle name) was born in Chicago on 2 May 1900. He was baptized at Geneva Lutheran Church on 26 October of that year. Arthur's father, Amandus Johnson, died when he was quite young. Art Johnson lived with his mother and uncle in St. Charles Township during his youth. He married Dora Nagel in Kane County on 25 July 1923. He and Dora moved to Wasco in the spring of 1927, when they purchased Anders Lofgren's home (see "Some Wasco Houses – Southeast Quarter"). Art Johnson was an auctioneer, and lived in St. Charles in the late 1940s and 1950s. They had two sons, Wesley and Kenneth Johnson.

Wesley A. Johnson, for whom the American Legion Post in Wasco was named, was born in St. Charles Township on 24 July 1924. His parents were Art and Dora Johnson of St. Charles. In January 1930, Wesley Johnson contracted whooping cough but recovered. Art Johnson's mother, Mathilda Johnson, had been living in Wasco since 1935. Wes graduated from St. Charles High School, and was a World War II veteran, "having seen service with the Troop Carrier Command in the Asiatic Theatre of operations." Wes Johnson married Elaine B. Andersen, who was born on 1 May 1926. In 1946, Wes and Elaine began occupying "their home in Wasco . . . which was vacated by the Gordon Swansons" the previous month. Johnson had just been discharged from Camp McCoy. In February 1948, Wesley Johnson purchased the "Frances-Mayme" grocery store in the Hummel Building from Frances and Mayme Anderson, who had operated it for the previous nine years. The store's grand re-opening was held on Saturday, 14 February 1948, at which refreshments were served. The store was called "Johnson's Cash Store" in newspaper advertisements. Wesley Johnson sold the grocery and market to Mr. and Mrs. D. E. Keiser of Geneva in January 1949.

Art Johnson as a boy - he is standing in front of his uncle's house in Wasco

Art Johnson, Auctioneer, advertisement from 1936

Wes Johnson re-enlisted in the U. S. Armed Forces during the Korean Conflict in the early 1950s. He began working as a State Trooper for Illinois State Police District 2 in Elgin shortly afterward. In December 1964, the Wesley Johnson family moved into their new house on Route 64, west of Wasco. Wesley A. Johnson, a past commander of the Wasco American Legion Post and of the Kane County American Legion, was fatally injured in an automobile accident on Route 47 near Elburn in May 1975. He was survived by his wife, his parents, two sons, a daughter, and two grandchildren. He was a member of St. Mark's Lutheran Church of St. Charles, the St. Charles Moose Lodge, the Elburn Lions Club, and the Fraternal Order of Police.

Wes Johnson with friends (including Ray Johnson and Marilyn Swanson) on his sixth birthday

Wes and Elaine Johnson, at the time of their marriage

Elaine and Wes Johnson at their store in Wasco, 1949

Kenneth Johnson, who was a Commander of the Wasco Post in 1960-61

The George Brown Family

George I. Brown, longtime Campton Township Assessor, was born on 24 May 1870 in Elbridge, Onondaga County, New York. He was a son of Samuel A. and Maria L. Brown. George came to Illinois at the time of his second marriage, and was a dairy farmer by occupation. The 1910 census shows him as aged thirty-nine, and his wife Lottie as aged thirty-five. Two sons from George's first marriage were in the household then: John K. Brown (aged five); and Arthur E. Brown (aged two). By 1920, sons "Jay" K. and Arthur remained in the household, and their younger half-brother George S. Brown as aged eight. The boys all attended Wasco School that year. Beginning in 1924, George I. Brown was elected as Campton Township's Assessor, an office he would hold for more than twenty years. In 1930, George listed his occupation as carpenter. His twenty-two-year-old son Arthur worked as a railroad carpenter that year, and was the only child remaining in the household.

On 24 May 1909, at "high noon," Lottie Stevens of Wasco married George Brown of Sennett, New York, at her parents' home, in a "very pretty and impressive wedding" which boasted over one hundred and twenty guests. Lottie's father, D. W. Stevens (see "The Stevens Family") was very well known in the region. At that time, Lottie was "a trained nurse"; for several years prior to her marriage, she had a "very successful service in Oak Park." She was a member of the Wasco Baptist Church, and throughout her life she had striven for "the betterment of the community" of Wasco. The bride wore a white satin dress and carried a large bouquet of white roses. The wedding's color scheme was pink and white, which "constituted the decorations everywhere." Rev. T. L. Ketman of Chicago, formerly a pastor at Wasco, performed the wedding ceremony. Miss Mildred Stevens, the bride's niece, played the piano during the wedding; Lottie's brother John Stevens "very ably acted in the capacity of master of ceremonies." Harold and Marion Stevens were the ring bearers.

George Brown had once worked as a teacher, but was a farmer at the time of his marriage to Lottie. The "happy couple departed for their home in Sennett" the day after their wedding. That morning, the Wasco Ladies Aid hosted a large breakfast with over one hundred in attendance. An issue of the *St. Charles Chronicle* from 3 December 1909 stated that George Brown and his family "from New York" had just come to Wasco "to make their home. Mrs. Brown was formerly Lottie Stevens." Lottie Stevens was very ill with a case of scarlet fever in the winter of 1907, and only returned home to Wasco after a five-week-long stay in the city of Chicago. In 1918, George I. and Lottie Brown were tenants on the 170-acre "Home Acres" farm owned by the Bergland family just east of Wasco. There were three children in the Brown household then: Keith, Arthur, and George Brown Jr.

George I. Brown traveled to the East Coast with his brother for three weeks in January 1927 and took a trip to Florida in November 1933. Three years later, he was hospitalized in Elgin for an extended period. The cause of the hospitalization a broken leg suffered when falling from a scaffold on the Bergland farm south of Wasco. He and his son Arthur had been doing work on a new barn there at the time of the accident, which occurred in October 1936. George visited his brother in Syracuse, New York, in November 1939. George Brown died in Kane County on 30 September 1946, and is buried in the Whitney Cemetery, beside his wife Lottie, who died on 21 May 1955. Lottie was a charter member of the Wasco Baptist Church. She was survived by three sons and nine grandchildren. Lottie's son Keith was a resident of Philadelphia, but sons Arthur and George remained in Wasco. See "Some Wasco Houses – Northwest Quarter" for further information on the Browns.

The Stevens Family

DeVolois W. Stevens, mentioned earlier in this work, was a leader in Wasco for most of his long life. Floyd Bergland wrote on Mr. Stevens' 100th birthday that "He has held every town office and has been most active in the local Baptist Church, which he helped build. Now he is feeble of body but still clear of mind. . . He still enjoys visiting with his friends and talking about his active and happy life." At that time (March 1943) Mr. Stevens was the only surviving member of Elgin G. A. R. Post #49. By 1941, he was the last survivor of Company G, 122nd New York Infantry, and was then the oldest settler in Campton Township. Stevens had twenty-four grandchildren and twenty-one great-grandchildren at that time.

During his 100th birthday celebration, D. W. Stevens told a *Chicago Tribune* reporter that "I'm going to keep on living until I help put the Republicans back in office." Stevens had been a Republican since the 1860s, served Campton Township as Supervisor, Assessor, Highway Commissioner, and School Trustee, unfailingly as a member of the G.O.P. In 1943 he also hoped to see World War II end, and discussed the difference between artillery of the Civil War and the then-current conflict with his grandson, Private John E. Stevens.

An 1860s photograph (CDV) of D. W. Stevens, later of Wasco

D. W. Stevens' great-grandfather was a captain in the Revolutionary War, and took part in the Boston Tea Party. His grandfather was a Colonel in the War of 1812. D. W. himself was born in Onondaga County, New York, and was a son of John and Catherine Stevens. He enlisted in Company G, 122nd New York Infantry, when he was nineteen. He took part in the battles of Fredericksburg, Antietam, the Wilderness, Gettysburg, and Williamsport, among many others. Not long after his discharge from the U. S. Army, D. W. and his wife Amelia moved to Campton Township. They had eight children and many grandchildren.

Amelia Stevens was called "the champion tomato raiser" in Wasco in 1889, when she grew a tomato weighing fully 1 ½ pounds! On 18 August 1907, when the Stevenses celebrated their forty-fifth wedding anniversary, they had no fewer than thirty-seven children, grandchildren, and nieces and nephews come visit them at their home near Wasco. The date corresponded with their youngest son Pary Stevens's seventh anniversary.

Fred C. Stevens, a son of D. W., moved away from Campton Township in March 1903. At that time, he relocated to his farm in Wisconsin. A farewell party was given for Fred and his wife Lulu (née Babbitt) in Wasco on the twenty-third of that month. Because it was a very stormy evening, attendance was lower than anticipated. Fred and Lulu were married in Kane County in November 1900. D. W. Stevens's sister from Syracuse, New York, visited him in Wasco in December 1905. In August 1913, D. W. Stevens returned to Wasco after a two-month stay with relatives in New York State.

D. W. Stevens of Wasco, visiting his regiment's monument at Gettysburg, Pennsylvania, 1930s

Fred Cornelius Stevens, who was a carpenter in the Wasco area for many years, later moved back to Kane County. He died in Elgin in September 1937, at the age of sixty. Fred was a member of the Wasco Baptist Church, Elgin Lodge 799 Loyal Order of the Moose, and the Modern Woodmen of America. He was survived by his father, three daughters, a son, and four grandchildren. Fred's immediate family lived in Elgin, but one of his three sisters (Mrs. George Brown) remained in Wasco. Fred's father D. W. Stevens died at the Stevens home in Wasco on 8 July 1943, at the age of one hundred. He was survived by two sons and three daughters, twenty grandchildren, and thirty-two great-grandchildren. DeVolois W. Stevens had been in failing health for the past several years prior to his death.

D. W. Stevens was born in Weedsport, Cayuga County, New York, and was a son of John A. and Catharine Stevens, both of whom were New York natives. D. W. married Amelia M. Hayden in New York State on 18 August 1862. They had a total of eight children. Of these, his daughter Lottie H., who married George I. Brown, was most associated with Wasco (see "The George Brown Family"). D. W. came to Campton Township in 1866, soon after the conclusion of the Civil War; his father had come to the township the previous year. His family farm was located on the south side of the present Silver Glen Road, east of Denker. He owned 148 ½ acres of land in 1892. Amelia (Hayden) Stevens died in 1923. Wasco schools were dismissed early on D. W.'s centennial birthday so that the sixty-some boys and girls there could sing to him. A radio dramatization of several events of his life was given on WLS on the evening of the 27th of March 1943. D. W. Stevens is buried in the Whitney Cemetery.

The Mather Family

Arnold Gylfe Mather of Wasco married Grace Bolcum of Campton Township at the home of the bride's parents, on Sunday, 4 April 1909. The Bolcum house was "prettily decorated in green and white, and a dainty lunch was served, following the ceremony." Only the immediate families were present at the wedding. Rev. McKittrick of the St. Charles Methodist Episcopal Church performed the ceremony. After a short honeymoon, the couple was to "reside in a cottage which the groom has recently purchased of Geo. Bergland" (see "Some Wasco Houses – Northeast Quarter"). At the time of the marriage, Grace Bolcum had worked for Peterson & Company for five years, and had "proved herself a most efficient clerk." Arnold Mather was then a manager of the Wasco Creamery for Sidney Wanzer & Sons of Chicago.

The gifts at the wedding "were many and beautiful." After starting a family, Mather began a new career following the First World War. In 1923, Arnold Mather sold McCormick-Deering Farm Machines.

Grace (Bolcum) Mather, with her sons Robert and Howard, in their Wasco home

Arnold Mather was born on 12 December 1872 in Finström, in the Åland Islands off the coast of Finland, and was a son of Karl Johan and Emilia Mether. The island on which Arnold was born is in the Gulf of Bothnia, about halfway between the mainland of Sweden and Finland, though it belonged to the latter nation. Mather arrived in the United States on 7 June 1902, at the age of twenty-nine. He was naturalized as a U. S. citizen on 7 February 1912, in Geneva. He worked for Sidney Wanzer & Sons Dairy for more than twenty years. In 1910, his position was "creamery foreman" and in 1918 and 1920 he was a creamery manager. The specific creamery that he managed was located on East 30th Street in Chicago. His World War I draft card mentions that he had blue eyes, sandy hair, was of medium height and build, and had a crippled right foot. For his first five years in the country, he lived in Chicago, and then moved to Wasco. Arnold was a member of the First Methodist Episcopal Church of St. Charles. His wife Grace was born in Plano, Kendall County, Illinois, on 31 March 1880. In November 1917, while the First World War raged, Grace was a representative of the Fox River Chapter of the American Red Cross. She was very involved in both fundraising and advocacy efforts during the war years.

On 1 May 1923, Arnold G. Mather purchased some property immediately east of his home from Harriet Austin. The purchase price was $10, and the sixty-six-foot-wide lot was vacant at the time. Mather passed away on 23 December 1936, at the age of sixty-four, following a severe heart attack. He was survived by his wife and their three sons: Robert Bolcum Mather (who married Nora Luther, and who lived in Chicago at the time of his father's death); Howard Arnold Mather (of Lombard, and later of Montgomery); and Lee Foch Mather (who married Mildred Northrup, and who lived in Wasco). Each of the Mather boys had one daughter.

Arnold Mather and his three sons, in 1923

The Mather boys by their home in Wasco, May 1924

Arnold Mather was an avid stamp collector and happily shared his hobby with his neighbor's son, George C. Bergland, who soon followed Mather in philately. Arnold's son Lee and his friend Lester Swanson were also interested in stamp collecting, as evidenced by their visit to a stamp collection display in Elgin in April 1937. Arnold G. Mather's funeral was held on 26 December 1936, at the family home in Wasco. Pall bearers were Elmer Peterson, Charles Ekstrom, Carl Meissner, Harry Marvin, Andrew Erickson, and Otto Karschnick. Rev. Robert Stephenson preached the funeral sermon, and vocalists at the funeral were Morris Whitney and Mrs. Robert B. Mather. Hymns sung at the service were "Beautiful Isle of

Somewhere" and "Going Home." Burial was in the Whitney Cemetery. Grace Mather died in Community Hospital, Geneva, on 1 September 1963.

Robert B. Mather was born in the family's new home in Wasco on 29 November 1909. During his early twenties, Robert was a machinist at their father's garage just steps west of the homestead. Robert Mather still lived in Kane County in 1938, but by 1940 he (along with his wife Nora and their young daughter) had moved to Ringslet, Emmett County, Iowa, where he worked as a salesman. Soon afterward, Robert worked for Babson Brothers, a catalog mail-order company in Chicago. He was employed by that firm for twenty-five years. In 1943, Robert and his family moved to Elgin. By the early 1950s, they were living on Gertrude Street in that city, and would stay there for many years. Robert B. Mather died in Harrisburg, Pennsylvania, on 6 January 1975. His wife Nora Matilda (Luther) Mather was born in Plato Township on 11 July 1912. She passed away in Ohio on 7 November 2001.

Howard A. Mather was born in Wasco on 18 June 1911. He attended Wasco School, and was a machinist at his father's garage in 1930. Howard married Margaret Elfreda Berg of St. Charles on 26 June 1935. At the wedding, the bride wore a white lace gown and carried a bouquet of white rosebuds and baby's breath. She carried a purse that belonged to Howard's grandmother, Mrs. C. W. Bolcum. Grace McWilliams was the Maid of Honor at the ceremony, and Robert Mather was Best Man. The groom's aunt, Mrs. Chester Bolcum, played the wedding march, while Elaine Ekstrom played "I Love You Truly" and "O Promise Me" on piano, accompanied by Dorothy Benson. Sixty friends and relatives attended the reception. Margaret Berg graduated from St. Charles High School and for the previous five years had taught elementary school at Wasco. Howard Mather worked for the Bowman Dairy Company. The couple moved to Lombard after their marriage. During the Second World War, Howard A. Mather served in the aviation branch of the U. S. Navy, and was stationed in the Aleutian Islands. He became an Aviation Machinist's Mate Second Class on 27 June 1943. The following December, while on leave, Howard met his brother Lee in San Francisco, and they drove home to Wasco for the Christmas holiday. Just after the war ended, Lee took over the management of the family's business while Howard got a job with the Clay Distributing Company in St. Charles. Howard Mather died on 19 July 1973 in Contra Costa, California.

Lee Mather of Wasco, circa 1944

Following his World War II service, Lee F. Mather of Wasco was a member of the National Association of Postmasters and the National League of District Postmasters of the United States. Lee was born on 18 January 1922, and married Mildred ("Millie") Northrop on 15 November 1947. Millie was born on 8 March 1926 and was a daughter of Merle and Nettie Northrup, and a granddaughter of Mr. and Mrs. James Roby of Wasco. Rev. Jesse T. Dodds officiated at the Mather-Northrop wedding. Millie graduated from Plato Center High School, and worked at Hawley Products in St. Charles. During the war Lee served in the U. S. Navy, on a submarine chaser the USS SC-1004, a ship which was built in California in 1942 and which was commissioned on 21 January 1943. Mather participated in the famous October 1944 Battle of Leyte Gulf, the largest naval conflict of World War II. Lee Mather was appointed acting Postmaster of Wasco in the summer of 1946 following the death of Floyd Bergland, who had held that job since 1924. Mather was Wasco's postmaster until 1949.

Mildred N. ("Millie") Mather in the 1940s

Lee Mather owned and operated the gas station and repair shop adjacent to the Mather store in Wasco, and was widely praised as an excellent mechanic. In December 1951, he was towing an auto transport truck and became stuck in the snow when crossing railroad tracks west of St. Charles. Mather put his World War II training "to good use" in the words of a newspaper article of the time, when he dove from the cab of his tow truck to avoid being struck by an oncoming eastbound train. Both he and the transport driver made it to safety and were unhurt. In 1964, the Mathers moved from the apartment above Lee's garage "to the home which was his mother's." An addition had been added to the back of the house, in which there was to be a kitchen and a family room. Lee ran the service station and store until exactly a week before his death, which occurred on 16 February 1992. Millie Mather, who helped Lee operate the service station for many years, was an active member of Wasco Ladies Aid and the American Legion Women's Auxiliary. Mildred and Lee had one daughter – Mary, who was a contributor to this work. Mildred N. Mather passed away in St. Charles on 7 June 1999 and is buried in Whitney Cemetery.

The Erickson Family

Andrew J. Erickson, the well-known Wasco blacksmith, was already working at his trade by June 1908. An article in the St. Charles *Valley Chronicle* from that time stated, under the heading of "Wasco News Items," that "Andrew Erickson, our thrifty and prosperous blacksmith here, and Grace Swanson, oldest daughter of Gust Swanson, were married in Rockford Saturday evening, June 20th. They will begin housekeeping at once in the rooms over the shop. They have the congratulations of friends, wishing them a prosperous and happy life." For information on Andrew and Grace Erickson see "Some Wasco Houses – Southeast Quarter," later in this work. The Ericksons had four children, one of whom (a daughter, Esther) died in infancy. The surviving children were Clayton, Harold, and Irma.

By the time he arrived in Wasco, Andrew Erickson had only been in the United States for a short time. He immigrated from Sweden via Liverpool, England, in April 1903, when he was twenty years old. Andrew John Erickson (whose father was named Eric Anderson) was born in Vatebo, Dalarnas län, Sweden, on 22 October 1882. He briefly lived in St. Charles before moving to Wasco (likely in 1906). Andrew married Grace H. Swanson in 1908 and their son Harold G. Erickson was born not long afterward. Grace was born in Lily Lake on 22 September 1891 and was the daughter of Gustav Herman and Ida Gertrude (Eddy) Swanson. The Ericksons moved into a house recently built by George Bergland (located just north of the store) in October 1909. Andrew J. Erickson became a U. S. citizen on 17 May 1911, when he was naturalized before the Kane County Circuit Court in Geneva. The family moved into their larger home just south of the Baptist Church in 1912.

Andrew was six feet tall, had a fair complexion, and had blue eyes and brown hair. He had a scar over the top of his left hand. The 1918 *Prairie Farmer's Directory of Kane County* lists Andrew Erickson as a blacksmith in Wasco, one of only three businesses listed in the village. He traveled to Sweden (to visit his mother and other relatives) during the winter of 1921-22 and returned to his home in Wasco in February of the latter year. He also visited Norway and Denmark during his travels. Erickson took out a newspaper ad in 1923, which stated that he did both "blacksmithing and horseshoeing" as well as welding. In 1930, the Ericksons had three children in the household: Harold (aged twenty-one); Clayton (aged twenty); and Irma (aged fourteen). Two lodgers were also in the household that year: Marshall Carlson, a painter; and Otto Olson, a blacksmith.

Andrew and Grace Erickson of Wasco, with their children Clayton, Harold, and Irma, in the early 1920s

Clayton V. Erickson was born in Wasco on 19 October 1909. Some sources give 1910 as his birth year, but this is incorrect, as he appears on the 1910 Campton Township census (taken that April) as a six-month-old infant. He was a salesman for a candy company in 1930, when he was still living at home. In 1931, he passed the examinations for the U. S. Navy and entered the Great Lakes Training Station. During his time in the Navy, Erickson was "one of the sailors called to duty in the big fire at Norfolk" in 1931. Clayton's closest friend in Wasco was Marshall ("Marsh") Carlson – they traveled together quite often in the late '20s and early '30s. On 29 October 1932, in San Diego, Clayton Erickson married Harriet Olaine. They moved to California immediately following their marriage. He and his wife then moved to Rockford by 1937, and remained there through the war and beyond. They had a son and a daughter, and they visited the family home in Wasco from time to time. Clayton Erickson died in Los Angeles, California, on 18 January 1968.

Irma Ruth Erickson, the youngest child of Andrew and Grace, was born in Wasco in December 1915. She was baptized at the Wasco Baptist Church, next door to her family's home. Like her older brothers, she attended the Wasco School. In 1930, Irma's brother Clayton Erickson was a salesman for a candy company. The oldest son, Harold, was a laborer. In 1931, Irma Erickson and two friends (Gordon Swanson and Frances Bloomquist) were returning home from having seen a show at the Arcada Theater in St. Charles, and ran into the Great Western railroad crossing signal in Wasco. The car stalled on the track, and shortly after the friends escaped the vehicle, the 9:15 passenger train crashed into it, leaving the car "a complete wreck." Although her father and mother had only completed eighth and seventh grades, respectively, Irma completed three years of high school (in St. Charles). In June 1935, Irma was badly injured while riding in an automobile with Joseph Anderson (a son of Simon Anderson, the founder of Colonial Ice Cream). Also in 1935, Irma Erickson was one of the nominees for the "Centennial Queen" contest to celebrate the hundredth year of Campton Township's settlement. When she was in her twenties, Irma worked ironing and pressing clothes; she began working in St. Charles in March 1937. She held a position with the Illinois Cleaners and Dyers in St. Charles in 1940. Irma Erickson moved away from Wasco in 1946, but frequently visited after that time.

Standing in this 1920s photograph are Margaret Burnell, Hedwig Peterson, Frances and Doryce Johnson, Jewel Brown, Irma Erickson, and Irene Austin. Seated are Blanche Allen, Faith Austin, and Mary Ellen Burr

Irma R. Erickson never married, and passed away on 19 September 2005, at Firwood Care Center in Batavia. She had lived there for ten years. Irma is well-remembered by long-time Wasco residents for her talent for baking – especially breads. Irma is buried with her family in the Whitney Cemetery.

Harold G. Erickson, Irma's brother, was born in Wasco on 17 August 1908. He worked at odd jobs and stayed at home through at least 1930. He worked in Rockford in 1928, and had a job with the Fuller Brush Company in 1935. Harold Erickson entertained the Dramatic Club at his home in the early 1930s, and traveled to Rockford fairly often to visit relatives. Harold moved to St. Charles by 1943. Later, he worked as a grave-digger and caretaker at the Whitney Cemetery. Harold G. Erickson lived in Geneva late in life, and died in Batavia on 27 June 1981. He is buried in the cemetery which he cared for.

Several of the same young ladies, in 1935. Gladys Bowgren (Queen) is seated second from right, with Jewel Brown at far right, Rita Ormond standing at center, and Faith Austin at far left, with Frances Johnson behind her

The Denker Family

Hugo Denker and his wife Frances (née Anderson) lived on a farm north of Wasco for most of their married life. Hugo was born in Chicago on 10 August 1892, and was a very tall man (6' 2"). His parents were Peter and Hilda (Svenson) Denker, both of whom were natives of Sweden. Peter, who was born in the village of Valinge on 13 August 1869, was a house carpenter, and immigrated to the U. S. in 1887. He married Hilda just four years later, on 26 September 1891, in Chicago, and was naturalized as a U. S. citizen in 1892. Hilda, whose maiden name is sometimes given as Swanson, was born in Sweden on 5 December 1869, and like her husband, immigrated as a teenager. The family lived in Chicago until the early years of the twentieth century. Peter and his brother Fred Denker (who immigrated in 1893) moved to Wasco in 1904. Fred was born in Sweden on 21 August 1876 and was a lifelong farmer. He lived with Peter throughout the 1910s and '20s, and never married. In 1918, the Denkers lived on the 207-acre "Homewood Farm" in Section 12, Campton Township.

The Denker farm was located on the west side of what is now Denker Road, reaching as far north as Silver Glen Road. Fred and Peter Denker "of the Township of Campton" purchased the property from Minerva, Paul, and Alice Warren on 29 October 1915 for $19,000. Peter and Hilda Denker celebrated their fiftieth anniversary with a large open house reception at their home. More than two hundred friends and relatives attended. A three-tier wedding cake was cut by their daughter-in-law and a buffet supper was served to members of the immediate family. Three grandchildren, Phyllis Denker, and Virginia and Owen Richmond, played a piano/violin piece for the honored guests. Prior to 1933, Peter Denker retired from the building/contracting business. After a lingering illness, Peter Denker passed away on his farm near Wasco on 23 January 1943. He was survived by his widow, two daughters, and a son, as well as by six grandchildren. There were also three siblings that survived him – a sister in Sweden, his brother Fred, and Mrs. Gust Anderson of Wasco. "Uncle" Fred Denker passed away on 30 August 1956 and is buried in the Garfield Cemetery.

After Peter Denker's death, Mrs. Hilda Denker moved to "town." She celebrated her seventy-seventh birthday at her home in Wasco in December 1946. A visitor was greeted on the occasion of Mrs. Denker's birthday by her daughter, "Miss Jennie Denker. . . formerly a teacher in the Geneva schools but [who] resigned this past year to take care of her mother." Mrs. Denker was born in Sweden, and was married in Chicago. She and her husband "later settled in Wasco where he was a contractor." The visitor (whose pseudonym was 'The Rambler') noted that "Mrs. Denker feels fortunate to have her two daughters . . . and one son living close to her home." She had six grandchildren – Peter and Phyllis Denker, and Virginia, Owen, Lowell, and Dean Richmond.

During World War I, Hugo Denker was a Private in Company C, 303rd Engineers. He was sent to France and returned to the United States via Bordeaux, sailing on 30 May 1919 aboard the U. S. S. Santa Olivia and arriving in Brooklyn on 10 June. He married Frances Anderson, one of CJ Anderson's eight daughters, in 1927. They had a daughter Phyllis Denker, who was born in Wasco in 1930, and a son Ralph Peter Denker, who was born four years later. Although the Denkers' property was known as "Homewood Farm" since the 1910s, Hugo and Fred Denker did not formally register this name with the state until May 1951. In 1957 or 1958, the Denkers moved to St. Charles. Hugo and Frances Denker, along with Jennie Denker and Amy (Denker) Richmond and her husband Frank, sold the Denker property to Betty W. Schmitz of Streamwood in February 1959. Hugo Denker was an active member of the Wasco American Legion Post. He lived at 103 N. Fourth Avenue in St. Charles at the time of his death, which occurred in Geneva on 5 June 1963. Like most of his family, Hugo Denker is buried in the Garfield Cemetery. He was survived by his widow, their daughter Phyllis (Denker) Turner, and their son R. Peter Denker.

On 20 April 1986, there was a large public antiques and collectibles auction at the American Legion building in Wasco. The items sold there belonged to Frances (Anderson) Denker and her daughter Phyllis. Frances had recently moved to a retirement home. Quite a bit of the furniture dated to the 1930s, but some was from the Victorian era or older. Frances Denker passed away on 28 August 1994, aged ninety-five.

Hugo had two younger siblings, Amy and Jennie Denker. Amy Denker was born in Chicago on 8 August 1894, and moved to the Wasco area with her parents when she was a child. Amy married Frank A. Richmond; they had a daughter and three sons. Frank was a builder in the area between the 1920s and 1960. He constructed milk sheds, barns, and houses in the area, including the home where he lived with his wife and their four children. Frank was born in Campton Township on 9 April 1888 and was its oldest continuous resident when he passed away on 16 May 1985. His parents were L. S. and Ella May (Flowers) Richmond; the family lived in Section 26, a mile and a half south of Wasco, where the Richmonds owned a seventy-acre farm. Frank

Amy Richmond, Elsie Schaefer, and Margaret Vanderhoof, as they appeared in the 1970s

fought in France during World War I and was a Corporal in the U. S. Army. He was later Clerk of the Wasco Consolidated School Board for fifteen years, and was a Trustee of the Kane County School Board. Amy was a member of the Wasco American Legion Auxiliary and she and her husband were members of Grace Lutheran Church of Lily Lake. She lived in the Wasco vicinity until 1978, when she moved to her daughter's home. Amy (Denker) Richmond passed away in Libertyville on 22 April 1979. She and Frank had four children, fourteen grandchildren, and six great-grandchildren. By the year 2000, only one of her four children remained in Illinois.

Jennie Denker was born in Chicago on 18 September 1895, and moved to the Wasco vicinity when quite young. She was confirmed at Grace Lutheran Church in Lily Lake in 1909. After graduating from high school, Jennie attended the DeKalb Teachers College for a time in the spring of 1931. She taught elementary school in Wasco, Elburn, and Geneva. She was an active teacher for more than thirty-five years. Jennie never married, and continued to live with her parents in the 1920s and '30s. She was an active member of Grace Lutheran Church, Lily Lake throughout her lifetime. She traveled throughout eastern Canada in September 1935. Jennie

Amy Denker of Wasco, about 1913

Denker was also active in Wasco's "Glad Game Club" in the 1940s. In May 1948, Jennie attended the annual meeting of the Rockford District Woman's Missionary Society, held in Batavia. Later in life, Jennie lived across the street from the Wasco Baptist Church. She moved to an apartment on Main Street in Batavia in November 1959. In the 1960s and later, she was active in the American Association of Retired Teachers. Jennie vacationed in Arizona in March 1961 and March 1968, and traveled to Freeport to see relatives in November 1971. She spent some time in Community Hospital, Geneva, after falling on some ice in January 1969. Jennie traveled to Iowa in October 1974 to visit the family of Dean Richmond. Jennie Denker passed away in Batavia on 18 June 1988, at the age of ninety-two. Her funeral services were held at Grace Lutheran Church, Lily Lake.

Amy's sister Jennie Denker, about 1913

Since their early childhood, John and Ella Olson, a nephew and niece of Peter and Hilda Denker, made their home with the Denker family. On 27 December 1941, Ella Olson married Evald Strom at the Denker home. Rev. John Melvin of Grace Lutheran Church performed the ceremony. Frances Denker played the wedding march. Ella's father, John Olson of Berwyn, was present. Jennie Denker was the Maid of Honor, and carried a bouquet of dark red roses. Allan Strom, the groom's brother, was Best Man. Ella had graduated from St. Charles High School and Northern Illinois Teachers College, and was a teacher in the Berwyn public schools. The groom,

R. Peter Denker, son of Hugo, in 1951

a graduate of Geneva High School, worked in the Lily Lake office of the Elburn Cooperative Company. The couple moved to Lily Lake immediately after their marriage. Ella (Olson) Strom was born on 14 August 1909, and passed away on 19 August 1969. Evald Strom died on 19 June 1981, at the age of seventy-two. Both are buried in the Lily Lake Cemetery.

In March 1960, Hugo Denker's son Ralph Peter, who was known by his middle name, moved "back to the farm where the Denkers made their home for so many years." He and his wife planned to have a large herd of dairy cows on the property as had been the case in the past. R. Peter Denker was born in Geneva on 7 June 1933, and graduated from St. Charles High School in 1951. R. Peter's father Hugo was recovering from surgery at Community Hospital, Geneva, soon after his son moved back to Campton Township. R. Peter Denker and his wife moved to Sterling, Illinois, in the late 1960s. They moved to Sauk City, Wisconsin, in the 1980s. Peter passed away in that locality on 6 September 2000.

The Bowgren Family

Oscar Emmanuel Bowgren was born in Sweden on 4 September 1880, and came to the United States with his parents as a child. His parents, Carl G. and Louisa Bowgren, left Västra Götaland, Sweden, in 1888. Most members of the Bowgren family settled in Geneva by 1891, and were members of the First Baptist Church there. Oscar began working for a piano factory nearby, and also engaged in farming. On 19 May 1904, Oscar Bowgren married Ida Skoglund. She was born in Småland, Sweden, on 24 April 1878, and was a daughter of Amandus and Caroline Skoglund. She came to the United States in 1886 and lived in New York for nine years before coming to Illinois.

After living in Geneva for a year after their marriage, Oscar and Ida Bowgren "decided to go farming and settled in Campton Township." They lived on what would later become the Jens and Christine Johnsen farm on Route 38, formerly owned by the Garfield family. Later the Bowgrens moved to New York State, where they farmed for eight years. They returned to Kane County in 1919. The Bowgrens rented the Alec Anderson farm in Campton Township in 1922 and 1923. They had six sons (Verner, Gordon, Stanley, Clifton, Hilton, and Charles) and one daughter (Gladys). Oscar died on 22 July 1936, as the result of an automobile accident. Ida Bowgren died in Geneva on 5 June 1950 (see "Some Wasco Houses – Northeast

Oscar Bowgren, around 1900

Quarter" for more information on the family). There were many members of the Bowgren family (Oscar had brothers Frank, John, Adolph, Otto, and Fritz), but most Bowgrens associated with Wasco are descended from Oscar and Ida. Bowgren Drive and Bowgren Circle in Campton Township (between Wasco and Elburn) were named for Oscar's brother Adolph, who moved there with his wife and family in the 1930s.

Oscar Bowgren's older brother August Wilhelm Bowgren is also associated with Campton Township, though not necessarily with Wasco. August worked for the U. S. Windmill Company of Batavia in the 1890s, and in 1903 he began farming. In March 1906, he moved onto the "Dick Garfield farm" on the present Route 38 and lived there with his large family for several years. August was born on 24 November 1868 in Skattegården, Västra Götaland, Sweden, and married Amanda Louisa Skoglund on 4 May 1895. Following August's death on 22 December 1914, the family moved to Geneva. In 1920, Amanda Bowgren was living with her three youngest daughters, Ruth, Alice, and Margaret. Amanda died at her daughter's house in St. Charles on 7 September 1936. She had lived in Geneva for the last twenty years of her life.

Ida Bowgren, around 1900. She and her husband would later settle in Wasco with their large family

Verner Bowgren, the oldest child of Oscar and Ida, was born in Campton Township on 2 July 1905 and grew up in Wasco. Verner was a farmer and was a member of the Wasco Baptist Church. He married Grace Patterson of Blackberry Township on 28 February 1936, in Geneva. They moved to her parents' farm near LaFox immediately following their marriage. Verner and Grace had two children, Ronald and Janice Bowgren. Later in life he was a Mason, and was a member of the Fox Valley Shriners. Verner and his family remained in LaFox for the rest of his life. The third annual Bowgren reunion was held at his home on 3 September 1944. Verner passed away on 16 May 1971 at his home in LaFox, and was survived by his wife, their two children, seven grandchildren, and his six siblings. Grace Bowgren passed away on her ninetieth birthday, 10 May 1999. She had ten great-grandchildren.

Gordon Allen Bowgren, the second child of Oscar and Ida, was born on 16 January 1907, and lived in Kane County throughout his life, with the exception of the time the family lived in New York State. Gordon was a tin cutter in a factory in 1930; he was living in Wasco with his parents and his four younger siblings at that time. In 1940, Gordon was a building carpenter, and was living at home in Wasco with his mother and two younger brothers. Gordon enlisted in the U. S. Navy on 14 January 1944. He enlisted in the city of Chicago, and was a Seaman 2nd Class by that spring. He was released from the service in October 1945. Gordon married Bernice L. Anderson of Geneva and was a member of the Geneva Lutheran Church and a charter member of the Wasco American Legion Post. Gordon and Bernice lived on Oakwood Drive in Geneva for thirty years. Gordon Bowgren passed away on 10 January 1978, following a long illness. He was survived by three children and three grandchildren, in addition to five siblings.

Stanley Oscar Bowgren, the third son of Oscar and Ida, was born on a farm on Route 38 in Campton Township on 24 June 1909. He attended Wasco School, and began working as a hired hand on area farms as a young man. Stan worked for Operadio in St. Charles for a short time, and met his future wife "at a farm dance." Stan Bowgren married Nina E. Williams on 5 June 1937, in St. Charles. They lived in an apartment over the State Bank in St. Charles until 1938, and then moved to Wasco.

Stan and Nina lived in Wasco for nearly all of their married life, and were active members of the Wasco Baptist Church. Stan served as a deacon there for many years. Both Stan and Nina were employed by St. Charles School District 303 for decades. Nina was a cook at the Wasco grade school and later worked at Denny's Den in Wasco. She and Stan had a son Terry (who was a contributor to this work), six grandchildren, and seven great-grandchildren. The Bowgrens raised cattle and chickens on their farm in Wasco, and delivered eggs throughout the region. Stan Bowgren retired in 1980; he passed away on 1 December 1995, at the age of eighty-six. Nina was born on 8 August 1915, and graduated from the school at Mooseheart. Her first job was with Operadio in St. Charles (now DuKane). She enjoyed gardening, traveling, crossword puzzles, sports, knitting, Bingo, dancing, crocheting, and (most of all) enjoying time with her family. She was a member of the Wasco Baptist Church, and Wasco Ladies Aid, and passed away at the age of ninety-one on 27 July 2007.

Clifton Alfred Bowgren, fourth child of Oscar and Ida, was born in the family's home on Route 38 in Campton Township on 15 May 1911. After graduating from St. Charles High School in 1930, Clifton worked for the Hawley Hat Factory in St. Charles. He took part in races at The Farm in the fall of 1934. In February 1936, he had his hand "badly burned when it became caught in the hat shaping machine." Clifton Bowgren attended the Century of Progress World's Fair in Chicago in October 1933. He and his brother Charles started Bowgren Trucking Company in the late 1930s. He was listed as an employee of The Farm in 1937, and as a truck driver in the 1940 census, when he was living at home with his mother and two brothers. Soon after his marriage to Jewel Brown, Cliff moved to his father-in-law's property just west of Wasco; he was there beginning in 1941. Cliff also farmed with his brother-in-law, John L. Brown. In May 1961, he entertained his brothers and sister and their spouses on his fiftieth birthday. The party was held at The Farm. Much later Cliff joined the real estate firm of Brannigar & Associates; he retired from that firm in May 1978. He was the chairman of the program committee of the LaFox Farmers Club in the early 1960s, and hosted that group many times in the 1960s and 1970s. Cliff Bowgren was appointed as an auditor on the Campton Town Board in 1972, the same year he obtained his real estate license. He was also a member of the Wasco Baptist Church, and was Superintendent of Garfield Cemetery (see "The Bert Brown Family for further

Stanley Bowgren outside of the family home in Wasco, 1930s

information on Clifton and his wife, Jewel (Brown) Bowgren). Clifton passed away at Delnor Community Hospital in Geneva on 5 November 1992. He was survived by his daughters Gay, Jan, and Joy, and eleven grandchildren.

Clifton and Jewel Bowgren's house at The Farm, about 1940

Fifth in the family of Oscar and Ida was Hilton Russell Bowgren, who was born on 16 July 1912 in Campville, Tioga County, New York. Hilton was close friends with Ellis Johnson of Wasco, and they traveled together to Chicago, Crystal Lake, and many nearby locations in the early 1930s. Hilton's brother Stanley took many trips with him during the Depression as well, such as to Detroit in July 1931. During the Kane County Centennial celebration in June 1936, Hilton Bowgren performed as a square dancer in the pageant "Milestones," performed in Geneva. Hilton married Margaret J. Dillenbach in October 1938, and they moved to Hinkley, DeKalb County, Illinois soon after their marriage. The 1940 census shows them living on a farm in Squaw Grove Township. After Margaret's death, Hilton married Anne Marie Watne. Hilton was an active member of St. Paul's United Church of Christ of Hinckley, and enjoyed golfing during his free time. Hilton died on 27 July 2003, and was survived by two sons (Jim and Dennis) and a stepdaughter (Christine) and four grandchildren.

Stanley and Nina Bowgren on their wedding day, in 1937

The 1943 Bowgren family reunion was held in Wasco, at the Judith Richmond house. Pictured are Adolph, August, Anna, and John Bowgren, with an unknown attendee, and Anna, Hulda, Ida, and Otto Bowgren

The Bowgren family in the 1940s. Clifton, Stanley, Babe, and Verner in the rear, with Hilton, Ida, Gladys, and Gordon in front

Charles Kenneth Bowgren was the youngest child in the family, and was known as "Babe" for most of his life. He was born in Geneva on 2 June 1920, but moved to Wasco with his family when he was an infant. He attended Wasco School, and in 1935-1936 Babe (who was 5' 11" tall) played on the undefeated Wasco basketball team. After graduating from Plato High School in 1939, he got a job as a laborer in an auto accessories facility. Babe Bowgren enlisted in the U. S. Marine Corps in 1943 as a Private First Class. On

13 February 1946, Charles Bowgren married Elizabeth Mary Weitl in Geneva. Her family lived on property that is now part of Pheasant Run Lodge in St. Charles. In May 1956, Charles Bowgren of Wasco applied to change the name of his trucking business from "Bowgren Brothers" to "Charles Bowgren." At the time he was transporting farm products, livestock, feeds, and coal within a fifty-mile radius of Wasco. Babe's brother Clifton left the business at that time. In 1959, the phone number for Charles Bowgren Trucking was "St. Charles 2110." Babe and Elizabeth were active in the LaFox Farmers Club in the 1960s and later. Elizabeth, who was an active member of the Wasco American Legion Auxiliary Post, started Bowgren Realty early that decade. She passed away on 21 August 1975, and was survived by six sons and a daughter. In May 1985, an auction/moving sale was held at Babe Bowgren's house at the corner of Route 64 and Snowbird Court, a mile west of Wasco. He then moved to St. Charles, where he spent the rest of his life. Charles K. Bowgren died in St. Charles on 27 June 2007.

In September 1964, many Bowgrens attended the Silver Anniversary celebration of John and Gladys (Bowgren) Olson of Wasco. The event was held at Grace Lutheran Church in Lily Lake, and was attended by some three hundred guests. Glady's brother Clifton, who was Best Man at the wedding, assisted in welcoming guests. Gladys's niece Gay Bowgren poured at the tea table, while another niece, Jan Bowgren served the cake. Joan and Joy Bowgren of Wasco attended the punch table. Beverly Bowgren of Geneva, a niece and goddaughter of the Olsons, circulated the guest book.

Clifton and Jewel (Brown) Bowgren's daughter Jan Rae Bowgren was born in St. Charles on 29 September 1945. She and her two sisters grew up in Wasco. Jan was an elementary school teacher, and married Stephen Cole. They moved to Texas, where Jan passed away on 28 November 1998. Clifton A. Bowgren was born in Campton Township on 15 May 1911, when his family lived on the Dick Garfield farm. He graduated from St. Charles High School, and not long afterward he and his brother Charles ("Babe") started the Bowgren Trucking Company. He married Jewel Brown in Wayne on 26 June 1940. For a time Bowgren farmed with his brother-in-law, John L. Brown, in Wasco. Later, Clifton joined a real estate firm, and was involved in the development of the Windings subdivision. He was a member of the LaFox Farmers' Club, the Wasco Baptist Church, and was Superintendent of Garfield Cemetery. Clifton Bowgren was struck by a car near his home, and died of his injuries two days later, on 5 November 1992, at Delnor Community Hospital in Geneva. Jewel A. Bowgren passed away on 10 February 2008, at the age of ninety-two, after falling ill at her daughter's home in South Carolina.

Jewel and Clifton Bowgren, around 1940

The last surviving sibling in the Bowgren family, Gladys Carolina (Bowgren) Olson passed away in Batavia on 11 July 2014, at the age of ninety-five. Gladys was born in New York State on 18 August 1918, and was the only girl in a family of seven children. Her parents returned to Wasco when she was quite young. She attended Wasco School and graduated from St. Charles High School in 1935. She sang in the choir and was a Sunday School teacher at Grace Lutheran Church, Lily Lake. She was a bookkeeper for Operadio in St. Charles, and also worked for Bergland & Company in Wasco. In 1967, Gladys took a job as a nurse's assistant in Geneva Community Hospital. She and John moved to Mountain Home, Arkansas, in

1972. Gladys enjoyed crocheting and knitting, loved animals, and was a gifted piano and organ player. She moved back to Illinois after her husband's death. Gladys Olson was survived by twenty-two nieces and nephews and scores of great- and great-great-nieces and nephews.

In June 2017, the Bowgren family celebrated its seventy-fifth annual family reunion at Wheeler Park in Geneva. Some sixty family members attended, coming from as far away as Florida and California. Ken Bowgren, who grew up in Wasco, is the family's archivist and genealogist. Attendees were descendants of siblings Oscar, Adolph, Otto, Emil, John, and Fritz Bowgren.

The Ekstrom Family

Charles Peter Ekstrom, who was a dairy farmer near Wasco for decades, was born in Helsingborg, Skåne län, Sweden, on 26 September 1872. His parents were Per Palsson Ekstrom and Johanna Johansson. The father was born in Sweden in 1840, and served in the Swedish army. As late as 1908, Per Ekstrom was still "engaged in farming in the land of his birth." He was called a "faithful and consistent member of the Lutheran church." Charles P. was the second of Per and Johanna Ekstrom's eleven children. Several of Charles's siblings (Gustaf, John E., and Joseph) remained in Sweden, while the others also emigrated to the United States. Charles's brother Fred Ekstrom, who was born on 26 July 1882, also came to Campton Township, and lived with him for years. Their brother Otto A. Ekstrom, who was born on 25 January 1886, also settled in the township. Charles P. Ekstrom attended school in Sweden until the age of fourteen, after which time he devoted himself "to his father's farming interests." At the age of twenty, in 1892, Charles P. Ekstrom came to the United States and settled in Kane County.

Charles P. and Lucy Ekstrom of Wasco, on their 55th Anniversary

On his farm, Charles P. Ekstrom raised hay and grain and was engaged in the dairy business. He had a herd of thirty cattle in the first decade of the twentieth century and raised Berkshire hogs, "of which he [made] a specialty." His wife Emma Louisa ("Lucy") Anderson was born in Campton Township on 28 October 1876. They were married in 1897. Charles and Lucy had three children in all. The oldest, Ester Olive Ekstrom, was born on 10 August 1899. She passed away on 6 January 1900. The second child in the family, Carl Elmer Ekstrom, was born on 8 December 1901. Politically, Charles P. Ekstrom was a Republican. Lucy (Anderson) Ekstrom had three sisters: Augusta Anderson (who was born on 31 May 1864); Amanda Josefina Anderson (who was born on 15 December 1868); and Emma Anderson (who was born on 22 December 1871, and who died in August 1872). The parents, Gustaf and Anna Christina (Johnson)

Anderson, came to the United States in 1869, and were farmers in Campton Township.

In 1920, Charles P. and Emma L. Ekstrom were living near the Bell, Bolcum, Larson, and Eddy families in the eastern part of Campton Township. Their two sons, Carl Elmer and Harold Paul Ekstrom, were in the household then, as was Lucy's eighty-four-year-old father, Gustaf ("Gust") Anderson. Lucy's mother had passed away in 1911, and Gust moved in with his daughter not long afterward. Gust Anderson passed away at the Ekstrom farm home on 13 June 1928. He had been born in Sweden on 25 February 1835, and came to Kane County from Sweden in 1869. He settled "on a small farm west of Wasco" at that time. Anderson's funeral services were conducted by Grace Lutheran Church, Lily Lake.

By 1930, the Ekstroms were living near Carl Olson and Frank Hagaman (in Wasco), and both Carl and Harold were still at home. Carl's wife Hazel was also living with the family then. Lucy (Anderson) Ekstrom was elected President of the Lily Lake Ladies Aid in December 1931. Her recipes for banana cake and date cookie bars were published in subsequent issues of the *Elburn Herald* from November 1934.

C. P. Ekstrom was a deacon of Grace Lutheran Church, Lily Lake. He passed away near Wasco on 29 September 1953. His wife Lucy passed away at Community Hospital, Geneva, after a brief illness, on 13 December 1960. She was survived by her two sons, five grandchildren, and a great-grandchild. For further information on his son Harold P. Ekstrom, see "Some Wasco Houses - Northwest Quarter."

Fred Ekstrom came to the United States in 1902 and was naturalized as a citizen in 1908. He married Julia O. Peterson on 28 July 1910, in Kane County. She was born on 14 September 1882, and died on 25 March 1913, less than three years into her marriage to Fred. They had one son, LaVern Ekstrom, who was born in Campton Township on 14 March 1911. During World War I, Fred Ekstrom rented Hickory Grove Farm in Section 21, Campton Township, which was owned by Mrs. Anna Anderson. This property was located on the present Route 64, two miles west of Wasco. After the war, on 22 February 1919, Fred married Ellen M. Steele, and they had five children. The children all attended Wasco School.

Harold Ekstrom's confirmation photo from Grace Lutheran Church, Lily Lake, 1929

In 1937, Fred and Ellen Ekstrom were renting 180 acres of the Chester Bolcum farm, two miles northeast of Wasco. They were still renting this farm in 1941, when their son LaVern was working as a farm hand there. Their oldest daughter Doris C. Ekstrom was then a student in the high school. The 1940 census gave Doris Ekstrom's occupation as a millinery cutter; her older brother and their father were listed as farmers. Ellen M. Ekstrom died on 14 January 1941, at the age of fifty-six, and is buried in the Whitney Cemetery. In 1942, according to his World War II draft card, Fred Ekstrom was 5' 10" tall, weighed 170 pounds, and had blue eyes and gray hair.

In 1947, Fred Ekstrom operated the "Flowing Spring Farm," owned by the Bolcum family. Fred later moved to Lily Lake, where he passed away on 3 March 1958. He was a member of Grace Lutheran Church, and was survived by three sons (LaVern, Ray, and Roger) and three daughters (Doris, Mary Ellen, and Gloria). There were thirteen grandchildren. Ray H. Ekstrom was a private during World War II and was reported missing in action in Italy, but was found to be alive shortly afterward. He rejoined his unit, and his wife Doris was told of his safe return on the first anniversary of their marriage, in October 1943.

Grace Lutheran Church, Lily Lake, of which so many Ekstroms were members

Carl E. ("Elmer") Ekstrom was born on 8 December 1901. On Saturday, 27 October 1928, Elmer Ekstrom married Hazel Ruth Johnson, who was born on the twelfth of the same month and year as her husband. She was the daughter of C. O. and Clara Johnson; their autumn wedding took place at the bride's home. Beatrice Johnson, the bride's cousin, played the wedding march, and Rev. Alburn Hemming performed the ceremony. Hazel's sister Dorothy Johnson was the bridesmaid, and Harold Peterson, the groom's cousin, was best man. Elmer operated a farm near Wasco until his retirement (in 1960) and then moved to Elburn. For twelve years, he operated the Elburn Feed Mill. Elmer and Hazel Ekstrom had three children: Darlene, Carl, and Wayne. Their son Wayne worked at the Wasco Blacksmith Shop for more than thirty years. Darlene was an active member of Grace Lutheran Church in Lily Lake. C. Elmer Ekstrom died at Community Hospital, Geneva, on 25 May 1973. He was buried in the Whitney Cemetery in Wasco.

Hazel R. Ekstrom passed away at her home in Elburn on 29 December 1986, at the age of eighty-five. She grew up on a farm on Burr Road, and met her future husband in their confirmation class at Grace Lutheran Church, Lily Lake. After their marriage they farmed on LaFox Road north of Wasco. They moved from the Ekstrom farm to Elburn in 1961. Hazel reported the Wasco news to the *St. Charles Chronicle* for years. She was survived by her daughter, two sons, seven grandchildren, and a great-granddaughter.

Ray H. Ekstrom, son of Fred and Ellen, was born in Wasco on 23 December 1919. He attended local schools and assisted on the family farm as a young man. Ray married Doris Lant in New York City on 17 October 1942, just before he left for basic training during the war. Ray served as a corporal in the 196th port battalion and was stationed throughout the European theater. After returning to Campton Township in 1945, he farmed for Dexter Norton. Later he worked on the Bolcum farm on Empire Road; in the mid-1950s Ray and Doris moved to Lily Lake, where he worked on the Ray Reed farm. Ray Ekstrom passed away at his home in Lily Lake on 2 February 2001. He was survived by three children, nine grandchildren, and six great-grandchildren.

Darlene (Ekstrom) Bohlin and her Sunday School class at Grace Lutheran Church, Lily Lake

The Jay Family

Lynn Leslie Jay was born in Aurora on 17 March 1891. His parents William Henry and Mary Etta Jay (both of whom were natives of Illinois) moved to Campton Township in 1909 or 1910. Lynn's father was a blacksmith, and later a farmer. The family moved to Cicero prior to the turn of the century, and from there to Kane County. In November 1913, however, Lynn Jay was living in Paw Paw, Michigan, when he visited friends in Wasco. Lynn married Lillian L. Kayner in Kane County on 22 December 1915. He claimed an exemption during the World War I draft because he had a wife and young daughter to support. In 1918, Lynn and Lillian Jay rented a forty-eight-acre farm in Section 24, Campton Township, from Frank Renwick. The Jays had one child (Evelyn) at that time.

By 1920, the Jays were living on a dairy farm near Wasco, and had two daughters, Evelyn (who was born in Campton Township on 21 May 1916) and Helen Jay (who was born on 1 September 1919). Lynn and Lillian's son Robert Benjamin Jay was born near Wasco on 8 July 1922. As an adult, Lynn Jay was 5' 6" tall, had blue-gray eyes and dark hair. Lynn and Lillian's daughter Margery was born on 18 September 1928, on the family's farm south of Wasco.

By 1930, there were four children in the Jay household: Evelyn (aged thirteen); Helen (aged ten); Robert (aged seven); and Margery (aged one). The three older children were all attending Wasco School that year. In March 1932, an important building on the farm of Lynn and Lillian Jay burned down. This was the Old Red Schoolhouse, which had been built in 1846, and which was relocated to the farm in 1906 by George Eddy, the previous owner of the Jay farm. The former school had been converted to a barn after it was moved to the property. The Jays also lost a silo and hen house at the time of this fire.

On 31 December 1935, Evelyn Elizabeth Jay, the oldest child in the family, married Leroy S. Hahn. The Hahns later moved to California. In November 1937, Helen Jay of Wasco married Lyle Rockwell of Elgin. A wedding supper was served in the home of the bride's parents, Lynn and Lillian Jay. After the marriage, the Rockwells moved to Elgin. Evelyn and Helen's only brother, Robert B. Jay (later known as "Senior" to many), began helping their father in the nursery in the 1930s. Robert helped Lynn expand Wasco Nursery in size and scope in the late 1930s and early 1940s. He joined the U. S. Army in January 1943. Robert purchased Wasco Nursery from the other members of his family in 1952.

The 1940 census of Campton Township indicates that Lynn Jay was (of course) working in the nursery industry; his specific occupation was given as "Landscaping." In the column asking for how many hours he had worked in a given week in March of that year, Lynn gave the response "84," which was probably accurate! His young daughter, Dorothy Jay, was shown in the household that year, in addition to the older children.

On 8 July 1942, in Kahoka, Missouri, Robert B. Jay married JoAnn Van der Hagen, daughter of Mr. and Mrs. Arthur Geldmeyer of St. Charles. Jay joined the U. S. Army in 1943 and was sent to the Pacific Theater. He was wounded in the Philippines and received the Purple Heart during his time in the service. Lynn and Lillian Jay

Helen Jay of Wasco, in 1932, with some of her classmates at the Wasco School

purchased the former McGowan home in Wasco in the fall of 1944, while the war was underway abroad. Roger W. Ekstrom of Wasco worked for Lynn Jay at Wasco Nursery from about 1942 until 1945 – the war years. Margery Jay of Wasco married John Horton of Elgin in November 1945. She later (in May 1960) married Lawrence W. Gauger of Wheaton. Margery's sister Helen (Jay) Rockwell was her Maid of Honor.

Throughout the 1940s, the Jay family spent their most of their vacations at their summer home in Webb Lake, Wisconsin. Lynn L. Jay passed away in Geneva on 18 October 1955; he is buried in the Whitney Cemetery. His widow Lillian (who was born on 20 November 1891) passed away in September 1986.

In May 1960, seventy-five Wasco residents gave Mr. and Mrs. Robert Jay a surprise housewarming party. The Jays were presented with "a lovely brass fireplace set and a purse." The evening was spent playing cards and ping pong, and visiting with friends. Four years after the housewarming, Robert B. Jay purchased a ninety-acre farm on Route 64. He moved business operations there in 1968. He and his wife retired in 2002.

Robert B. Jay of Wasco passed away on 26 September 2005, at the age of eighty-three. Bob Jay was a former Commander of the Wasco American Legion and was active in that group for many years. He was an avid outdoorsman, and enjoyed fishing, hiking, and hunting. He also enjoyed reading and woodworking. JoAnn Jay passed away on 8 August 2012. Bob and JoAnn had three children – Nancy, Robert, and Barb Jay; they also had four grandchildren, and three great-grandchildren.

The Langrill Family

Thomas Langrill of Wasco was born in Blackberry Township, Kane County, on 22 February 1871. He was a farmer in the Wasco area for thirty years and retired from that occupation in the mid-1920s. The Tom Langrill farm was located just north of Wasco, at the intersection of Burlington and Empire Roads. In the late 1920s, Langrill moved into the Nettie Anderson house and resided there for the rest of his life. The 1940 census shows him as one of four boarders then living in the Anderson home. He was not married and had no children. In 1946, Thomas Langrill was employed by the Stoner Water Softener Company in St. Charles. Fifty-nine acres of his former farm were sold at auction in February 1948. Thomas Langrill died at St. Joseph's Hospital, Elgin, on 29 September 1951.

Thomas's sister Emma Langrill (also of Wasco) was born in Kane County on 9 January 1877. She married Nicholas Heitz Jr. of Aurora in February 1905. Just one week after their marriage, the Heitz family moved to South Dakota. A third Langrill sibling connected with Wasco was James Langrill, who was one of the oldest children in the family. He was born in County Wicklow, Ireland, in 1864 or 1865; as an infant, he and his family immigrated to North America. They lived in Canada for a time, and then in New Jersey, but came to Kane County by 1870. The Langrills first settled in Kaneville Township, but moved to Blackberry Township soon afterward. The parents of all the Langrills of Wasco were Isaac and Hannah (Gilchrist) Langrill. James Langrill, who was a "common laborer" by occupation, died in Wasco on 25 November 1933. In fact, he was found dead, "seated in a chair at his home" at least three days after his passing.

Harriet Eddy of Wasco, in 1921

Another sister in the family, Mary Ann Langrill was also a Wasco resident. Mary Ann was born in Ireland on 18 July 1862, and came to the United States in 1866. She married C. M. Eddy in Kane County on 8 October 1890. Charles M. Eddy was a teamster, and was a native of Ohio. Their daughter Harriet M. ("Hattie") Eddy were born in Wasco on 24 April 1904, and her sister Gertrude V. Eddy was born the following year, on 19 April. Charles and Mary Ann also adopted a son, Wilford A. Eddy. In 1918, the Eddys rented the sixty-six-acre Langrill farm in Section 10, Campton Township, just over a mile north of Wasco. In 1920, Charles Eddy was employed as a farrier. In the late 1920s, Gertrude moved to St. Charles, and was joined by her sister Hattie soon afterward. Mary Ann and her adopted son moved to Ingalton, in Wayne Township, DuPage County, prior to 1930. Gertrude Eddy worked as a bookkeeper at a hardware store in 1940, when Hattie, who had attended three years of college, was a school teacher. Gertrude Eddy, who taught in Wasco when she was a young woman, moved to St. Charles in the 1950s. She married Douglas D. Langrill, a cousin, in 1950. Gertrude passed away in St. Charles on 30 November 1988.

Harriet Eddy, who taught school in Wasco in the 1920s and '30s, married Royal Tucker Morgan on 8 October 1947. He was born in Wheaton in 1888, and was Assistant Superintendent of Schools in DuPage County for thirty years. Royal passed away on 16 July 1964. Harried lived in St. Charles for many years; she died in DuPage County on 8 May 1993.

Grace Alice Vanderhoof was born in Campton Township (near Wasco) on 27 November 1897. Her parents were Frank and Kate (Hawley) Vanderhoof (see "The Vanderhoof Family," below). Grace married Howard L. Langrill, who was a son of Isaac Langrill Jr. Howard was born in Rolla, North Dakota, on 2 June 1900. They lived in West Chicago in 1928, Downers Grove in 1930, and in Genoa in 1935. Grace A. (Vanderhoof) Langrill died in San Diego, California, on 12 September 1949.

The Vanderhoof Family

The Vanderhoofs were a well-known family in the Wasco area for over a century, and the name is still familiar to long-time area residents. The pioneer of this family was Levi Vanderhoof, who was born in New York State in 1829. He married Esther Y. Terry, also a native of New York, on 2 December 1852. The family name was Dutch, and Levi's ancestors had resided in the American colonies since 1661, when Geertje Van Der Hoeven and her children sailed into New Amsterdam from Beesd, in the Netherlands. Levi Vanderhoof lived in Washtenaw County, Michigan in 1850, and his marriage took place there two year later. In 1856 the Vanderhoofs moved to Batavia, Kane County, Illinois. At the time of the 1860 census, there were three children in the family: Phylantha, aged seven; Frank, aged five; and Harlan, aged two. The two older children were born in Michigan. Levi Vanderhoof and his family moved to St. Charles by 1865, and to Campton Township in 1866. Their farm was located in the west half of Section 11 and the east half of Section 10, just over a mile north of the future site of Wasco. Levi Vanderhoof died on his farm during the first half of the year 1870.

Frank Vanderhoof, in the year 1872

Kate Hawley Vanderhoof, in the 1920s

Frank Vanderhoof worked on the family farm throughout the 1870s and 1880s. On 2 January 1895, Frank Vanderhoof "of Wasco" married Kate A. Hawley in Delaware County, Iowa. Frank continued to own and reside on his parents' farm in the southwest quarter of Section 11. The farm would be owned by the family until the 1950s, in fact, when it was sold to Joe Anderson. In 1918, Frank and Kate Vanderhoof owned 330 acres of land in Sections 10 & 11, Campton Township. Their two children, George and Grace, were in the household at that time. Frank Vanderhoof died in Campton Township, near Wasco, at 5:45 AM on 20 November 1925, at the age of sixty-nine. Sadly, this was his son's thirtieth birthday.

Frank Vanderhoof had a younger brother named Wirt Dexter Vanderhoof, who was born in 1867. Wirt lived long enough to witness the beginning of Wasco, but fell ill and died on 8 June 1893, at 11:15 in the morning. He is buried in the Whitney Cemetery not far from the family's home. Rev. Eddowes of Geneva preached at Wirt's funeral on Sunday, the tenth of June.

George and his sister Grace Vanderhoof, around 1903

George Levi Vanderhoof, the only son of Frank and Kate Vanderhoof, was born on the family farm just north of Wasco on 20 November 1895. He was born in the then-new Vanderhoof house, which had been built in the summer of 1891. George lived in or near Wasco his entire life. He graduated from St. Charles High School in 1913. On 4 September 1918, George entered the United States Army, and was sent to Georgia. There, he was assigned to the 6th Company, 1st Sappers Replacement Battalion, and was shipped overseas to France to fight in the Great War. He was released from his service in the Army on 14 July 1919, and returned home. He joined the American Legion at the time of its founding, in 1919. On 14 May 1927, George L. Vanderhoof married Emma Minnie Bolwahnn. She was born in Wasco on 30 June 1904, and was a daughter of Frank C. and Letitia (Meissner) Bolwahnn. George and Emma had a daughter, Lois Mae Vanderhoof, who was born on 10 October 1928. Emma and George separated that year, and were divorced in 1930. Emma and Lois moved to Glen Ellyn, and George stayed in the Wasco area. He farmed for some time, and then became a carpenter.

At the time of his first marriage, George Vanderhoof lived and worked on the family farm. The farm comprised more than one hundred and fifty acres at that time, located almost entirely on the north side of Burlington Road, just west of Corron Road. More than three years after his divorce, on 29 March 1934, George married Margaret Bartelt of Batavia, and they lived on the family farm until 1952. Then, they purchased the former Bergland home and moved to Wasco (see "Some Wasco Houses – Northwest Quarter"). Margaret was born on 14 October 1898; her mother Rosaline Bartelt was born in Campton Township. Margaret worked as a teacher for years, retiring from that line of work in 1959, when she opened a tea and coffee shop in Wasco. George worked as a carpenter with his friend Frank Richmond after his retirement from farming. George Vanderhoof had a passion for horses, and "rode them, broke them, drove and doctored them with a sincere and abiding passion." George served on the Whitney Cemetery Board and placed flags on all of the veterans' graves every Memorial Day. He was a member of Wasco's Wesley Johnson Legion Post 1195. George Vanderhoof was the region's last remaining World War I veteran when he passed away at Delnor Hospital on 28 May 1985. George was survived by his wife, a daughter from a previous marriage (Lois Vanderhoof Carty) and three grandchildren.

Margaret (Bartelt) Vanderhoof lived until the age of ninety-eight, and passed away in Geneva on 5 May 1997. She was born in Batavia Township, and was a daughter of John William and Rosaline (Alexander) Bartelt. She attended the Peck School, and then Batavia High School. Margaret took summer courses at DeKalb Normal School and graduated from there in 1926. She taught in the Chicago school system for thirty-six years, principally at the Shields School at 47th and Western. From the time of her marriage (in 1934) until 1952, she and George lived on the Vanderhoof farm on Burlington Road. Margaret ran a tea room in the Little House in Wasco for a short time (see the Scott/White House) and was the Wasco correspondent for the *Elburn Herald* for many years. Margaret Vanderhoof was a member of the Wes Johnson American Legion Auxiliary Post 1195, and attended the Geneva Methodist Church. She was survived by a sister, a brother, and her stepdaughter Lois.

Grace Vanderhoof in 1917

The Lathrop Family

Edwin Pruden Lathrop was one of the thirteen heads of household listed as Wasco residents in 1896. He was George Bergland's business partner for a time. Edwin Lathrop was born in Udina, Kane County, Illinois, on 3 October 1853. The Lathrops lived in Elgin in 1870, and in Hampshire Township in 1880. On 15 December 1880, in Kane County, Edwin married Hattie E. Rice, a daughter of James and Lucy Rice (see "The Rice Family"). He was still living in Wasco in the spring of 1901, when his parents (Alvin H. and Delia Lathrop) visited him from North Dakota. By 1910, Edwin and Hattie Lathrop were living in San Gabriel Township, Los Angeles County, California, with Hattie's parents, the Rices. They had moved there in 1907. E. P. Lathrop died in Los Angeles on 12 January 1918. Hattie returned to Illinois in 1946, and lived to the age of ninety.

The Hagaman Family

The Hagamans lived on the same farm just south of Wasco for over ninety years. "Captain" John George Hagaman was from Denmark, and his wife Eliza was a native of England. Mr. Hagaman, said to have been a sea captain, was easily the earliest European immigrant to settle in Campton Township, and died some time before 1859, perhaps as early as 1848. His name was given on the 1848 tax list, but he did not appear on the 1850 census of the township, although Eliza and her four children were listed. The family lived in New York State in the mid-1830s, but came to Illinois before 1840. John G. Hagaman acquired his Campton Township lands in February 1843 and March 1844, although he was a pre-emption claimant and thus was settled on the property prior to the completion of the government survey. The Hagamans were probably living in Campton Township by 1837. A map of Kane County from 1860 shows the 160-acre farm then belonging to the "E. Hogerman Heirs" [sic] on the east side of what is now LaFox Road, in Section 23, Campton Township. The property extended a full three-fourths of a mile from north to south, beginning just south of the site of the future Wasco School, continuing southward nearly to the point where Mill Creek crosses LaFox Road.

Elida Hagaman, the oldest child in the family, was born on 22 November 1833 according to her gravestone and death record, though censuses indicate a later year of birth. Her name has many spelling variations, with "Alida" being the most common. Elida was likely born in New York, though some censuses give Illinois as her birthplace. She lived with her mother and brothers in 1850, 1860, and 1870. Her occupation was given as "Raising Poultry" in the last-mentioned year, when she was listed as owning $1400 in real estate. She was in Campton Township with her brother Henry and his wife and child in 1880. Late in life (in 1888) Elida married John Swanson (not to be confused with John S. Swanson, mentioned earlier in this work). John was more than twenty years younger than his bride. They resided with Elida's brother Henry in Campton Township as late as 1910. She died in Wasco or St. Charles on 31 July 1930, and was buried in the Whitney Cemetery. Records of Bethlehem Lutheran Church give Elida's correct date of death, her gravestone being off by four days. John Swanson died in Geneva on 5 September 1946, aged eighty-eight.

Henry William Hagaman married Mary Jane Cooley in Kane County on 21 January 1866. She was born in March 1848, and was a daughter of Calvin and Charlotte Cooley. In 1880, Henry and Mary Hagaman lived near the Cooley and Chaffee families. They had one child at that time, William Henry ("Willie") Hagaman, aged three. They also had a daughter Clara Bessie Hagaman, who was born in 1882. Mary died in July 1898, and is buried in the Blackberry Cemetery on her parents' lot. Henry moved to Elgin after 1910, and passed away in Kane County on 3 September 1919, at the age of seventy-nine.

The 1870 Campton Township census shows Joseph and his brother John Hagaman as farmers, aged twenty-six and twenty-five, respectively. They in the same household, along with their mother, their older sister Elida, and John's new bride. In 1872, Joseph owned the northernmost forty acres of the farm, east of the Rice property, and John owned the southernmost thirty-seven acres. Their mother Eliza owned the eighty-three-acre central parcel, containing the house and outbuildings. She died on her farm on 31 December 1876, and is buried in the Whitney Cemetery. Joseph inherited his mother's farm, and had planted an orchard north of the home by the early 1890s. John purchased additional land directly east of his farm from the Norton family in April 1874, and then purchased another twenty acres from his brother in October 1885, bringing his farm to seventy-eight acres.

Mrs. Emma Jane (Scatliff) Hagaman, wife of Joseph, was born in New York City on 14 August 1842, and was a daughter of James and Jane Scatliff. She married Joseph on 20 October 1875. Joseph Hagaman was a farmer, and was born in Illinois in 1842. He put up a "power windmill" on his farm in September 1889. He died on his farm near Wasco two years later. He and Emma had no natural children of their own, but they adopted one child, Walter Spencer Hagaman, prior to 1880. He was born on 21 June 1873 in Mount

Vernon, New York. Walter left Wasco after the death of his adopted father, moving to Philadelphia, where he worked as a mechanical engineer. He returned to the area in 1922, and improved the Hagaman family's farm home greatly. Walter passed away in St. Charles on 1 May 1925.

In the first years of the twentieth century, Mrs. Hagaman and her mother went back and forth from Wasco to Chicago twice per year. Typically they would stay in Wasco during the summer and fall, and in Chicago during the winter and spring. Emma's mother, Jane Scatliff, died at the home of her daughter in August 1906. Mrs. Scatliff was eighty-seven years old, was survived by two sons and a daughter, and was a member of the Episcopal Church. In 1920, Emma Hagaman lived at #2720 Osgood Street, Chicago. Emma J. Hagaman passed away in that city on 4 March 1922, at the age of seventy-nine.

The Hagaman farms near Wasco, in 1904

Joseph's younger brother John Hagaman lived on the farm immediately south of his brother's land. John was born in May 1843, and was a Civil War veteran. He served as a Private in Company A, 67th Illinois Infantry, beginning on 13 June 1862. John Hagaman mustered into service in Chicago, and was a resident of Campton Township at the time. He was 5' 5" tall, had gray eyes, light hair, and a fair complexion. He married Mariam E. Ruddock in April 1870. Both were Illinois natives. Their children were George, Nellie, Hattie, and Mariam Hagaman. Initially, all the Hagamans, along with their widowed mother Eliza, lived in the same household south of Wasco. Soon after 1870, however, Joseph and John were living in separate (but nearby) homes. John and Mariam moved to Elgin in January 1890, or shortly afterward. They were living on Milwaukee Street in that city in 1900, when he listed his occupation as a farmer. Though their four children were all still living then, only their daughter Mariam, who was born in February 1879, was in the household. She was attending school at that time. John's son George Frank Hagaman married Jessie M. Price in Elgin on 30 September 1903. In April 1907, Mr. and Mrs. John Hagaman were "residing on their farm here [in Wasco] again." They later moved to California, where John died on 3 August 1932. His widow Mariam passed away two years later in Los Angeles County. In 1920, the Hagamans lived on Crestwood Avenue in Burbank. In 1930, they lived on Pasadena Avenue in the city of Los Angeles.

George and Jessie Hagaman had a daughter Florence, who was born in Elgin in 1904. The family lived in at #3430 Walnut Street, Chicago, in 1920. George was then a clerk for an oil company. He and Jessie moved to Los Angeles in 1921, and at that time he opened a grocery store. George died in Glendale, California, on 25 November 1934, at the age of seventy-three. Jessie, who was born in Connecticut on 27 May 1881, died in Los Angeles on 7 July 1968. George's sister Nellie Elizabeth Hagaman was born in Elgin on 4 May 1872. She moved to Wasco with her parents before 1880, and remained there until 1890, when the Hagamans moved to Elgin. Her marriage to Emery T. Moore took place in Winnebago County on 26 August 1904. They had a son Thomas, who was born in 1907, and a daughter Beatrice, who was born in 1912. The family moved to the city of St. Charles by 1910; Emery Moore worked there as a retail merchant. They were still in St. Charles in 1930, when Emery was selling farmland as a real estate agent. Emery died in that city on 27 October 1938, aged sixty-eight; Nellie passed away in the same locality on 19 February 1946.

In the spring of 1924, John Brischer moved onto the Walter Hagaman farm just south of Wasco. The previous tenant, J. Mason, was then retiring from farming.

Gerald W. Hagaman in 1947. His Marmion yearbook from that

The two Hagaman brothers later associated with Wasco were associated with Joseph's family, by way of adoption. Gerald W. ("Jerry") and Donald ("Don") Hagaman were sons of Frank W. and Florence (Fenner) Hagaman, who were born in Maryland and Pennsylvania, respectively. Frank's place of birth is occasionally given as Chicago/Cook County. His date of birth is given as 4 October 1894 or the same date in 1895. He was 5' 10" tall, and had brown eyes and brown hair. He was a World War I veteran. His obituary states that he moved to Philadelphia with his family at an early age, and returned to Illinois in 1922, settling in Wasco. Frank W. Hagaman was a candidate for Justice of the Peace on the Campton Township Republican ticket in April 1925, and again in March 1929. In 1930, Frank was serving a Justice of the Peace; ten years later, he was an advertising salesman. Frank had attended college for six years, and his wife was a high school graduate. In 1942, Frank was employed by Aurora radio station WMRO. He was a founding member of Wasco American Legion Post 1195, and was very active in the Post's activities and other groups such as the St. Charles Drum & Bugle Corps. Frank was an adopted son of Walter S. Hagaman, mentioned earlier, who in turn was an adopted son of Joseph.

In January 1935, Frank W. Hagaman sold his 120-acre family farm a half-mile south of Wasco to Floyd Bergland and his sister Florence Peterson. Mr. Hagaman parceled off the house and outbuildings just prior to the sale, however, and continued to live there with his son Jerry. A contemporary newspaper article asserted that the property had then been in his family for ninety-nine years, starting with a pre-emption claim to the land by his grandfather, John Hagaman, a Danish sea captain and one of the very first settlers of Campton Township. In 1936, Frank Hagaman was a judge at the bugle and drum contest held at the Illinois State Fair. The Bergland family owned all of the former Hagaman lands south of Wasco other than the four-acre parcel containing the house and outbuildings in the 1940s and '50s. In 1957, the owners of the four-acre parcel were Don and Karen Hagaman, and Frank and Florence Hagaman. Frank Hagaman died in St. Charles on 21 February 1961.

Gerald Hagaman attended Marmion Military Academy, and was a pitcher for the Wasco Cardinals baseball team in the mid-1940s. He was a "well-known square dance caller" for the Campton 4-H Square Dance Team in 1949 and 1950. In 1951, during the Korean War, he trained at Fort Leonard Wood. He married Marilyn Mueller of West Chicago in August 1954. Gerald Hagaman was then the organizational director of the DuPage County Farm Bureau in Wheaton; he and his wife moved to Geneva after their marriage. Jerry's brother Don graduated from St. Charles High School, and was later involved in coaching several sports in the Wasco area. Don Hagaman was most associated with Wasco baseball, especially in the 1960s and '70s. Don L. and Karen Hagaman, along with Don's mother Florence, sold their remaining lands south of Wasco in April 1971. The purchasers were Richard L. and Judy A. Nickla of Campton Township.

In the late 1970s, Florence Hagaman served as president of the St. Charles American Legion Post 342 Auxiliary. She was elected Senior Vice President of the Women's Relief Corps in St. Charles in 1973. She was a long-time member of Wasco Ladies Aid, and was active in the Wasco Auxiliary before moving to St. Charles. Her son Don and his family moved to Galva, Illinois, after leaving Wasco, while Jerry moved to Bloomington. Florence (Fenner) Hagaman died in Galva on 17 November 2005, aged ninety-eight.

The Anderson/Barber Family

Mary (Anderson) Barber was born on a farm west of Elburn on 2 July 1860. Her parents, Gunner and Ulrike Anderson, purchased a farm just over a mile west of Wasco when she was a young girl. Gunner Anderson "of Kaneville" purchased the southern half of his farm for $1000 on 7 March 1866. The present Town Hall Road was the western border of the property, which by 1872 was over 138 acres in size. In 1870, the Anderson family had four daughters in the household, including Olive, who was born on 30 June 1863. Olive passed away on 23 October 1877, and is buried in the Blackberry Cemetery.

By 1880, there were still three daughters (all teenagers) in the Anderson household: Mary V., Amanda M., and Annetta G. ("Nettie") Anderson. Amanda ("Mandy") Anderson died in 1889, at the age of twenty-five. The family's farm was expanded to the east due to a purchase of forty acres of forested land from James C. Rice in March 1891. The Anderson farm reached 200 acres in size by the turn of the century. Gunner Anderson passed away on his farm in Campton Township on 5 April 1905. He was a native of Norway, and his wife was born in Sweden in December 1825. Although the couple had six children, only one (Nettie G. Anderson, later of Wasco) was living on the farm by 1900. In 1913, Ulrike Anderson and her daughter moved into the house at the southwest corner of Route 64 and LaFox Road (see "Some Wasco Houses – Southwest Quarter"). Mrs. Gunner Anderson died in Wasco on 13 October 1914, at the age of eighty-eight. She had come to the United States from Sweden in 1853. She was survived by two daughters and six grandchildren. Her funeral was conducted from the Wasco Baptist Church.

The barns on the old Barber farm west of Wasco, in 1974

Mary V. Anderson married Carroll A. Barber at the Anderson home near Wasco on 28 June 1888. Over one hundred friends and relatives attended. Rev. Craven of Elgin performed the ceremony. The groom was employed by the McCormick Reaper Company, and the bride worked as a school teacher in Chicago at the time of the wedding. Carroll was born on 5 November 1853 and was a son of Calvin C. and Maria Louisa (Garfield) Barber of Blackberry Township, who were both New York natives. The Barber children were all born in Kane County, and were farmers. After their marriage, Carroll and Mary Barber lived on a farm near LaFox, in the northern part of Blackberry Township, while Mary's sister Nettie stayed on their parents' property west of Wasco. By 1910, the Barbers (who remained in Blackberry) had six children: Minnetta, Leslie C., John Kenneth, Hillis E., Furnald K., and Claron D. Barber. All of these children except Kenneth, who was known by his middle name, were still on the Blackberry farm in 1920. Some of these children later became associated with Wasco. Carroll Barber died in Blackberry Township on 23 May 1924.

Mary Barber in 1935, at the Campton Centennial

Following her husband's death, Mrs. Barber moved back to the Campton Township, moving in with her son Furnald. By 1940, Mary Barber had moved in with her sister Nettie Anderson, in Wasco. She lived there until 1948, when she moved to the Bellevue Home in Waterman, Illinois. She died there on 5 July 1949, at the age of eighty-nine. In her young adulthood, Mrs. Barber taught at the Old Red Schoolhouse south of Wasco. She also taught in Chicago for a time. She was very interested in education and was even on the Board of Education for Geneva for a term. Her funeral was held at the Wasco Baptist Church, with Dr. J. C. Murley of Northwestern University conducting the services. Mary (Anderson) Barber was survived by a daughter (Minnetta) and three sons (Hillis and Leslie of Wasco, and J. Kenneth Barber of Chicago). Mary's sister Nettie Anderson, mentioned throughout this work, also survived.

Hillis Barber was born in Campton Township on 7 February 1897. He was a veteran of World War I, and was later active in the Wasco American Legion Post 1195. He was employed as a building and architecture supervisor by Shaw-Metz and Associates of Chicago. His final job was supervising the construction of Chicago's iconic McCormick Place. Hillis Barber died in Delnor Hospital, St. Charles, on 19 August 1962. He was survived by his wife Elsa, one brother (Leslie, of East Lansing, Michigan) and one sister (J. Minnetta of Wasco) and was buried in the Garfield Cemetery.

Julia Minnetta Barber attended the University of Illinois in Champaign in 1914 and was a teacher by 1918. She and her brother Furnald lived in Champaign in 1920 and 1921; he was a student there, and she was a teacher. Minnetta Barber traveled to China in 1926, when she took a position as an instructor at Ginling College. In the early 1930s, Minnetta taught at Monticello Seminary in Godfrey, Illinois. She then did child guidance work in Kane County. Minnetta moved to Carbondale in the fall of 1936, when took a position teaching English at Southern Illinois State University. She remained in Carbondale through at least 1947.

Minnetta returned to the family's farm near Wasco by 1956. She spent most winters in Arizona beginning in the late 1960s. Minnetta Barber passed away on 14 September 1982, at the age of ninety-three.

In October 2015, the 1870s limestone smokehouse from the Barber farm near Wasco was moved to the Garfield Farm Museum. White Brothers Trucking of Wasco handled the transportation of the historic smokehouse; the building was lifted by means of a heavy crane onto the truck which transported it to its current location.

The Chrystal Family

Jennie Chrystal was born in Kane County on 1 May 1883, and was a daughter of James and Emma (Wadley) Chrystal. The Chrystal family's large farm was located just west of the village of Wasco, on both sides of Brown Road. They purchased this property from Charles L. Muir on 1 October 1902. The present Route 64 was the farm's southern boundary, and the Chicago Great Western railroad tracks marked its northern limit. It was immediately west of the Higgins farm. In May 1906, Jennie Chrystal entered the *St. Charles Chronicle's* "piano contest," as one of only two contestants from Wasco (the other was Olive Bolcum). Chrystal did not win, but was one of the top dozen finishers. The Chrystals visited relatives in Sycamore in August 1906, and both Harry and Jennie Chrystal attended a Chautauqua (an assembly with speakers, music, preaching, and entertainment) in that town during the visit. On 14 May 1908, Jennie married Fred Lake. Their wedding took place in St. Charles.

James Chrystal was a native of Montreal, Canada, and his wife Emma was born in Michigan. James was brought to the United States by his parents in 1854, and they initially settled in Burlington Township, Kane County. He and Emma were married in Kane County on 8 March 1876. The Chrystals lived on a farm in Virgil Township in 1880, when they had two young children: George, aged three; and James, aged four months. Not long after their daughter Jennie's marriage, the Chrystals sold their Wasco farm to Peter A. Peterson. This sale took place on 26 February 1910. The Chrystals moved further west, and were living alone on their farm near Lily Lake in 1920. James Chrystal died at his home in Campton Township on 15 May 1929, at the age of seventy-nine, and is buried in Lily Lake. He was survived by his wife, a daughter Jennie, and sons George C. Chrystal of Elburn, and sons Harold W. and Roy J. Chrystal of Lily Lake.

James and Emma Chrystal of Wasco, around 1904

Harry Wadley Chrystal, Jennie's younger brother, was a farmer in Lily Lake in 1918, and was a janitor at the Lily Lake School in 1930 and 1935. He was born in Virgil Township on 10 January 1886. Harry's wife Leola was born in Michigan on 8 June 1899. Roy James Chrystal, Harry's brother, was born in Virgil

Township on 1 May 1888. He was a barn carpenter in 1910, and a farmer in 1920. Roy's wife Lena (née Rasmussen) was from Illinois, though her parents were both from Denmark. Their daughter Ida Chrystal was born in Lily Lake on 13 October 1918. Jennie, Harry, and Roy's mother Emma Chrystal passed away in Lily Lake in April 1936, at the age of eighty.

Jennie Chrystal, prior to her marriage to Fred Lake

In 1910, Jennie (Chrystal) Lake was living with her husband on his parents' farm north of Wasco. Fred Benjamin Lake was a farmer, and was a long-time resident of Campton Township. Fred was born on the Lake farm on Burlington Road on 9 February 1886. He and Jennie had two daughters: Marion G. Lake, who was born on 21 August 1909; and Mildred, who was born in January 1911. Fred's brother Frank Lake, who was employed in the hardware and plumbing business, was also in the household at that time. Fred and Jennie moved to Elgin in the 1910s, and stayed there for many years. Fred sold his 160-acre farm near Lily Lake in November 1916. He was a salesman in the 1920s, and in 1930 was a "stationary engineer" for a coal company. Fred and Jennie were then living with their son Harold Fred Lake, who was born in Elgin on 18 November 1920.

The Lakes relocated to western McHenry County by 1929, when their daughter graduated from high school in that locality. They moved to Aurora by 1938. Fred worked as a salesman at that time, though the 1940 census listed him as a farm laborer. Fred and Jennie moved to Chicago in 1944, when he began a job with the Triangle Motor Rebuilding Company. He passed away in Marion, Illinois, on 12 September 1947, and is buried in the Whitney Cemetery. Fred was driving in Salem during a severe rainstorm when his car "skidded crosswise on the highway and was struck broadside by a delivery truck." He later died of his injuries. Fred's daughter Marion preceded him in death, on 1 September 1932. He was survived by his wife, their son Harold, their daughter Mildred (Lake) Stattner, and a sister, Zilpha (Lake) Brown of Wasco. Jennie Lake later moved to Linn County, Iowa, where she passed away on 5 April 1970.

The Harold Anderson Family

Harold Anderson's extensive farm was located immediately northwest of the village of Wasco, on both sides of Brown Road. The farm was previously owned by Harold's father-in-law Peter August Peterson, and prior to that by James Chrystal, and earlier still by Charles Probert. Much of the farm is now open space, including the Brown Road Meadows and Anderson Park, named for the family. Harold Gustaf August Anderson was born in Kungsbacka, Halland County, Sweden, on 3 February 1894. He came to the United States as a teenager, moved to Kane County, and married Ellen Peterson (daughter of P. A.

Peterson) on 26 February 1923. They met in church, as was typical for this time and place. Ellen was born in Kane County on 18 July 1900. She and Harold had two children - Robert P. and Ruth A. Anderson.

Ellen's father Peter August Peterson (formerly Perrson) was born in Skåne County, Sweden, on 29 May 1871, and was a son of Per and Assarina Peterson (this couple was listed as Per and Esrina Nelson in the 1900 Campton Township census). Peter's older brother Nels Peterson, who came to the United States in 1882, was a farmer on Beith Road in Campton Township, two miles southwest of Wasco. Peter August, who was more generally known by his middle name, immigrated in 1888, and married Bothilda Nelson a decade later. August and Bothilda's oldest daughter, Alice Peterson, was born on 28 May 1899. The family purchased their Wasco farm from James and Ellen Chrystal on 26 February 1910. P. August Peterson retired in 1920, and moved to #303 Park Avenue, on the east side of St. Charles. Peterson he died on 10 May 1931 at the Peter Denker home in Wasco. His wife preceded him on 14 September 1930. Both are buried in the Garfield Cemetery. They were survived by three daughters and a son (Paul M. Peterson) as well as by three grandchildren. Their daughter Alice had married Rudolph Mongerson on 28 June 1928. Alice and Ellen's sister Esther had married J. Lawrence McGowan on 18 June 1925.

Harold Anderson passed away on 24 April 1962, and was survived by his children, who lived nearby, and four grandchildren. Ellen Anderson died in St. Charles on 21 November 1989, at the age of eighty-nine. She was a charter member of the Home Circle of Grace Lutheran Church, Lily Lake. Ellen lived at the home farm until 1986, when she became a resident at the Pine View Care Center in St. Charles. She had five grandchildren and eight great-grandchildren. Her grandson Neal purchased the family farm in 1987.

Charles Probert standing outside his Wasco farm in the 1890s. The house, thought to have been built in 1849, and the surrounding property have both been owned by the Anderson family since 1910

Robert P. ("Bob") Anderson was born in St. Charles on 10 September 1924 and attended Wasco School as a young man. Bob graduated from St. Charles High School in 1941 and played first base for the Bergland Lumber Company's softball team during his teenage years. He was a skilled player, and considered trying out for the Chicago Cubs when he was a young man. He married Dolores Klotz in 1948, and they built a home on his parents' farm property. The Andersons sold their herd of dairy cattle in 1967, after which time Bob Anderson was elected Campton Township Assessor. In the April 1969 Campton Township election, in fact, Robert P. Anderson received sixty-seven votes out of a total of seventy-two cast!

Bob Anderson loved horses, and boarded them for twenty-five years following his time as a dairy farmer. Bob was appointed Campton Township Supervisor in 1985, and was voted into that office during the 1989 election. His goal that year was to keep the township "operating as a good cohesive unit of local government." He also sought to work toward the preservation of open space in the township, a goal which was achieved largely through his efforts some years later. The Andersons boarded horses and were active in both their church and community. Bob Anderson worked in various capacities at businesses in Batavia, Geneva, and Lily Lake. He was a faithful member of Grace Lutheran Church, Lily Lake, and passed away on 15 February 2007.

The "new" Bob & Dolly Anderson home on Brown Road, pictured soon after its completion in 1950

An aerial view of the Anderson farm from 1987

In the mid-1980s, Evergreen Valley Feed was located at the Anderson farm on Brown Road. The business was open from 9:00-6:00 daily but was closed on Sundays. The company sold Wayne Horse Feeds and other products. Bob's son Neal Anderson worked for his uncle Melvin Peterson at the Wasco Blacksmith Shop prior to his marriage. He engaged in dairying with his brother for five years, and then in 1986 began his career in commercial construction. Neal was the founder of Anderson Building Systems, and was elected as a Campton Township Trustee for two terms. He was then Campton Township Supervisor for eight years, and was a leader in the town's open space movement. He began a new business, Luau Coffee, in 2003, and in January 2018 Neal Anderson received Campton Hills' first Outstanding Citizen Award. He is currently serving on the Garfield Farm Museum Board, and was a contributor to this work.

More recently, the Anderson family's barn has been the location of Grace Lutheran Church of Lily Lake's "Christmas Barn Service" for most of the 2010s. Coffee and hot cocoa are served at this unique worship service, where hay bales serve in place of pews, and many Christmas songs both old and new are sung.

The Brown Road Meadows, formerly the eastern part of the Harold Anderson farm

The Ross Family

The Ross family's farm was located just one mile northwest of the center of Wasco for three generations. Access to the farmhouse was gained from the west side of Brown Road, along a long lane. The farm was located on both sides of the Chicago Great Western railroad tracks. John Ross purchased the original forty-acre parcel of the farm from Henry I. and Helen M. Lincoln of Franklin Grove on 31 January 1876. The purchase price was $1000. John and Britta ("Betsy") (Anderson) Ross sold a part of their property to the Minnesota & North Western Railroad Company on 14 July 1886. The Rosses were both still living in 1891, when they obtained a mortgage using their farm as collateral. That October, they had purchased an adjoining forty-acre parcel of property from Catharina Anderson. John and Betsy Ross were both born in Sweden in the 1830s, and came to the United States in 1869. John was deceased by January 1899, and it is very likely that he died on his eighty-acre farm near Wasco.

Alfred E. Ross was the next owner of the Ross farm in Wasco. His mother transferred ownership of the property to him in October 1916. Alfred was born in St. Charles on 14 September 1870, and married Anna C. Johnson in Kane County on 14 October 1897. By 1900, he was the only surviving child of John and Betsy. Alfred and Anna had four children that survived infancy: Helen F., Alvida E., Imon C. W., and Paul J. A. Ross. The Rosses ran their farm as a dairy in the early twentieth century. Alfred's mother was listed as "Bertha" on the 1910 and 1920 censuses. Alfred Ross died on the farm on 15 March 1922, at the age of fifty-one. His widow Anna survived until 8 January 1971. Their son Paul John Alfred Ross, his wife Mabel, Paul's brother Imon Carl William Ross (a bachelor), and Anna C. Ross (a widow) kept the Wasco farm until 31 August 1960, when they sold it to John N. and Marijo C. Basic. Paul and Mabel Ross had moved to Batavia by that time, but his mother and brother remained in Campton Township until then.

Helen F. Ross, daughter of Alfred and Anna, was born on the family farm on 22 October 1907. She married Einar Free, and they enjoyed more than sixty years of marriage. They had one daughter, Betty Free. Helen was diagnosed with lymphoma in 1975, but successfully overcame the disease. She passed away in Elgin on 28 August 2001. Her younger sister Alvida (Ross) Cordes, who was born in Wasco on 23 October 1909, passed away in Sun City, Arizona, on 3 December 1977.

The large barn on the "old Ross farm" in Wasco burned on 30 October 1975. The buildings there had been abandoned by the time of the fire.

The Theodore Johnson Family

Theodore Knut Johnson was born in Småland, Sweden, on 2 April 1882 and came to the United States when he was a teenager, in 1898. He and his wife Hilma Josephine Fritz, who immigrated in 1905, shortly before their marriage, which occurred in St. Charles on 9 February 1907. They had three children who were associated with Wasco for many years. These were: Beatrice Johnson, who was born on 8 December 1907; Gunnar Theodore Johnson, who was born in St. Charles Township on 25 April 1912; and Helen M. Johnson, who was born on 20 October 1917. The children all attended Wasco School. Beatrice was a music teacher in 1930, and her brother was a farm laborer. All three children were still living with their parents on the family farm near Wasco in 1940.

In the late 1910s and early '20s, the Johnson family rented the 118-acre Bergland farm just south of Wasco, on the east side of the present LaFox Road. The Hagaman farm was immediately north of this property. On 1 March 1936, Theodore and Hilma Johnson purchased property of their own – the former Emery and Ella Sharp farm on both sides of the present Town Hall Road, adjoining the Barber property. The parents remained here until the end of their lives. The mother in the family, Hilma (Fritz) Johnson, was born in Sweden on 29 September 1885. She her husband were members of Bethlehem Lutheran Church, and Hilma was active in Wasco Ladies Aid. She died at her home west of Wasco on 6 December 1961, after a lingering illness. Rev. J. David Ekstrom officiated at her funeral. She was survived by her husband, their three children, and two grandchildren. Hilma was also survived by six siblings, five of whom lived in Sweden.

Theodore Johnson was a farmer in Campton Township for more than fifty years. He passed away in Community Hospital, Geneva, on 26 January 1965. Rev. Arthur Holmer performed his funeral services; he and Hilma are buried in the Whitney Cemetery.

Beatrice Johnson's piano students appeared in a recital in the Wasco Church in June 1931, and again in October 1932. She was elected president of the Wasco Community Club in January 1932, and was also active in the U-Go-I-Go Club in the 1930s. She was the Secretary/Treasurer of that group in 1935. Beatrice played the piano and the organ at many local weddings and events in the 1930s, '40s, and later. She lived in the Nettie Anderson house for some time.

Gunnar T. Johnson graduated from Wasco School in June 1928. He never married, and had no children. Prior to his retirement he farmed near Wasco for many years. Like his parents, he was a member of Bethlehem Lutheran Church, St. Charles. Gunnar Johnson passed away in Geneva on 29 September 1992.

Edward R. Peterson, husband of Helen Johnson of Wasco

Helen Margaret Johnson of Wasco worked for the Cost Department of the Elgin Watch Factory when she married Edward R. Peterson of St. Charles in December 1948. Her sister Beatrice was the Maid of Honor at the wedding. Edward was born in St. Charles Township on 13 September 1915, and graduated from St. Charles High School in 1933. He was a son of John E. and Augusta (Anderson) Peterson. Ed started working in the Cost Accounting Department of the Elgin Watch Factory in 1939, and served in the U. S. Army for three-and-a-half years during World War II. He was in France and England during the war years and returned to civilian life in December 1945. Ed Peterson was a chief accountant at Plant 2 (Elgin Watch Company) in 1955. Edward and Helen lived on South Second Street in St. Charles for many years. Ed died on 15 January 1966, at the age of fifty. Helen worked for Universal Water Softener, and then for the American Livestock Insurance Company. She enjoyed painting in her free time. Helen's sister Beatrice Johnson died in Wasco on 22 September 1995. Helen (Johnson) Peterson passed away at Delnor Hospital in Geneva on 31 December 2016, at the age of ninety-nine. She had two daughters, one of whom survived her.

The Two Olson Families

John and Annette Olson came to Wasco in the early 1910s, after a residence in Chicago. Their children Ella Olson (who in 1941 married Evald Strom) and John A. Olson were well-known in the Wasco community for many years. Both Ella and John lived with Peter and Hilda Denker in 1920, when they were still attending school. Ella was later active in Grace Lutheran Church, Lily Lake, and passed away on 19 August 1963. She was survived by her husband, two sons, and a daughter. In 1930, John A. Olson was still living with the Denker family, near Wasco, and was then employed as a salesman for a lumber and coal yard (almost certainly Bergland's, as it was the only one in the vicinity). He was born in 1906, and married Gladys C. Bowgren in 1939. They moved to Mountain Home, Arkansas, in August 1972. John worked as an assistant director at Roller Funeral Home there. John Olson died in Mountain Home on 13 March 1995 (see "Some Wasco Houses – Southwest Quarter" for further information on John and Gladys).

Representatives of the two local Olson families: Ella Olson of Wasco, in May 1922 (left); and Florence Olson of the same place, in May 1929 (right)

There was another local man named John A. Olson, but this John Albert Olson was a farmer, and was born in Söderåkra, Sweden, on 8 March 1877. He and his future bride Olivia ("Olive") Larson came to the United States in 1900 and 1897, respectively, and were married in Kane County on 22 February 1902. Initially, John A. Olson was a farm hand on the Frank and Katie Vanderhoof farm on Burlington Road. John and Olive Olson were the parents of Edith Marie, Esther Elvira, Paul L., and Florence Ingrid Olson, who were born between 1902 and 1913; this Olson family lived on a farm just a mile north of Wasco. John was tall, fair, had blue eyes, and was missing two fingers on his left hand, the result of a farm accident in his youth. They formally joined Bethlehem Lutheran Church of St. Charles in June 1910. In 1918, John and Olive Olson, along with their four children, were renting the 160-acre Frank Bolwahnn farm in the east half of Section 10, Campton Township.

Edith, Paul, and Florence Olson were still living with their parents in 1930, on a farm north of Wasco. Paul was then working as a farm laborer. Edith Linea Maria Olson was born in St. Charles on 29 August 1902, and was baptized at Bethlehem Lutheran Church. She was confirmed at the same congregation in December 1915, and married William Hoffman in St. Charles on 8 November 1930. By 1940, they had children Luella, Alvin, Howard, and Gloria Hoffman, and were living on a farm near Wasco. Edith passed away on 30 October 1960, and is buried in Union Cemetery, St. Charles.

The John A. Olson of this family died in St. Charles on 16 April 1944, and his widow passed away there on 21 December 1947. They were still living near the Vanderhoofs and Bolwahnns in Campton Township as late as 1940. The two pioneer Olson families of Wasco do not appear to be closely related.

Esther Elvira Olson was born on 16 July 1904, and married Chester R. Johnson, an automobile mechanic. Chester was a son of Oscar and Myrtle Johnson, and was born in Wasco on 20 June 1901. Esther and Chester moved to Villa Park, in DuPage County, before 1930. Their son Kenneth was four years old at that time. By 1940, the family was living in the village of Maywood, in Cook County. Chester was then a service manager at a garage. The family later lived in Lily Lake. Esther (Olson) Johnson passed away in St. Charles on 24 December 1988. Chester died at Delnor Hospital, St. Charles, on 15 February 1989. They were survived by their son John Johnson of Aurora, as well as three grandchildren and two great-grandchildren.

Paul Albert Leonard Olson, son of John and Olive, was born in Campton Township on 28 November 1911. He was confirmed in 1925, and married Gladys M. Boyd of Elgin on 22 February 1941. They lived in Wasco until March 1945, when they moved to a dairy farm in Huntley. Paul Olson passed away on 17 April 1968, and Gladys died on 28 May 2001.

Florence Ingeborg Olson was born in Wasco on 15 November 1913. She was baptized on 17 October of the following year, at Bethlehem Lutheran Church, St. Charles. She was confirmed at Grace Lutheran Church, Lily Lake, in June 1927. In 1935, Florence married Philip A. Van Overmeiren. He worked for Moline Malleable Ironworks in 1950, when they lived on South 12th Street in St. Charles. They had children Roger F., Robert, and John Van Overmeiren. After Philip's death, Florence married Alvin M. Sizemore. Florence passed away in Aurora on 9 June 2003. She was survived by two children, five grandchildren, and four great-grandchildren.

Some Wasco Houses

Northwest Quarter

<u>40w774 Route 64</u> – the Rice/Johnson house. Joseph C. Rice of Wasco built this home shortly before 1904, probably in the year 1903. The Wasco column of the *St. Charles Chronicle* from mid-July 1903 stated that "J. C. Rice has begun the construction of a new tenant home," which most likely refers to this structure. It's located in the north half of the northwest quarter of Section 23, in Campton Township. At the time it was built, the home was on a small plot of land, surrounded on three sides by the farm of Horace Higgins. The home and property was sold by the Rice family to Solomon and Alex Johnson in February 1908. The Johnsons owned the house and lot for many decades, and lived in it for quite some time. The house seems to have been rented, though, in the early years. When Rev. Hand of the Wasco Baptist Church settled in Wasco in June 1908, he was to "occupy the Rice house." This must refer either to this house, or to the House of the Seven Gables across the street (the Rice family owned both homes). In October 1943, the four Johnsons that had long-owned the property (Alex, Ellen, Solomon, and Fern) briefly quit their claim to this parcel in favor of George and Hilda Hawkins. Immediately afterward, though, the Hawkinses sold the land back to two of the Johnsons – Solomon and Fern.

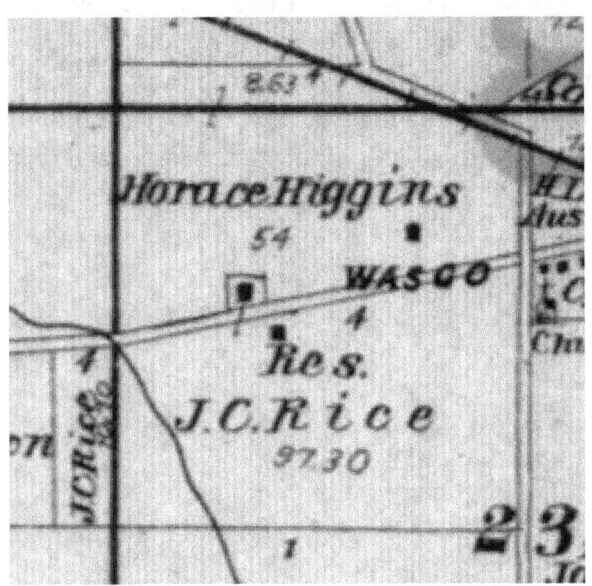
Western portion of Wasco, in 1904

In the 1960s and early '70s, the owners of record and the homes' occupants were Ellis R. and Frances M. Johnson and their daughter, all well-known Wasco residents (see "The Isaac Johnson Family"). In August 1974, the Johnsons sold to Stanley H. and Betty A. McConnaughay. The McConnaughay family had been residents of the St. Charles area beginning in 1934, when Stanley's parents, John Arthur and Florence McConnaughay, came to Kane County from Bluford, Jefferson County, Illinois. Stanley and Betty were married in July 1952. The Rice/Johnson house considered here was owned by Eugene L. Bushue and his wife Ardis from 1976 until 1982, and by Eugene and his second wife Dorothy from then until June 1997. The house has been owned by Deanna L. Palushik since 2010, and was previously owned by Andrew Hilgenberg & Danielle Avallone.

The Rice/Johnson house in 2018, looking northwest

The Rice/Johnson house in the 1960s, looking northeast

The present 40W774 Route 64 is visible on the far right of this c. 1910s photograph. The House of Seven Gables belonging to the Rice family is on the left. Viewer is looking west-southwest

Members of the Rice family outside their principal home (The House of Seven Gables) in Wasco, probably about 1905

40W754 Route 64 – the Ekstrom house. This one-story white frame house was built in 1953. The lot itself was sold to Harold P. and Lois J. Ekstrom in May 1952, by George and Hilda Hawkins. The home was owned by the Ekstroms for many decades and was sold to Travis Dexter in 2017. Harold P. Ekstrom was appointed as Wasco's Officer-in-Charles on 28 September 1973, and was made Postmaster on 5 January 1974. He served in that office for just over eleven years.

Harold Paul Ekstrom was born in Geneva on 20 June 1916, and was a son of Charles P. and Emma Louise (Anderson) Ekstrom. His father was born in Sweden, and his mother was a native of Illinois. They were married in Kane County on 21 August 1897. The family moved to a farm on Old LaFox Road, north of Route 64, and were residents there for many decades. C. P. died on 29 September 1953, and his widow on 13 December 1960. Harold attended Wasco School and St. Charles High School. During World War II, Harold was a Staff Sergeant for the U. S. Army Air Forces. In 1950, Harold and Lois lived on West State Street in Geneva, but moved back to Wasco three years later. Harold worked for the Bergland Company in Wasco, and later for Hummel & Company, as the lumber yard manager. He managed personal projects for Floyd H. Bergland, and at various times worked in the post office, lumberyard, and the hardware store in the Bergland building. During that time, he was a clerk in the Wasco Post Office, and as was stated above, became Postmaster. He married Lois Johnson in June 1949, and soon afterward they moved into their new home on Route 64. As postmaster, Ekstrom was described as being the "heart of the hamlet," and "ground zero for gossip and town news." He loved to talk, enjoyed company, had a good sense of humor, and knew everyone in Wasco. He retired from the post office in 1985. Harold passed away in Geneva on 12 March 2002. He was survived by his widow, two children, and three grandchildren. He was a member of Bethlehem Lutheran Church, St. Charles.

Harold Ekstrom, of Wasco. The photo, from the Bergland collection, dates to the 1940s

Harold Ekstrom, at his station in the Wasco Post Office, 1970s

The Ekstrom house in the 1960s

The Ekstrom house in 2018

40W738 Route 64 – the Carlson house. This one-story white frame house was built circa 1960. The lot itself was purchased by Kenneth Elnor and Alice (Engstrom) Carlson from George E. and Hilda Hawkins in October 1950. Ken Carlson was born in St. Charles in July 1926, and was a World War II veteran, having served in the Navy during that conflict. He worked at the Reber & Foley Service Station in St. Charles for many years. Alice's parents were Louis and Mable Engstrom. The house was owned by the family of Kenneth and Alice Carlson for decades, and then (beginning in the fall of 2014) by the Vincent Czernik family. The home was purchased in October 2016 by Joseph Pacione.

The Carlson house, shortly after its construction

The Carlson house in the 1990s

<u>40W718 Route 64</u> – the Hummel house. This one-story house, also a white frame structure, was built circa 1950. It was the home of Fred and Mary Lou Hummel for years. The Hummels moved to Campton Township in 1929, and purchased Bergland & Company in 1947. Fred E. Hummel lived in River Forest prior to coming to Kane County. He bought the 194-acre C. J. Anderson farm on Route 64 near Lily Lake (including the livestock and machinery) in November 1928. Fred and Mary Lou Hummel purchased the house lot on Route 64 from George and Hilda Hawkins in May 1949. Fred Jr. was the Secretary-Treasurer for the Elburn and Countryside Fire Protection District in the late 1950s, and in early 1960s he became President of the Board of Trustees of that organization. On 17 March 1949, Fred was appointed

Postmaster of Wasco, replacing Lee F. Mather, who had been temporarily filling that role since the death of Floyd Bergland. The home is now owned by the Fred Hummel Jr. Declaration of Trust.

The Hummel house, likely in the mid-1960s

The Hummel house in 2018

40W698 Route 64 – the Peterson house. This two-story brick home was known as the Peterson house for its original owners and occupants. It was built in the summer of 1930, and was first occupied by Elmer and Florence during the first week of December of the same year. The "Wasco News" column in the *Elburn Herald* from 29 May 1930 stated that "the foundation of the new home of Mr. and Mrs. Elmer Peterson is nearly completed. Work on the construction of the house will commence soon." The 4 December 1930 issue of the same paper stated that "Mr. and Mrs. Elmer Peterson are moving to their new home this week." In 1929, the property was sold to the Petersons by George E. Hawkins. The house was built immediately west of the old Hawkins family orchard. The home's first occupants were Elmer and Florence Peterson, and Florence's mother Louise Bergland. Previously, the family had lived in the Bergland home a quarter-mile to the east.

The Peterson home, as originally built, was an attractive two-story yellow brick building with a matching brick garage and chicken house. According to their nephew, the Petersons "took meticulous care of their property, and always had a manicured lawn and beautiful flower and vegetable gardens." The family always kept chickens, for both eggs and meat. The Petersons had a live-in Swedish helper, Lotten Swanberg, who was very close to the family. Florence was a successful business person, and invested in stocks, bonds, and property. She drove an Oldsmobile following her husband's death, and enjoyed a domino game called '42.'

The former Peterson house is presently owned by Daniel W. & Mary A. Clark, who have been there for more than ten years. The owners prior to them were Edwin and Barbara Dannewitz. The Dannewitz family had previously lived in DeKalb; they purchased from Lawrence E. and Betty J. Bishop in June 1975. The Bishops purchased from the Bergquist family in 1969, and moved in that June. They moved to California after selling their home in Wasco.

The Peterson house in Wasco, soon after its completion - the photo dates to about 1930

Florence Bergland Peterson and Lotten Swanberg, at the Peterson home, 1940s

Arthur W. Bergquist, who purchased the house from the Executors of the estate of the late Florence M. Peterson in February 1952, was born in 1900 in Blackberry Township. In June 1935, Arthur Bergquist of LaFox married Marie C. Daum of Lee, Illinois. Marie Bergquist was very active in community affairs in Wasco in the 1940s and later. She was involved in the Kane County Home Bureau, the Wednesday Card Club, the Bunco Club, the Red Cross, the Helping Hand Club, and the American Cancer Society. She entertained at her home quite frequently, and was a member of St. Gall's Church in Elburn. The Bergquists moved into their new home in Wasco on 11 March 1952. They did not have any children. Arthur died in Wasco on 15 February 1968. His wife Marie C. Bergquist passed away at St. Luke's Hospital in Chicago on 6 September 1968, at the age of sixty-three. On 25 October 1955, Arthur and Marie Bergquist purchased the vacant lot immediately east of the house from George and Hilda Hawkins. The house was owned by Elmer and Florence (Bergland) Peterson for several decades prior to the Bergquists' purchase. See "The Peterson Family" for further information on Elmer and Florence.

The Peterson house during World War II – from a color slide in the George Bergland collection

Florence (Bergland) Peterson and Lotten Swanberg outside the Peterson house in Wasco

The Peterson house in the 1960s

The Peterson house in 2018

<u>40W662 Route 64</u> – the "new" Hawkins house, which is located a good distance back from the roadway, was built between December 1970 and the summer of 1971. This brick ranch-style home was owned by George E. & Hilda A. (Berglund) Hawkins, and later by Leonard O. & Adele Hawkins. Mr. and Mrs. Leonard Hawkins moved into the home by the middle of August 1971. It is located on the largest land parcel now in Wasco, which comprises most of the northwestern quarter of the village. Leonard Hawkins died at St. Joseph's Hospital in Elgin on 9 December 1990, at the age of fifty-eight. He was born in Geneva on 28 January 1932. Leonard served on the Boards of the American Cancer Society, the Wasco Sanitary District, and Grace Lutheran Church of Lily Lake. For more than forty years, he farmed the family's land in Wasco. Leonard was Campton Township Assessor for sixteen years, and worked at First National Bank of Elgin and at Merchants National Bank of Aurora. He was survived by his wife Adele J. (Geske) Hawkins (who passed away in February 2016) and two children, Kimberlee and Todd Hawkins.

Giant haystack on the Hawkins farm in Wasco, 1910s

The "new" Hawkins house (rear view) in the 1980s

The "new" Hawkins house (front view) in the 1990s

The "new" Hawkins house in 2018

40W642 Route 64 – the "old" Hawkins house, an American Foursquare also known to Hawkins family members and neighbors as "Sionilli." It was built in 1917; the date of construction was carved into one of the concrete steps at the rear of the home. The house's name, which was chosen by Nels and Amanda Hawkins and their children, is Illinois spelled in reverse. The farm buildings are located to the north and northwest of the house – it was a working dairy farm for many years. The home is now owned by Carl & Kimberly Masters, who acquired it in 2017 from William P. and Cheryl K. Qualls. The Qualls family, formerly of Villa Park, purchased the house and property in May 1987 from an Illinois Regional Bank Trust. The Trust acquired the property from Harold R. and Arlynne M. Nickell in April 1982. The Nickells, who were previously living in Melrose Park, purchased the house in June 1979 from Jeffrey W. and Lorraine G. Hastings of Liberty, Missouri. Jeffrey Hastings served as a Trustee for the Wasco Sanitary District in the mid-1970s. The newly-reorganized Wasco 4-H Club was begun at this home in 1972. The Hastings family purchased the home from Leonard and Adele Hawkins on 23 July 1971. The Hawkins orchard was located to the west of the home, and the original home on the property was located slightly northwest of Sionilli. It was a simple frame building, lacking electricity and plumbing, and was taken down during the Great Depression. It had been built prior to Wasco's creation.

For information on George E. Hawkins and his parents, siblings, and children, see "The Hawkins Family" section of this work. George Hawkins was said to be the last local farmer to deliver his milk from his farm to the Wasco milk depot with a horse and wagon. In the 1930s, Don Swanson would walk from his family's home to the Hawkins farm to collect milk in an eight-quart milk pail. The Hawkins family kept Holstein cows, which were milked by hand in the barn. Milk was taken from the barn into the milk house where it was strained and placed in large galvanized milk cans. These containers were then placed in a large rectangular concrete tub. Cold water was pumped by means of a windmill from the nearby well into the concrete tub. After cooling during the morning, the milk was taken to the center of Wasco, and placed in a milk house, used by all nearby dairy farmers. The milk was taken from here to the Bowman Dairy Plant in River Forest to be pasteurized and bottled, for delivery to homes and stores.

The "old" Hawkins house, likely in the 1960s

The "old" Hawkins house, in 2018

One of the Hawkins farm's outbuildings, in the 1980s

The gambrel-roofed barn on the Hawkins farm, likely in the 1950s

<u>40W610 Route 64</u> – the Lottie Brown house, for many years occupied by her son Arthur Brown. Dating to the 1890s, this is one of Wasco's oldest homes. Lottie Brown, the last surviving charter member of the Wasco Baptist Church, died at the age of eighty on 21 May 1955. Her funeral services were conducted from the Wasco Church. Lottie (Stevens) was born in what would become Wasco, on 28 September 1874. She married George I. Brown at the Wasco Church in 1909 (see "The George Brown Family"). On 10 April 1922, for $3600, Lottie H. Brown purchased the house and lot described here from Alonzo D. Chaffee and his wife Phoebe. Phoebe's maiden name was Padelford, and she was from Almora, Kane County, Illinois. They had been married since October 1863. Around the time A. D. Chaffee sold his house to the Browns, he celebrated his seventieth birthday with many Wasco friends and neighbors gathering to congratulate him and wish him well. Alonzo Duane Chaffee passed away in 1924, and is buried in the New Hampshire Cemetery in Lily Lake.

Arthur Brown advertisement, circa 1960

The rear and east side of the Lottie Brown house, taken in the 1980s

The Brown house, in 2018

Mrs. Brown was survived by three sons: Keith of Philadelphia; and Arthur E. and George S. Brown of Wasco. She had nine grandchildren. At the time of Lottie Brown's death, the house was on 99/100 of an acre of land. Arthur Brown moved to New York State in the summer of 1976, after the sale of his home was finalized.

Since 1993, the Lottie Brown house has been owned by Craig and Johanna Hanson. Prior to that, it belonged to Michael R. and Barbara E. Martins; they purchased the house and property in 1989 from Paul M. and Judy K. Tower. The owners prior to the Towers were William G. and Cheryll O. Kinnett, who lived at the former Lottie Brown house in Wasco until June 1979. The Kinnetts were formerly of St. Charles and purchased from Arthur E. Brown himself on 12 June 1976.

Alonzo D. Chaffee of Campton Township, who probably built the Brown house, purchased the lot on which it stands from Horace S. and Martha Higgins on 3 June 1899. The purchase price for the lot (99/100 of an acre) was $237.60. The house may have been built at that time. It does not seem to appear on the 1892 Campton Township map, although a wagon shop is shown quite close to the house site.

Wedding of George and Lottie Brown, 1909. Ray Smith is at far left, and Maude Stevens is at right

George I. Brown was a farmer and a later a carpenter. He was born in New York State and moved to Wasco in the early twentieth century. He attended three years of college. George worked in general construction, but for some time his son Art worked as a carpenter for the railroad. He was also Campton Township Assessor for many years. George was tragically killed in an auto accident on 30 September 1946. George's son Art was injured in the accident, which occurred near Toledo, Ohio.

40W586 Route 64 – the Paul and Ethel Waterhouse house. The first building on this site, which was constructed by St. Charles native Algernon A. Burr, was built in the mid-1890s. The house was described as a "fine home," and a "handsome residence." It cost $5000 to build, an enormous sum for a home at that time. When the house was totally destroyed by fire in April 1901, it was considered a major loss for Wasco. The Burrs did not immediately rebuild on the site, and returned to St. Charles to live. Mr. Burr died in St. Charles in April of 1903. He had lived in Wasco for seven years. The 1900 census shows that three family members were in the home then: Algernon, who was a carpenter; Cornelia, who was born in Connecticut on 17 November 1846; and their only son, Arthur J. Burr, a teacher, who was born in St. Charles in 1876. Arthur moved to Chicago around the time that his parents' house was destroyed by fire, and he later moved to Missouri. In the 1920s, '30s, and '40s, Arthur Burr and his wife Mabelle owned a farm northeast of Wasco, just over the St. Charles Township border. Though Arthur and Mabelle lived and worked in St. Louis, they regularly "returned to their farm home for the summer months."

Algernon's widow Cornelia (Bartlett) Burr moved to St. Charles, and sold the Wasco property to Charles J. Waterhouse on 14 August 1912, for $1000. A new house (the present structure) seems to have been built on the property shortly before the sale. Waterhouse then moved his family into the present structure. Mrs. Burr passed away on 21 September 1921, and is buried in the Garfield Cemetery.

Algernon A. Burr, who lived in Wasco for seven years – at right, the only known image of the Burr house, painted c. 1899 – the house is only partly shown, and is at the extreme left edge of the painting

Paul Preston Waterhouse purchased the house and lot from his parents, Charlie J. and Sallie Waterhouse, on 22 April 1918, for $3800. The purchase price for the property was $1000, proving that the house was standing then. Paul P. Waterhouse was born in Neosho County, Kansas, on 9 March 1895. Paul married Ethel Coombes. They had no children. Paul was the depot agent for the Great Western Railroad in the 1930s. He drove a "Whippet" automobile, one of the smallest vehicles produced in North America at the time. In the late '30s and early '40s, Gloria Stewart and Don Swanson would practice singing duets in the home, with Ethel Waterhouse accompanying them on piano. This pair would often sing at the Wasco Baptist Church. Also see "The Waterhouse Family" for further information on Paul and Ethel.

Ethel (Coombes) Waterhouse was a teacher for forty-one years, and for most of her career she taught at Wasco School. She taught first grade just prior to her retirement. She had "a deep love of horses and an uncanny ability to handle them." For years she brought seeds and plants to her classroom, and her students would study their growth while caring for them. Her parents were born in Somersetshire, England. When Ethel was a teenager, her parents bought a farm north of Wasco, and she attended school there through her sophomore year, completing her studies at Geneva High School in 1914. Ethel received an elementary teaching certificate from DeKalb Normal School in 1916. In her early years of teaching, she would drive a horse and buggy to school, and would arrive early to "get the fires going" so that the classrooms would be warm by the time the students arrived. Ethel also taught Sunday School at Wasco Baptist Church for eighteen years. She retired from teaching in May 1959. Ethel Waterhouse passed away on 7 August 1970, at the age of seventy-five.

Paul P. Waterhouse owned his long-time home until June 1973. At that time, he sold the house and property to Austin J. and Joan Burke of the village of Addison. Mr. and Mrs. James Burke lived in the home while they built a new home on Anderson Road. Their daughter and son-in-law, Mr. and Mrs. David Hess, also lived in the home while they built a new home in The Windings. Three years later, in the fall of 1976, the Burkes sold to Robert T. and S. Frances Verkler, who moved to Wasco from South Holland, Illinois. The former Waterhouse house was then sold by S. Frances (formerly Verkler) Matz and her husband Ronald Matz to James E. and Eve F. Zahrndt**Error! Bookmark not defined.** in December 1986. Steven A. and Amy Cochran were the property's next owners. Since 2003, the house has been owned by the Judith C. Hines Trust of St. Charles.

Ethel Coombes and her brother William, as children

The Waterhouse house is known for its low-pitched roof, overall horizontal design, and spacious front porch. The historic garage behind the house is also remarkable for its hipped-roof design and south-facing dormer window. This structure is older than the house itself, and dates to the construction of the Burr house in the mid-1890s. It is visible in the late 1890s photograph of the Bergland house next door.

The Waterhouse house, as it appeared in the 1960s

The Waterhouse house in the 1990s

Ethel Waterhouse, with Olive and Bonnie Bergland, about 1936

<u>40W562 Route 64</u> – the Bergland/Vanderhoof House. This two-story Queen Anne style frame house was likely built in the spring and summer of 1894. Louise Bergland purchased the property on which the house was constructed in March of that year – she acquired part of the lot from Leonard and Emma White on the seventeenth of that month, and the other section of the lot from Horace S. Higgins just ten days later. Higgins was then a bachelor, and he sold his portion of the property to Bergland (who was "of Campton

Township" at the time of the deed) for $100. The Whites, who sold the smaller portion of the lot (comprising its eastern third), conveyed a one-eighth acre portion for just $40. The house was built in the Queen Anne style, which was very popular in Illinois in the mid-1890s. This local example of the style features asymmetrical design, verticality, decorated gables and porches, a hipped-roof turret topped by a finial, and an ashlar limestone foundation.

The oldest photograph of the Bergland house in Wasco. The photo dates to the late 1890s, and shows the house as it was originally constructed. Note the Burr/Waterhouse garage shown at the left of the photograph

As was recently stated, the house immediately west of the Bergland house (which preceded the Waterhouse House) burned to the ground in April 1901. The Bergland house was only saved at that time "by the most heroic efforts on the part of the villagers." The carriage house of the Burr house can be seen to the left of the Bergland house in the 1890s photo at left. George C. Bergland spent the last twenty years of his life in this house, and his widow and two children remained there for more than thirty years afterward. Louise Bergland owned the house and lot in January 1928, when Route 64 was widened and improved in Wasco. The property was deeded to Floyd H. Bergland in 1930. George and Bonnie Bergland, the only children of Floyd and Olive Bergland (see "The Bergland Family") grew up in this home and lived there until their father's death in 1946. On 17 March 1948, Floyd's widow Olive L. Bergland sold the house and property to Lee and Mercedes Boylan of St. Charles. A few years later, on 5 February 1951, Mercedes G. Boylan of Wasco, by then a widow, sold it to George L. and Margaret B. Vanderhoof of Campton Township.

The Bergland house contained a kitchen, dining room, living room, parlor, and den on the first floor. There were four bedrooms and a bathroom on the second floor, plus an attic and full basement. There were maple trees in front of the home in the 1930s and '40s, and large elms to the side and rear of the home. The Berglands kept extensive flower beds (particularly with irises and roses) in the back yard. In the northwest corner of the yard, there was a small white playhouse with green shutters. This small building was part of a float for Bergland & Company during the 1935 Campton Township Centennial Parade. During the parade, George C. Bergland and his cousin Phyllis Denker sat in chairs on either side of the front door of the 'home' on the float. The parade proceeded west down Route 64, ending at Campton Town Hall.

Painting of Wasco (detail) dating to c. 1899, showing the Bergland house

The Bergland house in the 1920s (left), and in the 1930s (right)

Side view of the Bergland house, perhaps in the 1950s

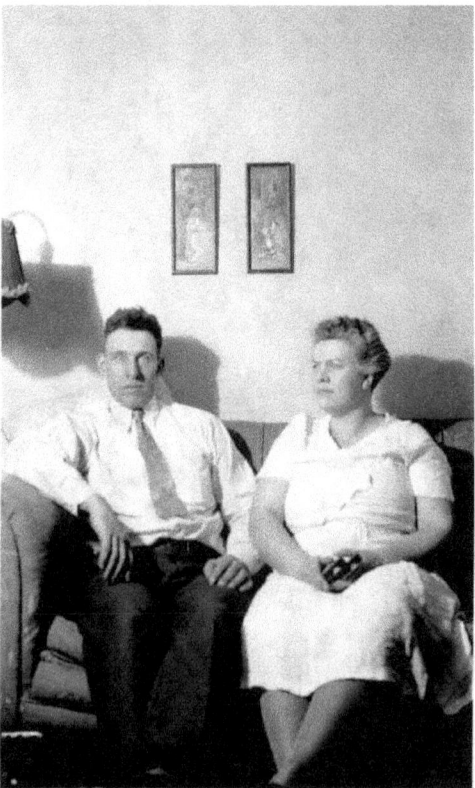
George, Margaret, and Kate Vanderhoof, in 1949 (left), and George and Margaret in the 1930s (right)

The Vanderhoofs owned the former Bergland house for just over thirty years. In July 1982, George and Margaret Vanderhoof sold the house and land to the Kane County Bank and Trust Company. The house is now owned by Robert and Milica Wolfgram, who purchased the property in December 1997 from the Old Second National Bank of Aurora (successor to the Kane County Bank and Trust Company).

The Bergland house in 2018

40W544 Route 64 – the Scott/White House. It is possible that this house was moved to its present site in the early days of Wasco. The building, at the latest, dates to the early 1890s (if built on the site) or before (if moved there then). On 9 January 1893, Leonard White of Campton Township purchased the half-acre property from William and May Ruddick/Ruddock of the same place. Since the purchase price was $600, there was almost certainly a building on the lot at the time. Ruddock had purchased the presumably vacant lot from Horace Higgins on the last day of July, 1890, for $50. The Ruddock family was from New York State, but came to DuPage County, Illinois, by the late 1840s. George and Fanny Ruddock owned a farm in Campton Township, near that of the Hagamans and Higginses, by 1870. George was William's father's brother. Mary Ruddock, one of George's daughters, married John Hagaman of Campton Township in April 1870. The Ruddock farm was located on the west side of the present LaFox Road, less than a mile south of Wasco. The northern edge of the Ruddock farm ran along the Rice farm's southern border. If the building was moved to Wasco, it was likely moved from the Ruddock farm.

Will Ruddock was Wasco's village blacksmith in February 1889. He welcomed a little girl (Jennie) into his family that month. Although William Ruddock does not seem to appear on the 1880 Campton Township census, his uncle and aunt George and Fanny Ruddock are listed with a daughter Delia Alice, and Delia's brother Erwin B. Ruddock was listed next door with his wife and young daughter. Since both John and Joseph Hagaman were listed immediately after both Ruddock households, it is clear that they were still living on their farm south of Wasco. The Ruddocks were also closely associated with the village of Winfield, in DuPage County, for many years. William J. Ruddock (later of Wasco) was born there in January 1859, and was a son of William and Ellen E. (Kemp) Ruddock. The Ruddocks had moved to the village of

Bloomingdale by 1870. After a rather brief residence in Wasco, William and May Ruddock moved to Chehalis County, Washington, by 1894. He continued working as a blacksmith in that region, and had a family of seven children by the turn of the century. Besides Jennie, those born in Wasco were: Benjamin, born in December 1890; and Bertha, born in October 1893. William's son and namesake was born in Illinois in October 1886. William J. Ruddock died in Tacoma, Washington, on 3 October 1940.

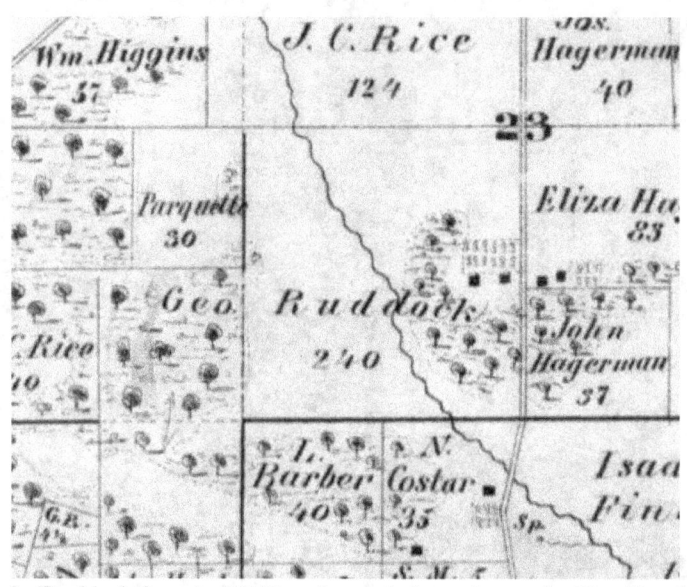

The location of the Ruddock farm in 1872 – the road shown is now LaFox Road, south of Wasco

Painting (detail) of Wasco, c. 1899, showing the Scott/White house

The 1892 map of Wasco shows a "B. Smith/Wagon Shop" located on or very near the site of the Scott/White house. Since William Ruddock, the house's owner until 1893, was a known blacksmith, and was later a teamster (see the 1910 census of Pierce County, Washington) is seems quite likely that Ruddock practiced his trade in this building which still stands near the center of Wasco. The Whites lived in the home from 1893 until their deaths several decades later.

In May 1909, one of the house's two principal occupants, Mrs. Emma M. White, was visiting her brother James Scott in Barton, North Dakota. C. Leonard White died in Wasco on 15 February 1927 (see "The Leonard White Family"). Beginning in 1938, following the death of Emma M. (Scott) White on 1 May of that year, Theo and Paul Scott lived in the home with their three sons (Leonard, Robert, and Beryl) and two daughters (Phyllis and Blanche). Paul was a building carpenter, and was born in Elburn on 8 April 1895. He was a nephew of Mrs. White, and lived in LaFox in the early 1920s. Theo, Paul's wife, was born in Batavia in 1897; her father, L. D. Wood, was Elburn's postmaster at one time. Paul and Theo were married in February 1923. The Scott family moved from Batavia to Wasco in June 1938. Around 1940, George Bergland raised pigeons in a converted chicken house owned by the Scott family. Paul H. Scott passed away in Wasco on 17 April 1952.

In July 1956, Theo Wood Scott and her children Blanche I. (Scott) Carlson, Beryl H. Scott, and Robert P. Scott sold the old Scott/White house to George and Margaret Vanderhoof, who lived next door. Mrs. Scott continued living in the house for a time, but paid a monthly rent (of $42) to the Vanderhoofs after the time of the sale. Mrs. Scott later moved to St. Charles. She celebrated her eightieth birthday in September 1977, with "several Wasco folks . . . in attendance."

For a brief time (between 1959 and 1963), there was a coffee shop/tea room in the building; it was known as "The Little House," and its "owner and chief cook" was Mrs. Vanderhoof. The establishment was known for hot breakfasts and lunches, homemade bread, sweet rolls, pies, and donuts. In the fall of 1960, Leonard and Agnes Valkenberg and family, who had immigrated from the Netherlands four years previously, moved into the Little House in Wasco. It was in this home, in February 1960, that members of the Wasco post of the American Legion held a special meeting to discuss moving and remodeling the Great Western Depot to a Legion Hall. The Legion also held installation ceremonies "in the big back yard at the Little House" in 1960, and enjoyed refreshments "at the long picnic tables" there. When Mrs.

The Little House coffee shop in Wasco, about 1961

Valkenberg took over the management of The Little House, she planned to "continue serving all home-made foods" and the "same delicious home-made doughnuts" as before. The Valkenbergs installed a serving counter in the building in the fall of 1961, "to help speed service." By June 1963, the building had "reverted to a residence," when Mrs. Hillis Barber moved into the building "formerly known as the Little House."

Once the restaurant ceased operations, the building went from being called the Little House to the Vanderhoof's little house. From 1967 to 1977, Rolland Woodraska "lived in the Vanderhoof's little house." Woodraska passed away in West Frankfort, Illinois, in March 1980. The "Vanderhoof little house" was redecorated during the summer of 1977 and was "ready for occupancy" that August. In 1978, Mr. and Mr. Steve Tobias occupied "the Vanderhoof's little house" in Wasco. The Vanderhoofs still owned the property in July 1982, when it was placed into the ownership of a Kane County Trust (No. 183). George Vanderhoof passed away in May 1985 and Margaret B. Vanderhoof followed him many years later, on 5 May 1997. After this time, the property was owned by a Trust overseen by the Kane County Bank. The Scott/White house is now a business and is the office for Great Western Properties. This real estate business is owned by Cody Salter, who founded it in 2005.

The Scott/White house, likely in the 1960s

The Scott/White house in the 1990s

The Scott/White house in 2018

<u>40W718 Route 64</u> – the Bergland/Hummel Store (see "Places of Business").

4N868 Old LaFox Road – the "Bergland/Hummel Cottage." The original "Bergland cottages" in Wasco were the two nearly-identical homes just east of Mather's store, but when those two buildings were sold to private owners (Mather and Meissner) in April 1909, this building was constructed. An article in the *St. Charles Chronicle* from 7 May 1909 states that "George Bergland has begun the construction of a new house," which is likely referring to the present 4N868 Old LaFox Road. The reference is certainly not to the Bergland home to the west, built in the 1890s, nor is it to either of the two original Bergland cottages, which had already been sold. The house in question was completed by mid-October 1909, at which time Andrew Erickson and his family occupied the dwelling. The home featured here has been a rental for most of its existence. In 1939, Ed Secylor and the Elfston family rented the home. In 1947, Mr. and Mrs. Vernon Bryant rented it. Bryant worked for Fred Hummel in the Wasco lumberyard. William Parson had lived in the Hummels' apartment there prior to the Bryant family. The Wren family moved out of the house "just north of Hummel's store" in May 1961.

The house is now owned by the Hummel family, who bought it from the Berglands in the mid-1940s. Like its near-twin to the north, it was built no later than 1910. The Stewart family also rented this home for a time.

The Bergland cottage, as it appears in 2018

The Bergland cottage appears in the background of this 1940s Swanson family photo, taken at Mather's

The old Bergland store, with the Bergland cottage visible to the right - the photo likely dates to before 1911

An undated (likely 1920s) view of the Bergland store, with the Bergland cottage visible to the north

A blurry image of the Bergland cottage in the 1960s

The Bergland cottage in the 1990s

4N878 Old LaFox Road – the McGowan/Leathers house. The home is thought to have been built in 1896, but a construction date of either 1904 or 1909 is equally likely. It is certainly older than the present Bergland store. The house is located on a small lot. It is the near-twin of the house to its immediate south and was said to have been built by George Bergland, or on his behalf. The lot on which the house is located was sold by the Berglands to Lawrence and Sarah McGowan "of the Town of Campton" on 21 February 1916. The purchase price of $1400 reflects the presence of a building then (also verified in early photographs). Lawrence and Sarah McGowan may have lived in the home prior to their purchase of the house and lot.

A very early (probably pre-1910) view of the three homes north of the Bergland Store

The McGowan/Leathers house in 2018

Lawrence McGowan, who came to Kane County with his parents, was born in New York State in July 1845, and was a Civil War veteran. He enlisted in the 52nd Illinois Volunteer Infantry, and was a participant in General Sherman's 1864 'March to the Sea.' McGowan married Sarah H. Hyre, and they had four children. In 1900 and in subsequent years, Mrs. McGowan occasionally visited her sister (Mrs. Harper) in Chicago. Lawrence McGowan passed away in the spring of 1920. A decade after her husband's death, Sarah McGowan sold the Wasco house to her daughter, Harriet J. (McGowan) Heath for $5 and "other good and valuable considerations." This transfer took place on 15 October 1930. Sarah reserved a life use of the house in the deed. Hattie Heath lived in Geneva at the time of this sale, and her siblings lived in Elgin and Lily Lake. "Grandma" McGowan fell ill in 1932, and her daughter Harriet cared for her. Sarah McGowan died at her home in Wasco on 15 January 1939, at the age of eighty-nine.

Harriet (McGowan) Heath of Elgin sold her late mother's home in Wasco to Lynn and Lillian Jay on 8 August 1944. The Wasco column from that time noted that "Lynn Jay has purchased the McGowan home." Mrs. Heath passed away not long afterward, in April 1945. Her death notice stated that she "used to live in Wasco." Lillian L. Jay sold the house and lot to Robert and Violet Leathers in March 1957, a year and a half after Lillian's husband's death. The Leathers family had occupied the house as renters for some time prior to the purchase.

Hattie McGowan and Ethel Coombes of Wasco, in the early 1910s

An article from August 1948 in the *Elburn Herald* stated that new residents in Wasco included the Leathers family. "They have moved into the house formerly occupied by the Aug family. The Leathers have two small children." At that time the family of Roy Aug, who had been in Wasco since at least 1944, moved to a farm northeast of the village, which was owned by John Coombes. Robert C. Leathers was born in Orchardville, Illinois, on 27 March 1916, and married Violet Lee in Geneva in October 1946. Robert had then recently completed his service in the U. S. Army, where he served as a Private First Class during World War II. He was later a punch press operator for Illinois Tool Works in South Elgin. The Leathers family sold their house in Wasco in the spring of 1979, and moved to Cisne, Illinois. Robert Leathers died at his home in Batavia in 2000.

A 1970s image of the McGowan/Leathers house

The McGowan/Leathers house, in 1983

In April 1979, Lester A. and Janis K. Gholson bought the McGowan/Leathers house from Robert C. and Violet Leathers for $31,500. The Gholsons sold the house three years later, to Rickey L. Bos of Sycamore. Since November 1984, the house has been owned by Arthur R. Schroeder. Schroeder was a trustee of the Wasco Sanitary District in the 1990s.

4N884 Old LaFox Road – the Probert/Whitney/Brown house. This two-story residence, which originally had a front clipped gable and an interesting variation of a Palladian-style second-story front window, was probably built in 1909, and was certainly standing by the mid-1910s. The one-third-acre lot on which the house was built was sold by the Austin family to Charles J. Waterhouse "of the village of Wasco" on 21 June 1909, for $150. The style of the home does not match those of the two to the south, thought to have been built around the same time. Charles Waterhouse probably either built this house himself or hired local carpenters to complete the task. Waterhouse sold the house and lot to Rachel C. (Whitney) Probert in May 1912, for $3000, and then he moved to the house and lot just west of the Bergland family's home. For a time in the 1920s and early '30s, Rachel's nephew Merrill Whitney and Merrill's son Morris lived in the home as well. Mrs. Probert owned the house until her death on 30 June 1934. Rachel Probert was the second wife of the late Charles L. Probert, and she was then the "oldest resident of the vicinity," and would have soon turned ninety-four years old. Her funeral was held from the Wasco Church (see "The Whitney Family" for further information on Rachel and her immediate family).

The Probert/Whitney/Brown house in 2018

The Probert/Whitney/Brown house in the 1990s - note the clipped gable then still present

A 1960s image of the Probert/Whitney/Brown house, with its original window arrangement

After Merrill Whitney's aunt's death, her house and property in Wasco were conveyed to him. The home was also associated with Dick Whitney, who was another nephew of Rachel (Whitney) Probert. Dick (who lived in Kansas City, Kansas, in 1929) was the son of John Whitney, Rachel's brother. In 1937, there was a lawsuit involving this property, the administrator of the late Rachel Probert's estate, and Richard Whitney. Arthur L. Paulson, Mrs. Probert's administrator, conveyed the property to Merrill Whitney in March 1937. The property was sold at public auction at that time, with Whitney being the high bidder; the amount bid was $1950. Merrill Whitney died in January 1944, and his house and property were then conveyed to his only son, Morris. Morris and Martha Whitney of Geneva formally sold the house to George and Martha Brown on 20 September 1951. The Browns lived there for more than twenty years.

George S. and Martha L. Brown of Wasco owned the house until they sold it to Lester A. and Janis K. Gholson (of St. Charles). This sale took place on 23 January 1973; Janis was a daughter of George and Martha, and was from Wasco. In fact, Janis's father George S. Brown was born in Wasco in 1911, and was a son of George I. and Lottie Brown (and was thus a brother of Art Brown). George attended two years of high school. His wife Martha lived in Kendall County prior to their marriage in the late 1930s. Their oldest son David Brown was born in 1939, and the following year George drove a truck for a local lumber company. In 1958 and 1960, George S. Brown was a driver for Nelson Brothers. The Gholsons, who owned the house to the immediate south after 1979, sold to Dennis J. and Holly Dewitte in August 1983. The Dewitte family sold the house and property to Dennis and Vicki Schmitz in January 1997.

The Probert/Whitney/Brown house is now owned by Lear Real Estate Enterprises (represented by Andre Radandt). Prior to 2009, it was owned by Didier Custom Homes, Inc. The Schmitz family (of Pickney, Michigan at the time of the sale) sold the house and property to Didier Custom Homes in July 2004.

4N902 Old LaFox Road – the Rediger/Maier house. This brick ranch was built in 1952. Dan W. and Bessie June Rediger were the home's first occupants, and had purchased the vacant property from the Hummel Company on 31 July 1952. The deed refers to the lot as being immediately south of "premises conveyed to Ethel L. Austin" in 1933 and 1934. Dan Rediger dug wells in the mid-1950s, and performed other related work. The Redigers sold the home to Earl Maier Jr. in January 1958. Earl Maier Jr. and his wife Roberta sold the house and property to Larry and Bonnie Danks in June 1969. The Maiers then moved to Wheaton. The home is still owned by Larry K. Danks, formerly of Wasco, but now of Minnesota.

The Rediger/Maier house, in 2018

The Rediger/Maier house in the 1990s

An obscured view of the Rediger/Maier house, likely 1960s

<u>4N920 Old LaFox Road</u> – the Downey/Austin house, one of the oldest in Wasco. This house was built prior to 1896, and perhaps as early as 1889. The home is now owned by Earl R. Smith, and has been for many years. On 3 April 1889, Harriet L. Austin purchased the property between the railroad and the present Route 64 from Norman L. Carpenter, for $700. She likely had the Austin home and store (in the same building) built soon afterward. In 1892, the Austin store and house site was owned by W. Austin – the structure was one of the first ten buildings built in Wasco.

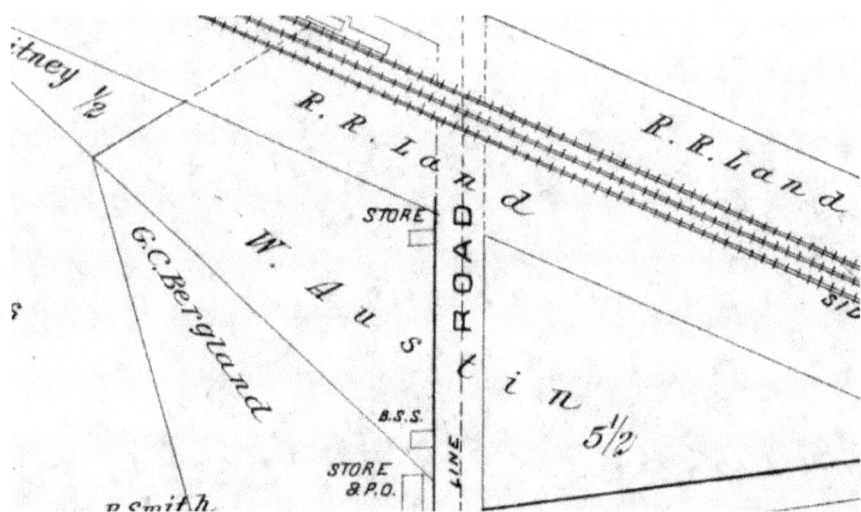
Austin family property in Wasco, 1892 - the store indicated is on the present site of 4N920 Old LaFox Road

On 7 June 1893, Harriet L. and Willard R. Austin began to subdivide their large Wasco property, selling the small lot immediately south of the railroad right-of-way, on the west side of the present LaFox Road, to Charles E. Hurd of Campton Township. The price was only $55, which indicates that Hurd was either a relative or close friend, or that there was no building on the lot at the time (even though one is shown on the 1892 map). Charles E. Hurd was the first railroad agent at Wasco, serving in that role between 1886 and 1888, and the family was active in the Wasco Baptist Church in the 1890s. On 30 May 1889, C. E. Hurd married Lou Foster of Crown Point, Indiana. As railroad agent, Hurd had "become a general favorite." Charles and Lou honeymooned in Minnesota, and made their home in Wasco. There was a Charles E. Hurd living in Chicago at the time of this purchase; since this man was a railroad conductor, he could be the same individual who purchased the Austin lot. It is certain that Charles E. Hurd (and his wife Lou A. Hurd) were living in the village of Maywood, in Cook County, in January 1903, when they sold their house and lot in Wasco to George H. Martin of Wasco. The *St. Charles Chronicle* noted that G. H. Martin purchased "the Hurd residence here" at the time. The purchase price was $1000. That summer, George quit his claim to the property in favor of his wife, Lillian M. Martin.

There was a "lawn social" given at the Wasco home of Mr. and Mrs. G. H. Martin in August 1903, which benefitted the Christian Endeavor Society (see "Important Social Organizations"). Ice cream and cake were served, and more than $10 was raised, which was put toward the purchase and installation of the new carpet in the Wasco Baptist Church. Mrs. G. H. Martin led the Christian Endeavor meeting during the third week of May, 1905.

George H. Martin was the Wasco railroad station agent for the Chicago Great Western until May 1906, when he was reassigned to Sycamore. He and his family left Wasco later that month, and for a time the Waterhouse family occupied the former Martin home. In July 1908, George H. Martin "of Malta" spent time with friends in Wasco – they rented the house during the latter part of their ownership. The Martins moved to Malta in February 1907, at which time Mr. Martin began a jewelry business there.

On 21 May 1909, Hattie A. (Downey) Marten "of the village of Wasco" purchased the lot and house now known as 4N920 Old LaFox Road. The sellers were Lillian M. Martin and her husband George H. Martin, who were then of Genoa, DeKalb County, Illinois. The buyers and sellers were not related. The purchase price was $1225, indicating that the house, which was on a quarter-acre-lot, was quite substantial for that time. The decennial census indicates that Hattie A. (Downey) Marten was living with her uncle John Whitney, near Wasco, in 1900, 1910, and 1920. She was her uncle's housekeeper, and had no surviving children. After her uncle's death in 1929, Hattie remarried and moved to Adrian, Michigan. An issue of the *St. Charles Chronicle* from 12 November 1909 indicates that "Mr. & Mrs. Downey of Appleton, Wisconsin have come

Hattie (Downey) Marten and her husband Charles, in the early 1890s. Hattie, who was born in Iowa, purchased her house in Wasco in 1909. Her parents occupied it from that time until their deaths in 1920. Hattie sold the house to Louise Austin in 1939

[to Wasco] to live, and will occupy the residence of their daughter, Mrs. Hattie Marten."

On 29 April 1939, Hattie A. (Downey) Marten Meach sold her house and lot just south of the railroad tracks to Ethel L. Austin of Wasco. Hattie, whose second husband was John J. Meach, was living in Adrian, Lenawee County, Michigan at the time of the sale. She was born in Buchanan County, Iowa, on 1 November 1869. Hattie's father, George A. Downey, was originally from Oswego County, New York. Her mother, Mary Ann (née Whitney) was from Campton Township. The Downey family moved to Campton Township in the late 1850s, but moved to Iowa soon after the Civil War. They also lived in Wisconsin for many years, but moved back to Kane County in the 1890s. George and Mary Ann (Whitney) Downey lived in St. Charles Township in 1900, but moved to Wasco a few years later. Ethel, who purchased from Meach, was the wife of Alvie Austin (see "The Austin Family").

The 1910 census shows that Hattie's parents, George and Mary A. Downey, were then living in Wasco. Since they were listed on the same page as Fred Swanson, Willard Austin, Charles Waterhouse, and Andrew Erickson, it is clear that they were living in the house their daughter would later sell to Mrs. Austin. In September 1913, Hattie Martin was in Wisconsin caring for her mother, who was visiting Hattie's brother there. In October 1919, Maggie (Downey) Copp of Michigan was in Wasco visiting her parents. George A. Downey died in Wasco on 9 April 1920. His wife Mary Ann had passed away just months before, on 14 January. In the fall of 1929, George and Mary's oldest son Charles Downey (who was then living in Michigan) visited Wasco and stayed at the John Whitney house. His sister's house may have been rented then. Hattie Meach died in Adrian, Michigan, on 11 July 1942.

Mary Ann (Whitney) Downey, in her rose garden in Wasco, just south of the railroad tracks. The Downey/Austin house is clearly visible in the background of the photo, which dates to about 1910

By September 1933, Ethel Austin was already occupying the premises which she would purchase outright less than six years later. Mrs. Austin was likely renting the home at this time, but may have had an agreement to purchase with Mrs. Meach. This is suggested in a deed from Edward and Maude Swanson, granting Mrs. Austin a narrow strip of land on the south and west sides of the parcel then still technically owned by Hattie (Downey) Meach.

An early 1910s, photograph of the Downey/Austin house, on the northwest side of Wasco. The couple in the buggy is very likely George and Mary Ann Downey

A member of the Swanson family, with the Downey/Austin house in the background, probably 1920s

The rear of the Downey/Austin house, in 1981

Earl R. Smith is the owner of the Downey/Austin house at the present time. He acquired the house and property in August 1977, from Ralph R. and Elsie E. Smith, his parents. Earl's brother Jimmy Lee Smith served as a medical specialist in the 9th Infantry Division in Vietnam in 1969. He was injured in September of that year, and was honorably discharged as a sergeant. Jimmy was awarded a Combat Medical Badge, a National Defense Service Medal, a Vietnam Service Medal, and a Purple Heart. Jimmy was married in December 1974, and later moved to Effingham, Illinois. His sister Kathy was married at Lily Lake Covenant Church in 1974. Jimmy and Kathy also had a sister Patricia, and a brother Bob. Ralph and Elsie (Elliott) Smith bought the house from the estate of the late Ethel Austin on 2 October 1967, for $6000. In the 1940s, '50s, and early 1960s, the Smith family lived in Flora, a small city in Clay County, Illinois.

The Downey/Austin house, as it appeared in 1996

The Downey/Austin house, in 2018

Ralph R. Smith of Wasco, who purchased the Austin house in 1967

The Downey/Austin house, as it appeared in the early 1960s

Southwest Quarter

<u>40W781 Route 64</u> – site of the House of Seven Gables, and the present Rice-Johnson barn. The property along the road, including the 1917 barn, is owned by Christine (Johnson) Brauer, a major contributor to this work. What would later become known as the Rice-Johnson farm was originally granted to two individuals following the completion of the government survey of Campton Township. The southern eighty acres (the south half of the northwest quarter of Section 23) went to Horace Bancroft in October 1845, who with his wife Arvilla sold to Timothy A. Wheeler ("of the County of Kane") in June 1849. The Bancrofts lived in St. Charles at the time of the sale. Wheeler almost immediately sold to John Tucker, and John R. and Margaret Tucker in turn sold this acreage to Joseph Rice on 24 November 1852. The sale price at that time was $125, or just over $1.56 per acre! The northern seventeen acres of the future Rice-Johnson farm were part of David Pattee's original land grant from 1843. At a very early date (before 1845) Pattee built a house on the north side of the road running through his property (the present Route 64, west of Wasco) and in March 1850 he and his wife Lucy sold the portion south of the road (and north of the eighty acres mentioned above) to Joseph Rice for $100.

Since both deeds mentioned above (although they were transacted years apart) were recorded in May of 1857, it is possible that Rice built a home on the property at that time. There was certainly a house on the property by April 1858, since that month Joseph and Sarah Rice sold the farm to their son James C. Rice, who immediately granted his parents a life lease to this land, for "their comfortable maintenance . . . during both of their natural lives." The property sale was for $1800, and all ninety-seven acres of the farm (in Section 23) were conveyed. The deed specifies that James C. Rice would reserve "the West half of the dwelling house." Whether there was a house on the land prior to 1857 is not known with certainty.

The House of Seven Gables, owned by the Rice family, and later by the Johnsons

A photograph showing the interior of the House of Seven Gables, dating to the decade of the 1900s

In the 1930s, Ellis Johnson would let the Swanson boys catch pigeons in his barn on Route 64. The boys had a notion that they could train these birds to be homing pigeons. The method used for their capture was to shine flashlights into the pigeons' eyes to blind them, and then to catch the birds and place them in burlap sacks. The pigeons would be relocated to the Edward Swanson barn, and released. They would be fed and watered, but the training was not successful. In the words of one of the Swanson boys, "when they were released, they flew away, never to return."

An undated (possibly 1910s) image of the Johnson farmhouse in Wasco

A clear image of the House of Seven Gables, perhaps from the 1920s

In one of the most significant losses to Wasco in recent decades, the historic House of the Seven Gables burned down on 11 July 1987 (see "The Isaac Johnson Family"). The building was completely destroyed, and many irreplaceable historic images, documents, textiles, and antiques were irreparably lost at that time.

40W731 Route 64 – the Ellis Johnson house. This brick ranch-style house was built in 1974. The Johnson family had moved into their previous home (across the street) in March 1944. Upon relocating to this house, Ellis and Frances Johnson were thrown a housewarming party in October 1974; the organizers of the event were Mr. and Mrs. Kenyon. The Johnsons received "a gift of two maple trees" from those in attendance. The McConnaughay family then moved into the former Johnson home. Frances Johnson died at Community Hospital on 28 November 1977, at the age of sixty-one. The estate sale for Ellis was held at his home "on the west end of town" in May 1993. Ellis and Frances's daughter still owns the property.

The Ellis R. Johnson house in 2018

The Ellis R. Johnson house in the mid-1990s

The Ellis R. Johnson house in 1974

<u>40W691 Route 64</u> – the Joel and Emma Hawkins house. This English Cottage-style house was built in 1938-39. The lot on which the building stands was sold by Solomon and Fern Johnson to Joel and Emma (Johnson) Hawkins on 7 September 1938. Like the Olson lot next door, the purchase price for the Hawkins lot was $1, plus "other good and valuable considerations." Both of the original owners of this home had deep Wasco roots and numerous close relatives living in close proximity. Emma Hawkins was Solomon Johnson's sister, and was the last of the Johnson siblings to survive. Joel Hawkins was born in Helsingborg, Skåne, Sweden, on 28 March 1882. He was a younger brother of Edward and Nels Peter Hawkins, and was thus an uncle of George and Mildred Hawkins of Wasco. Joel

Joel and Emma Hawkins of Wasco

Hawkins, who was often known as "Joe," came to the United States in 1901. Before moving to Wasco, Joel lived near the Corrons and Bolwahnns in the northeastern part of Campton Township. His wife Emma (Johnson) Hawkins, whom he married in the early 1930s, was also a native of Sweden. She had been married before, to an Olson, and had a son George, who was born on 23 February 1902. In 1910, Emma and George Olson lived with Thomas Langrill, just north of Wasco. Emma was serving as Langrill's housekeeper at that time. In 1920, George Olson, who was then seventeen, was living with his uncle John Johnson, in St. Charles Township. He was then working as a farm laborer. Ten years later, George was still in his uncle's household, working as a "laborer." Emma and Joel had no children together. Joel was 5' 4" tall, had hazel eyes, and weighed 140 pounds in 1942. He was a farmer for most of his life, and retired in 1937, shortly before building this home.

The Joel and Emma Hawkins house, likely 1960s

Emma and Joel Hawkins would spend Christmases across the street with the Johnson family of Wasco. Both Hawkinses were very quiet, and were "neat as pins." Emma Hawkins of Wasco passed away in Community Hospital, Geneva, on 1 March 1965. She was survived by her husband, and by their son George, who then lived in Valley View. Joel Hawkins, a member of Grace Lutheran Church of Lily Lake, sold his house in Wasco to his great-nephew Leonard Hawkins in December 1965. Joel died in Elgin on 26 August 1967.

The former Joel & Emma Hawkins house has been owned by Andrew J. and Caroline A. Wedick since 1998. Caroline Wedick is the volunteer coordinator at Fox Valley Hospice. The house's previous owners (beginning in

The Joel and Emma Hawkins house, in the mid-1990s

1994) were Michael and Michele Beecher, and prior to the Beechers the property was owned by S & C Revitalizers, Ltd. Leonard and Adele Hawkins, mentioned above, sold the house to Peter R. and Virginia Sparacio (of Bridgeview) in September 1970. The Sparacios owned the home for four years, and sold to the Jensens in the fall of 1974. The Spracio family then moved to Missouri, and the Jensens and their three children moved in. In May 1980, the Jensens sold the property to the Illinois Association of the Seventh Day Adventists. The Association of Seventh Day Adventists sold the house and property back to the Jensens in March 1989.

40W675 Route 64 – the John and Gladys (Bowgren) Olson house. The house was built in the summer and autumn of 1939. The parcel on which the house was constructed was sold by Solomon and Fern Johnson to John A. Olson and Gladys C. Bowgren; the date of the sale was 15 April 1939. The price paid by the purchasers was $1 "and other good and valuable considerations." John Olson was born in Chicago on 11 January 1906. His mother died when he was six years old, at which time John came to Wasco to live with his aunt and uncle, Pete and Hilda Denker (see "The Denker Family"). John Olson married Gladys Bowgren in "a pretty home wedding" on 16 September 1939, and the article describing their wedding noted that

"following a trip thru the east the couple will reside in their new home in Wasco." At the wedding ceremony, the bride's cousin Ruth Bowgren sang "I Love You Truly," and Miss Gladys Lundgren of Geneva played "Love's Old Sweet Song" on the piano. Gladys wore her mother's 1904 wedding dress, and carried a bouquet of white roses.

The Olson house in Wasco, as it appeared in 1977

The Olson house in 1996

The Olson house in 2018

Gladys (Bowgren) Olson, of Wasco

John Olson worked for Bergland Lumber of Wasco for twenty-two years, and then was employed with Owens-Illinois, a glass products company, in St. Charles for seventeen years. John was an active member of Grace Lutheran Church, Lily Lake, where he served as Sunday School Superintendent and Chairman of the Church Board. John and Gladys lived in Wasco until the fall of 1972, when they moved to Mountain Home, Baxter County, Arkansas. Meetings for the American Cancer Society were frequently held at the Olson family's home prior to that time. Since 2006, the house has been owned by Warren M. Peltier. The owners prior to him were Jeffrey N. and Bonnie J. Childs. The Childs family, who previously lived in St. Charles, purchased directly from John and Gladys Olson on 10 July 1972. Bonnie J. Childs (daughter of Jeffrey) graduated from Elgin Community College in 1978; her father was the choir director for St. Charles High School when the family purchased the Olson home. Jeff Childs wrote music for the organ, and was involved with Grace Lutheran Church, Lily Lake.

John and Gladys Olson in the 1940s, and Gladys Bowgren with her mother Ida, in 1937

<u>40W569 Route 64</u> – the John and Annie Coombes house. This one-story frame bungalow with both front and side dormers and hipped roof was built in 1923. The one-third-acre lot upon which the home sits was sold to John and Annie Coombes by Solomon and Alex Johnson (and their wives) on 5 June 1923. The Coombes' daughter and across-the-street neighbor was Ethel, who married Paul Waterhouse (see "The Waterhouse Family"). The original purchase price of the Coombes property in Wasco was $312.50.

John Coombes, who was born in Somersetshire, England, on 2 April 1868, married Annie Perkins in Kane County on 18 March 1892. He had come to the United States in 1885, and Annie immigrated three years later. Soon after his arrival, John Coombes farmed "in the Geneva countryside." John and Annie had two children – Ethel, just mentioned, and William James ("Willie") Coombes. Willie was born on 14 December 1892, probably in Blackberry Township, where the family lived at the time of the 1900 census. The Coombes family lived on a dairy farm in St. Charles Township in 1910 and

The Coombes house in 2018

1920. Willie Coombes contracted typhus after swimming in the Fox River, and passed away on 15 August 1921. John and Annie Coombes were living alone in their home in Wasco at the time of the 1930 and 1940 censuses. Annie was an active member of the Wasco Baptist Church, and was an excellent baker and cook. John Coombes died at his home in Wasco on 28 February 1951, and Annie passed away on 6 February 1962. John had a brother in Wheaton, a sister in Batavia, as well as four siblings who had remained in England. Annie's two brothers lived in the United States, but her sister lived in England. Both she and John, who were survived by their daughter, are buried in the Whitney Cemetery.

Thomas Mullally bought the former Coombes house from Patrick H. Collins in 2016. Patrick H. and Julia E. Collins, who ran the Collins Store, had purchased the home and from Vernon L. and Carol A. Critchfield in January 1974. The Critchfields moved to Wasco from Ramm Road (Virgil Township) in August 1966. They acquired the dwelling, which was then still known as the "Coombes house" directly from Ethel C. Waterhouse and her husband. The Critchfield family moved to Colorado after selling their home in Wasco.

The Coombes house in 1996

The Coombes house, likely in the 1950s

The Coombes family, with John and Annie Coombes at left, and Ethel Coombes Waterhouse near center-right

<u>40W553 Route 64</u> – the D. W. Stevens house. This clipped-gable 1 ½ story frame home is thought to have been built as early as 1914, but perhaps was not completed until 1918. The lot was sold by the Johnson brothers to D. W. Stevens on 15 November 1918, just days after the WWI Armistice was signed. The purchase price for the lot was $250. Mr. Stevens was Campton Township Assessor at that time. The home was certainly completed by February 1919, when it was mentioned in the *Elburn Herald*. There was a large celebration for D. W. Stevens's eighty-fifth birthday in March 1928; this was held at the Wasco church and was attended by one hundred and fifty guests. There were also significant celebrations held in Wasco for Mr. Stevens's ninetieth, ninety-fifth, and one-hundredth birthdays.

A faded image of the D. W. Stevens home from the 1960s

The D. W. Stevens house in the 1980s

The D. W. Stevens house, as it appears in 2018

In October 1943, Alfred A. and Emily J. Peterson purchased the former D. W. Stevens home, after selling their farm north of Wasco. On 29 November 1943, there was a large sale held at their former farm; the Petersons moved into their new home "in town" that December. Art Swanson then occupied their former farm property. The Petersons owned their Wasco home until December 1948, when they sold to Robert G. and Irene M. Holtz of St. Charles. Mr. Holtz was then a teacher in "the St. Charles school." The Holtzes moved into the home on 1 March 1949, not long before the birth of their daughter. James C. Minard of St. Charles purchased the former Stevens house from the Holtz family in June 1958. The Holtzes moved to St. Charles at that time.

Thomas Mullally is the home's current owner, and has been since 2010. Prior to that time, the house was owned by Christopher L. and Hope Collins. They purchased in 2003 from Katherine A. Jennings of Wasco. Jennings purchased the property in 1995 from D. A. and Gail Hanna. The Hannas bought the house nine years earlier (in 1986) from David J. and Mildred L. ("Millie") Sleeman, long-time Wasco residents. The Sleemans had owned the property since the fall of 1961. At that time, David Sleeman drove for St. Charles Kitchens; he and Millie had four children, and had been married since 1948. David Sleeman served in the U. S. Marine Corps during the Korean War in the early 1950s. The family enjoyed vacationing at Devil's Lake, Wisconsin, in the 1960s. In December 1964, Mrs. Sleeman and her daughter Linda were involved in a frightening accident at the center of Wasco, during which their car was struck by a large trailer truck, ricocheted into the gasoline pumps at the Mather Service Station, and burst into flames. Fred Hummel and Lee Mather helped extinguish the fire, and get the Sleemans to safety. Millie Sleeman was president of the Wasco American Legion Post Auxiliary in the early 1970s. The Sleemans' son Dwayne joined the U. S. Navy in October 1975, after graduating from St. Charles High School. He was a crewmember aboard the cruiser USS Chicago in 1979. David and Millie Sleeman moved to Florida after their retirement.

40W541 Route 64 – the Carpenter/Cray house. Cal and Edna (Carpenter) Cray owned this home for many years, but its original owner and occupant was Emma Carpenter, Edna's mother. The home was built between 1913 and 1914. Emma Carpenter of Campton Township purchased the quarter-acre lot on which the house was erected from the Johnson family, on 18 June 1914. The purchase price was $250. In December 1946, Mrs. Carpenter celebrated her ninety-fifth birthday with an open house at her long-time residence. She visited with some sixty friends, while "sitting in her favorite chair." A newspaper article stated that "she was dressed for the occasion and despite her years looked sprightly as she sat in the living room."

The earliest known photo of the Nettie Anderson and Cal Cray homes, Wasco, taken in 1915

Edna (Carpenter) Cray lived in her namesake house for most of her life. She was born on 9 August 1893, in Wasco, and moved to the 'new' house with her mother when in her early twenties, shortly after her father's death (see "The Carpenter Family"). The 1920 census shows just two individuals living in the home now designated 40W541 Route 64 – Emma Carpenter, who was then aged twenty-six, and her widowed mother, who was in her late sixties. Edna married Calvin Cray on 1 September 1926. The 1930 census shows three people in the household – Cal and Edna Cray, and Edna's mother Emma. Cal was then a carpenter for the railroad. He was also a well-known sheep shearer, and worked in "all manner of farming trades." Edna Cray was an active member of the Wasco Baptist Church, the Women's Relief Corps of St. Charles, the Daughters of the American Revolution, and the Wasco Ladies Aid. Barbara Louise and "Butchie" Beck made their home with the Cray family in 1946.

Edna Carpenter of Wasco, about 1913

Cal Cray of Wasco passed away in Elgin on 8 November 1976. He was eighty-nine years old, and his funeral was conducted from the Wasco Church. He and Edna had a daughter, Rose (Cray) Swichtenberg, and five grandchildren. Calvin Cray was born in Lone Tree, Iowa, and began shearing sheep in 1920. He lived for a time in Colorado, where he worked on cattle ranches. He also lived in Kansas, where he first entered the sheep-shearing business. That task was performed mostly in the spring, so for the rest of the year he worked on farms or did odd jobs. He came to Illinois in 1926, and roomed in St. Charles, where he met his future wife Edna. In his eighties, Cal still occasionally sheared sheep and did carpentry work. He was called "Wasco's oldest resident" in 1968, when he was eighty-two.

Cal's widow Edna R. Cray sold the house to the National Bank and Trust Company of Sycamore in December 1976. There was an auction held at the Cray home the last week of the previous month, when Mrs. Cray moved to Elgin. She later moved to Aurora. Edna passed away in at Community Hospital in Geneva on 19 November 1981, at the age of eighty-eight. The Cray house was extensively remodeled in the summer of 1977. Since at least 1981, the house has been owned by Richard W. and Linda L. Dillon. The Dillon family came from Kewanee, Illinois.

The Cal and Edna Cray house in the 1960s

The Cal Cray house in 2018

Cal Cray, 87, has been shearing sheep for 54 years and once traveled across the state to follow his trade. Today, he operates on the driveway at his Wasco home.

Two photographs of Cal Cray of Wasco, taken in his eighties

40W523 Route 64 – the Nettie Anderson house. Nettie G. Anderson was a noted artist of Wasco, and several of her painted teacups and plates are still in existence. Her 1 ½ story home with unusual fenestration, at the very heart of Wasco, was probably built between 1908 and 1911, although some sources imply that it is slightly older. When James C. Rice sold his extensive property in Wasco to the Johnson brothers, they (on 2 March 1908) in turn sold him the lot at the southwest corner of the present Route 64 and Old LaFox Roads. The lot was two chains wide, and two-and-a-half chains deep, and was conveyed for $125 (a surveyor's chain is sixty-six feet in length). Rice had by then already moved to the city of Los Angeles, however, and it is unclear if he ever lived in the home on this lot. The Rice heirs sold Nettie Anderson (noted as an unmarried woman in the deed) the parcel on which the house stands on 28 October 1911, for $200. On 18 June 1914, the Johnson family sold the lot immediately south of the house to Nettie Anderson, for $175.

On 30 October 1913, the Wasco community threw a housewarming party for "Mrs. Anderson and her daughter Nettie," who must have just moved into this house. Eighty friends attended, and the whole community gave the Andersons a gift of a dining room table and six chairs – George Scott, who lived across the street, presented the gift. Miss Eva Downey sang a solo at the housewarming party, and there was also other musical entertainment.

The Nettie Anderson house in 2018

During the 1930s and '40s, the house, now known for its red and white color scheme, was gray and was covered in stucco. Nettie Anderson, who owned the home for longer than anyone, was very active in the Wasco Baptist Church, the Community Club, and Wasco Ladies Aid. She was an avid gardener and beekeeper. Besides painting cups, saucers, and plates, Nettie also painted oil landscapes. She displayed many of these paintings on the walls of her home. One of her paintings hung in the Swanson house parlor. The painting used on the cover of this work, although not signed, may have been a very early example of her work. Nettie would also offer painting lessons to Wasco residents. She also had a horseshoe pit on her property, where local children would gather to play. When these games were completed, the horseshoes were always placed neatly together on Nettie's back steps.

Side view of the Nettie Anderson house, 1960s

In the 1940s, Beatrice Johnson lived in the Nettie Anderson home. She taught piano, charging $1 for a one-hour lesson. Sometimes her students left for their lessons in the middle of the school day and returned to Wasco School when the lessons were completed. More often than not, Nettie Anderson would turn off her hearing aid during these lessons so as to avoid having to listen to the novice students attempting to play scales!

John Burgeson passed away in the Nettie Anderson home in Wasco on 6 March 1946. He had lived in the home for twenty years. Burgeson was born in Sweden in 1859, and had come to the United States in the 1880s. He worked on several farms in and around Wasco for a time, and was once employed by the Roehlk Transfer Company. Charles Isaacson also lived in the Nettie Anderson home in the 1930s and '40s.

The small barn behind Nettie Anderson's house, as it appears today (2018)

Nettie Anderson of Wasco, in 1953

Nettie Anderson was severely injured in July 1949, when she accidentally ran an inch-long thorn from a raspberry bush into her wrist. In February 1950, Nettie took a trip to Florida, traveling with and her niece, Minetta (whose name was sometimes spelled Minnetta, or Minnette) Barber. In 1952, Nettie was the oldest member of the Kane-DeKalb Beekeepers Association, and was presented with an honorary life membership in that group. On 14 September of that same year, a large neighborhood auction was held at the Nettie Anderson home in Wasco. Art Johnson was the auctioneer, and the property being auctioned belonged to Nettie herself, but also to Minetta Barber, Paul Waterhouse, Cal Cray, George Vanderhoof, and Anne Mongerson.

On 15 December 1953, Nettie Anderson was tragically killed near her home in Wasco, after being struck by an automobile while crossing Route 64. Her funeral services were held at the Wasco Baptist Church. Annetta G. ("Nettie") Anderson was a daughter of Gunnar and Ulrika Anderson of Campton Township, and was born in Kane County on 24 June 1866. She was survived by a niece and three nephews.

Nettie's niece, Julia Minetta Barber, inherited her aunt's home and property. Barber taught English at the University of Illinois, Monticello College, and Southern Illinois University, and was a granddaughter of Gunnar Anderson, who moved to Campton Township in 1866. Minetta Barber was raised in LaFox, but moved to her family's farm west of Wasco in 1927. The original house on this farm burned in 1932. Minetta and her brother Furnald Barber bought that property in 1934, and she inherited it at her brother's death in 1947. Minetta Barber sold the farm property to the Kane County Forest Preserve in 1974, although she kept lifetime occupancy there.

In 1955, Miss Barber sold her aunt's former "town" property at 40W523 Route 64, to Dean and Vesper Clopton of Wasco. By 1962, some of the former Nettie Anderson property was owned by a trust, Wasco Incorporated. Since 1987, the home has been owned by the Fred E. Hummel Family Trust. Fred E. Hummel Jr. purchased the home and property from Robert M. Birkinbine, Sandra Kay Mulvey, and Tracy Lynn Anderson. Bob Birkinbine, who was president of the Wasco School PTO in the 1970s, had purchased the property in 1978 from the First National Bank of Geneva.

Minetta Barber in May 1974

4N788 Old LaFox Road – the Esther, Effie, and Rose Johnson house. This white two-story house, built in the American Foursquare style, was constructed in 1916. The lot on which the home was built was sold by Solomon, Fern, Alex, and Ellen Johnson to Isaac Mongerson on 22 March 1915. The purchase price was $425. Soon afterward, Isaac's sister Anna L. (Mongerson) Johnson came into possession of the property. Anna was born in Småland, Sweden, on 20 September 1857, and came to the United States in 1870. In 1880, she was living in St. Charles with her parents and three brothers. Anna married August Johnson in Kane County on 7 February 1885. August G. Johnson was born in Sweden on 17 February 1852. In December 1894, August Johnson bought the 165-acre Isaac and V. Celestia Finley farm located on the present LaFox Road, between the Mongerson and Hagaman farms. By then the Finleys had moved to Franklin County, Kansas. The Johnsons, who paid $8085 for the property, had four children, all of whom were in school in 1900. The oldest child, and only son, Carl E. Johnson, was born in February 1886. In 1910, Carl was listed a farm laborer on the home farm. His sister Esther was already a public school teacher by then; all four children were living at home. In 1918, the Johnson property was known as "Grand View Farm." August G. Johnson had been in Kane County since 1869.

The 1920 census shows all four Johnson children living with their parents on the farm just south of Wasco. Since the Miller and Mongerson families were listed on either side of the Johnsons, they were still residing on the farm rather than at this home, "in town." None of the children, who were then in their twenties and thirties, were married. Carl worked on the farm, and Esther was teaching high school. Rose was listed as a "house keeper." Their father August Johnson passed away at home on 7 October 1924. Sisters Esther, Rose, and Effie Johnson, all daughters of Anna and August, entertained the Glad Game Club at their home in Wasco in March 1928 and June 1936 (see "Important Social Organizations"). The 1930 census shows Carl as the head of the household; his mother and sisters were all still together in the Johnson home. Esther was still teaching then, and was also listed with the same profession ten years later. By 1940, Mrs. Anna Louise (Mongerson) Johnson (aged eighty-three), was still in the household. Mrs. Johnson passed away on 17 July 1942, "at her Campton Township home," after eighteen years as a widow.

The Esther, Effie, and Rose Johnson House, Wasco, in 2018

The Esther, Effie, and Rose Johnson house was rented to the family of Norman and Gertrude (Parsons) McKay beginning in 1939. Prior to that, the McKays were living in Elgin, where Norman was employed by the Elgin Machine Works. The two McKay children, Nancy and Dennis, attended Wasco School. In 1940, Norman McKay was a cabinet assembler, and was living in Wasco. They stayed in the area for most of that decade, and returned to Elgin when the Johnson sisters moved into the home.

The Johnson sisters moved from Wasco to Batavia in 1961, and again rented their long-time Wasco home. Esther Johnson, who taught school in Wasco for forty years, passed away at her home on South Washington Street, Batavia, on 10 June 1966. She was a member of the Batavia Evangelical Covenant Church. Her sister Effie, who was born on 29 November 1892, was the youngest in the family. Effie, who was active in Wasco Ladies Aid, died in Batavia on 21 November 1967.

The Johnson house as it appeared in the 1960s

In 1943, Miss Rose Johnson was the vice president of Wasco Ladies Aid, and her sister Esther was that group's Flower Fund Treasurer. Rose J. Johnson was born in Kane County on 15 March 1891, and moved to the Wasco area when she was three years old. Rose spent nearly seventy years of her life in Wasco, most of it on the farm just south of the village. The August and Annie Johnson farmhouse and barn are still standing on the east side of LaFox Road, and are now part of the Fox Mill Community Center. In March 1955, Mr. and Mrs. Verner Granquist moved to this property, known as "the Esther Johnson farm located south of Wasco on the blacktop road." Carl E. Johnson, who had remained on the family's farm when his sisters moved closer to town, passed away in 1953. His sister Rose kept house for him for many years.

Rose Johnson, the last survivor of the three Johnson sisters of Wasco, moved to Batavia in the early 1960s. She died there on 22 September 1973, at the age of eighty-two, and was buried in Garfield Cemetery. In her will, Rose Johnson agreed to convey her Wasco house to David V. and Marjorie E. Granquist, after a certain amount was paid to her estate – this agreement in fact dated back to 1961, when Rose's sisters were still alive. In her will, Rose also gave a large bequest to the Evangelical Covenant Church of Batavia, who took title to the house as part of this bequest. The Granquists purchased the house and lot from the church in December 1980. The house, which sits on a lovely treed lot, has been owned by Andrew C. Lenkaitis since 2007. The previous owners were Thomas & Patti Fitzsimmons; they purchased from Marjorie E. Granquist in 2006.

4N768 Old LaFox Road – the Mongerson/Santell house, also known as the "Santell Prairie Home." This structure was made a Kane County Landmark in 2007. This brick two-story Prairie-style house was built in 1923; Frank Richmond is thought to have been its principal builder. The lot on which the house stands was sold by Andrew and Grace Erickson to Andrew J. Mongerson on 7 March 1923. The sale price was $275. Mongerson also purchased a small strip of land south of the home from the Johnson brothers in April 1927, for $10. When she was young, Nancy Mongerson would stop by this home, and would enjoy her grandmother's homemade root beer when the school day concluded. The Mongerson family owned the home until May 1968, when the Mongerson heirs sold it to Henry and Amy L. Verhaeghe. Thomas and Jane Allen Allen purchased the property and house from the Verhaeghes on 16 November 1968. The home's next owner was Reed C. Klein, who bought the property in November 1975. Since 1986, the home has been owned by Sam & Beth Santell. Sam Santell, who passed away in April 2006, was a regional land planner for Kane County, and was instrumental in creating the 2020 Land Resource Management Plan.

Andrew and Augusta Mongerson of Wasco

An image from the 1960s of the Mongerson/Santell house

The Mongerson/Santell House, on Old LaFox Road in Wasco

<u>4N748 Old LaFox Road</u>– the Denker/Untz house. This two-story brick house with a hipped roof was built in either 1926 or 1928. The lot itself was conveyed to brothers Fred and Peter Denker by Solomon Johnson and others on 4 April 1927. Since the selling price was $10, it seems that the lot would have been vacant at that time, but an article in the "Wasco" column of the *Elburn Herald* from December 1926 states that "The Denkers expect to get into their new home at Wasco about Christmas." The article does not specify which Denkers were moving to a new home, but there were only two Denker households in Campton Township in 1930 – Hugo and Frances, who seem to have been on the farm on Denker Road then (Vesta Bell was listed immediately before them) and Peter and Hilda, who lived with Peter's brother Fred. Peter was then retired, but had recently been a carpenter, and the low purchase price for the lot may reflect his likely construction of the house prior to the recording of the deed with the Johnsons. John A. Olson, who would later marry Gladys Bowgren, was living with the Denkers in 1930. Olson was working as a salesman for the Bergland lumber and coal yard.

Jennie Denker, who never married, lived in the Denker home in Wasco for a time, but later moved to Batavia. Jennie was born on 18 September 1895, and lived until the summer of 1988. Jennie owned the house and property until February 1963, when she sold to the Untz family. Leo G. and Marjorie Untz and their family lived in the home beginning at that time. Leo Untz sold and installed carpet, linoleum, and floor tile. Leo George Untz was born in La Salle County, Illinois, in 1923, and married Marjorie Mattis in West Brooklyn, Illinois, in December 1945. Mrs. Untz set up a beauty parlor in her home in the spring of 1960. She was said to be "doing a nice job of keeping the Wasco women trim looking" soon afterward. Leo (who was known to some as "Butch") passed away in Missouri in 2016. The Untzes left Wasco in the spring of 1975, settling in Arkansas. John T. Karametsos, the proprietor of the Wasco Inn, which opened in 1973, purchased the home from Mr. Untz, and his family has owned the home since that time.

Harriet McGowan and Jennie Denker, at the old Wasco School where they taught

The Denker/Untz House in Wasco, which was built in the 1920s

4N732 Old LaFox Road – the Ekstrom/Swanson house. This one-story frame house was built by Peter Denker; the year of construction is not known, but the house is thought to date to 1930 or slightly earlier. It is sometimes considered to be the "last house in Wasco" when going south from the post office. The property itself was sold by the Johnson brothers to Lucy E. Ekstrom "of the Township of Campton" on 26 April 1939. The sale price was $1 and "other valuable considerations." Emma Louise ("Lucy") Anderson had married Charles Ekstrom in Kane County on 21 August 1897 (see "The Ekstrom Family"). In 1930, the Ekstrom family consisted of Charles P. and his wife E. Louise, and their sons Carl and Harold. Carl's wife Hazel R. was also in the household at that time. A newspaper column in the "Wasco News" section of the *Elburn Herald* from early November 1928 stated that "Mr. and Mrs. Charles Ekstrom are moving into their new home," and it is possible that this house is the one referred to here.

The Ekstrom/Swanson house, in Wasco, in 2018

The Swanson house as it appeared in the 1960s

Charles P. Ekstrom was born in Sweden, and came to the U. S. in 1892. His wife was a daughter of Gustaf Anderson, who came from Sweden to the United States in 1869. Before moving to the house, the Ekstroms lived on a dairy farm in Wasco, near the Bolcum, Larson, and Eddy families. In November 1953, Lucy E. Ekstrom, "sometimes known as Emma L. Ekstrom, a widow" deeded her long-time home to her sons Elmer and Harold. She included that she reserved "the life use, enjoyment and income" from the said properties conveyed. Lucy Ekstrom passed away on 13 December 1960.

The former Ekstrom house has been owned by Richard G. ("Dick") Swanson for well over fifty years. In fact, he's resided in the house since 1961, when he acquired the home and property from Harold and Lois Ekstrom. Dick's parents Gordon E. and Rose S. (Wilkerson) Swanson were long-time Wasco residents. Gordon was born on 31 August 1916, and Rose on 22 November 1915. In August 1961, Mr. and Mrs. Kenneth Johnson sold their house in Rainbow Hills (a small unincorporated community near Peck Road and Route 64 in St. Charles Township) and "moved into Dick Swanson's house, the former home of Mrs. Chas. Ekstrom." The Johnsons lived there temporarily while their new home was being built.

Edward, Maude, Lester, Gordon, and Wallace Swanson, in Wasco

Northeast Quarter

40W214 Wasco Road – the Terry and Joan Bowgren house. This single-story frame house was designed in 1972, and built the following year. The parcel on which the house is located was conveyed to Terry and Joan by Terry's parents, Stanley and Nina Bowgren, in April 1972. The home is located on the former site of the Carpenter/Bowgren cherry orchard. The Bowgren family has lived in the home since its construction. They are contributors to this work.

The Terry and Joan Bowgren house, built in 1973

40W228 Wasco Road – the Carpenter/Bowgren house. This upright-and-wing style vernacular frame house pre-dates the construction of the Minnesota and Northwestern Railroad, and is the oldest house on its original site in Wasco. It is thought to date to 1881, but may be slightly newer or older. The site was certainly vacant in 1860, when the property was still a part of the western edge of the John Whitney farm. The property later comprising the thirty-six-acre Carpenter farm was sold to William L. Slate in August 1870, and by 1873 there was a house on the land, either on or very close to the present house site. William L. Slate had married Ellen Williams in Kane County on 23 March 1865. Slate obtained a mortgage in October 1872, and may have built his house then. "D. Slate" (possibly William's brother) is shown as occupying the property early in 1873. William L. and Ellen Slate (of Aurora) sold the new house and land to Norman L. Carpenter on 17 September 1873, for $1800. The property was still owned by Norman L. Carpenter in the mid-1880s, when Wasco was created. The house appears on the 1892 Wasco map, with an orchard shown just to the east. The Carpenters owned the property throughout the decades of the 1900s and the 1910s. Norman L. Carpenter died in April 1914, at the age of seventy-one.

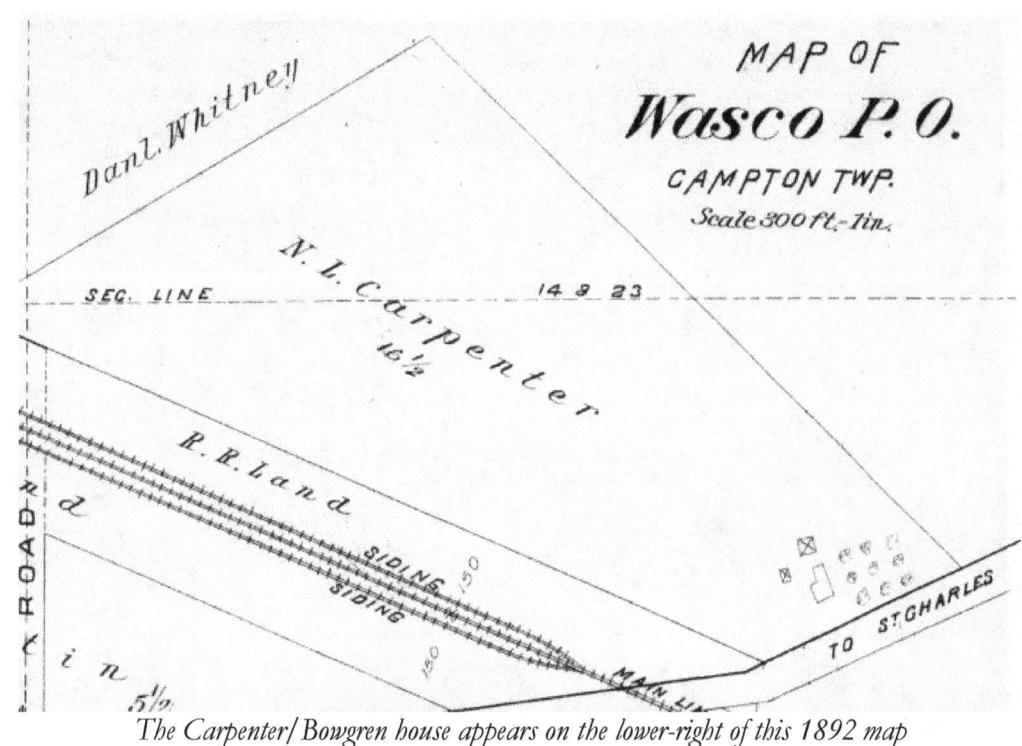

The Carpenter/Bowgren house appears on the lower-right of this 1892 map

On 16 June 1916, Norman Carpenter's widow Emma and his daughter Edna sold their interest in the family's Wasco farm to Nellie V. (Carpenter) Cherry and Nettie (Carpenter) VanWambeke of Elgin, Emma's half-sisters, for $1350. In 1918, H. T. and Alberta VanWambeke rented the twenty-three-acre "Cherry Farm" as it was then called, from Mrs. Cherry and Mrs. VanWambeke, his sister-in-law. The Carpenter heirs (who by then had moved to Los Angeles) sold the farmhouse and property to Oscar E. and Ida Bowgren "of the town of St. Charles" on 16 February 1925. The price paid in the deed was recorded as "ten dollars and other good and valuable considerations." The grantors agreed to pay the taxes for 1924 as part of the sale of the property. It is possible that the Bowgrens moved onto the farm prior to their purchase, since on 13 November 1924 the *Elburn Herald* stated that "the large barn on the Bogren [sic] farm near Wasco was destroyed by fire early Tuesday evening."

Oscar and Ida Bowgren lived in the former Carpenter house for many years; they and later their sons kept Hereford beef cattle on the property. One barn on the site (now razed) was hauled to Wasco from the Fabyan Estate in Geneva. Oscar Bowgren was killed in an accident at McDonald and Dittman Road on 22 July 1936. Mr. Bowgren was hauling lumber at the time of the accident. His employer (George Bergland, who owned the Wasco lumberyard) paid off the family's mortgage after Bowgren's tragic death. Elmer Johnson of Wasco was in the truck with Mr. Bowgren at the time of the accident. Both men were pinned under the load of lumber, which caught on fire. Local farmers took both men to the Community Hospital in Geneva, where Oscar Bowgren died from his burns and injuries.

In 1940, Ida Bowgren was living in the house with her children Gordon, Clifton, and Charles (see "The Bowgren Family"). Ida's daughter Gladys, who married John Olson the previous year, had only recently moved to her newly-built home at the present 40W675 Route 64. The Carpenter/Bowgren house was owned by the Bowgrens until it was purchased by the Lenkaitis family in 2016.

The Bowgren family of Wasco, including Oscar (right), Ida (left), and Stan (center). Hilton is on the left, front.

The Carpenter/Bowgren house, as it appears in 2018

The Bowgren house as it appeared in the 1990s

The Bowgren house in Wasco, likely 1950s

The Bowgren house on Wasco Road, probably in the 1940s

An early photograph of the Bowgren house in Wasco, likely circa 1924

Gladys and Babe Bowgren, with their father Oscar at right, outside the Bowgren house in Wasco (1920s)

The winter of 1936, with the Bowgren house in the background

40W238 Wasco Road – the Stan and Nina Bowgren house. This home, built in 1938, is known as a "West Chicago House." This home style was pre-fabricated, and was popular during the Great Depression. The home was built shortly after Stan and Nina's marriage, which took place in June 1937. Charles K. ("Babe") Bowgren bought this small one-story framed house from his brother when his term in the Armed Services was complete. The deed was dated 27 December 1946. Babe added on to the house. In May 1956, Babe and his wife Elizabeth sold the property back to his brother Stanley O. Bowgren, and his wife Nina. Stan Bowgren drove a school bus for many years, and his wife was a cook in the Wasco school cafeteria. Babe Bowgren worked at Burgess-Norton in the late 1960s.

The Bowgren family owned the home for nearly all of its existence. Joan and Terry Bowgren sold the house to the Lenkaitis family in December 2016.

The Stan and Nine Bowgren House, in 2018

An aerial view of the Bowgren property on Wwsco Road, likely 1960s

Both of the Bowgren houses in Wasco are visible in this photo, likely taken in the early 1940s

Bowgren friends and relatives, outside the Stan and Nina Bowgren House, 1940

The Stan and Nina Bowgren house, soon after its construction

Site of 4N995 Old LaFox Road - Fred and Caroline Swanson owned a house located near the Annie Nelson house, immediately north of the curve in LaFox Road, where Section 23 meets Section 14. The half-acre property adjoined the right-of-way of the railroad, and lay along the old Whitney/Carpenter claim line. Fred Swanson had acquired half of this parcel from Norman and Emma Carpenter on 7 June 1893. He built a house there not long afterward, and the house stood until at least the 1970s. The Swansons were there for several decades, up through and including the 1930s. Half of the land was part of the estate of Charles M. Eddy (who died on 5 January 1929) and was purchased by Fred Swanson, who had owned the other half for decades prior. Fred A. Swanson of Campton Township died on 12 October 1931, at the age of seventy-three. His wife Carrie E. (Roesner) Swanson lived until 1957. Both are buried in the Whitney Cemetery. Caroline E. Swanson of Campton Township sold the family's house and land (which was "known as the Fred Swanson property") to Dan W. Rediger in June 1956, but reserved a life estate on the property. Rediger was still the owner of record in 1964. It may be this house that was rented by the Redigers to the Hendry family beginning in the summer of 1961.

Swanson family members have tentatively identified this photograph as showing Fred and Carrie Swanson (left) with another couple

In December 1967, Dan Rediger "destroyed the big old barn on his place by fire recently with the help of the fire department" but it is possible that the barn referred to was on Rediger's property on Burlington Road, which he purchased in the summer of 1960. Melvin L. Peterson purchased the LaFox Road property from the Dan and Bessie Rediger in November 1969. Shortly afterward, Melvin Peterson built the new Wasco Blacksmith Shop immediately east of the old home.

Site of 4N965 Old LaFox Road – the former Eddy family/Annie Nelson house. Formerly located near the curve in the road, down a lane, this house was torn down many years ago. The Eddy family owned the small parcel here, and built a house on it around 1907, when they bought the land from the Carpenter family. The Eddys owned the property but rented the house on it for an extended period. They were the lot's formal owners until the two daughters of Mary Eddy (Gertrude Viola Eddy of St. Charles and Harriett Mae (Eddy) Morgan of West Chicago) sold the site to Philo G. and Carolyn J. Plummer in December 1947. The property was located north of the railroad's right-of-way, and immediately east of Fred Swanson's property. Annie Nelson, who was a midwife, and who delivered several Wasco children in the 1930s, rented the house beginning around 1931. She later moved to a house on the north side of Old Burlington Road, near Bergland Home Acres. She was born in 1892, and lived in Plato Township prior to coming to Wasco. She had children including Alma, Arthur, Ada, Arnold, Helen, Elmer, Donald, Margaret, and Verner.

Wesley Newton Plummer, who bought the Eddy house and lot, was born in Campton Township on 1 October 1883. He had moved to Tacoma County, Washington before 1914. Plummer and his family sold their land in Wasco to Alfred E. and Jane E. VanWinkle in September 1963. The VanWinkles sold the property to Melvin L. Peterson in November 1969, shortly before he built his new blacksmith shop nearby. An article from the *Elburn Herald* from March 1975 stated that "the old house at the railroad crossing in Wasco which was known as the Eddy house years ago is now being torn down." This of course is a reference to the home at this site. The Annie Nelson home site is now occupied by the Wasco Business Center buildings (4N949, 4N951, 4N953, and 4N955 Old LaFox Road).

<u>Site of 4N931 Old LaFox Road</u> – the former John Oslund/Marsh Carlson house was located here. The home resembled a long shed, and contained two apartments. It was oriented in an east-west direction, and was a frame structure; it may have been originally built by the Swanson family as an outbuilding. The structure was converted to a residence in the fall of 1934. Prior to that year, the building served as "[Arnold] Mather's machine house," which were "remodeled into comfortable living rooms." The two men who lived in the house the longest, and who were also its original occupants, were John Oslund and Marsh Carlson.

John Oslund was born in Sweden on 8 December 1872. He came to the United States in 1891, and worked for many years as a farmer, and later as a cement contractor. In 1894, Oslund was a charter member of the Lily Lake Mission Covenant Church. He never married, and had no children. John Oslund worked as a farm laborer for his brother-in-law, Alfred Peterson, in 1900. In March 1909, Oslund purchased a farm one mile northwest of Wasco; the property was located on the north side of the present Brown Road, and extended northward to what is now Empire Road. He owned this property until his death. Later part of this property was developed into the King's Mill Subdivision; another part of the property contained the western half of Lake Campton. He was living on his farm in 1910, with several members of the Swanson family. John Oslund performed miscellaneous road and ditching work for Campton Township in the 1910s. In 1920, Oslund was a farm laborer for Charles J. and Hilda Anderson on their dairy farm west of Wasco. A decade later, Oslund boarded with Edward and Maude Swanson in the family homestead. John Oslund moved into the house being considered here in November 1934. In August 1940, John Oslund was one of three men who set posts for the new Kane County radio tower located in Campton Township. Oslund passed away in Wasco on 3 January 1948. On 5 June 1948, the John Oslund farm near Wasco, then containing 144.5 acres of land, was auctioned off to the highest bidder. The dairy barn, dwelling, and outbuildings were all then "in good repair."

Marshall Ellis ("Marsh") Carlson of Wasco was born in Chicago on 15 December 1883, and was a son of Charles and Lottie Carlson. When he was a teenager, Marsh Carlson worked as a farm laborer for John and Emma Anderson in Campton Township. As early as 1906, Marshall worked for Wanzer Brothers Dairy in his city of birth. In 1910, he was a farm laborer for Charles J. and Hilda Anderson, and was living on their farm. By 1918, he was a farmer, and was blind in his left eye. In 1930, Marshall was living in the Andrew and Grace Erickson house in Wasco. Marsh was then aged forty-six, and was a painter. He was single, and was born in Illinois. Marsh Carlson moved into this home late in 1934, when its conversion to a residence was completed. Carlson remained at the home in the 1940s, and was then living alone in his apartment. He died in 1951. The home seems to have been demolished in the 1980s.

<u>4N901 Old LaFox Road</u> – the Higgins/Austin/Swanson Family home, built circa 1895. According to oral tradition in the Swanson family, a previous house on or near this site burned down, and this house was

then built. The original house was thought to have been owned by Van Rensselaer and Lucy Higgins. In the late 1880s, they moved from their farmhouse on Route 64 "into town," a distance of less than a thousand feet! When the "new" (present) house was built, its early occupants were Harriet (Higgins) Austin, her husband Willard Austin, and their four children – Maude, Alvie, Flossie, and Rollie. In later years, Alvie moved across the street, and Rollie moved to Chicago. Maude remained in the house, living there with her husband Edward Swanson, and then with their three boys. Maude lived in this home her entire life. Two of her children moved away, but her son Lester Swanson remained in the old homestead. Lester was a veteran of World War II and was associated with the home for decades (see "The Swanson Family").

Wallace Swanson outside of the Swanson house in Wasco, 1913

The Swanson home in Wasco, probably early 1960s

A view of the Swanson house in 2018

The Swanson house is certainly among the oldest buildings in Wasco. During the Depression, the property fell into foreclosure, but was purchased at auction by Edward and Maude Swanson. The auction took place at the east door of the Kane County Courthouse in Geneva on 25 July 1933. At that time, the Swanson property consisted of 5.58 acres of land in Wasco, located on both sides of the present Old LaFox Road, between Route 64 and the railroad right-of-way. The Swansons sold most of their property on the west side of LaFox Road to George Hawkins in November 1934, but retained the three-acre parcel on the east side. Lester Swanson lived in the old family home until his death in February 1996. The family's antique spinning wheel is still in the possession of a descendant. An antique quilt owned by the family, marked with the names of dozens of early Wasco settlers, was donated to Garfield Farm Museum by Don Swanson in 2017. The Swanson garden plot was located just to the south of the family home.

A professional line drawing of the Swanson house from 2002

Maude L. (Austin) Swanson passed away on 23 December 1947, at the age of sixty-six. Her husband Edward had preceded her on 11 June of that year; both are buried in the Whitney Cemetery. Their sons were Wallace Austin, Gordon Edward, and Lester Lewellyn Swanson, all of whom were born in Wasco. Wallace, the oldest son, was born on 5 August 1907. The *St. Charles Chronicle* offered the fact that his weight at birth was ten pounds! He attended the Wasco School, and on 12 July 1928, married Louise Martha Gerdau in Elgin. They had six children, the oldest of whom (Wallace Jr.) was born in 1930. The family lived in Campton Township, near the Alfred and Alma Swanson farm, at that time; Wallace drove a gravel truck. Soon afterward, Wallace and his family moved back to the Swanson homestead in Wasco. In 1940, Wallace and Louise lived in Wasco with their children; Wallace was still a truck driver at that time. By November 1949, Wallace and Louise were divorced, and Wallace (who was then living in Chicago) quit his claim to the Swanson property in Wasco in favor of his son Wallace A. Swanson Jr. Wallace Swanson was later a general mechanic, and married Dorothy Slimm. He died in Valparaiso, Indiana, on 12 February 1973.

The Swanson house in August 1996

Lester Swanson's truck, in Wasco, 1930s

Wallace A. Swanson of Wasco as a young boy (left); Wallace and Louise Swanson, with their children Wallace Jr., Donald, Robert, Charlene, and Ralph, about 1940 (right)

Joan Folgers has owned the former Swanson home for more than twenty years. A floral business, Gardens & Gatherings, was located here in recent years. Folgers first opened her shop in the year 2000. Joan and her husband had owned a wholesale greenhouse in West Chicago for ten years prior to opening the shop. They spent four years renovating the former Swanson house, which had not been painted for several decades prior to their purchase of the structure. In 2004, Gardens & Gatherings offered "a full array of gift wares, candles, and silk custom floral arrangements." They also carried a full array of fresh flowers for all occasions. They grew and sold thousands of poinsettias at that time, and worked with several local schools who used the plants in their fundraisers.

The Swanson house in Wasco, 1910s

Site of 4N879 Old LaFox Road – this was the location of the former Andrew Erickson/Wasco blacksmith shop (see "Significant Institutions & Places of Business") and the Wasco milk stand. Just south of the blacksmith shop, and north of Mather's garage, stood a milk collection stand. It was an open structure to which local farmers brought their milk each morning in twenty-gallon metal containers, some by truck, and some by horse and wagon. These containers would then be shipped aboard the milk trains. After 1945, bulk milk trucks began coming directly to farms, and pumped or siphoned milk from the farmers' bulk coolers. Prior to bulk coolers, farmers used to pump cool water into open tanks in their milk houses, to keep the milk cool after the day's milking. Perhaps the last local farmer to deliver milk by means of horse and wagon was George Hawkins. Each morning, as Mr. Hawkins drove his team of horses from his farm to the milk stand, he would hang a gallon pail of whole milk on a hook on the utility post at the end of the Bergland family's driveway. The Berglands would skim the cream from the milk for whipping, and would refrigerate and use the milk itself.

Dorothy Corron wrote that the milk stand was a "gray, frame can-shanty" and was located "between Mather's garage and the blacksmith shop." Her description was written in the 1960s but recalls events of several decades prior. Trucks from each farm generally converged at Wasco between 7:00 and 9:00 each morning, loaded with multiple cans of milk. The cans were transferred to a large semi-trailer parked across from Bergland's store in preparation of the haul to Chicago. Empty cans, returned from the prior day's trip, were stacked in the milk stand. Each farmer "picked up his portion of the empties before returning to his farm to tackle the chores of the day."

Wasco farmers lining up to deposit their milk in the milk stand, 1910s

40W484 Route 64 – the Mather Store and Service Station. Formerly the farm/machine implement business of Elmer Peterson, this building has been a place of business in Wasco for more than a century (see "Johnson's Store/Larson's Garage/Mather's Gas Station" for information on this building).

Site of 40W470 Route 64 – the former Augusta Meissner house. This house, located on a one-third acre lot, was likely built circa 1904. The site was vacant in 1892, but there was a house built just to the east (before 1909) which was the twin of this home. A brief sentence in the "Wasco Items" column of the *St. Charles Chronicle* from 26 August 1904 likely gives a first reference to this home: "George Bergland has begun the erection of a new house." The house just east of this one was probably built very soon afterward. These two homes were originally known as the "Bergland cottages." Both must have been completed by October 1907, since that month John Conroy and his new bride "immediately began housekeeping in one of Bergland's Cottages." Conroy was a night operator for the Chicago Great Western railroad. George and Louise Bergland sold the lot containing the western Bergland cottage to Augusta Meissner (Minnie's mother) on 30 March 1909. The purchase price of $1100 also proves that a house was already standing at that time. Augusta's husband Charles Meissner had died in 1905. A 1908 Kane County history referred to Augusta as "Gussie, the wife of Charles Misner [sic], who lives at Wasco in this county." Augusta's father was Louis Kammrad, who came to the United States from Germany in 1882.

Charles Meissner was living on a farm four miles west of Wasco when he was killed on 1 November 1905. Mr. Meissner, then forty-six years old, was "unloading milk at the creamery" in Wasco when the team of horses hitched to his milk wagon became frightened "at steam escaping from the factory" and suddenly leaped, kicking Charles Meissner in the head and fracturing his skull. Meissner was carried to the home of Charles Bliss, where he died of his injuries three hours later. He left a wife and four children, all of whom moved to Wasco very shortly after his tragic death.

Augusta (Kammrad) Meissner was born in Ramitz, Mecklenburg-Vorpommern, Germany in November 1862. She came to the United States in May 1882, and married Charles Meissner in Kane County on 30 September 1884. They had four children: Letitia, who was born in May 1885, and who married Frank C. Bolwahnn on 19 November 1903; Augusta, who was born in May 1888, and who married Robert M. Corron; Carl William, who was born on 20 November 1894, and who married Irene Kahn; and Minnie M. Meissner, who was born on 25 February 1901, and who married Henry Tiedemann. The family lived in Plato Township in 1900. After her marriage, Letitia moved to the Bolwahnn farm on the present Burlington Road, two miles northwest of Wasco. By 1910, Augusta Meissner and her two younger children were living in the village of Wasco, in their new home next to the Mathers. Both of the Meissner children attended Wasco School that year; it had opened just four years before. By 1920, only Augusta and Minnie remained in the family's home in Wasco. Carl and Irene were married in Kane County on 22 July of that year, and they then moved to the 160-acre dairy farm south of Plato Center owned by Carl's mother. Carl was active in the Wasco Pure Milk Association for many years, and served as that group's Secretary in 1934. Carl remained in Plato Township for the rest of his life, and passed away in 1950.

Carl and Letitia Meissner, as children, 1890s

Augusta Meissner was still the homeowner of the present 40W450 Route 64 in February 1928, when the road was improved and widened. In fact, the Meissner family owned the property up through 1950, the year following Augusta's death. Minnie Meissner moved to Elgin by 1924, but frequently visited her mother in Wasco, often spending a week with her at a time. Minnie worked for the Ackemann Brothers department store in Elgin, and married quite late in life. Augusta Meissner was ill for a nine-month period leading up to July 1946; during that period she lived with her daughter Letitia on her family's farm near Wasco. Mrs. Meissner passed away on 9 October

1949, at her daughter Letitia's house, aged eighty-six. She was buried in Plato Center. On 5 September 1950, Letitia (Meissner) Bolwahnn, along with her sisters Minnie Meissner and Augusta (Meissner) Corron and their sister-in-law Irene Meissner, sold their late mother's house and land to Robert B. and JoAnn Jay. In April 1953, the Jays sold the house to Pete and Jane Bohr. The Bohr family had moved to Wasco in the mid-1940s, and ran a restaurant and bar in town known as Bohr's Tavern. Peter J. Bohr was born in Iowa in 1903, and lived in Wasco until about 1955, when he moved to Joliet, and later to Aurora.

Augusta (Meissner) Corron, "Grandma" Augusta (Kammrad) Meissner, Flora and Jayne Norton, Grandma Norton, Minnie Meissner, and Dexter Norton Jr., in 1938

In June 1955, Pete and Jane Bohr (who were then living in Joliet) sold their house in Wasco to John A. and M. Joan Larson of Campton Township. The Larsons, who previously lived in St. Charles Township, sold to Pearl V. Dorr, a widow, on 22 July 1960. Pearl Dorr Schuetz and her husband Harold (briefly) sold the property to Jack E. and Wilma Jean Williams of Campton Township in January 1966, but the Williamses conveyed the land and house back to Pearl V. Dorr that October. In September 1973, Pearl and her husband Ralph F. Stelle finally sold the home to Lee and Mildred Mather, whose garage and store were immediately to the west. Pearl was born in Iowa on 8 July 1909, and lived on South Seventh Avenue in St. Charles in 1940. She later moved to Macoupin County, Illinois, where she died on 8 May 1989.

The Augusta Meissner house (white, with one-story porch) in Wasco, 1915

On 20 October 1992, Mildred N. Mather sold 40W450 and 40W470 Route 64 to Outbound Investors Corporation of Geneva. The building was torn down later that decade. The present brick commercial structure on the site was built in 2003.

Minnie Meissner (left) and her sister Augusta (Meissner) Corron, of Wasco

Site of 40W450 Route 64 – site of the Arnold and Grace Mather house. The property on which this home was built (likely in 1904, or shortly afterward) was sold by Willard & Harriet Austin family to George Bergland on 30 July 1904. Bergland paid $164 for the half-acre lot at that time. The home was built at or near the same time as the Meissner house, just west of it. Both "Bergland cottages" were sold almost simultaneously. On 9 April 1909, the Berglands sold the eastern of the two cottages, with its lot, to Arnold Mather, for $1000. In April 1921, Harriet Austin (then a widow) sold a narrow strip of land along the eastern border of the property (fifteen feet wide and one hundred and sixty-five feet deep) to Arnold G. Mather for $56.25. The Mathers still owned the property in 1928, and in fact would own it for nearly all of its existence. In 1930, Arnold and Grace Mather were living in the home with their three sons: Robert, Howard, and Lee. Only Grace and Lee remained there in 1940. For information on the individuals that occupied the home, see "The Mather Family."

Nora Mather, the widow of Robert, quit her claim to the family's home at 40W450 Route 64 in favor of Mildred N. Mather just prior to the sale of the house and land. After selling her property in Wasco in October 1992, Mildred N. Mather moved to Sedgewick Circle, in St. Charles. She passed away on 7 June 1999, at the age of seventy-three, and is buried in the Whitney Cemetery. When Lee Mather died in 1992, they owned a 44.5 acre farm on Bolcum Road in Campton Township. The Mather home in Wasco was razed prior to 2002.

Robert and Howard Mather in 1915, with their mother visible behind the carriage wheel

Arnold, Howard, and Robert Mather of Wasco, in 1915

An undated photo of Lee Mather's truck, with the Mather home in the background, perhaps 1930s

The Mather house, likely in the 1960s

The Mather house in later years, likely 1980s

Site of 40W422 Route 64 – site of the Gordon and Rose Swanson house. This home, which incorporated a small two-room structure moved to the site, was built on the land once owned by Charles A. Swanson and his family, who lived on the east side of LaFox Road. The house here on Route 64 was constructed on a small lot of land deeded by Maude L. and Edward A. Swanson to their son Gordon Swanson, and his wife Rose, in November 1944. The lot, which was seventy feet wide, was sold to them for $10 and other valuable considerations. The Swansons added a kitchen and three bedrooms to the older structure they had moved there, and improved the place tremendously. During the war, Gordon Swanson aided the war effort by hauling paper collected in local scrap drives to Aurora. Gordon had lost his left hand in a corn shredder accident in January 1935, when he was eighteen years old. He and Rose were just starting a family when this house was expanded. The property was owned by the Swansons until it was sold to a bank, which razed the house. Old Second National Bank now owns this property. The bank's groundbreaking ceremony took place in September 1990.

Gordon and Rose Swanson in the late 1930s

Kane County Bank opened their "long-awaited Wasco branch" on 16 September 1991. Dean Capes was the bank's president at that time, and Thomas Geske of St. Charles was the branch manager. This was the first bank ever to open in Wasco in its long history. The bank branch offered safety deposit boxes, sales of bonds and travelers checks, and an ATM for after-hours use. The lobby was open from 9:00 AM to 4:00 PM on weekdays, with extended hours on Fridays. The first week the bank was open, two horseback riders came through the drive-up lanes to make deposits! A merger between Old Second and Kane County Bank and Trust took place in 1991-1992. In September 1994, Dean Capes, Vice Chairman of the Board for the Kane County Bank and Trust Company, was made manager of the bank's Wasco branch.

The Gordon and Rose Swanson house, in the 1960s

The bank under construction, in 1991

Old Second Bank as it appears in 2018

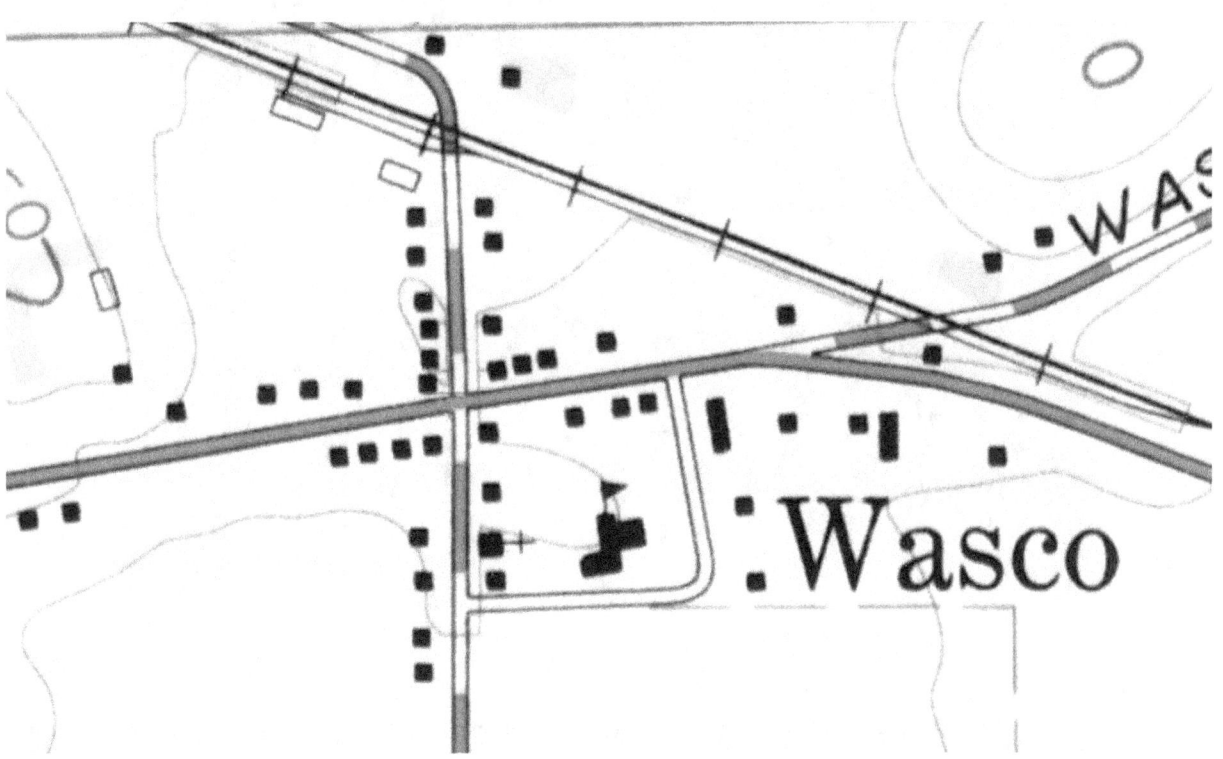

A topographic map of Wasco from 1964 - the Gordon and Rose Swanson house is shown near the center of the map

Southeast Quarter

<u>4N767 Old LaFox Road</u> - the Andrew and Grace Erickson House. Beginning in November 1955, this home was used as the parsonage of the Wasco Baptist Church. Previously, it was occupied for many years by Arnold and Grace Erickson and their children. The property on which the house was built, located just south of the land belonging to the church proper, was sold by Chester W. and Cassie Bolcum to A. J. Erickson on 29 February 1912, for $125. In December 1912, Andrew and Grace Erickson took out a mortgage for $1000 from George Bergland, using this property as collateral. The house was built at that time. The Bolcums had purchased the lot from James C. and Lucy M. Rice in October 1905, for $107.50, but had not improved the land during their ownership. The Ericksons paid off their mortgage in January 1916, not long after George Bergland's death. In February 1919, Grace Erickson became the property's sole legal owner, when her husband sold her his interest in the house and land for $1, and other valuable considerations.

The Andrew and Grace Erickson house, as it appears in 2018

The house and lot briefly passed from the Erickson family's ownership in November 1941, when Andrew and Grace sold it to Blanche Allen. She immediately quit her claim to the property, however, and it seems that the Ericksons stayed in the home. Blanche was born in Campton Township in 1916, and was unmarried at the time of her purchase (she was called a "spinster" in the deed, even though she was in her twenties at the time!) and was from Wasco. Her father, Ennis H. Allen, had owned the large farm on the east side of Wasco since 1902, when he purchased it from Isaac Barber. On 22 May 1946, at Bethlehem Lutheran Church in St. Charles, Blanche Allen of Wasco married Wesley E. Knudson of Blue Island, Illinois. They lived on the E. H. Allen farm following their marriage. Blanche and Wesley Knudson still owned nearly all of the east half of the northeast quarter of Section 23 throughout the 1950s and as late as the mid-1960s. Their property ran from the south side of the present Wasco Road southward, beyond the railroad, covering both sides of Route 64, and more than twelve hundred feet further south.

On 11 November 1955, Andrew J. Erickson, then a widower living in Geneva Township, sold his old home in Wasco to Julius Wynthein, Stanley Bowgren, and Roscoe Pierce, the Trustees of the Baptist Church of Wasco, and to their successors in trust. The sale was transacted for $10 and other valuable considerations. The former Erickson house and property is still owned by the church today.

A 1917 photo of the newly-built Erickson house, with the Wasco Baptist Church to the immediate north

<u>4N783 Old LaFox Road</u> – the Wasco Baptist Church, which was covered earlier in this work.

<u>4N805 Old LaFox Road</u> – the Maud Richmond House. This Cape Cod style house was built in 1937 by Frank Richmond, for his sister Maud. Previously, "Bergland Hall" (built circa 1893) was located on the site. Bergland Hall (sometimes called Millen Hall) was used by the public as a meeting place. The Rice family first sold the quarter-acre parcel to George C. Bergland on 5 July 1893. The purchase price was $50. Bergland Hall was a popular meeting place through 1907 at least, but it seems to have disappeared by the late 1910s. Whether it was destroyed by fire or another cause has not been definitely established. The property where the Hall formerly stood was sold by the Bergland family (Floyd, Olive, and Louisa, along with Florence and Elmer Peterson) to Maud C. Richmond on 2 January 1937, for a token sum. The legal description placed it between lots previously conveyed to the Millen family, and to the "Baptist Church at Wasco." Maud Richmond was unmarried; her brother Frank Richmond was a local builder, who constructed several homes on LaFox Road south of Route 64 beginning in the 1920s.

Maud Richmond of Wasco passed away in St. Charles in July 1964. She was born on a farm in Campton Township on 7 August 1892, and lived in the area her entire life. Maud was preceded in death by a sister and two brothers, and was survived by her brother Frank Richmond.

This early 1920s photo was taken near the steps of the Wasco Baptist Church, looking northeast; Bergland Hall would have stood in the field shown here; the Millen garage and house are in the background

In July 1961, the Maud Richmond house was sold by David F. and Joanne L. Allen to C. Russell and Glory Nelson Nystrom of Geneva. Local newspapers of that era state, however, that "Mr. and Mrs. Sam Gray and two children" moved into "Maude Richmond's former home" in the spring of 1961, after they purchased from the Allens. According to county records, though, the Nystroms sold to Donald I. and Mary Gray in August 1966. The Grays in turn sold to James F. and Ruth V. Clapper in 1971. The Clapper family owned the house for over a decade; they sold it to Gerald A. Chouinard of Elburn in 1984. The house is now owned by Jack E. Anderson, who purchased it from Gregory and Catherine Chouinard in 2004.

Maud Richmond, in the dark coat, standing just north of her house in Wasco. The Wasco Baptist Church is visible in the background

Front view of the Maud Richmond house, near the Baptist Church in Wasco

40W483 Route 64 – the Will & Mary Millen House. Also see "The Millen Family" for information on the builders and first residents of the home. Some consider this house to be "the first house in Wasco." Although the Carpenter/Bowgren house is probably older, the village did not yet exist when it was constructed. Likewise, the Scott/White house and the Mitchell/Morter house, both of which may also predate the Millen house, may have been moved to their present locations from outside the village. The Millen house is thought to be the first house built in Wasco after the construction of the railroad and the creation of the village. The structure was likely built in the year 1887. The property on which the house was built, consisting of a half-acre of land, was sold by James C. and Maria L. Rice to C. W. Millen "of the Town of Campton" on 4 April 1887. The purchase price was $50. Articles in the St. Charles *Valley Chronicle* from June 1908 show that C. W. Millen of Wasco was already remodeling his residence then – it had been standing for more than twenty years by that time.

The Millen family still owned the house and property in the spring of 1928, when Route 64 was widened and improved. In fact, the family owned the home through June 1943, when the heirs of the late C. W. Millen (who lived in the house until his death in 1930) sold the property to Lynn L. and Lillian Jay. The heirs of the late C. W. Millen included Charles W. and Evangeline Millen, Earl V. and Ella Millen, Mattie A. (Millen) Agnew and her husband Chauncey, and Charlotte W. (Millen) Bartlett and her husband Walter. The house was later owned by the Leathers family for quite some time.

Lynn L. Jay passed away in October 1955, and at that time his widow Lillian signed a document soon afterwards authorizing the Geneva Building and Loan Association to direct their loan attached to this property to Dale M. and Novella V. Leathers (of Wasco). The Leathers family had lived in Orchard, Wayne County, Illinois in the 1940s, and had moved to Geneva by 1950. Dale was then a foreman for the

Insulation Products Company of North Aurora. Dale and Novella Leathers formally purchased their house in Wasco from Lillian Jay in November 1961. Dale M. Leathers passed away in April 1983. Five years after her husband's death, Novella V. Leathers sold the property to the Mish family. Since that time, the Will & Mary Millen house in Wasco has been owned by Louis and Joy Mish.

The Millen house in Wasco, as it appeared in 1915

View of the Millen house today (2018), looking northeast

The same view of the Millen house, approximately ninety years ago

40W459 Route 64 – the Mitchell/Morter House. This small one-story house was built further north in Campton Township prior to 1888, moved to the new village that year, and was significantly remodeled in 1948. The one-third acre lot on which the house stands was originally conveyed by James and Maria Rice to George Bergland on 21 April 1888. George Bergland's daughter wrote in the 1930s that "Mr. Bergland also moved a small frame house from North of Wasco and erected it in the village as a home for the station agent. This was the first house in the village, the old Mitchell house, which has recently been remodeled by Harold Mortor."

The purchase price for the village lot was $50 – it seems that Bergland must have moved a house to the site very soon afterward. Bergland rented the home for years, and finally sold it to Mrs. Bertha Hiser "of the Town of Campton" on 11 July 1904. Since the purchase price was $500 then, there was certainly still a building on the lot at that time. In 1900, Bertha Hiser (who married William A. Hiser in Kane County in April 1898) was living with her parents, Jonas G. and Mary T. Blank, in Wayne Township, DuPage County. Bertha was born in Illinois in December 1872; the family ran a dairy farm for many years. Will Hiser had a brother, Frank, who lived in St. Charles; Frank visited Will Hiser in Wasco in the summer of 1905. The Hisers moved from Wasco to St. Charles in March 1907, when Mr. Hiser accepted a job as "blacksmith and farm hand" at the St. Charles Industrial School.

For part of 1907 and 1908, Rollie V. Austin rented the Hiser house in Wasco. In November 1908, Ed Swanson and his family began occupying the home, when Rollie Austin moved to the Rice house. The Swansons rented the home for a short time only. In May 1909, William Hiser "moved his family back to their home in Wasco." Hiser was employed as a blacksmith at the [St. Charles] School for Boys. The Hisers (who moved to Wayne) sold the house on Route 64 in Wasco to Eva Mitchell (of Elburn) on 29 May 1911, for $400. Mrs. Eva Mitchell, a widow, still owned the property in 1928. She would sometimes close her Wasco home during the winters, and would go and live with her daughter until the spring. Eva (Covey)

Mitchell (of Wasco) died at her daughter's home on 7 February 1940. She was eighty-eight years old. The Mitchell estate sold the home in May 1948; in the meantime, it was rented.

Detail of a late 1920s photograph taken at the corner of the Mather building, showing the Mitchell/Morter house before it was drastically changed. The man featured was identified as Charles, surname unknown.

Part of the Mitchell/Morter house (at left) is visible in this early 1910s photo of the Millen house next door

The Mitchell/Morter house, in 2018

The Mitchell/Morter house in the 1960s

The new owners of the Mitchell home were Harold Morter Jr. and his wife Donna. A local newspaper article from August 1948 stated that "Mr. and Mrs. Bob Morter and small son, Terry, have moved into their newly remodeled home in Wasco. The Morters are formerly of St. Charles and about a year ago purchased the home known to many as the Mitchell home and completely remodeled the place." There may have been a fire in the building shortly before, which destroyed the upper part of the structure, as the roof appears much lower at present than is indicated in earlier photographs. In April 1949, Harold Morter Jr. conveyed the house and property to his parents, Harold and Mabel C. Morter of St. Charles. In September 1964, the Morters sold the house and land to Otto B. and Rose E. Mueller of Naperville. Theodore ("Dusty") and Shirley Reinert rented the Morter/Mueller home for many years. The Reinerts lived in St. Charles in 1950, when Dusty worked for Operadio. They moved to Wasco later that decade, and finally relocated to Cambridge, Wisconsin, in 1992. Dennis and Cheryl Tischhauser sold the home to the Essex family in the summer of 2014, after having owned the property for over twenty years. Steven and Laura Essex owned the home until February 2017. The present owner is Kevin Decorte.

<u>40W441 Route 64</u> – the Gust Swanson House. This two-story cross-gable frame house was built in 1888, and therefore is nearly as old as the Millen house two doors to the west. An *Elgin Advocate* column from February 1888 stated that "Gus Swanson is to erect a fine residence this coming spring. He is getting the material on the ground." Another column in the same paper from the second week of December 1888 stated that "Gus Swanson has completed his new house and will soon occupy it." The deed creating the present parcel dates to 21 April 1888, when James C. and Maria Rice sold the property to Gust Swanson "of the Town of Campton." The original purchase price was $50, and the house was built soon after the deed was recorded. Gust Swanson died (still owning the house) in December 1896.

The Gust Swanson house in Wasco, in 2018

Following Gust Swanson's death, the house and property went to his son Claus A. Swanson, who was born in Sweden in 1857. Claus's wife was Emma C. (Anderson) Swanson, who was born in August 1866. Claus and Emma had four children, two of whom (Claude A. and Ila E. Swanson) died rather young. The family (consisting of the parents and their two surviving children, Mildred and Norvid, as well as Emma's widowed mother Anna Anderson) still owned the home in the 1910s. Norvid Swanson of Wasco studied agriculture at the University of Illinois between 1912 and 1916. He married Louise Mattie Redborg on 19 March 1921. They lived in St. Charles in the late 1920s, but for a short time they rented the "Bergland cottage" in Wasco.

The Gust Swanson house in the 1990s

On 9 June 1932, Claus A. and Emma C. Swanson deeded their house and property in Wasco to their son Norvid R. Swanson, and their daughter Mildred E. (Swanson) Olson (also see "The Gustaf Swanson Family" section of this work). Norvid lived in Wasco at the time of the aforementioned deed, but Mildred was living with her husband and family in St. Charles. The other grantor in the deed was Claus's unmarried brother Charles J. Swanson. In March 1933, Norvid and his wife Louise moved to the Swanson Brothers' farm in Campton Township. By late 1936, they had moved to South Third Street in St. Charles, and remained there during World War II. Norvid and his sister Mildred, along with their spouses, sold the home and property to William Massolle Jr. on 14 October 1943. In the mid-1950s, Norvid Swanson worked as a teller for the Merchants' National Bank, and lived in Batavia.

In June 1948, William and Muriel Massolle sold the former Gust Swanson house to Adrian and Mary Jane Landreth of St. Charles for $5500. The Landreths lived in the old house for years. Adrian W. Landreth was born in 1915, and was a Sergeant in the U. S. Army during World War II. In 1950, his

The rear of the Gust Swanson house in the 1960s

wife Mary Jane Landreth was a clerk for the Operadio Manufacturing Company. Much later, the Landreths moved to Effingham County, Illinois. In October 1990, Adrian W. and Mary Jane Landreth sold their house in Wasco to John and Mary Messina, who owned the house until selling to the present owners. Since June 2005, the house has been owned by Warren & Leslie Peltier of St. Charles.

40W425 Route 64 – the Johnson/Lofgren House. This frame house was built in the mid-to-late 1890s, and is among the oldest in Wasco. It was painted blue for many years, though it was originally white, and the house was recently remodeled. The main gable is parallel to the street. The property was conveyed from the Rice family to Charley Johnson "of the Town of Campton" on 7 October 1896. The purchase price was

The Johnson/Lofgren house in 2018

$80. Since Johnson took out a $300 mortgage the following year, using the property as collateral, it is likely that the house was built then or shortly before. The deed was subject to a notable provision; namely, "provided always that the sale of any intoxicating liquors by any grantee on said premises will render this deed void."

The first mortgage, which was loaned to Johnson by George Bergland, mentioned a "1 ½ story house" already standing on the lot in 1897. This loan was paid off by February 1900. Johnson took out another mortgage on the property in 1910, this one from P. A.

Peterson. This mortgage was satisfied in August 1915, several months after Mr. Peterson's death. On 14 May 1918, for $1600, Charley Johnson (a lifelong bachelor) sold the property and house to Anders G. Lofgren of Wasco. Lofgren, a native of Sweden and a local farmer, lived there with his wife Johanna for just under a decade. One of their daughters, Anna Wilhelmina ("Minnie") Lofgren, who was born in 1884, married Elmer Peterson of Rockford in June 1907. The marriage took place at the parents' home in Wasco. The Petersons lived in Rockford for a time and had two daughters. He is not to be confused with the other Elmer Peterson mentioned in this work, who married into the Bergland family.

The Johnson/Lofgren house in 1999

The Johnson/Lofgren house as it appeared in the 1950s

Art and Dora Johnson of Wasco

The Lofgren family's house and property were included on the June 1926 petition "for the organization of . . . the Fox River Conservancy District." The purpose of the district was for river control, sanitation, and the development of a reliable water supply. On 4 April 1927, Anders G. Lofgren, a widower living in Wasco, sold the house to Arthur R. Johnson (also of Wasco) for $10. In February 1928, Arthur and Dorothy Johnson sold a sliver of land on the northern edge of their property to the People of the State of Illinois for the improvement and paving of Route 64. Anders G. ("Andrew") Lofgren died in Wasco on 27 May 1931, at the home of his son-in-law, Elmer Peterson. Lofgren was seventy-eight years old at the time of his death; he is buried in the Whitney Cemetery.

Arthur R. Johnson and his wife Dora lived in their house in Wasco for more than a decade. In February 1939, William Parsons moved "to the Arthur Johnson house in Wasco." The Johnsons obtained a mortgage on the property in March 1939; Carl H. Olson was the lender – the amount was $1500. This mortgage was repaid in 1941. Arthur and Dora Johnson sold the home and property to Frank S. and Bessie L. Skeen of Blackberry Township on 31 December 1943. By 1950, Art and Dora Johnson had moved to St. Charles, where he worked as a city policeman.

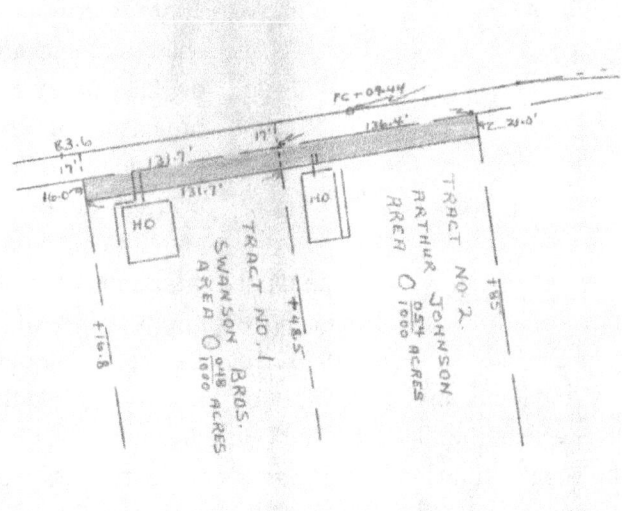

Survey of lands conveyed from Art Johnson to the People of the State of Illinois in 1928

Frank and Bessie Skeen sold their house to Axel N. and Minnie (Deckert) Anderson of Campton Township on 10 December 1948. Minnie was born on 20 August 1885 and was a daughter of William and Louisa Deckert of Lily Lake. She married Axel Anderson, a native of Sweden and a Kane County farmer, on 9 March 1910. The wedding took place at Bethlehem Lutheran Church, St. Charles. Axel was attended by his brother, William C. Anderson. Axel Anderson was born in Sweden on 8 October 1884, and immigrated in 1903, coming directly to Kane County. The Andersons farmed until their retirement in 1948, when they moved to Wasco. The couple had three children: William August, Hazel Alice, and Myrtle Florence Anderson.

Myrtle Anderson was born on 6 February 1925, in Campton Township, and married Henry A. Feltgen, Jr. in 1953, before moving to St. Charles. She passed away in Geneva on 6 September 2006 and was buried in the Blackberry Cemetery. Myrtle's older sister Hazel married Howard Berglund, and moved to Hickman Mils, Missouri. She was born on 27 February 1915 and attended Wasco School. She died in Kansas City, Missouri, on 27 November 2002. William A. Anderson was born on 4 March 1911, and was a forger in an auto parts factory in 1940. He moved to Crystal Lake, and later lived in Hebron. William died in Moorsville, Indiana, on 8 January 1988. Axel Anderson was custodian for the Kane County Livestock Center from 1953 to 1957. The Anderson family celebrated their fiftieth anniversary in March 1960 with an open house held at the Wasco School.

Axel and Minnie Anderson of Wasco, in 1960

Minnie Anderson attended the Deckert family reunions for many years, and in 1959 and later she was often the eldest family member present. Minnie's father, William F. Deckert, who was a native of Saxony, had come to the United States aboard the "Egypt Monarch" which sailed from London on 25 June 1883. His wife Louisa followed with the oldest children the next year. There were nine children that survived childhood, including Minnie, who was born on 20 August 1885. She was the chief organizer of the 1960 Deckert family reunion, held in Elburn. Minnie passed away in Kane County two days after her eightieth birthday. Axel Anderson of Wasco died on 4 March 1967, at the age of eighty-two. The family's house in Wasco was put up for sale shortly afterward. The purchasers were John S. and Ethel L. Bowman, of Wayne. After several years in Wasco, the Bowmans sold to Harold G. Miller Jr. in July 1975. Ten years later, Harold and Vikki Miller sold the house and property to Mary Ann Davy. In April 1988, Robert E. Davy, Jr. sold the Johnson/Lofgren house to Mary Ann and Samuel R. Owensby. In July 2001, the Owensbys sold to Preston and Wesley Scroggin of DuPage Lighting, Inc. Some say the Johnson/Lofgren house in Wasco is (or was) haunted. The house is still owned by Wesley Scroggin.

40W411 Route 64 – the Mathilda Johnson House. This one-story white frame house at the corner of Route 64 and School Street was built in 1935. Matilda's brothers (see "The Isaac Johnson Family") helped finance the construction costs. The house was later owned by Mathilda's only son, Arthur Johnson. Art and Dora Johnson (see above) sold the house and land to their son and daughter-in-law, Wesley A. and Elaine B. Johnson of Campton Township, on 21 March 1957. The house was rented for some years. The Johnsons sold to Everett S. Larson Jr. of Campton Township in April 1959. Everett and his wife Marcia Larson sold the house and land to Elizabeth A. Burnell in July 1964. The house is now owned by Rosemary (Burnell) Crain, whose grandparents, Frank and Rose Lorang, were early Elburn settlers.

The Mathilda Johnson house, in 2018

The rear of the Mathilda Johnson house, in the 1960s

The rear of the Mathilda Johnson house, likely in the 1940s

4N793 School Street – the Chuck and Gen White House. Charles M. White secured the lot on which this house was built on 4 October 1950; it was part of a larger tract purchased by Charles and his brother Joseph in 1947. Chuck and Genevieve ("Gen") (Gassmann) White were married on 8 February 1947, in St. Charles; they honeymooned at the St. Charles Hotel. Gen was born in Chicago on 25 December 1924. Their house in Wasco was completed early in 1951. Chuck and Gen White lived in Wasco for more than twenty years, and then moved to Patch Grove, Wisconsin. They had five children: Jim, Mary Jane, Susan, Barbara, and Roberta White, and eleven grandchildren. Genevieve M. White passed away in Patch Grove on 18 May 2005, at the age of eighty. She enjoyed sewing, hosting parties, and playing euchre.

Charles M. White, who was born in Batavia on 27 February 1922, passed away in Niles, Michigan, on 19 March 2015, at the age of ninety-three. During his long career at White Brothers Trucking (see "Significant Institutions & Places of Business") Chuck White and his employees "hauled millions of feet of concrete conduit, thousands of miles of concrete pipe, thousands of concrete and steel beams used for bridges and buildings, millions of tons of machinery," and countless of oversize and overweight loads of all descriptions. After moving to Wisconsin in the 1970s, Chuck White operated several farms, until his true retirement in 2009. The Chuck and Gen White house is now owned by the White Brothers Trucking Company and serves as their business office.

Chuck and Gen White, with their Matron of Honor and Best Man behind them

The Chuck and Gen White house, in 2018 - Business office for White Brothers Trucking

<u>4N763 School Street</u> – the Joe and Phyllis White House. Joseph N. White was born in 1920, and was the oldest son of John P. and Mary White, who lived in Batavia Township in 1940. Joe White was a truck driver that year. After graduating from high school, Joe enlisted in the U. S. Army Air Corps on 1 July 1940. After the end of the war in 1945, Joe returned home to Kane County. He took out a mortgage in August 1948, and began construction of this home in Wasco. The house was placed on a 150' x 200' lot carved out of the White brothers' property, purchased the previous year. The one-story home was completed in 1949. Joe White died in November 1957, leaving his wife Phyllis and their daughters Devra, Cheryl, Connie, and Jodi. Joe was also survived by his parents (who lived in Batavia) and his grandmother, Martha White of Aurora.

In April 1962, Phyllis White and her second husband William Dillon sold the house and property to Werner F. and Ruth M. Ladewig of Campton Township. The Dillons lived in Tulsa, Oklahoma at that time. Ladewig was later a co-owner of L. and M. Power & Equipment Inc. in DeKalb. The Ladewigs sold to Albert and Lorraine Mueller of St. Charles Township in October 1966. The Muellers owned the house and property for more than twenty years. In the fall of 1989, Albert Mueller of St. Charles sold the property in question to Samuel R. and Mary Ann Owensby. In August 1999, the Owensbys sold 4N763 School Street to James and Virginia White, whose family had built the house half a century before. So, the Joe

Joe White of Wasco, about 1945

and Phyllis White house on School Street is now (again) owned by the White family.   Jim White, the son of Chuck, now lives in Wisconsin.

The Joe and Phyllis White house, about 1961

The Joe and Phyllis White house, in 2018

Site of 40W331 Route 64 – the former Harvey and Alma Cole house was located east of the present site of the Fox River & Countryside Fire & Rescue building, and immediately west of the Wasco Inn. The Coles moved to Wasco in the fall of 1950, purchasing property on the south side of Route 64 from Lathrop J. and Patricia J. Hunt of St. Charles. Their parcel of land had 129' of frontage, and was 199' in depth. Earlier, the Coles lived in North Aurora, where Harvey F. Cole was a welder for the Austin-Western Company. In the 1960s, Alma A. Cole was a member of a knitting club called the "Knit Wits." She and Nina Bowgren were involved in an automobile accident in March 1971; the women were on their way to Rochelle, Illinois at the time. The Coles had a son, John Harvey Cole, who was married in Hinckley, Illinois, in 1962, and a daughter, Carol Ann, who was married the following year. The Cole property in Wasco was sold by the

Coles to White Brothers Trucking in March 1964. A newspaper article from the time stated that the company was "located adjacent to them."

The oldest part of the Cole house was built as a one-story frame garage in the late 1920s, or slightly later, and the building was expanded to two stories (and was converted to a residence) in 1949. Until December 1948, the parcel of land containing the Cole house was owned by Clarence W. and Elaine L. Raasch, who were then living in St. Charles. At that time the Raasches sold the land and house to Victor E. and Irene M. Thomas of Geneva. A Kane County Court case from 1949 stated that Victor Thomas had recently "purchased a garage building and filling station in Wasco," and this property is in fact the property in question. In August 1950, the Thomases (who were then

The Cole house, as it appeared about 1961

living in Campton Township) sold their property to Lathrop Hunt, who only owned it for a short time before selling it to the Coles, who used the property as a dwelling (see "The Wasco Garage" for the early history of the property). The building seems to have been demolished in 1977 or 1978.

Site of 40W299 Route 64 – the former Raasch house was located east of the Wasco Inn, on the south side of Route 64. The former house site is now occupied by a gas station. Clarence W. and Elaine L. Raasch purchased property here from Harry and Marjorie Travis in July 1945, and likely had their home constructed at that time. Prior to that summer, the Raasches were residents of Sycamore, in DeKalb County, but relocated to Wasco immediately. An article from August 1945 stated that "Mr. and Mrs. C. Raasch are the new owners of the garage formerly owned by the Harry Travis family." Clarence Raasch was born in Oak Park on 18 August 1918, and served in the U. S. Army during World War II. He married Elaine Langbartels on 23 June 1945, in Steger, Illinois. Elaine was born on 22 February 1921. Clarence worked as a Teamster mechanic, and was a member of the American Legion Post 1195. Clarence and Elaine Raasch had two sons and two daughters: Rick,

Elaine Raasch in 1988

Danny, Melanie, and Denise. In June 1970, Clarence and Elaine Raasch celebrated their twenty-fifth anniversary at the Wasco Legion Hall.

The Raasch family sold some of their property to Peter J. and Jane M. Bohr (see "Travis Tavern/Bohr's Tavern") on 23 August 1948. They sold the parcel they were using as a "garage building and filling station in Wasco" to Victor E. and Irene Thomas in December of that year (see "Site of 40W331 Route 64"). The Denny family purchased an adjoining parcel of land here from the Raasches in February 1952. Mrs. Raasch, who at one time served as president of the local American Legion Auxiliary, occasionally entertained the Wasco Knitting Club and the Shrinking Matrons at her home in the 1960s. The Raasch family moved from Wasco to their home in Florida in April 1980. They had sold their home and property to the Karametsos family in November 1979. For a few years after their purchase of the Raasch house, the Karametsos family ran a pizza parlor from the building. The structure suffered a fire in 1985, and was demolished. The Marathon gas station on the site, which is owned by Western Trail Outpost LLC of Hinckley, was built in 2012-13. That company purchased the property from the American Bank and Trust Company of Geneva in 2011. The site was vacant for more than twenty-five years after the Raasch house was razed.

Clarence W. Raasch, a past Commander of the American Legion Post in Wasco

The Raasch house in Wasco, in the 1960s

Significant Institutions & Places of Business

The Bergland/Hummel Lumberyard

The Bergland Lumberyard was located on the west side of Old LaFox Road, immediately south of the Chicago Great Western railroad tracks. One would enter the yard from the east, and for many years the yard contained three buildings. There was a large in-ground truck scale on the site, used for weighing coal and grain. The yard had large bins containing field tiles, coal, and other products. Besides wood products, coal and animal and poultry feed were also sold here. There was a feed mill on site for grinding feed products that local farmers would buy or sell. West of the buildings was a livestock area, used mainly to hold cattle, pigs, and steers that were destined for shipment to the Chicago stockyards. A fatal accident occurred immediately north of the lumberyard's entrance in October 1930, when local farmer David H. Marshall was struck by a Chicago-bound Great Western freight train while attempting to cross the tracks. His load of lumber was "scattered along the tracks for some distance," and the driver was instantly killed. The buildings at the lumberyard were "completely modernized" in 1936 by the Berglands. A newspaper article dating from 1937, for the fiftieth anniversary of the "general store owned by Bergland and Co." asserted that "while the Wasco store deals in foodstuffs and other supplies, their main business is lumber. In addition to the yards at Wasco, they have yards at Glen Ellyn." Floyd H. Bergland was then in charge of the business.

In the spring of 1947, the lumberyard was sold to Fred Hummel, who continued to own and operate it through April 1976. Harold Ekstrom (who was first hired by the Berglands, and who assisted in the post office, lumber yard, and the hardware store) managed the lumberyard for many years during the Hummel family's ownership. The Hummels moved to Elmhurst when they relinquished ownership of the business; the remaining stock from the store and lumberyard were sold at a largely-attended public auction on Saturday, 10 April 1976. Bill Olesen, who grew up in Lily Lake, worked at the Hummel Lumberyard from the early 1960s until August 1980. Lawrence J. ("Tuffy") Faber worked there in the 1970s.

Following the 1976 auction, a woodworking shop opened in one of the buildings at the former lumberyard for a time. Mark Johnson was the proprietor of the shop "in the old lumber yard in Wasco" in September of that year. The Porter Brothers purchased the lumberyard in 1976, and made extensive repairs there that summer, and put in a new well. Richard B. Porter of St. Charles obtained a mortgage at that time, using his new property as collateral. The property was known as 4N944 LaFox Road, Wasco, by 1984, at which time Porter was still the parcel's owner. Ownership of the parcel was transferred to a trust that year.

In the 1980s, the Argo Manufacturing Company (Pace Machinery and Fittings Inc.) facility was built on the western portion of this site. Argo, which was started as a machinery business by John Mitson in the 1940s, makes lightweight aluminum jacks, pit equipment, high-performance automobile brakes, and many other items. The business was moved from Franklin Park to Wasco in 1983. The large building on the eastern end of the former lumberyard was built in 1988, not long after the original buildings from the Bergland era were removed. The property is now owned by North Star Trust Company of Chicago.

The Bergland Lumberyard, about 1943

George Bergland on his father's horse, EJ - the Alvie Austin house is seen in the background near EJ's tail, with the Bergland Lumber Yard to the left of the frame

Bergland lumber, likely in the 1950s

The Bergland Lumberyard, likely early 1960s

The Original Bergland Store

Prior to the construction of the present Bergland/Hummel store, there was an earlier frame building on the same site. This building was oriented north-south, and was of the "false-front" style of vernacular architecture popular in the last third of the nineteenth century. The main two-story building was three window bays wide (east-west) with a one-story addition on the west. A porch roof covered the main entrance, which was flanked with two large windows. There was another door on the eastern side of the front of the building, which may have given access to the second story. The building was either built on its site in 1887 or 1888, or was moved there at that time. The building to the immediate north of the first Bergland store was moved across the street before 1908, and this site was replaced with the two nearly-identical cottages shown in later photographs. The old store was moved slightly west (and was retained) when the new store was built in the early 1910s. Both buildings stood side-by-side for a time, but the older building was removed or demolished prior to 1918.

The oldest extant photograph of the original Bergland store, taken in the early 1890s

George C. Bergland was shown as the owner of the old Bergland store property on the 1892 Wasco map, but he had only very recently obtained title to the property when the map was created. On 1 July 1892, Bergland paid John V. and Charlotte Millen $1500 for the half-acre lot which had been earlier taken out of the extreme southeastern corner of the Higgins farm. The original Bergland store building, labeled as "Store & P.O." is shown on the map. Since John V. Millen was a carpenter, owned the lot on which the store was built at the time of its construction, and was living in Campton Township at the time he sold to Bergland, it is very likely that Millen built the old Bergland store. Thus even though Bergland (not Millen) is known to have conducted business in the old store as early as 1888, it is unlikely that Bergland built the store himself. The Millens were from New Jersey, and came to Kane County in the 1850s. J. V. Millen had purchased property directly from Horace Higgins, on 29 March 1887. This purchase price of $50 conveyed a vacant parcel of land – the store was probably built on Millen's new half-acre parcel by the end of that calendar year. J. V. Millen is known to have built a large barn for Albert Lemon "on his farm near Gray Willow" in the summer of 1888, and a new barn for J. H. Delancey the previous winter.

It is clear that there was an apartment located over the post office in the old Bergland Store. In September 1903, for example, the rooms "above the post office" were then being "occupied by Mr. Green and [his] family." Green was the night operator for the Chicago Great Western Railroad. There were likely two apartments there, in fact, since by October 1903, Merritt Whitney and his wife were occupying "the rooms over the store" recently vacated by S. Bergquist. William Babbitt rented the rooms after Merritt Whitney. In May 1905, Merrill Whitney and his wife were occupying the "rooms over Bergland's store." Beginning in March 1907, William Bryant and his family were occupying the "rooms over the store that Mr. Babbitt vacated."

Painting of Wasco (detail) showing the old Bergland store, circa 1899

Bergland purchased the triangular parcel of land immediately north and east of the store lot (but still on the west side of the present Old LaFox Road) on 30 July 1906. On that date, Bergland "of Wasco" paid $875 to John A. and Augusta Carlson of St. Charles Township, in exchange for two small triangular parcels of land at the northwest corner of the intersection of what is now Route 64 and LaFox Road (described in the deed as a "road running North and South through Wasco Station"). Bergland would build one of his Wasco "cottages" on this property soon after the deed was recorded.

John August Carlson, who sold to Bergland, lived in or near Wasco in 1900. He was a farmer, was born in Sweden on 16 February 1863, and came to the United States in 1891. His wife Augusta (Johnson) Carlson was born in August 1864; they were married in Kane County on 8 April 1893. They had no children. The Carlsons left Wasco after selling the property to Mr. Bergland. John A. Carlson passed away at his home on Jefferson Avenue in St. Charles on 13 April 1942.

The Carlsons were only owners of the Bergland cottage lot for a brief time. They acquired the two adjoining parcels (the larger piece being just a quarter-acre in size) on 24 January 1906, for $900. The previous owners were Benjamin R. and Elizabeth M. ("Lizzie") Kayner of Campton Township. The Kayners were married in Cook County on 6 October 1890. Elizabeth's maiden name was Schwab, and she was born in Chicago in 1863. In the 1910s, '20s and '30s, the Kayners owned a fifty-four-acre dairy farm, located three miles northeast of Wasco. Their property was just north of the present Silver Glen Road, near the St. Charles Township line. Ben was a blacksmith before he was a farmer; he was born in Ohio in November 1864. His daughter Lillian, who was born in St. Charles in November 1891, later married Lynn L. Jay. Elizabeth Kayner died on the family's farm home north of Wasco on 6 January 1940; she had lived there for forty years. She was survived by her daughter Lillian (Kayner) Jay, five grandchildren, and two great-grandchildren. The Kayners are buried in the Whitney Cemetery.

The old Bergland store in Wasco, probably taken about 1906

There were two other early owners of the Bergland cottage lot which should be mentioned here. B. R. Kayner purchased the property (for the second time) in November 1902, from Christ and Ida Burgeson. The purchase price was $900. One Christ Burgeson (with a wife Ida) was born in Västra Götaland, Sweden, on 18 May 1861. Christian A. Burgeson came to the U. S. in 1879, and on 20 October 1891, in Chicago, he married Ida M. Almberg. He was a boiler maker, and lived in Chicago in 1900. On 15 April 1901, for $800, Christ Burgeson (of Chicago) purchased the Bergland store lot from the Kayners, to whom he would later sell the land. A newspaper article from 19 April 1901 stated that Burgeson was going to "go into the business here immediately." The Kayners moved to Orangevale, California very soon after selling their property. Burgeson immediately obtained a mortgage upon his purchase, from Charles Mongerson of Campton Township. The Kayners had earlier (in January 1900) obtained a mortgage on the property. They were living in "the town of Wasco" at the time.

The old Bergland store in Wasco, in the decade of the 1900s

The original purchase of the Bergland cottage lot took place in November 1891. Harriet L. and Willard R. Austin parceled off a quarter-acre of their seven-acre property (encompassing the north half of Wasco) to Charles Simons on 7 November 1891. The purchase price was $50; the buyer and sellers were all residents of Campton Township. Charles and Melissa Simons immediately obtained a $150 mortgage using this property as collateral. The lender was Daniel McDonald. The Simons family owned the property (according to deeds on record) for six years. In November 1897, the Kayners purchased the two adjoining parcels of property on which the old Bergland store stood. The first parcel was sold to them by Charles and Melissa A. Simons of Cloverdale, in DuPage County. This parcel, containing the store, sold for $750. Willard R. and Harriet Austin sold the second of two adjoining parcels to Kayner, "of the Town of Campton." The purchase price for this irregular quadrilateral of land just north of the store, was sold for $50. B. R. Kayner "of the village of Wasco" obtained a mortgage, using this property as collateral, the same week as his purchase.

In March 1905, Kayner resumed his former duties as Wasco's blacksmith. In February 1906, B. R. Kayner purchased a farm north and east of Wasco from J. A. Carlson. This property was close to the present Silver Glen Road. George C. Scott conducted a farm auction at the Ben Kayner property northeast of Wasco on 31 January 1913. Kayner lived until 1948.

In November 1905, there was a library of seventy volumes kept at Bergland's store. It was managed by the Mothers' Club and was open to the public every Friday. It is thought to have been the first significant lending library in Wasco. No known local newspapers mention the demolition or relocation of the old Bergland store, which must have occurred some time after the first months of 1910, but prior to the end of 1916. The building appears in several photographs known to date to the early 1910s.

This photograph, showing the old and new Bergland stores side-by-side, was taken prior to 1914 (likely circa 1912)

The Bergland/Hummel Store

The present brick building was built around 1912 or 1913. Since that time, the building has been split into two halves on the ground floor. For most of the twentieth century, there was a grocery store and meat market on the west side of the building, and a hardware store and post office on the east side. Frances and Mamie Anderson (two sisters, neither of whom ever married) operated the grocery store in this building for years. The Anderson sisters lived near the intersection of Route 47 and McDonald Road, in "Chicken Grove." At the store, shelves along the west wall contained all types of canned fruits and vegetables, and many other items as well. There was also a display case for cut meats, milk, and cheese, and a walk-in cooler behind the showcase. This cooler, located at the rear of the grocery area, usually contained a half or quarter beef. Meat was cut, chopped, ground, or sliced to order on a round wooden chopping block, and weighed on an overhead hanging scale. The interior of the grocery store was painted a cream color for many years. There was a storage room in the back of the grocery area. The building's basement housed barrels of linseed oil, vinegar, kerosene, and other liquids, which were sold to customers who brought their own containers for these products.

The wooden chopping block from the Bergland store

The grocery store in the west half of the Bergland store had a center aisle with canned and dry goods shelved on either side. Items such as flour, sugar, coffee beans, and oatmeal were in large pull-out bins, and would be packaged and weighed in whatever amounts the customer required. Coffee was ground upon purchase by a sizeable Star Mill hand grinder. Payments in the grocery store were handled by means of a large cash register located there. Access to the store building was via both front and rear doors. There was a long wooden bench outside the front entrance for the customers. They often sat, smoked, and talked there, from the store's earliest days. The glass-walled post office was located just inside the store's rear east entrance. Behind the glass wall was a series of over one hundred post office boxes; each had a painted black number on its outer face. Behind this wall of boxes was an enclosure containing a desk for the postmaster. On his right there was a window through which a clerk would hand the postmaster mail and payments. The postmaster's roll-top desk was located behind the post office enclosure in a small space; there was also a large floor-to-ceiling safe located here. There was a window facing east nearby, and a door to the south, leading into the hardware section of the building.

With the advent of the automobile in the area in the late 1910s and early '20s, two gasoline pumps were installed in front of the Bergland store. Neither has survived, although there was still a single pump present as late as World War II. The Bergland family's retail interests in Wasco were under the name *Bergland & Company*, which was managed by George C. Bergland from 1887 until his death in 1914.

George's son Floyd H. Bergland then managed the company for more than thirty years. Floyd's management was only interrupted, in fact, during the years he was away at college and when he served in the U. S. Army. His older sister Florence (Bergland) Peterson managed the company at that time. The interior of the Bergland store was remodeled and painted in September 1936, and occasionally afterward. Over the years, farmers would often bring their produce, particularly eggs, into the store for resale to customers. Before they could be sold, however, the eggs would have to be "candled." If the egg was clear upon being placed above a hole in a store's wooden light box, it could be sold. If not, the egg was returned to the farmer.

The hardware store in the Bergland/Hummel building had a row of shelves along the east wall from the front to the back. These shelves contained paint, nails, tools, and a wide variety of miscellaneous items. The post office and postmaster's office were located in an area at the rear of the store. There was a north-south aisle near the offices, and people could enter the back door of the store to gain access to their post office boxes located here. Louise M. Swanson's

Frances Anderson, outside the Bergland store in Wasco

box number was 45, and Maude and Edward Swanson's number was 76. Stairs accessing the basement were located on the north wall of the building. Large burlap bags of ground grain were stored there.

Carl Peterson, Peter Johnson, and Arthur Bolcum outside the Bergland Store, November 1917

The probate inventory of George C. Bergland was filed in Kane County in December 1914. At that time, Bergland's property, including the store, was bequeathed to his wife and their two children. In 1935, an advertisement for Bergland & Company of Wasco stated that it was then "Campton's Oldest Business House – We Sold to Your Grandfather, We Sold to Your Father, We Want to Sell to You." Floyd Bergland became the firm's sole owner in 1937, after which time the company "enjoyed rapid expansion under his management." Floyd had obtained full title to the store property from his mother, sister, and brother-in-law on 3 July 1937. Louise Bergland of Wasco died at Community Hospital, Geneva, on 11 October 1938. After her son Floyd Bergland's death in May 1946, the family's store and business was sold out of the family. The business dealt in "lumber and building supplies, hardware, coal and feed" at that time.

Advertisement of Bergland & Company, December 1937

The Bergland store and business was sold to Hummel & Company by the heirs of Floyd H. Bergland on 3 March 1947. It was "one of the largest business transactions of recent years in this vicinity" according to the *Elburn Herald*. Mr. Hummel had been a resident of Campton Township since 1929. He had lived on the "Rainbow Dairy Farm" near Wasco for a time prior to his purchase of the Bergland store. When Fred Hummel Jr. returned from Korea in May 1947, he was immediately associated with his father in the new family business. John Olson and Harold Ekstrom worked for the company at the time, and continued in their positions after the Hummels assumed ownership. The Berglands wrote that Mr. Hummel's "understanding and interest, and his acquaintance with [the community's] needs, will ensure a continuance of the pleasant relations that have existed for many years." In the spring of 1960 (as well as for several years before and afterward) Hummel's had several hundred baby chicks sent there each spring "by parcel post." The chicks made "cheerful sounds" and reminded the customers of the season of new life. The chicks were sold to the local farmers, who then raised them. The Hummel family ran the business until 1976.

Wesley A. Johnson purchased the grocery store in the Hummel Building from Frances and Mayme Anderson in February 1948. They had run the store for the previous nine years. A close look at an interior view of the Bergland store taken during Johnson's ownership reveals several recognizable products for sale: Coca Cola, Quaker Oats, Wheaties, Grape Nuts, Red Dot potato chips, Monarch coffee, and O-Cedar mops. Mr. and Mrs. D. E. Keiser of Geneva purchased the store and market from Johnson in January 1949. From 1951 to 1963, Mr. and Mrs. Fred Bree ran the grocery store in the Hummel building. In 1959, Fred and Bernice installed "a beautiful new open front freezer case" in which to display meats and cheeses for sale. Upon closing the grocery business, Fred began working for a bank in West Chicago.

Interior of the Bergland store, with Wes Johnson at center, in January 1949

Another interior view of the store from the same period, looking south

The interior of the Bergland/Hummel store, possibly 1960s

The second floor of the Bergland/Hummel store contained two apartments. One was located on the east side of this floor, and the other on the west. Both contained a kitchen, dining room, living room, and bedrooms. Some of the occupants of these apartments were Nelly Westfield, William Parson, and Frank Wickizer and his wife. Mertell (Whitney) Wickizer and her husband Loren also lived in an apartment over the store in the pre-war years. The earliest-known occupants of the "rooms over Bergland's store" were Mr. and Mrs. Edward Swanson, who moved in during the month of October 1913.

George Bergland's "new" store, as it appeared in the 1910s, with the old store to the west still visible, and the future Mather's service station on the right half of the photo

The Bergland store and Wasco post office, soon after the opening of the new building, 1910s

The Bergland Store, in the early 1920s

The Bergland store in the 1930s, looking northeast

Bergland's store in Wasco, about 1943

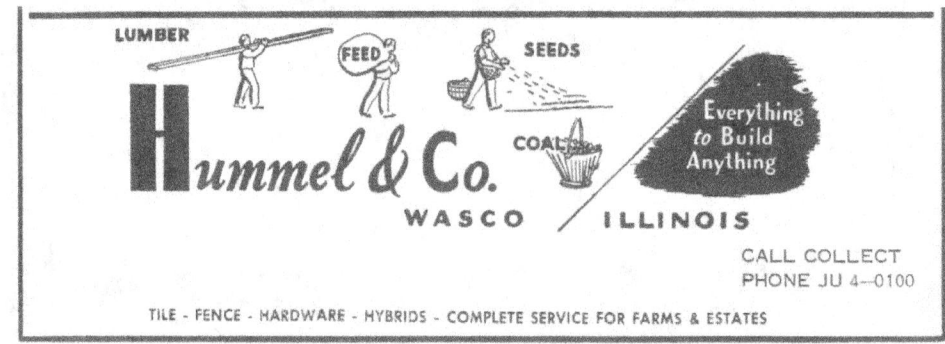
Ad for Hummel & Company, Wasco, circa 1960

The Hummel store, perhaps in the late 1950s

Hummel's store, in the late 1960s

The west side of the Bergland/Hummel store in 2018

The successor to Hummel's store was the Collins General Store, which operated in the same building for twenty-one years (see "A Brief Decade-by-Decade History of Wasco - The 1980s"). Patrick and Julie Collins held a "going away party" in October 2001, after selling their grocery store and retiring. In more recent years, "The Corner Store" occupied the east half of the Bergland building. The store sold pastries, chocolate, candy, newspapers, and more. It was owned by Kathy Munyon and Patty Mika and closed in October 2008. The Wasco Post Office has been located in the building since it was built. Before that, the local post office was located in the original frame Bergland store. Karen's Quilt and Bead Shop now [2018] occupies the east half of the Bergland building. The building's address is 40W514 Route 64.

Erickson's Blacksmith Shop

Besides the railroad and the Bergland store, the local blacksmith shop was arguably the most important business in Wasco's early history. The building housing the blacksmith shop was originally located on the west side of the present LaFox Road, just north of the original Bergland store. The 1892 map of Wasco shows the building in that location, and it is also shown there in an early 1890s photograph. The building was likely built in 1887 or 1888. When George Bergland built the two identical cottages to the north of his old store (sometime between 1896 and 1908, but likely circa 1904) the blacksmith shop was moved almost exactly across the street, and was turned around one hundred and eighty degrees. Will Ruddock was Wasco's "village blacksmith" in February 1889 and may have been the first to work in the building. B. R. Kayner served as Wasco's blacksmith beginning in 1905, although he must have worked in this trade some time earlier, since the St. Charles Chronicle mentions him as "returning" to his "duties as blacksmith in Wasco" then. The local blacksmith would have shod horses, sharpened plows, repaired farm equipment, fixed wagon wheels, and much more. Every local farmer would have visited the Wasco blacksmith shop on a more or less regular basis.

Beginning in May 1906, Ed Swanson of Wasco kept a barber shop in the rooms over the blacksmith shop. The shop may have been closed or relocated by December, though, since during that month W. C. Bryant and his family were occupying the "rooms over the blacksmith shop." Bryant was employed in the nearby creamery. Another possibility is that Swanson's shop was located in a second blacksmith shop in Wasco. For a short time in the 1890s, and perhaps as late as the decade of the 1900s, another blacksmith shop (which doubled as a wagon shop) was located on the Higgins property, a short distance west of the original Bergland store. This shop, which was either razed or moved by the 1910s, was built after 1886 and is shown on the 1892 map.

Andrew Erickson, who operated the local blacksmith shop for nearly fifty years, moved to Wasco in 1908 and began working at his trade in the blacksmith shop building (also see "The Erickson Family"). Erickson was born in Sweden in 1882 and came to the United States in 1903. The person that ran the blacksmith shop prior to Erickson seems to have been William A. Hiser, for in March 1904, in the "Wasco Items" column of the *St. Charles Chronicle*, there was a line stating that "Mr. Hiser, formerly a resident of St. Charles, runs the blacksmith shop here." The Hisers had not been in Wasco for long, though, since in 1900 they were listed in the census as being residents of Wayne Township, DuPage County.

Local farmers would bring their horses into the first floor of the Erickson blacksmith shop; they would then be fitted for shoes, and Mr. Erickson would nail the shoes in place. Nearly all local farmers had draft horses that required rather frequent shoeing. Erickson would make the shoes himself from heating iron in a furnace. He had a large anvil to help shape the shoes. The shop also had a large room used for storage. On the north side of the shop there was a set of stairs leading to the second floor, which contained three rooms. One room was a small kitchen, and another was a bedroom. Walter Denison lived in this apartment for a time, and kept a barber shop in the building. Denison erected a barber pole on the west side of the Erickson blacksmith shop building during his tenancy there. A column from the *Elgin Advocate* from December 1888 stated that "Wm Denison, who has a great desire to see Wasco a town, has started a barber shop. Will is death on hair." Herman Meyer was the blacksmith shop's proprietor for a time.

As has already been stated, Andrew J. Erickson was already working as a blacksmith in Wasco by 1908. Immediately following his marriage, he and Grace moved into the rooms over the blacksmith shop. The property on which Andrew Erickson ran his blacksmith shop was sold to him by George and Louise Bergland, on 2 August 1911. Since the price paid was $1000, and the lot size was under a quarter-acre, the building was of course already standing at that time.

In November 1933, the short-lived Wasco Athletic Club had its offices in "the apartment over the A. J. Erickson blacksmith shop." Robert Cowan was the group's President, and George Perkins was its Vice President. The final officer of the club was Palmer Johnson, who served as Secretary/Treasurer. Erickson operated his shop downstairs throughout the 1910s, 1920s, 1930s, and for most of the 1940s.

Besides conducting his usual business, Mr. Erickson also held a turkey raffle each November for many years. Many Wasco residents would gather at the shop for this raffle – they would buy a ticket and place their bets on a particular number. A wheel would be spun, and whoever's number came up would win the turkey. These gatherings were quite popular in the 1930s and '40s. A small ice house (demolished long ago) was located just south of the blacksmith shop. Here, local families would bring their milk, which was collected by the Kubinec Company in the 1930s. The milk was placed aboard the eastbound milk train, bound for processing in River Forest, and then for sale in Chicago.

The only known photograph showing the Wasco blacksmith shop on its original site - the photo dates to the early 1890s, and the large doors on the first floor of the building (below the sign) are just visible

The Erickson Blacksmith shop, at its second location, on the east side of LaFox Road, about 1920

Painting of Wasco (detail) showing the old blacksmith shop, c. 1899

The Andrew Erickson Blacksmith Shop, Wasco, 1910s

Andrew and Grace Erickson finally sold the shop building to Philo and Carolyn Plummer in August 1948. Around the same time, Erickson sold the blacksmith business itself to Dan Rediger, who replaced the old coal forge with an electric welder. Rediger, who also sharpened lawnmower blades in addition to performing more traditional blacksmith work, sold the business to Melvin Peterson in 1952. Andrew J. Erickson died in Wasco on 12 December 1956. His wife Grace (Swanson) Erickson passed away on 18 May 1950. On 30 July 1954, the Plummers quit their claim to the property in favor of Roy L. and Ellen S.

Peterson of St. Charles. In July 1965, the owners of the building and property were Roy and Ellen Peterson, and their son Melvin L. Peterson, of St. Charles. The Petersons sold to Walter C. and Mary A. Foulkes, and Charles D. Foulkes, in October 1971. In 1975, the Foulkes family quit their claim to the property in favor of Constance L. Madsen of St. Charles. The former Erickson blacksmith shop was demolished in the summer of 2002. The parcel which once contained the Wasco Blacksmith Shop is now owned by 40W484 LLC of St. Charles. This company purchased the property through a Sheriff's Deed in November 2013, after the previous owner (Westbound Station LLC) fell into foreclosure.

Roy L. Peterson is on the right in this 1956 photograph. His siblings Clarence, Mabel, and Earl are also pictured

A late 1950s photograph of the Erickson blacksmith shop

The former Erickson blacksmith shop, in the mid-1990s

The former Erickson blacksmith shop, not long before its demolition - photo dates to c. 2000

The Wasco Blacksmith Shop

The next incarnation of a blacksmith shop in Wasco was Melvin Peterson's blacksmith shop. Peterson purchased the business from Dan Rediger, a welder, in 1952. Horses were still being shod there on a fairly regular basis at that time. The shop could repair and/or fabricate anything made out of metal. Melvin Peterson had learned blacksmithing while working on Colonel Baker's farm (now Pheasant Run Resort) in St. Charles in the late 1930s. Peterson fixed military equipment and continued welding during World War II, when he served on the St. Charles Civil Defense Team.

Advertisement for Melvin Peterson's Wasco Blacksmith Shop, circa 1961

Tom Peterson in the new blacksmith shop, Wasco, about 1970

The new Wasco blacksmith shop, in August 1970

In 1969, Melvin Peterson purchased the Rediger and VanWinkle homes just north of the railroad tracks in Wasco. These properties together comprised approximately three-and-a-half acres of land, and soon after his purchase, Peterson constructed his new 60' x 144' building, shown above. Melvin's son Tom (who was then a student at Bradley University) designed and laid out the new all-steel building. The structure contained a parts room, an office, a lunch room, a repair area, and a show room. Various wrought iron goods (such as furniture) were on display here. The Bagge and Swanson Trucking Company of Wasco made the building's two entrances. The grand opening of the new building took place in the summer of 1970.

An article on the Wasco Blacksmith Shop from May 1970 praised the quality of the ornamental iron work being produced there. Some of the shop's products included fireplace fixtures, railings, window guards, stairways, gates, furniture, and grilles. Peterson employed eight men in 1970, and operated a service truck which was almost constantly being used. In the 1980s, the shop sold quite a number of lawn mowers, trimmers, snow blowers, and other yard equipment. All types of welding could be done at the shop, and all varieties of industrial, automotive, and agricultural equipment could be repaired there. Melvin's wife Ruth Peterson, daughter of Harold Anderson, assisted her husband in the business, and also worked for the State Bank of St. Charles prior to her retirement. Wayne Ekstrom worked at the Wasco Blacksmith Shop for thirty years, and knew "nearly everyone in Wasco."

Advertisement from Wasco Lawn & Power, 1992

Melvin Peterson retired in the late 1980s, and finally sold the business to Ted Frerichs in 1992. Frerichs had worked at the blacksmith shop for seven years prior to his purchase; with the acquisition he inherited a collection of "antique tools, 20th century metalworking machines, a gas forge, and a 389-pound anvil."

The anvil continued to get daily use throughout the 1990s. Ted retired in 2012, and passed away later that year. The former Wasco Blacksmith Shop (at 4N953 LaFox Road) was renamed Wasco Lawn & Power in February 1992. Bob Adams and Dan Lee acquired the business in 1991; they introduced a new line of snowmobiles and related equipment in 1994. Wasco Lawn & Power opens at 8:00 AM six days a week and is still located at 4N969 Old LaFox Road in Wasco. They are the Fox Valley's largest independent lawn and snow equipment center. Bob Adams has run the business for many years.

Johnson's Store/Larson's Garage/Mather's Gas Station

On the northeast corner of Route 64 and LaFox Road is one of Wasco's oldest commercial buildings. The structure dates to just before the turn of the twentieth century – this two-story frame structure was completed in the spring of 1897. On 2 April 1896, Harriet L. (Higgins) Austin and her husband Willard sold the property on which the store was built to Oscar Johnson "of the County of Kane." Johnson paid $125 for the half-acre property, located at the heart of Wasco. On 20 May 1897, Oscar M. Johnson took out a mortgage from "Mal" [Melvin] Whitney, using his newly-acquired property as collateral. The deed mentions a "Two Storey Building 24 x 40 feet used as a store and dwelling." Johnson took out a second mortgage from Whitney in July 1897.

On 4 March 1898, Oscar M. Johnson took out a third mortgage (this time from John Whitney) and again used this property as collateral. O. M. Johnson, then still a bachelor, sold the encumbered property less than a month later. The purchaser was Andrew Johnson "of the Town of Campton," and the price paid was $1100. The property was then subject to three mortgages, totaling well over $600. Oscar Magnus Johnson was born in Sweden on 18 October 1874 and came to the United States as a boy. He married Myrtie Reed "near Plato Center" on 7 November 1900, in Kane County, and lived in Campton Township for the rest of his life. They had a baby boy, born in Wasco, in June 1901. Oscar Johnson retired from farming in 1932 and moved to Lily Lake. He passed away in 1959 and is buried in the Lily Lake Cemetery.

Andrew and Mary Johnson of Campton Township sold their building to John W. Larson of the city of Geneva on 16 January 1899. Larson paid $1400 for the property, and he and his wife Hilma immediately took out a large mortgage (for $900, at 6% interest) from Thomas B. Stewart of Lily Lake. The mortgage was not repaid in full, and foreclosure proceedings took place in 1901. John W. Larson (of Geneva) sold his interest in the Wasco property to his trustees at that time; this deed specifically mentions his "store stock, goods and wares, merchandise and property situated in the store building on the said property at Wasco, Illinois." The Trustees soon sold out to John T. Peterson and Frank Sandholm, also of Geneva. Frank Sandholm died shortly afterward, and Peterson and the Sandholm heirs then sold (on 30 April 1904, for $2000) the property to George Bergland of Wasco.

An article in the *St. Charles Chronicle* from early July 1904 stated that Elmer Peterson had "for some time run the store opposite Mr. Bergland's, and with such a degree of aggressiveness that at last he possesses as his wife the daughter and bookkeeper of his competitor." Elmer Peterson had just married Florence Bergland in "one of the prettiest home weddings ever witnesses in Wasco."

During Bergland's ownership of this building, his son-in-law Elmer Peterson ran a farm implement business on the first floor. Peterson also sold automobiles from time to time, probably starting in the early 1910s. Following George C. Bergland's death in 1914, the property was passed along to his heirs. The 1918 Wasco business directory had just three entries – one was "Peterson Elmer T - Implements." Elmer Peterson retired from the business around 1920. The Bergland family sold the building and lot to Albert V. Larson on 29 July 1920. The price paid was $2500. This amount was considerably less than the value of the property, but the deed conveyed an important stipulation – until 1 January 1940 (almost twenty years after the sale) no building on the property was to be used to sell "the goods and chattels commonly sold in a general Country store, such as staple groceries, meats, hardware, dry goods, and clothing, boots and shoes" but language in the deed specified that there was no restriction on "using said premises . . . as a garage and a place wherein may be sold . . . automobile accessories." In other words, the Berglands sold at a loss but guaranteed not having a rival store across the street.

The building that would later house Mather's Gas Station. The photo dates to the 1910s

Albert V. Larson, who opened the garage in the Mather building, was born on a farm in Campton Township on 5 August 1885. His parents, John and Ida Larson, were both Swedish immigrants, and purchased a farm on Corron Road in the 1890s. Albert attended the Stone schoolhouse on Silver Glen Road, and then St. Charles High School. He married Anna A. Johnson in Cook County on 27 August 1906, and by 1910 they were living in Wasco, near the Whites and Berglands. Albert's occupation was given as "Laborer – odd jobs" at that time. A 1908 biographical sketch of his father stated that August was then engaged in "carpentering" and was living "near Wasco." In June 1914 and again in November 1915 Albert V. Larson was paid by Campton Township for work he did on building culverts – other local residents were paid for grading, ditching, supplying and hauling gravel, and similar work. The frame addition to the east of the original building was constructed sometime between 1915 and 1921. The 1920 census listed Larson's occupation as "Proprietor – garage." The garage in the Mather building must have opened that year. By 1921, the garage sold tires, oil, and automotive supplies.

On 5 June 1924, Albert and Anna Larson sold their garage and property in Wasco to John Larson of Sycamore, for $4000. Soon afterward, Albert and Anna Larson moved from Wasco to Estes Avenue in Chicago. He was employed there as an auto mechanic for a cab company. Anna worked as a laundress. They had no children. In 1942, Albert was living on West Chase Avenue in Chicago. He had blue eyes, brown hair, a ruddy complexion, and was 5'9" tall, and weighed 200 pounds.

It is Arnold and Grace Mather who are most associated with the gas station and convenience store in this historic Wasco building. Arnold Mather was a manager for the Wanzer Dairy Company throughout the 1910s, and for most of the previous decade as well. He retired from this position in the 1920s, and began running an implement business. By the fall of 1923, he was actively selling McCormick-Deering farm machines. The Mathers completed their purchase of the building and property from John Larson (of Sycamore) on 1 November 1929. In the spring of 1930, the first floor of the building's southwest corner was "angled" and three gasoline pumps were installed there. Each pump was surmounted by either a red, white, or blue crown. In July 1931, Arnold and Grace Mather signed a lease with Standard Oil Company, an Indiana Corporation. The lease made reference to fifteen square feet of space in Mather's garage, "immediately adjacent" to the property leased. This space was for storage of oil "and for the use of the second party's attendants." The property was already, by 1929, in use as a filling station. The lease with Standard Oil continued through the fall of 1934. The lease also makes reference to the cost of remodeling the front of the service station (a project which cost some $1500).

Larson's Garage, about 1921, before the corner was reconfigured

In October 1929, Arnold G. Mather was listed in a local newspaper as the garage's new proprietor. The three gasoline pumps outside of Mather's were in place by the end of 1930. During the Depression, the Mathers' store sold candy, ice cream, Coca-Cola, Orange Crush and other drinks, newspapers (the *Elgin Courier*, the *Aurora Beacon News*, the *Chicago Sun Times*, the *Daily Herald*, etc.), and many other items. During the war years, Grace Mather would pump gasoline when her son Lee was in the Army. Upon his return, Lee would perform automobile repair, lawnmower repair, and similar work. In the 1930s, "Shorty" Anderson lived in the apartment above the store. Shorty drove a Ford Model A. Beginning in 1932, Grace Mather began working as a local agent for the *Elgin Daily Courier-News*, and continued in that role until at least 1948. The 1940 census listed Grace Mather as a "Store Keeper" for a filling station. By then her two older sons had moved away, but her son Lee was in the household, working as an attendant at the gas station. During World War II and afterward, Grace Mather was also a correspondent for the *Elburn Herald*. She sold over three hundred newspapers from her store every Sunday in 1946, since that was the day that the largest number of local farmers brought in their milk to the depot just north of the store. She ran both the grocery and the filling station while her two sons were away during the war. Mather's sold Red Crown gasoline for many years.

In 1930, Howard and Robert Mather (Arnold and Grace's older sons) were both working as machinists in the family's garage, which was attached to the east side of the store building. The garage served as a Chicago Motor Club Service Station, and sold batteries, tires, and auto parts. The Mathers performed oil

The Mather Garage, about 1929, shortly before the building's first floor was altered

changes and both major and minor repairs. In the 1940s, the phone number there was St. Charles 4071-R-2. Lee Mather became more and more associated with the garage after his older brothers moved away. Lee operated the business until a week before his death, which occurred in 1992 (see "The Mather Family" for further information).

A 1940s photo of the interior of the Mather store shows the following products for sale, among others: Dolly Madison cakes; Cracker Jacks; Kool Aid; Gold Medal enriched flour; F & F cough lozenges; Switzer's licorice; Arm & Hammer baking soda; Rose-Dale canned pumpkin; Quaker oats; Argo corn starch; Flavor-kist marshmallow toppers; work gloves; La Palina cigars; Butter Nut bread; Coca Cola; Dr. Pepper; Life Savers; Beech Nut gum; Clark bars; Oh Henry!; Milky Way; Nabisco saltines; Salada tea; Calumet baking powder; Campbell's soup; Kuehmann's potato chips; Brooks catsup; Dr. Lyon's tooth powder; Tums antacid; and canned corn. In the 1950s other products for sale in the store included Morton salt, Hills Brothers coffee, French's mustard, Dolly Madison cakes, Cracker Jacks, and dozens more items of all varieties.

Grace B. Mather sold the corner store and property to Gertrude E. Stover of Elgin, in January 1958. However, Miss Stover (who was not married) immediately quit her claim to the property in favor of Grace and Lee Mather, for $10 and other valuable considerations. In September 1964, Grace B.

The Mather service station in the summer of 1930

371

Mather, along with her son Lee F. and Lee's wife Mildred N. Mather, all sold their property to Gertrude E. Stover of Elgin, but again Stover immediately quit her claim in favor of the Mathers. Elgin city directories from the 1950s and '60s show that Gertrude E. Stover was a stenographer and later the office manager for Kirkland Brady McQueen and Churchill, a local law firm. In April 1964, Lee and Mildred Mather (and their daughter) moved from their apartment above the store into the home which had been Lee's mother's, just two buildings east of the garage. The home had been newly-remodeled at that time.

Mather's Gas Station in the 1930s

Grace Mather with two of her granddaughters, mid-1940s, with the Mather store's exterior visible

Grace Mather in the Mather store, 1940s

Gordon Bowgren outside of Mather's Gas Station, in 1948

Lee Mather in his garage, adjoining the store to the east, 1940s

Mather's Service Station, likely 1950s

Mather's building in 1996

Mather's building after the removal of the eastern addition, early 2000s – note the "missing" section of the first floor

The Wanzer Dairy/King's Mill

The Wanzer Dairy building is the oldest structure now in Wasco, although it was not built on its present site but was moved there from further north. The small parcel of land on which the building sits was deeded from James C. and Lucy M. Rice "of the village of Wasco" to A. Nolting (of Elgin) on 28 October 1897. Nolting paid $100 for the half-acre lot, which lay between the southern edge of the right-of-way of the Chicago Great Western Railroad and the north side of the present Route 64. A. Nolting and his wife Sophia (who were still "of the city of Elgin") sold the property containing the newly-relocated building to I. Shoudy and F. L. Melville of Rockford for $4475, on 18 July 1901. This deed mentions the property and "the Creamery thereon" and "all machinery belonging therewith." Shoudy and Melville sold to George Bergland on 21 October of that year, but just three days later, he sold the property and creamery to Sidney Wanzer, William B. Wanzer, and Howard H. Wanzer of the City of Chicago. Bergland's 1914 obituary stated that he "induced the I. H. Wanzer company to establish a bottling plant" in Wasco.

The McPartland family, who was owned the building for the better part of a century, relates the story that the building was moved to its present site "with horses and skids" when the stream on which the former grist mill sat (actually a branch of Ferson Creek) was "dammed to make Fisher's lake." The method of the move is probably accurate, but the reason for the move does not seem to be. Oral tradition states that the building's move took place around 1890, although the lack of a structure on the building's present site on the 1892 map (although the "Creamery" is shown on the 1904 map) combined with the deed records suggests that the move took place significantly later in the decade of the 1890s. Also, the move seems to have preceded the creation of Fisher's lake/Lake Campton by many years. The lake is not shown on maps created as late as 1948, and does not seem to be mentioned in print until the mid-1950s.

The Wanzer Creamery as it appeared in 1915. Robert and Howard Mather are the children in the photograph

There was a struggle between Wasco-area farmers and the Wanzer Dairy in September 1913. After initially agreeing to pay $1.90 per can for milk, the Wanzers then posted a "buy" price of $1.75. The farmers "were up in arms, held a meeting and appointed a committee to write an ultimatum to the company." The farmers refused to sell at the lower price, and insisted they would bypass Wasco and find a market at Virgil, St. Charles, or Elburn instead. There were Bowman and Borden plants there that would pay the higher price.

In April 1916, four large automobiles owned by men representing the Milk Producers Association "blocked the roads leading to the Sidney Wanzer milk factory" at Wasco. Before the cars arrived, one-third of the local producers had already delivered. The other two-thirds were held up, and were "induced to return home with full milk cans."

In April 1922, William B. Wanzer, Howard H. Wanzer, H. Stanley Wanzer, Sidney Wanzer III, F. B. Wanzer, E. B. Wanzer, and Louis M. Hill, all of the City of Chicago, sold their interest in the Wanzer Dairy property in Wasco to Sidney Wanzer & Sons, Incorporated. William B. Wanzer, the President of Sidney Wanzer & Sons, lived on Normal Parkway in Chicago, and died on 21 May 1932. He was one of Chicago's leading figures in the dairy industry, both as President of the Milk Dealers' Bottle Exchange and a member of the Milk Dealers' Association. As a young boy, William B. Wanzer began working for his father, Sidney Wanzer, in the company he founded in the 1870s.

King's Mill, as it appears in 2018

Sidney Wanzer & Sons deeded one-third of an acre of land to the People of the State of Illinois in March 1928, when the present Route 64 was widened and improved. In December 1929, the corporation deeded the property to Arthur C. and Madge Anderson of Wasco. In September 1951, the Andersons sold the land and dairy building to John W. De Gignac of Campton Township. De Gignac, a bachelor, took out a mortgage on the property in 1953. In February 1955, he sold out to Lorraine Fifield of Chicago; Fifield sold her newly-acquired Wasco property almost immediately to Kathleen Nord of St. Charles. The De Gignac family lived in Oak Park in the 1920s and '30s, and in Chicago prior to that time. During that era, Mr. De Gignac made shipping boxes, and then furniture, for Marshall Field & Company, and for Sears & Roebuck. In 1962, Nora E. De Gignac and her husband Haydon sold their home, and they moved "into the apartment above their wood working shop." The shop seems to have been located in the present King's Mill building.

A very early view of the Wanzer Dairy, in Wasco

By 1964, the owners of the former Wanzer Dairy building were Haydon and Nora De Gignac, as well as Haydon McParltand, who is the property's present owner. In October 1965, the De Gignacs sold their interest in the property to their grandson, Richard Haydon McPartland of Elmhurst. In 1969, McPartland began the repair and restoration of the historic King's Mill/Wanzer Dairy building.

In the early 1990s, Haydon and Kathleen McPartland's four children worked at King's Mill in various capacities. The McPartlands were widely known then for restoring fine antiques, and for repairing and reupholstering furniture. One of the company's earlier jobs included refinishing a suite at the Drake Hotel in Chicago "in preparation for a visit by Princess Margaret" of Britain. They also repaired a leather-top table for the British Consulate in Chicago (the table arrived at King's Mill in a limousine). King's Mill also carried (and carries) Oriental rugs and upholstery fabrics. As Haydon McPartland once said of his business, "We want to be busy, but not too busy. . . We don't advertise. We just do good work and trust the Lord to bring in the customers."

Haydon McPartland of Elmhurst, in the early 1950s. His family has owned King's Mill for many years

Travis Tavern/Bohr's Tavern/Denny's Den

In the 1930s and early '40s, Marjorie Travis of Wasco operated a sandwich shop and sometime tavern, whose front room contained a long single bar with seats. She would serve food and beverages here, as well as beer, and for about a decade the shop operated as one of two restaurants in Wasco. It was located near her husband's auto repair shop/garage (see "The Wasco Garage") which he had run since 1924.

Harry Travis purchased this property, which contained more than two acres of land, in the late 1920s. In September 1928, the Wasco column of the *St. Charles Chronicle* noted that "Mr. and Mrs. Harry Travis are now nicely settled in rooms over the garage."

On 3 October 1929, Harry E. Travis entered into a lease with the Shell Petroleum Corporation, and agreed to operate a service station on his property "in a business-like manner and will at all times endeavor to promote and increase the sale of gasoline at said station." Travis agreed to pay, as rent, one half cent per gallon for all gasoline sold over a two-year period. The premises were also to be used as an automobile service station. The lease also listed Travis's right to paint all buildings on his property "in Shell colors" – namely, yellow, white, and red. In 1931, Travis entered into a new lease for his gas station and garage, this time with The Texas Company, popularly known was Texaco. The service station building was then 24' x 20' in size, and contained two pumps and a one-thousand-gallon underground tank. The lease with Texaco was renewed in 1933, after a second underground tank had been installed.

Advertisement for Denny's Tavern, December 1951

Just after World War II, the Travis family sold the sandwich shop to Pete Bohr, a Greyhound bus driver. Pete Bohr's Tavern was located on the east side of Wasco, on the south side of Route 64. It was open by 1947, but no earlier than 1945, as that year was when the Bohrs moved to Wasco (from Chicago). The Bohrs moved into the former Lynn Jay house in May 1945. In the late 1940s, the Bohrs hired Louise Swanson, who prepared the fish for the very popular Friday night fish fry held at the tavern. In May 1950, the tavern was sold to the Denny family. Della (Mancini) Denny was born in May 1913 and moved from LaSalle, Illinois, to Wasco in 1950.

The Dennys enlarged and remodeled the restaurant in 1958. They specialized in fish, spaghetti, Italian beef, and chicken dinners, as well as their homemade chili and soups. Lyle ("Swish") Johnson was the bartender at Denny's Den just after this era, and continued tending bar after the establishment was sold. Ads from the early 1970s stated that Denny's Den was "Old in Tradition" but "New in Ideas." Their soup, hot sandwiches, and chili were popular lunch options. The Dennys lived in a small apartment behind the restaurant/tavern and worked there day after day for twenty-three years. In May 1973, Mr. and Mrs. Peter Denny sold Denny's Tavern, which was also known as "Denny's Den," and moved to Wisconsin. Peter J. Denny died at his home in that state on 13 October 1987, at the age of seventy-five. Pete was born in Iowa, grew up in Peru, Illinois, and opened his restaurant in Wasco after more than a decade in the tavern business. His widow Della passed away on 21 October 2012, at the age of ninety-nine.

The Wasco Inn

The Wasco Inn, located at 40W301 Route 64, was the next incarnation of the former Denny's Den. Owners were John and Athina Karametsos and their family; their daughters Georgia, Vicki, and Margie worked there for many years. The family purchased the property directly from the Dennys, and opened the Wasco Inn on 1 April 1973. It was famous for its prime rib, chicken dinners, pasta, sirloin steak sandwiches, and deep-fried perch, among other dishes. The Karametsos family initially lived in the home attached to the south side of the tavern. From its opening until the early 1980s, the restaurant used the slogan "We Invented Home Cooking." The restaurant's co-owner John Karametsos was tragically killed in an auto accident on Route 64 in June 1980. His widow Athina, who was once called the "Greek Matriarch of Wasco," remodeled and improved the restaurant in 1993, when it had been open for twenty years. Athina, who was a native of Lidoriki, Greece, was born in 1937, and fled her village (which was burned) during World War II. She came to the United States in the late 1950s. She and John settled in Chicago in 1961, at the time of their marriage, and moved to Lisle in 1969.

Already by the mid-1970s, the Wasco Inn was well-known for its fish, spaghetti, chicken dinners, steaks, and cocktails. The establishment had many "regulars" and was open daily until late in the evening. The restaurant was extensively remodeled and improved in 1993. The restaurant's interior was completely updated, but the menu was not significantly changed. Karametsos wanted "all the families that come here with their kids to feel comfortable" and had been planning the renovation for three years.

In 1994, the Wasco Inn was described in a newspaper article as "a welcome find for bikers on the St. Charles bike path and touring antiquers." It had an all-wood dining room, a "long, spacious bar with pine walls," electric beer signs, a jukebox, television sets, and was still being run by Athina Karametsos and her daughters and sons-in-law. John Cappos, a cousin, was the soup and daily specials chef then. He had worked for the restaurant since 1978, and was the daytime head chef in the 1990s. Gary Wren, who started at the restaurant as a teenager, was head chef for the dinner hour.

The Wasco Inn, as it appeared in the 1970s

Steak, chicken, and fried fish were the best-selling dinners, and some specialties included lobster tail, Grecian chicken, ribeye steak, gyros, Italian beef, and shish kebab. The new décor was helping to attract some of the younger couples moving into nearby housing developments. Madeline A. ("Maddie") Van De Veire worked most of her life as a waitress, and was very well known in the area. She served customers at The Farm, then at Denny's Den, and later at the Wasco Inn. She was employed by the last-mentioned restaurant until it closed. Athina Karametsos, the Wasco Inn's co-founder, passed away on 22 January 1998, at the age of sixty.

The house and garage attached to the Wasco Inn, pictured in October 1976

*The newly-renovated Wasco Inn as it appeared in July 1993 –
compare with the photo from the 1970s, taken from more or less the same perspective*

After the Wasco Inn closed in 1999, Taylor Street Pizza and Dairy Queen opened in the building which formerly housed the restaurant. On 31 August 2003, Luau Coffee (founded by Campton Township native Neal Anderson) opened in the location between these two businesses, at 40W301 Route 64. In 2017, Luau Coffee moved across the street and a bit west, to their present location at 40W450 Route 64. Margie Karametsos (one of John and Athina's daughters) still owns the property, which consists of three adjoining parcels and one building.

One of the last ads for the Wasco Inn, February 1999

The stores at 40W301 Route 64, including Dairy Queen and Taylor Street Pizza, as they appear in 2018

The Wasco Garage

In 1924, Harry Travis and Lawrence McGowan were the two proprietors of the Wasco Garage. In fact, they had just purchased their ownership interest in the garage that spring from "Mr. Larson," who had operated it in Wasco "for several years." The establishment was still known as the "Travis Garage" in April 1928. Harry Travis was already an auto mechanic at the time of the 1920 census, when he and two other men were boarding with Mrs. Harriet Austin, in Wasco. Harry was born in Campton Township on 1

Harry Travis of Wasco, about twenty-three years before he purchased the local garage

February 1899 and was a son of Frank and Nora (Mitchell) Travis, who came to Kane County in 1887. The Travis family owned a 64 ½ acre farm in Section 4, Campton Township, in 1918. The farm was located on the east side of Dittman Road, and had frontage on Burlington and Silver Glen Roads as well. The Travis children attended Gray Willow School, which was surrounded on three sides by the family's land. Harry married his wife Marjorie L. Beard of St. Charles on 2 August 1928. By that time, he was selling automotive accessories from his garage, and was repairing vehicles of all types.

In 1930, Harry Travis was a machinist at the Wasco Garage; Marjorie was then working as a waitress at a lunch stand. They had an infant daughter (named June) at that time, and later had a son named Kenneth. Harry listed his occupation as a mechanic, and his place of employment as a "service station" in 1940. Travis still lived in Wasco in 1941, when he traveled to Wisconsin for a fishing trip with Andrew Erickson and Elnor Carlson. He died in St. Charles in June 1981. Arthur Brown worked in the Travis Garage in 1931. In August 1945, Harry Travis sold the Wasco Garage to Clarence Raasch. The Travis family moved to Elgin, where Harry got a job as a mechanic for Phillips Auto Parts. Harry Travis enjoyed fishing, and often took trips to Wisconsin to pursue this interest. He died in St. Charles in June 1981. The one-story garage building, which was greatly expanded with a two-story residential addition in 1949, was later owned by Harvey and Alma Cole, who moved to Wasco in 1950 (see "Some Wasco Houses – Southeast Quarter"). It was used as a residence from that time until its demolition in the 1970s.

The Farm Restaurant

Located just west of Wasco, on the south side of Route 64, The Farm Restaurant (sometimes known as The Farm Inn) was opened by Bert Brown and his family in 1932. For several years prior to that, beginning in 1925, the Browns had operated a vegetable stand on the site. Bert and Zilpha Brown opened their property to local businesses and organizations for picnics after 1928, taking advantage of the "grassy hills and shade trees" on their extensive property. By 1930 (in addition to fresh vegetables) eggs, sandwiches, and refreshments were being sold from the stand, in the next few years the Browns' family business was dramatically expanded and diversified. In the 1930s The Farm Restaurant served "The Best of Food Cooked Country Style" with a fish fry available every Friday, and Blumer beer on draft at the bar. In the early years, Bert and Zilpha's daughter Jewel was "in charge of the dining room."

During most summers in the 1930s, The Farm was also a gathering spot for Sunday auto races, which drew very large crowds. There was also music and dancing in a pavilion on the property. Bert was an enterprising businessman, and his children Jewel and John were both closely connected with The Farm

Restaurant from its beginning. By the late 1930s, "picnic parties" were held at The Farm several times per week, and frequently drew regular crowds from as far away as Chicago. After seeing some visitors playing baseball on the picnic grounds, Bert Brown invested in the construction of an authentic baseball diamond on the property. He later had two swimming pools built on the site. Races, picnics, parties, and hundreds of special events were held at The Farm in the pre-World War II years. Local newspapers of the 1930s advertised fried chicken at the farm for 35¢ and a steak plate for a dime more. "Peg's Blue Moon Orchestra" was the most popular musical entertainment at The Farm in that era.

The original vegetable stand at The Farm, in 1930

During the Depression, groups from the Moline Malleable Iron Works Company, the Pure Milk Association, the Turner Brass Works, and more gathered for annual outings at The Farm. A half-mile dirt race track was built there, and modified Model T's known as "flivvers" raced at The Farm on Sunday afternoons. Crowds of over two thousand people often gathered for these races. Drivers from the Tri-Cities, Aurora, Sycamore, Elgin, and Chicago participated. In September 1933, the Wasco Baseball Club sponsored a dance at The Farm, charging a quarter for admission. Music was performed by "the Vagabond band." Besides a baseball game and the dance itself, other entertainment included an auto race, at which Bob Mather was a flagman. The racers that day included Verner Bowgren of Wasco. The race track was improved during the 1934-35 season, and typical admission in that era was thirty-five cents.

While the 1933 Chicago World's Fair was underway, Bert Brown hung canvas sacks over his fence to prevent passers-by from seeing a free race or show (a row of poplar trees was planted there shortly afterward, in order to accomplish the same goal). Admission was most often 25¢ at that time. By the early 1930s, the original vegetable stand at The Farm had been converted to a sandwich stand, and then was made into a restaurant with live entertainment. Nearby concession stands sold pop and hamburgers for a nickel each. Bert's son John took care of farming the land around the 'entertainment' portion of the property. The produce grown there was used in the restaurant. Horseback riding, boxing matches, and horseshoe-throwing contests all took place at The Farm, and motorcycle races were held over the hills on the Brown's property. The open-air dance floor on the hill behind the restaurant was very popular during the summer in particular, but was used in all good weather. A new dance floor was opened there on 23 June 1936. Dance instructors from Chicago sometimes came to the events held there, which included a jitterbug contest with a $5 first prize.

A number of cottages were built on the grounds of The Farm to accommodate overnight guests, and the bandstand near the dance floor enjoyed regular use. During the winter, skiing took place on the property. In the basement of the restaurant, a World War I-style French cantina known as 'The Dugout,' later renamed 'the Subterranean Tap Room,' was built complete with sandbags and military helmets for decoration. Food was served there on tin plates to add to the place's authenticity. Nettie Pow How's Hawaiian Trio and Edmund O'Clair's Radio Orchestra provided entertainment both upstairs and downstairs during and just after The Dugout's grand opening.

A large number of events were held at The Farm's "Picnic Grove" in the late 1930s. For example, on Sunday, 22 August 1937, a gathering of employees of the Modern Steel Equipment Company was held there – this was their first annual picnic. The flyer advertising the event gives the location as "one mile west of Wasco." Free soft drinks and ice cream were given out during the event, which culminated in a dance at 8:45 PM. Events went on all day, beginning at 10:00 that morning. Drawings were held for prizes ranging from an electric toaster to a ton of coal! A mixed relay race was held, with men and women over forty participating, and a concert was held featuring the State Champion Geneva Community High School Band. On 18 September 1938, Kane County's Annual Milk Day (sponsored by the Pure Milk Association) was held at The Farm. The drawing held that day included prizes such as a chair and footstool, a Lanz hay fork, and one "pure bred Hampshire gilt." Miss Marie Wynthein was chosen Queen of the Pure Milk Day Picnic, and there was plenty of "free milk for all." On New Year's Eve, 1938, a floor show took place at The Farm, featuring Col. Bob Nelson, America's "pioneer radio auctioneer." Musical acts included Bea Scharpenter, with "bewitching songs and a guitar." The cover charge was $1 per person. On 5 August 1939, the Moline Malleable Iron Company held its fourth annual picnic at The Farm. The event ran from 1:00 to 10:00 PM, and was open to the company's employees and their families. There were refreshments for all, plus dancing, a balloon race, a three-legged race, a pie-eating contest, a tug-o-war, a needle-threading contest, and a married versus single men's softball game.

An auto race at The Farm, probably in 1934

Several accidents took place at the race track just east of The Farm, such as on 31 May 1936, when a car careened off the track and into the Brown's adjoining gravel pit. There was a fatal accident there in July

1936, when a twenty-eight-year-old Chicago driver was killed when his car skidded and overturned during a time trial. The Kane County Republican Central Committee held a barbeque at The Farm in October 1936, which drew a very large crowd. Some entertainment held at The Farm during that same time period included a show by Lester Oman and his Marionettes, music from The Backyard Follies (featuring Dixie Lee), and singing and accordion accompaniment by "Lorraine and Harry." Baseball games continued to be played at The Farm throughout the 1930s. The Browns sold the restaurant to Ruth and Jerry Daum, who came to Wasco from Plano in the fall of 1948. John Gerald Daum was a World War II veteran and was a charter member of the Wasco American Legion Post.

In 1935, the annual Wasco school picnic was held at The Farm. The first several Kane County Milk Days were held there beginning in 1938. In June 1939, a Brown Swiss Cattle Show was held at The Farm, at which nearly one hundred animals were exhibited and judged. Seven northeastern Illinois counties participated in the show, which also included a 4-H Calf Club event, and many cash prizes. On 4 September 1939, the Pure Milk Association held its second annual Kane County Milk Day picnic on The Farm. The event included agricultural talks, a prize competition, and a recreational program. In the summer of 1939, Peg's Blue Moon Orchestra continued to entertain at The Farm, and "Judge" F. W. Hagaman "directed the nocturnal activities" from The Dugout. Movies were shown, horseback riding on private bridle paths was available, and the outdoor dance pavilion was used regularly. The outdoor pool was under construction that summer, though several cabins were already available for overnight guests. An article from that era asked "If you doubt Bert Brown's popularity ask yourself how a man could start with a hamburger stand and a gas pump, seven years ago, and experience such phenomenal growth if he didn't have something worth a few miles of driving."

After Prohibition ended in 1933, Bert Brown brought a mahogany bar from Monroe, Wisconsin to his restaurant at The Farm. "Golden Glow" beer, brewed in Monroe by the Blumer Brewing Corporation, was on tap at the bar then, and Leon Mack was the bartender. On 4 May 1941, the fourth annual Tourist Trophy motorcycle race was held on the racecourse at The Farm. This event, which began at 2:00

Motorcycle race at The Farm, just west of Wasco, 1930s

PM that day, was sponsored by the Fox Valley Motorcycle Club. It was one of the last major events held at The Farm, since the onset of World War II meant a shift in people's focus and a concerted effort to support the war effort. Bert retired during the war years, and both of his children married and began families of their own. By the late 1940s, he and Zilpha leased The Farm's restaurant to others, and the local attractions faded away, one after another. Ruth Garaghty successfully ran the restaurant starting in the late 1940s.

A large crowd gathered at The Farm, early 1930s

Ruth N. (Oakland) Daum Garaghty worked at the restaurant longer than anyone else and was widely known in the area. She started cooking and baking at The Farm in 1948 and continued to work there until declining health forced her to retire some thirty years later. In the 1950s, she operated the restaurant "with the help of her faithful employees." She married Joseph Garaghty on 13 February 1955. They worked together at The Farm for twenty years. In 1965, June Ekstrom began working for the Garaghtys at The Farm Restaurant. For nineteen years, June was the "friendly and gracious hostess that patrons and owners alike counted on" at that establishment. June passed away in December 1984.

A 1940s image of the bar at The Farm

A fire at The Farm in 1971 led to the replacement of nearly all of the restaurant's interior, and after that time only the frame of the main dining room remained from the Brown's original building. The Garaghtys retired in 1977 due to declining health. Ruth passed away in Geneva on 5 October 1984, at the age of seventy-two. She was survived by her daughter and four grandchildren. Her husband E. Joseph Garaghty died in Newark, New Jersey, on 20 February 1985.

The Wasco American Legion held its Christmas dinner at The Farm restaurant in 1960. The Pure Milk Association continued to hold their annual meetings and dinners at The Farm for decades. In November 1966, for example, Robert Johnsen of St. Charles was re-elected president of that organization's St. Charles local. Friday fish fries were very popular at the Farm Inn throughout the 1960s and '70s. The Farm Restaurant had a complete remodeling in 1971, after the fire, and celebrated a "Grand Opening" on 18 May that year. Several contractors extended their congratulations to Joe and Ruth Garaghty "for continuing their tradition of serving fine foods and beverages" in the area.

In 1977, fried haddock with a tossed salad, rolls and butter, and a baked potato, cost $3.25 at The Farm Inn. During that era, the dining room was open 11:00 AM to 11:00 PM Monday through Thursday, 11:00 AM to midnight on Friday and Saturday, and from noon to 10:00 PM on Sunday. On every day except Sunday, the cocktail lounge at the Farm Inn was open two hours later than the restaurant.

The Olde Farm Inn operated in the building during the second half of the 1980s. Beginning in November 1991, when the restaurant had its grand (re-) opening, Dave Walradt owned the Silverado Grill at the site. The Silverado was a "Texas-style saloon and grill," which specialized in T-bone steaks, chili, and burgers. Niko's Lodge opened in the same building beginning in November 2006, after a ten-month renovation. The Lodge on 64 (formerly the Lodge Bar & Grill), located at 41W379 Route 64, now operates on the site. Aaron and Kristie Perez purchased the restaurant late in 2012, and made many improvements to the facility. These included a new mural in the entryway, the installation of a rotisserie oven behind the host station, and an overhaul of the menu. The Lodge is known for its homemade appetizers, and American fare such as steaks, burgers, seafood, pasta, and salad.

The Farm, in about 1938

White Brothers Trucking

This multigenerational Wasco-based business was founded by brothers Joseph and Charles M. ("Chuck") White in 1939, and has been in continuous operation ever since. Joe and Chuck grew up in Aurora, where their father operated a fruit and vegetable stand. The White brothers began their careers with a $25 second-hand truck, used to haul livestock and loads of vegetables. They would also occasionally haul furniture. The business grew from year to year, and by the mid-1960s their fleet included one hundred tractors, one hundred and fifty trailers, and twenty forklifts. The vehicles were all designed to move heavy loads. At that time White Brothers had terminals at South Beloit, Illinois, Dayton, Ohio, Amherst, Ohio, and Hattiesburg, Mississippi. Trucks operating out of the Wasco depot were dispatched by radio. The company owned a one-hundred-and-sixty-foot transmission tower to aid in this effort. By that decade the company specialized in road building equipment, steel girders, and concrete pipe, among other heavy loads. To supply and properly maintain its fleet, White Brothers opened Wasco Truck Repair Company.

The White brothers purchased over six acres of land east of the Wasco School from Solomon and Fern Johnson of Wasco on 5 September 1947. Joseph and Phyllis White, and Charles and Genevieve White were already Campton Township residents at that time. The company's offices are located at the southeast corner of Route 64 and School Street. The main commercial building was built in 1947. White Brothers Trucking obtained title to its property in Wasco (which was deeded to it by founders Joseph and Charles White) on 1 February 1954. The company provides heavy-haul services and over-the-road flatbed trucking. It transports steel beams, railcars, generators, oversize pipe, containers, construction equipment, and other large and heavy loads.

Joe White died of leukemia in 1957, at the age of thirty-seven. Chuck White directed the company's operations following his brother's death. Chuck's wife Genevieve sometimes drove a truck herself in the early days and helped build the Wasco terminal. Donald Hamm was a driver for White Brothers in the 1950s, and later became a dispatcher there. In more recent years, Hamm was the company's vice president, and general manager. Ralph Immer was general sales manager in the mid-1960s, and Kenneth Anselment was general manager. During his vacations, Chuck White enjoyed fishing in Canada, and hunting deer and antelope in Wyoming. In 1984, Chuck's son James ("Jim") White took over the company.

In 1996, White Brothers Trucking of Wasco received the Fleet Safety Improvement Award, sponsored by the Transportation Group of the Specialized Carriers and Rigging Association. Members of the group engage in heavy specialized transportation, machinery moving, steel hauling, crane rental, and more. Two years earlier, Jim White was elected to the SC&RA's Board of Directors. White Brothers Trucking was one of just four specialized transportation companies having zero accidents in 1993; they also received the Fleet Safety Improvement Award in 1994.

In June 2007, after twenty-five years running the company, Jim White retired as president. He was succeeded by Don Renner, who had previously been White Brothers Trucking's sales manager, and who had worked for the company since 1993. At the time of White's retirement, the company owned and operated fifteen trucks, employed twelve drivers, and contracted with nearly three dozen independent operators making deliveries throughout the country. In 2016, White Brothers Trucking sold some of their property in Wasco to Camm Leasing Services, LLC, of Dundee. The company still owns the large vacant parcel of land north of Campton Centre and south of the businesses along Route 64.

One of the White Brothers Trucking Company's long stepdeck trucks

Wasco Nursery

Wasco Nursery has been in business since 1925. The nursery's first location was on the west side of LaFox Road, a half-mile south of Wasco, and the business was originally known as the "Jay & Ingle Nursery." The founder of the business was Lynn Leslie Jay, a farmer who began his foray into the nursery field by growing "hardy trees with local roots." Jay was born in Aurora in 1891, and his family moved to Campton Township shortly before 1910 (see "The Jay Family"). Jay's plants and trees soon gained a reputation of being high in quality and very hearty. Lynn Jay was advertising in local newspapers as early as 1930. That year, he was selling trees, shrubs, and evergreens at bargain prices. Shrubs were priced as low as thirty cents apiece. Lynn and Lillian Jay of Wasco originally purchased their farm in the southwest quarter of Section 23, Campton Township, on 18 February 1925. The property originally contained thirty-five acres of land. Its previous owner was George Eddy of Elgin.

The Jays sold the northern part of their acreage on LaFox Road to Anton Glomp in June 1939; Glomp had been renting the property since 1934, but shortly after his purchase Glomp sold the land to Louis A. and Olive Brodhage. Also in 1939, the Jays entered into an agreement with Western United Gas and Electric Company to remove three box elder trees along LaFox Road (then called "State Aid Route 16") which were interfering with the electric lines running on the western side of the road. In the late 1930s, Lynn's son Robert ("Bob") Jay began working for the family's nursery business. Both Jays were widely respected for their horticultural expertise. Bob Jay served in the Pacific Theater during World War II, and returned to the business after the war's conclusion in 1945. Bob purchased the business in 1952. In the late 1960s, Bob Jay purchased a ninety-acre property on the south side of Route 64, west of Town Hall Road. He moved the business to this location in 1968.

In 1940, Lynn L. Jay's occupation on the Campton Township census was "Landscaping – Nursery." He was then living with his

Lynn Jay, in the fields of his farm in Wasco

wife Lillian, their three children (Robert, Marjorie, and Dorothy) and the children's maternal grandfather Ben Kayner. That year, Wasco Nursery was selling five-foot fruit trees for seventy-five cents! Lynn and Lillian Jay sold the farm south of Wasco to their son Robert M. B. Jay and his wife JoAnn on 19 October 1942.

In 1946, Julius Verhaeghe drove the bus for Wasco School, and picked up Dorothy Jay in front of the Wasco Nursery, "which was operated by her parents." In 1947, Wasco Nursery offered seven-foot spruce trees for sale for $8 apiece. They also sold, at that time, a "fine line of shade trees, fir trees, and shrubs" as well as landscaping services. Their phone number was St. Charles 4091-R-1.

Wasco Nursery truck, in the early 1940s

In 1954, an advertisement for the Wasco Nursey asked patrons to "drive out to Wasco where you may choose from thousands" of trees and shrubs. Six-foot tall junipers were for sale for $7 each, and nine-foot Chinese elms were the same price. Robert and Joann Jay purchased some additional land for their growing nursery business in March 1956. This parcel was on the south side of their farm on LaFox Road, and was previously owned by William C. Miller of St. Charles. The Jays purchased a ninety-acre farm on the south side of Route 64 in 1964, and moved business operations there four years later.

The spring of 1970 marked "the first full season for the Wasco Nursery at their new location" on Route 64. Bob and Joann Jay (and their son Bob) were then putting in "many long hours working to get everything ready for their customers" according to a Wasco newsletter from the period. The expanded sales yard featured trees, shrubs, bushes, and flowers, with ample parking nearby.

In the early 1970s, Bob Jay's son Robert L. ("RL") Jay took an active role in Wasco Nursery, and began the company's greenhouse operations. He also significantly enlarged the retail sales yard, and expanded the company's landscape design services. RL purchased the business from his father in 1987. In 1989, Jay bought a twenty-acre parcel in Virgil Township to grow plants and trees sold by the nursery. In 2002, another forty-acre farm was purchased by the business to help keep up with growing demand. Wasco

Nursery's current owner, Matt Zerby, began working for the company in 1992; he purchased half of the business from RL in 2005, and the other half seven years later.

Thomas McIlvaine began working at Wasco Nursery in 1974. In 2004, he grew a 591-pound pumpkin there, which he took to the Illinois State Fair that fall. His pumpkin, which took eight men to move, won a fifth-place ribbon and prize at the fair. To grow the prize pumpkin, he used mushroom compost, water, fertilizer, and a "secret recipe" of chemicals. The pumpkin was given a plywood shelter to protect it from wind, direct sun, and rain. In 2008, McIlvaine exceeded his previous record by growing a 709-pound pumpkin which was fifty inches wide. In 2009, this record too was surpassed, when the Wasco Nursery landscaper managed to grow a pumpkin which weighed 1,148 pounds. Some new ingredients used in the fertilizer that year included fish, seaweed, and crab shells. The enormous pumpkin was displayed at the nursery until November and attracted the interest of thousands of visitors. By then McIlvaine, popularly known as the "Pumpkin Man," had been growing giant pumpkins for fourteen years. The grower broke his own record in 2014, when he produced a pumpkin weighing 1,241 pounds. McIlvaine used more than three tons of fresh cow manure to help grow the record-setting Atlantic Giant pumpkin that year.

The nursery is now located at 41W781 Route 64 in Wasco. It features a state-of-the-art 7200 square foot greenhouse (built in 2003) and the nursery offers heated storage space for tropical plants during the winter months. Today, Wasco Nursery's garden gift shop is open year-round, and its ten-acre retail garden center is the largest in the region. Wasco Nursery consists of three separate farms totaling nearly one hundred and sixty acres of land. The nursery is "focused in their mission to provide area residents with high-quality, locally-grown plant and landscape material, expert advice and professional installation and design services." The art gallery in the nursery's Education Center features the work of artists who interpret nature using a variety of media. Sharon Schmidt is the gallery's curator. Besides plants, flowers, and trees of all types, Wasco Nursery also sells mulch, compost, soil, statuary, pottery, fountains, and all materials needed for water features. They offer tree removal, tree planting, landscape design, and many other related services. Matt Zerby, who is still [2018] serving as owner and president, proudly boasts that Wasco Nursery has a "bigger selection of trees, shrubs, perennials, annuals, herbs, and vegetables than any other garden center in northern Illinois."

A recent aerial view of Wasco Nursery

Fox River & Countryside Fire & Rescue

Located at 40W361 Route 64, Fox River & Countryside Fire & Rescue has been in Wasco since the beginning of May 2011. In fact, the official opening of the newly-completed "Fire Station 1" took place at 12:01 AM on the first day of that month, shortly after the final contracts for staffing the district were approved. The lot on which the station was built had been previously owned by James White of White Brothers Trucking. As early as June 2008, the St. Charles Countryside Fire Protection District Board called for architectural proposals for "a new fire station in the Wasco area." Officials stated that a new station in the district's western end would both improve response times and positively impact services. A successful referendum was needed before construction on the new station could begin. The Fire & Rescue district covers almost forty square miles, and its population is over twenty-five thousand people. Besides fire suppression and fire prevention, the district provides emergency medical services. Their primary response areas cover the unincorporated regions of St. Charles and Campton Townships, and the incorporated villages of Wayne and Campton Hills.

One of the fire trucks at Fox River & Countryside Fire & Rescue, in Wasco

A 2018 image of Fox River & Countryside Fire & Rescue, in Wasco

Trellis Farm & Garden

Located at 40W296 Wasco Road, Trellis Farm & Garden has been in business in Wasco for nearly a decade. They sell items such as horse feed and grooming supplies, birdhouses and bird feeders, dog and cat food, wild bird seed, birdbaths, chicken coops, hay cubes, gardening tools, propane, water softener salt, and much more. It is a family-run business, with a knowledgeable staff. Just Animals Wellness Clinic uses their location to host low-cost programs, including on flea and tick control, microchipping, and vaccinations.

Trellis Feed & Supply in 2018

Trailside Automotive Repair

Opened in August 2012, Trailside Automotive Repair has as its goal "to be a top-notch automotive repair shop where customer service is always number one." They offer service, repair, and maintenance of all makes and models of cars and trucks. Mark and Theresa Shoup are the business's owners. They are located at 40W288 Wasco Road.

Trailside Automotive Repair in 2018

Country Gas/Suburban Propane

Country Gas was located at 40W370 in Wasco from 1987 until the mid-2010s; they were succeeded by Suburban Propane, which remains at that location. Country Gas was a propane supplier, and was formerly known as National Butane Gas of Wasco. National Butane, in turn, opened in the late 1940s, and was run by Albert F. Birch and his brothers Robert and William for many years. National Butane Gas was headquartered on Peyton Street in Geneva in the pre-World War II years. Their motto in 1941 was to give "the people, beyond the reach of city gas all the advantages of modern gas service." Their fuel was used for both cooking and heating, and "for practically every purpose for which any gas is employed." In 1948, when National Butane Gas moved to Wasco, they advertised to local farmers, stating the new availability of butane carburetors for tractors. They were also offering heating and cooking installations at that time. In the mid-1960s, National Butane Gas was still gearing its local advertising towards farmers – one headline from 1964 was "Farmers, for Corn Drying use Economical National Gas."

FARMERS!
NOW AVAILABLE

BUTANE CARBURETORS
FOR
TRACTORS
PLENTY OF GAS — CHEAPER THAN GASOLINE
WRITE OR PHONE FOR INFORMATION
HEATING AND COOKING INSTALLATIONS

NATIONAL BUTANE GAS CO.
Wasco, Illinois
Phone: St. Charles 138

Advertisement for National Butane Gas, 1948

Country Gas itself was started not in Wasco but in Crystal Lake. Its founder was Leonard W. Petersohn, who started a propane business from his home in the 1950s. The present business was organized in 1963; Len Petersohn was President of the Illinois Propane Gas Association in the mid-1980s. He passed away in Hoffman Estates in 2001. Suburban Propane acquired the Wasco property in April 2018.

The Country Gas storage building in the 1980s

Country Gas's main building in the 1990s

Suburban Propane in 2018

Local Sports

Although every sport conceivable has been played in Wasco at some point during its long history (Wasco even had a "Horse Shoe pitching team" that traveled to Wisconsin in September 1939) it seems clear that the sports with the biggest and most sustained impact in the village have been baseball and, more recently, softball. Other sports enjoyed brief periods of popularity, however. Edna Bolcum of Wasco played on the first girls' basketball team in St. Charles in 1907, and the team's games were covered in detail in the local press. Wasco had a football team in the early 1920s and later. Bowling was extremely popular locally in the 1950s. Still, no sports have played so major and enduring a role in Wasco as "America's pastime" and its younger sister sport, softball.

Boys Baseball

St. Charles established a "base ball" club in the summer of 1888. By the end of July, the team had played five games, and had a record of two wins and three losses. Teams emerged in Elgin, Aurora, Geneva, and other Kane County settlements around the same time. Some of the players on the St. Charles team had origins in Campton Township, and a few may have even resided in Wasco, although no thorough list of early players has been located. The teams were mostly informal, and players came and went rather frequently, as their schedules, jobs, and schooling allowed.

Not to be outdone by their neighbors to the east, the very first settlers of Wasco also formed a baseball team in June 1888. There was even a "diamond at Wasco" by the end of that month. The existence of the first Wasco team and diamond are proven by several entries in the *Elgin Advocate* from that month and the next, such as when "The St. Charles boys beat the Wasco ball tossers" 16 to 14, or when "the Elgin watch factory base ball club beat the Wascos 16 to 22." Also that July, the "St. Charles base ball club played the Wascos," with the Wasco team winning. As a consequence of the win, "tin pans made . . . the music." By the spring of 1889, there was even a "Wasco Ladies' Base Ball club" with "seven vigorous looking young ladies" as members. An observer wrote of them that they looked "as if they could make a three-base hit every time." The Wasco baseball team played clubs from East Plato and the Elgin Watch Factory in August 1889. It is very likely that baseball teams continued to play in the area for the remaining years of the nineteenth century, and into the twentieth.

There was another baseball team in Wasco as early as October 1923 – from its early days it was affiliated with the local school. Wasco played Lily Lake that year, and perhaps others. Other local teams by 1926 included those at Kaneville, Plato Center, Elburn, West Chicago, St. Charles, LaFox, Virgil, Aurora, and Batavia. In 1929, the local team was composed of players then attending Wasco School (which then had two high school grades). In 1931, the Wasco baseball team "crossed bats with" the team from West Chicago, "the LaFox boys," and the "strong Glen Ellyn Pros." The Nelson Lake Cardinals (who played at the Nelson Lake ball park) were undefeated that year. The Wasco team played at home "at the Brown diamond" (on or The Farm on the south side of Route 64). By October 1931, "the popular 'Farm' baseball field on highway 64, west of Wasco" was the site of a baseball tournament. The field had lately been made popular "by the generosity of Mr. [Bert] Brown." The swimming pool and picnic grounds there were also extremely popular at that time. There were ten players on the Wasco baseball team in 1931: three Johnsons, plus one each from the Bowgren, Whitney, Linquist, Corron, Till, Foulkes, and Claeys families.

In early April 1932, fifteen young men at the Wasco School expressed their interest to their teacher, Mr. Lindgren, for forming a baseball team that season. Interest in the team was higher than usual since the school offered no track and field that year. The boys hoped for "a few games with other schools" by the summer, and their team was soon organized. By the summer of that year, Wasco was playing a team from Virgil Township, and "the Aurora Boulevard nine," and scores often reached double digits. There was a baseball tournament played at The Farm over two weeks in September 1932, "before a large crowd." In the summer of 1933, the Wasco baseball team played (and defeated) the "St. Charles Merchants' team" as well as a team from LaFox. In October 1933, Wasco's married men's ball team lost to the single men's team with a score of sixteen to five. In 1934, they played teams as far away as Elmhurst. Their home field was by then definitively located at the Farm, just west of Wasco.

Baseball being played at The Farm, west of Wasco, around 1930

Locals described Wasco as a "baseball village" during the pre-World War II years. Many summer evenings, "the boys would gather at the Wasco School baseball field" for a game. In the late '30s and early '40s, some of those that typically showed up to play were: John Mongerson, Ben Goldenstein, Herman Meyer, Wally Swanson, Bob and Don Swanson, Jerry and Don Hagaman, Kenny Carlson, Billy Crooke, and Kenny Johnson. These were pickup games, and sometimes the local boys played teams from Plato Center, Lily Lake, or St. Charles. Often the players would drive to St. Charles after the games, and would go to Colonial for ice cream.

Cal and Robert Corron in their Wasco baseball uniforms, 1932

The Bergland Lumber Company sponsored a local softball team for a number of years. In the early 1940s, Robert P. Anderson of Wasco (who would later go on to coach Wasco Little League teams) served as the team's first baseman. The team often played in Pottawatomie Park, in St. Charles. Members of the Bergland softball team gathered at the St. Charles Country Club in November 1945, at an event hosted by their sponsor, Floyd Bergland. Fred Hummel, who took over Bergland and Company in 1947, sponsored a Wasco softball team in the fall of 1948.

The Wasco Cardinals softball team was organized in June 1945. The team was for boys aged fifteen and younger, and the team's first coach was Ben Goldenstein. Their first games were played against Plato Center, Lily Lake, St. Charles, and the Geneva and LaFox 4-H softball teams. The team achieved their eleventh win by late July 1945. Ken Travis was the team's star pitcher that year. In early August 1946, the Cardinals softball team had a record of ten wins and three losses. Some of the players for the Wasco team that year were Stewart Johnson, Jim Reber, Don Chakas, Ben Goldenstein, and Jerry Hagaman. In June 1947 the Cardinals team was made up "of high school players from St. Charles and Wasco." They started their third season that month, "with victories over Fox Valley and Burger Drugs of St. Charles." The games were held in Pottawatomie Park in St. Charles. Jim Reber led the Wasco Cardinals in hitting that season, with Herm Meyer not far behind. Stewart Johnson and Ben Goldenstein also played on that year's team. The Cardinals also played Lily Lake, Geneva, LaFox, and the Hilltopper and Elgin 4-H softball teams. The team does not seem to have lasted more than three or four seasons.

An undated photo of the Bergland Lumber softball team

In September 1948, the Wasco School's baseball team played their first game of the season against Lily Lake. Wesley Johnson coached the Wasco team that year. Following this season, however, there was little in the way of organized baseball or softball in Wasco for ten-year period.

The Wasco American Legion Post began sponsoring several local baseball programs beginning in 1959. The Wasco Post provided equipment for "the elementary age school boys of the community" starting that May, the same month that the Auxiliary hired Don Hagaman to coach and manage the players. In 1968 Babe Bowgren described the program as "one in which we are all proud." The Post awarded a scholarship to Lily Lake resident Willis ("Willy") Crook that fall, which allowed him to attend the Mickey Owen Baseball School in Miller, Missouri. In 1970, so many boys came out for the baseball program that the Babe Ruth League team had to be divided in two. The teams were known as Babe Ruth Leagues I & II, and most of the players were (of course) from Wasco. In April 1972, registration for Little League baseball was held at the Wasco Legion Hall. All boys in the Wasco School between the ages of eight and sixteen were eligible to play. The Wasco American Legion continued to run a baseball league until the early 1980s. The Legion's old baseball diamond was adopted as the first field used by Wasco Baseball when that program was established in 1988. During the summer of 1999, there was an attempt to recreate a Wasco American Legion baseball team, but the effort was short-lived.

Some Wasco Baseball players, including Tom Corron and Kirk Anderson, circa 1966

The Wasco baseball team, in the "Twilight Little League," June 1966. The coach is Don Hagaman. The front row has the following players: John Ball, K. C. Johnson, Kirk Anderson, Chuck Bowgren, Dwayne Schmitt, John Valkenburg, Mark Johnson, Tom Corron, and Steve Hahn. Back row: Bill Vermaat, Mike O'Connell, Ross Lauger, Jeff Swanson, Jeff Sleeman, Bob Fleming, Kyle Hanson, and Bill Cooke.

The Wasco baseball team, in the early 1970s.

The current Wasco Baseball program was established in 1988. Its full name is the "Wasco American Legion Baseball League," and the organization is run by a Board of Directors and an Executive Committee. Its goal is "to firmly implant in the boys and girls of the community the ideals of good sportsmanship, teamwork, honesty, loyalty, courage, and respect for authority, within the environment of our baseball sports program." One of the program's three founders was Sam Gallucci, who ran the league when it was first established and for many years afterward. The first season there were forty-three boys playing on three teams. The second year the number of teams doubled, and by the third year there were eleven teams in the league. Just a decade later, there were nearly ninety teams at all age levels playing for Wasco Baseball. Today, the program offers six leagues, ranging from Pee Wee to Colt, and offers participation for children ages four to eighteen. Wasco Baseball's President is Jim Hudmon, and its Vice President is Paul Stephens.

The baseball fields that adjoin the old Wasco Depot were renovated in the year 2000, thanks to more than $20,000 in donations by the Wasco Baseball league. New fencing was erected, a new backstop was built, and a traditional grass infield was installed for use during 2001 season. In the summer of 2001, the field was renamed Wasco American Legion Field No. 1. The field was in use as a baseball diamond as early as 1967. By the end of the 2001 season, Wasco Baseball had eighty-eight teams playing on eighteen fields. Nine-tenths of the players that year lived in Campton Township. Former Campton Township Supervisor Ed Malek threw out the first pitch on the newly-renovated field in June 2001. In July 2001, Wasco Baseball's fourteen-year-old travel team swept three regional tournaments, winning the Geneva Swedish Days Tournament, the Father's Day Tournament, and the Batavia Invitational.

Wasco Baseball's LaFox Fields were built by the summer of 2000. They are located on the west side of LaFox Road, at the curve, southwest of Wasco Elementary School. The two eastern fields were purchased by Campton Township from the Wasco Sanitary District in 2004. The two western fields are located on property owned by the Kane County Forest Preserve.

In July 2008, both the 12U Wasco Wolverines and the Wasco Warriors traveled to New York State for the Cooperstown Dreams Park National Invitational Tournament. Wasco Baseball had sent a 12U team to the tournament since 1996, but it was only in 2008 that the organization was awarded two bids in the invitation-only competition. The previous two Wasco teams to travel to the tournament made it as far as the quarterfinals before being eliminated; the tournament features some of the best baseball programs in the nation, and participation in it is for many players nothing less than a life-changing experience.

In late July 2012, the Elite Sports Training Center opened in St. Charles. This indoor facility, which features batting cages widely utilized by the local baseball and softball community, caters to players in local leagues such as Wasco Baseball and Wasco Fast-Pitch Softball, among others. In 2014, Wasco Baseball began a new partnership with St. Charles North High School's baseball program. The high school agreed to hand-pick two coaches to work with Wasco's top travel teams at the thirteen and fourteen-year-old levels. Up until that time, fathers of various players had exclusively served as coaches at all levels. The move to outside coaching came at a time when almost two thousand players participated in Wasco Baseball's in-house and travel programs at all age levels.

LaFox Fields Recreational Area in Wasco

Girls Softball

The Wasco Girls Fastpitch Softball League was established in 1988, at a time when the population of the Wasco area was growing rapidly. The league is one that exemplifies both transformation and positive growth. It was formed in large part due to the success of the Wasco Boys Baseball program run by Sam Gallucci. As the local population grew, so did the need for an organization to help support, challenge, and cultivate the abilities of local female athletes. Within a few years, it became evident that because of the wide array of talent and competitive drive amongst area players, there was a demand for both travel and recreational leagues to be established in Wasco.

The local softball program participated in the Rural Kane County Softball League, and after only a short time many talented girls began signing up for Wasco softball. With every passing year, the local softball program grew in size, and before long the Wasco Girls Fastpitch Softball League boasted more than twenty teams, playing in six different age groups. More than three hundred girls played in the league yearly, receiving excellent training and instruction. In the early 1990s, Joe and Traci Medina helped expand the program, and arranged for the Wasco teams to compete with those in the West Suburban Softball League. In 1995, Joe Garbarski helped found the Wasco Diamonds, a travel team comprised of players from the Wasco Girls Softball League. Players selected for the Diamonds were determined through tryouts; 1996 was their first full season. Their first two softball fields were built the following year, in Anderson Park, through the joint efforts of Coach Garbarski, Campton Township officials, a large number of volunteers, and the players themselves. The Wasco Diamonds' official colors (royal blue, black, and white) were selected in 1998.

In 1994, the first all-star female softball team from Wasco entered a local tournament, and the demands of a fully travel-based organization swiftly became evident to all those involved. Realizing this, Joe Garbarski led the charge for an exclusively travel league, and by 1998 established a respectable program complete with home fields and a growing positive reputation. For most of the 1990s, Wasco Girls Fastpitch Softball players utilized the three fields adjoining Verhaeghe Park, just east of the intersection of Burlington Road and Silver Glen Road. There were 283 players in the league in the summer of 1998. At that time Mike Serritella was serving as the softball league's president.

The Wasco Diamonds, 16U Team, in 2017-18

While the Diamonds grew their organization, Wasco's recreational softball league gained a new leader in Sue Sobieski. In 1998, Sobieski became the league's president and she immediately began improving and expanding the organization. The growth was swift, and with the help of hundreds of volunteers, Wasco Girls Fastpitch Softball has grown to become one of the largest and most respected recreational leagues in the state.

By 2000, the Wasco Diamonds fielded teams at four age levels, the oldest being sixteen and under (16U). The program saw continued improvement at that time, as many more players came to tryouts, and as more league teams qualified for participation in national tournaments. By 2002, there were seventy girls playing for the Wasco Diamonds, representing twenty area schools. The next year, the Wasco Diamonds

Golf Outing (the organization's main fundraiser) began, and continues today. In 2004, the Diamonds had seven teams playing across five age levels, and high-place finishes in national tournaments became the norm rather than the exception. By the summer of 2006, the Wasco Diamonds' 16U team had made two appearances in the Amateur Softball Association's National Tournament. That year, the 12U team (coached by John Djukic) traveled to the national tournament as well. Their record going into the ASA tournament in July 2006 was 61-8.

A girls' league which used to have just a few teams at each level has now expanded into a vast and prized cornerstone of the local community. More than forty-five teams, with girls from pre-K to high school play in the spring/summer leagues as well as a fall league in a given year. Garbarski, the Wasco Diamond's founder and first president, retired from the latter position in August 2007, after thirteen years of leadership. After his tenth season, Field 1 at Campton Township Community Park was named Garbarski Field in his honor. As a coach, Garbarski had accumulated over three hundred and fifty wins by that time, and Wasco Diamonds teams had won over forty tournament championships. Greg Trusso took over as Diamonds president at that time.

Some happy players for the Wasco Warriors, with their coaches

The Wasco Diamonds gained their first national title in July 2008, when the 12U team won the United States Specialty Sports Association World Series in St. Louis, Missouri. The Diamonds had eight wins and no losses in the tournament, and outscored their opponents by a total of 76-14! Coach Bill Morrow particularly credited the team's pitching for their wins; the Diamonds' pitchers allowed the fewest runs of any team playing in the tournament. Morrow also praised each player for the incredible effort they put forth throughout the series, and spoke of the value of playing teams from multiple states. The tournament was for girls aged eleven and under, and every player on the 12U Diamonds was no older than eleven at the time of the series.

The Wasco Warriors "light travel" teams were formed in 2012 and have won numerous Class C tournaments under an incredible all-volunteer coaching staff. In recent years, they were even featured in a national commercial.   In July 2016, the Wasco Diamonds 13U team won the U. S. Specialty Sports Association Open Division National Championship. They won eight straight games to clinch the title. Top players for the team that year included Sam Keller, Mady Johnson, Sydney Eby, Abby Smith, Rylee Levine, Jaylee Pfau, and Lily Bakulski. The team was coached by Jordan Smith.

Today, the Wasco Diamonds Traveling Fastpitch Softball Program prepares players for competition at the collegiate level, while placing emphasis on teamwork, skills development, and sportsmanship. The organization boasts highly-competitive teams, and utilizes a state-of-the-art private training facility in nearby Elburn. Over a period of more than twenty years, the Wasco Diamonds' teams have enjoyed tremendous success at both the regional and national levels. The 2018-19 season will prove to be exciting and eventful, as It will witness the merger of the Wasco league with both the St Charles Silver Hawks and the Dennison Silver Hawks. While the organization is constantly changing, growing, and bettering itself, it has never lost sight of the core of the program - the girls. Sobieski, Krause, Kudlicki, Serratella, and the hundreds of other of volunteers who have called Wasco Fastpitch their home have never lost sight of the main goal to empower, promote, uplift, and challenge their female athletes.

After a two-run double, Wasco Girls Fastpitch claimed first place in the 2016 Fall Classic

Wasco Girls Fastpitch went on to win the 2017 10U Championship

Important Social Organizations

The Wasco History Club

Although short-lived, the Wasco History Club seems to have been the second-largest social organization of the early twentieth century (the largest and most important being Wasco Ladies Aid). The History Club was in existence as early as 1907, and seems to have been comprised solely of young unmarried adults in Wasco. They had entertainments at members' homes, Bergland hall, and other community gathering spots. When Arnold and Grace Mather were married in 1909, both had been "most loyal and faithful members" of the club for the previous two years. The History Club surprised them at their new home after their honeymoon, and read a poem on "Good Old Friendship" before presenting them with a monetary gift. Despite their newly-married status, both Mathers were "retained as honorary members of the club" by a unanimous vote of the remaining membership. The club was in existence through the World War I years, but seems to have dissolved by the beginning of the 1920s.

Modern Woodmen of America

Perhaps the first fraternal organization to be established in Wasco was Lodge no. 1771 of the Modern Woodmen of America. It was well-established in Wasco by 1896, when the local chapter had thirty-three members. This group first met on the second and fourth Saturdays of every month. This Modern Woodmen of America was founded in Lyons, Iowa, in 1883. Members were exclusively men between the ages of eighteen and forty-five. The Wasco chapter had an active membership in 1903, and often appeared at funerals of one of their members "in a body." The Modern Woodmen hosted an oyster supper in LaFox in October 1905 and were active throughout the region. The Woodmen put on a play at Bergland's Hall in Wasco in May 1907, which raised $58 over two days. Pary Stevens and John McGowan were the two Wasco residents attending the M.W.A. picnic in Rockford in June 1907.

In the 1910s, Kane County politicians often appealed to local supporters of the Modern Woodmen of America. There was a large Modern Woodman picnic held in St. Charles in August 1913. In the 1910s and '20s, officers of the M.W.A. held titles such as "Venerable Council," "Worthy Advisor," and Banker. The group would often give financial benefits to the widows and families of long-time members, taken out of annual dues paid into the organization's treasury. The Wasco chapter seems to have become inactive by the late 1920s. The village of Kaneville had an active chapter of the Modern Woodmen of America for many years after the Wasco chapter ceased having regular meetings.

In an undated postcard (circa 1909) sent to Fern Bell by her brother Glen, he wrote "it pays to be a woodman, you see how good the woodmen were to mother when father got hurt."

The logo of the Modern Woodmen of America in the early twentieth century

Fern Lillian Bell married Solomon Johnson in June 1911, so the postcard must predate this event. Their father was John W. Bell, who was an active local member of the Modern Woodmen of America.

The Woman's Christian Temperance Union

Wasco had an active membership in this nationwide temperance society in the early twentieth century. Women in the Norton, Higgins, and Warren families, and others, were members, and from time to time attended regional conventions in Chicago, Geneva, Aurora, or Elgin. The Woman's Christian Temperance Union (WCTU) held a "silver medal contest" in Lily Lake in late February 1901, which was attended by many Wasco wives and mothers. The WCTU held a concert in the Wasco Church in August 1904, featuring a ladies' quartet from Chicago. Mrs. Higgins of Wasco met with the WCTU in March and September 1905. Mrs. Carpenter, Mrs. Warren, and Mrs. Bergland (all of Wasco) attended the WCTU convention in Chicago that fall. Mrs. Emma A. Stewart of Elgin was elected President of the Kane County WCTU at the convention held in that city during the fall of 1905. Minerva Warren of Wasco was appointed superintendent of the "Mothers meeting and cradle roll" committee at that time, while other women were in charge of such committees as "Temperance literature" and "Prison and Jail work."

In October 1905, the Wasco WCTU held a religious service at the newly-opened St. Charles Boys' Home. A month later, they held a similar service at the Girls' Home in Geneva. A WCTU dinner was held at Margaret Norton's house, just east of Wasco, in January 1906. The group held an essay contest and musical entertainment at the Wasco Church the next month, charging a fifteen-cent admission. The topic was "The Effects of Anti-Narcotics" and the winner of the written competition was Edna Bolcum. Gladys Fisher took second prize, and Charlotte Millen third. Mr. Ellsworth and Mrs. Higgins of Wasco, among others, supplied the music.

The early logo for the WCTU

In May 1906, Mrs. H. S. Higgins and Minerva Warren of Wasco attended the WCTU convention in Geneva. In September of that year, the Wasco WCTU held an oratorical contest at the local church. Floyd Bergland won for the seniors, and Grace Shaft for the juniors. Other competitors included Selma Metzger, Gertrude Bolcum, Mae DeLaney, Charlie Millen, Harriet McGowan, Edna Carpenter, Ellen Nelson, and Paul Scott. Those from Wasco attending the September 1906 WCTU convention in Aurora were Mrs. Higgins, Mrs. Carpenter, Mrs. Bergland, Minerva Warren, and Miss Norton. Mrs. Mary E. Kuhl, state president of the WCTU, spoke to members in Wasco on 1 May 1907. The WCTU entertained the St. Charles Union at the Wasco Church in early August of that year; the entertainment was followed by a devotional worship service.

In October 1913, Margaret Norton entertained several members of the WCTU at her home just east of Wasco. That same month, more than four hundred delegates from all over Illinois attended a statewide WCTU convention in Springfield. Attendees were promoting a statewide campaign against saloons. These efforts, of course, eventually culminated in the passage of the Eighteenth Amendment to the U. S.

Constitution by Congress in 1917. Illinois ratified this amendment on 14 January 1919; prohibition was in effect for the next eleven years. In October 1919, Emma Carpenter represented Wasco when she attended the Kane County WCTU convention in Elgin.

In June 1925, all the WCTU branches in Kane County participated in a joint picnic in Geneva. One of the region's largest branches was the St. Charles division. In February 1927, some Wasco-area residents involved in the organization were Emma Carpenter, Edna Cray, and Emma Fischer.

In May 1931, Mrs. Carpenter hosted a St. Charles WCTU meeting at her home; in fact, in the later years it seems that all of the Wasco participants in this organization were formally part of the group's St. Charles chapter. When the WCTU served refreshments at Martha Higgins' birthday party in Geneva in December 1933, several Wasco women attended the event. That same month, nation-wide prohibition was lifted with the passage and ratification of the Twenty-First Amendment. One of the last-documented meetings of the WCTU in Wasco took place in June 1938, with at least Mrs. Cray, Mrs. Carpenter, and Mrs. Elmer Peterson as hostesses.

The Christian Endeavor Society

Various young men and women active in the Wasco Baptist Church were also members of an organization called the Christian Endeavor Society (CES). This group was founded in New England in 1881, and a branch existed in Wasco as early as 1903, and perhaps during the previous decade as well. The group is a nondenominational young person's evangelical society, whose goal is "to promote an earnest Christian life among its members, to increase their mutual acquaintanceship, and to make them more useful in the service of God." In August 1903, the CES held an ice cream fundraiser at the Martin house in Wasco, and the money raised at that event went toward the new carpet in the Wasco Church. In 1904, some of the local leaders of the society, which met every Sunday, included Nettie Anderson, Maude Austin. Clara Stevens, Charlotte Millen, Mrs. E. C. Chaffee, Mrs. G. H. Martin, and Mrs. Higgins. Willard R. Austin, E. S. Chaffee, and J. I. Ellsworth were three of the handful of male leaders of the society meetings mentioned in early newspapers. Some of their membership attended a Christian Endeavor convention held in Dundee that year. The group gave a "literary social" at Bergland's Hall in February 1904 – all those who attended were asked to recite a quote or interesting fact about either Washington, Lowell, Lincoln, or Longfellow. D. W. Stevens and J. I. Ellsworth both led Christian Endeavor meetings in Wasco in March 1905; the following month Pastor Peterson (of the Wasco Baptist Church) was a Christian Endeavor Society leader. Harriet Garfield was an active member at that time as well.

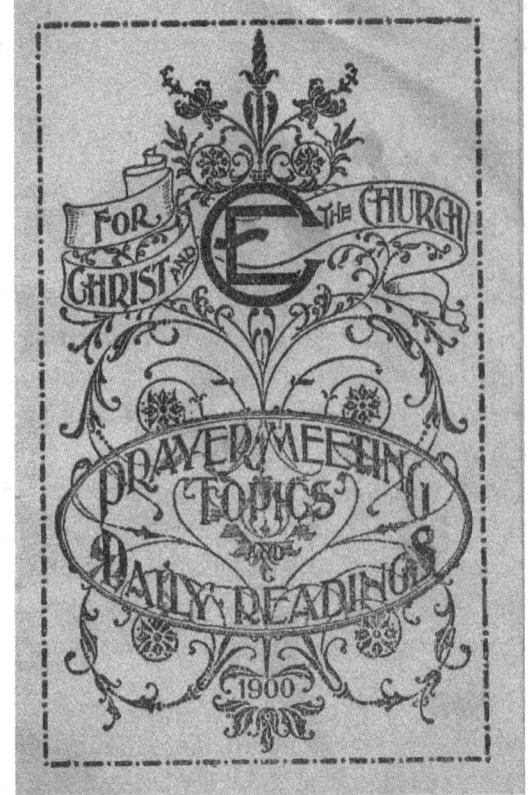

Christian Endeavor booklet from 1900

In May 1905, the Christian Endeavor Society of Wasco held a "Literary Social" in Bergland's Hall. Everyone attending was asked to "represent a book," or else face a fine of one dime! Ice cream and cake were for sale at the event for fifteen cents. The WCTU attended the Christian Endeavor meeting in early June of that year. Leaders of the Christian Endeavor meetings in the summer of 1905 included Edith Cass, Mrs. E. S. Chaffee, Ida Sharp, Charlotte Millen, Mrs. Higgins, Olive Bolcum, Nettie Anderson, and Lottie Stevens. Florence Peterson led a Christian Endeavor Society meeting later that fall, as did Mrs. A. D. Chaffee, Carolyn Plummer, C. W. Millen, and Flossie Austin.

Some leaders of Wasco's Christian Endeavor Society in 1906 included Mrs. A. D. Chaffee, Olive Bolcum, Edna Bolcum, Maude Austin, E. S. Chaffee, J. I. Ellsworth, Mr. Pillins, Carolyn Plummer, Flossie Austin, Mrs. E. H. Allen, Mrs. E. T. Peterson, Jennie Garfield, Edna Crubaugh, and Fred Nelson. In August 1906, the Christian Endeavor society had a "Consecration service" at the Wasco Church; the service was conducted by Rev. C. Thompson of Elburn. The society held a "Measuring social" at the Bolcum home in August 1906, and a watermelon social at the E. H. Allen house that October. J. I. Ellsworth was elected President of the Wasco Christian Endeavor Society in January 1907. Mrs. Higgins was Vice President, while Flossie Austin was the group's Secretary, and Edna Bolcum was its Treasurer.

Mrs. E. T. Peterson led the Christian Endeavor Society meeting in February 1907 which had the theme "Missions in India." Flossie Austin was the meeting leader the following month, Grace Bolcum led in May, Jennie Garfield in June, C. J. Waterhouse in July, and Magdalene Lorang in August of the same year. The society continued to be active for the next several years but seems to have faded away in Wasco prior to the first World War.

Wasco Ladies Aid

The Wasco Ladies Aid has been mentioned many times throughout this work, but a few more lines here may be of some interest. The Wasco Ladies Aid is the oldest existing social organization in Campton Township, and has been meeting regularly since 1890. That year, Rev. William Lane of Lily Lake took steps to organize the Wasco Church. That summer, Rev. Lane "wisely proposed that the Wasco women should organize for work, and it was he who wrote the original Constitution and By-laws forming the Wasco Ladies Aid," according to Phebe Chaffee, a founding member. When the Wasco Church was dedicated the following November, the Ladies Aid "served dinner and supper to all at the depot."

In 1896, the first edition of the *Wasco Ladies Cook Book* was published. The book was revised and reprinted in 1913. A few copies still exist, having been passed down from one generation to the next, and are owned by current Wasco Ladies Aid members. The Ladies Aid created many beautiful quilts in that era (and still do) for the benefit of missions and charitable institutions. For more than a century, Ladies Aid meetings have featured the singing of hymns. In the early

Signature of Phebe Chaffee, a founder of Wasco Ladies Aid

years, the 1782 hymn "Blest Be The Tie That Binds," written by a Baptist clergyman, was sung more frequently than any other.

In June 1901, the Ladies Aid had its first 'tea' of the season, held in Bergland's Hall in Wasco. Their July tea was held at Miss Nettie Anderson's, and the following month it was held at Mrs. J. W. Bell's home. The ladies have been engaged in quilting since at least 1909, and often hosted suppers to benefit the Wasco Baptist Church (sixty-five attended one in March 1910). They had a sewing committee very early in the twentieth century. Their presentation of the play "Breezy Point" in April 1904 was extremely popular, and proved to be a significant fundraiser for that time. In almost all cases, the funds raised went directly to the Wasco Baptist Church. The Ladies Aid received six new members during the winter of 1904, and membership seemed to fluctuate between fifteen and thirty active members at any given time. Funds raised by the Ladies Aid in 1903 went toward the new church carpet. The Ladies Aid hosted a Harvest Home Dinner in J. Bell's grove near Wasco in September 1903, raising $32 for the Wasco Church. The Ladies Aid held a "pumpkin social" in Bergland's Hall in October 1903. They hosted a "New England supper" (also in Bergland's Hall) in late October 1904, which brought $31 into their treasury. The Ladies Aid's "harvest home festival" held at the John Bell grove near Wasco that fall took in just over $141.

Some of the founders of Wasco Ladies Aid, during the decade of the 1900s. Back row: Etta Fischer, Nettie Anderson, Mary Millen, _____ , Vesta Bell, Lena McGowan, Flossie Austin, Kate Vanderhoof, and Florence Peterson. Front row: _____ , Emma Carpenter, Martha Higgins(?), Mrs. D. W. Stevens(?), Anna Bergland, _____ .

In the spring of 1905, many Ladies Aid events were held at the homes of Mrs. D. W. Stevens and Mrs. George Bergland. That summer, Mrs. E. P. Lathrop, Harriet Garfield, and Mrs. C. W. Millen hosted Ladies Aid meetings. The Harvest Home Festival that year was held on 24 August, in Bell's Grove, northeast of

Wasco. The Ladies Aid gave a "lawn social" at H. T. Fisher's farm in September 1905, where they served ice cream and cake for fifteen cents. This fundraiser featured the "Wasco orchestra and band" and raised $14 total. Josephine Whitney entertained the Ladies Aid at her residence in November of that year, and Mrs. Frank Vanderhoof followed the next month, with a noon luncheon at her farm home.

On 11 November 1905, the Wasco Ladies Aid held a New England supper at Bergland Hall, which was widely attended. Mrs. Mertie Webb, Mrs. Daniel Whitney, and Mrs. E. H. Allen were hosts of other Ladies Aid events that season. In January 1906, the newly-elected Ladies Aid officers were: Nettie Anderson (President); Mrs. Frank Vanderhoof (Vice President); and Mrs. Merrill Whitney (Secretary/Treasurer). Mrs. J. W. Bell, Mrs. Ellsworth, Mrs. N. L. Carpenter, Harriet Garfield, Mrs. H. T. Fisher, and Mrs. C. W. Millen all entertained the Ladies Aid later in 1906.

On the first and second day of June, 1906, the Wasco Ladies Aid put on a play entitled "Miss Fearless and Company" in Bergland's Hall. Josephine Whitney played the lead role, and the other actors were Etta Fisher, Mertell Wickizer, Anna Allen, Lillian Martin, Florence Peterson, Nettie Anderson, and Carrie Swanson. Admission to see the production was twenty-five cents. The play raised $55 in two days and was so popular that an encore performance was given in Lily Lake later that month, bringing in another $12. Mrs. Fred Swanson entertained the Ladies Aid in September 1906, and Mrs. L. White and Mrs. Merrill Whitney hosted the next month.

Some members of the Wasco Ladies Aid, in 1909, getting ready to can grapes. Left to right: Mary Millen, Mary Ann Downey, Mrs. Chaffee, Louisa Bergland, Vesta Bell, Florence Peterson, Lillie Whitney, and Mrs. Newberry

Hosts of various Wasco Ladies Aid events in 1907 included Mrs. C. W. Millen, Nettie Anderson, Mrs. A. D. Chaffee, Mrs. Frank Vanderhoof, Mrs. George Bergland, Mrs. J. W. Bell, Margaret Norton, Mrs. Ellsworth, and Mrs. Carpenter. That February the Ladies held a "Carpet-rag social" at Mrs. Bergland's house, during which each attendee was asked to bring a "ball of carpet rags, with her name in the center." Dinner was served, and friends were invited to attend. The Ladies Aid put on a three-act play entitled "Our Folks" in the spring of 1907. Charles J. Waterhouse had the leading role in the production, which raised $46.60. Other local actors included Marshall Carlson, Fred Lake, Elmer T. Peterson, Roy Chrystal, Etta Fischer, Charlotte Millen, Jenny Chrystal, Carrie Swanson, and Anna Allen. The Ladies Aid sponsored an ice cream social at the Frank Vanderhoof farm in July 1907, selling cake and ice cream for fifteen cents. Mrs. N. L. Carpenter hosted the Ladies Aid meeting at her home later that summer.

In November 1913, the Wasco Ladies Aid sponsored a bazaar at the church, during which "Rugs, aprons, home cookery, and candy will be on sale." The Ladies also offered a 25¢ supper after the bazaar. That year, "Mesdames McGowan, Millen, and Peterson" were frequent entertainers at Ladies Aid events.

The Harvest Home Supper was still being run by the Wasco Ladies Aid in November 1915 and drew attendees from well beyond just Wasco. The Ladies Aid dinner in March 1916 raised $9. It was held at the house of Mrs. John Ramm, and was "pretty well attended." Mrs. George Muirhead of Plato Center, along with the Elgin Quartet, gave an entertainment on 13 July 1917, under the auspices of the Wasco Ladies Aid. The event was held in the Wasco Church. In February 1919, the Ladies Aid put on a short play entitled "How I Earned My Dollar" at the Wasco Church. A sum totaling $45 was raised, "a part of which was given to missions." The original records of the Wasco Ladies Aid, including the 1890 constitution creating the group, were lost some time prior to 1924, and have never been recovered.

In September 1924, the Wasco Ladies Aid gave a "fruit shower" for Mrs. Harry L. [Anna] Sharp, who had been ill for some time. Mrs. Sharp had "always been active in the society," and to show their appreciation for her long-time support, the Ladies gave gifts of quarts of fruit, jelly, and canned vegetables.

In March 1928, the Ladies Aid celebrated the thirty-fifth wedding anniversary of Mr. and Mrs. John McGowan. The couple was given a beautiful plant as a gift, and refreshments were served in the Wasco Church parlor. The group hosted a tea at the church in May of that year, and again the next month, with Mrs. Roy Sharp as chairman. The Ladies Aid also served a dinner in the Wasco Church parlor on 25 October. On 15 November 1928, the Ladies Aid served a chicken dinner at the church. The 1928 Wasco Ladies Aid Christmas party was held at the home of Fern Johnson.

During the Depression, The Wasco Ladies Aid often served tea at the Wasco Church on Thursday afternoons. Mrs. A. J. Mongerson chaired the committee in charge of these events in the early 1930s. Mrs. Peter Denker hosted the Ladies Aid in December 1929. That month, the Ladies Aid served refreshments at the Golden Wedding celebration for Mr. and Mrs. C. W. Millen. Florence Peterson hosted a Ladies Aid dinner in October 1930. Mrs. George Hawkins hosted the November 1931 Ladies Aid meeting. In June 1933, the following Ladies Aid officers were elected: Fern Johnson (President); Rose Johnson (Vice President); Ann Mongerson (Secretary); Mrs. Mertell Wickizer (Treasurer); and Edna Cray (Assistant Secretary).

At the 1933 Ladies Aid Christmas party, held in the church, there was "a Christmas tree for the children and a chicken supper for members and their families." Mrs. Albert Richmond joined as a new member of the Ladies Aid in September 1935. In March 1936, the Wasco Ladies Aid hosted a community-wide ninety-third birthday dinner for D. W. Stevens, a charter member of the Wasco Church. Over one hundred and fifty guests attended this celebration. A similar event was held every year afterwards until Mr. Stevens was no longer able to participate in public functions. In June 1936, the following Ladies Aid officers were elected: Olive Bergland (president); Ann Mongerson (vice president); Jude Richmond (treasurer); and Edna Cray (secretary). Mrs. Mertell Wickizer was outgoing president. In the fall of 1939, Mrs. Florence Peterson and Mrs. Robert Perkins were among the most active Ladies Aid members. Donations were made in this era to the Red Cross, the Polio Fund, and to assist those affected by floods.

For many years the Ladies Aid organized "Family Night" suppers near the holidays, and "Harvest Home" dinners each fall. All community members were welcome at these gatherings. In the 1940s, food donations were collected at the latter event, and would be brought to the Baptist Children's Home in Maywood. Members would also hem dish towels for the Children's Home, and would send eggs to the residents there at Easter time. During World War II, the Wasco Ladies Aid participated in a large-scale canning drive. Members also sent care packages to the servicemen from Wasco who were serving abroad.

In May 1945, a committee was appointed to create a new constitution for the Ladies Aid. This document, which is still in effect, states that the purpose of the organization is to "cooperate with the Baptist Church of Wasco, in helping to maintain the building and its furnishings" and to "assist in other benevolent purposes." The last surviving founding member of the Ladies Aid, Nettie Anderson, died in 1953, after sixty-three years of active membership. As has been stated, the Wasco Ladies Aid paid for many goods and services during the first several decades of the twentieth century, including janitorial services at the church, fuel and repair bills, lawn care, piano tuning, insurance, new pews, and much more. They purchased small chairs for the Sunday School when that group was reorganized in 1941. Members of the Ladies Aid thoroughly cleaned the Wasco Church every spring – half of the membership would work on the auditorium, and the other half would clean the basement. On these days, lunch was served at noon, followed by a short devotional.

After 1949, the Wasco Ladies Aid sent gifts of money and garden seeds to Jack Brown's Bear Track Mission (now known as the Kentucky Mountain Mission) in Beattyville, Lee County, Kentucky. Many bandages for cancer patients were knitted and rolled in the 1950s and '60s, often under the supervision of Minnie Anderson. Mrs. A. J. Erickson hosted the Ladies Aid meeting in January 1950; Florence Peterson hosted the meeting that March. Mrs. Theodore [Hilma] Johnson hosted the Ladies Aid meeting in July 1959. The meeting took place in the Wasco Church that September, and at the home of Mrs. Skeen the following month. Edna Cray hosted a meeting late that year.

The Wasco Ladies Aid met at The Little House in July 1961 for a dessert luncheon. Later they reconvened in the "cool church basement" to make bandages for the Cancer Society. In December 1961, the annual Ladies Aid Christmas party was held at the home of Mrs. Hillis Barber. Mrs. Axel Anderson hosted the Ladies Aid meeting in February 1962, Mrs. Frank Hagaman hosted that May, and Mrs. Stanley Bowgren in July. In 1962, the Christmas party was held at the home of Mrs. Robert Corron. Mrs. Chalberg of Campton Hills hosted the 1964 Christmas luncheon, at which twenty-two members and guests were present. The afternoon was spent singing carols, visiting, and looking at Mrs. Dexter Norton's collection of old Christmas cards.

In March 1964, the Wasco Ladies Aid met at the home of Ruth Chalberg. They spent the afternoon "tearing old sheets into strips" and rolling them into bandages for the Cancer Society. The Aid members were always glad to receive donations of old sheets for this purpose. The next month, the Ladies met at the home of Mrs. Dexter Norton, and held a silent auction. In November 1965, the Ladies Aid celebrated their 75th Anniversary with a tea held at the Wasco Church. During the second half of the 1960s, meetings were held in the homes of the Johnson sisters, Edna Fischer, Flora Norton, Lucinda Corron, Marjorie Anderson, Frances Denker, Florence Hagaman, and others. Silent auctions were frequent during that era.

On 1 October 1970, the Ladies Aid held a salad luncheon to celebrate their 80th anniversary. In the 1970s, the group met at the homes of its members, as per the group's tradition. Some hosts during that decade were Nina Bowgren, Jewel Bowgren, Edna Fischer, Lucinda Corron, Flora Norton, Frances Denker, Anne Kautz, Anne Hassel, Olive Hamilton, and Dolly Bolcum, among others. The Ladies Aid sold coffee and lemonade at the Campton Township Bicentennial celebration in 1976 and had their annual Christmas luncheon at the Mill Race Inn in Geneva that December. The party was held at Karen's in Geneva in 1975. The Wasco Ladies Aid gathered at the Hotel Baker in St. Charles for that occasion in 1972, 1974, 1977, and 1979. The Ladies held a picnic in the LeRoy Oakes Forest Preserve for several years, including in June 1978 and July 1979. In September 1979, the Ladies enjoyed a brunch held on Nina Bowgren's deck.

Louise Wilkison, a senior member of the Wasco Ladies Aid, passed away on 18 August 1986, just weeks before her 100th birthday. Louise lived in Batavia before moving to Wasco to be with her daughter, Rose (Wilkison) Swanson.

The Wasco Ladies Aid has remained very active in the twenty-first century, and is fast approaching its 129th year of continuous existence. It has raised money for literally hundreds of good causes throughout the years. Contributions in 2017 went to the Living Well Cancer Center, the Salvation Army, the Corron Farm Preservation Society, Garfield Farm, the Elder Day Center, and Fox Valley Food for Health. Current [2018] officers are Joy Larson (President); Joan Bowgren (Treasurer); and Joy Nelson (Secretary). The group remains a vibrant and enjoyable social organization; members continue to join the group, which meets nearly every month.

Members of the Wasco Ladies meeting at the Lenkaitis Farm north of Wasco, August 2018. From left, Joy Nelson, Joy Larson, Chris Brauer, Ginny Waller, Ellie Peterson, Nancy Haire, Pat Hollis, Nancy Warner, Lois Burgess, and Kathy Peterson

The Pollyanna Club

For about a decade, beginning in 1929, members of the Pollyanna Club met in Wasco. The club's name comes from the bestselling 1913 novel *Pollyanna* by Eleanor Porter, in which the main character has an unfailingly optimistic outlook. The book is also the source of the name of the Glad Game Club, mentioned below. In the book, Pollyanna always tries to find the positive in a given situation, no matter how bleak it may appear at first glance; she calls this process, which she learned from her father, "the Glad Game."

The Pollyanna Club of Wasco was meeting by March 1929, with the Johnson sisters as members. In December 1929, the group held a roast chicken dinner in the Wasco Church. After the meal, "games were played until old Santa himself arrived with his pack of gifts." There were eighty attendees; the church dining room was decorated with a Christmas theme. During the last week of June, 1930, the Pollyanna Club held its annual picnic at Johnson's Mound, near Batavia. In August 1933, members of the club played the card game "42" at one of their meetings. Members at that time were Hazel Ekstrom, Ethel Waterhouse, Mrs. Reuben [Rose] Verner, and Edna Cray.

Two of the other members named in local newspapers a short time later were Mrs. Lawrence McGowan and Mrs. Norvid Swanson, who hosted events in October and November 1933, respectively. Mathilda Johnson of Wasco entertained the Pollyanna Club earlier that year. Members in 1934 included Lotten Swanberg, Nettie Anderson, Frances Anderson, Florence Peterson, Mrs. Elnor Bell, Maud Richmond, and Florence and Ellen Mongerson. In December 1935, the Pollyanna Club held its Christmas party at the New England Tea Room in Batavia. In 1937, the group's Christmas party took place at the Hotel Baker in St. Charles. Again, the game "42" was played "with honors going to Miss Esther Johnson and Hugo Denker." Edna Cray and Emma Vanderhoof were active members in March 1938.

The Wasco Glad Game Club

Another social organization in Wasco, called the Glad Game Club, existed in the 1920s, '30s, and '40s. It was limited to female membership. The club was meeting by August 1924, when it held its annual picnic dinner in Lord's Park, Elgin. Mae Swanson hosted one of the group's events in June 1927. In 1928, active members included Florence and Ellen Mongerson, Maude Richmond, as well as the wives of Norvid Swanson, Everett Smith, Elmer Peterson, and Carl Olson, among others. The club's annual Christmas party was held at the home of Kate Vanderhoof in December 1928 – some fifty women were present, and "a very fine dinner was served." Each member invited either a friend, or their mother. Christmas gifts were exchanged then, and all present "reported a fine time. The Wasco Glad Game Club can do things up right." Santa Claus appeared at the Glad Game Club's 1929 Christmas party, which "was great fun for the children," with "everyone saying what a great time they had." In 1929 and 1930, the club occasionally met at the homes of either Nettie Anderson, Mildred Johnson, Frances Denker, Olive Bergland, or Edna Cray. Officers in 1930 included Lotten Swanberg (President), Bessie Baggs (Vice President), and Frances Anderson (Secretary).

In October 1930, the club threw a bridal shower for one of its members, Miss Anne Askeland. The decorations were in autumn colors, "with orange and green predominating." The Anderson sisters, Louisa Swanson, Frances Denker, Hilda Hawkins, and Florence Hagaman were active members in 1931. The 1932 Christmas party, which included "a fine program and very nice refreshments," was held in the parlor of the Wasco Church. Jenny Denker hosted the Club at their regular meeting in March 1933, and Mildred Johnson hosted in September 1934. Other active members then were Hilda Hawkins, Emma Vanderhoof, and Edith Hoffman. Grace Perkins entertained the Wasco Glad Game Club at her home in October 1935, and Clara Anderson of St. Charles hosted in May 1936. In August 1936, the Glad Game Club met at the home of Hazel Ekstrom. Ethel Waterhouse and Rose Verner were active members at that time. Officers in 1937 were Grace Peterson, Jennie Denker, and Rose Johnson.

Florence and Ellen Mongerson, early members of the Wasco Glad Game Club

In 1939, members of the Glad Game Club included Alice Mongerson, Ellen Anderson, and Esther McGowan. During the early war years, the Glad Game Club continued to meet, but the group seems to have disbanded by 1944. Although some of its later members (such as Mildred Olson) were from St. Charles, and others (Esther McGowan, for example) lived in Lily Lake, most continued to be Wasco residents. Amy Richmond, Nettie Anderson, and Jenny Denker continued to be active in the club at that time. Dinners were occasionally held in Batavia or Elburn. Annual picnics in the pre-war years were often held at Johnson's Mound.

Wasco Mothers' Club

This group existed in the early years of the twentieth century. The Wasco Mothers' Club was dedicated (in part) to educating its members in a number of fields, including politics, social progress, and famous activist women of the past. The Mothers' Club existed as early as 1905, and Mrs. A. D. Chaffee was one of its original members. Mrs. George Bergland was also a charter member, as was Mrs. A. A. Burr. Mrs. Warren entertained the Mothers' Club meeting in September 1905, at which Mrs. Heffernan of the Chicago Congress of Mothers addressed the ladies of Wasco. Mrs. J. I. Delaney hosted the Wasco Mothers' Club in November 1905, and Mrs. Frank [Emma] Brown was the host the following month. Mrs. Daniel Whitney hosted the club in January 1906, Mrs. H. T. Fisher hosted in February, and Mrs. E. H. Allen followed as host that March.

The Mothers' Club of Wasco held a well-attended "Pound social" at the home of C. W. Bolcum in April 1906, in which they raised the sum of twenty dollars. Mrs. August Fischer of St. Charles hosted the Wasco Mothers' Club in June 1906, and Mrs. H. S. Higgins of Wasco was the host the next month. Mrs. Bolcum was again the host in September, and Mrs. Burr hosted in October. Mrs. William Kimble hosted the Wasco Mothers' Club the following winter. Mrs. George Bergland hosted a Mothers' Club meeting in March 1907, and Mrs. H. T. Fisher followed her that May. Those attending that particular meeting included Mrs. Frank Plummer, Mrs. F. Schlager, Mrs. Will Plummer of Elgin, and Mrs. Gust Fischer of St. Charles.

Mrs. Cassie Bolcum is shown here (center) with her husband Chester and their family – Edna, Olive, Bessie, and Art in the back row, and Esther, Chester, Grace, Myrtle, and Gertrude seated in front

In 1911-1912, Mrs. John I. Delancy was President of the Wasco Mothers' Club, and Mrs. John Bell was Treasurer. Other members included Mrs. Frank Brown, Mrs. Ennis Allen, Mrs. Theodore Fischer, Libby R. McCarthy, Mrs. Blanchard, Mrs. Lambert, Mrs. C. W. Bolcum, Mrs. Norton, and Mrs. John McGowan. Mrs. L. E. Wickizer and Emma J. Hagaman entertained the Mother's Club in September 1913. In February 1916, Mrs. Bangs of Chicago addressed the Wasco Mothers' Club. The group seems to have become inactive by the end of World War I.

The Wasco Mothers' Club existed in a new form in the late 1950s. The Mothers' Club of Wasco School came into being in 1952. The group wrote a cookbook in 1957 and began the barbeque supper the following year. The Mother's Club (renamed the Wasco Parents' and Teachers' Club in the mid-1960s) raised thousands of dollars for the school. Some of the group's early purchases were filing cabinets, coat racks, mimeograph machines, and a film projector. In 1959, some Mothers' Club members included Mrs. Robert Johnsen (President), Mrs. Roger Ekstrom, Mrs. Allan Egner, Mrs. Kenneth Carlson, Mrs. Lee Mather, Mrs. Mrs. Ralph Voss, Mrs. C. W. Raasch, Mrs. Malcolm Ball, Mrs. George Olson, Mrs. Gordon Anderson, Mrs. Wesley Johnson, Mrs. Fred Hummel Jr., and Mrs. Howard Turner. In 1962, the club held a "guest meeting at the Wasco school" featuring a Swiss exchange student. In 1963, Mrs. Turner, vice president of the club, presented the Cub Scout pack flag and membership charter "to the Cub Scouts of Wasco." The group was also referred to as "The Wasco Mothers and Teachers Club" throughout that period.

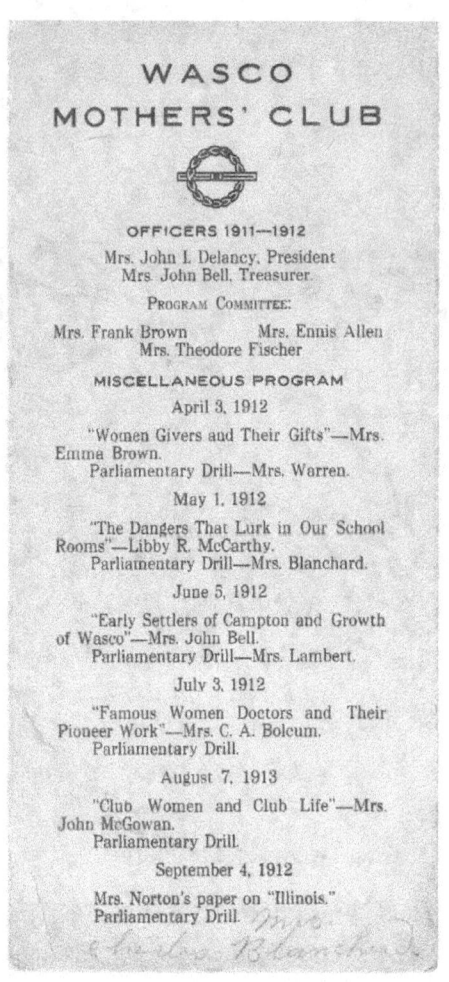

Card from the Wasco Mothers' Club, 1912

The Wasco Home Bureau

The Wasco Home Bureau was active in the 1930s and '40s, and was a local unit of the Kane County Home Bureau. Its members focused on learning about how to improve the home, and homemaking in general. In May 1931, Campton Township women who were interested in the group were invited to an informative meeting, which was hosted by Nona M. Schwarz, Kane County Home Advisor. The proposed new Home Bureau unit invited include women of Wasco, Lily Lake, and the entire township to participate. The meeting was held on the eighth of that month, and the new unit was organized that very afternoon. Miss Schwarz received calls at the Home Bureau office in Geneva at the time of the Campton unit's organization. A few years later, the Lily Lake and Wasco units began meeting separately.

In February 1938, Gertrude Bekman, "home advisor," gave the lesson to the group. Her topic was "Social Diseases." In May of that year, the Bureau met at the home of Lavina Christenson, and selected the following officers: Mrs. Everette Johnson (Unit Chairman); Edna Cray (Vice Chairman); Mrs. George Hawkins (Secretary & Treasurer). In November 1939, the Home Bureau met at the Scott house in Wasco – Gertrude Fields spoke on the topic "Special Meals for Guests." Another topic of that era was "interesting table center pieces." The Wasco Home Bureau also sponsored the Silver Clover 4-H Club of Wasco in

1939. Mrs. Fields chaperoned the girls during their trip to the Kane County Livestock Exposition in November of that year.

In 1940, the Wasco Home Bureau held a "500 card and Bunco party" at the Wasco School. They served a barbeque luncheon, and at their regular meeting discussed the topic "homemaking in other lands." Active members then included Mrs. James Rees, Mrs. Paul Scott, Edna Cray, Mrs. George Hawkins, Mrs. Everett Johnson, Mrs. Leonard Askeland, Mrs. George Reed, Miss Ila Johnson, Mrs. Preston Gee, and Mrs. Al Richmond. Other topics of discussion that year included "floors and woodwork" and "home making in Denmark." Several members of the Wasco Home Bureau put on a play entitled "Christmas Barricade" in December 1940. This performance was given an "A" rating in the Kane County music-drama contest held that season. The group was still active in 1942, but their activities lessened in frequency during the later years of World War II. Some topics presented during the war included "the year's food needs" and "timely topics on gardening." Attendance at the group's monthly meetings usually fluctuated between ten and twenty participants.

The Wasco/Campton 4-H Club

This organization was very active in the area between the 1930s and the 1950s. The first incarnation of the Wasco 4-H Club met periodically as early as 1934, but was not formally organized until two years later. The first eight girls joined the Wasco 4-H Club in June 1936. Miss Gertrude Beekman of Geneva, Bureau advisor, and Mrs. Brundage of LaFox assisted in formally organizing the chapter that month. Miss Della Scott of Wasco was club leader, while Ethel Bell Johnson of Wasco was president. Vice president was Arlene Gustafson, while Helen Shepard of St. Charles was secretary and treasurer. Betty Marie Carlson of Wasco was publicity chairman. The first meeting took place on 6 June at the home of Mrs. E. White. A "clothing course" was immediately begun.

One of the Wasco 4-H Club's earliest large-scale events took place in 1937, when the group sponsored a "Winter Project Achievement Day" held in early April of that year. Members discussed livestock and farming, as well as home economics, but also played games and held dances. The newly-named Silver Clover 4-H Club met at the Wasco School in May 1939. Officers elected at that time were: June Olson (president); Leona Olsen (vice president); Margery Jay (secretary and treasurer); Eleanor Johnson (reporter); and Phyllis Scott (recreation leader). The group's name was selected by the members; their first sewing project was discussed at that meeting. Harriet M. Eddy and Mrs. Leonard Askeland were the club's adult leaders then. Attendance at 4-H events in Wasco waned after 1940, though, and the group ceased meeting for a time.

The Wasco 4-H Club was formally reorganized in the immediate postwar years. They held their first formal meeting on Wednesday, 22 January 1947, when Nancy Mongerson was elected Club President. Dean Richmond was elected Vice President then, and Barbara Larson was elected as Secretary. Don Hagaman was chosen to be the group's "Reporter." At the initial meeting, Kane County 4-H Adviser Robert J. Howard explained "the organization and purposes of 4-H Club work." Mrs. L. R. Larson acted as the new group's first local adviser. The Wasco 4-H Club briefly sponsored a baseball team in the late 1940s. The group attended the Illinois State Fair in August 1947, and several of its livestock entries won awards. Melvin Johnson of Wasco was a winner in the Holstein group that year.

The Campton 4-H Club was formed in March 1948 through the unification of the Lily Lake and Wasco 4-H Clubs, whose merger was facilitated by Lowell Richmond. In its early years, one of the leaders of the Wasco 4-H Club was Don Hagaman; another was Wally Brown. Dean Richmond was acting president of the Wasco group in July 1947. In December of that year, Donald Swanson was elected as the group's President; René Verhaeghe as Vice President; Melvin Johnson as Program Chairman; Joy Fisher as Secretary; Dexter Norton Jr. as Treasurer; Barbara Larson as Pianist; Lowell Richmond as Photographer; and Lory Jonatat as Reporter.

The unified group frequently met at the Wasco School, and a good number of its members were from Wasco itself. In February 1948, the Lily Lake and Wasco 4-H Clubs held their first joint function at a "box social" held at the former "Campton Town House." Boxes prepared by the "mothers and daughters of the group" were auctioned off by Adolph Mongerson and Stanley Bowgren. Total receipts for the evening amounted to over $74, and the event was hailed as a "great success." The Campton Town Hall was then being painted and redecorated to accommodate future meetings of the Campton 4-H Club. Jeffy Hagaman was Club leader in 1949; he also directed the group's square dance team at that time. The group also conducted garden tours. The Campton 4-H Club was renamed the Wasco 4-H Club in December 1950 but continued to be known by both names for several years. The group continued to meet at the Wasco School. They conducted a rummage sale on 18 November of that year, which brought in $105. The Wasco 4-H Club began organizing a basketball team that winter. They received the blue award from the National Recreation and Rural Arts group then, as well as a plaque from the Illinois Agricultural Association. In Home Economics the club had twelve county honor project members in 1950, and thirteen honor members in agriculture.

Elwood Hultine was still the group's President in April 1951. Jerry Hagaman was an active leader then, and some girls in the organization at that time were Barbara Norton, Carol Bateman, Rose Cray, Phyllis Bowgren, Marjorie Weier, Evelyn Raplus, and Marjorie Carlson. Clara Raplus was elected president of the Campton 4-H in September 1954. Mary Anna Mattson was vice president then. Carolyn Synnott was home economic secretary, and Susan Smith was agriculture secretary. Meetings usually opened with the Pledge of Allegiance followed by the 4-H Pledge. Rummage sales and Christmas parties occurred yearly throughout the 1950s. Some active members in 1955, besides those just mentioned, included John Schudel, Jerry Kline, Joan Murray, Loretta Meyers, Ronald Hartmann, Laurence Dibblee, Beverly Brown, Gordon Jacobson, Dale Hartmann, Carolyn Brown, and Barbara Norton.

Gary Johnson was the group's President in August 1958. Eileen Strom, Linda Collins, Helen Abram, Nancy Wessels, Beverly Brown, Betty Sizemore, Judy DuBois, Sharon Gee, Pat McCornack, and Carolyn Synnott were active members then. Active boys at the time included Paul Johnson, Wolfgang Smalius, Tom Bricher, Ron Hartmann, Harry Weir, and Gerald Van Thurnout. Topics of interest ranged from sheep and livestock to subjects such as "when to pick corn and beans," cooking, sewing, table setting, tractor maintenance, soil types, and "how to wash your hands correctly." The Campton 4-H Club sponsored the Farm-City Week Banquet in Elburn in November 1959 and the following year.

The "new" Wasco 4-H Club was created in May 1972, at the home of Mrs. Jeffrey Hastings. Anyone from the age of nine to nineteen was invited to participate. The group was called the "4-H Wasco Winners Club" in March 1975, when its members took part in a public speaking contest held at the Kane County Fairgrounds. In 1978, Mickie Baert and Darlene and Rick Collins of Wasco were chosen as three of the top twenty 4-H members in Kane County. The Wasco Winners exhibited and took home several prizes at the

1985 Kane County Fair. Exhibit categories that year included food, arts and crafts, child care, photography, horses, beef, sheep, swine, goats, poultry, rabbits, dogs, and mechanical science.

Several members of the Goodrich family won awards for the Wasco Winners at the 1990 Kane County Fair. The Wasco Winners 4-H Club celebrated National Dairy Month in June 1997 by visiting the Community Crisis Center in Elgin and entertaining the children there with milk-themed games. Michelle Braddock of St. Charles was president of the Wasco Winners then. Kathleen Ann Robinson was Club Leader for the Wasco Winners for several years prior to her death in December 2007.

The Wasco Community Club

This organization was most active between the 1920s and 1950s. They were associated with one-act plays, dramas, musical and other community entertainments, card parties, and other local events. The group existed at least as early as February 1923. In April 1927, the group they sponsored a musical performance at the Wasco Church, featuring Mrs. Mabel Martin on violin, plus the St. Charles Troubadours male quartet. In December 1930, the Wasco Community Club presented "Bishop's Candlesticks" in a Kane County one-act play contest. In 1931, Morris Whitney, Harriet Eddy, and Howard Mather comprised the Program Committee of the Wasco Community Club. All three of these individuals (plus Arthur Brown and Margaret Berg) had acted in the play the previous year.

The Community Club hosted a "Dad's Night" at the Wasco Church in March 1933, which featured a debate as well as vocal and instrumental music. In January 1934, Stanley Bowgren was elected as the Community Club's Secretary and Treasurer, Lotten Swanberg was elected Vice President, and Morris Whitney was elected President. In March 1934, Ida Harley gave a reading at a Wasco Community Club meeting. The Club sponsored a debate on the National Recovery Administration in April 1934. Beatrice and Helen Johnson played a piano duet preceding the debate, which was judged by Adolph Mongerson and two others.

In April 1935, the Wasco Community Club, in conjunction with the high school students, put on a play entitled "The Pampered Darling." The group's officers that year were: Dexter Norton (President); Ralph Wilkison (Vice President); and "Miss Helga" (Secretary/Treasurer). In 1937, the Wasco Community Club had the following committees: Entertainment (Robert Corron, Rose Johnson, and Francis Anderson); Refreshments (Mildred Johnson, Mr. and Mrs. George Hawkins, and Mr. and Mrs. Carl Olson). In the spring and summer of 1937, Ellen Mongerson was in charge of the entertainment at the Wasco Community Club's successive themed meetings: "British night," "German night," and "Swedish night." Paul Waterhouse and John Goldenstein were active in the group then; it met the first Friday of every month. In November 1937, the Wasco Community Club held a special event at the Wasco Church, which included violin selections of Mr. Gullotta, a "Punch and Judy" puppet show, and a "chalk talk." Robert Corron was the program's chairman, and was assisted by Frances Anderson and Rose Johnson. Elva Garfield played piano at a group event in 1938. The Community Club's topic of discussion in March 1938 was "Women of the Bible."

Kane County Farm Advisor Arthur Johnson addressed the Wasco Community Club in February 1939. Stanley Bowgren was the group's Chairman in May 1940. The Club held a picnic in Olson Woods on the Fourth of July, 1941. The group met most often at the Wasco Church. In October 1941, the WCC invited an attorney from Batavia to address their meeting. The club sponsored a speaker from the Illinois State Training School for Boys in March 1942. The previous month's speaker was School Superintendent Harry M. Coultrap of Geneva. Frank Hagaman was elected President of the Wasco Community Club in December 1948. Mrs. Jack Horlock was elected Vice President, and Joseph Burn was elected Treasurer.

In June 1951, the Wasco Community Club sponsored an ice cream social at the Wasco Grade School. Kurt Jonatat was the club's President at that time. They held a "cake auction" at the school in February 1952, and a card party there in April 1953. The club sponsored a square dance and masquerade (with lunch and prizes) held in the Wasco School gym on 24 October 1953.

Robert Corron, active member of the Wasco Community Club, in 1933

The Fortnightly Card Club

This group is not to be confused with Elburn's Fortnightly Club, which had an entirely different purpose. The Wasco group simply met bi-weekly to play cards, while the Elburn group was linked to the Chicago Fortnightly Club, which first originated in the 1870s as a place for women to have intellectual lives when they were largely denied access to universities. The Fortnightly Clubs of Chicago paired literary study and social concern, and held frequent debates and lectures. Wasco's Fortnightly Card Club was active in the 1930s and early '40s, and its members included Olive Bergland, Ellen Johnson, Fern Johnson, Josephine Perkins, Augusta Mongerson, and Annie Coombes.

The Shrinking Matrons

This humorously-named coffee club for women was popular in Wasco in the 1960s. It began meeting as early as 1963 and continued to meet through the early 1970s. Mrs. William Divine entertained the Shrinking Matrons at her home in April 1963, and Anne Van Bogaert and Mrs. John Schafer both entertained the following month. The ladies enjoyed "black coffee and much good talk" together at their meetings, which often occurred twice per month. Mrs. Clarence Raasch entertained the group that November. The group's first coffee hour in 1964 took place in January at the home of Mrs. Jay Johnsen. In May 1964, some of its members included Mrs. George Vanderhoof, Mrs. Joe Van Bogaert, Mrs. David Sleeman, Mrs. Fred Hummel Jr., Mrs. Clifton Bowgren, Mrs. Robert Anderson, and Misses Edna and Delia Mungerson. In December 1964, the Shrinking Matrons each brought a dozen Christmas cookies to the group's "coffee meeting" held at the home of Mrs. John Schaefer. The meeting was spent eating the samples and copying one another's recipes. In January 1965 Mrs. George Vanderhoof hosted the group, when several members reported "loss of poundage." Alice Carlson was host in May 1966. Mrs. Vanderhoof hosted one of the group's last formal meetings, in May 1972. By May 1977, the group no longer existed, although "the members of the little coffee club formerly known as the Shrinking Matrons" met at Mrs. Kenneth Carlson's house then. The occasion prompting this meeting was a visit from Elsie Schaefer of California (formerly of Wasco).

The U-Go-I-Go Club

Lily Lake also had a branch of this club, which seems to have been entirely social (and local) in origin. The social dice game Bunco was often played (and refreshments served) at U-Go-I-Go meetings. Membership in the early years seems to have mainly consisted of young women. In the spring of 1929, the club was already meeting. Two early members of Wasco's U-Go-I-Go Club were Doris and Myrtle Johnson, who were active that year. Members in the fall of 1931 included Misses Helga and Rose Strom. A Mothers and Daughters Banquet was held in May of that year at the Wasco Church. In August 1932, the club held a picnic in Wing Park, in Elgin. Members of U-Go-I-Go met at the home of Beatrice Johnson in June 1933, and at the home of Ella Olson in November of that year. Florence Olson hosted the club in August 1934, and Frances Johnson did so in January 1937. The U-Go-I-Go Mothers and Daughters Banquet was held at Thornapple Lodge in St. Charles in May 1935. In May 1936, members of the club

Rose Strom, who, with her sister Helga, were members of the U-Go-I-Go Club

"entertained their mothers at a dinner at the Pioneer House, Elgin." Frances Johnson hosted the U-Go-I-Go Club's meeting in January 1937.

On 15 May 1937, the U-Go-I-Go Club of Wasco held its annual Mothers and Daughters Banquet at Stonewall Lodge in Elburn. Twenty-four attendees were present, including Miss Esther Johnson, Helen and Rose Strom, Doris Johnson, Mrs. Peter Denker, Mrs. Axel Johnson, Mrs. C. O. Peterson, Miss Pauline Peterson, and Mrs. Ella Olson. A four-course-dinner was served, singing took place, and the group played Bunco. The club met less regularly after 1940. In February 1946, Mrs. Ellis Johnson entertained the club at her home. In December 1949 the U-Go-I-Club had their Christmas party at the home of Mrs. Ella Strom in Lily Lake.

The U-Go-I-Go Club seems to have faded out of existence by 1957, since that year an article in the Elburn Herald used the past tense when it stated that years earlier "Wasco had a club called the U-Go-I-Go club." The club (or a reincarnation of the club) was extant as late as March 1972, however, when Vera Larson of St. Charles hosted one of its meetings.

The Pure Milk Association (Wasco Local)

Development of a northern Illinois milk-producers' cooperative began in the mid-1920s. By the fall of 1925, there was an ordinance being considered for passage in Chicago which was to require that all milk sold in the city come from herds certified to be free from tuberculosis. W. C. McQueen was the Kane County representative at an initial meeting of dairy experts favorable to the creation of a cooperative to address such an ordinance, and was one of eight men sent out by the Dairy Department of the Illinois Agricultural Association in order to determine public sentiment at a county level for a Pure Milk Association. McQueen found Kane County farmers to be very favorable to the idea, and became one of the founders of the newly-organized Pure Milk Association in January 1926. The Wasco local of the Pure Milk Association was set up a short time later, perhaps in 1929, when membership in the Association was skyrocketing. The Pure Milk Association handled milk sales, promotion, quality checks, and surplus milk handling, among other services.

The Wasco local elected the following officers in December 1933: Ludwig Covalsky (President); Joseph Bagge (Vice President); Carl Meissner (Secretary); Harold Anderson (Treasurer); and Gust Anderson (Local Director). In 1936, some men associated with the Wasco Pure Milk Association were Albert Richmond, Elmer Ekstrom, and the aforementioned Harold Anderson. William Hoffman of Wasco was elected Director of the Wasco local at the annual meeting of the PMA held in January 1940. The PMA sponsored a "neatest farm" contest in the fall of 1940, which drew sixty-three competitors in Kane County. Nearly all of the participating farmers were members of Pure Milk Association locals.

Program cover of the Pure Milk Association's "Kane County Milk Day," 1939

On 9 December 1941, the Wasco Pure Milk local held its annual supper at the Farm. That year, the Pure Milk Association was Chicagoland's largest dairy cooperative. After the war ended, the PMA fought hard to raise regional milk prices, arguing that "food did help to win the war and it can help to write the peace." The group's 1948 annual meeting was held in the Sherman Hotel, Chicago, and was attended by more than twenty-five hundred dairy farmers, all PMA members. This was the group's twenty-third annual meeting; by then the group represented more than fourteen thousand dairy farmers in Illinois, Wisconsin, Indiana, and Michigan. In December 1949, seventy people attended the Pure Milk Association's local banquet held in the basement of the Wasco Church. Mr. Thomsen of Denmark was the evening's speaker. The Wasco local was still in existence in 1969, when the entire Association became part of the Associated Milk Producers. The PMA remained active throughout the 1950s and '60s. In July 1952, more than eight hundred farmers in Kane County were members of District 9 of the Pure Milk Association. The PMA's total membership stood at more than fourteen thousand at that time. C. W. Bolcum Jr. of Campton Township was the PMA's District 9 director from at least 1952 to 1966.

In 1951, PMA members had marketed more than a billion (!) pounds of milk, valued at nearly $82 million. The group guaranteed a market for milk every day, barring strikes and floods, and the PMA's significant cash reserve guaranteed payment for the product as well. They owned twelve plants outright and worked with other cooperatives handling milk also. The Pure Milk Association also guaranteed payment for damage to farm buildings by fire or windstorm. In 1953, the PMA looked into the possibility of initiating bulk milk pickups.

There were thirteen locals in District 9 in 1962; that year the annual meeting, which drew more than two hundred dairy farmers and their wives, took place in Legion Hall, St. Charles. In 1961, there were fourteen locals, including Wasco. Some three hundred and fifty members and spouses attended the annual meeting that year, at which C. W. Bolcum Jr. was unanimously re-elected to the PMA's Board of Directors. In September 1965, the PMA's annual fall delegate meeting took place at Pheasant Run Lodge near St. Charles. In 1966, Robert Johnsen was re-elected president of the St. Charles local at the group's annual meeting, which was held at The Farm in Wasco. In 1967 and again in 1969, Robert C. Corron was elected as president of the Wasco local. Leonard Hawkins of Wasco was elected delegate in both of those years as well. The PMA was an extremely powerful regional cooperative for decades, and, like all locals, the PMA's Wasco branch offered numerous financial benefits to its membership.

The Wasco American Legion

Although referenced in many other places throughout this work, Wasco American Legion Post No. 1195 deserves another mention here. The post was first organized in 1946, by Frank Hagaman, and began with seventeen veterans. Five veterans were from the First World War, and the other twelve were from the Second. Some charter members included George Vanderhoof, Rudolph Mongerson, Hugo Denker, and Frank Richmond. Joe White was the unit's first Commander, beginning in 1949. In August 1949, the following officers were elected: Joseph White (Commander); Frank Richmond (Senior Vice-Commander); Wesley Johnson (Junior Vice-Commander); Frank Hagaman (Adjutant); Douglas Kaiser (Finance Officer); Bob Scott (Chaplain); and Willis Johnson (Sergeant-at-Arms). The Executive Committee that year also included members George Vanderhoof, Raymond Fischer, Vic Thomas, Lee Mather, and Lloyd Reichter.

The Wasco Legion Auxiliary, sometimes known as the Ladies Auxiliary, was organized in 1954. The Auxiliary held an annual rummage and bake sale (with a refreshment booth) throughout the late 1950s and early '60s. Proceeds from the sales were used to advance "the work on the Post Home" which was described in 1961 as "a do-it-yourself project the Legion and the Auxiliary have been busy about for some time." The Auxiliary's first President was Elaine Johnson, who was succeeded by Liz Bowgren in 1955, and Phyllis White in 1956. The next three Presidents were Barbara Sanderson, Elaine Raasch, and Mildred Mather.

Officers of the Wasco American Legion Post in 1961 were: Dean Clopton (Commander); Mark K. Anderson (Senior Vice Commander); Clarence Raasch (Junior Vice Commander); Harold Ekstrom (Adjutant); Gordon Bowgren (Chaplain); James Hatzis (Sergeant-at-Arms). Flea markets were held at the Legion Post in later years.

The groundbreaking for the American Legion Post's new home, on 18 February 1960. Ed Schneider and Claire Miller are standing on the machine, with Frank Richmond, Robert Jay, George Vanderhoof, Gordon Bowgren, Frank Hagaman, Harold Ekstrom, Clarence Raasch, and Wes Johnson pictured left to right.

Beginning in 1958, the Wasco American Legion Post sponsored a boys' baseball team, and in that era they sponsored several educational programs on Flag Day, and purchased markers for veterans' graves. The Post was known for throwing Halloween and Christmas parties, and for hosting potluck dinners for the Wasco community. In 1961, the Post planted a tree on the Wasco School grounds as a memorial to Joseph White, the Post's first commander. The Post held spring and fall auctions at that time, as well as occasional bake sales and rummage sales with the help of the Auxiliary, in order to raise money for their causes.

In April 1960, members of the Wasco American Legion Post sold non-interest-bearing bonds to help finance the relocation of the Great Western Depot building onto property they had just purchased on the Charles Ekstrom farm, adjoining the railroad to the north. They first broke ground at the new site on 18 February 1960. The first ground broken was by Clarence Raasch, Commander, Wes Johnson, past Commander, and Gordon Bowgren, Chaplain. The Post building was described as being built on the "LaFox blacktop," now Old LaFox Road, "along the Chicago Great Western railway." Ed Schneider of Elgin did the excavation, and (with the help of the Muehlfelts of Wheaton) moved the building to the new site. Frank Richmond served as architect and contractor. In December 1961, the Post sponsored a turkey sale and card party "in their new home." The building was dedicated as a memorial to all veterans of Campton Township.

Two views of the Wasco American Legion Post from September 1960

Work being done to place the former Wasco Depot on its new site, September 1960

The former Wasco Depot was known as the American Legion Home throughout the 1960s and early '70s. The Wasco Legion Auxiliary was active throughout the Post's existence, and hosted frequent fundraisers to benefit the veterans and the community at large. In 1972, the Post had two surviving veterans of World War I – Frank Richmond and George Vanderhoof. That year, Lucinda Corron presented the Legion a "picture of the original building, the old Wasco depot." Officers of the Auxiliary in 1972 were: Liz Bowgren (President); Sandy DeBruycker (First Vice President); Donna Jorgensen (Second Vice President); Millie Sleeman (Secretary); Joan Bowgren (Historian); Donna Morter (Sergeant-at-Arms); Roberta Van De Veire (Chaplain); and Violet Begerman (Treasurer).

The American Legion Home in Wasco was renamed the Wesley A. Johnson Memorial Legion Hall in December 1975, in honor of its late commander. William Huber was Post commander at that time. When Frank Richmond of Wasco turned ninety in April 1978, his birthday was celebrated by an open house held at the Legion Hall. In 1979, the Legion Post hosted a steak dinner in honor of the Auxiliary's twenty-fifth year. Charter Auxiliary members who were still active then included Lois Ekstrom, JoAnn Jay, Elaine Johnson, Elaine Raasch, Barbara Sanderson, Elsie Schaefer, and Margaret Vanderhoof. Fifty-five people attended the event, and those preparing the meal were Mr. and Mrs. Bob Morter, Barbara Sanderson, Bill Huber, and Bob Scott.

Frank Richmond and George Vanderhoof on the Fiftieth anniversary of the American Legion, in 1969

In March 1999, Campton Township agreed to purchase the Wasco American Legion Post building for $170,000. According to Township Supervisor Ed Malek, the purchase removed a financial burden from the Post itself, and provided it "with the resources to assist their members." The Post's members were allowed to continue meeting in the building, and did so until the Post was dissolved three years later.

The final newsletter of the Wesley Johnson Memorial Legion Post No. 1195 was mailed to its members on 25 April 2002. It was written by John G. Person of the Farewell Committee, and concerned the dispersal of Post funds and the retirement of the colors. American Legion posts in Geneva, Elburn, and St. Charles were each given $15,000 at the dissolution of the Wasco Post, and the balance of the assets were "invested with the St. Charles American Legion Post #342 scholarship fund," which marked the creation of a perpetual scholarship with the investment of approximately $83,000. Post 1195's final dinner was held at Sorrento's Ranch on the south side of Route 64, west of Route 47, on Thursday, 23 May 2002.

The Wesley A. Johnson Memorial Legion Hall, as it appeared in 1983

The last officers of the Wasco Ladies Auxiliary (elected in 2002) were: Joan Bowgren (President); Trudy Huber (1st Vice President); Angie Huber (2nd Vice President); Rita Geske (Secretary); Elisa Bowgren (Treasurer); Lois Ekstrom (Chaplain); Barb Sanderson (Historian); and Ruth Kacirek (Sergeant-at-Arms).

Bibliography

"15 Year Awards." *Elgin Watch Word*. February 1955: 17.

"300 Honor Olsons on 25th Anniversary." *Elburn Herald*. 17 September 1964: 2.

"4-H Club Organized in Wasco." *Elburn Herald*. 31 January 1947: 1.

"4-H'ers win at Fair." *Elburn Herald*. 22 July 1982: 10.

"'A' Award for Home Bureau Play." *Elburn Herald*. 9 January 1941: 1.

"A Double Deal." *Chicago Tribune*. 1 October 1994: WC25.

"A New Departure." *Valley Chronicle*. St. Charles, IL. 5 August 1887: 1.

"About Folks You Know." *Elgin Advocate*. 20 April 1889: 5.

"About People You Know From Wasco and Vicinity." *Elburn Herald*. 1 April 1937: 1.

"About People You Know In and About Wasco." *Elburn Herald*. 9 June 1938: 5.

"About People You Know Over in Wasco Community." *Elburn Herald*. 21 October 1937: 1.

"Action in the Twilight League." *Elburn Herald*. 23 June 1966: 4.

Affidavit of Earl V. Millen. Kane County Deed Book 1187:596.

Affidavit of Lillian L. Jay. Kane County Deed Book 2111:156.

"After 21 years, Collins store changes hands." *Elburn Herald*. 18 October 2001: 16.

American Legion Post No. 1195 archives. Joan Bowgren collection, Wasco, IL.

"AMPO forms new district, elect officers, delegates." *Elburn Herald*. 26 February 1970: 1.

Anders, Jeremy. "Wasco Diamonds win 1st national title." *Kane County Chronicle*. 23 July 2008.

Anderson, Neal. Photo collection (1890-1990). Wasco, IL.

Anderson, Paul F. Photo collection (1965-1975). St. Charles, IL.

"Arctic Blast hits at Wasco Lawn & Power." *Elburn Herald*. 15 December 1994: 23.

"Area 4-H Clubs take trophies & ribbons home from Kane Co. Fair." *Elburn Herald*. 15 August 1985: 14.

"Area 4-H'ers win at Ill. State Fair." *Elburn Herald*. 19 August 1982: 12.

Atlas of Kane County, Illinois. Chicago: D. W. Ensign & Co., 1892.

Atlas-Plat Book of Kane County, Illinois. Rockford, IL: The Thrift Press, 1927.

"Art. Johnson, Auctioneer." Advertisement. *Elburn Herald*. 30 January 1936: 8.

"Auction." *Elburn Herald*. 2 January 1914: 5; 21 February 1957: 8.

"Auction!" *Elburn Herald*. 13 February 1919: 4; 21 June 1973: 4.

"Auction – Leonard Hawkins – Wasco, Ill." *Elburn Herald*. 1 February 1973: 5.

Aurora, Kane County, Illinois, City Directory, 1954. Aurora, IL: Finch & McCullough, 1954.

Baker, Wayne. "Open-air sewage treatment plan raises stink." *Chicago Tribune*. 27 April 1994: A5.

"Bank branch groundbreaking." *Elburn Herald*. 20 September 1990: 3.

Barnes, Sarah. "KC Bank branch opens in Wasco." *Elburn Herald*. 19 September 1991: 1.

_____. "Silverado Adds Texas Flair." *Elburn Herald*. 21 November 1991: 14.

Bartelt, Edith. "Wasco and LaFox." *Elburn Herald*. 6 December 1962: 6.

Bartlett, Linda. Photo collection (1930-1960). Cody, WY.

"Base Ball Tournament." *Elburn Herald*. 2 July 1931: 1.

"Baseball Finale." *Elburn Herald*. 2 August 1973: 3.

Bateman, Newton, and Paul Selby. *Historical Encyclopedia of Illinois and History of Kane County*. Chicago: Munsell Publishing Company, 1904.

"Bean Appetit serves up coffee lovers." *Elburn Herald*. 14 June 2001: 20.

"Bean There . . . Run That 5K." *Elburn Herald*. 20 October 2005: 25.

Bell-Graham Elementary School. "About Us." bellgrahamd303.org. May 2018.

Bethlehem Lutheran Church Confirmation Photo, 1908. Bethlehem Church Archives. St. Charles, IL.

Bergland, Floyd H. "Daily Reminder, 1908." unpublished MS. Wasco, IL.

Bergland, George. Photo and slide collection (1870-1960). St. Charles, IL.

Bergland, George. Personal Memoir. Unpublished MS. St. Charles, IL.

"Bergland & Company" advertisement. *Elburn Herald*. 22 October 1936: 15; 23 December 1937: 4.

"Best New Year Wishes, Denny's Tavern." Advertisement. *Elburn Herald*. 27 December 1951: 4.

"Big Red Cross Drive in Elburn Starts Monday." *Elburn Herald*. 16 May 1916: 1.

The Biographical Record of Kane County, Illinois. Chicago: The S. J. Clarke Publishing Company, 1898.

Bilyk, Jonathan. "Sage Creek latest to open doors at Randall, 64." *Kane County Chronicle*. 14 December 2007.

_____. "Trucking business changes." *Kane County Chronicle*. 21 June 2007.

_____. "Work to begin on gas station in Campton Hills." *Kane County Chronicle*. 11 May 2012: 9.

Bourbon, Steve. "Elite Sports Training center to make opening." *Kane County Chronicle*. 28 July 2012: 24.

Bowgren, Charles. "Public Notice, State of Illinois, County of Kane." *Elburn Herald*. 24 May 1956: 13.

Bowgren, Jewel. "Wasco & LaFox." *Elburn Herald*. 17 May 1973: 9; 30 January 1975: 11; 6 September 1979: 5.

Bowgren, Mrs. Clifton [Jewel]. "Wasco & LaFox." *Elburn Herald*. 30 January 1969: 3; 13 March 1969: 3; 29 January 1970: 3; 2 March 1972: 2; 17 May 1973: 9.

Bowgren, Mrs. Verner. "Wasco & LaFox." *Elburn Herald*. 13 March 1952: 4.

Bowgren, Terry and Joan. Photo and document collection. (1895-1980). Wasco, IL.

"Boys 1913 Corn Club Wins Special Honors." *Elburn Herald*. 6 May 1915: 1.

Brack-Johnson, Ann. "Old Church to transplant roots to new home." *Daily Herald*. 22 February 1998.

Brauer, Chris. Photo Collection (1860-1970). Wasco, IL.

"Bulk Milk Pickups Seen By Kane County Farmers." *Elburn Herald*. 7 May 1953: 8.

Burd, Valerie. "Family True to the Finish." *Chicago Tribune*. 15 September 1991: B10.

"Business Women to meet at Wasco Inn on Sept. 23." *Elburn Herald*. 17 September 1981: 2.

California Voter Registrations, 1900-1968. Los Angeles County. Database. Ancestry.com. August 2018.

"Campton." *Geneva Republican*. 11 July 1891: 2.

"Campton." *The Valley Chronicle* [St. Charles, IL]. 20 August 1886: 4; 3 September 1886: 1; 17 September 1886: 8; 8 October 1886: 4; 22 October 1886: 8; 12 November 1886: 8; 19 November 1886: 4; 17 December 1886: 1; 24 December 1886; 31 December 1886: 4; 14 January 1887: 1; 4 March 1887: 4; 11 March 1887: 8; 25 March 1887: 1; 1 April 1887: 4; 15 April 1887: 1; 13 May 1887: 1; 27 May 1887: 8; 3 June 1887: 4; 17 June 1887: 4; 1 July 1887: 4; 15 July 1887: 4; 29 July 1887: 1; 12 August 1887: 1; 19 August 1887: 8; 26 August 1887: 8; 9 September 1887: 1; 30 September 1887: 5; 11 November 1887: 4; 16 December 1887: 4; 6 January 1888: 4; 17 February 1888: 4; 23 March 1888, p. 8; 30 March 1888, p. 4; 27 April 1888, p. 4; 11 May 1888, p. 1; 8 June 1888, p. 7; 15 June 1888, p. 1; 13 July 1888, p. 8.

"Campton 4-H." *Elburn Herald*. 30 September 1954: 10; 28 April 1955: 5.

"Campton 4-H Club Meets." *Elburn Herald*. 12 June 1958: 4; 28 August 1958: 2.

"Campton 4-H News." *Elburn Herald*. 2 December 1954: 3; 3 January 1957: 1.

"Campton 4-H Notes." *Elburn Herald*. 31 March 1955: 3.

"Campton Dance Team at WLS Barn Dance in Chicago." *Elburn Herald*. 25 November 1949: 1.

"Campton Makes Big Sale of War Stamps." *Elburn Herald*. 23 May 1918: 4.

Campton Township Assessor's Office. File collection, assessment records. Wasco, IL.

"Campton Township Initiatives Move Forward." *Elburn Herald*. 3 August 2000: 8.

"Campton Township's Sesquicentennial Parade." *Elburn Herald*. 10 October 1985: 5.

"Campton Treasurer's Annual Statement." *Elburn Herald*. 22 April 1915: 4.

"Candidate Profiles – Campton Township." *Elburn Herald*. 23 March 1989: 14.

"Capes to manage Kane County Bank's Wasco branch." *Elburn Herald*. 8 September 1994: 17.

Census records of Kane County (1850-1940). Database. Ancestry.com. September 2018.

Centennial of Wasco Baptist Church, 1891-1991. Wasco, IL: n. p., 1991.

Chicago and North Western Railroad Employment Records, 1935-1970. Database. Ancestry.com. April 2018.

"Chicago Company Low Bidder on Hospital Addition." *Elburn Herald*. 24 March 1955: 5.

Chicago Great Western Railway Company Plat [1893]. Kane County Deed Book 316: 381.

Chicago Metropolitan Agency for Planning. "Village of Campton Hills Comprehensive Plan." cmap.illinois.gov, 2012. July 2018.

Chroust, Kevin. "Cooperstown Bound." *Kane County Chronicle*. 12 July 2008.

"Col. George C. Scott, Champion Auctioneer." *Elburn Herald*. 31 January 1913: 4.

"Community Club." *Elburn Herald*. 3 December 1949: 6; 3 May 1951: 4.

"Community Hospital Opens Drive in Wasco." *Elburn Herald*. 15 July 1954: 5.

"Community to Honor Departing Soldiers." *Elburn Herald*. 23 August 1917: 1.

Considine, Mike. "Wasco baseball field gets new name." *Daily Herald*. 25 June 2001.

Corron, Dorothy. "History of Wasco School & Barbeque." Unpublished MS. 1968.

"Corron to seek Recorder nomination." *Elburn Herald*. 15 October 1987: 15.

Corron, Tom. Photo collection (1860-1970). Fort Wayne, IN.

"County Board OKs 737-acre Development Near Wasco." *Chicago Tribune*. 10 September 1992: C3.

"County and Vicinity News." *Valley Chronicle*. St. Charles, IL. 5 November 1886: 1; 18 March 1887: 8.

Craft, Mrs. D. "Lily Lake." *Elburn Herald*. 14 June 1946: 5; 1 March 1956: 5.

Craft, Mrs. Maurice. "Lily Lake." *Elburn Herald*. 30 January 1948: 7; 14 March 1957: 9; 26 February 1976: 4; 1 November 1976: 4.

Crawford, William B. and Wes Smith. "Restauranteur sentenced for laundering funds." *Chicago Tribune*. 19 December 1986: A2.

Cunningham, Heather. "An anchor for Township Campton to renovate old depot for use as a community center." *Daily Herald*. 5 October 2000.

_____. "Garden shop owners realize dream." *Daily Herald*. 2 April 2004.

"D. E. Keisers Purchase Wasco Store." *Elburn Herald*. 28 January 1949: 1.

"Dairyman Pleads 'Fair Play'; Has Faith In Milk Purity." *Chicago Tribune*. 13 February 1909: 8.

"Dairyman's Yes To Pure Milk." *Chicago Tribune*. 6 February 1909: 8.

Danahey, Mike. "Preservationists seeking to restore, move a one-room 1852 schoolhouse in Campton Township." *Chicago Tribune*. 15 March 2018: online.

Daniels, Mary. "Queen of the Fleas." *Chicago Tribune*. 22 January 1989: CC14.

"Dates Fixed for One Act Playlet Contest." *Elburn Herald*. 11 December 1930: 1.

Dauskurdas, Sherri. "Rooted in community." *Kane County Chronicle*. 7 April 2015.

"Death Erases Last Name On Elgin G.A.R. Roll." *Chicago Tribune*. 9 July 1943: 12.

"Deckert Reunion." *Elburn Herald*. 22 September 1960: 3.

Deed from A. J. Erickson to George Bergland. Kane County Deed Book 503:180.

Deed from A. J. Erickson et al. to Grace Erickson. Kane County Deed Book 635:447.

Deed from A. Nolting et al. to I. Shoudy et al. Kane County Deed Book 414:340.

Deed from Albert V. Larson et al. to John Larson. Kane County Deed Book 744:276.

Deed from Alex Johnson et al. to Lucy E. Ekstrom. Kane County Deed Book 1062:497.

Deed from Alonzo Chaffee et al. to Lottie H. Brown. Kane County Deed Book 710: 148.

Deed from Anders G. Lofgren to Arthur R. Johnson. Kane County Deed Book 846:268.

Deed from Andrew J. Erickson et al. to Philo G. Plummer et al. Kane County Deed Book 1421: 409.

Deed from Andrew J. Erickson to Julius Wynthein et al. Kane County Deed Book 1771:59.

Deed from Andrew J. Erickson et al. to Andrew J. Mongerson. Kane County Deed Book 710:212.

Deed from Andrew Johnson et al. to John W. Larson. Kane County Deed Book 383:570.

Deed from Arthur C. Anderson et al. to John W. De Gignac. Kane County Deed Book 1555:240.

Deed from Arthur E. Brown to William Gary Kinnett et al. Kane County Recorder Doc. #1367954.

Deed from Arthur L. Paulson to Merrill Whitney. Kane County Recorder 1047: 397.

Deed from Arthur R. Johnson et al. to Carl H. Olson. Kane County Deed Book 1057: 584.

Deed from Arthur R. Johnson et al. to Charles J. Dau. Kane County Deed Book 1067:174.

Deed from Arthur R. Johnson et al. to Frank S. Skeen et al. Kane County Deed Book 1198:336.

Deed from Arthur R. Johnson et al. to People of the State of Illinois. Kane County Deed Book 909: 123.

Deed from Arthur R. Johnson et al. to Wesley A. Johnson et al. Kane County Deed Book 1840:7.

Deed from Benjamin R. Kayner to Christ Burgeson. Kane County Deed Book 379: 91.

Deed from Benjamin R. Kayner to John A. Carlson. Kane County Deed Book 450: 471.

Deed from Bessie M. Stevens et al. to Alfred A. Peterson et al. Kane County Deed Book 1208: 33.

Deed from Blanche Allen to Andrew J. Erickson. Kane County Deed Book 1159:65.

Deed from Bradley V. Foss to Gunner Anderson. Kane County Deed Book 93: 145.

Deed from C. A. Darnell to George Bergland. Kane County Deed Book 530: 37.

Deed from C. Russell Nystrom et al. to Donald I. Gray et al. Kane County Deed Book 2361:544.

Deed from Carl E. Peterson et al. to Charles P. Ekstrom. Kane County Deed Book 623: 615.

Deed from Caroline E. Swanson to Dan W. Rediger et al. Kane County Deed Book 1797:137.

Deed from Charles E. Hurd to George H. Martin. Kane County Deed Book 427:347.

Deed from Charles F. Field et al. to John T. Peterson et al. Kane County Deed Book 409:171.

Deed from Charles K. Bowgren et al. to Stanley O. Bowgren et al. Kane County Deed Book 1800: 297.

Deed from Charles Simons et al. to Benjamin R. Kayner. Kane County Deed Book 374: 450.

Deed from Charlie Jameson Waterhouse to Paul P. Waterhouse. Kane County Deed Book 627: 159.

Deed from Charley Johnson to P. A. Peterson. Kane County Deed Book 503: 48.

Deed from Charley Johnson to Anders G. Lofgren. Kane County Deed Book 627:230.

Deed from Charley Johnson to George Bergland. Kane County Deed 274: 384.

Deed from Chester W. Bolcum et al. to A. J. Erickson. Kane County Deed Book 540:456.

Deed from Chester W. Bolcum to Nils Hawkins. Kane County Deed Book 507: 358.

Deed from Christ Burgeson et al. to B. R. Kayner. Kane County Deed Book 427: 107.

Deed from Christ Burgeson et al. to Charles Mungerson. Kane County Deed Book 274: 532.

Deed from Clarence W. Raasch et al. to Peter J. Bohr et al. Kane County Deed Book 1421:177.

Deed from Clarence W. Raasch et al. to Victor E. Thomas et al. Kane County Deed Book 1435:293.

Deed from Claus Swanson et al. to Norvid R. Swanson et al. Kane County Deed Book 923:209.

Deed from Cornelia Burr to Charlie J. Waterhouse. Kane County Deed Book 550: 214.

Deed from the County of Kane to the Trustees of the Wasco Cemetery Association. Kane County Deed Book 359: 614.

Deed from Dan W. Rediger et al. to Earl Maier Jr. et al. Kane County Deed Book 1881: 411.

Deed from Dan W. Rediger et al. to Melvin L. Peterson et al. Kane County Deed Book 2566:534.

Deed from Dana E. Rice et al. to William L. Slate. Kane County Deed Book 120:429.

Deed from David F. Allen et al. to C. Russell Nystrom et al. Kane County Deed Book 2093:124.

Deed from David Pattee to Joseph Rice. Kane County Deed Book 46: 298.

Deed from David Pattee to William Higgins. Kane County Deed Book 114: 137.

Deed from Donald I. Gray et al. to James F. Clapper et al. Kane County Deed Book 2652: 71.

Deed from Earl Maier Jr. et al. to Larry K. Danks et al. Kane County Deed Book 2525: 267.

Deed from Earl V. Millen to Lynn L. Jay et al. Kane County Deed Book 1036:302.

Deed from Edna R. Cray to the National Bank & Trust Company of Sycamore. Kane County Deed Book Doc. No. 1593008.

Deed from Edward Swanson et al. to Ethel L. Austin. Kane County Deed Book 985:598.

Deed from Edward Swanson et al. to George Hawkins. Kane County Deed Book 997:125.

Deed from Ellen J. Mongerson et al. to Henry Verhaeghe et al. Kane County Deed Book 2458:103.

Deed from Elida Hagerman [Hagaman] to George Bergland. Kane County Deed Book 176: 402.

Deed from Emma A. Swarthout to Nettie Anderson. Kane County Deed Book 541: 216.

Deed from Emma Carpenter et al. to Nettie VanWambeke et al. Kane County Deed Book 611: 116.

Deed from Ethel C. Waterhouse et al. to Vernon L. Critchfield. Kane County Deed Book 2362: 34.

Deed from Everett S. Larson Jr. et al. to Elizabeth A. Burnell. Kane County Deed Book 2246:242.

Deed from the First National Bank of Chicago et al. to Arthur W. Bergquist. Kane County Deed Book 1570:221.

Deed from Florence M. Peterson et al. to Floyd H. Bergland. Kane County Deed Book 1052: 298.

Deed from Floyd H. Bergland et al. to Albert V. Larson. Kane County Deed Book 652:534.

Deed from Floyd H. Bergland et al. to Lawrence McGowan et al. Kane County Deed Book 602:252.

Deed from Floyd H. Bergland et al. to Maud C. Richmond. Kane County Deed Book 862: 439.

Deed from Frank J. Brown et al. to Herbert J. Brown. Kane County Deed Book 879: 165.

Deed from Frank S. Skeen et al. to Axel N. Anderson et al. Kane County Deed Book 1433:499.

Deed from Fred E. Hummel to Richard B. Porter. Kane County Deed Book. Record No. 1361791.

Deed from Fred Swanson to Caroline E. Swanson. Kane County Deed Book 928:40.

Deed from George Bergland et al. to Arnold Mather. Kane County Deed Book 530: 515.

Deed from George Bergland et al. to Andrew Erickson. Kane County Deed Book 536:79.

Deed from George Bergland et al. to Augusta Meissner. Kane County Deed Book 499: 451.

Deed from George Bergland et al. to Bertha Hiser. Kane County Deed Book 440: 263.

Deed from George Bergland et al. to Sidney Wanzer et al. Kane County Deed Book 414:409.

Deed from George Eddy to Lynn L. Jay. Kane County Deed Book 771: 105.

Deed from George E. Hawkins et al. to Arthur W. Bergquist et al. Kane County Deed Book 1769:122.

Deed from George E. Hawkins et al. to Solomon Johnson et al. Kane County Deed Book 1198:218.

Deed from George S. Brown et al. to Lester A. Gholson et al. Kane County Deed Book 2828: 118.

Deed from Grace B. Mather to Gertrude E. Stover. Kane County Deed Book 1879:423.

Deed from Grace Erickson et al. to Blanche Allen. Kane County Deed Book 1158: 430.

Deed from H. Theo. Fischer to the Wasco Cemetery Association. Kane County Deed Book 2708: 131.

Deed from Harold P. Ekstrom et al. to Richard G. Swanson. Kane County Deed Book 2075: 51.

Deed from Harriet Austin to Arnold G. Mather. Kane County Deed Book 687: 586 and 719: 97.

Deed from Harriet Austin to Charles Simon. Kane County Deed Book 308: 313.

Deed from Harriet J. Heath to Lynn L. Jay et al. Kane County Deed Book 1218: 231.

Deed from Harriet L. Austin et al. to Benjamin R. Kayner. Kane County Deed Book 371: 613.

Deed from Harriet L. Austin et al. to Charles E. Hurd. Kane County Deed Book 332: 151

Deed from Harriet L. Austin et al. to Oscar Johnson. Kane County Deed Book 356: 302.

Deed from Harry Travis et al. to Clarence W. Raasch et al. Kane County Deed Book 1233: 404.

Deed from Hattie A. Meach et al. to Ethel L. Austin. Kane County Deed Book 1062:475.

Deed from Henry I. Lincoln et al. to John Ross. Kane County Deed Book 157: 475.

Deed from Horace Bancroft to Timothy Wheeler. Kane County Deed Book 14: 450.

Deed from Horace Higgins to J. V. Millen. Kane County Deed Book 248: 551.

Deed from Horace S. Higgins et al. to Chester W. Bolcum. Kane County Deed Book 507: 359.

Deed from Horace S. Higgins to Louise Bergland. Kane County Deed Book 345:47.

Deed from Hummel & Co. to Dan W. Rediger et al. Kane County Deed Book 1586: 63.

Deed from Irene H. Ramer to Ralph R. Smith et al. Kane County Deed Book 2423: 469.

Deed from Isaac Finley et al. to August Johnson. Kane County Deed Book 347: 88.

Deed from James C. Rise et al. to Trustees of the Baptist Church at Wasco. Kane County Deed Book 311:36.

Deed from James C. Rice to Joseph Rice et al. Kane County Deed Book 93: 583.

Deed from James C. Rice et al. to C. W. Millen. Kane County Deed Book 264: 590.

Deed from James C. Rice et al. to Charley Johnson. Kane County Deed Book 365: 634.

Deed from James C. Rice et al. to Chester W. Bolcum. Kane County Deed Book 450:9.

Deed from James C. Rice et al. to George Berland. Kane County Deed Book 264: 606.

Deed from James C. Rice et al. to George Bergland. Kane County Deed Book 332: 300.

Deed from James C. Rice et al. to Gust Swanson. Kane County Deed Book 264: 607.

Deed from James C. Rice et al. to Solomon Johnson et al. Kane County Deed Book 494: 35.

Deed from James C. Rice et al. to Trustees of Schools of T40N R7E 3d P.M. Kane County Deed Book 449:590.

Deed from James Chrystal et al. to Frank J. Brown. Kane County Deed Book 443: 164.

Deed from Jennie Denker to Leo Untz. Kane County Deed Book 2167: 179.

Deed from Joanne Heisten to Roy L. Peterson et al. Kane County Deed Book 2299:144.

Deed from Joel Hawkins to Leonard Hawkins. Kane County Deed Book 2324:520.

Deed from John A. Carlson et al. to George C. Bergland. Kane County Deed Book 468: 300.

Deed from John A. Larson et al. to Pearl V. Dorr. Kane County Deed Book 2033:480.

Deed from John Elliott to August W. Fischer. Kane County Deed Book 106:409.

Deed from John Gustav Fischer et al. to H. Theo. Fischer. Kane County Deed Book 780:428.

Deed from John Hagaman to George and Louisa Bergland. Kane County Deed Book 429: 133.

Deed from John Larson to Arnold G. Mather et al. Kane County Deed Book 916:224.

Deed from John R. Tucker et al. to Joseph Rice. Kane County Deed Book 46: 297.

Deed from John Ross et al. to the Minnesota & North Western Railroad Company. Kane County Deed Book 243: 120.

Deed from John S. Swanson et al. to Alfred Swanson. Kane County Deed Book 499: 589.

Deed from John V. Millen to George C. Bergland. Kane County Deed Book 315: 197.

Deed from John W. Larson et al. to Thomas B. Stewart. Kane County Deed Book 380:342.

Deed from John W. Larson to Charles F. Field et al. Kane County Deed Book 410:299.

Deed from John Whitney to the Trustees of the Wasco Cemetery Association. Kane County Deed Book 378: 456 and 602: 562.

Deed from Joseph Rice et al. to James C. Rice. Kane County Deed Book 104: 77.

Deed from Julia Minnetta Barber to Dean W. Clopton et al. Kane County Deed Book 1728: 552.

Deed from Lawrence E. Bishop et al. to Edwin A. Dannewitz. Kane County Recorder Doc. 1332811.

Deed from Lee F. Mather et al. to Gertrude E. Stover. Kane County Deed Book 2252:277.

Deed from Leonard O. Hawkins et al. to Peter R. Sparacio et al. Kane County Deed Book 2610: 19.

Deed from Leonard O. Hawkins et al. to Jeffrey W. Hastings et al. Kane County Deed Book 2682: 450.

Deed from Leonard White et al. to Louise Bergland. Kane County Deed Book 345:48.

Deed from Lester A. Gholson to Dennis J. Dewitte et al. Kane County Recorder Doc. No. 1651428.

Deed from Letitia Bolwahnn et al. to Robert B. Jay et al. Kane County Deed Book 1517:181.

Deed from Lillian L. Jay to Dale M. Leathers et al. Kane County Deed Book 2111:171.

Deed from Lillian L. Jay to Robert Leathers et al. Kane County Deed Book 1840: 317.

Deed from Lillian M. Martin et al. to Hattie A. Marten. Kane County Deed Book 506:489.

Deed from Lorraine Fifield to Kathleen Nord. Kane County Deed Book 1741:481.

Deed from Louise Bergland to the People of the State of Illinois. Kane County Deed Book 909:109.

Deed from Lucy E. Ekstrom to Elmer Ekstrom et al. Kane County Deed Book 1660: 108.

Deed from Lucy Higgins et al. to William Higgins. Kane County Deed Book 105: 270.

Deed from Lucy Higgins to Horace Higgins. Kane County Deed Book 158: 268.

Deed from Lynn L. Jay et al. to Anton Glomp. Kane County Deed Book 1089: 46.

Deed from Lynn L. Jay et al. to Robert M. B. Jay et al. Kane County Deed Book 1159: 362.

Deed from Mary M. Morgan et al. to Philo G. Plummer et al. Kane County Deed Book 1387:22.

Deed from Maude L. Swanson et al. to Gordon Swanson et al. Kane County Deed Book 1218:359.

Deed from Mercedes G. Boylan to George L. Vanderhoof et al. Kane County Deed Book 1574:160.

Deed from Morris Whitney et al. to George S. Brown et al. Kane County Deed Book 1556: 543.

Deed from Myrtle Florence Feltgren et al. to John S. Bowman et al. Kane County Deed Book 2410:81.

Deed from N. L. Carpenter et al. to Fred Swanson. Kane County Deed Book 332:105.

Deed from Nettie VanWambeke et al. to Oscar E. Bowgren et al. Kane County Deed Book 681: 377.

Deed from Norman Carpenter et al. to Minnesota & North Western Railroad Company. Kane County Deed Book 243: 196.

Deed from Norman Carpenter to Harriet Austin. Kane County Deed Book 270: 331.

Deed from Norvid R. Swanson et al. to William Massolle Jr. Kane County Deed Book 1184:402.

Deed from O. M. Johnson to John Whitney. Kane County Deed Book 363:634.

Deed from Olive L. Bergland et al. to Hummel & Company. Kane County Deed Book 1337: 544.

Deed from Olive L. Bergland to Lee Boylan et al. Kane County Deed Book 1402:447.

Deed from Oscar M. Johnson to Andrew Johnson. Kane County Deed Book 375:229.

Deed from Oscar M. Johnson to Mal Whitney. Kane County Deed Book 274:382.

Deed from Oscar M. Johnson to Malvin Whitney. Kane County Deed Book 274:388.

Deed from Paul J. Ross et al. to John N. Basic. Kane County Deed Book 2040: 535.

Deed from Paul P. Waterhouse to Austin J. Burke et al. Kane County Deed Book 2875:444.

Deed from Pearl V. Schuetz to Jack E. Williams et al. Kane County Deed Book 2330:239.

Deed from Peter J. Bohr to John A. Larson et al. Kane County Deed Book 1749:473.

Deed from Phyllis White Dillon to Werner F. Ladewig et al. Kane County Deed Book 2127:629.

Deed from Ralph R. Smith et al. to Earl R. Smith. Kane County Recorder Doc. No. 1419303.

Deed from Raymond P. Fischer et al. to Downers Grove National Bank. Kane County Deed Book 2238:123.

Deed from Robert B. Jay et al. to Peter J. Bohr et al. Kane County Deed Book 1640:431.

Deed from Roy L. Peterson et al. to Walter C. Foulkes et al. Kane County Deed Book 2704:381.

Deed from Sarah McGowan to Harriett J. Heath. Kane County Deed Book 928:221.

Deed from Sidney Wanzer & Sons, Inc. to Arthur C. Anderson et al. Kane County Deed Book 894:420.

Deed from Sidney Wanzer & Sons, Inc. to the People of the State of Illinois. Kane County Deed Book 909:310.

Deed from Solomon Johnson et al. to Andrew J. Mongerson. Kane County Deed Book 866: 567.

Deed from Solomon Johnson et al. to DeVolois Stevens. Kane County Deed Book 636: 85.

Deed from Solomon Johnson et al. to Emma Carpenter. Kane County Deed Book 574: 387.

Deed from Solomon Johnson et al. to Fred and Peter Denker. Kane County Deed Book 869: 79.

Deed from Solomon Johnson et al. to Isaac Mongerson. Kane County Deed Book 585: 499.

Deed from Solomon Johnson et al. to James C. Rice. Kane County Deed Book 494: 32.

Deed from Solomon Johnson et al. to Joel and Emma Hawkins. Kane County Deed Book 1071:508.

Deed from Solomon Johnson et al. to John A. Olson and Gladys C. Bowgren. Kane County Deed Book 1096:105.

Deed from Solomon Johnson et al. to John and Annie Coombes. Kane County Deed Book 787: 199.

Deed from Solomon Johnson et al. to Joseph White et al. Kane County Deed Book 1365:429.

Deed from Solomon Johnson et al. to Nettie Anderson. Kane County Deed Book 821: 436.

Deed from Stanley V. Bowgren et al. to Charles K. Bowgren et al. Kane County Deed Book 1331:63.

Deed from Stanley O. Bowgren et al. to Terry K. Bowgren et al. Kane County Deed Book 2746:476.

Deed from Theo Wood Scott et al. to George Vanderhoof et al. Kane County Deed Book 1803: 82.

Deed from Vernon L. Critchfield to Patrick H. Collins et al. Kane County Deed Book 2925: 536.

Deed from Werner F. Ladewig et al. to Albert Mueller et al. Kane County Deed Book 2368:344.

Deed from Wesley A. Johnson et al. to Everett D. Larson Jr. Kane County Deed Book 1957:529.

Deed from Wesley N. Plummer et al. to Alfred E. VanWinkle et al. Kane County Deed Book 2563:252.

Deed from Willard R. Austin et al. to George Bergland. Kane County Deed Book 440: 354.

Deed from William B. Wanzer et al. to Sidney Wanzer & Sons, Inc. Kane County Deed Book 688:580.

Deed from William C. Miller to Lynn L. Jay et al. Kane County Deed Book 1786: 604.

Deed from William H. Hess et al. to Smitt Swanson. Kane County Deed Book 191: 127.

Deed from William Higgins et al. to Lucy Higgins. Kane County Deed Book 132: 175.

Deed from William Hiser et al. to Eva Mitchell. Kane County Deed Book 531: 403.

Deed from William L. Slate et al. to Norman L. Carpenter. Kane County Deed Book 144:251.

Deed from William Massolle Jr. et al. to Adrian Landreth et al. Kane County Deed Book 1412:249.

Deed from William Ruddick et al. to Leonard White. Kane County Deed Book 321: 380.

"Denkers Celebrate Golden Wedding." *Elburn Herald*. 2 October 1941: 4.

"Denny's Tavern." Advertisement. *Elburn Herald*. 6 November 1958: 7; 7 January 1960: 11.

"Diamonds 18U team takes 2nd in AAA National tourney." *Elburn Herald*. 7 August 2003: 31.

"District 303 schools win excellence awards." *Kane County Chronicle*. 1 February 2012: 2.

Divine, Lois V. "LaFox." *Elburn Herald*. 12 March 1936: 4.

"Doings at Wasco." *Elburn Herald*. 7 April 1927: 1; 18 August 1927: 5; 19 January 1928: 5; 8 March 1928: 5; 29 March 1928: 8; 26 April 1928: 8; 17 May 1928: 5; 21 June 1928: 5; 2 August 1928: 5.

Donavin, Denise Perry. "Township exploring historic district status for Wasco." *Daily Herald*. 17 September 2002.

_____. "Richmonds Reunite at Garfield Farm." *Elburn Herald*. 31 August 2000: 15.

Donovan, Deborah. "A sense of community – builders strive for 'home-town' feeling in two developments." *Daily Herald*. 22 November 1997.

Dorfman, Brad. "School Playground Called a 'Sewer.'" *Chicago Tribune*. 18 July 1990: D3.

"East Campton." *Valley Chronicle* [St. Charles, IL]. 29 June 1888: 4.

"Educator of the Year Award nominees set." *Kane County Chronicle*. 24 April 2012: 13.

"Elburn Local Jottings." *Elburn Herald*. 12 July 1917: 1.

"Elburn Local Notes." *Elburn Herald*. 16 May 1913: 4.

"Elburn Locals." *Elburn Herald*. 17 December 1914: 4; 6 May 1915: 8; 1 March 1917: 8; 13 December 1917: 8.

"Elgin G.A.R. Vet, 100, Living for G.O.P Comeback." *Chicago Tribune*. 22 March 1943: 25.

Evans, William W. *Kane County Gazetteer and Directory, 1896-97*. Geneva, IL: Kane County Directory Company, 1896.

Evans' Elgin City Directory, 1933-34. Elgin, IL: Evans Directory Service, 1934.

Evans' Elgin City Directory, 1935-36. Elgin, IL: Evans Directory Service, 1936.

Evans' Elgin City Directory, 1937-38. Elgin, IL: Evans Directory Service, 1938.

Evans' Elgin City Directory, 1939. Elgin, IL: Evans Directory Service, 1939.

Evans' Elgin City Directory, 1941. Elgin, IL: Evans Directory Service, 1941.

Fabbre, Alicia. "Campton Trustees reject town center proposal." *Daily Herald*. 11 March 1999.

_____. "Developers would build 'a brand-new Wasco.'" *Daily Herald*. 17 July 1998.

_____. "New School for Fox Mill subdivision gets green light." *Daily Herald*. 15 September 1998.

_____. "New School may be named for administrators." *Daily Herald*. 16 February 2000.

_____. "Not a bend in the road anymore – The Campton Crossings development will alter the look and feel of tiny Wasco, but some look forward to the conveniences." *Daily Herald*. 22 February 1999.

_____. "Schools open doors for new year." *Daily Herald*. 8 September 1998.

_____. "Softball president argues against using fields for school." *Daily Herald*. 15 July 1998.

_____. "Wasco School students make case for new playground." *Daily Herald*. 30 January 1998.

"Family Reunion." *Elburn Herald*. 10 September 1959: 10.

"Farm Advisors Hold Office Days." *Elburn Herald*. 6 January 1921: 5.

"Farm-City Banquet will be in Elburn." *Elburn Herald*. 19 November 1959: 1.

"Farm Inn." Advertisement. *Elburn Herald*. 12 May 1977: 2.

"Farmers Dump Milk in Fight To Raise Price." *Chicago Tribune*. 2 October 1935: 3.

"Farmers Sign Milk Scale." *Chicago Tribune*. 17 September 1909: 13.

"Fine Wasco Residence Burned." *St. Charles Chronicle.* 12 April 1901: 1.

"Fifteen Years Ago." *Elburn Herald*, 23 December 1949: 14.

Fiftieth Anniversary, The Baptist Church of Wasco. Wasco, IL: Wasco Baptist Church, 1941.

"Fire at Wasco Last Week." *Elburn Herald*. 24 March 1932: 1.

"Fireman's Dance and Banquet Largely Attended." *Elburn Herald*. 7 October 1915: 1.

"Five Fox River Towns Arrange Celebrations." *Chicago Tribune*. 3 September 1939: 2.

Flanagan, Sheri. Swanson/Austin Photo collection (1880-1960). Batavia, IL.

"Flea Market – Wasco American Legion." Advertisement. *Elburn Herald*. 23 May 1974: 11.

Fleming, Leonard N. "Geneva volunteer keeps proving that age is no barrier." *Chicago Tribune*. 26 December 1991: C1.

"Forest Preserve promotes bike safety during National Night Out." *Elburn Herald*. 28 July 2011: 17A.

"Former Wasco Resident Passes Away in Chicago." *Elburn Herald*. 19 November 1948: 1.

Foster, Mike. "Wasco shows flavor of oneness." *St. Charles Chronicle*. 12 July 1983.

"Fox River & Countryside Fire District meeting set for Saturday night." *Kane County Chronicle*. 28 April 2011: 4.

Frankowski, Mike. Wasco Fastpitch photos (2010s). Campton Hills, IL.

Garbarski, Joe. "History of the Wasco Diamonds." 2013. www.wdfastpitch.com/history. August 2018.

"Gerald Hagaman Weds West Chicago Girl; Will Live in Geneva." *Elburn Herald*. 9 September 1954: 1.

Gibbons, Adam D. and M. Heidi. Photo collection (1860-2018). Geneva, IL.

Gibula, Gary. "St. Charles schools told to brace for big influx." *Chicago Tribune*. 16 June 2004: 2W4.

"Gladys Bowgren and John Olson married." *Elburn Herald*. 21 September 1939: 1.

Goode, Janet A. "Wasco Orange Crushers defeat Elburn Hawks for championship." *Elburn Herald*. 20 July 1989: 4.

Goodyear, Sarah Jane. "Wasco Residents Fly Flags Proudly." *Chicago Tribune*. 24 March 1968: A3.

Grace, Joe. "That's a lot of pumpkin pie." *Kane County Chronicle*. 23 October 2008.

"Grace Lutheran Church Christmas Eve Service." *Elburn Herald*. 24 December 2015: 21.

"Grace Lutheran Church Elects New Officers." *Elburn Herald*. 22 January 1942: 5.

Guyer, Kathy. "Coffee Corner." *Kane County Chronicle*. 12 January 2000: B1.

Haase, Roald. "Commercial centers expanding to former farmland." *Kane County Chronicle*. 24 January 2007.

_____. "Niko's Lodge opens doors in Wasco." *Kane County Chronicle*. 25 November 2006.

_____. "Old Towne Finds 'new town' right place to expand." *Kane County Chronicle*. 31 December 2004.

_____. "Wasco-Campton area hot for retail development." *Kane County Chronicle*. 5 September 2004.

"Hagaman Farm in Family Since 1836 Sold Recently." *Elburn Herald*. 10 January 1935: 4.

Hagaman, Mrs. Frank. "Wasco." *Elburn Herald*. 22 July 1949: 7; 12 August 1949: 5; 26 August 1949: 6; 14 October 1949: 6; 4 November 1949: 4; 18 November 1949: 6; 2 December 1949: 9; 9 December 1949: 12; 16 December 1949: 12; 6 January 1950: 19; 27 January 1950: 11; 24 February 1950: 6; 24 March 1950: 16.

"Happy 100th Birthday, Wasco School." *Kane County Chronicle*. 23 September 2006: 13.

Harms, Michael. "Coffee house brings paradise to Wasco." *Elburn Herald*. 18 September 2003: 5.

"Hello Wasco – Welcome LaFox." *Elburn Herald*. 21 May 1959: 1.

"Here at Last." Valley Chronicle. St. Charles, IL. 31 December 1886: 5.

Heun, Dave. "St. Charles' Melvin Peterson is a walking history book." *Daily Herald*. 8 August 2010.

Hitzeman, Harry. "Campton Hills' Fall Fest about building traditions." *Daily Herald*. 31 August 2018: 3.

"Hold Motorcycle Races Near Wasco, Ill. Today." *Chicago Tribune*. 4 May 1941: B5.

"Holiday Rites Unite Couple." *Elburn Herald*. 1 January 1942: 1.

"Honor Adolph Mongersons at Wasco Open House." *Elburn Herald*. 1 December 1955: 9.

"Hummel & Company." Advertisement. *Elburn Herald*. 28 February 1957: 5.

"Hurt in a Runaway." *Valley Chronicle* [St. Charles]. 9 July 1897: 4.

Husffeldt, Lee. "Hobby steers St. Charles man into auto racing business." *Daily Herald*. 23 March 1998.

_____. "Wasco gets ready for new season." *Daily Herald*. 4 February 1988.

Illinois Civil War Muster and Descriptive Rolls Detail Report. Illinois State Archives. Database. www.ilsos.gov. September 2018.

Illinois Marriage Index, 1860-1920. Database. Ancestry.com. September 2018.

Illinois Deaths and Stillbirths Index, 1916-1947. Database. Ancestry.com. August 2018.

"In the Country." *Valley Chronicle* [St. Charles, IL]. 8 October 1886: 1.

Johnson, Joan, ed. "Booming Businesses in Wasco." Newsletter. Privately printed, 1970.

Johnson, Phyllis. Photo collection (1860-1950). Burlington, IL.

Joslyn, R. Waite, and Frank W. Joslyn. *History of Kane County, Illinois*. Chicago: The Pioneer Publishing Co., 1908.

Kane County, Illinois, Rural and Business Directory, 1924-1925. Chicago, IL: McDonough Company, 1924.

Kane County Property Tax Map. Kane County Illinois GIS Technologies. kanegis.maps.arcgis.com. October 2018.

"Kane-DeKalb Beekeepers Meet at Morrill Farm." *Elburn Herald*. 7 August 1952: 9.

"Kane Little Ten Forms Conference." *Elburn Herald*. 6 May 1920: 1.

"Kaneville." *Elburn Herald*. 11 July 1913: 5.

"KC Bank & Trust merger complete." *Elburn Herald*. 12 March 1992: 6.

Koonce, Izetta K. Copp and Kenneth W. Copp Jr. Photo collection (1870-1960). Eustis, FL.

Kuleta, Gene. "Improved Water System to Aid Homes, Firefighters." *Chicago Tribune*. 12 May 1997: 3.

Kunz, Tona. "Wasco developer riled over unexpected stores." *Daily Herald*. 20 September 2001.

"LaFox." *Elburn Herald*. 22 October 1914: 5; 17 February 1916: 1; 18 June 1948: 7.

"LaFox Farmers Club To Hold Card Party." *Elburn Herald*. 6 March 1958: 5.

"LaFox Notes." *Elburn Herald*. 25 April 1918: 5; 29 August 1918: 5.

"LaFox People You Know and What They Are Doing." *Elburn Herald*. 8 March 1934: 1.

"LaFox Wins Tournament at 'The Farm' Wasco." *Elburn Herald*. 22 September 1932: 1.

Lagattolla, Al. "A star with a shovel." *Kane County Chronicle*. 20 November 2013: 34.

Landreth, Mary Jane, ed. "The Wasco News." Newsletter. Wasco, IL: Wasco American Legion Auxiliary, 1966-1970.

"Large Crowd Attends Wasco Open House, School Dedication." *Elburn Herald*. 20 November 1952: 1.

"Large Farm Sold Near Lily Lake." *Elburn Herald*, 8 November 1928: 8.

Larson, Mrs. L. W. "Wasco." *Elburn Herald*. 19 November 1948: 9; 24 December 1948: 12.

Lassiter, Dawn. "Meat is our main thing." *Kane County Chronicle*. 19 September 2004.

"Last Elgin Civil War Vet Feted on 98th Birthday." *Chicago Tribune*. 23 March 1941: 13.

"Learns on Her Wedding Anniversary Mate is Alive." *Chicago Tribune*. 17 October 1943: 25.

Lease from Arnold G. Mather et al. to Standard Oil Company. Kane County Deed Book 958:50.

Lease from H. E. Travis to the Texas Company. Kane County Deed Book 947:434; also Book 975:505.

Lease from Harry E. Travis et al. to Shell Petroleum Corporation. Kane County Deed Book 918:25.

"Legion Post 1195 honors Auxiliary's 25th year." *Elburn Herald*. 16 August 1979: 6.

"Let Contracts for St. Charles School Annexes." *Chicago Tribune*. 4 January 1951: A4.

"Lily Lake." *Elburn Herald*. 25 March 1915: 5; 3 June 1915: 4; 4 November 1915: 5; 23 November 1916: 5; 3 February 1927: 4; 20 August 1931: 5; 16 November 1967: 9.

"Lily Lake." *Valley Chronicle* [St. Charles, IL]. 4 May 1888: 4.

"Lily Lake." *St. Charles Chronicle*. 10 December 1931: 7; 19 January 1939: 5; 16 February 1939: 4; 21 March 1940: 4; 2 December 1943: 3.

"Lily Lake Items." *Elburn Herald*. 30 November 1922: 5; 18 October 1923: 5; 25 October 1923: 5; 10 April 1924: 1; 13 November 1924: 4; 27 May 1926: 5.

"Lily Lake Milk May Come to Elburn." *Elburn Herald*. 26 September 1913: 1.

"Lily Lake Mission Church in Fortieth Anniversary." *Elburn Herald*. 12 July 1934: 1.

"Limestone smokehouse removed from preserve." *Kane County Chronicle*. 20 November 2015: 21.

"Little League Season Begins." *Elburn Herald*. 7 June 1962: 5.

"Little Milk is Delivered at Wasco." *Elburn Herald*. 6 April 1916: 1.

"Local 4-H Clubs Among Winners at State Fair." *Elburn Herald*. 15 August 1947: 1.

"Local couple re-launches The Lodge on 64." *Elburn Herald*. 21 March 2013: 7A.

"Local Men Elected Directors of PMA." *Elburn Herald*. 18 January 1962: 6.

"Lord of Life Lutheran Church Calendar." *Elburn Herald*. 21 November 1991: 3.

"Lord of Life to break ground." *Elburn Herald*. 23 July 1992: 5.

"Louis C. Horner, Attorney, Dies After Collision." *Chicago Tribune*. 10 May 1936: 9.

"Lumber Truck and Auto Burn in Crash." Chicago Tribune. 23 July 1936: 4.

Lynch, Maureen. "Area now on softball map." *Kane County Chronicle*. 17 July 2006.

Malek, Ed. "Township to Purchase Wasco Legion Hall." Campton Township Newsletter (March 1999). volume 3, issue 1: 2.

"Man Instantly Killed by Fast Freight Train." *Elburn Herald*. 16 October 1930: 1.

"Maple Park Takes Title." *Elburn Herald*. 21 July 1966: 4.

"Marriage Licenses." *Chicago Tribune*. 22 October 1898: 5.

Mask, Teresa. "Board eyes options for throngs of new pupils." *Daily Herald*. 15 September 1996.

Mather, Mary. Photo collection (1890-1970). Wasco, IL.

Meltzer, Erica. "Campton Township tax hike successful." *Daily Herald*. 4 April 2001.

"Men In Service." *Elburn Herald*. 26 July 1979: 8.

Menchaca, Charles. "St. Charles residents continue plea to keep Lincoln, Wasco schools open." *Kane County Chronicle*. 12 December 2015: 14.

"Milk Producers Union." *Chicago Tribune*. 9 September 1887: 2.

Miller, Judith. "Kane County board highlights." *Elburn Herald*. 11 August 1994: 3.

"Money In Peddling Milk." Chicago Tribune. 28 October 1899: 14.

"National Butane Gas." *Elburn Herald*. 3 April 1941: 7.

National Butane Gas advertisement. *Elburn Herald*. 4 June 1948: 5; 29 October 1964: 16.

Nelson, Christopher. "Wasco district's water rated best-tasting." *Kane County Chronicle*. 17 December 2004.

Nelson, Joy. Photo collection (1860-1965). Geneva, IL.

"New Corporations." Chicago Tribune. 14 April 1897: 10.

"No New Cases in Cattle Plague in This Community." *Elburn Herald*. 11 February 1915: 1.

"North Campton." *The Valley Chronicle* [St. Charles, IL]. 10 December 1886: 4; 7 January 1887: 1; 24 January 1887: 8; 20 May 1887: 1; 23 September 1887: 4.

"Nursery Bargains." Wasco Nursery advertisement. *Elburn Herald*. 18 April 1940: 8.

"Nursery Stock." Wasco Nursery advertisement. *Elburn Herald*. 10 April 1934: 8.

Obituary of Albert F. Birch. *Elburn Herald*. 25 October 1990: 4.

Obituary of Alfred Swanson. *Elburn Herald*. 27 June 1940: 8.

Obituary of Algernon A. Burr. *St. Charles Chronicle*. 1 May 1903: 1.

Obituary of Amanda W. Hawkins. *St. Charles Chronicle*. 28 April 1921: 1.

Obituary of Amy Denker Richmond. *Elburn Herald*. 3 May 1979: 10.

Obituary of Andrew Mongerson. *Elburn Herald*. 8 November 1951: 1.

Obituary of Anna C. Brown. *Daily Herald*. 30 March 1999.

Obituary of Anna Johnson. *Elburn Herald*. 23 July 1942: 7.

Obituary of Anne Mongerson Kautz. *Chicago Tribune*. 24 December 1998: 5.

Obituary of Athina Karametsos. *Elburn Herald*. 29 January 1998: 9.

Obituary of August J. Fischer. *St. Charles Chronicle*. 31 May 1907: 1.

Obituary of C. Elmer Ekstrom. *Elburn Herald*. 31 May 1973: 5.

Obituary of Calvin Cray. *Elburn Herald*. 11 November 1976: 13.

Obituary of Calvin M. Corron. *Elburn Herald*. 8 May 1986 4.

Obituary of Charles J. Anderson. *Elburn Herald*. 10 November 1944: 3.

Obituary of Charles W. Millen. *Elburn Herald*, 15 May 1930: 1.

Obituary of Chester R. Johnson. *Elburn Herald*. 23 February 1989: 5.

Obituary of Clara Anderson. *Elburn Herald*. 5 September 1940: 4.

Obituary of Claus A. Swanson. *Geneva Republican.* 11 June 1943: 5.

Obituary of Clifton A. Bowgren. *Elburn Herald*. 12 November 1992: 18.

Obituary of Edna R. Cray. *Elburn Herald*. 26 November 1981: 3.

Obituary of Elizabeth Bowgren. *Elburn Herald*. 28 August 1975: 4.

Obituary of Elizabeth Kayner. *Elburn Herald*. 11 January 1940: 5.

Obituary of Ellen Anderson. *Elburn Herald*. 30 November 1989: 7.

Obituary of Elsia Elliott Murray. *Elburn Herald*. 30 September 1926: 1.

Obituary of Emma Swarthout. *Geneva Republican*. 23 February 1940: 1.

Obituary of Esther Johnson. *Elburn Herald*. 16 June 1966: 3.

Obituary of Ethel Austin. *Elburn Herald*, 3 December 1964: 6.

Obituary of Ethel C. Waterhouse. *Elburn Herald*. 13 August 1970: 6.

Obituary of Eva Mitchell. *Elburn Herald*, 8 February 1940: 8.

Obituary of Frank W. Hagaman. *Elburn Herald*. 23 February 1961: 1.

Obituary of Fred B. Lake. *Elburn Herald*. 18 September 1947: 1.

Obituary of Fred C. Stevens. *Elburn Herald*. 9 September 1937: 4.

Obituary of Fred Ekstrom. *Elburn Herald*. 6 March 1958: 5.

Obituary of Genevieve M. White. *Kane County Chronicle*. 10 July 2005.

Obituary of George Bergland. *Geneva Republican*. 14 November 1914: 1.

Obituary of George L. Higgins. *The True Republican* [Sycamore, Illinois]. 25 July 1923: 1.

Obituary of George L. Vanderhoof. *Elburn Herald*. 30 May 1985: 4.

Obituary of Gladys C. Olson. *Daily Herald*. 17 July 2014: 31.

Obituary of Gladys M. Olson. *Daily Herald*. 30 May 2001.

Obituary of Gordon A. Bowgren. *Elburn Herald*. 19 January 1978: 8.

Obituary of Gordon E. Swanson. *Elburn Herald*. 5 January 1984: 3.

Obituary of Gunnar T. Johnson. *Elburn Herald*. 8 October 1992: 14.

Obituary of Harold P. Ekstrom. *Daily Herald*. 14 March 2002.

Obituary of Hattie E. Lathrop. *Geneva Republican*. 16 July 1948: 1.

Obituary of Hazel R. Ekstrom. *Elburn Herald*. 1 January 1987: 4.

Obituary of Harriet Austin. *Elburn Herald*, 26 September 1929: 7.

Obituary of Helen F. Free. *Daily Herald*. 30 August 2001.

Obituary of Herbert Brown. *Elburn Herald*. 10 December 1970: 4.

Obituary of Hillis Barber. *Elburn Herald*. 23 August 1962: 13.

Obituary of Hilma Johnson. *Elburn Herald*. 21 December 1961: 8.

Obituary of Hugo Denker. *Elburn Herald*. 13 June 1963: 2.

Obituary of Irma R. Erickson. *Kane County Chronicle*. 21 September 2005.

Obituary of J. C. Johnson. *St. Charles Chronicle*. 9 November 1906: 1.

Obituary of James Chrystal. *Elburn Herald*. 23 May 1929: 1.

Obituary of James Langrill. *Elburn Herald*. 30 November 1933: 1.

Obituary of Jan R. Cole. *Daily Herald*. 4 December 1998.

Obituary of Janice L. Stahl. *Daily Herald*, 13 July 2017.

Obituary of Jennie Denker. *Elburn Herald*, 23 June 1988: 5.

Obituary of Jerry Daum. *Elburn Herald*. 12 February 1953: 1.

Obituary of Jewel A. Bowgren. *Elburn Herald*. 14 February 2008: 14.

Obituary of Joel Hawkins. *Elburn Herald*. 31 August 1967: 3.

Obituary of Johana Peterson. *St. Charles Chronicle*. 15 March 1901: 1.

Obituary of John Coombes. *Elburn Herald*. 9 March 1951: 1.

Obituary of John L. Brown. *Elburn Herald*. 26 December 1991: 4.

Obituary of John M. Johnson. *Elburn Herald*. 11 January 1940: 4.

Obituary of John Olson. *Elburn Herald*, 23 March 1995: 11.

Obituary of John Whitney. *Elburn Herald*. 17 October 1929: 1.

Obituary of Joseph White. *Elburn Herald*. 7 November 1957: 8.

Obituary of Josephine Whitney. *St. Charles Chronicle*. 6 May 1910: 1.

Obituary of Leonard Hawkins. *Elburn Herald*, 13 December 1990: 4.

Obituary of Leonard W. Petersohn. *Chicago Tribune*. 30 October 2001: 8.

Obituary of Leonard White. *Elburn Herald*. 24 February 1927: 5.

Obituary of Lester L. Swanson. *Elburn Herald*. 15 February 1996: 9.

Obituary of Lottie Brown. *Elburn Herald*. 26 May 1955: 5.

Obituary of Louise Bergland. Geneva Republican, 14 October 1938: 5; and *Elburn Herald*, 13 October 1938: 4.

Obituary of Louise Wilkison. *Elburn Herald*. 21 August 1986: 3.

Obituary of Lucy Ekstrom. *Elburn Herald*. 22 December 1960: 6.

Obituary of Madeline A. Van De Veire. *Kane County Chronicle*. 3 July 2006.

Obituary of Margaret B. Vanderhoof. *Elburn Herald*. 8 May 1997: 10.

Obituary of Margaret N. Hawkins. *Daily Herald*. 20 October 1998.

Obituary of Marie C. Bergquist. *Elburn Herald*, 12 September 1968: 2.

Obituary of Marion Lake. *Elburn Herald*. 8 September 1932: 8.

Obituary of Mary Barber. *Elburn Herald*. 8 July 1949: 1.

Obituary of Maud Richmond. *Elburn Herald*. 30 July 1964: 7.

Obituary of Mildred N. Mather. *Daily Herald*. 9 June 1999.

Obituary of Nettie Anderson. *Elburn Herald*. 17 December 1953: 3.

Obituary of Norman L. Carpenter. *Elburn Herald*. 1 May 1914: 5.

Obituary of Norvid Swanson. *Elburn Herald*, 28 December 1972: 11.

Obituary of Olive Bergland Hamilton. *Elburn Herald*. 9 August 1984: 7.

Obituary of Oscar M. Johnson. *Elburn Herald*. 30 April 1959: 8.

Obituary of Peter A. Peterson. *Elburn Herald*. 27 August 1987: 7.

Obituary of Peter August Peterson. *Elburn Herald*. 14 May 1931: 1.

Obituary of Peter Bohr. *Elburn Herald*, 31 August 1961: 12.

Obituary of Peter Denker. *Elburn Herald*. 28 January 1943: 4.

Obituary of Ray H. Ekstrom. *Elburn Herald*. 8 February 2001: 11.

Obituary of Raymond Johnson. *Elburn Herald*. 27 August 1992: 13.

Obituary of Robert B. Jay. *Elburn Herald*. 29 September 2005: 23.

Obituary of Robert P. Anderson. *Elburn Herald*. 22 February 2007: 4B.

Obituary of Rose S. Swanson. *Elburn Herald*. 3 August 1989: 7.

Obituary of Ruth N. Garaghty. *Elburn Herald*. 11 October 1984: 6.

Obituary of Sam Santell. *Chicago Tribune*. 23 April 2006: 4C5.

Obituary of Sarah C. Rice. *Elgin Advocate*. 25 May 1889: 8.

Obituary of Stanley O. Bowgren. *Elburn Herald*. 7 December 1995: 9.

Obituary of Thomas Langrill. *Elburn Herald*. 4 October 1951: 1.

Obituary of Ulrike Anderson. *Elburn Herald*. 15 October 1914: 1.

Obituary of Verner Bowgren. *Elburn Herald*. 20 May 1971: 5.

Obituary of Vesta Bell. *Elburn Herald*. 19 November 1931: 1.

Obituary of Wallace A. Swanson Jr. *Elburn Herald*. 28 February 1991: 4.

Obituary of Wesley A. Johnson. *Elburn Herald*. 8 May 1975: 16.

Obituary of William A. Austin. Sycamore True Republican. 23 November 1910.

Obituary of Zilpha K. Brown. *Elburn Herald*. 7 July 1977: 7.

"Old Neighbors' Day is Annual Event at Wasco." *Elburn Herald*, 24 October 1913: 4.

"One Dead, 30 Hurt In Train Wreck." *Chicago Tribune*. 19 January 1903: 2.

"Our History." Wasco Nursery. www.wasconursery.com. April 2018.

"Paul Scott Weds." *Elburn Herald*. 22 February 1923: 8.

Peterson, Florence Mabel (Bergland), "Genealogy of George Charles Bergland and Bonnie Louise Bergland." Notebook. Wasco, IL: n.p., 1939.

Peterson, Florence, and Fern Johnson. *Historical Sketch [of the Wasco Baptist Church]*. Wasco, IL: n. p., 1941.

Pierce, Victoria. "Lights, camera, gangland action!" *Kane County Chronicle*. 8 October 1993: 1, 11.

Pilat, Roxanne. "At tiny post offices, it's nostalgia that delivers." *Chicago Tribune*. 27 March 1994: A7.

"Plant Now." Advertisement for Wasco Nursery. *Elburn Herald*. 2 May 1947: 8.

Plat of Campton Oak Farms subdivision [Campton Township]. Kane County Plat Book 48:47.

Plat of Deer Run Creek subdivision [Campton Township]. Kane County Plat Book 72:38.

"Plow Contest Victor Makes It Two in Week." *Chicago Tribune*. 22 September 1940: 20.

"PMA Meets in Chicago on March 20." *Elburn Herald*. 12 March 1948: 6.

"PMA 'Neatest Farm' Winners." *Elburn Herald*. 5 September 1940: 1.

"PMA Picks Delegates." *Elburn Herald*. 9 September 1965: 3.

"PMA Re-elects Bolcum at Annual Meeting." *Elburn Herald*. 26 January 1961: 10.

"PMA Seeks Raises in the Price of Milk." *Elburn Herald*. 22 February 1946: 6.

Polk's Elgin City Directory (1959). R. L. Polk & Company, St. Louis, MO, 1959.

Polk's Elgin City Directory (1960). R. L. Polk & Company, St. Louis, MO, 1960.

Polk's St. Charles, Batavia, and Geneva Directory (1950). R. L. Polk & Company, St. Louis, MO, 1950.

Polk's St. Charles, Batavia, and Geneva Directory (1956). R. L. Polk & Company, St. Louis, MO, 1956.

Polk's St. Charles, Batavia, and Geneva Directory (1958). R. L. Polk & Company, St. Louis, MO, 1958.

Polk's St. Charles, Batavia, and Geneva Directory (1960). R. L. Polk & Company, St. Louis, MO, 1960.

Prairie Farmer's Reliable Directory of Farmers and Breeders, Kane County, Illinois. Chicago: Prairie Farmer Publishing Company, 1918.

Presecky, William. "Campton Hills? Voters to Decide." *Chicago Tribune*. 10 January 2007: 9.

_____. "100 ash trees facing ax in Kane." *Chicago Tribune*. 13 March 2008: 3.

"Pretty in Pink Champs." *Elburn Herald*. 31 October 2013: 16.

"Pretty Wedding at Wasco Thursday." *Elburn Herald*. 13 October 1927: 8.

"Public Auction – Antiques-Collectibles-Victorian." *Elburn Herald*. 17 April 1986: 10.

"Pure Milk Group has over 800 Members in Kane County Local." *Elburn Herald*. 3 July 1952: 8.

"Pure Milk Locals." *Elburn Herald*. 6 November 1969: 7.

"Pure Milk Locals elect new officers." *Elburn Herald*. 19 October 1967: 8.

"Quality Nursery Stock." *Elburn Herald*. 21 October 1954: 8.

Quit Claim of George H. Martin to Lillian M. Martin. Kane County Deed Book 422:250.

Quit Claim of Kathleen Nord et al. to Nora E. De Gignac. Kane County Deed Book 2018:516.

Quit Claim of Louise Swarthout to Julius Wynthein et al. Kane County Deed Book 1736:225.

Quit Claim of Louella Tappan et al. to Julius Wynthein et al. Kane County Deed Book 1736:226.

Quit Claim of Philo G. Plummer et al. to Roy L. Peterson et al. Kane County Deed Book 1693:495.

Quit Claim of Solomon Johnson et al. to George E. Hawkins et al. Kane County Deed Book 1190:403.

Quit Claim of Wallace A. Swanson Sr. to Wallace A. Swanson Jr. Kane County Deed Book 1479:365.

"Races at 'The Farm' Near Wasco Labor Day." *Elburn Herald*. 23 August 1934: 1.

"Railroad Awards." *Valley Chronicle* [St. Charles, IL]. 13 August 1886: 1.

"Railroad Banquet." *Valley Chronicle* [St. Charles, IL]. 31 December 1886: 5.

"Railway Matters." *Valley Chronicle* [St. Charles, IL]. 15 October 1886: 4.

"Ramblings." *Elburn Herald*. 20 September 1946: 4; 25 October 1946: 1; 1 November 1946: 6; 6 December 1946: 4.

Ranstrom, Verla. "Forest Preserve to shed old barn." *Elgin Courier-News*. 28 May 1974: 18.

"Reach for the Sky." *Kane County Chronicle*. 20 September 2005.

"Realignment of Streets Will Close Wasco Road." *Chicago Tribune*. 15 June 1994: B3.

"Referendums." *Chicago Tribune*. 19 March 1992: 25; 10 April 2009: 3; 21 March 2012: 6.

"Reward Top Achievement at Kane 4-H Rally Night." *Elburn Herald*. 9 November 1978: 14.

Rhodebeck, Ashley. "Campton residents get vision of town center, Wasco area." *Kane County Chronicle*. 14 October 2011: 2.

Rice, William. "Countryside Chic." *Chicago Tribune*. 29 May 1994: SM18.

Rutkowsky, Barbara. "Wasco." *Elburn Herald*. 27 February 1948: 6; 26 March 1948: 15.

"Saints' Halo 1951." Yearbook. St. Charles High School. St. Charles, IL: 1951.

Schelkopf, Eric. "Old Towne Pub Wasco becoming popular music place." *Kane County Chronicle*. 24 June 2015: 10.

_____. "St. Charles man grows 1,148 pound pumpkin." *Kane County Chronicle*. 8 October 2009.

Schlueter, Tom. "It's the Great Pumpkin on display." *Kane County Chronicle*. 15 October 2004.

Schmit, Kevin. "Influx of Saints will help Post 342." *Daily Herald*. 25 June 1999.

"School Notes." *Elburn Herald*. 1 May 1924: 8.

Schory, Brenda. "Bowgrens of Geneva to host 75th consecutive family reunion." *Kane County Chronicle*. 6 June 2017. Online.

_____. "Cupcake shop a sweet dream come true." *Kane County Chronicle*. 3 February 2010: 16.

_____. "Preservation Society to celebrate Old Wasco Days at Corron Farm." *Kane County Chronicle*. 28 June 2011: 8.

_____. "St. Charles School District 303 eyes closing three schools in cost-savings measure." *Kane County Chronicle*. 9 September 2015: 2.

_____. "Wasco Nursery displays half-ton pumpkins." *Kane County Chronicle*. 17 October 2014: 9.

_____. "Wasco Sanitary District will remain independent." *Kane County Chronicle*. 18 October 2007.

_____. "Zip codes plentiful in Campton Hills." *Kane County Chronicle*. 26 May 2008.

Schwab, Jay. "Wasco Baseball enthused about partnership." *Kane County Chronicle*. 25 July 2014: 15.

Scott, Della. "Wasco News." *Elburn Herald*. 9 December 1937: 5.

Scott, Gregory. "Board chooses school redistricting option that moves fewest number of children." *Chicago Tribune*. 3 June 1994: B3.

"Second Graders Send Hope to Katrina Victims." *Kane County Chronicle*. 13 September 2005.

"Second Victim of Auto-Truck Crash is Dead." *Chicago Tribune*. 24 July 1936: 10.

"Series of Evangelistic Services To Be Held in Wasco Baptist Church." *Elburn Herald*. 23 February 1956: 7.

"Show Atomic Film at Wasco Church." *Elburn Herald*. 26 June 1952: 4.

Sjostrom, Joseph. "Kane Farmland Lures Developers." *Chicago Tribune*. 6 December 1989: D10.

Sloboda, Ashley. "D-303 Facing Questions about future of Middle Schools." *Geneva Republican*. 18 February 2016. News: 5.

_____. "Vote keeps schools open in St. Charles School District 303." *Kane County Chronicle*. 12 January 2016: 6.

Slowik, Ted. "D303 to decide in January whether to close schools." *Chicago Tribune*. 24 December 2015: 1.

Smith, Patsy. "Message to the Residents." *Village of Campton Hills Newsletter*. March 2008: 1

Smith, Leslie Mann. "The Anvil Chorus Blacksmith's Work Today is Ornamental, Not Utilitarian." *Chicago Tribune*. 30 June 1995: 8.

"Social, Achievement Day Planned This Weekend in Wasco Community." *Elburn Herald*. 5 July 1951: 1.

"Softball, Fastpitch registration." *Elburn Herald*. 30 January 1997: 6.

"St. Charles." *Elgin Advocate*. 27 April 1889: 7.

St. Charles Biographical Directory, and Census Report, 1885. Chicago: J. F. Wilcox, 1885.

"St. Charles Moves in Construction Plan for Schools." *Chicago Tribune*. 5 November 1970: W7.

Stewart, Beverly. "Heartland Cuisine, the new Farm Inn becomes Olde." *Chicago Tribune*. 15 January 1989: N5.

Strom, Mrs. C. E. "Wasco News." *Elburn Herald*. 15 November 1934: 5; 24 January 1935: 5; 31 January 1935: 5; 28 March 1935: 5; 4 April 1935: 5.

"Suburban [Election] Results." *Chicago Tribune*. 4 November 2004: 11.

Sulski, Jim. "Explosive Growth is Moving West." *Chicago Tribune*. 16 March 2000: 13.

Swanson, Carrie. "Wasco News." *Elburn Herald*. 9 May 1935: 5; 23 May 1935: 5.

Swanson, Don. Photo collection (1880-1965). Geneva, IL.

Swanson, Don. "Wasco Memories, 1933-1952." Unpublished MS. Geneva, IL. 2018.

Swanson, Maude. "About People You Know From Wasco and Vicinity." *Elburn Herald*. 18 March 1937: 1.

Swanson, Maude. "Wasco News." *Elburn Herald*. 29 August 1935: 4; 5 September 1935: 4; 3 October 1935: 5; 10 October 1935: 5; 21 November 1935: 6; 5 December 1935: 10; 12 December 1935: 7; 20 February 1936: 8; 7 March 1936: 8; 14 May 1936: 4; 21 May 1936: 4; 11 June 1936: 10; 18 June 1936: 8; 13 August 1936: 8; 27 August 1936: 5; 10 September 1936: 7; 5 November 1936: 5; 21 November 1935: 6; 21 January 1937: 8; 28 January 1937: 8; 25 March 1937: 4; 15 April 1937: 4.

"Tabulation of Voting Tuesday in Kane County." *Elburn Herald*. 10 November 1950: 5.

Tebo, Meg. "Pupils Put Own Work Into Playground." *Chicago Tribune*. 17 February 1998: 3.

Tebo, Meg. "District is Planning to Build New School at Fox Mill Site." *Chicago Tribune*. 16 September 1998: 7A.

Thayer, Kate. "Fire board seeks architects for proposed station." *Kane County Chronicle*. 24 June 2008.

Thayer, Patty. "Face lift enhances family dining at the Wasco Inn." *Kane County Chronicle*. 20 August 1993: 14.

"The Farm on Highway Sixty-Four is Popular." *Elburn Herald*. 1 October 1931: 1.

"This Week's Recipes." *Elburn Herald*. 15 November 1934: 4; 22 November 1934: 4.

"Three Pioneers Die Suddenly." *Elburn Herald*, 17 October 1916: 1.

"Three Townships in Two Episodes." *Elburn Herald*. 18 June 1936: 1.

"Treasurer's Annual Report" [Campton Township]. *Elburn Herald*. 13 April 1916: 4.

Tri-annual Atlas & Plat Book. Rockford Map Publishers, Distributed by the Kane County Farm Bureau. St. Charles, IL: 1964.

20th Century Atlas of Kane County, Illinois. Chicago: Middle West Publishing Company, 1904.

Umphlett, James and Betty Jane. Photo collection (1900-1980). Cody, WY.

"U-Go-I-Go Banquet held at Stonewall Lodge." *Elburn Herald*. 20 May 1937: 1.

"U. of Illinois Cow Sets Brown Swiss Butterfat Record." *Chicago Tribune*. 5 March 1937: 23.

U. S. Army Transport Service, Passenger Lists, 1910-1939. Database. Ancestry.com. July 2018.

U. S. City Directories, 1822-1995. Database. Ancestry.com. June 2018.

U. S. Evangelical Lutheran Church in America, Swedish American Church Records, 1800-1946. Database. Ancestry.com. September 2018.

U. S. Geological Survey. USGS Historical Topographic Map Explorer. historicalmaps.arcgis.com. September 2018.

U. S. Passport Applications, 1795-1925. Database. Ancestry.com. August 2018.

United States Department of the Interior. "Geneva [Illinois] Quadrangle." Washington, DC: U. S. Geological Survey: 1948.

Unzicker, Tim. "1 man hurt in spectacular Wasco propane explosion." *Geneva Republican*. 3 March 1994: 24.

"Vacation Bible School." *Elburn Herald*. 4 August 1988: 5.

Vanderhoof, Margaret. "Tragedy Averted as 8 Escape Injury In Truck-Auto Accident at Wasco." *Elburn Herald*. 31 December 1964: 9.

Vanderhoof, Mrs. George [Margaret]. "Wasco & LaFox." *Elburn Herald*. 3 September 1959: 7; 10 September 1959: 6; 24 September 1959: 10; 1 October 1959: 3; 8 October 1959: 6; 22 October 1959: 6; 12 November 1959: 12; 7 January 1960: 6; 11 February 1960: 4; 3 March 1960: 6; 31 March 1960: 3; 28 April 1960: 4; 26 May 1960: 10; 28 July 1960: 2; 18 August 1960: 6; 15 September 1960: 4; 6 October 1960: 10; 13 October 1960: 3; 22 December 1960: 16; 9 March 1961: 8; 30 March 1961: 13; 25 May 1961: 4; 13 July 1961: 6; 20 July 1961: 6; 24 August 1961: 4; 7 September 1961: 6; 19 October 1961: 2; 9 November 1961: 8; 23 November 1961: 7; 30 November 1961: 4; 15 February 1962: 6; 8 March 1962: 14; 19 April 1962: 2; 31 May 1962: 3; 5 July 1962: 5; 30 August 1962: 2; 27 September 1962: 3; 10 January 1963: 6; 21 February 1963: 14; 14 March 1963: 6; 16 May 1963: 12; 23 May 1963: 7; 30 May 1963: 8; 6 June 1963: 8; 27 June 1963: 2; 1 August 1963: 4; 7 November 1963: 19; 5 December 1963: 11; 5 March 1964: 4; 16 April 1964: 11; 28 May 1964: 11; 10 December 1964: 10; 24 December 1964: 13; 25 February 1965: 11; 30 September 1965: 6; 5 May 1966: 7; 12 May 1966: 3; 19 May 1966: 5; 1 September 1966: 3; 17 November 1966: 1; 22 December 1966: 20; 20 June 1968: 2; 1 May 1969: 4; 5 June 1969: 9; 19 June 1969: 6; 26 June 1969: 7; 16 October 1969: 2; 23 October 1969: 7; 13 November 1969: 9; 11 December 1969: 5; 18 December 1969: 11; 12 November 1970: 6; 19 November 1970: 4; 10

December 1970: 4; 6 May 1971: 4; 1 July 1971: 7; 19 August 1971: 5; 2 December 1971: 2; 6 April 1972: 8; 13 April 1972: 2; 11 May 1972: 4; 20 July 1972: 2; 3 August 1972: 8; 10 August 1972: 5; 31 August 1972: 8; 16 November 1972: 4; 5 April 1973: 10; 4 October 1973: 4; 15 November 1973: 4; 21 February 1974: 5; 2 May 1974: 6; 23 May 1974: 4; 4 July 1974: 6; 10 October 1974: 6; 21 November 1974: 9; 13 March 1975: 5; 24 April 1975: 6; 6 November 1975: 7; 20 November 1975: 6; 17 June 1976: 11; 24 June 1976: 14; 26 August 1976: 16; 2 September 1976: 12; 16 September 1976: 8; 25 November 1976: 9; 2 December 1976: 9; 28 April 1977: 5; 12 May 1977: 15; 16 June 1977: 7; 11 August 1977: 13; 6 September 1977: 10; 22 September 1977: 7; 1 December 1977: 8; 8 December 1977: 8; 15 December 1977: 8; 30 March 1978: 18; 27 April 1978: 14; 4 May 1978: 18; 22 June 1978: 12; 16 November 1978: 5; 26 April 1979: 10; 17 May 1979: 5; 13 March 1980: 7; 27 March 1980: 13.

"Virgil." *Elburn Herald*. 16 March 1916: 5.

"Voting Totals." *St. Charles Chronicle*. 16 November 1900: 1.

Walker, Chris. "Enthusiasts cruise into Wasco for Model Car Indoor event." *Kane County Chronicle*. 30 January 2018.

"Was a Disastrous Storm." *Elgin Advocate*. 3 August 1889: 6.

"Wasco." *Elburn Herald*. 21 November 1913: 3; 9 October 1919: 5; 10 February 1921: 5; 1 February 1923: 5; 26 July 1923: 4; 6 March 1924: 1; 24 April 1941: 4; 10 July 1941: 8; 16 October 1941: 4; 4 December 1941: 2; 5 March 1942: 3; 16 April 1942: 2; 11 June 1942: 6; 12 November 1942: 7; 13 May 1943: 4; 10 June 1943: 8; 9 September 1943: 2; 23 September 1943: 8; 14 October 1943: 7; 2 March 1944: 8; 28 December 1945: 3; 1 February 1946: 4; 14 May 1948: 7; 27 August 1948: 7; 17 September 1948: 6; 1 July 1949: 5; 3 May 1951: 4.

"Wasco." *Elgin Advocate*. 6 August 1887: 8; 10 September 1887: 8; 3 December 1887: 4; 17 December 1887: 8; 7 January 1888: 8; 28 January 1888: 8; 4 February 1888: 8; 11 February 1888: 8; 10 March 1888: 8; 31 March 1888: 8; 21 April 1888: 8; 5 May 1888: 8; 16 June 1888: 5; 23 June 1888: 8; 30 June 1888: 8; 11 August 1888: 4; 18 August 1888: 8; 8 September 1888: 3; 8 December 1888: 8; 16 February 1889: 8; 23 February 1889: 6; 8 June 1889: 8; 29 June 1889: 5; 7 July 1889: 8; 10 August 1889: 8; 31 August 1889: 8; 21 September 1889: 8; 12 October 1889: 10; 2 November 1889: 8; 14 December 1889: 6; 21 December 1889: 8.

"Wasco 12U takes home Woodstock crown." *Elburn Herald*. 14 July 2005: 30.

"Wasco American Legion Baseball League Constitution & By-Laws." www.wascobaseball.com. April 2018.

"Wasco American Legion Breaks Ground for Post Home." *St. Charles Chronicle*. 24 February 1960: 1.

"Wasco & LaFox." *Elburn Herald*. 28 May 1959: 10; 18 June 1959: 10; 16 July 1959: 9; 23 July 1959: 3; 24 December 1959: 12; 6 July 1961: 6; 21 September 1961: 12; 19 July 1962: 9; 4 April 1963: 8; 22 August 1963: 10; 28 January 1965: 2; 4 May 1967: 7; 14 December 1967: 7; 5 October 1972: 9; 8 April 1976: 7; 31 August 1978: 16; 10 April 1980: 16; 12 June 1980: 6; 26 June 1980: 6; 21 August 1980: 6.

"Wasco and LaFox News." *Elburn Herald*. 23 December 1965: 12.

"Wasco Baptist Church." Advertisement. *Elburn Herald*. 22 October 1987: 14.

"Wasco Baseball." *Elburn Herald*. 5 September 1974: 13.

"Wasco Blacksmith Shop." *Elburn Herald*. 7 May 1970: 8.

"Wasco Cardinals Seek Softball Games." *Elburn Herald*. 22 June 1945: 6.

"Wasco Cardinals Start Season With Two Wins." *Elburn Herald*. 20 June 1947: 7.

"Wasco Cardinals Win Third Straight Game." *Elburn Herald*. 9 August 1946: 7.

"Wasco Christmas Bazaar to feature Santa's Secret Shop for children." *Elburn Herald*. 5 December 1974: 7.

"Wasco Church Presents 'Skid Row' Movies." *Elburn Herald*. 28 January 1954: 7.

"Wasco Community Club Debate Program Friday." *Elburn Herald*. 5 April 1934: 1.

"Wasco Community Club meets Friday evening." *Elburn Herald*. 12 February 1942: 4.

"Wasco Community Club to Feature British Night." *Elburn Herald*. 22 April 1937: 1.

"Wasco Community Club to hear Farm Advisor." *Elburn Herald*. 9 February 1939: 4.

"Wasco Community Club to meet Friday Nov. 5th." *Elburn Herald*. 4 November 1937: 1.

"Wasco Diamonds announce inaugural golf outing." *Elburn Herald*. 29 May 2003: 22.

"Wasco Diamonds Fastpitch." *Elburn Herald*. 24 June 1999: 14.

Wasco Diamonds Fastpitch Softball. website. www.wdfastpitch.com. August 2018.

"Wasco Diamonds Open 15th Season." *Elburn Herald*. 12 March 2009: 9.

"Wasco Diamonds Win USSSA National Title." *Geneva Republican*. 4 August 2016. Sports: 7.

"Wasco Dramatic Club Gives 'The Yellow Shadow.'" *Elburn Herald*. 14 March 1935: 1.

Wasco Elementary School photograph and document collection (1906-2018). Wasco, IL.

"Wasco 4-H Club." *Elburn Herald*. 2 January 1948: 7; 15 December 1950: 7; 27 April 1951: 5.

"Wasco Girls Fastpitch." *Elburn Herald*. 2 July 1998: 23.

"Wasco Girls fastpitch softball standings." *Elburn Herald*. 4 June 1998: 22.

"Wasco Girls Fastpitch Softball Winter Clinic." *Elburn Herald*. 4 March 1999: 21.

"Wasco Gives Farewell Party for Fourteen Drafted Men." *Elburn Herald*. 27 June 1918: 5.

"Wasco Has Country Fair This Day." *Elburn Herald*. 26 August 1915: 1.

"Wasco High School." *Elburn Herald*. 25 May 1939: 1.

"Wasco Home Bureau News." *Elburn Herald*. 2 April 1942: 7; 12 March 1942: 6.

"Wasco House burns to a shell." *Elburn Herald*. 16 July 1987: 4.

"Wasco Inn." Advertisement. *Elburn Herald*. 25 February 1999: 12.

"Wasco Items." *Elburn Herald*. 13 February 1919: 4; 2 September 1920: 5; 15 September 1921: 5; 7 August 1924: 4; 25 September 1924: 4.

"Wasco Items." *St. Charles Chronicle*. 15 May 1903: 8; 5 June 1903: 8; 26 June 1903: 8; 17 July 1903: 8; 31 July 1903: 8; 7 August 1903: 8; 14 August 1903: 8; 21 August 1903: 8; 11 September 1903: 8;

25 September 1903: 8; 9 October 1903: 8; 20 November 1903: 8; 4 December 1903: 8; 15 January 1904: 8; 22 January 1904: 8; 29 January 1904: 8; 12 February 1904: 8; 18 March 1904: 8; 25 March 1904: 8; 1 April 1904: 8; 15 April 1904: 8; 22 April 1904: 8; 6 May 1904: 8; 13 May 1904: 8; 20 May 1904: 8; 10 June 1904: 8; 1 July 1904: 8; 22 July 1904: 8; 5 August 1904: 4; 12 August 1904: 4; 19 August 1904: 8; 26 August 1904: 8; 2 September 1904: 8; 23 September 1904: 8; 7 October 1904: 8; 28 October 1904: 8; 4 November 1904: 8; 11 November 1904: 1; 18 November 1904: 8; 2 December 1904: 4; 16 December 1904: 8; 3 February 1905: 8; 17 February 1905: 8; 24 February 1905: 8; 3 March 1905: 8; 10 March 1905: 8; 17 March 1905: 8; 24 March 1905: 8; 31 March 1905: 8; 14 April 1905: 8; 12 May 1905: 8; 19 May 1905: 8; 2 June 1905: 8; 9 June 1905: 8; 16 June 1905: 8; 23 June 1905:8; 14 July 1905: 8; 4 August 1905: 8; 11 August 1905: 8; 18 August 1905: 8; 1 September 1905: 8; 8 September 1905: 8; 15 September 1905: 8; 22 September 1905: 8; 29 September 1905: 8; 6 October 1905: 8; 13 October 1905: 12; 20 October 1905: 8; 27 October 1905: 8; 3 November 1905: 8; 10 November 1905: 8; 24 November 1905: 1; 1 December 1905: 8; 5 January 1906: 8; 19 January 1906: 8; 26 January 1906: 1; 2 February 1906: 8; 9 February 1906: 8; 16 February 1906: 8; 23 February 1906: 1; 2 March 1906: 8; 9 March 1906: 8; 16 March 1906: 8; 23 March 1906: 8; 30 March 1906: 8; 6 April 1906: 8; 20 April 1906: 6; 27 April 1906: 1; 4 May 1906: 8; 11 May 1906: 8; 18 May 1906: 1; 25 May 1906: 8; 1 June 1906: 8; 8 June 1906: 8; 15 June 1906: 8; 22 June 1906: 8; 29 June 1906: 8; 13 July 1906: 4; 20 July 1906: 8; 3 August 1906: 8; 10 August 1906: 8; 17 August 1906: 8; 24 August 1906: 8; 31 August 1906: 8; 7 September 1906: 8; 21 September 1906: 8; 28 September 1906: 8; 5 October 1906: 8; 12 October 1906: 8; 26 October 1906: 1; 9 November 19061: 1; 16 November 1906: 1; 23 November 1906: 8; 7 December 1906: 8; 14 December 1906: 8; 28 December 1906: 8; 18 July 1913: 8; 25 July 1913: 8; 8 August 1913: 8; 22 August 1913: 8; 29 August 1913: 8; 5 September 1913: 8; 26 September 1913: 8; 3 October 1913: 8; 10 October 1913: 1; 31 October 1913: 8; 7 November 1913: 8; 21 November 1913: 8; 26 December 1913: 8.

"Wasco Legion to Move, Convert Depot to Hall." *Elburn Herald*. 21 January 1960: 1.

"Wasco Legion Sponsors Dance Saturday, Nov. 5." *Elburn Herald*. 27 October 1955: 1.

"Wasco Legion Sponsors Public Auction Sunday." *Elburn Herald*. 20 October 1955: 1.

"Wasco Legion Sponsors Sale." *Elburn Herald*. 9 June 1955: 1.

"Wasco Met Sad Defeat." *Elburn Herald*. 22 February 1917: 8.

"Wasco News." *Elburn Herald*. 9 September 1920: 4; 9 December 1926: 10; 27 January 1927: 5; 17 February 1927: 1; 19 May 1927: 8; 9 June 1927: 5; 6 September 1928: 5; 27 September 1928: 4; 11 October 1928: 4; 25 October 1928: 10; 8 November 1928: 5; 15 November 1928: 10; 13 December 1928: 8; 20 December 1928: 9; 27 December 1928: 8; 10 January 1929: 5; 31 January 1929: 4; 7 February 1929: 4; 14 March 1929: 4; 18 April 1929: 7; 6 June 1929: 4; 18 July 1929: 4; 15 August 1929: 9; 12 September 1929: 5; 3 October 1929: 5; 7 November 1929: 4; 12 December 1929: 11; 19 December 1929: 8; 23 January 1930: 5; 6 February 1930: 5; 29 May 1930: 5; 5 June 1930: 5; 3 July 1930: 5; 25 September 1930: 7; 2 October 1930: 4; 16 October 1930: 5; 23 October 1930: 7; 6 November 1930: 5; 20 November 1930: 4; 4 December 1930: 4; 11 December 1930: 9; 22 January 1931: 4; 12 February 1931: 5; 7 May 1931: 5; 21 May 1931: 5; 28 May 1931: 5; 4 June 1931: 5; 16 July 1931: 5; 23 July 1931: 5; 3 September 1931: 5; 10 September 1931: 5; 29 October 1931: 8; 26 November 1931: 5; 26 May 1932: 4; 2 June 1932: 4; 7 July 1932: 5; 28 July 1932: 4; 18 August 1932: 5; 25 August 1932: 5; 8 September 1932: 5; 20 October 1932: 5; 10 November 1932: 4; 22 December 1932: 5; 19 January 1933: 4; 9 February 1933: 5; 2 March 1933: 5; 9 March 1933: 4; 20 April 1933: 5; 22 June 1933: 8; 10 August 1933: 5; 31 August 1933: 8; 5 October 1933: 8; 12

October 1933: 4; 2 November 1933: 4; 16 November 1933: 4; 14 December 1933: 4; 11 January 1934: 5; 16 August 1934: 5; 30 August 1934: 4; 13 September 1934: 5; 27 September 1934: 5; 6 June 1935: 4; 12 December 1935: 7; 7 March 1936: 8; 18 June 1936: 8; 22 October 1936: 5; 2 September 1937: 4; 30 September 1937: 4; 4 November 1937: 5; 25 November 1937: 5; 3 February 1938: 8; 3 March 1938: 5; 17 March 1938: 5; 19 May 1938: 5; 26 May 1938: 4; 9 June 1938: 5; 30 June 1938: 8; 16 March 1939: 8; 25 May 1939: 8; 13 July 1939: 5; 31 August 1939: 5; 28 September 1939: 5; 12 October 1939: 8; 2 November 1939: 5; 16 November 1939: 4; 25 January 1940: 4; 13 February 1940: 7; 4 April 1940: 9; 2 May 1940: 4; 16 May 1940: 4; 8 August 1940: 8.

"Wasco News." *St. Charles Chronicle*. 1 March 1901: 8; 15 March 1901: 8; 22 March 1901: 10; 12 April 1901: 8; 19 April 1901: 10; 3 May 1901: 8; 17 May 1901: 8; 24 May 1901: 8; 31 May 1901: 6; 7 June 1901: 10; 28 June 1901: 10; 5 August 1901: 4; 21 November 1902: 8; 12 December 1902: 10; 19 December 1902: 14; 9 January 1903: 6; 16 January 1903: 8; 23 January 1903: 8; 30 January 1903: 8; 6 February 1903: 8; 27 February 1903: 8; 3 April 1903: 10; 10 April 1903: 10.

"Wasco News Items." *St. Charles Chronicle*. 11 January 1907: 10; 18 January 1907: 8; 25 January 1907: 8; 1 February 1907: 8; 8 February 1907: 8; 15 February 1907: 8; 22 February 1907: 8; 1 March 1907: 8; 15 March 1907: 8; 22 March 1907: 4; 29 March 1907: 1; 4 April 1907: 8; 26 April 1907: 1; 3 May 1907: 4; 10 May 1907: 8; 17 May 1907: 8; 31 May 1907: 1; 14 June 1907: 8; 28 June 1907: 1; 12 July 1907: 8; 19 July 1907: 10; 26 July 1907: 8; 2 August 1907: 8; 9 August 1907: 8; 16 August 1907: 1; 23 August 1907: 10; 20 September 1907: 8; 4 October 1907: 8; 18 October 1907: 8; 8 November 1907: 8; 29 November 1907: 8; 6 December 1907: 8; 13 December 1907: 8; 20 December 1907; 10 January 1908: 8; 7 February 1908: 8; 14 February 1908: 8; 28 February 1908: 8; 6 March 1908: 8; 20 March 1908: 8; 10 April 1908: 8; 24 April 1908: 8; 24 July 1908: 8; 31 July 1908: 8; 21 August 1908: 8; 11 September 1908: 8; 25 September 1908: 8; 2 October 1908: 8; 23 October 1908: 8; 30 October 1908: 8; 6 November 1908: 8; 13 November 1908: 8; 11 December 1908: 8; 1 January 1909: 8; 15 January 1909: 8; 29 January 1909: 8; 5 February 1909: 8; 26 February 1909: 8; 5 March 1909: 8; 9 April 1909; 23 April 1909: 8; 7 May 1909: 8; 14 May 1909: 8; 28 May 1909: 8; 4 June 1909: 8; 18 June 1909: 8; 30 July 1909: 8; 13 August 1909: 8; 17 September 1909: 8; 24 September 1909: 8; 12 November 1909: 9; 3 December 1909: 8; 17 December 1909: 8; 31 December 1909: 8; 7 January 1910: 8; 14 January 1910: 8; 25 February 1910: 8; 29 April 1910: 8; 13 May 1910: 8; 27 May 1910: 1; 3 June 1910: 8; 10 June 1910: 8; 17 June 1910: 8.

"Wasco News Notes." *Elburn Herald*. 30 January 1919: 4.

"Wasco News of Interest." *Elburn Herald*. 5 April 1934: 1.

Wasco Nursery & Garden Center. Facebook page. www.facebook.com/WascoNursery. August 2018.

"Wasco Party." *St. Charles Chronicle*. 28 November 1902: 1.

"Wasco Pastor Quits to Work in Store." *Elburn Herald*. 24 September 1914: 5.

"Wasco Revolutionary Bar-B-Que is May 15." *Elburn Herald*. 6 May 1976: 11.

"Wasco Sanitary District settles complaint." *Kane County Chronicle*. 7 May 2010.

"Wasco School Addition Delayed." *Elburn Herald*. 3 September 1959: 7.

"Wasco School Presents Operetta Friday Night." *Elburn Herald*. 23 April 1942: 8.

"Wasco School Program Cast is Listed." *Elburn Herald*. 21 December 1945: 6.

"Wasco School to observe American Heritage Days." *Elburn Herald*. 5 March 1981: 5.

"Wasco Scouts to hold pizza bash this Saturday." *Elburn Herald*. 9 April 1981: 7.

"Wasco Takes Little League Crown." *Elburn Herald*. 29 July 1965: 8.

"Wasco Train Wreck Attracts Visitors." *Elburn Herald*. 14 April 1950: 4.

"Wasco U14 traveling takes two tourneys." *Elburn Herald*. 16 July 1998: 15.

"Welcome Back to The Farm Restaurant." *Elburn Herald*. 13 May 1971: 9.

Wells, Ryan. "Family recipes add spice to pizza parlor." *Elburn Herald*. 17 May 2001: 19.

"Wesley Johnson Purchases Wasco Grocery Store." *Elburn Herald*. 13 February 1948: 7.

White Brothers Trucking [website]. www.whitebrotherstrucking.com. March 2018.

"White Brothers Trucking receives safety award." *Elburn Herald*. 6 June 1996: 19.

"White Brothers – Wasco's Quiet Giant." *Elburn Herald*. 25 February 1965: 1.

"White elected to international board." *Elburn Herald*. 2 June 1994: 5.

Wickizer, Mrs. L. E. "Wasco." *Elburn Herald*, 4 August 1944: 4; 18 August 1944: 3; 1 September 1944: 3; 29 December 1944: 5; 20 April 1945: 4; 11 May 1945: 4; 13 July 1945: 3; 27 July 1945: 4; 24 August 1945: 3; 16 November 1945: 4; 21 December 1945: 14; 15 February 1946: 5; 31 May 1946: 5; 5 July 1946: 5; 16 August 1946: 7; 11 October 1946: 5; 22 November 1946: 8; 6 December 1946: 7; 4 April 1947: 11; 21 March 1947: 9; 4 April 1947: 11; 23 May 1947: 7; 30 May 1947: 6; 25 July 1947: 9; 24 October 1947: 6.

Willyard, Mrs. Russel H. "Locals." *Elburn Herald*. 28 November 1957: 6.

"Winter Plant Storage" [Wasco Nursery advertisement]. *Kane County Chronicle*. 13 October 2016. News:17.

Winterhalter, Ella. "Lily Lake." *Elburn Herald*. 6 October 1944: 6.

World War II Draft Registration Cards [United States]. Ancestry.com. Database. August 2018.

Yue, Loraine. "Shops placing late bets on holiday items." *Chicago Tribune*. 29 July 2003: 3.

"Zip Code Number Helps Zip Mail to its Destination." *Chicago Tribune*. 13 December 1964: N12.

Surname Index

Abhalter 105
Abrahamson 98, 141, 142, 173
Abram 420
Ackerlund 190
Adams 368
Addams 127
Agnew 22, 109, 168, 169
Aiken 161
Aldridge 53
Alexander 221
Allen ... 27, 33, 47, 82, 97, 128, 164, 178, 183, 299, 326, 328, 409, 411, 412, 416, 417
Almberg 350
Andersen 192
Anderson ... 11, 15, 25, 27, 29, 32, 34, 36, 38, 50, 61, 66, 85, 90, 95, 98, 110, 130, 133, 134, 136, 147, 149, 150, 151, 152, 153, 154, 167, 177, 181, 192, 201, 203, 204, 205, 208, 213, 214, 218, 220, 225, 226, 228, 231, 233, 239, 241, 294, 295, 296, 302, 303, 312, 328, 334, 337, 352, 370, 377, 381, 400, 408, 409, 411, 413, 415, 416, 417, 421, 422, 424, 425
Askeland 93, 94, 416, 419
Atchison 127
Auer 93
Aug 99, 269
Austin ... 13, 19, 25, 29, 32, 35, 83, 111, 112, 113, 114, 115, 117, 118, 119, 125, 128, 140, 168, 270, 273, 274, 276, 277, 278, 279, 313, 315, 331, 351, 368, 382, 408, 409
Avallone 236
Babbage 138
Babbitt 161, 162, 196, 349
Backberg 31
Baert 420
Bagg 84
Bagge 30, 98, 424
Baggs 415
Baird 147
Baker 131
Bakulski 405
Baldwin 11
Ball 45, 48, 400, 417
Bancroft 280

Barber ... 10, 21, 34, 52, 77, 81, 108, 127, 176, 225, 226, 262, 296, 326, 413
Barrett 98
Bartelt 220, 221
Bartlett 16, 17, 20, 168, 169, 253, 329
Basic 50, 232
Bateman 95, 420
Bauerlein 86
Bayless 89
Beard 383
Beecher 285
Beekman 419
Begerman 49, 427
Beith 10, 17
Bekman 418
Bell 14, 15, 19, 20, 21, 25, 30, 65, 89, 90, 102, 108, 153, 154, 156, 167, 168, 186, 214, 300, 407, 410, 411, 415, 417
Benjamen 121
Benson 37, 95, 97, 185
Bent 186
Bentley 121
Berg 89, 97, 128, 200, 421
Bergland ... 15, 18, 19, 20, 21, 22, 25, 27, 29, 32, 36, 37, 39, 40, 74, 83, 84, 85, 99, 108, 110, 113, 120, 121, 123, 124, 126, 127, 128, 129, 131, 133, 135, 137, 140, 144, 151, 152, 153, 160, 163, 165, 167, 183, 195, 196, 197, 199, 201, 221, 239, 242, 243, 244, 255, 256, 257, 259, 261, 264, 266, 267, 270, 286, 300, 305, 317, 320, 326, 327, 331, 336, 345, 348, 349, 351, 352, 358, 360, 368, 399, 406, 407, 411, 413, 415, 416, 422
Berglund 142, 143, 246, 338
Bergquist 243, 244, 349
Besser 32
Bingham 113, 139
Birch 395
Birk 102
Birkinbine 296
Bishop 175, 243
Blackman 164, 166
Blanchard 417
Blank 331
Blecker 73

Blood 58, 160
Bloomquist 203
Bogue 158
Bohr 42, 319, 344, 379
Bolcum ... 19, 23, 24, 25, 27, 33, 34, 83, 89, 90, 109, 126, 128, 197, 200, 214, 215, 227, 303, 326, 407, 409, 414, 417, 425
Bolwahnn 38, 97, 220, 234, 284, 318, 319
Boose 58
Bos 270
Bowgren ... 31, 33, 35, 37, 39, 42, 47, 49, 50, 55, 84, 86, 94, 95, 97, 98, 99, 118, 145, 164, 207, 209, 212, 233, 285, 300, 304, 305, 309, 327, 384, 398, 399, 400, 414, 420, 421, 422, 425, 426, 427
Bowman 338
Boyd 235
Boylan 256
Braddock 421
Brauer 280, 414
Bree 354
Bricher 420
Brischer 224
Brodhage 390
Brown ... 15, 22, 24, 25, 26, 27, 32, 35, 40, 46, 51, 53, 56, 85, 86, 92, 97, 99, 127, 129, 138, 140, 172, 173, 175, 176, 188, 195, 197, 210, 212, 250, 252, 270, 272, 383, 386, 397, 416, 417, 420, 421
Brundage 419
Bryant 118, 264, 349, 361
Bullock 42
Bumgarner 51
Burgeson 186, 295, 350
Burgess 414
Burke 254
Burleson 129
Burn 422
Burnell 338
Burnidge 69
Burr .. 20, 21, 27, 29, 81, 165, 252, 253, 416, 417
Bushue 236
Byerhoff 32
Caldwell 157
Calhoon 99
Capes 323
Cappos 380
Carden 42
Carlson ... 25, 27, 30, 32, 84, 86, 92, 98, 99, 120, 126, 129, 149, 150, 164, 202, 240, 261, 312, 349, 351, 383, 398, 412, 417, 419, 420, 423
Carpenter ... 6, 9, 11, 13, 14, 19, 25, 32, 113, 124, 157, 165, 168, 179, 181, 274, 291, 304, 305, 311, 407, 408, 411, 412
Carty 221
Cass 409
Catnaugh 138
Caustin 16
Cavoltsky 84
Cellini 68
Chaffee ... 9, 11, 15, 17, 19, 22, 25, 80, 81, 82, 83, 88, 107, 150, 151, 157, 158, 250, 252, 408, 409, 411, 416
Chakas 399
Chancellor 181
Chapman 115
Cherry 168, 179, 305
Childs 286
Chouinard 328
Christenson 418
Chrystal 25, 27, 227, 228, 412
Claeys 398
Clapper 328
Clark 243
Claus 51
Cleveland 18
Clopton 77, 296, 425
Close 27, 98
Clutterbuck 109
Cochran 254
Cole 212, 342, 383
Collins 55, 288, 290, 360, 420
Cook 167
Cooke 400
Cooley 222
Coombes 29, 178, 253, 287, 422
Coombs 32
Cooper 167
Copp 276
Cordes 232
Corron ... 29, 42, 47, 49, 52, 56, 70, 73, 84, 98, 284, 317, 319, 398, 400, 413, 414, 421, 425, 427
Coughlin 18
Coultrap 178, 422
Covalsky 424
Covey 331

Cowan	361
Coy	25, 89
Craft	109
Crain	338
Craven	226
Cray	40, 42, 53, 84, 86, 181, 291, 293, 296, 408, 412, 413, 415, 418, 419, 420
Critchfield	52, 288
Crook	49, 84, 91, 128, 399
Crooke	398
Crosby	11
Crubaugh	409
Cunningham	99
Czernik	240
Dabbs	172
Dallesasse	190
Danks	273
Dannewitz	243
Darflinger	51
Daum	244, 386
Davis	86, 188
Davy	338
Day	66
Dayton	189
De Gignac	377
Dean	90
DeBruycker	427
Deckert	44, 337
Decorte	333
Delancey	349
Delancy	417
Delaney	416
DeLaney	407
Deletkanic	84
Denison	361
Denker	29, 40, 43, 90, 92, 99, 151, 204, 205, 206, 229, 256, 285, 300, 301, 302, 412, 414, 415, 416, 423, 425
Denny	52, 344, 379
Denson	138
Dent	83
Devitt	105
Dewitte	272
Dexter	239
Dibblee	42, 420
Dillenbach	210
Dillon	292, 341
Divine	422
Djukic	404
Dodds	200
Dorr	319
Dowling	78
Downey	91, 275, 276, 294
Downs	48
DuBois	420
Duddridge	30
Dunham	16
Durant	9
Eby	405
Eckstrom	144, 145
Eddy	11, 18, 32, 34, 38, 53, 89, 91, 92, 93, 98, 128, 135, 147, 163, 168, 201, 214, 216, 218, 303, 311, 390, 419, 421
Edwards	41
Egner	417
Einwich	51
Ekdahl	27
Ekstrom	24, 27, 29, 30, 33, 50, 55, 76, 92, 95, 97, 98, 99, 126, 129, 141, 149, 151, 199, 213, 214, 217, 232, 239, 302, 303, 345, 367, 415, 416, 417, 424, 426, 428
Elfston	264
Elliot	107
Elliott	84, 85, 181, 278
Ellsworth	25, 83, 92, 103, 128, 407, 408, 409, 411
Elvin	92
Engstrom	240
Enquist	37
Erdman	102
Erickson	25, 29, 32, 34, 35, 40, 67, 84, 85, 96, 97, 109, 199, 201, 202, 203, 264, 276, 312, 317, 326, 327, 361, 363, 383, 413
Espel	142
Essex	333
Eyles	154
Faber	345
Fabyan	305
Feldmann	58, 87
Feltgen	338
Fenner	224, 225
Ferson	185
Fessenden	183
Fields	418
Fifield	377
Finley	297

Fischer...22, 24, 51, 81, 84, 85, 97, 164, 181, 182, 183, 184, 408, 412, 414, 417, 425
Fisher.. 33, 41, 127, 183, 407, 411, 416, 417, 420
Fitzsimmons 298
Fleming 51, 400
Flinn 23
Folgers 316
Foulkes 364, 398
Francisco 79
Franzen 142
Free 232
Fremont 111
Frerichs 367
Freundlich 102
Frey 155
Fritz 232
Fuller 11
Gallucci 401, 402
Garaghty 387, 388
Garbarski 403
Garfield...15, 54, 79, 81, 85, 207, 208, 212, 226, 408, 409, 410, 411
Gassmann 340
Gauger 217
Gee 419, 420
Geldmeyer 217
Gerdau 120, 315
Geske 246, 323, 428
Gholson 270, 272
Gibson 153
Gilbert 79
Gilchrist 218
Glasco 119
Glomp 390
Goldenstein...85, 86, 99, 131, 164, 398, 399, 421
Goodrich 421
Gordon 49
Graham 65, 102, 103, 151
Granquist 298
Gray 51, 328
Green 349
Gross 53
Gullotta 421
Gustafson 98, 100, 419
Guthrie 90
Hagaman...13, 19, 25, 31, 33, 40, 42, 45, 48, 49, 99, 128, 150, 157, 214, 223, 259, 386, 398, 399, 400, 414, 416, 417, 419, 420, 422, 425, 426
Hahn 217, 400
Haire 414
Håkansson 141
Hall 89
Hamer 109
Hamilton 11, 151, 414
Hamm 389
Hand 25, 83, 236
Hanna 290
Hansen 102
Hanson 49, 145, 252, 400
Harkness 83, 181
Harley 86, 87, 99, 421
Harper 268
Harris 102
Harrison 17, 92, 127
Harroldson 147
Hartman 27
Hartmann 420
Hassel 414
Hastings 248, 420
Hatch 98, 99
Hatzis 47, 425
Hawkins...22, 32, 33, 40, 47, 49, 91, 92, 95, 128, 141, 142, 144, 145, 168, 191, 236, 239, 240, 241, 243, 244, 246, 248, 250, 283, 285, 314, 317, 412, 416, 418, 419, 421, 425
Hawley 219
Hayden 197
Heath 15, 268
Hedberg 30
Heffernan 416
Heitz 218
Hemming 215
Hempt 30
Henry 99
Hess 136, 254
Heuertz 47
Hibbeler 49
Higgins...13, 19, 25, 32, 83, 88, 111, 113, 114, 118, 120, 124, 128, 138, 139, 140, 157, 159, 227, 236, 252, 255, 259, 313, 368, 407, 408, 409, 417
Hilburn 115
Hilgenberg 236
Hill 32

Hines 254
Hiser 331, 361
Hitchcock 9
Hoagland 8
Hoffman 416, 424
Hollis 414
Holmer 133, 232
Holmquist 30, 90
Holst 121
Holtz 290
Horan 85, 94, 95
Horlock 422
Horning 60
Horton 217
Howard 419
Huber 428
Hudmon 401
Hultine 42, 420
Hummel...44, 55, 192, 239, 241, 264, 273, 291, 296, 345, 353, 354, 359, 399, 417, 422
Hurd 15, 20, 74, 81, 128, 274
Hyde 87
Hyre 268
Idarius 171
Idleman 140
Isaacson 32
Jablonski 56
Jackson 180
Jacobson 420
James 156
Jarot 65
Jay...33, 34, 37, 49, 84, 95, 98, 216, 217, 218, 269, 319, 329, 350, 390, 391, 419, 428
Jennings 39, 290
Jensen 285
Jenson 30, 95
Jessup 134
Jewell 164
Johansson 213
Johnsen 84, 98, 207, 388, 417, 422
Johnson...6, 20, 22, 27, 28, 29, 30, 31, 32, 34, 36, 39, 40, 41, 42, 45, 47, 49, 50, 51, 52, 56, 57, 60, 77, 84, 85, 86, 89, 90, 91, 92, 94, 95, 98, 99, 100, 102, 108, 114, 121, 126, 129, 137, 143, 144, 155, 159, 164, 167, 179, 183, 185, 186, 187, 188, 191, 192, 210, 213, 215, 232, 234, 236, 239, 280, 282, 285, 287, 289, 291, 294, 295, 297, 298, 302, 303, 335, 337, 338, 345, 349, 361, 368, 389, 398, 399, 400, 405, 407, 412, 413, 414, 415, 416, 417, 418, 419, 420, 421, 422, 423, 425, 426, 428
Jonatat 420, 422
Jonson 150
Jordan 130
Jorgenson 49, 102
Joshua 44
Judy 65
Kacirek 428
Kahn 318
Kaiser 30, 425
Kammrad 318
Karametsos 55, 301, 344, 380, 381
Karschnick 199
Kautz 414
Kayner 90, 216, 349, 350, 360, 391
Keiser 192
Keller 405
Kelley 15
Kellogg 124
Kemp 135, 259
Kenyon 282
Keplar 130
Ketman 19, 81, 195
Killoran 164
Kimble 82, 417
Kingsmill 179
Kinnear 172
Kinnett 252
Kinney 188
Klasing 43, 44
Klein 299
Klotz 229
Knudson 326
Krause 405
Kudlicki 405
Kuhl 407
Kwasniewski 66
Kyle 8, 14
Ladewig 341
Lake...15, 22, 25, 27, 127, 128, 145, 172, 175, 227, 228, 412
Lamb 178
Lambert 417
Landreth 50, 335
Lane 79, 81, 409
Langbartels 343

Langrill 32, 166, 218
Lant 215
Larsen 103, 104
Larson ... 30, 32, 92, 99, 155, 163, 183, 214, 234, 303, 319, 338, 368, 369, 370, 382, 414, 419, 420, 423
Lathrop 20, 159, 221, 410
Lauger 400
Leahy 22
Leathers 50, 51, 267, 269, 329
Ledbetter 50
Lee 269, 368
Lemon 349
Lenkaitis 298, 305, 309
Levine 405
Licher 164
Lillibridge 175
Lincoln 231
Lind 29
Lindgren 398
Lindquist 95
Linquist 398
Littlejohn 30
Lively 92
Lockhart 145
Lofgren 33, 90, 192, 336, 337
Loop 190
Lorang 338, 409
Lundgren 285
Luther 198, 200
Mack 386
Madsen 364
Maier 273
Malek 65, 401, 428
Malmberg 25
Mancini 379
Mann 143
Mapes 90
Marshall 345
Marten 275
Mårtensson 141
Martin 74, 149, 161, 275, 408, 411
Martins 252
Marvin 95, 97, 199
Mason 224
Massolle 335
Masters 248
Mather ... 33, 41, 67, 84, 98, 197, 199, 242, 264, 291, 312, 317, 319, 320, 321, 370, 372, 384, 406, 417, 421, 425
Mattis 301
Mattson 420
Matz 254
Mazur 61
McCarthy 417
McClure 107
McConnaughay 236
McCornack 420
McDonald 15, 99, 351
McGillivray 79, 81, 155
McGowan ... 25, 28, 33, 34, 49, 91, 92, 217, 229, 268, 269, 382, 406, 407, 412, 415, 416, 417
McKay 42, 84, 297
McKinley 175
McKittrick 197
McMahon 60
McPartland 376, 378
McQueen 424
McWilliams 200
Meach 276, 277
Meager 25, 27
Meanger 103
Medina 402
Meissner .. 33, 199, 220, 264, 317, 318, 320, 424
Melville 90
Melvin 206
Meredith 115
Merrell 102
Messina 335
Mether 198
Metzger 407
Meyer 99, 361, 398, 399
Meyers 420
Mika 360
Millen ... 14, 19, 20, 22, 24, 25, 33, 81, 91, 92, 109, 125, 126, 167, 168, 169, 171, 327, 329, 334, 348, 407, 408, 409, 411, 412
Miller 33, 87, 109, 110, 181, 338, 391, 426
Mills 115
Minard 290
Mish 330
Mitchell 331, 383
Mitson 345
Mongerson ... 6, 11, 23, 25, 28, 30, 33, 34, 42, 43, 47, 90, 91, 93, 101, 126, 128, 130, 229, 296,

  297, 299, 350, 398, 412, 413, 415, 416, 419, 420, 421, 422, 425
Moody 15
Morgan 159, 183, 219, 311
Morrison 103
Morrow 404
Morter 331, 333, 427, 428
Muehlfelt 426
Mueller 224, 333, 341
Muir 147, 227
Muirhead 412
Mullally 288, 290
Muller 24
Mulvey 296
Mungerson 136, 422
Munyon 55, 360
Murley 226
Murphy 163, 186
Murray 420
Nagel 192
Nagy 64
Nash 91, 92, 114
Nelson...98, 120, 141, 229, 272, 311, 312, 407, 409, 414
New 129
Newberry 23
Newton 17
Nibel 172
Nichols 99, 179
Nickell 248
Nickla 225
Nolting 376
Norris 6, 130
Norton...17, 33, 42, 84, 99, 109, 128, 149, 164, 179, 181, 215, 407, 411, 413, 414, 417, 420
Nystrom 328
O'Connell 49
O'Connell, ... 400
Oakland 387
Oberhart 145
Olaine 202
Olesen 345
Olsen 419
Olson...34, 40, 50, 92, 94, 95, 96, 98, 129, 135, 164, 202, 206, 214, 233, 235, 283, 284, 285, 286, 300, 305, 334, 415, 416, 417, 419, 421, 423
Osborne 28, 84, 91, 98
Oslund 33, 118, 312
Outhouse 11, 14
Owensby 338, 341
Pacione 240
Padelford 250
Paetz 188, 189
Paige 86
Palushik 236
Parson 137, 264, 356
Parsons 297
Pattee 13, 64, 138, 157, 162, 280
Patterson 208
Paulson 272
Pease 93
Peck 113
Pelley 41, 46, 76
Peltier 286, 335
Pepple 58, 87
Perch 38
Perez 388
Perkins 128, 178, 287, 361, 413, 416, 422
Person 428
Peters 99
Petersohn 395
Peterson...11, 15, 21, 22, 25, 29, 30, 31, 33, 40, 47, 50, 56, 57, 81, 82, 83, 90, 92, 98, 108, 109, 120, 126, 127, 128, 129, 134, 147, 148, 149, 150, 155, 183, 185, 191, 199, 214, 215, 227, 228, 233, 243, 244, 290, 311, 312, 317, 353, 364, 366, 368, 408, 409, 411, 412, 413, 414, 415, 416, 423
Pfau 405
Pierce 86, 327
Pillins 409
Plummer...15, 85, 147, 149, 182, 183, 311, 312, 363, 409, 417
Porter 415
Potter 43, 84
Powell 11, 27, 182, 184
Prendergast 45, 100
Price 223
Probert...10, 11, 15, 33, 118, 147, 162, 163, 228, 270, 272
Quackenbush 88, 107
Qualls 248
Quist 115
Raasch...47, 50, 52, 71, 77, 343, 383, 417, 422, 425, 426, 428

Raczkiewicz	105
Radandt	273
Rambow	115
Ramer	115
Ramm	412
Ranstead	121
Raplus	420
Rasmussen	186, 189, 228
Reber	399
Redborg	134, 334
Rediger	44, 86, 273, 311, 363, 366, 367
Reed	215, 368, 419
Rees	86, 165, 419
Reichter	425
Reinert	333
Renner	389
Renwick	33, 216
Rice	13, 19, 20, 25, 57, 79, 86, 87, 138, 147, 157, 158, 186, 221, 225, 236, 259, 280, 294, 327, 329, 331, 334, 335, 376
Richmond	29, 30, 34, 36, 42, 50, 53, 84, 85, 99, 204, 205, 206, 220, 298, 327, 412, 413, 415, 419, 420, 424, 425, 428
Robinson	49, 164, 165, 421
Roby	200
Rockwell	217
Roesner	311
Rollins	99
Ross	11, 95, 231, 232
Royce	173
Ruddick	259
Ruddock	223, 259, 360
Russell	50
Rylander	149
Saelens	92
Salter	262
Sanderson	50, 425, 428
Sandholm	368
Santell	67, 299
Saperston	128
Sarbaugh	118, 154
Scatliff	222
Schaefer	47, 77, 86, 422, 423
Schafer	422
Scherman	141
Schlager	417
Schmidt	45
Schmitt	400
Schmitz	205, 272, 273
Schneider	426
Schroeder	270
Schudel	420
Schuetz	319
Schultz	97
Schwab	349
Schwarz	418
Scott	37, 91, 128, 164, 165, 166, 261, 294, 351, 407, 419, 425, 428
Scroggin	338
Secylor	264
Selden	20
Serratella	405
Serritella	403
Shaft	407
Sharp	30, 88, 89, 115, 165, 232, 409, 412
Shaver	15
Shott	39
Shoudy	376
Shrader	27
Simmons	183
Simon	20, 125
Simons	351
Sizemore	235, 420
Skala	49, 56, 98
Skeen	337, 413
Skoglund	27, 207
Slate	157, 304
Sleeman	50, 291, 400, 422, 427
Slimm	315
Smalius	420
Smith	68, 70, 274, 278, 405, 415, 420
Sobieski	72, 405
Soderquist	29
Spaak	152
Spalten	49, 51
Sparacio	285
Spence	161
Spencer	177
Spriet	145
St. John	83
Stahl	73, 102
Stattner	228
Steele	214
Stelle	319
Stephens	130, 401
Stephenson	199

Stevens...15, 19, 21, 33, 79, 80, 81, 83, 85, 88, 108, 110, 165, 195, 196, 250, 289, 290, 406, 408, 409
Stewart 128, 253, 264, 368, 407
Stickney 12
Stokke 73, 106
Stover 371
Strom 50, 94, 98, 206, 233, 420, 423
Svenson 204
Swanberg 33, 124, 243, 415, 421
Swanson...11, 20, 22, 25, 27, 33, 39, 42, 49, 50, 75, 90, 91, 95, 97, 99, 109, 114, 118, 119, 123, 125, 126, 128, 133, 134, 135, 136, 137, 147, 163, 164, 192, 199, 201, 203, 248, 253, 276, 277, 281, 290, 294, 303, 311, 312, 314, 315, 323, 331, 334, 356, 361, 379, 398, 400, 411, 412, 414, 415, 420
Swarthout 86, 159, 168
Swichtenberg 292
Synnott 42, 420
Taft 128
Tanner 109
Tappan 86
Tarnow 95, 97
Taylor 105
Tengwald 143, 168
Terry 219
Thomas 344, 425
Thompson 43, 56, 89, 99, 409
Thomsen 40, 424
Thornton 179, 183
Thorpe 156
Thull 51
Thurber 25, 89
Tiedemann 318
Till 398
Tobias 262
Tope 67
Torstenson 152
Tower 252
Travis 33, 92, 378, 379, 382, 399
Tredup 99
Troyer 65
Trusso 404
Tucker 280
Turner 205, 417
Ullman 110
Untz 50, 300, 301

Valkenberg 261
Valkenburg 400
Van Bogaert 47, 99, 422
Van De Veire 49, 380, 427
Van der Hagen 217
Van Der Hoeven 219
Van Overmeiren 235
Van Thurnout 420
Vanderbruggen 118
Vanderhoof...6, 22, 25, 27, 29, 30, 31, 46, 49, 50, 56, 77, 88, 90, 91, 109, 126, 128, 145, 173, 219, 221, 234, 256, 258, 261, 262, 296, 411, 415, 422, 425, 427, 428
Vandervolgen 11
Vandervolk 144
VanWambeke 180, 305
VanWinkle 312, 367
Verhaeghe 44, 50, 85, 99, 299, 391, 420
Verkler 54, 254
Vermaat 400
Verner 415, 416
Volpp 163
Voss 417
Wadley 227
Wait 161
Waite 17
Wakeman 99
Walker 11
Waller 414
Wallin 78
Walradt 388
Walters 115
Walton 169
Wanzer 25, 197, 312, 376, 377
Ward...14, 15, 40, 41, 108, 153, 155, 167, 180, 188
Warne 115
Warner 101, 102, 414
Warren... 25, 27, 28, 83, 154, 173, 204, 407, 416
Waterhouse...25, 33, 34, 42, 43, 45, 74, 84, 92, 93, 97, 99, 100, 109, 165, 176, 177, 178, 179, 252, 253, 254, 255, 270, 276, 287, 296, 412, 415, 416, 421
Waters 98
Watkins 15
Webb 89, 90, 163, 169, 411
Wedick 284
Weier 420

Weir 420
Weiss 69
Weitl 212
Wessberg 33
Wessels 420
Westbrook 45
Westfield 161, 356
Wheadon 33
Wheeler 280
White...17, 20, 21, 25, 33, 42, 44, 46, 111, 126, 139, 140, 154, 164, 165, 166, 179, 255, 259, 261, 340, 342, 389, 393, 411, 419, 425
Whitney...13, 19, 20, 22, 25, 26, 27, 33, 34, 38, 89, 91, 92, 107, 108, 109, 118, 128, 160, 161, 163, 164, 168, 181, 182, 199, 270, 272, 275, 276, 304, 349, 356, 368, 398, 411, 416, 421
Wickenden 38
Wickizer...34, 109, 163, 164, 179, 356, 411, 412, 417
Wiegel 86
Wilcox 91, 92
Wilkerson 303
Wilkinson 88
Wilkison 84, 95, 98, 119, 414, 421
Williams 89, 98, 209, 319
Wilson 185
Wing 98
Wojnicki 63
Wolfgram 259
Wood 261
Woodraska 262
Worth 10
Wredling 99
Wren 380
Wright 168, 169
Wynthein 84, 85, 86, 98, 327, 385
Yahnke 61
Young 164
Zahrndt 254
Zerby 392
Zobjeck 50
Zwirn 67

About the Author

Adam D. Gibbons is an author and private tutor in Geneva, Illinois. He lives on the east side in the former Snow family farmhouse, which just celebrated its 180th birthday this past May. He is a graduate of Northwestern University (Bachelor of Arts, History) and Wake Forest University (Master of Arts, History) and had been a genealogist since the age of thirteen. For several years, Adam worked as a fact-checker and researcher for an educational publishing company in Evanston, Illinois. He has lived in the Chicago area since 1993, other than two years in Winston-Salem, North Carolina. Adam keeps a daily journal that has run over 10,100 continuous days, whose entries (put together) exceed three and a half million words. His family lived in New York State for fourteen generations. When he is not writing books or tutoring, he may be found taking his son and daughter to play and violin practice, volleyball and tennis lessons, and a wide variety of school and church events. His wife Heidi is a photographer and an elementary school teacher in Geneva. So far, their children have not adopted Adam and Heidi's love of history, but both enjoy math, animals, seeing new places, and reading! Adam has had the pleasure of serving as the President of the Board of Directors for Preservation Partners of the Fox Valley for the past three years, and has held a Board seat with that organization for just over a decade. Adam is a Life Member of the Western New York Genealogical Society, conducts historic home research in the Fox Valley, and is the owner of Old Adage Press. He enjoys gardening, reading, travel, collecting antiques, and spending time with his family. He is also a home-bound tutor for three local school districts, and specializes in tutoring math, history, and all areas of the ACT, SAT, and GRE. Adam can be reached at gibbons0529@gmail.com.

www.ingramcontent.com/pod-product-compliance
Lightning Source LLC
Chambersburg PA
CBHW051358070526
44584CB00023B/3202